£30

MESOPOTAMIA AND THE EAST

An Archaeological and Historical Study
of Foreign Relations *ca.* 3400 – 2000 BC

Timothy Potts

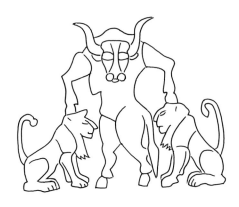

Oxford University Committee for Archaeology
Monograph 37

Published by the Oxford University Committee for Archaeology
Institute of Archaeology
Beaumont Street
Oxford

Distributed by Oxbow Books
Park End Place, Oxford OX1 1HN

Distributed in North America by
The David Brown Book Company
PO Box 511, Oakville, CT 06779

ISBN 0 947816 37 2

Printed in Great Britain at
Cambridge University Press

For Olivia

Contents

Chapter 4: Metals and Metalwork   143

Chapter 5: Stones and Stonework

Chapter 6: Stone Vessels   217

Chapter 7: Conclusions

Acknowledgements

The research for this study was undertaken while a Research Lecturer and British Academy Post-Doctoral Fellow at Christ Church, Oxford. Museum study for chapter 6 was funded by the British School of Archaeology in Iraq (Iraq Museum) and the British Institute of Persian Studies (Louvre). Publication was made possible by a subvention from the British Academy. To all of these institutions I am grateful for their support.

Many people have contributed to this study through discussion or comments on earlier drafts. I am particularly grateful to J.A. Black, D. Frayne, P. Michalowski and P. Steinkeller for comments on chapters 1 and 3, and to S. Dalley, Th. Jacobsen and N. Yoffee for views on philological and historical matters. I owe a special debt to P.R.S. Moorey who was supervisor of the D.Phil. thesis from which this study grew and has since continued to give generously of his time and expertise. J.-J. Glassner, N. Postgate, D. T. Potts, and P. Steinkeller made available articles in press and P. Kjærum supplied information on unpublished material from Failaka. Other assistance was provided by H. Baker, E. Carter and A.R. Green. All line drawings are by Tessa Rickards.

I am grateful also to the staff of the museums who facilitated access to their collections: P. Amiet, B. André and A. Caubet (Louvre), H. Behrens, M. de Schauensee and A. Sjöberg (University Museum, Philadelphia), J.E. Curtis and T.C. Mitchell (British Museum), P.R.S. Moorey (Ashmolean Museum), V. Donbaz (Istanbul) and the staff of the Iraq Museum, Baghdad.

Notes for the Reader

1. References in the text

References follow the Harvard system except for philological works which are cited according to their standard abbreviations as follows:

ABC   A.K. Grayson, *Assyrian and Babylonian Chronicles*, Texts from Cuneiform Sources V, New York, 1975.

ABWI   H. Steible, *Die altsumerischen Bau- und Weihinschriften*, FAOS 5, Wiesbaden, 1982.

AHw   W. von Soden, *Akkadisches Handwörterbuch*, Wiesbaden, 1965-1981.

AKI   I.J. Gelb & B. Kienast, *Die altakkadischen Königsinschriften des dritten Jahrtausand v. Chr.*, FAOS 7, Stuttgart, 1990.

ARI 1   A.K. Grayson, *Assyrian Royal Inscriptions 1: From the Beginning to Ashur-resha-ishi I*, Wiesbaden, 1972.

CA   J. Cooper, *The Curse of Agade*, 1983.

CT   Various authors, *Cuneiform Texts from Babylonian Tablets in the British Museum*, London.

DP   F.-M. Allotte de la Füye, *Documents présargoniques*, Paris, 1908 (DP 1-68), 1909 (DP 145-265), 1913 (DP 266-467), 1920 (DP 468-669).

EE   *Enmerkar and Ensuhkešdanna* (edited Berlin 1979).

EL   *Enmerkar and Lugalbanda* (edited Wilcke 1969, Jacobsen 1987).

ELA   *Enmerkar and the Lord of Aratta* (edited S. Cohen 1973, Jacobsen 1987).

EN   *Enki and Ninhursag* (edited Attinger 1984).

EWO   *Enki and the World Order* (edited Benito 1969, Kramer & Maier 1989).

H*h*   HAR-ra: *hubullu* (edited *MSL XI*).

IRSA   E. Sollberger & J.-R. Kupper, *Inscriptions royales sumériennes et akkadiennes*, Paris, 1971.

ITT   Various authors, *Inventaire des tablettes de Tello ...*, Paris, 1910-1921.

LAK   A. Diemel, *Liste der archaischen Keilschriftzeichen*, Die Inschriften von Fara I, Leipzig, 1922.

LGN   Early Dynastic List of Geographical Names (edited Biggs 1974: 71-78, Pettinato 1978, *MEE 3*: 229-39).

LH   *Lugalbanda in Hurrumkurra* (unedited).

Lipšur   *lipšur* litanies (edited Reiner 1956).

LSU   *Lament over Sumer and Ur* (edited Michalowski 1989).

MAD   I.J. Gelb, *Materials for the Assyrian Dictionary*, 5 vols, Chicago, 1952-1970.

MDP   Various authors, *Mémoires de la Délégation en Perse*, Paris.

MEE   Various editors, *Materiali Epigrafici di Ebla*, Istituto Universitario di Napoli, Seminario di Studi Asiatici, Naples.

MSL   Various editors, *Materials for the Sumerian Lexicon*, Rome.

MVN   Various editors, *Materiali per il vocabulario neosumerico*, Rome 1974-.

NBWI   H. Steible, *Die neusumerischen Bau- und Weihinschriften*, FAOS 9, Stuttgart, 1991.

PSD   *Philadelphia Sumerian Dictionary*, Philadelphia.

RÉC   F. Thureau-Dangin, *Récherches sur l'origin de l'écriture cunéiform*, Paris 1898.

RGTC 1   D.O. Edzard, G. Farber & E. Sollberger, *Répertoire géographique des textes cunéiformes, Band 1: Die Orts- und Gewässernamen der präsargonischen und sargonischen Zeit*, Weisbaden, 1977.

RGTC 2   D.O Edzard & G. Farber, *Répertoire géographique des textes cunéiformes, Band 2: Die Orts- und Gewässernamen der 3. Dynastie von Ur,* Wiesbaden, 1974.

RGTC 3   B. Groneberg, *Répertoire géographique des textes cunéiformes, Band 3: Die Orts- und Gewässernamen der altbabylonischen Zeit,* Wiesbaden 1980.

RGTC 5 K. Nashef, *Répertoire géographique des textes cunéiformes, Band 5: Die Orts- und Gewässernamen der mittelbabylonischen und mittelassyrischen Zeit,* Wiesbaden 1982.

RTC F. Thureau-Dangin, *Recueil des tablettes chaldéennes*, Paris, 1903.

SARI I J.S. Cooper, *Sumerian and Akkadian Royal Inscriptions I: Presargonic Inscriptions,* New Haven, 1986.

SKL *The Sumerian King List* (edited Jacobsen 1939).

ŠL A. Deimel, *Šumerisches Lexikon*, IV vols, Rome 1925-50.

TLB Various editors, *Tabulae Cuneiformes a F. M. Th. de Liagre Böhl collectae*, Leiden 1954-.

UET Various editors, *Ur Excavations: Texts,* London & Philadelphia 1928-.

VS 14 W. Förtsch, *Altbabylonische Wirtschaftstexte aus der Zeit Lugalanda's und Urukagina's*, Vorderasiatische Schriftdenkmäler, Leipzig, 1916.

2. Royal and Dedication Inscriptions

References to third-millennium building, dedication and royal inscriptions follow the listings in *ABWI, NBWI, AKI* and *SARI I*. In *AKI*, references to "D" and "S" refer to year dates and cylinder seal inscriptions respectively.

3. Other Abbreviations

(a) Periods

JN	Jemdet Nasr	OB	Old Babylonian
ED	Early Dynastic	MA	Middle Assyrian
OAkk	Old Akkadian	NA	Neo-Assyrian
OA	Old Assyrian	NB	Neo-Babylonian

(b) Royal Names (for year names and royal inscriptions)

Man	Maništušu	Š	Šulgi
NS	Naram-Sin	AS	Amar-Suen
SkS	Šarkališarri	ŠS	Šu-Sin
		IS	Ibbi-Sin

(c) Miscellaneous

Akk.	Akkadian
GN	geographical name
PN	personal name
Sum.	Sumerian

4. Transliteration of Sumerian and Akkadian

Sumerian is transliterated in **bold**, Akkadian in *italics*. The phoneme ḫ/ḫ is always rendered h/ḫ. Restorations are shown in square brackets [.....], additions in normal brackets (.....).

List of Figures and Tables

Figures

Tables

Introduction

1. MESOPOTAMIA AND FOREIGN RELATIONS

Foreign relations have long been a central concern of archaeological and historical study of ancient Mesopotamia. The lack of any general synthesis, such as exist for Egypt and many other regions of the Near East,[1] is not a reflection of the subject's immaturity but rather of its scale and complexity. Situated at the geographical centre of the Near East, Mesopotamia shares borders or direct sea-links with virtually all other major areas of ancient settlement – the Gulf states to the south-east, Iran to the east, Anatolia to the north and Syro-Palestine to the west, this last giving access by land to Egypt. Only to the south-west, in the barren wastes of northern Saudi Arabia, was there a vast nothingness.

Centrality brought with it certain economic and political advantages, but also its share of liabilities. Potentially the most influential region of the Near East, Mesopotamia was also at greatest risk of being overwhelmed; a possible threat to all, she was also exposed to attack on almost every front, as is illustrated by the succession of invaders who punctuate Mesopotamian history: Gutians, Elamites, Šimaškians, Kassites, Medes and Persians from the east; Amorites, Hittites and Aramaeans from the north and west, to name only the most obvious. In many ways Mesopotamia represents the antithesis of Egypt, the other great power centre of pre-classical antiquity, whose historical independence and cultural introversion derived largely from her geographical isolation.

A number of economic and political factors combined to stimulate interaction between Mesopotamia and surrounding regions. Blessed with great agricultural richness capable of supporting a large concentrated population, but virtually devoid of natural resources, the settlements of the Tigris-Euphrates alluvium were forced to import virtually all raw materials other than clay, reeds and some stones. The resulting trade in metals and most timbers and stones ensured Mesopotamia's place as a significant economic force in the Near East and kept her in regular contact with neighbouring territories. Likewise, the early emergence of Sumer and Akkad as major military powers saw the lowlands playing a key rôle in inter-regional political developments. Along with Egypt, Mesopotamia represented one of the two perennial foci of political power in the ancient Near East, and generally much the more imperialistic.

For many years the accidents of discovery focused modern scholars' attention on Mesopotamia's more distant contact with Late Predynastic Egypt, where Sumerian influence was seen to have played a rôle in that region's rapid progress towards civilization,[2] and with the cities of the Indus valley. In both instances it was clear from the outset that contact must have been established by sea, though in the case of Egypt it was (and still is) unclear whether boats sailed east around Arabia, or down the Levant from northern Syria.[3] Evidence of Sumerian land-based contact, on the

---

[1] For Egypt W. Helck's substantial study, *Die Beziehungen Ägyptens zu Vorderasien im 3. und 2. Jahrtausend v. Chr.*, Wiesbaden, 1962 and for Palestine J.B. Hennessy's *The Foreign Relations of Palestine during the Early Bronze Age*, London, 1967. For Mesopotamia, the closest equivalent so far is the Rencontre proceedings, Nissen & Renger (eds) 1982 and, for early relations with Iran, Curtis ed. 1993.

[2] Frankfort 1951: 100-11.

[3] Moorey 1990; Teissier 1987.

other hand, remained sporadic and geographically limited. Historical evidence seemed inconclusive at best. A few great warriors claimed to have reached the Mediterranean, but they were regarded as exceptional; even Sargon's claim to have marched to Purushanda in inner Anatolia was treated with scepticism. As for the east, since Elam was equated essentially with Susiana, the Sumero-Akkadian expeditions recounted in third-millennium inscriptions were not envisaged as penetrating much beyond Khuzistan. Up to the 1960s, archaeological evidence was equally equivocal. The plateau remained largely unknown. Tepe Hissar, the only major highland site contemporary with the empires of third-millennium Mesopotamia, provided nothing to suggest more than remote and indirect acquaintance with the lowlands. Tepe Sialk, whose final occupation belonged to the preceding Proto-Elamite period, can be seen in retrospect to have held a clue to the real extent of late-fourth- and early-third-millennium interaction. But in isolation its significance could not be fully appreciated. Interpretation and speculation centred around trade. Typological or other connections were argued to derive ultimately from overland trade bringing highland raw materials (copper in the case of Sialk) into the lowlands.

   This view of Mesopotamia's eastern relations was completely transformed by the explosion of fieldwork undertaken in Iran during the late 1960s and 70s. Widespread excavations at sites across the plateau by teams from the United States (Chogha Mish, Godin Tepe, Tal-i Malyan, Tepe Yahya, Tal-i Iblis, Tepe Hissar), Italy (Shahr-i Sokhta, Tepe Hissar), France (Susa, Tal-i Jalyan) and Iran (Shahdad) brought to light much new evidence of highland-lowland relations, and allowed older evidence from Mesopotamia to be reappraised. From the perspective of the present investigation three chief developments may be noted. First, highland Iran was shown to have supported major urban centres (Anšan, Shahr-i Sokhta) as early as the third millennium which might be expected to have had dealing with Mesopotamia on terms of approximate equality. Secondly, the intensity and geographical range of cultural influence, especially in the Proto-Elamite period, proved to be much greater than anticipated, extending far beyond the Zagros onto the Iranian plateau. Thirdly, evidence accumulated from Iran and beyond of a previously unsuspected exchange network dating to the later third millennium along which metalwork, stonework and other finished artefacts were distributed across vast areas from Bactria through central Iran to Susa. The origin of much of the metalwork in particular, previously classed at Susa with the 'Luristan bronzes', became apparent during the 1970s through the plundering of thousands of graves in southern Bactria. The recognition of Bactria as a major manufacturing centre, actively involved in third-millennium inter-regional exchange, marked the beginning of a further departure in the study of Greater Iran, whose full implications have only recently begun to be assessed.

   Appreciation of the greater scope of inter-regional interaction revived interest also in neighbouring southern Turkmenia where many years of excavation by Soviet scholars, previously reported almost exclusively in Russian, had remained largely outside the purview of Near Eastern studies. Translations and syntheses of recent Soviet research have made this material more widely known.[4] With revisions in the dating of the crucial Namazga sequence, developments in Central Asia were shown to have more nearly kept pace with those in the Near East. Meanwhile, the Belgian mission to Luristan (Pusht-i Kuh) was at last providing a secure archaeological context for some of the early 'Luristan bronzes', confirming that the consumption of

---

[4]   Masson & Sarianidi 1972; Kohl ed. 1981; *idem* 1984; Sarianidi 1986.

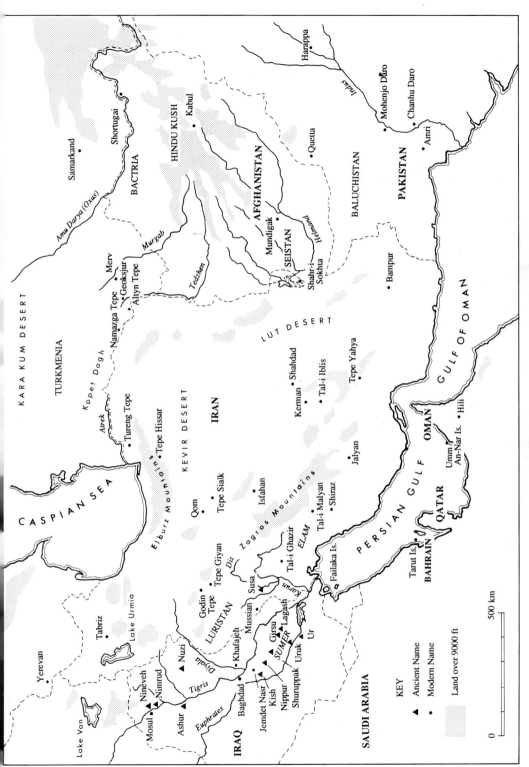

Figure 1. Map showing principal sites of third-millennium Mesopotamia and Greater Iran.

copperwork by nomadic tribesmen had begun by the early third millennium, and that types distinctive of 'Luristan' were being produced by the late Early Dynastic period.

With the closure of Iran to western expeditions at the end of the 1970s field-work shifted into neighbouring regions, particularly the Gulf States, where the pioneering excavations of the Danish expedition already provided a framework for investigation. Discoveries in eastern Arabia and the off-shore islands have elucidated many aspects of Sumerian trade with these regions, previously known only from textual sources. Important aspects of this research have been the confimation that the large copper reserves of Oman were exploited for trade with Mesopotamia (and elsewhere?) as early as the third millennium and that Oman was the homeland of the distinctive *série récente* soft stone vessels widely traded along the Gulf to Sumer.[5]

The major rôle played by American scholars in the expansion of Iranian archaeology had a decisive influence also on the lines of its interpretation and the direction of much secondary research. An increasing proportion of the younger scholars working in Iran came from the anthropologically-oriented training which had become prominent in the wake of the 'new archaeology' of the 1960s. Iran thus became (and remains today) one of the few regions of the Near East where the aims and aspirations of this ambitious programme have been seriously applied. Traditional typological studies were eschewed, or became a prelude to the real business of comparative investigation perceived as the explanation of social processes. Sophisticated interpretive frameworks ('models') and a range of scientific techniques ('inter-disciplinary studies') were brought to bear on the analysis of the processes and structures underlying and regulating ancient culture, both internal developments and regional phenomena. Much speculation centred around trade and exchange which were preceived as crucial factors in the emergence of complex society and in the spread of bureaucratic practices beyond the alluvium.[6] More generally, trade came to be viewed by many as the corner-stone of highland-lowland relations throughout antiquity, determining the nature and extent of contact between the peoples of the Mesopotamian plains and the Iranian plateau. Earlier suppositions that the Sumerians had imported raw materials from Iran were given sharper definition in the light of the new archaeological evidence. The existence of an extensive trade in stones, metals, timber and so on from the newly discovered urban centres of highland Iran to the resourceless cities of the plains, resulting, according to some scholars, in a mutual "economic dependence", acquired virtually the status of an accepted datum.

The impact of these novel approaches and interpretations was not restricted to the American academic community. International colloquia bear testimony to the increasing influence of these ideas, especially on the work of the long-established French mission at Susa, and on the Italians at Shahr-i Sokhta where Marxian elements also played a part.[7] Not only the younger scholars were affected. Something of the same spirit – a readiness to explain archaeological patterns in terms of sociological or economic processes – pervades the recent work of Pierre Amiet, including his major synthesis *L'âge des échanges inter-iraniens, 3500-1700 avant J.-C.*

The results of archaeological investigation stimulated fresh research on the historical geography of Iran, also yielding unexpected results. A major development,

---

5   For reviews of this work see generally D.T. Potts 1990 and (for Oman) Tosi 1989a.
6   Johnson 1973; Wright and Johnson 1975; Alden 1982 with bibliog.
7   Deshayes (ed.) 1977; *Paléorient 4* (1978): 131ff.; *Paléorient 11/2* (1985).

which shifted the focus of Iranian toponymy dramatically eastwards, was the identification of Tal-i Malyan as the Elamite capital of Elam (Anšan). This inspired radical reassessments of third-millennium historical geography and of historical evidence for the extent of Mesopotamian political and military penetration of the east.[8]

2. SCOPE AND NATURE OF THE PRESENT STUDY

The present study attempts to assess the nature and extent of southern Mesopotamia's relations with the east in the light of this much expanded body of archaeological and historical evidence. By 'the east' is meant Iran, South-Central Asia (southern Turkmenia, Margiana, Bactria) and the Indo-Iranian borderlands (Afghanistan, Pakistan) as far as the Indus Valley. The time-range considered is the third millennium BC with an extension back into the late fourth millennium to include the Uruk IV period and the 'Proto-Elamite phenomenon'. The end-date of 2000 BC, though corresponding to a major historical break in Mesopotamia, is somewhat arbitrary from the viewpoint of the east. Due to considerations of space, the account has not been continued down to the archaeologically more natural cut-off point of *ca.* 1800/1700 BC.

In geographical terms, emphasis is laid on the areas which have seen important recent developments, particularly highland Iran, Bactria and the Gulf states. The need to treat at length the sea-borne Indus trade is alleviated by numerous recent studies of this topic.[9] Trade along the Gulf represented a major component of Sumer's eastern supply network, and must be taken into account in any assessment of the scale and nature of overland trade with Iran. Many of the same materials were theoretically accessible through Gulf shipping and Iranian caravan. A recurrent theme of this study is the question of how much came through each channel.

Within these geographical and chronological parameters aspects of Mesopotamia's eastern relations have been selected for investigation according to the availability of relevant data and the emphasis of recent research. Most of the present study is concerned with what may be broadly defined as political and economic relations. Early political relations with the east have not previously been the subject of detailed examination. Mesopotamian and Elamite political histories have been written, but no study which provides a connected narrative of relations between the two. The basis for such an account begins in the Early Dynastic III period when strictly 'historical' texts begin to appear. These become more abundant (and sporadically more reliable) as the millennium progresses, though there are still many serious lacunae. To the extent that any general theme may be gleaned it is one of endemic animosity and opportunistic hostility.

Economic relations between Mesopotamia and the east constitute a less well defined complex of subjects which have received widespread attention in recent years. The bulk of the present study is concerned, directly or indirectly, with various aspects of this theme. What materials were traded between Greater Iran and Mesopotamia, and by which means? How, if at all, did trade relate to politics? And

---

[8] Steinkeller 1982; *idem* in press [b]; Stolper 1982; Vallat 1985.
[9] Ratnagar 1981 (a convenient synthesis of material up to 1980, though sometimes unreliable on the Mesopotamian evidence); see also studies in G.L. Possehl (ed.), *Harappan Civilization: A Contemporary Perspective*, Delhi 1982; Lal & Gupta eds 1984; Jarrige ed. 1988.

what was its economic importance? Much recent work ascribes to overland trade with highland Iran a significant place in the Mesopotamian economy. Is this sustained by a broad assessment of the presently available evidence?

Both textual and archaeological evidence are crucial to a better understanding of these issues. Recent research by anthropologically-oriented scholars has sometimes suffered from a preoccupation with ever more 'sophisticated' analyses of the archaeological data at the expense of documentary information. This is particularly unfortunate in the present case, since the concerns of the relevant texts often supplement the archaeological data, providing evidence of precious materials and perishable commodities which do not generally survive on archaeological sites. Moreover, the chronological distributions of these different lines of evidence, as presently preserved, are largely complementary. Traces of Sumerian 'presence' abroad (in Egypt, the Upper Euphrates, Iran and the Gulf) date principally to the late fourth and early third millennia, while textual evidence of long-distance contact concentrates significantly later, in the Akkadian and Ur III periods. The dangers of relying exclusively on archaeological data are well illustrated by the pattern of evidence in Oman, whose material culture in the later third millennium, when Sumerian trade with Magan was most intense, was oriented decisively to Baluchistan and regions further east, *i.e.* away from Sumer.[10] Likewise in Bahrain, with the redating of the Barbar Temple to the very end of the third millennium, there is virtually no evidence of Sumerian influence on the local material culture before the Ur III period, long after trade with Sumer had begun.[11] Wherever possible, the present study attempts to integrate the available archaeological evidence with the results of textually-based historical and philological research in the conviction that this provides the best hope for a balanced appraisal.

Mesopotamia relied on foreign supplies for almost all raw materials except mud and reeds, which she possessed in abundance. Metals, timber and most stones, as well as many animals and secondary products (resins, perfumes, oils, some hides *etc.*) had to be imported. The presence of each of these materials, whether attested through textual or archaeological evidence, has something to contribute to the broad picture of Mesopotamia's economic relations; and all would deserve attention in a comprehensive investigation. Restrictions of space, however, have prevented such a broad review here. The present study concentrates on those materials and artefact types which have proven, with hindsight, to contribute most to an understanding of Mesopotamia's relations with the east – *viz.* metals and metalwork, and stones and stonework. A separate chapter is devoted to stone vessels, one of the few categories of finished goods that can be demonstrated to have been exchanged in any quantity.

Pottery, which formed the basis of most early studies of Mesopotamian-Iranian relations,[12] is considered here only in connection with the Late Uruk and Proto-Elamite periods since, after that time, Mesopotamian and highland Iranian ceramics followed essentially separate paths. This is illustrated most dramatically by the prevalence of various painted wares in Iran, from the northern Zagros through Luristan and Susiana (Susian 'second style') to south-central Iran (Jalyan, Yahya) and Baluchistan ('Kulli ware'), while the pottery of contemporary Mesopotamia is typically plain and drab, or decorated with incision alone. Exchange of pottery between lowlands and highlands after the Jemdet Nasr/Early Dynastic I period is

---

10   Cleuziou 1986: 148; Weisgerber 1984/85: 9.
11   D.T. Potts 1990: 168-72 (redating); there is only a single possibly JN-type polychrome sherd from north of the Barbar Temple, and a JN seal from Hajjar (*idem* in press [b]).
12   *E.g.* McCown 1942; *idem* 1954; Le Breton 1957; Dyson 1965.

virtually unattested.[13] There is an important point in this, but it is a negative one that can be stated briefly: third-millennium Mesopotamia and Iran formed essentially separate ceramic 'universes', thus mirroring in their pottery the ethnic gulf between the Sumero-Semitic lowlands and the mixed non-Sumerian, non-Semitic inhabitants of highland Iran. In gross terms, 'pottery' and 'peoples' correlate.

The interruption of field-work in Iran has provided an opportunity for assessment and interpretation of the wealth of new material brought to light. As well as field reports, a number of more general synthetic works have recently appeared, of which two are particularly relevant: P. Amiet's *L'âge des échanges inter-iraniens* (1986) and E. Carter and M. Stolper's *Elam: Surveys of Political History and Archaeology* (1984). The focus of Carter and Stolper is exclusively Elamite, though relations with other regions to the east and west are noted periodically. Amiet covers a much wider geographical range from Susa across Iran to Bactria and, as in the present study, he is directly concerned with evidence for inter-regional exchange and other cultural connections. However, neither study systematically includes Mesopotamia, which lies outside the defined purview of Carter and Stolper, and was excluded from the Iranian network of third-millennium regional exchange which constitutes Amiet's primary theme. When Mesopotamia does appear in these works, it is from the Iranian perspective. In this they differ essentially from the present study which adopts a Mesopotamian viewpoint and looks east.

3. GEOGRAPHICAL TERMINOLOGY

The political and cultural heartland of Mesopotamia in the period considered here lay in the south of the country. The focus of power shifted from Sumer to Akkad and back again, but these vacillations are rarely relevant to the theme of this study. Therefore, unless otherwise specified, 'Mesopotamia' should be understood to mean 'southern Mesopotamia' (*i.e.* Babylonia) and 'Sumer' should be read as elliptical for 'Sumer-Akkad'. Due to ignorance of the ancient toponymy of the eastern highlands, the conventional modern or Greek names are used. 'Greater Iran' is used to refer to Iran and the adjacent highland regions from South-Central Asia through Afghanistan to Baluchistan.

---

[13] A few Susian/Luristan 'second style' jars are reported from Sumer: Cros 1910-14: 310, fig. 20; de Genouillac 1934: pl. 34:2a,c; Woolley 1934: 387, pl. 186a; *idem* 1955: pl. 26b; Hansen 1973: 69. Interestingly, in the Late Uruk to ED I period pottery itself, or the influence of painted styles, seems to have moved both ways: Late Uruk types (bevelled rim bowls, four-lugged jars *etc.*) are found through Susiana into the highlands (Sialk, Godin, Iblis, Yahya); and the highland-derived JN polychrome ware and ED I 'scarlet ware' extend west into lowland Mesopotamia (Sumer, Diyala).

Chapter 1

Historical Geography of Greater Iran

1. PEOPLES AND PLACES OF GREATER IRAN

Unlike Mesopotamia, where an abundance of texts provides a sound basis for the study of ancient toponymy, the historical geography of third-millennium Iran remains very poorly known. Many Iranian place names are attested in contemporary Sumero-Akkadian royal inscriptions, geographical lists, archival texts and literary compositions as well as in later geographical lists;[1] but, except for Susa, whose biblical connections ensured the preservation of its ancient identity, only one highland centre has been precisely located. That is the Elamite capital Anšan, identified on the basis of cuneiform texts from the site as Tal-i Malyan in Fars.[2] The rest of the eastern highlands remain, from an historical point of view, *terra incognita*.

This ignorance is due chiefly to the dearth of native Iranian documents, a fact which may be attributed only partly to lack of excavation. The primary factor is that bureaucratic literacy seems not to have been as prevalent in third-millennium Iran as in the Mesopotamian lowlands. Excluding the Proto-Elamite texts, which cannot yet be properly read, only a handful of third-millennium Iranian sites have produced texts, and all of them except Anšan are concentrated in the extreme south-west of the country.

Similar problems have been alleviated elsewhere in the semitic Near East (notably Palestine) by the preservation of ancient site names in modern toponyms. In Iran, however, a succession of Indo-European incursions has largely eradicated the earlier Elamite and other native designations. Apart from Susa (Sum. šu-šín, šušin(a), Akk. *šu-šín*) and a few other possible exceptions[3] the modern site names bear little recognisable relation to the ancient toponymy.

By default, therefore, the much larger body of Mesopotamian documentation has become the chief point of reference for the geo-political configuration of early Iran. But this creates other problems. The Sumerocentric orientation of these texts inevitably introduces biases, for which allowance must be made if a balanced picture is to be drawn. In the first place, their range of interest is limited to states with which

---

[1] *LGN*: 1-30 (Road to Hamazi?), 73, 75, 77/178, 203, 230, 237 (Urua [?], Zigini, Uruaz, Der, Lulubum, Nawar), 271-289 (area of Zamua?) (Pettinato 1978; Steinkeller 1986: 37-39; Frayne in press [a]); *ED Names & Professions List*: Biggs 1974: 67 ll. 191, 193 (Zigini, Arawa); *ED God List*: *ibid.*: no. 82 obv. iii:18f. (Elam, Aratta); *Literary Text*: *ibid*. no. 132 ii (URUxAZ); *Lexical Lists*: Deimel 1923: no. 23 obv. ii:12 = Green & Nissen 1987: pl. 38 W21208, 8+16++, i:4 (= entry 30), p. 279 no. 499 (Susa). For later geographical lists see *MSL XI*. On Aratta note also below notes 8, 11.

[2] Reiner 1973.

[3] 'Magan' may be reflected in modern 'Makran', so-named after its inhabitants who are called *Maka* in Old Persian and *Makai* in Greek (Eilers 1983). Note also Frayne's (in press [a]: chart 17) discussion of what he identifies as the 'road to Hamazi' in the *LGN*: 1-30, suggesting that modern Kurdish toponyms retain vestiges of 3rd-mill. GNs; however, since his identifications are sometimes based on these similarities the case can easily become circular.

the Sumerians and Akkadians had military, diplomatic or economic relations. Thus the frequency with which a place is mentioned is a function not only of its importance (an assumption which contributed to the misperception of Susa, rather than Anšan, as the capital of Elam) but also of its proximity. More distant states, even very powerful ones, may be mentioned only rarely, and some no doubt are still not attested at all. Secondly, the accuracy of the geographical information that can be extracted from these citations is often questionable. This is true particularly of royal inscriptions and literary compositions whose historical and geographical fidelity may often have been compromised to propagandistic or literary ends.

Throughout recorded history the border between Mesopotamia and Iran has represented a major ethno-linguistic division. Thus in the third millennium, Sumerian-Akkadian settlement was restricted essentially to the alluvium, while the uplands to the north and east supported a heterogeneous collection of non-Sumerian, non-Semitic peoples. As western Semites (notably the Amorites) from Syria infiltrated southern Mesopotamia during the latter part of the third millennium they too stopped at the edge of the Tigris-Euphrates floodplain. To this day the highlands remain linguistically and ethnically a different world, dominated since the first millennium BC by Indo-Europeans.

From the Mesopotamian perspective, therefore, any highland represented foreign territory, a fact reflected directly in the etymologies of some key Sumerian and Akkadian terms. The Sumerian word for "mountain" (kur) served also for "foreign land" and hence as an appelative for "foreigner", literally a "man of the mountain" (lú kur).[4] Likewise, in the Akkadian and Ur III periods the Akkadian word for "east", *šadium*, came to mean also "foreigner".[5]

Of the eastern peoples attested in third-millennium Mesopotamian documents only the Elamites have left written records of their own. More or less closely associated with Elam, and probably also located in southern Iran, were the peoples of Marhaši, Šimaški, Pašime, Zahara and other regions whose linguistic and ethnic affiliations remain obscure; the only clues lie in the personal and geographical names preserved in Sumerian and Elamite documents. The territory to the north and north-east of Sumer, in the mountains from northern Luristan and Kurdistan around to northern Syria, came increasingly to be dominated in the third millennium by the Hurrians. Other peoples of the Zagros mountains are known only from rare royal inscriptions in Akkadian (the Lulubi and Guti) or just as names.

The following discussion sets out the evidence regarding the locations of the more important eastern toponyms attested in Mesopotamian sources. It is unclear in most cases whether these represent regions or cities, since this distinction is rarely made explicit. The general place-name determinative ki is ambiguous; unless the word for "city" (uru) or "land" (kur) is prefixed – and that is rarely the case[6] – there is no way of telling whether a city or region is intended. To complicate matters further, in some cases a region may be specified by reference to its major city, as the "land(s) [ma-da or *ma-at*] of GN". Thus, as well as the "city Anšan" there appears the "land(s)

---

4   Limet 1972: 124. In the Archaic Uruk texts this seems also to mean "slave" (Klengel 1980-83: 244).
5   Steinkeller 1980; *cf.* Frayne 1992: 627 who prefers "highlander".
6   In 3rd-mill. non-literary texts the principal non-Mesopotamian places specified as uru, 'city', are Anšan, Šariphum (Trans-Tigridian?) and Tišidi (*RGTC 1*: 247; *RGTC 2*: 312 and s.v. places cited). As kur, 'foreign lands', appear Subir, Martu, Elam, Dilmun, Magan and Meluhha (*RGTC 1*: 243; *RGTC 2*: 309 and s.v.; geographical lists [*MSL XI*: 54f.] mention also Tidnum, Gutium, Marhaši, Lulubi and many others). Many more places are qualified as ma-da/*ma-at*, also translated as 'land(s)', perhaps with the sense 'territories [of city X]'. These include the foreign places Šimaški (LÚ.SU.A), Sigriš and Zabšali (both in Šimaški), Anšan, Awan, Elam, Gutium, Hamazi and Susa.

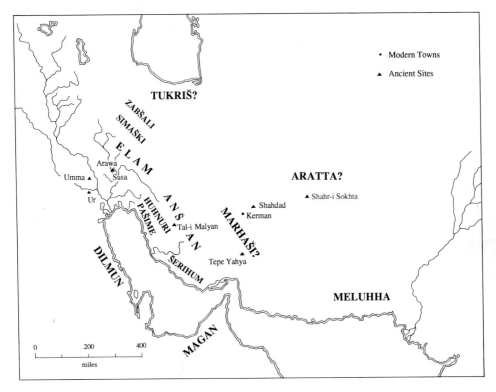

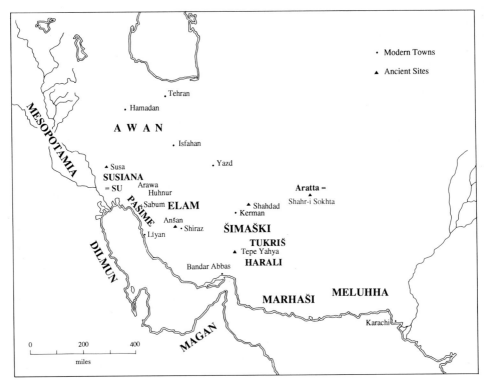

Figure 2.   *Recent reconstructions of the historical geography of third-millennium Iran by Steinkeller (top) and Vallat (bottom).*

of Anšan".[7] On a more general level, this prevents the segregation of names into different levels of the toponomic hierarchy, and thus the determination of which terms are mutually exclusive in reference and which may be subsumed under one another. It is clear from the few well defined cases that in addition to names for towns and cities there were also terms for regions of varying size and definition, for tribal and other ethnically-based territories, as well as for nation-states, empires and transnational entities – the equivalents of such modern terms as the "Low Countries", the "Maghreb", "Latin America", "Europe" – but for the vast majority of toponyms we have no secure basis for deciding into which of these categories they belong and thus for assessing appropriately their 'association' with other regional designations. Mesopotamian scribes may sometimes have blurred distinctions which were not important or relevant to them but which represent genuine ethnic or political divisions. Thus NIM, "Elam(ite)", seems sometimes to have been used with the general sense of "(eastern) highland(er)", and was therefore applied to people whom a true Elamite from Anšan would hardly have regarded as kin.

(a) Aratta

Excluding dubious references in the Archaic texts from Uruk,[8] the toponym Aratta is not attested in non-literary cuneiform documents until the first millennium BC.[9] That the Sumerians of the third millennium believed in a city[10] of this name, however, is indicated by a handful of early literary and lexical texts in which Aratta features, often with the place-name determinative.[11] More details are provided by the famous cycle of narrative poems set in proto-historical times (approximately Early Dynastic II in archaeological terms) which centre around the rivalry between Uruk

---

7   Gudea Stat. B vi:64; IS9 date formula; *RGTC 2*: 10.
8   Green 1980; Nissen 1985b: 228f. Green reads the signs KUR+RU[(ki)], which occur in the subscripts of a group of administrative accounts, as 'Aratta' (Green 1980: 10, 16f.). However, a reading 'Šuruppak', written in later periods SU.KUR.RU[ki], is also possible (*ibid.* and n. 53). In one instance (text no. 21) the signs are accompanied by another which Green reads LAMxKUR (*ibid.*: 17). This yields LAMxKUR.KUR+RU which approximates to the standard writing of Aratta. The parallels cited as grounds for reading the signs in question as LAMxKUR (*ibid.*: 17 n. 98) do not, however, require this value rather than SUxKUR. In view of the nature of the texts (temple administration of livestock) and the occurrence of the toponym KUR+RU in other Archaic texts in association with Sumerian officials (*ibid.*: 10), 'Šuruppak' would seem the more plausible reading. Michalowski (1988: 161 comm. to l. 14) likewise takes the LAMxKUR.RU in Abu Salabikh texts to be Šuruppak.
9   Written syllabically and logographically as LAM.KUR.RU[(ki)] or LAMxKUR.RU[(ki)]; references cited in S. Cohen 1973: 61 n. 90; Wilcke 1969: 40. Note also in later times the Aratrioi near Arachosia in the *Periplus of the Erythraean Sea*, 47 (*cf.* Hansman 1978: 334). The place in southern Babylonia listed by Ptolemy *Geography* V 20 does not represent a plausible Greek transliteration of 'Aratta' as is sometimes claimed (*cf.* Kramer 1932: 119).
10 The tradition of its seven multi-coloured walls (*ELA*: 286f.; *EL*: 413-6; *cf.* S. Cohen 1973: 56 n. 68) suggests a city rather than a regional entity.
11 An ED literary compositions mentioning Aratta is known from Abu Salabikh (Biggs 1974: no. 278, V´5), Ebla (Edzard 1984: nos 20-21, A xi 4 = B xii 3) and possibly Mari (Durant & Bonechi in press); and another is preserved in two Ur III copies at Nippur (Michalowski 1988). A lugal aratta appears in an ED God List (Biggs 1974: no. 82 obv. iii:19). The word aratta[(ki)] also occurs in 3rd-mill. lexical texts, although rarely as a geographical designation. In the Fara texts aratta (without ki) denotes a type of bronze vessel (*LAK* 190; Deimel 1923: no. 20 (VAT 12625) vi 6 11 rev 3; improved readings in Limet 1960: 254 [leaving l. 11 untransliterated]; *cf. ŠL II*: 839 sub 436(1)); while in Gudea Cyl. A xxvii:2 aratta[ki] may be a genuine GN (thus translations of Michalowski 1986: 133 n. 3, Jacobsen 1987: 422) or perhaps serves as an epithet of the place-name Keš, meaning 'glorious', 'venerable' or suchlike (Kramer 1932: 118; Sjöberg *et al.* 1969: 70; *cf.* trans. Alster 1975: 103). The latter reading of this and other passages where aratta[ki] occurs with Keš is based on a 1st-mill. vocabulary where aratta[ki] is given the Akkadian equivalents *kabtu* and *tanadatum* (Diri 88f. and Proto-Diri 547a; *cf.* Kramer 1932: 117f.; Sjöberg *et al.* 1969: 70; *ŠL II*: 436, 4c; *CAD*: s.v. *kabtu* 3). This usage apparently derives from the city's prodigious wealth which was celebrated in Sumerian epics long after direct contact had ceased.

and highland Aratta under Enmerkar and his son Lugalbanda, second and third rulers of Uruk I.[12] In *Enmerkar and Lugalbanda*, Enmerkar leads an army to Aratta and lays siege to the city itself.[13] Most preserved copies of these compositions are Old Babylonian in date but the stories were no doubt composed in the third millennium.[14] On the cumulative weight of this evidence, the probability – though it can be put no more strongly than that – is that such a place existed.[15]

The first-millennium references to Aratta are best accommodated by a location within Mesopotamia[16] and cannot bear on the position of the like-named third-millennium city, which the Sumerian poems portray in clear, albeit general, terms as a distant place, an "inaccessible summit", "in the midst of the (eastern) highlands where the sun rises".[17] Attempts to locate the earlier Aratta have thus been based on the evidence of the epics themselves, in particular the description of the route followed by the messenger from Uruk, and the presumed source areas of the raw materials to which the Arattans had access.

As described in the poems, the long and difficult route to Aratta,[18] supposedly known only to merchants and military guides,[19] passed first through Susa, Sabum (= Agha Jari in eastern Khuzistan?)[20] and other unlocated places[21] and thence on to the mountain land of Anšan. Within (or perhaps beyond)[22] Anšan seven mountains were crossed before reaching Aratta itself. At some point, perhaps after the mountains, the road passed on to a "flatland".[23]

The epics of the Enmerkar-Lugalbanda cycle reflect the great fascination and envy with which the Sumerians regarded Aratta's phenomenal abundance of precious stones and metals. In these compositions it is particularly associated with gold, silver, tin (?) and above all lapis lazuli,[24] which was so common that Aratta is described as the "mountain of bright lapis lazuli" and its temple, appropriately called "the house of lapis lazuli" (é-za-gin-na(-ak)), was said to be made of it.[25] The task of the people of Aratta is stated as being "to ply with gold and bright lapis lazuli" (or: "gold, silver and lapis lazuli") and they are admonished to "[cut] the pure lapis lazuli from the lumps" and, more generally, to "[bring down] ... the mountain stones from

---

[12] Principal editions are: *ELA* – S. Cohen 1973, Jabobsen 1987: 280-319 (trans.); *EL* – Wilcke 1969, Jacobsen 1987: 322-44 (trans.); *EE* – Berlin 1979; *LH* – Hallo 1983 (all with further references), whose line numberings are followed here.

[13] Falkowitz 1983: 106f.; Alster 1990: 62 n. 16, 65-67.

[14] One Ur III text (of *LH*) is known (S. Cohen 1973: 10, n. 19; edn. by Hallo 1983); see also the ED compositions cited above note 11.

[15] *Cf.* Michalowski 1986: 133: "the most plausible conclusion is that Aratta never existed at all, that it is a mythological invention ..." and Moorey 1993, questioning whether Aratta and other Iranian lands were not for the Sumerians a kind of El Dorado – a distant mythical land of vast riches.

[16] S. Cohen 1973: 61; *cf.* Unger 1928: 140. HAR-gud equates Aratta specifically with *māt suhi* (*MSL XI*: 35 l. 12) which lies on the Middle Euphrates (Ismail *et al.* 1983: 193).

[17] S. Cohen 1973: 57, n. 73; Michalowski 1988: 157.

[18] Described in *ELA*: 73-6, 164-9, 108-14, 509-10; *EL*: 342-4; *cf.* Wilcke 1969: 29-40; S. Cohen 1973: 57f.

[19] S. Cohen 1973: 32 n. 20, 58, n. 81; *cf.* A. Shaffer 1983: 307f. n. 4; Kramer 1987: 12.

[20] Vallat 1985: 53; *cf.* Wilcke 1969: 35. Frayne (in press [a]) argues that there were four places of this name and suggests for this one the region of Lake Zeribor (and for the others: in Agha Jari; on the Euphrates; and on the Lower Zab).

[21] They are, in sequence, the Zubi/Black mountain, Mt Sabum and the "Mountain Cave" (Hurrumkurrak); *cf.* Wilcke 1969: 29-40.

[22] That they are within Anšan seems to be the implication of *EL*: 342-44 (Wilcke 1969: 35; Jacobsen 1987: 341); *cf.* Hansman 1978: 332 *contra* Majidzadeh 1976: 107.

[23] S. Cohen 1973: 53f., 58, n. 80; Wilcke 1969: 213f.

[24] *ELA*: 16-19, 26, 38-41, 49-50, 80-81, 124-27, 481-85, 618-19; *EL*: 409-10.

[25] *ELA*: 481, 26, 559.

their mountain (sources)", implying that Arattans could and did mine these materials themselves.[26]

These indications suffice to establish a location in highland Iran east of Anšan (centred on Malyan), but attempts to refine the equation further – *e.g.* identifying it with Shahr-i Sokhta – depend upon dubiously literal interpretations of the epic sources.[27] In particular, the description of the route to Aratta is not an historical itinerary, as is assumed by identifications of the "seven mountains" with particular ranges in Fars or Kerman,[28] but a formulaic expression of the Sumerian poets' (not necessarily accurate) geographical 'world-view'.[29] That Aratta was thought to lie beyond Anšan is clear enough, and this much they may be expected to have got right. But until the boundaries of third-millennium Anšan, *i.e.* Elam, are defined more closely this leaves a great deal of scope. Likewise, as regards the Arattans' connection with raw materials, close localisation is not yet possible since even lapis lazuli, the rarest of their commodities, may have come from sources which are now depleted or unknown. Also, the poets may have failed to distinguish – and perhaps were in no position to distinguish – between genuine source areas and entrepôts where, as archaeological evidence attests, blocks of lapis were cut down and worked along routes in both southern and northern Iran (Shahr-i Sokhta and Tepe Hissar) at considerable distances from the mines of Badakhshan.[30] Aratta's association with tin[31] is too tenuous to warrant any argument concerning the recently discovered deposits of this metal in Afghanistan.

Aratta is once implied to be accessible from Uruk by boat, a detail which, if confirmed, would require a complete revision of all present suggestions.[32]

(b) Elam

Throughout the third millennium and long after, Elam represented the most important and powerful of Sumer's eastern neighbours. The relationship between the two was always precariously equivocal, a *status quo* of nervous mutual respect being punctuated by periods of alternating rapprochement and hostility, not infrequently culminating in full-scale war. At times a truce or even an alliance might be struck, but more often the two great powers were at loggerheads. Mesopotamian rulers from Eannatum on proved their mettle by "conquering" Elam, and the Elamites for their part were ever ready to descend on the lowlands in times of weakness. This they did with devastating effectiveness in the last years of the third millennium, destroying a political and cultural pre-eminence which the Sumerians never regained.

Elam is also much the best known of the third-millennium kingdoms of the east, thanks to extensive excavation in Susiana and, more recently, at Anšan in Fars; and also due to the fact that the Elamites, alone of Sumer's neighbours, were a literate society.[33] Using first the still undeciphered Proto-Elamite pictographic and linear

---

26   *ELA*: 618f. (*cf.* S. Cohen 1973: 286), 40, 50.

27   See previously Herrmann 1968 (south or south-east of the Caspian); Majidzadeh 1976, 1982: 66 (Kerman); Sarianidi 1971 (Badakhshan); Hansman 1978, Steinkeller 1982: fig. 2, Vallat 1985 (Shahr-i Sokhta); S. Cohen 1973 (Hamadan-Nehavend-Kermanshah-Sanandaj); Kramer 1963: 269, 275 (bewtween Lake Urmia and the Caspian).

28   Majidzadeh 1976, Hansman 1978.

29   Berlin 1983: 22, 24.

30   Shahr-i Sokhta – Tosi 1974, Tosi & Piperno 1973. Hissar – Bulgarelli 1979.

31   *ELA*: 17.

32   *ELA*: 148f. (*cf.* S. Cohen 1973: 52 n. 41, 56); *cf.* Kramer 1977: 61 n. 16. It is interesting in this connection that the Karkeh River was known to the Assyrians in the 1st mill. as the "lapis lazuli river", the *uqnû* (Speiser 1967: 31-33).

33   Others (*e.g.* the Guti) have left rare monumental inscriptions only.

scripts,[34] and, from the Akkadian period, Mesopotamian cuneiform, the Elamites kept records which largely parallel the concerns of scribes to the west: the administration of daily affairs and the celebration of royal achievements. But the language of the Elamite texts is quite different, being related neither to Sumerian nor Akkadian, nor indeed to any other known language.[35] Through these texts, supplemented by more copious Mesopotamian documentation, where "Elamites" and "Susians" are often mentioned as traders and other free travellers as well as prisoners and conscript labourers, a skeletal picture of Elamite society and political history has been reconstructed.[36]

For many years the almost exclusive concentration of archaeological work on Susa led naturally, but mistakenly, to the assumption that that site was the capital and geographical focus of Elam in the third and second millennia, as was certainly the case in the Persian period. Elam was thus identified directly with Susiana, and the material culture of Susa was taken as paradigmatic of Elam in general.[37]

The identification of Tal-i Malyan in Fars as the city of Anšan, for much of its history the Elamite capital, enormously expanded the geographical horizons of Elam and inspired Vallat's thorough reinterpretation of the geography and structure of the Elamite federation.[38] Through analysis of Elamite titulature, and circumstantial evidence from popular religion, onomastics *etc.*, Vallat demonstrated that Susa, far from being the geographical and political centre of Elam, lay at the very western periphery, its lowland position being virtually unique among major Elamite centres.[39] This is reflected in the "alternance and duality" of Susian material culture and ethnic make-up, at once both Elamite and Mesopotamian.[40] Susian names were predominantly Sumero-Semitic; before the thirteenth century, Elamite deities were out-numbered by Mesopotamian ones; and, most indicative of all, there were virtually no Elamite texts at Susa after the Proto-Elamite period – for almost a thousand years, such Susian documentation as exists employs Sumerian and Akkadian. Susiana's separation from Elam proper is reflected in the titulature of the Sukkalmah period (early second millennium) which knew both a "sukkal of Elam and Šimaški" and a "sukkal of Susa", and perhaps also in the second-millennium geographical designation *šu-še-en*, which Vallat sees not as a variant writing of *šu-šu-un*, "Susa", but as a designation for "Susiana" in distinction to "Elam".[41]

Elam, on the other hand, was essentially a highland entity. This too is reflected in the logogram used to write its name in Sumerian and Akkadian, NIM meaning

---

[34] Stolper 1984: 7f.
[35] Caucasian and Dravidian connections (McAlpine 1981) have been suggested but remain unproven; see generally Reiner 1969.
[36] Stolper 1984; Hinz 1972; Sigrist & Butz 1986: 31.
[37] *E.g.* Amiet 1966.
[38] Reiner 1973 (previously Hansman 1972); Vallat 1980. While this identification has been universally accepted it should be noted that the inscriptions concerned date to the 12th century BC. A residual question mark hangs over the identification of 3rd-mill. Anšan since survey and excavation at the site indicate that Malyan, and indeed the rest of the Kur valley, was devoid of permanent settlement from *ca.* 2800/2600 to 2200 BC, precisely the period when Anšan becomes prominent in historical sources: "Such population as still remained in Fars followed the pastoral nomadic way of life, leaving the fields of Anshan barren until the beginning of the Kaftari Phase, late in the 3rd mill." (Sumner 1989: 135f.). This remains a glaring enigma.
[39] Of other major Elamite cities, only Awan may confidently be located in the lowlands. Both are conspicuously absent among places supplying NIM, "highlanders" in Ur III texts (Fish 1955; *RGTC 2*: 311).
[40] Amiet 1979a.
[41] Vallat 1980: 3.

literally "high, elevated".[42] Elam was thus the "highland" and its people were "highlanders". Gudea's reference to the "Susians of Susiana and the Elamites of Elam" therefore reflects a genuine and important distinction, albeit one which Mesopotamian scribes elsewhere blur over.[43] Anšan was the primary capital of Elam proper and the two toponyms may therefore alternate in royal titles and other contexts.[44] Documents at Anšan were written in Elamite[45] and the pantheon was not supplemented by deities from Susa or Akkad.

Various other places were closely associated with Elam, some even serving as the seats of 'Elamite' dynasties. On this basis Elam is often regarded as having constituted a federation of states, rather than a single polity.[46] Most recently Vallat has argued that a distinction should be drawn between an 'Elamite Kingdom' proper, consisting of Anšan and its territory, and an 'Elamite Empire', including also various combinations of these other regions. The two most prominant confederates were Awan and Šimaški, which feature in the titles of third and early second millennium Elamite rulers at Susa. An Old Babylonian school text from that site records two sets of twelve names which it designates respectively as "kings of Awan" and "kings of Šimaški" (Fig. 4).[47] Although the parallel equi-numerous listings are clearly schematic, contemporary references to some of these rulers confirm that the tradition preserved by the king list is essentially historical. The Dynasty of Awan, familiar from the *Sumerian King List* and Akkadian royal inscriptions, was the earlier, its later rulers being contemporary with the kings of Agade and early Ur III.[48] The last named, Puzur-Inšušinak, has left inscriptions in linear Elamite (Stolper's "Proto-Elamite B") and Akkadian at Susa, of which he was also the governor. The location of Awan remains unclear; perhaps also in Susiana.[49] Šimaški, the nominal seat of the second dynasty, was a highland region perhaps as remote as Kerman (see below p. 32). The dynasty was founded in the course of the Ur III empire, which one of its members (probably Kindattu) was instrumental in destroying. Three Šimaškian kings are attested at Susa by contemporary building, votive and seal inscriptions, one of them – Idadu – being accorded the title "King of Šimaški and Elam".[50]

The extent of the Elamite empire, though clearly much greater than was envisaged twenty years ago, remains difficult to define in any detail. It included at least the territory on the road from Susa through the town of Huhnuri (region of

---

[42] The Elamite name was *ha-da-am-ti*, which Hinz suggests be analysed as "god's land", from *hal*, "land" and *tamt*, "(gracious) lord" (Hinz 1971: 644; Hinz & Koch 1987: I 594 (*hal*), 584 (*ha-da-am-ti*)). Damerow & Englund 1989: 1 n. 1 suggest that **elam** may be an Akkadianized rendering of both Sumerian and Elamite terms influenced by *elûm*, "to be high".

[43] Cyl. A xv:6f. *Cf.* the ED III Lagaš account texts citing maritime merchants who brought goods by boat from "Elam", which can here only be Susiana (M. Lambert 1954: 64f. DP 423; Leemans 1960: 175). On the other hand, as well as the specific geo-political entity of Elam, NIM seems often to have been used by Sumerian scribes more generally to refer to any "(eastern) highland(er)" (Zadock 1987: 3f.).

[44] *E.g.* in descriptions of Huhnuri as "the 'bolt' of Anšan/Elam" (Vallat 1980: 4).

[45] The only foreign-language texts, both in OB script, are a Sumerian document and a school text (language unidentified) from Kaftari levels (late 3rd-early 2nd mill.) (Stolper 1976: 90).

[46] *E.g.* Hinz 1971: 648.

[47] Scheil 1932: iv.

[48] *RGTC 1, 2*: s.v. The 9th king, Hišepratep, is probably the Hisibrasini whose son (Luhišan) was captured by Sargon. The 11th king, Hita, is perhaps the co-signatory of the Naram-Sin treaty; the text is damaged at the crucial point. Puzur-Inšušinak, the last king, has recently been convincingly assigned to the early Ur III period (Steinkeller 1989).

[49] *RGTC 2*: 20.

[50] Stolper 1982: 44.

Behbehan?),[51] known as "the 'bolt' of Anšan/Elam",[52] to Anšan. Vallat takes the eastern limit of Elam to be defined by the western border of the Kavir-Lut deserts southwards to the Gulf, but there is no hard evidence: ceramic parallels ('Susa II' style) extending to Jalyan and a linear Elamite inscription at Shahdad are uncertain guides at best.[53] The definition of the southern boundary also remains vague. Economic texts indicate that Elam (perhaps only Susiana?) could be approached by boat but there is no indication how much of the Iranian coastline was Elamite. Positive evidence exists only for the port of Bushire where sporadic inscriptions of Šimut-wartaš, Humbanumena and other rulers evidence Elamite control from the eighteenth century on.[54] But since the earlier attribution of one Bushire inscription to the Akkadian period is doubtful,[55] third-millennium control of this region cannot be proved. Steinkeller argues that Bushire represented the southern limit of ancient Pašime, which oscillated between Elamite and Mesopotamian control in the later third millennium (below p. 19). In the north-west some negative indication of the limits of Elam is provided by references to the Guti, Lulubi and other non-Elamite (?) peoples who seem to have inhabited the Central Zagros, probably as far south as Luristan.

The Elamite hegemony was not static but expanded and contracted as Elam's political fortunes rose and fell. The one point at which we are given a more precise definition is around the turn of the third/second millennia in the reign of Išbi-Erra of Isin. This is immediately after the collapse of Ur when Elam's power may be presumed to have been near its height.[56] The source is a praise-hymn to Išbi-Erra which describes the kingdom of the Šimaškian-Elamite king Kindattu (almost certainly the ruler responsible for the destruction of Ur) as stretching:

> [from] Pašime, the 'breast' (i.e. coast) of the sea (= Persian Gulf), [to] the border of Zabša[li] (and) [from] Arawa, the 'lock' of Elam, [to] the border of Marha[ši][57]

The locations of these places (except Arawa) are discussed below.[58] Here it may be noted that they are much less clearly fixed than is Elam itself, and that most suggestions for their placement also depend on this passage (in particular the implied contiguity with heartland Elam and the pairing – along axes? – of "from X to Y"). Steinkeller takes the Pašime-Zabšali axis to extend from the head of the Gulf through Fars some way towards the Caspian Sea and the Arawa-Marhaši axis to

---

[51] Duchene (1986) argues for a location near Arrajan in the region of Behbehan, where the Susa-Anšan road enters the highlands. Huhnuri is associated with Sabum and Pašime (*ibid.*: 68f.). *Cf.* previously *RGTC 2*: 77f.; Hinz 1975: 448 (Qal'e-ye Toll, 20 km south of Izeh/Malamir).

[52] This may involve a pun, *huhn* (*hu-hu-un*) being Elamite for "wall" (Hinz 1975: 488).

[53] Vallat 1985: 50; Miroschedji 1974 (Jalyan); Hiebert & Lamberg-Karlovsky 1992: fig. 4 (Shahdad).

[54] Pézard 1914: 39-92. This dating assumes that the untitled Šimut-wartaš at Bushire is the sukkal of that name. Humbanumena dates to the 13th century.

[55] Reiner 1965.

[56] *Cf.* Vallat 1990: 122, extending Elam under the sukkalmahs from the Persian Gulf to the Caspian Sea and from the Mesopotamian border to the Lut Desert.

[57] van Dijk 1978; translation after Steinkeller 1982: 240.

[58] Arawa is almost certainly to be identified with Urua ((ú)URUxA(a); Ebla *LGN*: *ar-ù*[ki]), probably located in north-west Khuzistan (Steinkeller 1982: 244-46; Frayne in press [a]: LGN 73). Conquered first by Eannatum (*AWBI*: Ean. 2=*SARI I*: La. 3.5) and Sargon (C7:Beischr. [c]; D-2-3), Urua maintained strong commercial contacts with Sumer (especially Lagaš), later becoming an Ur III province ruled by an appointed ensi (Šulgi-zimi, attested from Šulgi to Šu-Sin) and paying taxes to Ur (Steinkeller 1982: nn. 27-29 for further details).

extend from the Mesopotamian-Iranian border to central or eastern Iran.[59] It is not certain, however, that this definition of Šimaškian Elam is inclusive rather than exclusive; for as well as places which may elsewhere be treated as part of Elam (Arawa, Zabšali, Pašime) it also includes one land (Marhaši) which was not. Might Išbi-Erra have sought to inflate his own victory over Kindattu by exaggerating the Elamite's earlier dominion?

(c) Zahara

The toponym Zahara occurs only in the Akkadian period and exclusively in royal inscriptions, apparently lying outside the range of direct economic and diplomatic contact and diplomacy. Zahara had apparently ceased to exist as an integral political entity (or at least no longer fell within the Mesopotamian purview) by Ur III times when references cease.

An inscription of Rimuš relates a major expedition against Elam, Parahšum and Zahara, whose leader (GÌR.NITÁ) is called Sargabi.[60] The association with Elam (the two armies assembled together "in the midst of Parahšum") is the only indication of Zahara's location given in this account. It is again paired with Elam in the year names of Šarkališarri describing a campaign against "Elam and Zahara opposite (*in pūti*) Akšak".[61] While this reference to Akšak, located on the Tigris south of the Diyala confluence,[62] fixes the site of engagement, it does not help with the location of Elam or Zahara.

In the present state of knowledge therefore a location for Zahara somewhere on the periphery of Elam seems most likely, but a more precise judgement is not yet possible.[63]

(d) Pašime / Mišime

Information relating to Pašime (Sumerian Mišime) has recently been collected by Steinkeller and will be only briefly reviewed here.[64] The land or city of Mišime (it only ever has the ki determinative) is first mentioned in Mesopotamian sources by Eannatum, who claims to have conquered the place in a campaign against Elam, in which he also attacked Uruaz and Arua.[65] It was probably not until the Akkadian period, however, that Pašime was directly ruled by Mesopotamia. Under Maništušu the place had an Akkadian governor, Ilšurabi, whose son appears among the witnesses on the Obelisk of Maništušu.[66] Šulgi later married a daughter to the ruler of Pašime, one Šuddabani, an act which Steinkeller sees as part of a vassal relationship.[67] Later, under Amar-Suen or Šu-Sin, perhaps after having revolted from Sumerian control, Pašime was incorporated into the Ur III state. Although there is no record of its conquest, Pašime appears among the many regions administered by Arad-Nanna.[68] A Drehem text records the sheep of Pašime delivered (as taxes) by the

---

[59] Steinkeller 1982.
[60] Rimuš C6.
[61] D-25-26.
[62] *RGTC 1*: s.v.; Frayne in press [a]: LGN99 suggests Tell Sinker on the ancient course of the Tigris north-west of Baghdad.
[63] *Cf. RGTC 1*: s.v. and end maps, which place it in the mountains immediately north-west of Susiana.
[64] Steinkeller 1982: 240-43.
[65] *ABWI*: Ean.2 iv:12-19.
[66] Scheil 1900: 16 A xiv:14-17. Note also the "[...] ensi Mišime" (late Sargonic?) (Steinkeller 1982: 242 n. 16).
[67] Steinkeller 1982: 241f., n. 16.
[68] Steinkeller (1982: 242 n. 17) suggests that its conquest may have occurred as part of Amar-Suen's campaign against Huhnuri.

"chancellor" (sukkalmah), *i.e.* Arad-Nanna, in ŠS6.[69] However, with the collapse of Ur it fell to the Šimaškian-Elamite king Kindattu, of whose empire it formed one of the limits in the praise-hymn to Išbi-Erra.

Described there as "the breast (*i.e.* coast) of the sea (=Persian Gulf)", Pašime is paired with "the border of Zabša[li]" as opposite extremities of Kindattu's broad hegemony. A coastal position at the head of the Gulf, not far from Sumerian Apišal, is confirmed by archival texts.[70] A Lagaš text citing "Elamites (NIM) of Huhnuri and Pašime, who came from Huhnuri" suggests a frontier with this Elamite bordertown, elsewhere called "the 'bolt' of Elam".[71] Steinkeller suggests a territory extending from southern Khuzistan along the Gulf coast as far as Bushire.[72]

Closely associated with Elam in historical inscriptions, Pašime may have been an Elamite-speaking region but there is no direct evidence as to its linguistic or ethnic character.

(e) Lulubum

The Lulubi[73] appear in Mesopotamian historical and literary documents as a people of the eastern mountains, the frequent object of military operations but not effectively brought under lowland control until Assyrian times.[74] First mentioned in the Akkadian period,[75] they continue to feature intermittently in descriptions of eastern campaigns into Neo-Assyrian times, although from the Old Babylonian period on the term was used also as a more general designation for eastern mountain folk and thus becomes of less precision for historical purposes.[76] Even in the later third millennium there can be no guarantee that the term always retained precisely the same ethnic and geographical designation.

Evidence of contact with Lulubum begins in the reign of Naram-Sin who waged war "in the mountains of Lulubum",[77] presumably conquering the peoples he encountered there and celebrated in his famous victory stele from Sippar, later taken to Susa. The Gutian king Erridupizir claims to have suppressed a rebellion in Lulubum when it was inspired to revolt by Simurrum.[78] Soon thereafter Lagaš texts dating to the dynasty of Gudea refer to foreigners, including a Lulubian and the "'sons' of Šimbišhu" (*cf.* Šimpišhuk, father of Puzur-Inšušinak), who are perhaps prisoners of war from an eastern campaign of Ur-Nammu and Gudea.[79] In any case, Šulgi claims the defeat of Lulubum (along with Simurrum, Urbilum and Karahar) in his years 25, 44 and 45. These other places are associated with Hurrians and such an affiliation cannot be excluded for Lulubum, although it is not among the places linked to people bearing Hurrian names.[80] Like the others, it paid taxes (gún) to Ur.[81] A damaged section of a Šu-Sin text describing a campaign against Šimaški includes among the labels of the defeated enemy leaders one "Waburtum, [e]nsi of

---

69 *TLB 3*: 34 v:8´,12´.
70 *E.g.* an Umma text mentions the "personnel of the roadhouse of the coast of Pašime" (Steinkeller 1982: 242f., n. 18).
71 *ITT 5*: 8212.
72 Steinkeller 1982: 242f.
73 Surveys by Klengel 1965, 1988.
74 Klengel 1965: 362 [Assurnasirpal II]).
75 A place Luluban in the Ebla *LGN* (no. 230) is tentatively identified by Steinkeller as Lulubum (1986: 39).
76 Klengel 1965: 354.
77 NS 4; see below p. 111.
78 *AKI*: Gutium C2, C3.
79 *RTC* 249, *MVN* 10: 92; Steinkeller 1988a: 53, n. 21.
80 Michalowski 1986: 146f.
81 Steinkeller 1987: n. 56.

Inscription

Figure 3. Rock relief of Anubanini at Sarpol-i Zohab. Late third to early second millennium.

[Lu?]lubum.[82] If correctly restored, this would imply that Lulubum had fallen under the control of Šimaški, forcing Šu-Sin to reassert Sumerian sovereignty.

In historical-literary compositions Lulubum, under a king named [...-a]-el/Lapana-ila, is included among the foreign lands which revolted against Naram-Sin.[83]

There is so far no positive evidence as to the nature of the Lulubian language or culture beyond the brief references of Mesopotamian literature and the rock reliefs at Darband-i Gawr, Sarpol-i Zohab and Darband-i Ramgan.[84] While they are listed in literary compositions among eastern enemies the Lulubi are not charicatured in the vitriolic terms reserved for the Gutians, Amorites and others, perhaps because they

---

[82] Ur C2: Beischr. h.
[83] Grayson & Sollberger 1976: Text L i:4´ (Lullûm); *cf.* Hittite version Güterbock 1938: 68 l. 10 (Lulliui).
[84] Klengel 1965: 350 with bibliog.; Kutscher 1989: BT2+3 (Erridupizir). Rock reliefs: Börker-Klähn 1982: nos 30-32, 34, N34; *AKI*: Varia 6, 7.

were not implicated in the major invasions which disrupted Mesopotamian life in the later third millennium.[85]

In Akkadian times there seems to have been close contact between the the the peoples of Lulubum and Gasur (later Nuzi), where it is referred to as Lulubuna. Other Sargonic texts mention sheep, goats and cattle from Lulubum, in exchange for which the Mesopotamians traded grain. Falkenstein suggested that the *lu-lu-bu-(na)ki* mentioned in Ur III texts from Lagaš represents a colony of these same people (perhaps POWs?), residing somewhere within the state of Lagaš.[86]

The location of Lulubum can be defined with greater confidence than any other Zagros kingdom thanks to the rock relief of "Anubanini, mighty king, king of Lulubum" preserved at Sarpol-i Zohab on the Khorasan Road, 140 kilometres west of Kermanshah (Fig. 3). This monument provides at least one fixed point for the territory of Lulubum in the late third or second millennium (the date of Anubanini cannot be more precisely prescribed), though whether at the centre (as usually assumed) or on the periphery cannot be determined. The area of Suleimaniyah is often cited as the region's focus.[87]

(f) The 'Hurrian frontier'[88]

The non-Semitic, non-Indo-European Hurrians are first attested in the late third millennium on the hilly northern and north-eastern fringes of Mesopotamia. By the mid second millennium they had spread westwards as far as Anatolia, Palestine and even Egypt, where these roving newcommers had a considerable impact on Near Eastern literature, religion and perhaps also material culture.[89] Syria became the focus of Hurrian settlement and the base of their second-millennium empire Mitanni. The first-millennium empire of Urartu around Lake Van seems to have coalesced principally from their descendents.[90]

It is only the easternmost Hurrians, who are also the earliest attested, who concern us here, those settled at the eastern end of what Hallo has called the 'Hurrian frontier' – the band of uplands stretching from the upper reaches of the Diyala through Urbilum and the Upper Tigris to the Upper Habur.[91]

As a people and culture the early Hurrians remain poorly known: their language is unrelated to any other except Urartian;[92] they are not characterised in any detail in Sumerian and Akkadian literature; and their art and material culture remain difficult to differentiate from that of the other Near Eastern peoples of the regions they inhabited.[93] Early studies of Hurrian history were confused by the Mesopotamians' sometimes interchangable use of the terms "Hurrian" and "Subarian" (the latter further confused by modern scholars with the "Su-people" (LÚ.SU(.A)), now read

---

[85] Except perhaps as the Umman Manda, led by the sons of (the Gutian king?) Anubanini, who are "people with sheldrake bodies, men with raven faces" (Gurney 1955: l. 31, translat. Cooper 1983a: 31).

[86] Klengel 1965: 351; *RGTC 2*: 112. Klengel 1988: 164. Falkenstein 1966: I 34.

[87] *E.g.* Klengel 1965: 350.

[88] For a recent survey of the Hurrians see Wilhelm 1989.

[89] Moorey 1989.

[90] Against the traditional assumption that the Urartians are the descendents of the Hurrians, some scholars now regard them as a separate branch (*e.g.* Wilhelm 1989: 4).

[91] Hallo, placing Simurrum in the Upper Diyala, began the frontier there; but since new evidence suggests that Simurrum, "which clearly represented the gateway to Hurrian territory from the Mesopotamian point of view" (Hallo 1978: 72), may lie further north on the Lower Zab (al Fouadi 1978 and below, main text), so perhaps should be the beginning of the Hurrian frontier. *Cf.* Wilhelm 1989: 7.

[92] The only plausible connections are with the North-East Caucasian group (Edzard 1975; Diakonoff & Starostin 1986; Greppin 1991: 721f. n. 11).

[93] Stein in Wilhelm 1989; Moorey 1989.

"Šimaški"), leading many scholars for long to identify the two. While the area of Hurrian settlement largely overlaps with the region known in the third millennium as Subir/Subartu, the ethnicon "Hurrian" is ultimately an independent designation which had its own criteria of application.

Leaving aside possible Hurrian etymologies for some Sumerian words,[94] which may indicate an early third millennium presence, the earliest clearly Hurrian personal and geographical names appear in Old Akkadian inscriptions which seem to place them to the north and north-east of Mesopotamia. A very fragmentary inscription of Narm-Sin describes a campaign against Subir (Subartu) in which most of the reconstructable names are Hurrian.[95] Of a total of forty-nine names only one, Azuhinum, is mentioned elsewhere.[96] It occurs in a year name of Naram-Sin: "the year Naram-Sin was victorious in a campaign against Subir in Azuhinum and captured Dahišatal". Unfortunately, this is not a decisive fixed point for there is evidence of two places of this name: one in the Habur, the other on the Lower Zab near Nuzi. Fadhil and Wilhelm assume that the one near Nuzi is meant here but Michalowski reserves judgement.[97] In the 'Great Revolt', a literary composition describing a revolt against Naram-Sin (below pp. 114-16), Simurrum, which was a major Hurrian centre in Ur III times, has a ruler with the Hurrian name Puttimatal.[98] An inscription of the Ur III or Isin-Larsa ruler of Simurrum Iddin-Sin found at Bitwata on the upper reaches of the Lower Zab north of the Raniya plain near the Iranian border (now the Dukan Lake)[99] may indicate that Simurrum was located near there, rather than south of the Diyala (as Hallo). Frayne attributes one of the Sarpol-i Zohab reliefs to Iddin-Sin or his son.[100]

There are isolated references to people with Hurrian names in southern Mesopotamia at Nippur, Girsu and possibly Umma at this time.[101] Possible Hurrian names at Old Akkadian Gasur (Nuzi) are rare and inconclusive.[102] Suggested Hurrian elements among the Eblaite pantheon are unlikely.[103]

Considerable numbers of Hurrians were brought back to Sumer as prisoners of war in the wake of campaigns against the Hurrian frontier and subsequently appear there in account texts, especially as labourers.[104] They were apparently quick to adapt to Mesopotamian life and the next generation often took Sumerian names. But Hurrian merchants, messengers and other free visitors also appear and a significant number of Hurrians seem to have been peacefully absorbed into Mesopotamian

---

[94] *E.g.* tabira, "copper worker" (Wilhelm 1989: 8f.).
[95] Michalowski 1986b. The royal name is lost but the attribution is soundly based on the epithets "he who shattered the might of Subir" and "king of the four quarters" (Michalowski 1986a: 4).
[96] Michalowski 1986a: 10f.; possibly also [H]a-su-ba-an-šè, the Hašu'anum of OAkk administrative texts which seems to lie east of the Tigris.
[97] D-13. For location: *RGTC 3*: 27f. (Habur), Lewy 1968: 162; Fadhil 1983: 72; Wilhelm 1989: 8 (Lower Zab); Michalowski 1986a: 11.
[98] Grayson & Sollberger 1976: 120 G29. Note however that a year name of the king records the ensi of Simurrum with the non-Hurrian name Baba (D-12). Other 3rd-mill. rulers of Simurrum are: under Erridupizir, Kanišba king of Simurrum (Kutscher 1989: BT2+3); and under Šulgi, Tabban-Darah ensi of Simurrum (Hallo 1978: 74f.). See also following note.
[99] al Fouadi 1978; for early Isin date see Frayne 1992: 634f. Interestingly, neither Iddin-Sin nor his son Zabazuna have Hurrian names.
[100] Varia 7; Frayne 1992: 634.
[101] Michalowski 1986: 139 n. 16.
[102] Gelb 1944: 52f.
[103] Astour 1978:3; *cf.* Archi 1979-80: 171.
[104] Gelb 1973: 79f. A group from Simanum was settled in the neighbourhood of Nippur by Šu-Sin (Civil 1967: 36; Gelb 1973: 76f., 91f.). Note also 113 women and 59 children from Šariphum (Gelb 1973: 75f.).

society, where they could rise to become scribes and other high-status officials.[105] Many Hurrians were also employed as officials in the administration of the highland provinces.[106]

Scattered clues allow a broad definition of the geographical pattern of early Hurrian settlement. In the Akkadian or Post-Akkadian period[107] a ruler with the Hurrian name Atalšen (or Arišen) claimed the title "King of Urkiš and Nawar". Urkiš, later a major cult centre of the Hurrian god Kumarbi, is most plausibly located at Tell Amuda on the Syrian-Turkish border.[108] Nawar was previously identified with Assyrian Namri/Namar in the Zagros mountains but recent discoveries have shown that there was a Nawar in the Habur region, very probably at Tell Brak, and this must now be considered the more probable location in this context.[109] More questionable historically is the reference in a late Hittite-Hurrian ritual text from Hattuša, purporting to describe events in the Old Akkadian period, to a king of Tukriš with the Hurrian name Kiklipatal.[110]

References to Hurrian geographical and personal names proliferate in the Ur III period, by which time the area of Hurrian settlement can confidently be charted in a broad arc from the headwaters of the Diyala north-west to the upper Habur, an area of principally dry-farming land above the 400mm isohyet. The southern part of this arc, as far north as Urbilum (and occasionally to Simanum near the Syrian border), became the primary arena of military activity in Neo-Sumerian times. From midway through the reign of Šulgi, year names, royal inscriptions, messenger texts and other archival documents record a regular exchange of messengers, as well as military expeditions and occasionally the betrothal of a royal daughter from Sumer to a patchwork of Hurrian principalities, many of which were eventually brought under Sumerian control and paid taxes to Ur.[111] Prominent among the toponyms – moving roughly southeast to north-west – are: Karahar, Simurrum, Harši, Kimaš, Humurti, Šašrum, Šetirša, Gumaraši, Hibilat, Urbilum (Arbela), Simanum, Mardaman and Šerši.[112] Lulubum also appears with Simurrum, Karahar and Urbilum as the object of Šulgi's attack (Š44-45) but whether it too was Hurrian remains unclear (above p. 20). Ninua (Nineveh) had a Hurrian leader – Tišatal – under Šu-Sin.[113] Another Tišatal was ruler (*endan*) of Urkiš and now (Ur III?) inscribes a foundation inscription in Hurrian, the earliest extant full text in this language.[114]

From the preponderance of Hurrian geographical and personal names associated with this region,[115] it seems likely that the population was predominantly

---

[105] Already in the Sargonic period a stone tablet from Nippur cites the Hurrian names Tupin and Šehrinewri (or Šehrinibri), perhaps ex-POWs (Gelb 1959: 187; Edzard & Kammenhuber 1972-75: 509).

[106] *E.g.* the Ur III general of Arrapha, Hašibatal, who had a son named Puzur-Šulgi who married a woman called Ninhedu (Limet 1972: 134).

[107] The text concerned (Varia 16) cannot be closely dated, but Atalšen's curse formula parallels that of Sargonic kings, so it must be contemporary or later than that dynasty (Wilhelm 1989: 9 [probably late Gutian-early Ur III]; Michalowski 1986: 138f. [Sargonic, Ur III or later]; Frayne 1992: 635 [Ur III]).

[108] *RGTC 2*: 224.

[109] *E.g.* Hallo 1978: 71, n. 4; Oates 1987: 188f. (Brak). More recently an OAkk seal has been recovered citing 'Nagar'. This GN also occurs on another Brak sealing with Hurrian names while the standard later form 'Nawar' appears on a tablet from the Mitanni Palace.

[110] Kammmenhuber 1976: 166f.; Wilhelm 1989: 9f.

[111] Hallo 1978; Steinkeller 1987. For an outline of these campaigns see below pp. 131-33.

[112] For suggested locations see *RGTC 1-2*: s.v.; Hallo 1978: map and *passim*; Steinkeller 1987: 38, map.

[113] Whiting 1976.

[114] Perrot & Nougayrol 1948.

[115] Gelb 1944: 112-14; Goetze 1953a:; Limet 1972: 135-37; Hallo 1978: 72 n. 16; Michalowski 1986: 146f.; Kutscher 1989: 70.

Hurrian.[116] This can be confirmed on a sounder onomastic basis when archives from the region become available in the early second millennium. These attest heavy Hurrian settlement from Shemsharra westwards to Tell Rimah, Chagar Bazar and Alalakh.

(g) Kimaš

The land of Kimaš[117] occurs in Sargonic and later Mesopotamian sources as a highland region of Iran within the general orbit of Elamite influence, if not always fully under its control. Puzur-Inšušinak claims to have supressed a rebellion in Kimaš and Hu-urti (Hurtum).[118] These same places and Harši were the objects of Šulgi's campaigns in years 46 to 48. But the Elamites maintained control of the region at least sporadically during the Ur III period since a certain Hun-NI.NI uses the joint title "ensi of Kimaš and šagin (GÌR.NITÁ) of the land of Elam".[119]

Kimaš is most often mentioned in the context of Ur III diplomatic missions and economic exchanges. It is one of the most frequently cited places in the 'Messenger Texts' and "highlanders" (NIM, here "troops"?) from Kimaš are also well attested.[120] Outside diplomacy, the chief interest of Kimaš for Mesopotamia lay in trade, especially as a supplier of cattle.[121]

Regarding location, the principal clues are: Kimaš's close association with Elam in the titles of Hun-NI.NI (though with the re-siting of Anšan this now allows greater scope than was previously recognised); Gudea's claim to have imported copper from Abullat in Kimaš;[122] and Šulgi's association of Kimaš with Hu-urti and Harši.[123] If Kimaš was really a copper source zone, and not just an entrepôt, a location for Gudea's Abullat near the mines of the Tiyari mountains north of Amadiyeh is possible.[124] Šulgi's conquest places Kimaš in the broadly Hurrian realm, though how far east this extended is unclear. Hun-NI.NI's dual title covering both Kimaš and Elam expands rather than limits the options.[125] Steinkeller includes Kimaš within the territory of Gutium, assuming this to be a broader toponym (see below).

(h) Gutium[126]

The Gutians, a fierce Zagros people, occupy the centre stage of third-millennium Mesopotamian history only once but their impact was swift and epochal nonetheless, bringing the once-mighty kingdom of Akkad to an end and effecting the first recorded wholesale invasion of southern Mesopotamia. Not surprisingly, this had a lasting effect on the Mesopotamian consciousness and the Gutians are reviled in Mesopotamian literature as the paradigm of bestial, uncivilised mountain-dwellers:

---

[116] *Cf.* Michalowski 1986: 139, arguing that geographical names are more conclusive evidence of Hurrian settlement than personal names.

[117] Usually ki-maš[ki], once preceded by *ma-at* (*RGTC 2*: 100).

[118] *AKI*: Elam 2.

[119] Edzard & Röllig 1976-80: 593. An unnamed "ensi of Kimaš" (*RGTC 2*: 100) perhaps also refers to the same ruler.

[120] *RGTC 2*: 100f.; Fish 1954; *idem* 1955: s.v.

[121] Edzard & Röllig 1976-80. They suggest that the Hunhili who supplies cattle is identical with Hun-NI.NI.

[122] Cyl. A, xvi: 15; Stat. B vi: 22.

[123] Geographical texts listing Kimaš between Ulmaš and Kiabrig (*MSL XI*: 141 ii:10-12) and between ki-ma-AN[ki] and Marhaši (*ibid.*: 57 iii: 93-95) are unhelpful.

[124] Moorey 1985: 9. This would approximate to the older view which locates Kimaš between the Hamrin and the Lower Zab (*RGTC 2*: 101 with references).

[125] *Cf.* Steinkeller (1988: 201, n. 31) who places Kimaš, along with Hu-urti, "in the western section of the modern province of Kermanshah, around the towns of Shahabad and Kermanshah".

[126] For a general survey of the Gutians see Hallo 1971.

> Not classed among people, not reckoned as part of the land,
> Gutium, people who know no inhibitions,
> With human instinct but canine intelligence and monkey's features ...[127]

A letter of Ibbi-Sin echoes this description: "He (Enlil) raised to the shepherdship of the land / Monkeys who came down from the mountains". Elsewhere they are "serpents of the mountains" (Utuhegal), "dogs" and "stupid people"; they are "not flesh and blood" and "oppressive people without instruction in divine worship".[128]

Historical-literary compositions, known from Old Babylonian and later copies, associate the Guti principally with Naram-Sin.[129] One fragmentary text describes a campaign by the king of Agade against a host of foreign forces, chief amongst them king Gula-AN of Gutium, while in the *Cuthaean Legend of Naram-Sin* Gutium is itself invaded by the Umman Manda.[130] Their most famous appearance is as the agents of divine retribution against the hubris of Naram-Sin in the *Curse of Agade* and the 'Weidner Chronicle'.[131] As yet, however, there is nothing in Naram-Sin's contemporary inscriptions to confirm these stories which very likely telescope events from the reigns of his successors. While providing useful general indications of where later tradition placed the Gutian homeland they cannot safely be used for historical-geographical purposes.

The Gutians are first attested in contemporary documents under Šarkališarri, who claims to have captured their king (A)šarlag.[132] A letter probably dating to his reign shows that they were already disrupting lowland agriculture and grazing.[133] These raids (and probably those of other eastern peoples) intensified in the years following the king's death, eventually undermining Akkadian control over all but the region of Agade north to Ešnunna (below pp. 119-21). After devastating, and to some extent occupying, much of Sumer for fifty years, the Gutians were evicted by Utuhegal of Uruk.

Despite their apparently barbarous ways, the Gutian kings adopted Mesopotamian manners and practices, writing royal inscription in Akkadian (La-arab) and even dedicating statues to Enlil in Nippur (Erridupizir). The Babylonians regarded the Gutian language as "confused".[134] It is distinguished from the language of Subartu (*i.e.* Hurrian) by Hammurabi,[135] and interpreters are recorded as early as Sargonic times but since only a few Gutian words are preserved it is impossible to say even in general terms which linguistic category it belongs to.[136] Of Gutian material culture there is no recognisable evidence either in Mesopotamia[137] or in Iran, unless Vanden Berghe's speculative identification of the people buried in individual stone-lined graves in Luristan is accepted.[138]

---

[127] *CA*: 154-56; *cf.* translation in Jacobsen 1987: 368.
[128] *LSU*; *Uruk Lament*; Cooper 1983a: 31 with references.
[129] Propagandistic compositions also include Gutium among the regions ruled by Lugalannemundu of Adab (Güterbock 1934: 40-47; Edzard 1957: 32; below p. 92 n. 31) and Sargon of Akkad (Grayson 1974-77: l. 15; below p. 100 n. 72).
[130] Grayson & Sollberger 1976: Text L; Gurney 1955: l. 56.
[131] Cooper 1983a; *ABC*: Chron. 19:54-57.
[132] D-27.
[133] Oppenheim 1967: 71f. no. 2; Foster 1990a.
[134] *CAD*: s.v. *egeru* 1d.
[135] Gadd & Legrain 1928: no. 146 iii-iv.
[136] Hallo 1971: 719.
[137] Attempts have occasionally been made to identify stylistically unusual art works as Gutian but there is no basis for such judgements.
[138] Vanden Berghe 1973a: 29.

Contemporary non-literary third-millennium documents provide no direct evidence for the location of Gutium.[139] The recorded produce of Gutium – cattle and oil – mentioned in Old Akkadian texts is of little help, as are Old Babylonian lexical lists citing Gutian figs, chariots, carnelian and wool, especialy since some of these are variously described as "Amorite".[140] The *Curse of Agade* has Enlil bringing the Gutians "out of the (eastern) mountains",[141] which provides at least a general link with the more explicit traditions of the second and first millennia. The existence of a few Ur III fragments of the *Curse of Agade* shows that this composition was composed in the third millennium, perhaps in the immediate aftermath of the invasion.[142]

A newly published historical-literary inscription of Ur-Nammu, composed in Ur III times, describes Gutium acting in concert with Zimudar and refers to "the district of Guti (and) Zimudar".[143] Later, in a broken context, the text refers also to a place called Tulium. These associations, though not explicit, imply a location for Gutium in the same general vicinity as these other toponyms. Zimudar, the eastern terminus of the Ur III "Amorite Wall", must lie somewhere in the Diyala region.[144] Tulium seems to belong in the same general area,[145] thus supporting a location for Gutium near the junction of the Jebel Hamrin and the Diyala river.

The matter becomes more complicated if, as is assumed by Steinkeller, the territory referred to as "Gutium" was also designated in part or whole by other narrower toponyms.[146] As with "Amurru", "Gutium" may have served as a general, ethnically-based name for an area within which particular regions were given more specific designations. Locating Gutium within the triangle formed by Kermanshah, Suleimaniyeh and Kirkuk, Steinkeller suggests that this area comprised the lands of Harši, Hu(m)urti and Karahar – all places familiar as the object of campaigns by the kings of Ur. He also regards Kimaš, the land conquered (along with Hu(m)urti by Puzur-Inšušinak, as part of the Gutian heartland.

Historical-literary compositions relating to the third millennium cite Gutium formulaically between Subartu (Subir) and Elam.[147] As with Subartu, "Gutium" became an increasingly general term, probably less attached to any specific ethnic, tribal or cultural entity, during the second and first millennium and evidence from these periods is therefore of little help.[148]

Of the later historical-literary compositions, the most specific regarding geography is also unfortunately one of the latest and least reliable – the *Sargon Geography*. This lists Gutium after Lulubum, Armanum and Akkad (here probably the Diyala) and before Niqqu and Der (Badra).[149] It further specifies the borders of Gutium as Abul-Adad (on the north?)[150] and Hallaba (on the south?), but the location of these places is unknown. The text later defines one of the borders of the land of Edamaruz as "Tergan of Gutium", presumably its northern border since a text of

---

[139] Archaeological and other evidence for Gutians to the north-west of Mesopotamia cited by Hallo 1971: 719 is equivocal.
[140] Hallo 1971: 713, 716f.
[141] *CA*: 157.
[142] Cooper 1983a: 11.
[143] Civil 1985: 28f.
[144] Michalowski 1978: 36-38; *RGTC 2*: s.v. Simudar. Also now attested in the Ebla *LGN* (*MEE 3*: 230 31).
[145] Frayne (in press [a]) suggests a location on the Diyala in the Hamrin basin.
[146] Steinkeller in press [b]
[147] *The Cuthaean Legand of Naram-Sin*: 55-58; Goetze 1934: 43 (Lugalannemundu).
[148] Hallo 1971: 716-18.
[149] Grayson 1974-77: ll. 12-17.
[150] This place is also cited as a border of Akkad.

Samsuiluna places Edamaruz between Gutium and Elam.[151] Siting this "Tergan of Gutium" at Lu(b)ti on the modern Tauq Çai, Hallo concludes that Gutium lay astride the Lower Zab, approximately between the 35th and 36th parallels.[152]

(i) Marhaši / Parahšum

The land of Marhaši (Akkadian Parahšum)[153] appears in historical and administrative documents only from the Akkadian to Old Babylonian periods[154] (though it continues to feature in literary, scientific and lexical compositions until the end of cuneiform civilization).[155] As a geo-political entity, therefore, Marhaši is restricted to the later third and early second millennia; that, at any rate, is when it fell within the Mesopotamian political horizon.

The references of these periods suggest a major highland power at the periphery of direct military and diplomatic contact with Mesopotamia. Marhaši seems to represent the easternmost limit of the Akkadian kings' land-based military ventures, being "conquered" both by Sargon and by Rimuš, in the latter case on Marhašian soil. Although too distant to be brought under direct control by these kings or their successors at Ur, Marhaši was evidently close enough for regular diplomatic contact to be strategically desirable and logistically feasible. Not infrequently between the reigns of Amar-Suen and Ibbi-Sin Marhašian messengers were dispatched to the court at Ur, where they resided sometimes for a year or more;[156] and occasionally the ruler of Marhaši would travel there himself.[157] Šarkališarri as crown prince, or his son, may have travelled to Marhaši to marry a Marhašian princess[158] and at least one later Marhašian ruler was given the hand of the Sumerian king's (Šulgi's) daughter,[159] inspiring the adoption of names compounded with "Šulgi" by some Marhašians.[160] In Ur III times groups of Marhašian NIM – here probably soldiers[161] – were deployed by the Sumerians in the eastern highlands and rarely in Sumer itself.

In Sumerian literary and lexical texts Marhaši is cited in company with distant exotic lands such as Magan and Meluhha,[162] though the particular order of places in such listings need not reflect their relative proximity (as assumed by Vallat).[163] It was the source of certain plants,[164] animals[165] and stones,[166] these latter including duh-

---

[151] *IRSA*: IVC7e.

[152] Hallo 1971: 719.

[153] For this reading see Steinkeller 1982: 237f. n. 1.

[154] Discounting the plagiaristic claim to the conquest of Marhaši by Kurigalzu II (Steinkeller 1982: 263 n. 99).

[155] Steinkeller 1982: 263.

[156] Sargonic texts from Susa recording the disbursement of flour to Marhašians *(MDP 14*: 23; Foster in press) may relate to the provisioning of earlier messengers *en route* to Akkad.

[157] Fish 1954: s.v. Marhaši; Steinkeller 1982: 260f., n. 95. Journeys by Marhašian messengers are not nearly as frequent as those of, *e.g.*, Šimaškians, but their presence in Sumer is attested for nearly all of the Ur III period from late in the reign of Šulgi.

[158] Westenholz 1987a: nos 133, 154, p. 97.

[159] Š18; Sigrist & Gomi 1991: 321.

[160] Michalowski 1987: 67 n. 48.

[161] Steinkeller 1982: 261f.

[162] *Ibid*: 247-49.

[163] Vallat 1985: 52.

[164] These include SUM.SIKIL 'shallots' which grow in Baluchistan (Vallat 1985: 52).

[165] The dìm-šáh/*margû*, possibly a type of bear, a Marhašian 'dog' and Marhašian 'sheep' (Steinkeller 1982: 248, 252; *CAD*: s.v. *margû* A). The association of Marhaši with "the monkeys, the elephants, the zebu (Cooper 1983a: water buffalo), and other beasts of exotic lands" in *The Curse of Agade* is dubious (Steinkeller 1982: 252f.; *cf.* translation of Cooper 1983a: 51). If, as Steinkeller argues, that composition attributes these animals specifically to Marhaši, then (as Vallat 1985: 51 points out) a location in Baluchistan, if not further east, is indicated; hardly as far west as Steinkeller's Kerman.

[166] Steinkeller 1982: 249-54.

ši-a (Akk. *dušû*), perhaps a type of agate,[167] *marhašu*, perhaps chlorite/steatite,[168] a type of carnelian "speckled with yellow"[169] and "precious stones".[170] These materials all have wide distributions on the Iranian plateau.[171] More promising is the lapis lazuli "which is full of green spots", which was believed to come from Marhaši.[172] This may be turquoise, or perhaps the greener variety of lapis recently discovered in the Quetta valley (below p. 210). A "speckled dog of Meluhha" came to Ibbi-Sin from Marhaši.[173]

Although Marhaši is consistently listed separately from, and thus lay outside, the land of Elam,[174] this latter region provides the chief point of reference for its location in royal inscriptions of the Akkadian empire.[175] It was as an ally of Elam that Marhaši was conquered both by Sargon and by Rimuš (in addition to other places defeated only by one or the other); and Naram-Sin claimed to have conquered "the totality of the land of Elam as far as Marhaši" indicating that it had a border with Elam, presumably on its eastern flank.[176] Not surprisingly, a significant proportion of Marhašian personal names are Elamite.

Two texts may provide more precise clues. The first, whose relevance has not previously been explored, is preserved in a group of inscriptions describing an eastern campaign of Rimuš.[177] The king first claims victory over Abalgamaš, king of Parahšum, and then recounts what seem to be further successes against the forces of Zahara and Elam[178] when these "assembled for battle in the midst of Parahšum". Rimuš next recounts the enemy casualties – 16,212 killed and 4,216 captured – and the leaders who were taken prisoner: Emahsini king of Elam, "all the [...] of Elam", Sidgau the šakkanakku of Parahšum, and Sargapi the šakkanakku of Zahara. This enumeration is followed immediately by the localisation "between Awan and Susa at the Upper River", apparently referring back to the capture of the highland leaders.[179] Since this event is related as a direct consequence of the victory over Zahara and Elam, it is natural to suppose that the battleground and place of capture were not far removed from each other. In that case it would follow that Awan and Susa – the reference points for the enemy leaders' apprehension – serves here to specify a

---

167 *Ibid.*: 249f.; Vallat 1985: 52; Heimpel 1988: 199.
168 A Sargonic royal inscription (Frayne 1984: 24f., ll. 72f.) shows that, in addition to small containers, inlay work and figurines (Steinkeller 1982: 251; Maxwell-Hyslop 1989: 131), *marhašu* was used for foundation tablets (*narua*), of which a number of steatite/chlorite examples have been found. Van Dijk's translation "marcassite" seems less probable (van Dijk 1983: 129).
169 H*h* xvi:129 (Pettinato 1972: 153); *abnu šikinšu* 9 (Horowitz 1992: 114).
170 Attinger 1984: 13.
171 Steinkeller 1982: 251f.; below pp. 177ff.
172 Steinkeller 1982: 250.
173 *Ibid.*: 253 n. 60.
174 Vallat 1985: 52.
175 For previous views on the location of Marhaši see references collected in Steinkeller 1982: 238f. n. 3; add Vallat 1985: 52 (Iranian Baluchistan).
176 NS C3:6-10; *cf.* Vallat 1985: 52 and below.
177 Rimuš C6, C8, C10.
178 The parallel account Rimuš C10:10f. adds here [Gu]pin and [Me]luhha.
179 Rimuš C6:43-48. That it is to this capture that the localisation refers (and not, as Hirsch 1963: 62f. translates, the events which follow) is proven by the newly published version Rimuš C10:19-29, where this phrase comes at the beginning of the sentence as normal syntax requires. It should be noted, however, that the parallel accounts (Rimuš C6:38-48; C8:9-18), where the localisation seems to come after the verb, remain grammatically problematical and no completely satisfactory interpretation of these passages has been offered. (In C8 Kienast translates it as a freestanding sentence semantically unrelated to either event.) Fortunately, the geographical issue is not much affected, for the only other event to which the locative phrase might relate – the heaping up of a tumulus which is described in the following lines – would likewise have taken place near the battleground and capture of the enemy leaders. See further T.F. Potts 1989: 128f. n. 20.

location close to "the midst of Parahšum" – the location of the battle – and thus that Parahšum, like Awan and Susa, is to be sought somewhere in south-western Iran.[180]

Against this, however, must be weighed the evidence of the second text, the praise poem of Išbi-Erra (above p. 17), which (like the evidence of plants, animals *etc.*) suggests a more eastern location. Referring to the empire of Kindattu around 2,000 BC, the hymn describes the king's dominion as stretching:

> [from] Pašime, the 'breast' (*i.e.* coast) of the sea (Persian Gulf), [to] the border of Zabša[li] (and) [from] Arawa, the 'lock' of Elam, [to] the border of Marha[ši]

On the assumption that this passage defines Kindattu's realm in terms of roughly north-south and east-west axes,[181] it has been used to fix the locations of both Marhaši and Šimaški (of which Zabšali formed a part; see below). Steinkeller, following van Dijk, argues that Pašime on the coast must represent the southern boundary of Kindattu's realm, in which case Zabšali would represent the northern extension and Arawa and Marhaši would define the limits along the east-west axis.[182] But Steinkeller reverses van Dijk's traditional placement of Marhaši at the western boundary with Arawa to the east on the ground that Arawa, the 'lock', *i.e.* entrance, to Elam, must be at the western (Mesopotamian) end of that land, and is probably to be identified with better-known Urua, a city not far from Sumer in north-western Khuzistan.[183] Hence Marhaši must lie at the eastern extremity of Elam, more precisely, according to Steinkeller, in eastern Fars or Kerman.[184]

Steinkeller argues compellingly that such a placement is more consistent with the general indications of other sources (summarized above), but his use of the Išbi-Erra poem as the foundation of this position is problematic. It is not at all clear that a Mesopotamian would most naturally describe the limits of an unfamiliar area in terms of cardinal points or axes, a practice which has meaning and utility only in the context of reasonably accurate maps. The Mesopotamian, without such a frame of reference, would perhaps be as likely to describe territorial limits in terms of familiar landmarks, routes or some other element of his 'mental map'.[185] In this context "from X to Y" need not mark any particular axis, but rather the first and last points (within the region concerned) along some familiar landroute. That this was indeed the intention of Išbi-Erra's poet is supported by Steinkeller's well-argued case for locating both Pašime and Arawa close to Sumer, and by the latter's description as the 'lock' of

---

[180] Possible support for such a location comes from an inscription of Ilum-muttabbil of Der (modern Badra) relating a victory over "the armies of Anšan, Elam and Šimaški" and describing the king as the "*ri-eṣ* of Parahšum" (Frayne 1990: 677f.). This is usually read "ally" (literally "helper", *rīsum*) following von Soden, *AHw.* 972 s.v. *rēsu*, 2(c). But why would Der strike an alliance with Parahšum/Marhaši in what seems to have been an otherwise exclusively Iranian conflict? Whatever the answer – and none is obvious – it is difficult to envisage a relatively minor city like Der forming an alliance with a major highland state that was not a close neighbour, able to exert direct and effective pressure on its military activities. This would imply a westerly location for Marhaši extending into the Zagros. Note however that Gelb (*MAD 3*: 233) read the word in question not as "ally" but as "smiter" (*rīsum*, from the verb *rāsum*). This reading, although a hapax (the participle in OB is usually uncontracted *ra-'i-iṣ*), would be grammatically unobjectionable (closely paralleling the use of SAG.GIŠ.RA for "conqueror") and perhaps makes better contextual sense. Again, however, it is difficult to imagine Der "smiting" a land far into Iran, unless Marhaši was part of the Elam-Šimaški alliance fighting outside its own territory.

[181] van Dijk 1978: 197.

[182] Steinkeller 1982: 239f.

[183] Above note 58.

[184] Steinkeller: 255; *idem* 1989a: 381. *Cf.* Maxwell-Hyslop 1989: 130-33, who supports this view on archaeological grounds, including within the borders of Marhaši the sites of Tepe Yahya, Shahdad and Shahr-i Sokhta.

[185] *Cf.* Michalowski 1986: 131 on figurative geography and territorial usages.

Elam, *i.e.* the first Elamite place on the road from Sumer. These would thus represent the first major staging posts within Greater Elam along two major routes into Iran. Since Arawa (*i.e.* Urua) can not yet be closely fixed,[186] and the direction of the route passing through it is unknown, the scope for placing the Marhaši terminus remains very great.

In the context of such uncertainty, negative evidence which allows some regions to be excluded from consideration takes on greater importance. Marhaši is conspicuously absent from the places conquered by Ur III kings along the 'Hurrian frontier' of the Zagros mountains north and north-west of the Diyala (below pp. 131-33), and this region may thereby be excluded.[187] On the other hand, reports of Ur III conquests to the east (Huhnuri, Anšan and Šimaški) are so few and brief (mainly in year formulae) that Marhaši's absence from them cannot be given any definite significance. The names of people identified as Marhašians in Ur III documents include a proportion that are Elamite and possibly Hurrian[188] but cannot otherwise be classified.

(j) Šimaški and the "Su-people"

New light has recently been thrown on the question of Šimaški by Steinkeller's demonstration that LÚ.SU(.A)[(ki)], previously read as the ethnicon "Su-people", is an alternative writing of "Šimaški" favoured by the scribes of Drehem.[189] Thus the many references to the "Su-people" as the object of raids by Ur III kings and as allies of the Elamites in the eventual destruction of Sumer, need to be reinterpreted as references to Šimaški(ans). Steinkeller's identification is accepted here but the logographic writing LÚ.SU(.A) is indicated in cases where the account depends exclusively on this reading.

The toponym Šimaški occurs in Mesopotamian and Elamite inscriptions (these also in Akkadian) from the late Akkadian to Old Babylonian periods.[190] In Mesopotamian documents it is most common in Ur III administrative texts where Šimaški is often cited as the origin of messengers and groups of NIM, "Elamites" or "highlanders". In Ur III and Old Babylonian royal inscriptions and year names Šimaški appears as the object of occasional military campaigns, the most significant being the conquest by Šu-Sin (below pp. 129-31). In literature, the Šimaškians (LÚ.SU(.A)[ki]) are portrayed in graphic terms as uncivilized tent-dwellers, a recurrent motif in describing foreign enemies which obscures what was probably a largely sedentary and sophisticated culture:

> The Šimaškians (LÚ.SU-e[ki]), who do not consecrate nugig and lukur priestesses in the places of the gods,
> Whose population is as numerous as grass, whose seed is widespread,
> Who lives in a tent, and knows not the places of the gods,

---

[186] Steinkeller 1982: 246, suggesting north-west Khuzistan.
[187] *Cf.* Steinkeller 1982: 247.
[188] Elamite: *ibid.*: 262 n. 97; Vallat 1985: 52. Hurrian: *e.g.* Arwilukpi the king ("man") of Marhaši in AS1 (Steinkeller 1982: n. 96) (*cf.* Hurrian *erwi*, "king" [Gelb 1944: 82]); *cf.* also from later literary sources Hupšumkipi, the king of Marhaši in *The Great Revolt* against Naram-Sin (Grayson & Sollberger 1976:; Gelb 1944: 55) and Tišš[i]enki, king of Marhaši in the Hittite Naram-sin text (Güterbock 1938: 68 1. 12´; *cf.* Hurrian *tiš* [Gelb 1944: 112]).
[189] Steinkeller 1988; *idem* 1990.
[190] Stolper 1982; Steinkeller 1988: 197, nn. 1, 2. After the Old Babylonian period Šimaški appears only in geographical lists.

Figure 4. Susa exercise tablet with list of kings of Awan and Šimaški. Sukkalmah period. 8.2 x 6.4 cm.

Who mates just like an animal, and knows not how to make offerings of
flour,
(Even) the evil namtar demon and the dangerous asag demon do not (dare
to) approach him,
One who, profaning the name of god, violates taboos ...[191]

According to an Old Babylonian king list from Susa (Fig. 4), Šimaški was the
nominal seat of the dynasty which ruled Elam around the turn of the third/second
millennia. The tablet, a school exercise text,[192] lists two dynasties of twelve kings
each, the first and earlier described as kings of Awan, the second as "twelve
Šimaškian kings". The order and other details of the list are questionable, but the
general historicity of a Šimaškian dynasty is confirmed by Mesopotamian documents

---

[191] Letter-prayer to Sin-Iddinam, translation after Michalowski 1986: 132.
[192] Scheil 1932: iv.

of the Ur III to Isin-Larsa periods, which mention a number of the "Šimaškian kings" and allow them to be correlated with local rulers from Šulgi (year 46) to Gungunum.[193] Best known of the eastern dynasts is Kindattu, the 'Elamite' who, according to Sumerian tradition, administered the *coup de grâce* to Ibbi-Sin and the Ur III empire. Under Kindattu's rule – the highpoint of Elamite power – the Šimaškian state held sway from Anšan to Susiana (and briefly even at Ur itself); or, as the praise-hymn to Išbi-Erra describes Kindattu's empire, "[from] Pašime, the 'breast' of the sea, [to] the border of Zabša[li] (and) [from] Arawa, the 'lock' of Elam, [to] the border of Marha[ši]". Šimaškian control over heartland Elam is confirmed by references to Kindattu (or his son), and later to Ebarti II, as "king of Anšan", and to the second king of the Susa list, Tazitta, as the "man of Anšan".[194] Not surprisingly, a significant proportion of the recognisable Šimaškian (LÚ.SU(.A)) names are Elamite.[195]

Judging by Mesopotamian sources, the Šimaškian state had come into being by *ca.* 2040 BC and lasted till *ca.* 1900 BC, when it was superseded by rulers who styled themselves in Sumerian manner as sukkalmahs, though these too were probably members of the same extended royal family.[196] While only one extant inscription from Susa dating to the period of the Šimaškian dynasty refers to Šimaški explicitly,[197] it is very prominent in the titulature of the succeeding Sukkalmah period when a "sukkal of Elam and Šimaški" (along with one of Susa and perhaps others) stood directly below the "grand regent" (sukkalmah).

Historical evidence for the location of Šimaški, reviewed by Stolper and Vallat, needs now to be modified in the light of Steinkeller's LÚ.SU(.A)-Šimaški identification and the newly published inscriptions of Šu-Sin.[198] Šu-Sin's accounts of his Šimaškian campaigns indicate that Šimaški consisted of at least six (perhaps as many as fifteen) regions,[199] chief amongst them being Zabšali.[200] The six which are qualified as "lands" were ruled (in the Sumerian scribe's terminology) by "great ensis" (énsi-gal-gal), the "cities" by ordinary ensis.[201] Although nominally the seat of an Elamite dynasty, with sovereigns bearing Elamite names,[202] the standard Elamite royal title "king/sukkal of Elam and Šimaški"[203] suggests that Šimaški was not part of Elam proper,[204] *i.e.* according to Vallat, not part of the *Kingdom* of Elam. As a source of NIM it was almost certainly a mountain land.[205] Its rulers, perhaps originally from Anšan, only later settled in Susa, there founding the dynasty of the sukkalmahs.[206]

---

[193] Stolper 1982: 49-56; Steinkeller 1988: 201f.
[194] Stolper 1982: 47, 50.
[195] Gelb 1940: 101-04; Vallat 1980: 9.
[196] Stolper 1982: 54-56; Grillot & Glassner 1991.
[197] In the title of Idadu, seventh king of Šimaški in the Susa king list, "king of Šimaški and Elam" (Scheil 1913: 26). Note also the reference in Puzur-Inšušinak's inscription (*AKI*: Elam 2:104-09) below p. 123.
[198] Stolper 1982: 45f.; Vallat 1985: 50; Kutscher 1989: BT4; *AKI*: Ur C2.
[199] 14 regions (15 including Zabšali) are listed as "Šimaški (LÚ.SU^{ki}), the lands of Zabšali" in BT4 ii:14-34 (Kutscher 1989: 90; below p.130). This list suggests that the 6+ places cited at BT4 viii:26-29 (*ibid.*: 91; *AKI*: Ur C2:23-25; Oelsner 1989: 407f.), listed immediately after the subtotal "together 6 lands (of Šimaški)", were likewise Šimaškian, since all of them occur (in the same order) midway through the longer list of 15. *Cf.* Kutscher 1989: 100, who regards only the six "lands" of BT4 viii:16-22 as Šimaški proper.
[200] Whether, like Anšan, Šimaški was also the name of a city is unclear.
[201] BT4 iii:24-29.
[202] Vallat 1985: 50; M. Lambert 1979: 35.
[203] See above note 197 for Idadu "king of Šimaški and Elam". The rulers of the Sukkalmah Period call themselves "sukkal of Elam and Šimaški". Is the reversal of order significant?
[204] *Cf.* the apposition of Susiana and Elam in Gudea Cyl. A xv:6f.
[205] Fish 1955; *RGTC 2*: 182; Stolper 1982: 52 n. 34; Vallat 1985: 50.
[206] Stolper 1982: 54f.

A number of indications suggest that Šimaški lay relatively close to Mesopotamia, though not within the bounds of direct Sumero-Akkadian rule (except perhaps under Šu-Sin).[207] It was within range of frequent diplomatic contact in the Ur III period, being one of the most oft-cited origins and destinations of messengers.[208] It was also a feasible military target, close enough to Susa to be intimidated by Puzur-Inšušinak in the early Ur III period, and to be the subject of Mesopotamian conquests from Šulgi (year formula 47) to Ilum-muttabbil of Der (*ca.* 1980 BC).[209]

Royal inscriptions commemorating these campaigns provide some more precise clues. Puzur-Inšušinak mentions the submission of Šimaški in the context of a campaign against Kimaš (above p. 24) and Hu-urti. Significantly, these are the same places whose later conquest by Šulgi are accompanied in the same or immediately succeeding years by archival references to the "booty of Šimaški (LÚ.SU(.A))", presumably from the same campaigns.[210] "What this suggests", as Steinkeller points out, "is that LÚ.SU(.A) was adjacent to Kimaš, Hu-urti, and Harši", which places he locates in western Kermanshah around Shahabad and Kermanshah. For Šimaški itself Steinkeller suggests the regions further south and east in modern Luristan and Fars; a similar conclusion was reached previously by Stolper.[211]

A recently published Sumerian account of Šu-Sin's Šimaški campaign allows this range to be more closely defined when it describes how "at that time, Šimaški, (which comprises?)[212] the lands of Zabšali, rose like locusts from the borders of Anšan up to the Upper Sea (=Caspian Sea? or Lake Urmia?)".[213] This suggests that Šimaški lay essentially to the north of, and shared a border with, Anšan in Fars. That it extended all the way to Lake Urmia or the Caspian – here the most likely identification of the "Upper Sea"[214] – implies a broader hegemony than previously envisaged but need not be merely royal bombast.[215]

---

[207] For previous discussion see Kupper 1969: 24ff. and Hinz 1971: 654 (near Khoramabad); Miroschedji 1980: 138 (south-east Khuzistan and the adjoining mountains); Vallat 1980: 8f.; *idem* 1985: 50-52 (eastern Fars or Kerman); Stolper 1982: 45f. and Steinkeller 1988 (north of Khuzistan or Fars). The old identifications of LÚ.SU(.A) with Subir/Subartu in northern Mesopotamia (Gelb 1944) and Sutium (Kramer) have been soundly rejected (Steinkeller 1988: 197f. with further refs.).

[208] Fish 1954: s.v.; *RGTC 2*: 182.

[209] References collected in *RGTC 2*: 171-74; Owen 1981: 261 s.v. Su/Su-a (add *AKI*: Elam 2). The historical evidence is reviewed by Stolper 1984: 16-23; note also the conquests of LÚ.SU(.A) from Š47 to IE13 (Steinkeller 1988: 197, n. 1, 201, n. 31; *IRSA*: IIIA4e, IIIA4g) and the associated references to LÚ.SU(.A) booty (next note).

[210] Booty recorded in Š47, the year after the defeat of Kimaš and Hu-urti (Š46 year formula), and Š48, the same year named for campaigns against Harši, Kimaš and Hu-urti (Steinkeller 1988: 201, n. 31).

[211] Steinkeller 1988: 201, n. 31; Stolper 1982: 45f.; 1984: 20. Stolper's argument is based principally on the description of Kindattu's empire in the praise-hymn of Išbi-Erra, discussed above in connection with Elam and Marhaši. Like Steinkeller and van Dijk, Stolper assumes that, in the description of Kindattu's empire, "the axis Bašime-on-the-sea – Zabšali [= part of Šimaški] is approximately south to north" and therefore concludes that Zabšali must lie "immediately to the north of 'Elam'. Hence: those parts of Šimaškian territory exposed to contact with Mesopotamian states lay amongst the valley systems to the north of Khuzistan and/or Fars" (Stolper 1982: 46), more precisely in the Burujird valley (Stolper 1984: 20). While the doubts expressed above about interpreting Išbi-Erra's description in terms of cardinal points apply here also, Stolper's conclusion is consistent with the other evidence presented here. Less convincing is Henrickson's (1984) attempt to trace the development of the Šimaškian state in the varying patterns of expansion and isolation of late 3rd and 2nd mill. pottery in the central Zagros.

[212] Thus Steinkeller reconstructs although the text is not explicit.

[213] Kutscher 1989: BT4 ii:14-20; translation after Steinkeller 1990: 10.

[214] Steinkeller assumes that this refers to the Caspian Sea. However, note "Subir on the borders of the Upper Sea" (Kärki 1986: ŠS20b:rs i´9´) which Civil takes to be Lake Urmia (Civil 1967: 37, ll. 5´-11´), and MA references to Lake Van as the *tâmtu elenîtu* (*RGTC 5*: 319).

[215] Possible support for this view may lie in the inclusion of a toponym Sigriš among the lands of Šimaški (*AKI*: Ur C2: 17; Kutscher 1989: BT4 ii:23, viii:17). A land with this name is placed by NA texts in Median

An alternative scheme which places Šimaški farther east in modern Kerman has been suggested by Vallat and recently supported on glyptic grounds by Stève.[216] The basis of Vallat's view is the standard opposition of the two sukkals: one of "Elam and Šimaški" and another of "Susa". This, he claims, shows that "Simaški devrait, comme l'Elam, appartenir à la partie orientale de la confédération". (A location between Susa and Anšan is excluded since this position is occupied by Huhnuri, the 'bolt' of Anšan/Elam.) "On peut donc imaginer que Simaški est situé à l'Est de l'Elam, c'est-à-dire dans l'actuelle province de Kerman".

Elamite titulature, however, is as likely to reflect the particularities of contemporary power politics as any geographical facts and thus provides a very uncertain guide at best to ancient toponymy. Moreover, a location in Kerman does not accord well with Šimaški's association with the western lands of Kimaš, Hu-urti and Harši.[217]

The glyptic evidence is at present no more compelling. Stève's placement of Šimaški between Anšan and the eastern border of modern Iran depends on the attribution of a group of cylinder seals in a syncretistic Iranian-Bactrian-Harappan style to Kerman. One seal bearing the inscription of "[Ebar]at, king of Ši[maški]",[218] is the only explicit link with Šimaški, the others being grouped around it on stylistic grounds. None, however, has a reliable provenance and it is by no means certain, as Stève assumes, that the likely arena for such a coming together of Iranian, Central Asian and Harappan elements is restricted to Kerman, or even to eastern Iran. Metalwork as far west as Susa has affiliations with these same regions (below pp. 168-76).

On balance, therefore, a location for Šimaški in western Iran, stretching from Anšan north towards the Caspian Sea and westward into Luristan, seems presently more likely.

(k) Dilmun, Magan and Meluhha

The location of this triad has been debated extensively in recent years[219] and will be reviewed here only briefly. All three were maritime states and relations with Sumer were effected almost exclusively by sea-craft which were known (presumably after their places of origin and/or type of construction) as Dilmun-boats, Magan-boats and Meluhha-boats.[220] Again, all three were principally important to Mesopotamia as trading partners, for the materials and objects they produced or passed on from further afield. Dilmun also held an important place in Sumerian mythology.[221] Not only exotic materials, crafts and animals, but also large quantities of copper came from these places, especially Magan. Magan and Dilmun appear only exceptionally

territory, which at that time continued past Behistun to Hamadan and beyond (Stolper 1982: 45f., n. 16). However, there is no proof that the 3rd- and 1st-mill. homonyms refer to the same place.
[216] Vallat 1980: 8f.; *idem* 1985: 50-52; Stève 1989.
[217] Since Steinkeller's reading of LÚ.SU(.A) as "Šimaški", Vallat's view also sits uneasily with his own arguments for locating the "Su-people" in Susiana (Vallat 1980: 9; *idem* 1985: 53).
[218] Stève 1989: seal A.
[219] Pettinato 1972: 99-101 reviews the literature up to 1970. Since then note particularly Sollberger 1970; Hansman 1973; Thapar 1975; During-Caspers & Govindakutty 1978; Ratnagar 1981: 68-71; Alster 1983; D.T. Potts 1983a; *idem* 1990; Michalowski 1988; Heimpel 1987 [edition of Mesopotamian sources]; *idem*: 1988; Glassner 1989.
[220] Heimpel 1987: 37f., 70ff. *passim*; Westenholz 1987a: nos 128, 132, 140; *cf.* Ratnagar 1981: 23, 39, 68f. Sargon claims that in his reign Meluhha-, Magan-, and Dilmun-boats docked at the key of Agade (Sargon C2:11-16). Note also the bronze models of Dilmun-boats dedicated at ED III Lagaš (Heimpel 1987: nos 11, 12; *DP.* nos 69, 70; *VS 14*: no. 13; Bauer 1972: 460f.).
[221] Kramer 1963a; Alster 1983.

(and Meluhha not at all) in diplomatic records (notably the messenger texts) and very rarely as the objects of military actions. The only definite encounter in the third millennium is Naram-Sin's conquest of Magan.[222] None seems ever to have been brought under lasting Mesopotamian rule.[223]

The canonical sequence, Dilmun-Magan-Meluhha, has always been taken to indicate their relative proximity to Sumer. As things stand, it also reflects the increasing degree of uncertainty which attaches to more precise localisations.

Dilmun appears in Sumerian texts far the earliest of the three.[224] It is now almost unanimously identified with Bahrain, less often with Failaka.[225] Some who accept the Bahrain identification take it to apply also (at some periods) to the adjacent Arabian littoral.[226] In the early Islamic period it seems to have included all of the Arabian coastline from Kuwait to Oman. Kramer extends third-millennium Dilmun all the way to the Indus, but such gross ambiguity would have rendered the term virtually useless as a geographical specification for economic and other practical affairs, and the equation should probably not be extended beyond Bahrain or Qatar.[227]

The locations of Magan and Meluhha rest less securely on documentary testimony concerning their exports to Sumer. Magan's principal resource was copper. The identification with Oman, proposed by Peake in 1928, has derived much support in the last decade from accumulating evidence of large-scale smelting of Omani copper in the third millennium.[228] 'Booty' vessels from Magan include both *série récente* chlorite, known to have been made in Oman, and calcite vessels which derive rather from Iran (see below Ch. 6, Sect. 2). The possibility that the term included also or only the opposite Iranian coastline has been suggested.[229] This cannot be excluded, but the logic of geographical semantics is against it. Apart from the practical confusion such equivocation would cause, a state encompassing territory on both sides of the Gulf represents an unlikely administrative prospect at this date. The hundred-kilometer-wide Straits of Hormuz constitute a major barrier to communication, and would have seriously inhibited any form of effective political or military hegemony.

Meluhha was known to the Sumerians as the source of many exotic commodities including ivory, gold, tin, copper, lapis lazuli, carnelian, various kinds of wood and a kind of bird (haia) usually identified as the peacock.[230] Most important

---

[222] Note also: 1) Maništušu's campaign to the "silver mines" on the "other side" of the "Lower Sea" (Persian Gulf), perhaps to be identified as Magan; 2) the inclusion of Meluhha (and Gupin) among the opponents of Rimuš in one redaction of a Nippur inscription (Rimuš C10); and 3) the substitution of the same place name (instead of Šerihum) in the NB 'Cruciform Monument' of Maništušu (below pp. 101, 103-05).

[223] The reference to an ensi of Magan under Amar-Suen is insufficient to prove that this land formed a province of the Ur III empire, as suggested by D.T. Potts 1990: 144.

[224] First in the Archaic Texts from Uruk (Englund 1983a; Nissen 1985b; *idem* 1986a; D.T. Potts 1990: 86f.) and later at Archaic Ur, Fara, Abu Salabikh and Ebla (Englund 1983a: 36; Pettinato 1983; Hruška 1983; D.T. Potts 1990: 87f.). Note, however, that doubts have recently been expressed by Glassner (in press) and Michalowski (1988a: 100f.) that this early Dilmun is really the distant land of later literature rather than a synonymous local place. Glassner points out that the Ur references occur in the context of land allotments, where one would expect only local Sumerian toponyms. Likewise, Howard-Carter (1987: 61) locates the Dilmun of Archaic (and possibly ED) times in the area of Qurnah near the Tigris-Euphrates confluence. The 'Dilmun shekel' at Ebla is probably to be read something like 'standard shekel' and thus should be deleted from the list of early connections (Archi 1987; Michalowski 1988a: 100f.).

[225] D.T. Potts 1983a.

[226] D.T. Potts 1990: 17, 85f.

[227] Kramer 1963a; *cf.* Alster 1983.

[228] Weisgerber 1981; Hauptmann 1985; D.T. Potts 1990: 119-25.

[229] D.T. Potts 1986b; Eilers in Leemans 1960a: 29 n. 1.

[230] Full lists of Meluhhan exports are given in Pettinato 1972: 116f., 162-166; Ratnagar 1981: 70f.

are ivory and ebony which cannot be accommodated short of the Indus (or Africa). Such a location is consistent also with the references to Meluhhan tin (AN.NA) and lapis lazuli (^{na_4}za-gìn, *uqnû*), both present in considerable quantities in Afghanistan, which represents the closest confirmed source to Mesopotamia (below pp. 208-10). In the case of lapis, confirmation of Harappan procurement has been provided at Shortugai on the Oxus river.

 Archaeological evidence confirms the existence of contacts between Sumer and the islands down the Gulf to Oman and the mouth of the Indus.[231] The possibility of major lacunae in this data advises caution in any attempt to narrow further the range of identifications deduced from textual evidence; but the incontrovertible fact that direct or indirect relations of some kind had been established between Sumer, the Gulf states and the Indus suffices to throw the balance of probability heavily against those Sumerologists who would identify third-millennium Magan with Nubia, and Meluhha with Ethiopia and the Somali coast or the Yemen, where there is no comparable evidence of contact at this date.[232]

 References in Ur III texts from Lagaš-Girsu suggest that peoples somehow connected with Magan, Meluhha and other eastern lands were settled in villages in Sumer. Most intriguing are the references to the "village of Meluhha (é-duru$_5$ me-luh-ha$^{(ki)}$)". The three named citizens/inhabitants (dumu) of this village bear Sumerian names, and the town seems to function as a normal unit of local agricultural production. But its name, once written with the place determinative ki, suggests to Parpola *et al.* that it was originally (in Akkadian times?) a trading settlement whose inhabitants were subsequently acculturized.[233]

 Other villages mentioned in Ur III Lagaš documents include a "village of the Magan people (lú-má-gan^{ki})", a "village of the Elamites (NIM-e-ne)", a place called "Lulubuna" (*cf.* Lulubum) and a "village of the travelling merchants (ga-eš$_8$)".[234] Falkenstein interpreted these villages, all in the province of Lagaš-Girsu, as colonies of the specified foreigners.[235]

2. ROUTES OF COMMUNICATION

(a) River and Sea Routes

 Throughout antiquity the superior speed and economy of water transport encouraged trade by boat rather than caravan, especially for large quantities and bulky goods.[236] Sumer, which owed its existence to the rivers flowing through it and

---

[231] The extensive literature on this subject is reviewed in the comprehensive studies by Ratnagar 1981 and D.T. Potts 1990.

[232] Jacobsen 1960: 184 n. 16; Kramer 1963: 276f.; *cf.* Leemans 1960a: 17-30. The evidence of contact cited by Jacobsen is restricted to the late Predynastic period (late 4th mill.), and there is nothing later till the Tôd treasure, probably sealed in the reign of Amenemhet II. All authorities agree that these toponyms apply to places in Africa from the late 2nd mill. On the view adopted here (Leemans 1960a: 30), this transfer occurred only after memory of the true location of these places had been lost; they were then conveniently applied to regions which produced some of the same materials (ivory, ebony, carnelian, gold *etc.*).

[233] Parpola *et al.* 1977: 145, 150; 136 text 3, ii:1.

[234] *Ibid.*: 145f. Note in this connection the people identified as coming from all three places – presumably traders or messengers – recorded as receiving oil at Sargonic Susa (Foster in press: n. 21; *MDP 14*: 42).

[235] Falkenstein 1966: 26f., 34; *cf.* Limet 1972: 134.

[236] According to the calculations of Jones (1966: 311), on the basis of prices in the Edict of Diocletian (AD 301) "It was ... cheaper to transport wheat from one end of the empire to the other by sea than to cart it

was connected by them to the open waters of the Persian Gulf, was certainly no exception. From the time of the earliest records, trade within Babylonia and with the east was carried on principally by boat.[237] Leemans' comments on the Old Babylonian period apply equally to the third millennium:

> The waterways were the natural routes in southern Mesopotamia and the Babylonians had adapted their economy to this fact. The quay, the *karum*, was everywhere the place where trade was carried on ... Boats are mentioned frequently in the texts, transport animals, especially donkeys, relatively rarely.[238]

The Tigris and Euphrates Rivers also served as the principal arteries of trade and communication between Babylonia and the north-west. The Tigris is navigable by modern native craft to Mosul, beyond which only downstream traffic is possible. The slower-flowing Euphrates is negotiable well into Syria and rafts can penetrate eastern Anatolia.[239] Downstream raft traffic is feasible from the headwaters of both rivers.[240] The Late Uruk settlements along the Euphrates (and Tigris?) illustrate the importance of these waterways as means of communication and cultural expansion from at least the mid fourth millennium. Old Babylonian itineraries indicate that caravans to the north-west usually preferred the Tigris route where grazing was better, and then cut across the Jazireh.[241]

Khuzistan was equally well served by waterways: the Kerkheh, the Diz, with its tributary the Shaur, and the Karun – the last being the largest river and the only one which has been navigable in modern times.[242] Susa lies on the modern Shaur which probably follows an ancient course of the Kerkheh.[243] By the second millennium, and perhaps much earlier, the Kerkheh seems to have flowed into the Diz which in turn joined the Karun, thereby issuing into the Gulf.[244] Susa was therefore easily accessible by boat from Sumer, and records show that this was indeed the preferred form of transport from at least the third millennium. The alternative overland trail to the Tigris at modern Amara took approximately three days.[245]

The fast-flowing tributaries of the Kharkeh, Diz and Karun rivers pass through treacherous gorges which render them little use for communication;[246] at most they may have provided fast downstream transport for light, manoeuverable craft. Likewise, of the Tigris' affluents in Kurdistan and Azerbaijan only the Diyala affords

---

[237] seventy-five miles". Note also D.T. Potts' calculation (1984: 266 n. 118) that a load of salt requiring 10 to 12 pack equids would have taken up just over one-third the cargo space of a 3rd-mill. ship.

[237] ED III documents from Girsu demonstrate river trade between Lagaš and 'Elam' (M. Lambert 1953: 64), here presumably meaning Susiana. Ur III texts likewise record river-trade between Lagaš and Susa (Leemans 1960: 175).

[238] Leemans 1960a: 34.

[239] Mason *et al.* 1944: 559, 561.

[240] Herodotus I 194 reports how the Armenians built round river craft from animal skins, willow and reeds for transporting wine and equids to Babylon. The largest carried as much as 500 talents.

[241] Leemans 1960a: 31, 33; Hallo 1964: 66, 69, *contra* Goetze 1953a: 56f.

[242] Mason *et al.* 1945: 581; Fisher (ed.) 1968: 553; *idem* 1971: 301.

[243] Kirkby 1977: 276.

[244] This is apparently the most ancient pattern of drainage evidenced by surviving meander patterns, which Kirby dates between *ca.* 1500 BC and AD 500 (Kirby 1977: 276-79). The situation may have been considerably different in the 3rd mill., however, when the crucial shift from an aggrading regime with multiple shifting channels to a more stable incising regime had not yet taken place. Kirby dates this changeover to some time between 1500 and 500 BC (*ibid.*: 282).

[245] Hinz 1972: 20.

[246] Brice 1966: 170.

access for the eastward journey into the Zagros foothills. Small modern craft followed this river early this century to Baquba[247] and shallow-draught ancient craft could doubtless penetrate further; but at some point it would be necessary to take to land.

To the south-east the Euphrates linked Sumer with the Gulf and the lands beyond – the Indus and perhaps also Egypt. Very important for trade were the settlements and emporia along the eastern coast of the Arabian peninsula and the nearby islands of Failaka, Tarut and Bahrain.[248] The easier and more direct passage to the Indus, however, was along the Iranian side of the Gulf.[249] The principal ports, from which roads still run inland today, are Bushire and Bandar Abbas/Minab. Bushire was probably a third millennium settlement and may have acted as a port for Anšan. The area of Minab also was almost certainly a port area for the cities of Kerman[250] to which it was connected by a direct route (below, land-route (8)). Trade between Kerman and Sumer would have been easier by Gulf shipping than over land.

Disembarking further east on the Makran coast there are several good harbours[251] whence it is possible to strike inland from Harappan ports along routes to Baluchistan and the few sizeable centres like Bampur.[252] The eastern terminus of the Gulf route seems to have been the mouth of the Indus and Gujarat.

(b) Land Routes [253]

Land communication and transport between Mesopotamia and highland Iran (Fig. 5) was severely limited by geography, climate and the availablility of water. Unlike the northern and western highlands, to which the Tigris and Euphrates provide convenient riverine access, there is no easy way from the Mesopotamian alluvium onto the Iranian plateau. Difficult though they are, the long tracks through the Zagros provide the only means of access. Running in parallel chains north-west to south-east, these mountains present a formidable barrier to all east-bound traffic. In the winter, heavy snow-falls render them virtually impassable. The terrain of the onward journey across the plateau is less difficult but water is scarce. Caravans have to follow the line of the oases, avoiding the great central deserts – the Dasht-i Kavir and the Dasht-i Lut. These factors greatly circumscribed the possible routes further east. Traffic across the plateau had two broad options: a northern route (the 'Great Khorasan Road') or a southern route (the 'Royal Road' through Anšan). Both were active in the third millennium.

(1) 'The Great Khorasan Road' and branching routes. From classical antiquity, and no doubt also in the third millennium, the main road from Mesopotamia across Iran followed the line of the 'Great Khorasan Road', as it was called by the Arab geographers.[254] Beginning in northern Babylonia this route follows the Diyala into the mountains at Qasr-i-Shirin and then turns south-east through the Zagros Gates to Shahabad; thence north-east through the fertile plains of the Qareh Su and Gamas Ab by modern Kermanshah, Behistun, Kangavar and Assadabad; thereafter

---

[247] Mason *et al.* 1944: 559.
[248] On the sea routes to these islands see Alster 1983: 47f.; Ratnagar 1981: 72ff.
[249] Ratnagar 1981: 74ff.
[250] Chamlou 1972: 84, 111.
[251] Brice 1966: 172.
[252] Ratnagar 1981: 48f.; Frye 1984: 13. In early Medieval times, merchandise from the Gulf was unloaded at Chah Bahar Bay and continued eastwards by land along the Kej Valley, since the sea route to the Indus in the summer monsoon could be too dangerous (Brice 1966: 172).
[253] Previous general discussions, taking into account the archaeological evidence, include Dyson 1965: 215f.; Stein 1940: *passim*; E. Henrickson 1975: 7-10; R. Henrickson 1986: 1-4; Majedzadeh 1982: 59.
[254] Le Strange 1905: 61ff.

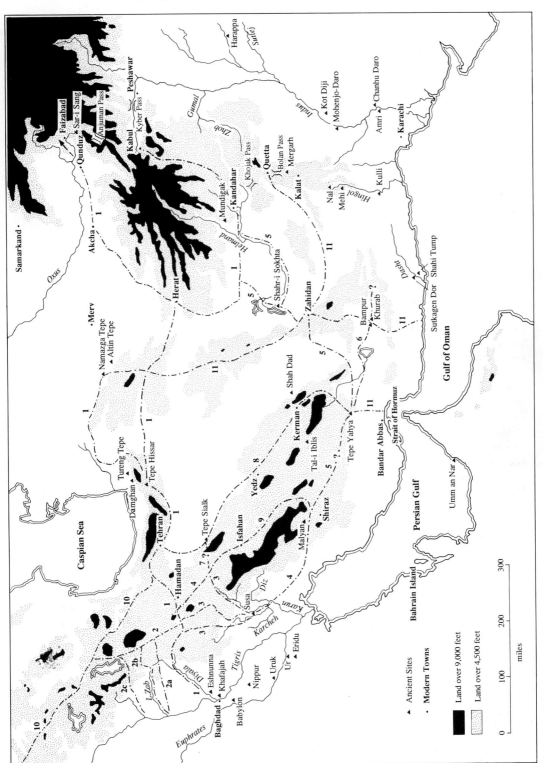

Figure 5.   Map showing major routes of communication from Mesopotamia eastwards across Greater Iran.

around the Kuh-i Alwand to Hamadan and on to Teheran where it meets the road from Tabriz and Trebizond (route (10) below).[255] From Teheran the road skirts the northern edge of the Dasht-i Kavir to Meshed[256] whence brances split off in various directions. Some routes lead south-east into Afghanistan via Herat around either side of the Hazarajat and thence via the Khyber, Gomal or Bolan Passes into the Indus Valley; others run south following the oases of the eastern mountain chain to Makran, with a side branch leading to Seistan.[257]

In the third millennium, however, the importance of the Khorasan Road probably derived more from the access it provided north and east from Khorasan over the rolling plateaux of the Binalud and Kopet Dagh mountains to the settlements of southern Turkmenistan, Margiana and Bactria. The towns along the northern piedmont of the Kopet Dagh (Anau, Namazga-tepe , Altyn-tepe *etc.*) could be reached most directly from the Meshed region by travelling north via Quchan to Ashkhabad; or by splitting from the Khorasan Road earlier, crossing the Elburz into the Gurgan plain and thus approaching from the west.[258] North-east from Meshed there are no major barriers to communication with the settlements of the Tedjen (Geoksjur, Khapuz) and Murghab deltas (Kelleli, Taip, Togolok, Gonur), though water is scarce in these sandy deserts. The Bactrian centres of the Oxus plains further east (Dashli oasis, Farukhabad, Sapallitepe, Mazar-i Sharif) are most easily reached not via the Tedjen but by skirting the Uzbekistan desert to the south along the piedmont of the Binalud and Hazarajut mountains where water is more plentiful. Following the Oxus still further into the Pamirs, the Harappan outpost of Shortugai would be reached.

On the basis of changing patterns in the ceramic evidence Levine and Young suggest that the westernmost stretch of the Khorasan road from Mesopotamia into the highlands may have been blocked in the Early Dynastic II-III period.[259] This would tie in with indications of highland-lowland frontier hostilities in the immediately preceding period, notably the construction of fortifications in the Hamrin at Razuk, Abu Qasim, Madhur, Gubba and Suleimeh.

(2) The Northern Zagros Routes.   In the Neo-Assyrian period access to Iran from northern Mesopotamia was achieved along three main routes which were probably already in use in the third millennium.[260] The southernmost route (Fig. 5, route (2a)) runs almost due east from Kirkuk through Kurdistan to Sulaimaniya and Sanandaj. From there a road leads south to the Khorasan Road and Behistun. The middle route (2b) is reached from the Lower Zab or Arbil, and leads east through southern Azerbaijan to Rania and Saqqiz, from where a road runs south through Kurdistan to Sanandaj, there meeting the southern route. The most northern route (2c), runs north-east from Arbil past Ruwandiz through Azerbaijan to the southern Urmia basin, and thence north to Tabriz. From there a continuation leads south-east, joining the Khorasan Road at Qazvin/Teheran.[261] A network of cross roads connects these and other routes of the northern Zagros at numerous points. Thus, while there is no major Azerbaijani thoroughfare comparable to the Great Khorasan Road, a

[255] Brice 1966: 90f.; *cf.* Frye 1984: 11.
[256] Brice 1966: 193.
[257] *Ibid.*: 179, 189.
[258] *Ibid.*: 177f.
[259] Levine & Young 1987: 50, 52.
[260] Levine 1973: 5-14, figs 1-2; *idem* 1974: 99-104, fig. 1.
[261] Frye 1984: 11; le Strange 1905: Map 1.

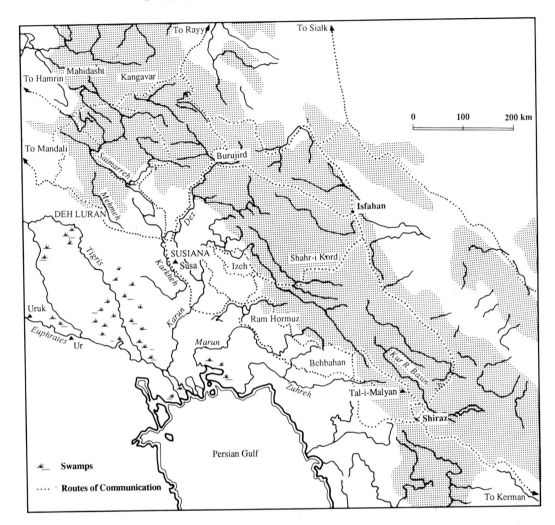

Figure 6. Map showing major routes of communication in south-western Iran.

number of tracks provide access. Given sufficient political or economic incentive, regular lowland contact with this region was entirely feasible.

(3) Routes through Susiana to Luristan. The most southern point of entry into highland Iran from Mesopotamia is through the network of roads commanded by Susa. These provide natural passage not only into the southern Zagros and Fars but also north to Luristan and the Khorasan Road. The boat trip from Sumer via the Karun was usually preferred to the journey up the Tigris and then overland to Der (Badra). While the onward journey from Der had to skirt the Kebir Kuh,[262] access to Luristan from Susa could more simply follow the northwest-southeast orientation of the mountain chains.

---

[262] Goff 1968: 108.

   Various natural routes still used by the migratory tribes run through Luristan to the fertile plains along the Khorasan Road. They keep mainly to the broad river valleys of the Diz and particularly to the Karkheh and its affluents, the Simareh, Qareh Su, Gamas Ab and Kashkan; but the crossings generally take the dry passes (kotals) rather than the treacherous river gorges.[263] The main tribal route into the highlands follows the Karkheh and Kashkan Rivers to Khurramabad and thence via Haršin to the Khorasan Road at Behistun or Kangavar. Other roads follow the Diz through Burujird to Hamadan or Kangavar, and (a poorer route) along the Simareh through Hulailan to Shahabad.[264]

(4) The 'Royal Road' to Anšan.   Perhaps the most important route eastwards from Sumer in the third millennium was the road leading through Fars to Anšan, the highland capital of Elam. In Achaemenid times this was the 'Royal Road' connecting Babylonia and Susa with Persepolis and Pasargadae. Various routes passing through the ancient settlements (Chogha Mish, Ghazir *etc.*) and the modern towns (Shushtar, Behbehan, Basht, Fahlian), or along the rivers (Marun, Zoreh), have been suggested but there are as yet no informative ancient itineraries, such as exist for the north-western routes, to choose between them.[265] From Sumer the most direct overland route probably ran straight across southern Khuzistan by-passing Susa and joining the Susa road somewhere near Behbehan. The coast nearest this city is also a likely point of disembarkation for Sumerian cargo or travellers going to Anšan; the track to Anšan from Bushire via the Shahpur valley[266] is almost as long and harder. Some Ur III 'messenger texts' suggest that the route from Girsu and Ur to Anšan ran by Nippur, and not through Susa, but the evidence is inconclusive.[267] Like Fars, Kerman supported a number of settlements at this time (*e.g.* Shahdad, Tal-i Iblis, Tepe Yahya), some of which may have maintained regular contact with Sumer. The positions of ancient sites like Jalyan and Tepe Yahya along possible extensions of the 'Royal Road' into southern Kerman suggest that easy communications continued at least that far east.

Various other routes across Iran have been suggested to account for trade and various associations in material culture.[268] Although feasible on geographical grounds, the question of their use and importance in the third millennium must be assessed in the light of archaeological evidence – in the first instance the existence of ancient sites along the proposed route. However, since few highland regions have been systematically surveyed[269] the absence of known sites does not preclude the existence of an active thoroughfare. The availability of water restricted third-millennium equid caravans more than camels, and many of the routes feasible for the latter can be excluded on this basis. The principal routes which have been suggested are:

---

263   E. Henrickson 1985: 7f.; R. Henrickson 1986: 1-4; Brice 1966: 169f.
264   Brice 1966: 170; R. Henrickson 1984: 100 n. 3; *idem* 1986: 1-4.
265   Stein 1940; Hinz 1972: 20; Alden 1982: figs 4-6; Carter 1984: 105, 107, fig. 4. Itineraries: Goetze 1953a; Hallo 1964.
266   Brice 1966: 171.
267   Gordon 1960: 132 n. 63. The itineraries given in these texts indicate only the places that the messenger has been, not necessarily which ones are on the natural routes to which other places.
268   *E.g.* Tosi & Piperno 1973: 16 [map]; Tosi 1974: fig. 1; *idem* 1974b: fig. 1; Alden 1982: figs 4-6; Hansman 1972: 103; Maxwell-Hyslop 1982: 31. Some simply trace the modern highways (*e.g.* Carter and Stolper 1984: fig. 4) a practice which, as Frye notes (1984: 10), is not always valid.
269   Carter 1984: fig. 4.

(5) Kerman-Seistan-Afghanistan.   This route would continue from the eastern end of the 'Royal Road' in southern Kerman north-east around the southern end of the Dasht-i Lut[270] and over the bleak eastern range to Seistan. From there routes continue up the Khash Rud and Helmand into Afghanistan, meeting the Herat-Kandahar road.[271]

(6) Kerman-Baluchistan-Indus.   That some traffic continued east from Fars through Kerman and on to Baluchistan and the Indus has also been suggested.[272] Most traffic this far east, however, probably took the sea passage (see above).

(7) Susa-Sialk-Teheran.   A connection between Susa, Sialk and thence to the area of modern Teheran is often assumed.[273] Though no modern thoroughfare serves this need directly, an ancient road may have existed.[274] It would have been slow and difficult, however, running directly counter to the mountain chains, and close by some of the highest peaks.

(8) Teheran-Sialk-Bandar Abbas/Zahedan.   The eastern fringe of the Kerman range, before giving way to the eastern deserts, provides a natural corridor for travel between the north-west plateau, crossing the Great Khorasan Road at Teheran, continuing south-east via Sialk to Kerman (Shahdad). From there it is possible to continue south through the Tang-i Zindan defile at the eastern end of the Zagros chain to Tepe Yahya and the coast (Bandar Abbas/Minab), whence some of the traffic using this route probably originated.[275]

(9) Kangavar-Isfahan-Shiraz.   This is today the principal highway along the middle ranges of the Zagros chain. Quitting the Khorasan Road at Kangavar, it passes by Godin Tepe and Tepe Giyan and on through the Burujird valley to Isfahan[276] before sweeping around to the south-west to Shiraz. In the third millennium this would have led to Anšan, joining up with the 'Royal Road'.

(10) Trebizond-Tabriz-Qazvin/Teheran-Khorasan-Central Asia.   In later periods this route, splitting off from the Khorasan Road at Teheran and running north-west through Azerbaijan and eastern Kurdistan to the Black Sea, was the most important artery of trade across Iran.[277] Its importance in the third millennium remains to be established.

(11) Meshed-Zahidan-Makran/Quetta.   From Meshed it is possible to travel south along the oases of the eastern range (Qain, Birjand) to Zahedan and thence into the fertile region of Sarhad. From Sarhad roads continue south by the Guinak Pass to Makran or turn east through northern Baluchistan, finally sweeping north-east to Quetta and the Indus Valley.[278]

---

[270] *Cf.* Brice 1966: 195.
[271] Alden 1982: fig. 5; Tosi 1974: fig. 1.
[272] *E.g.* M. Lambert 1974: 14; Maxwell-Hyslop 1989: 129.
[273] *E.g.* Alden 1982: fig. 5; Tosi 1974: fig. 1; Carter 1984: fig. 4.
[274] Carter & Stolper 1984: fig. 4 simply trace the circuitous modern route up the Diz then via Burujird, Malayer, Arak and Khomey.
[275] Brice 1966: 172.
[276] R. Henrickson 1986: 1.
[277] Frye 1984: 10.
[278] Brice 1966: 188-90, 197.

3. MEANS OF TRANSPORT

Trade and other contact with the east was constrained not only by the routes of communication but also by the forms of travel and the means of bulk transport available in the third millennium. The types of boats used on the Tigris-Euphrates rivers and along the Gulf, as well as their capacities, itineraries and speeds, have been reviewed by Ratnagar,[279] and need not be repeated here. Regarding land travel, however, some discussion is required, since the more careful retrieval of faunal remains on Near Eastern sites and improvements in methods of identification have recently yielded significant new evidence.

(a) Beasts of Burden

(1) EQUIDS. Before the popularisation of the camel in the late second millennium (see below) the principal beasts of burden in the Near East were various kinds of equid. Three species were present in Mesopotamia and Iran.

(i) Hemiones ('onagers'): These were present in two sub-species, the now extinct 'Syrian onager' (*Equus hemionus hemippus*), native to the lowlands and hilly flanks of Greater Mesopotamia, and the 'Persian onager' (*Equus hemionus onager*) which inhabited the Iranian plateau and lands further east.[280] Hemiones were hunted in Mesopotamia and Iran for their meat and hides, as they had been over the Near East for millennia.[281] To the Sumerians they were the 'equid of the steppe/desert' (anše-eden-na), under which name they appear from Early Dynastic I onwards.[282] Hemiones were long thought to have been the principal domestic equid of the Sumerians, but more recent investigations suggest that they cannot be fully domesticated – a fact which explains their conspicuous absence from lists of work-equids in third-millennium texts.[283] Nonetheless, documentary evidence shows that they were captured and kept in a semi-wild state from at least Early Dynastic IIIa for cross-breeding with domestic equids (see below).

(ii) Asses: The domestic ass or donkey (*Equus asinus*) was used as a pack animal in Palestine already in Chalcolithic times,[284] and was probably introduced by the early third millennium into Iran, the Gulf and Mesopotamia, where the term anše, attested as early as the Archaic Uruk texts, has plausibly been assigned this meaning.[285] In the later third millennium further qualifications (ANŠE.DUN.GI [Early Dynastic III], ANŠE.LIBIR [Akkadian – Ur III]) were added to distinguish the ass from other equids.[286] Ass-like animals are often represented in Sumerian art and recently devised tests suggest that most if not all of the domestic equid skeletons from third

---

[279] Ratnagar 1981: 157-72, 178-82.
[280] The 'Persian onager', though now restricted to higher altitudes (Clutton-Brock 1981: 101), may have also inhabited the Mesopotamian piedmont in antiquity (Zarins 1976: 76, 79, 81, 84, 141; Zarins 1978a: 16).
[281] Zarins 1976: 61ff.; *idem* 1986: 178f.; Postgate 1986: 199; Gibson 1987: 472.
[282] Postgate 1986: 196.
[283] Zarins 1978a: 16f.; Clutton-Brock 1981: 98-101. Texts: Zarins 1986: 188.
[284] C. Epstein 1985: 59.
[285] Zarins 1978a: 3; Postgate 1986: 200f. The ancestor of the Mesopotamian/Iranian ass may have been a local Asiatic species, not the African wild ass (*E. africanus africanus*) as long believed (Zarins 1986: 176f.; Clutton-Brock 1986: 212; *cf.* Clutton-Brock 1981: 98f.). For the ass in the Gulf see D.T. Potts 1993b: 180, 182, 188.
[286] Postgate 1986: 196, whose readings are followed here.

millennium burials, previously regarded as hemiones, are actually asses (or ass ×
hemione crosses).[287]

(iii) **Horses:** Present evidence suggests that the horse (*Equus caballus caballus*) was
introduced into Mesopotamia as a domesticate from the northern steppes only in the
late third millennium,[288] the date of the first plausible illustrations.[289] While asses,
hemiones and crosses are mentioned in Early Dynastic texts, the Akkadian term *sisû*
(appearing first in an inscription of the Gutian king Erridupizir)[290] and Ur III anše-zi-
zi are the earliest definite designations for 'horse'.[291] The Neo-Sumerian term is
replaced in the early second millennium by anše-kur-ra = *sisû*, which remains
thereafter the standard designation. There is no osteological evidence of the horse in
Mesopotamia until the Isin-Larsa period[292] but horse bones, some perhaps from wild
animals, are found from the late fourth and early third millennia in Palestine,[293]
Anatolia[294] and possibly Iran[295] and Central Asia.[296] As the later Sumerian name
implies, the horse was an animal of the highlands (kur). Naturally at home in the
temperate grass- and forest-steppes of the north, it was not well suited to the extreme
climate of the alluvial plains. As in later periods, stocks must have been regularly
replenished, probably from Anatolia, Syria or Iran.[297]

All these equids can inter-breed, and the offspring, though usually sterile, are
often stronger and better suited for work than their parents.[298] The relatively minor
morphological differences between hybrids and their parents makes identification on

---

[287] Asses in art: Clutton-Brock 1981:99. Ass remains definitely occur at Abu Salabikh (Clutton-Brock 1986:
209, 211f.); probably at Nippur, Kish, Razuk and Madhhur (Clutton-Brock 1986: 210, 218; Zarins 1986:
170f., 173f.). Previous identifications, as yet unconfirmed by these methods, were made at Tell Asmar
(one bone; Zarins 1976: 182), Lagaš (*ibid.*), Susa D (*ibid.*; *idem* 1986: 179), Anšan (Banesh – Kaftari
phases; Zeder 1984: 289 n. 50), Shah Tepe IIA (Ur III – OB) (H. Epstein 1971: 570; Zarins 1976: 183) and
Alaça Hüyük (*ca.* 2400-2200; *ibid.*: 182). Note also a "domesticated donkey" at Gonur in Margiana, *ca.*
2000 BC (Sarianidi 1993: 35).

[288] Sherratt 1981: 272f. The case advanced by Zarins (1976; 1978a; 1986) for a much earlier (late 4th or
early 3rd mill.) introduction has not been generally accepted (*cf.* Postgate 1986).

[289] Rein-ring from Til Barsip in Syria, *ca.* 2500-2350 (Thureau-Dangin & Dunand 1936: no. 32, pl. XXXI; *cf.*
Zarins 1976: 295ff.); shell inlay from Susa (Amiet 1966: fig. 143). The usual identification of the latter as
a Przewalskii horse (*e.g.* Moorey 1970: 38) raises the interesting question of whether the natural range of
this animal, usually thought to have been restricted to the continental steppe-lands of Central Asia,
extended also to south-west Iran. If so, could this be a centre of early domestication? Sollberger 1984: 12
regards the Proto-Elamite sign for equid as "an equid's head with a mane typical of Equus Przewalskii"
which he considers "at home" in Elam.

[290] $si\text{-}se_x(SU_4?)$ (Kutscher 1989: BT2 vi:8; Frayne 1992: 632 reads ANŠE.si-s[i]-šu-nu). Note that this animal
is listed separately from the "asses", imere(ANŠE[e?]) (*ibid.*: vi:7).

[291] Alternatively, Zarins (above note 288) takes various equid terms occuring from ED I, identified by Postgate
as asses (see above), to refer to types of horses. The anše-kur on a Jemdet Nasr tablet, sometimes
regarded as evidence for early horses, is probably to be read 'male equid/ass' (Postgate 1986: 201 n. 27).

[292] Zarins 1986:180.

[293] Arad (EB II); Zarins 1986: 180.

[294] Zarins 1986: 179f. with bibliog. The sites concerned are: Norşuntepe, Tülintepe, Arslan Tepe, Tepeçik,
Demirci Hüyük (Chalcolithic-EB I). Later evidence comes from Selenkhahiyeh in Syria (late 3rd mill.) and
Korüçütepe (Old Hittite) (Zarins 1976: 187f.; *idem* 1986: 179f.; Littauer & Crouwel 1979: 41 nn. 16, 17;
Mellaart 1981: 137).

[295] This evidence may be questionable since it is omitted by Zarins 1986:179f.: Geoy Tepe M (Chalcolithic)
(Burton-Brown 1951: 29; Zarins 1976: 197); Susa D, Cart Burials (Zarins 1976: 188f.; *cf.* Zarins 1986:
168f.). Also possibly Chogha Mish (Proto-Elamite) (Zarins 1976: 187). The horse bones reported from 5th
and late-4th mill. Iblis (levels I and IV) (Zarins 1976: 185ff.; Littauer & Crouwel 1979: 24f.) are
questionable. The report of possible horse bones at Godin IV (early 3rd mill.) (Littauer & Crouwel 1979: 24
n. 46) has not been confirmed.

[296] Kelleli 1, Taip and Takhirbai 3 in Margiana; Namazga-tepe Tekken-tepe in southern Turkmenia; all late
3rd – early 2nd mill. (Kohl 1987: 22).

[297] For two speculative routes of entry see Zarins 1976: 197f.

[298] Clutton-Brock 1981: 94. However, modern tests suggest that ass x hemione hybrids may be unruly and
difficult to mannage (Clutton-Brock 1986: 200, n. 22).

the basis of osteological or pictorial evidence extremely difficult.[299] A Proto-Elamite tablet from Susa showing equids with three different kinds of mane (upright, falling, maneless) may suggest the presence of at least that many species/breeds in the alluvium near the beginning to the third millennium.[300] Later documentary evidence is more illuminating. Texts of the Early Dynastic IIIa to Ur III period in Mesopotamia and from Ebla mention a hybrid (anše-BARxAN), almost certainly ass x hemione, which was preferred for chariots and cost up to six times more than pure-bred asses.[301] There is presently no evidence of horse hybrids until the second millennium,[302] when mules are attested in contemporary documents and in bones from Korüçütepe in Turkey,[303] but the probability of breeding from Ur III times, when horses first became available in significant numbers, cannot be excluded.

There is no direct evidence from contemporary representations or documents as to which of these equids were used as pack animals in third-millennium Mesopotamia. The loading of grain onto 'horses' (anše-kur-kur-ra) for transport from Uruk to Aratta in *Enmerkar and the Lord of Aratta* line 127 is probably anachronistic.[304] Šu-Sin loaded the booty of Zabšali in highland Iran onto pack-asses (anše-bar) for transport to Ur.[305] In the Old Assyrian period asses (ANŠE, *emarum*), very rarely horses, were used as carriers in the trade with Cappadocia.[306] This may reflect earlier practice but it would be surprising if the superior speed, strength and endurance of the horse/ass/hemione hybrids (especially the mule) over the pure-bred asses and horses had not already been recognized and exploited.

(2) CAMELS. Although dromedaries are occasionally illustrated in Mesopotamia and surrounding regions from the Ubaid period on,[307] no representations suggest that the animals were yet domesticated. Camels do not appear in third-millennium texts (except perhaps in a Proto-Elamite text from Chogha Mish).[308] Suggestions that dromedaries were domesticated by the early third millennium in Egypt, south and south-east Arabia remain unconfirmed.[309] Both dromedaries and 'Bactrian' camels were known to Old Babylonian scribes, and the latter at least seem by then to have been tamed to the point of being milked.[310] Clear evidence of widespread use of domestic camels for transport, however, does not appear until the later second millennium, when dromedaries were introduced in large numbers by the Aramaeans.[311]

---

[299] Littauer & Crouwel 1979: 23, 25f.; Clutton-Brock 1981: 91, 95ff.; Clutton-Brock 1986.

[300] Amiet 1966: fig. 50b.

[301] Postgate 1986: 196f.; Zarins 1986: 184ff.

[302] No mule bones have been identified among the 3rd mill. remains which have been recently re-examined (Clutton-Brock 1986: 208).

[303] Texts: Postgate 1986: 196. Bones: Zarins 1976: 200f.

[304] S. Cohen 1973: 118, 192f.

[305] *IRSA*: IIIA4e; Kutscher 1989: BT4 v:13; Landsberger 1965: 292.

[306] Veenhof 1972: 1 n. 2.

[307] Evidence collected in Brentjes 1960, H. Epstein 1971: 567ff., 581 and Bulliet 1975: 46, nn. 42, 43 (note that the plaque showing a [? camel] rider [Bulliet's fig. 10] is from Tell Asmar not Ur). Add the Jemdet Nasr seal with a 'Bactrian' camel reported by Tosi 1974: 163 and the dromedary on a stamp seal from Gonur (Sarianidi 1993: 34, pl. VIIIg). For Egypt (figurines, reliefs, pot-protomes, hair) see H. Epstein 1971: 558ff. (some dates incorrect), Ripinsky 1985; for Umm an-Nar (bones, reliefs) see Tosi 1974: 162; Hoch 1979: 607ff.

[308] Ripinsky 1985: 134 n. 3.

[309] H. Epstein 1971: 571ff.; Ripinsky 1975; *idem* 1985; Bulliet 1975: 56; Compagnoni & Tosi 1978: 100f.; *cf.* Zarins 1978a.

[310] *CAD*: s.v. *ibilu*.

[311] Evidence collected in H. Epstein, Brentjes loci cit. and Bulliet 1975: 60ff. (note that the Byblos 'foundation deposits' from which comes the bronze figurine [Bulliet fig. 16] are mainly 2nd [not 3rd] mill., as is probably this piece) and, for patriarchal associations, 35ff., 58 and Barnett 1985: 17. A copper camel

Camel bones, probably from dromedaries, excavated in third-millennium houses on Umm an-Nar island must, if local, be from domesticated herds; otherwise, captured wild beasts may have been brought across for slaughtering.[312] Frifelt suggests that camels were used to bring copper across Oman from the eastern mountains to Umm an-Nar.[313] Their bones have been found at a number of sites in Oman as well as early second millennium Failaka.[314]

Iran, on the other hand, probably fell within the distribution of the wild 'Bactrian' camel.[315] There is some evidence to suggest that these had been domesticated in adjacent southern Turkmenia and perhaps at Shahr-i Sokhta by mid-millennium.[316] There is as yet no proof of their use as pack animals at that date, but this remains a strong probability.

Camel bones first appear in the Indus Valley on Mature Harappan sites by which time they were domesticated. Although osteological data is equivocal the likelihood is that they were Bactrian.[317]

(3) BOVIDS. Domestic bovids were present in both Mesopotamia and Iran and may have been used ocasionally as beasts of burden, though they are less suited to this task than to the draught (see below).

(b) Wheeled vehicles

Scattered evidence from Mesopotamia (Fig. 38), Iran, Central Asia and the Indus indicates that wheeled vehicles of various forms were widely employed for a range of purposes in the third millennium.[318] However, they must have been restricted to relatively flat open ground – the lowland alluvium, the broad intermontane valleys and the open rolling plateaux.[319] They would have been entirely unsuitable for transporting goods through the rugged Zagros mountains, as is confirmed by the lack of references to carts or other land vehicles in trade texts of the third millennium.[320]

(c) Ridden animals

(i) *Equids*. The equids used as pack animals could also serve as riding beasts for fast light transport. Firm evidence of equid-riding in Mesopotamia does not begin

---

amulet is reported from Sargonic Girsu; de Genouillac 1934: 89 (TG 956). Of particular interest are the camels ridden (?) on the two Syrian seals: Porada 1977, 18th century BC ('Bactrian') and Brentjes 1960: 30 fig. 3, mid-2nd mill. (?) (dromedary).

[312] Hoch 1979: 591, 607-13.
[313] Frifelt 1975.
[314] D.T. Potts 1993b: 182, 188, 194.
[315] Clutton-Brock 1981: 126.
[316] See generally Bulliet 1975: 148ff., H. Epstein 1971: 569f. Bones have been recovered beginning in the late 3rd mill. at Shah-tepe in the Atrak Valley; in the 4th – 3rd millennia at Anau-tepe, Altyn-tepe, Ulug-tepe, Hapuz-tepe, Chong-tepe and Namazga-tepe in south Turkmenia; further east, in the late 3rd mill. at Harappa and Mohenjo Daro; and south in 3rd mill. Oman (loc. cit.; Tosi 1974: 162; Campagnoni & Tosi 1978: 99f.). At Shahr-i Sokhta Tosi takes the presence of bones, woven hair, dung and a possibly camelid figurine in phases 6-7 (*ca.* 2700-2500 BC) to indicate an early stage of domestication (Campagnoni & Tosi 1978).
[317] Meadow 1984.
[318] Littauer & Crouwel 1979: 31ff., 44ff.; Calmeyer 1969: 8f., 11f., 20, Taf. 1:3; Schmidt 1937: 199, fig. 118; Lisitsina 1981: 354-56; Masson & Kiiatkina 1981: 115; Kohl 1984: 114; *idem*. 1987: 22; Amiet 1986b: 16, Taf. 8-9.
[319] Littauer & Crouwel 1979: 35.
[320] Likewise in the OA Cappadocian trade, carts were used occasionally for large loads but only within Anatolia (Veenhof 1972: 1). Note however *ELA*: 278 "as to the relief grain due to us (in Aratta), let him not load it into carts".

until the Early Dynastic III/Akkadian period,[321] but it almost certainly began earlier. Likewise, though there are no contemporary illustrations of riding in Iran and Central Asia it was surely practised there too. Asses and mules, whose hooves are tougher than horses,[322] would have provided the best mounts for travel through the rocky passes of the Zagros into the eastern highlands.

(ii) *Camels*. If Bactrian camels were perhaps already domesticated in Iran, southern Turkmenia and the Indus (see above), there is still no pictorial evidence that they were ridden. Similarly, in Mesopotamia, aside from an Ur III-Old Babylonian plaque from Khafajeh, which may show a ridden camel (or an equid?),[323] there are no pre-second-millennium illustrations.

4. CHRONOLOGY

Table 1.1 summarises the chronology adopted in this study. Table 2.1 provides a more detailed comparative stratigraphy of the recent excavations at Susa.

It should be emphasised that the comparative stratigraphy and chronology of Greater Iran in the third-millennium is still very poorly known. This applies especially to sites dug in the first half of this century when stratigraphical controls were primative or non-existant (Susa, Tepe Sialk, Tepe Giyan, Tepe Hissar), and to material retrieved in clandestine excavations (Luristan, Bactria). Typological connections, still the primary basis of all relative chronologies, can indicate only very approximate correlations across such a vast area. Radiocarbon determinations are rarely numerous or consistent enough to provide a viable independent framework.[324]

Two areas of particular uncertainty which directly affect this study relate to Tepe Yahya and southern Turkmenia. The high Yahya chronology originally proposed by the excavator has been progressively lowered in the light of observations by Amiet and others. The most thorough and radical revision is by D.T. Potts, who convincingly down-dates periods IVC1, IVB (and by implication also IVA) by almost half a millennium (below pp. 260f.).[325]

Regarding Namazga Tepe, the original type-site for southern Turkmenia (and by extension also for Margiana and Bactria) the Soviet chronology[326] is generally agreed to be too low, but revised estimates incorporating C14 evidence still differ by as much as four hundred years.[327]

Both views on these issues are represented in Table 1.1.

---

[321] Littauer & Crouwel 1979: 34f., 45f. Pictorial evidence is collected in Moorey 1970 (add Owen 1991: no. 271, frontispiece). The earliest representations seem to be an ED III-Akkadian seal impression from Kish (Buchanan 1966: no. 290b) and an Akkadian gold fillet from Ur (Woolley 1934: pl. 139; probably not an equid). Note also the ED IIIb burial of a man with an *E. hemionus onager* (his mount?) at Lagaš (Zarins 1986: 171). For documentary evidence (Ur III ra-gab, 'riders') see Salonen 1956: 224ff.; Zarins 1976: 419f. The ED IIIa *Instructions of Šuruppak* warns: "Don't purchase a hemione (if you are intending) to buy a riding animal (u_5)" (Biggs 1974: 60 vi:4f.; Zarins 1986: 188). Messengers at Mari rode donkeys (*imeru/emaru*) (Leemans 1960: 134; Salonen 1956: 56-58).

[322] Littauer & Crouwel 1979: 12.

[323] Frankfort *et al.* 1940: 212, fig. 126:f.; Bulliet 1975: 46.

[324] Schacht 1987: 190f.; Dyson 1987: 675-78 (Hissar II/Proto-Elamite horizon); Brentjes 1986 (Turkmenia); Voigt & Dyson in press; Sarianidi 1993: 36 (Gonur Tepe, Margiana).

[325] Amiet 1976: 24, n. 4; D.T. Potts in press [a].

[326] Masson & Sarianidi 1972; Sarianidi 1993: 36 (Margiana).

[327] Amiet 1986: 187f.; 190-204; *idem* 1987: 175; Kohl 1981: xxviii-xxxi; *idem* 1984: 209-36; Brentjes 1986; Carter 1991: 169; Hiebert & Lamberg-Karlovsky 1992.

Table 1.1 is based upon the following sources (*'cf.'* indicates an alternative view):

Mesopotamia.	Porada 1965; Hansen 1965; *idem* in press; Wright & Johnson 1975 (Uruk phasing); Vértesalji & Kolbus 1985: 91-97, fig. H; Wright 1980 (C14 dates); Brinkman in Oppenheim 1977: 335f.; *cf.* Huber 1982.
Susa.	Carter 1984: fig. 15; Amiet 1986: 12f.
Tepe Farukhabad.	Wright ed. 1981: Table 2; Carter 1984: fig. 15; *cf.* Haerinck 1987.
Luristan	(Pusht-i Kuh cemeteries). Vanden Berghe & Haerinck 1984; Haerinck 1987; *cf.* Vanden Berge 1972; *idem* 1982.
Godin Tepe.	R. Henrickson 1985: Table 1; *idem* 1987: fig. 64; *cf.* Haerinck 1987: n. 119; Dyson 1987.
Tepe Giyan.	R. Henrickson 1985; *idem* 1986; Dyson 1965 (phase V only).
Tepe Sialk.	Amiet 1985; *idem* 1986: 41, 61ff.; Dyson 1987.
Tal-i Malyan (Anšan)	Amiet 1986: 12f.; Alden 1982: fig. 2, table 2; Carter 1984: fig. 15; *cf.* Sumner 1986: 199 n. 2; *idem* 1988: 313-16.
Tal-i Iblis.	Tosi 1979: Table 1; Carter 1984: fig. 15; *cf.* Caldwell ed. 1967: 21ff., fig. 2.
Shahdad.	Amiet 1986: 12f., 134; Salvatori & Vidale 1982: 135f.
Tepe Yahya.	Left column: Amiet 1986: 12f.; *idem* 1976: 24, n. 4; *cf.* Lamberg-Karlovsky 1972: 89; *idem* 1977: 35; Kohl 1975: 18; Carter 1984: fig. 15. Right column: D.T. Potts in press [a]; *cf.* Bovington *et al.* 1983: 351 (C14 dates); Beale 1986: 11.
Shahr-i Sokhta.	Amiet 1986: 12f.; Tosi 1979: Table 1; Biscioni *et al.* 1977: 84; *cf.* Bovington *et al.* 1983.
Bampur.	Amiet 1986: 12f.; *cf.* de Cardi 1970: Table 2; Tosi 1979: Table 1.
Tepe Hissar.	Left column: Tosi 1979: Table 1; Amiet 1986: 185. Right column: Bovington *et al.* 1974 (C14 dates); Dyson 1987; Yule 1982: Abb. 3.
Tureng Tepe.	Amiet 1986: 12f.; Deshayes 1970: 208; *idem* 1975; *idem* 1976; *cf.* Yule 1982: Abb. 3.
Mundigak.	de Cardi 1984: Table 9.1; Tosi 1979: Table 1; *cf.* Allchin & Allchin 1982: fig. 5:17.
Mehrgarh.	Jarrige & Lechevallier 1979: 533f.; Lechevallier 1984: 46, Table 7.6; *cf.* Allchin & Allchin 1982: fig. 5:17.
Indus Valley.	Allchin & Allchin 1982: fig. 5:17.
Namazga Tepe.	Left column: Amiet 1986: 12f., 187f. Right column: Kohl 1981: xxviii-xxxi; *idem* 1984: 209-36.
Margiana.	Amiet 1986: 190; Pottier 1984: 54.
Bactria.	Amiet 1986: 190-204; Pottier 1984: 54f.
Oman.	Cleuziou 1989; Cleuziou & Tosi 1989; D.T. Potts 1990; *idem* 1993b.
Bahrain.	D.T. Potts 1990.

Mesopotamia		Iran									
BC	PERIOD	SUSA	FARUKH-ABAD	LURISTAN	GODIN TEPE	TEPE GIYAN	TEPE SIALK	TAL-I MALYAN	TAL-I IBLIS	SHAH-DAD	TEPE YAHYA
			A B			Dyson Henrick-son		ABC TUV			L-K. D.Potts Amiet
1800		Sukkalmahs			III2						
	Isin-				- - - - -			Kaftari			
	Larsa	V.R. I									
1900	(2004-1792)	3	14		Gap			I			IVA
		4	15								
2000		Dyn. of				IVA					1
	Ur III	Šimaški 5			III4					IVA	2
	(2112-	Susa V			IVC			?			3
2100	2004)	Puzur- 6	18		Gap			↓			IVB 4
	Guti	Inšušinak						?			5
		7			Gap			- - - -			6
2200	↑		- -?- -				?				
	Akkadian	8			IVB					1	IVC1
	(2334-	Dyn. of						Gap		2	
2300	2154)	Awan ?			III5		?			3	
		Susa IV			Gap					IVB	
2400	ED IIIB	9	Gap							4	
		10								Area B	5
2500					IVA	?				6	Gap
	ED IIIA	11			III6						
2600		12	- - -?- - -					- -?- - - -?-			Gap
		13	11 19	III							
		14									
2700	ED II	15						Late			
								Banesh			
		Acrop. I 16						II			
2800	ED I	13 17		II	Gap						
			5 20					II III			
		14a-b 18	6 21		IV		IV2	Late-Midd.			1
2900	Jemdet	Susa III						Banesh		IVC IVC2	
	Nasr	15							VI		
3000		16 Proto-		I	VIA V		IV1	III			2
	(Uruk III)	Elamite									
		?								C	
3100			17 27		VD			Early-Midd.		- - - -	
		17 Late	18 28					Banesh			
	Late Uruk	Uruk						IV			
3200	(VII-IV)	18							V	Gap Gap	
		Susa II	20 31			III6-7		Early		A	
		19	21 32		VIB VC2			Banesh			
3300	Middle	Middle					↓	(Anšan			
	Uruk	Uruk						founded)			VA
	(XII-VIII)										

Table 1.1 Comparative chronology of Greater Iran adopted in this study.

		Greater Indus					Central Asia			Gulf		
SHAHR-I SOKHTA	BAMPUR	TEPE HISSAR	TURENG TEPE	MUNDI-GAK	MEHR-GARH	INDUS VALLEY	NAMAZGA TEPE	MARGIAN A	BACTRIA	OMAN	BAHRAIN	BC
		Amiet / Dyson, Yule				- - -?- - -	Amiet Kohl			Hili 8 Tombs		
			- - -?- -				VI	Gonor	Djarkutan	↑ Wadi Suq	Babar III	1800
	VI	IIIC	IIIC2					Kelleli ? ↓	Sapali ? ↓	III	City II	1900
IV (0-2)						Mature Indus	V / VI			II g	Babar I-II	2000
	V	IIIC / IIIB	IIIB		VIII	Indus				II f	Babar Temp. I	2100
		IIIA	IV3					- - -?- - -	- - -?- - -	II e / Umm an-Nar	City I	2200
III (3-4)	IV1-3	IIIA			- - -?- - -		V			II d		2300
										II c2		2400
	III	IIB IIIB	IIB		VII		IV			II c1		2500
II (5-7)	II					Early				II b		2600
	I			IV2		Indus	IV			II a		2700
		IIIA		IV1						Hafit / I c		2800
		Late		III	VI	Pre				I b		2900
I (8-10)		IIA / II	IIA			Indus	III					3000
		Middle								I a		3100
		Terminal					III					3200
		IC / I		II								3300
				V		II						

Chapter 2

Sumer and the Proto-Elamites

1. THE 'PROTO-ELAMITE PHENOMENON'

Before the mid-fourth millennium, southern Mesopotamia's relations with Iran – as far as these may be gleaned from traded materials and typological parallels – play a secondary role to those with Upper Mesopotamia and, in the Ubaid period, the Gulf. Parallels between Mesopotamian and Iranian pottery, glyptic and metalwork can be demonstrated during Neolithic and Chalcolithic times,[1] but, outside Susiana, there is little to suggest more than irregular, largely indirect contact such as would be expected in adjacent regions with complementary natural resources.

Already Susa is something of a special case. Geographically part of the lowlands, this city was more able to participate in developments further west and clearly did so from the beginning of her history. During the Susa I period, monumental building programmes, fully the equal of any in Sumer, and the development of sealing practices to identify and secure property, are evidence that Susa, like Sumer, was the focus of administrative and social advances which seem to be associated with early 'state' formation.[2]

But none of this is any preparation for the explosion in Mesopotamian-Iranian relations that was to follow. In strikingly clear and unambiguous terms, the archaeological record of the late fourth and third millennia illustrates the transposition of Late Uruk-Jemdet Nasr (and later Proto-Elamite) culture far outside its original homeland into the surrounding highlands. This great expansion in the limits of Sumerian[3] influence and control represents a dramatic shift in the nature and intensity of relations with Iran and other neighbours. In the extent of demonstrable colonisation and wholesale cultural penetration of foreign territories the Late Uruk/Proto-Elamite expansion remains unparalleled in the archaeological record until Achaemenid times.

In the north-west a number of settlements whose purely Sumerian material culture compels us to regard them as colonies, were established along the Great Bend of the Euphrates.[4] Sumerian settlement probably continued as far north as Hassek Hüyük and traces of Late Uruk material culture are found even further

---

[1]   Dyson 1965; Voigt & Dyson in press; Caldwell 1976.
[2]   Amiet 1986: 36f. (buildings); *ibid.*: 43f. (sealing); Wright & Johnson 1985.
[3]   This term is used here for convenience although it is not until the Uruk III period that grammatical indications identify the language of the Archaic texts as Sumerian (Nissen 1985: 354f.).
[4]   Excavated sites include Habuba Kabira (Strommenger 1980), Qannas (Finet 1979; *idem* 1983), Jebel Aruda (van Driel & van Driel-Murray 1979; *idem* 1983), Carchemish (Woolley & Barnett 1952). See generally Algaze 1986b.

upstream into Anatolia.[5] There was almost certainly a similar colony at Nineveh and perhaps at other points along the Tigris;[6] and Uruk-related material is found between the rivers at Tell Brak[7] and elsewhere in Assyria.[8] Recent reports suggest the possibility of Late Ubaid or Uruk colonies associated with copper working in Transcaucasia.[9]

The Sumerians also dominated the territory eastwards into Susiana, where the Susa II culture is now virtually indistinguishable from that of contemporary Late Uruk Sumer. As Algaze has stated, "in the later part of the Uruk period the Susiana plain was culturally as much a part of the Mesopotamian world as the alluvium itself".[10] Colonies[11] of this lowland culture were established in the highlands where they have been excavated at Godin Tepe and Tepe Sialk. Late Uruk pottery is known from surveys of many more sites as far east as Tal-i Iblis VI-IV and Tepe Yahya VA.[12] As in the north-west, these seem to have been relatively isolated outposts.[13]

To the south-east there is accumulating evidence of Sumerian presence along the Gulf littoral, mainly in the form of pottery. While most parallels are with Jemdet Nasr to Early Dynastic material, a clay bulla-like object and drooping spouted vessel sherds from Dhahran in eastern Arabia may date back to the Late Uruk period.[14]

The end of the Uruk IV period seems to have represented something of a crisis in Sumerian foreign relations, witnessing a complete withdrawal from the north-west, where the Euphrates colonies were abandoned.[15] Likewise in the east, Chogha Mish was abandoned and Godin was occupied by 'Yanik' intruders who had no links with the lowlands.[16] At Susa the Uruk-related culture was replaced by the distinctive Proto-Elamite (Susa III) assemblage (Fig. 7:12-17), so-named from the script which first appears in these levels. The specific ceramic, glyptic and other links of the Susa III culture are primarily with the Iranian plateau (especially Tal-i Malyan). However, some lowland connections are still apparent in the pottery, and particularly in Proto-Elamite bureaucracy which likewise involved extensive use of writing and sealing.

---

[5]   Hassek Hüyük (Behm-Blanke *et al.* 1981), Samsat (Ozdogan 1977: 130-34), Kurban Hüyük (Algaze 1986), Arslantepe, Degimentepe, Koruçutepe and Tepecik (Esin 1982; Mellaart 1982: 8). See generally Algaze 1986a; *idem* 1986b; Mellink 1992: 134f.

[6]   Collon & Reade 1983 (numerical tablet and tag bulla); Algaze 1986 (bevelled-rim bowls, monumental architecture *etc.*); *idem* 1986b.

[7]   Mallowan 1947.

[8]   Algaze 1986a; *idem* 1986b; *idem* 1989; Sürenhagen 1986. In general, connections are strongest at the river sites; inland sites like Gawra and Abu Danne are conspicuously lacking in lowland connections (Mellaart 1982: 9; Algaze 1986a: 131).

[9]   Kohl in Algaze 1989: 597f.

[10] Algaze 1986: 20-22. Algaze argues that Sumer colonized Susiana in the Susa II period thus establishing a 'formal empire', in contrast to the 'informal empire' represented by settlements along the Euphrates. *Cf.* Nissen 1985a: 39 who notes the difficulty of assuming that the population of south-western Iran during the Uruk period differed substantially from that of earlier and later periods, when highland Iranian traits are more noticeable.

[11] *Cf.* the distinction between enclaves, stations and outposts in Algaze 1989.

[12] Bevelled-rim bowls and spouted jars occur at Iblis VI-IV in Kerman (Caldwell ed. 1967: 23-25, 111-201) and at Yahya VA (Lamberg-Karlovsky 1972: 97; *idem* 1973: 304f.). Surveys of 900 sites in the Mahidasht and Kermanshah regions of the Central Zagros identified 11 sites with bevelled-rim bowls. Two, where these represented 5% and 19% of the total repertory, may be Uruk outposts like Godin (Young 1986: 219f.). Lesser quantities of bevelled-rim bowls were collected at a few other sites in the Kangavar valley (*ibid.*: 218) and at Tepe Giyan (*ibid.*: 220).

[13] No bevelled-rim bowls have been found in surveys of the Burujird and Assadabad valleys and the Hamadan and Malayer plains (Young 1986: 220) suggesting that Godin may have been unique in eastern Luristan.

[14] D.T. Potts 1993b: 180f.

[15] Algaze 1986b: Ch. 5.

[16] Young 1986: 221.

Late Uruk Period

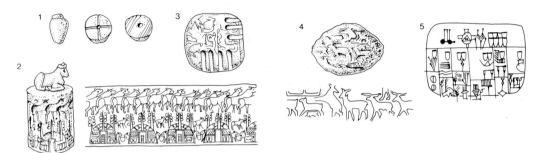

Susa II Period (= Late Uruk)

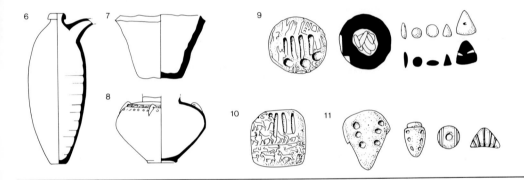

Susa III Period (= Jemdet Nasr)

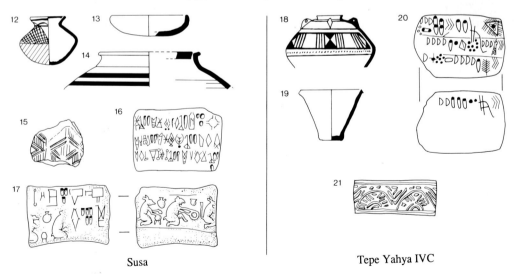

Susa

Tepe Yahya IVC

Figure 7. Late Uruk period assemblages from Sumer (2, 5), Habuba Kabira (1, 3, 4) and Susa (6-11). Proto-Elamite assemblages from Susa (12-17) and Tepe Yahya (18-21). Not to scale.

Evidence of these practices is found over an even greater area of Iran than the Susa II sites, from Susa north-east to Tepe Sialk (and possibly Tepe Hissar), and across Fars (Tal-i Malyan) and Kerman (Tepe Yahya) to Seistan (Shahr-i Sokhta) in the east.[17] There are also clues that Proto-Elamite artefacts may have reached Egypt, like Uruk ones before them: notably cylinder seals and perhaps also impressed tablets.[18]

The appearance of identical administrative practices, glyptic and pottery in the Susa II-III periods, at sites which previously show no evidence of specific material cultural links, has come to be known as the 'Proto-Elamite phenomenon'. An explanation of this phenomenon, and its relationship with Protoliterate Sumer, presents the first major task for any study of early Mesopotamian-Iranian relations.

Proto-Elamite culture was first encountered in the late nineteenth century by French excavators at *Susa* and that site remains the principal point of reference. In the early excavations, from which most available material derives, there was no rigorous stratigraphical separation of the Proto-Elamite and earlier Uruk-related assemblages. Le Breton established what distinctions could be justified on the basis of the original records, assigning the Proto-Elamite material to his periods Cb-Dd/c/d; but it was not until the excavations of Le Brun on the Acropole that a reliable stratigraphical sequence was established, separating the Late Uruk (Susa II) from the Proto-Elamite (Susa III), thereby allowing the more numerous 'unstratified' finds to be dated.[19]

The Susa II pottery from Acropole I:22-17 includes a number of standard Late Uruk types: bevelled rim bowl, 'flower pots', four-lugged jars with incised shoulder decoration, drooping spouts *etc.* (Fig. 7:6-8).[20] As in Middle-Late Uruk Sumer, this period also saw the introduction of cylinder seals (level 20) and envelope bullae containing clay 'tokens' (Fig. 7:9). The bullae were impressed with stamp or cylinder seals and (from level 18) sometimes also tokens corresponding in types and number to those enclosed (Fig. 10). Tablets occur also (Fig. 7:10), but unlike Uruk IV, where a pictographic script was in use, only 'numerical' tablets are attested.

In the Acropolis sounding there is a stratigraphical break, perhaps indicating a short period of abandonment, before the Susa III or Proto-Elamite period proper begins,[21] represented by Acropolis I: 16-13/11 and Ville Royale I:18-13.[22] Although a few pottery forms continue, the material culture in general is noticeably different from the preceding period. Bricks and hearth types, as well as the bulk of the pottery (Fig 7:12-14), are now markedly different and relate to forms familiar from Tal-i

---

[17] Suggestions that incised markings on Central Asian figurines and ceramics were inspired by the Proto-Elamite script remain unconfirmed.

[18] For cylinder seals see Teissier 1987. An unprovenanced Egyptian ivory/shell label (Scharff 1929: no. 113, Taf. 22) bears an animal frieze reminiscent of Proto-Elamite glyptic, circular markings resembling numerical signs, and a pictogramme resembling the proto-Egyptian sign for a plough. Pittman (n.d. [2]) suggests that an Egyptian craftsman had copied a sealed numerical tablet, probably without knowing what it was.

[19] Le Breton 1957; Le Brun 1971; *idem* 1978. However, some types, notably the more elaborate painted pottery previously recovered in funerary contexts, are entirely lacking.

[20] Le Brun 1978: 183, fig. 32; Amiet 1986: 55.

[21] Le Brun 1971: 210f.; *idem* 1978: 57f.; Dittmann 1986: 171f., 175; *cf.* Stève & Gasche 1971: 10. An erosion layer above level 17, paralleled by the final collapse and abandonment of the high terrace (Canal 1978a: 50) – where there is a similar erosion layer (Stève & Gasche 1971: 10, plan 2, coupe c; plan 7, coupe 4) – may indicate a significant break at Susa at this time (Dyson 1987: 648f.). *Cf.* Strommenger (1980: 483f.) who argues for a "long interval", starting level 16 in the ED I period.

[22] Carter 1980. There is no generally agreed starting point for the Proto-Elamite period. Some (*e.g.* Carter 1984: 115f.) still include the late Susa II levels (Acropole I:18-17) in the Proto-Elamite period. But it is now more common to restrict this to the Susa III period; or more generally to levels in which pictographic Proto-Elamite tablets occur. To avoid ambiguity this latter is here sometimes referred to as the "Proto-Elamite period proper".

TABLE 2.1
The Comparative Stratigraphy of Recent Excavations at Susa[1]

PERIOD	ACROPOLE	ACROP. I	ACROP. II	VILLE ROYALE I	MESOPOTAMIA
Susa I	A2	27	11		*Late Ubaid -*
		23	7		*Early Uruk*
3500------					
		22	6		
		21	5		*Middle Uruk*
		20	4		
Susa II		19	3		
		- - - - - - -	- - - - - -		- - - - - - - - - - -
		18	2		
					Late Uruk
		17	1		
3100------					
		gap?			
		- - - - - - -			*Jemdet Nasr*
		16			
Proto-		15			
Elamite		14b			
		- - - - - - -			- - - - - - - - - - -
Susa III		14a		18	
		13		17	*Early Dynastic I*
				16	
				15	- - - - - - - - - - -
				14	
				13	*Early Dynastic II*
2600------					
	4	10?		12	
				11	
	3			10	*Early Dynastic III*
				9	
Susa IV				- - - ? - - -	- - - - - - - - - - -
Awan	2			8	*Akkadian*
Dynasty					
				- - - - - -	- - - - - - - - - - -
	1			7	
2150------					*Post-Akkadian*
Puzur-			VILLE	6	
Inšušinak			ROYALE B		- - - - - - - - - - -
Susa V				5	*Ur III*
Šimaški			VII	4	
Dynasty				- - - - - -	- - - - - - - - - - -
2000			VI	3	*Isin-Larsa*

Notes
1 Based upon stratigraphical reports and studies as follows ('cf.' indicates an alternative view): **Acropole** - Stève & Gasche 1971; *cf.* Van Loon 1981; Haerinck 1987. **Acropole I** - Le Brun 1971; *idem* 1978. **Acropole II** - Canal 1978a; *idem* 1978b. **Ville Royale I** - Carter 1978; *idem* 1980; *idem* 1984: fig. 15. Ville Royale B - Gasche 1973.

Malyan on the plateau.[23] The elaborate painted wares with Diyala connections, typical of the Deh Luran, are rare at Susa.[24] The glyptic too is now dominated by

---

23   Wright 1987: 147.

native Iranian styles.[25] The most distinctive style is characterised by animals in human attitudes (Fig. 7:17; *cf.* Fig. 23) typically rendered by deep lines outlining the animals' component parts (Fig. 9), or more rarely by naturalistic, well-rounded carving deriving from the fine Uruk IV style, though now with different subjects (Figs 7:17; 8). This naturalistic style is particularly prominent on tablets which, in Acropole I:16 and after, are inscribed in the Proto-Elamite script (Figs 7:16-17; 8). Sealings from doors (usually 'Piedmont style'; Fig. 7:15), jars and tags continue, but bullae and tokens disappear. The contexts of these finds are modest, presumably private buildings, in contrast to Uruk where administrative documents seem to be concentrated in the large temple complexes.[26]

The Susa Acropole sequence has been described in some detail since the ceramic, glyptic and tablet typologies established there form the basis of the relative chronology of Proto-Elamite sites across Iran and, more importantly, of the major division of the Proto-Elamite period into a lowland-dominated phase (Susa II) and a highland-dominated phase (Susa III, the Proto-Elamite period proper). The significant historical consequences of this division will be discussed later. For the purposes of the present study, the material from the other Proto-Elamite sites of Khuzistan and highland Iran, reviewed in a number of recent works, may be dealt with more summarily.[27]

Excavated sites belonging to the earlier Proto-Elamite phase with Uruk IV/Susa II-related pottery (bevelled-rim bowls, four-lugged jars and drooping-spout jars *etc.*), glyptic, sealings (from jars, doors, tags *etc.*), envelope bullae and 'numerical' tablets include Chogha Mish in Susiana,[28] Tal-i Ghazir in the Ram Hormuz plain,[29] Godin Tepe V in the Kangavar valley of northern Luristan[30] and probably also Tepe Sialk IV1 on the plateau.[31] Tal-i Malyan was certainly occupied during this period but the relevant levels (Early Banesh) have not been excavated.[32]

Occupation continued uninterrupted into the developed Proto-Elamite phase at Ghazir, Tepe Sialk IVC2, Tal-i Malyan (Middle Banesh)[33] and Susa. Chogha Mish, on the other hand, was abandoned, and Godin Tepe was burned and re-occupied after a gap by Yanik-culture intruders from the north.[34] Further east at Tepe Yahya IVC2 and Shahr-i Sokhta I,[35] where there is no evidence of earlier lowland

---

[24]   Gautier & Lampre 1905: 73-80; Carter 1984: 120, n. 103.
[25]   Amiet 1972: 129-33, 142-45; *idem* 1973; *idem* 1986: 98-101.
[26]   There are however exceptions which are repeatedly overlooked in statements that contrast the evidence from Susa and Uruk (*e.g.* Schmandt-Besserat 1981: 325). Numerical and pictographic tablets were found at Uruk in excavations of apparently domestic architecture far outside the temple compounds in square O XI-XII (Heinrich 1934: 14, Taf. 14:b, d). Schmandt-Besserat's arguments (1986: 107) that the buildings excavated at Susa also represent public administrative complexes (perhaps oil warehouses) are unconvincing.
[27]   Alden 1982; Carter 1984: 115-32; Amiet 1986: 51-73, 91-119.
[28]   Kantor 1975; *idem* 1976; *idem* 1976a; *idem* 1977; *idem* 1979; Delougaz & Kantor 1972; *idem* 1973.
[29]   Caldwell 1968; Carter 1984: 121f.
[30]   Weiss & Young 1975; Young 1986.
[31]   Ghirshman 1938; Amiet 1985; *idem* 1986: 67-69. Amiet (1985: 309) argues for dating Sialk IV1 to the Late Uruk period and IV2 to the Proto-Elamite period (Susa III). Early features have also been noted by Dittmann (1986: 184f.) and Young (1986: 221 n. 23). Previously, Sialk IV was often dated entirely to the Proto-Elamite period proper (*e.g.* Alden 1982, who incorrectly places IV2 before IV1).
[32]   Sumner 1974; *idem* 1976; *idem* 1977; *idem* 1986; Sumner ed. 1980.
[33]   Terminology of the Banesh phases follows Sumner 1986: 199 n. 2, collapsing some of Alden's (1982) finer distinctions.
[34]   Young 1986: 212, 222.
[35]   Lamberg-Karlovsky 1970; *idem* 1971; *idem* 1972; *idem* 1973; *idem* 1977; Lamberg-Karlovsky & Tosi 1973; Lamberg-Karlovsky *et al.* 1976a; Tucci ed. 1977; Tosi ed. 1983 (with extensive earlier bibliography).

1

2

Figure 8.   Proto-Elamite tablet from Susa (1) and detail of cylinder seal impression (2). 21.0 x 26.7 cm.

Figure 9. Impression of Proto-Elamite cylinder seal from Susa. Ht. 3.2 cm.

colonies,[36] the Proto-Elamite culture appears in fully developed form.[37] Likewise, a number of tablet blanks, clay tokens and a clay tag with three "non-Proto-Elamite signs", impressed bullae and a Piedmont Style seal may indicate Proto-Elamite penetration as far as north-east Iran.[38]

All these mature Proto-Elamite settlements share a common repertory of administrative documents including tablets in the Proto-Elamite script, seal-impressed bullae, and sealings from doors, jars, sacks, tags *etc.* Sites as far east as Tepe Yahya have also yielded small quantities of Jemdet Nasr-Early Dynastic I-related pottery, particularly bevelled-rim bowls, 'conical cups/solid footed goblets', and polychrome jars (Fig. 7:18-21). More of the pottery, however, is now distinctive to the highlands, especially Middle Banesh Tal-i Malyan. The appearance of Banesh-related ceramics throughout south-central Iran and in the lowlands of Khuzistan (Fig. 7:12-14) has been taken to indicate a change in the cultural orientation of the Proto-Elamite settlements away from Sumer to highland Iran, particularly Fars. The new Proto-Elamite pictographic script (see below) and the employment of a native Iranian glyptic also distinguish Proto-Elamite culture from that of Jemdet Nasr-Early Dynastic II Sumer. 'Piedmon-style' glazed steatite cylinder seals and impressions are one of the few types common to both regions, occurring from Sumer right across Iran to Sokhta.[39] Their homeland, previously identified as the Zagros piedmont, may rather be highland Proto-Elam.[40]

Certain areas are conspicuously excluded from Proto-Elamite control. Throughout the Susa II-III periods the pottery and funerary customs of the Deh Luran plain (Tepe Farukhabad, Khazineh, Mussian, Aliabad)[41] relate directly to Sumer and especially the Diyala-Hamrin region, rather than to Susiana. Sumerian

---

[36]   Note, however, that Lamberg-Karlovsky (1972: 97; *idem* 1973: 304f.) states that lowland-related pottery (bevelled-rim bowls, spouted jars) begins in Yahya VA.

[37]   Surface surveys at Shahdad suggest that that site also was occupied during the Proto-Elamite period but no diagnostic finds are reported (Salvatori & Vidale 1982).

[38]   Dyson 1987: 658-60 (Tepe Hissar).

[39]   Amiet 1979.

[40]   Le Breton 1957: 108; Amiet 1986: 99.

[41]   Gautier & Lampre 1905; Wright ed. 1981.

common wares predominate and Jemdet Nasr-Early Dynastic II-related polychrome pottery, rare at Susa, occurs frequently in funerary contexts.[42] There are no Proto-Elamite tablets or other distinctive Proto-Elamite markers.

Likewise, eastern Luristan (Kangavar, Nehevend, Assadabad valleys), the Hamadan plain and other areas occupied by the Transcaucasian 'Yanik' culture at the end of the Susa II period show no further contact with the lowlands or with Proto-Elam.[43] On a broader scale, there are no known lowland or Proto-Elamite colonies in Baluchistan, and north-eastern Iran so far shows only limited evidence of contact: the evidence from Hissar cited above and a cylinder seal in Proto-Elamite style from Bactria.[44] The true extent of contact in this direction remains to be established.

2. SETTLEMENT PATTERNS AND DEMOGRAPHIC CHANGE

Extensive surface surveys in Sumer and Akkad, Susiana, the Deh Luran plain, the Izeh plain, the Ram Hormuz plain and the Kur River basin provide a basis for tracing the broad pattern of demographic change during the late fourth and early third millennia.[45] Although the evidence is very uneven (Table 2.2), with many areas remaining unexplored, the results in the regions investigated have some important implications, and, provided the limitations of the data are recognised, constitute a legitimate avenue of enquiry.[46]

The Late Uruk period in Sumer witnessed dramatic urban expansion. Around Uruk itself, total settlement area increased by 121%. Nippur and Ur/Eridu, on the other hand, decreased by 45% and 60% respectively.[47] The net result was a much larger and more concentrated population centred on Uruk. At the end of the Uruk period, though the major centres continued to grow, a large number of sites were abandoned and new ones established, both in the periphery (Ur, Diyala) and in the Uruk heartland, perhaps reflecting major demographic and social disruptions.[48] There was a further doubling of settlement in the Uruk region from the Jemdet Nasr to Early Dynastic I periods, this time not at the expense of the surrounding regions. Uruk itself reached 200 hectares, five times the size of any other contemporary Mesopotamian settlement.

---

[42]   Carter 1984: 120; Wright ed. 1981; Carter 1984: 120.
[43]   Young 1986: 219, 221.
[44]   Amiet 1977: fig. 22; *idem* 1986: 115.
[45]   Sumer-Akkad – Adams & Nissen 1972; Adams 1981; Wright 1981b. Susiana – Adams 1962; Johnson 1973; Schacht 1987; Alden 1982. Deh Luran – Wright ed. 1981: 181-85. Izeh Plain – Wright ed. 1979: 69; Sajjidi 1979. Ram Hormuz – Wright 1987. Kur basin – Sumner 1972; Alden 1982.
[46]   The site areas of the larger, more important settlements such as Susa and Tal-i Malyan are the most difficult to estimate because of later occupation; yet incorrect estimates of these could significantly obscure the overall trends. Note the discrepancies concerning the settlement area of Susa during Susa I (Johnson 1975: 21; *idem* 1985: 25 [10 ha.]; Weiss 1977: 356f. [27 ha.]), late Susa II (Algaze 1986b: 20f. n. 10) and Susa III (below in main text); and regarding Late Uruk Susiana (Wright 1987: 151, Table 26 [53 ha.]; Alden 1982; *idem* 1987: 164, Table 29 [62 ha.]) and the Proto-Elamite Izeh plain (Wright loc. cit. [33 ha.]; Alden loc. cit. [51.6 ha.]). (Wright's estimates are followed in this study.) *Cf.* also the general warnings of Young 1986: 222f. Similarly, at Tal-i Malyan it is interesting to note that of the four operations where Banesh pottery was recovered in excavation and the surface pottery is recorded (operations ABC, TUV, F26 and XX; Sumner 1980: 6-10), only one (TUV) had Banesh ceramics on the surface. The others are recorded as having scatters of Kaftari material only. As excavation proved, TUV is the only one of the four areas not reoccupied during this period. Thus, in these cases at least, the surface pottery reflected only the latest period of occupation.
[47]   Adams 1981: 69; Wright 1981: 325-27.
[48]   Postgate 1986a: 93.

TABLE 2.2

The Settlement of Sumer and Iran in the Late Fourth to Early Third Millennia
Total Areas of Occupation from Survey Data[1]

	SOUTHERN MESOPOTAMIA				LOWLAND IRAN		HIGHLAND IRAN	
	Ur-Eridu Region	Uruk Region [2]	Nippur-Adab Region [2]	Diyala Region [2]	Susiana Plain		Kur River Basin, Fars	
Early/Midd. *Uruk*	50(?) ha [0][3]	138 ha [1]	290 ha [2]	very low	*Middle Uruk*	127 ha [0]	*not related*	
Late Uruk	18(?) ha [0]	306 ha [1]	160 ha [1]	some growth	*Late Uruk*	62 ha [0]	*Early Banesh*	26 ha [0]
Jemdet Nasr	53 ha [0]	328+ ha[4] [3]	142+ha [1]	120(?) ha [0][6]	*Early Susa III*	17 ha [0]	*Late Midd. Banesh*	62 ha [1]
Early Dynastic	34 ha [0]	690 ha [2,1]	170 ha [2]	200(?) ha [0][6]	*Midd./Late Susa III*	15 ha [0]	*Late Banesh*	57 ha [1]
SOURCE:[5]	Wright	Adams	Adams	estimate[6]		Johnson		Alden

Notes
1 After Wright 1987: 164, table 29.
2 Areas reduced by 20% to compensate for Adams' method of estimation (Adams 1981: Chap. 3, n. 6).
3 Numbers in brackets denote the number of small (40-199 ha) and (where appropriate) large (200+ ha) urban centres in each region.
4 After Adams and Nissen 1972: fig. 7, with the area of Uruk estimated at 100 ha.
5 After Wright 1981: 325-27, Adams 1981: 69-88, Johnson 1973: 101, 145, Alden unpubl. PhD dissertation, tab. 48.
6 These data estimated from Adams 1965 are of dubious accuracy. In this 1957-58 survey, occupations were defined only as "Warka-Protoliterate" (Uruk-Jemdet Nasr) and "Early Dynastic" (I-III inclusive) and site areas were often exaggerated (Adams 1965: 125, 183). Still, these estimates at least indicate the scale of occupation and growth. Since no town in the region was larger than 33 ha (Adams 1965: 42), the Diyala had no urban centres comparable in scale to those found in other regions.

Contemporary Susiana and southern highland Iran seem to present the opposite phenomenon of population decline, which has led to the suggestion of a movement between Susiana and Sumer,[49] though why this should have occurred remains unclear.[50] The population of Susiana expanded from the Early to Middle Uruk periods, when Susa itself covered *ca.* 25 hectares.[51] In Late Uruk, the settlement area of Susiana dropped by 58% to *ca.* 53 hectares, this consisting mainly of Susa, Abu Fanduweh and Chogha Mish.[52] The Deh Luran plain also declined at this time by 66%, a total of only 3 hectares. In the Izeh plain only a single Middle Uruk settlement has been identified, and none at all in Late Uruk. The Ram Hormuz plain and most of Luristan seem also to have been completely deserted at this time.[53]

In the succeeding Susa III period the depopulation of Susiana continued. The total settlement area fell by more than half to 17 hectares (assigning 11 ha. for Susa)

49 Johnson 1973: 156; *idem* 1975: 337 (to Mesopotamia); Adams 1981: 69-75; Wright & Johnson 1985: 28f.; Dittmann 1986: 182f. This may be affected particularly by the greater area of settlement at Susa postulated by Dittmann 1986: 182f.
50 Alden 1987: 161.
51 Johnson 1973: 71; Alden 1982: 617-20, 622; Wright & Johnson 1985: 27f.
52 Johnson 1973: 67-69, 143-52; Alden 1982: 618; *cf.* Algaze 1986b: 20f., n. 10 suggesting a much larger area (40 ha.) for late Uruk Susa.
53 Wright ed. 1981: 181-85 (Deh Luran); Wright ed. 1979: 59, 69 (Izeh); Johnson 1982: 629; Wright 1987: 147 (Raz Hormuz).

consisting of 31 sites, most of them, as in Sumer, new foundations.[54] Susa, though still the largest settlement on the plain, shrank significantly to between 21 and 10 hectares[55] and Chogh Mish was now completely abandoned. Besides Susa, only two sites of over three hectares are known in central Khuzistan.[56] The bulk of the remaining sites (78%) are located in a triangle bounded by the Dez and Shureh rivers, up to 17 km distant. Alden interprets these as seasonal occupations by small groups of herders, and attributes the decline of urban Susiana to military or political pressure from Sumer.[57] Wright likewise suggests "conflict within and between (the) regions" of Susiana and its neighbours, but not necessarily an increase of nomadism.[58]

At the north-west and south-east extremes of Khuzistan the situation was very different. In the Deh Luran plain, where the ceramics connect with Sumer,[59] the population increased in Susa III times, as in Sumer itself, from 3 to 31 hectares.[60] Tepe Mussian reached 14 hectares – in the same range as Susa – and was perhaps already fortified.[61] The previously deserted Izeh plain now supported 12 Proto-Elamite settlements – perhaps winter grazing sites – with a total area of 33 hectares, the largest site of 12.6 hectares being comparable to Susa, and making this the most densely settled region of Proto-Elam.[62] The four largest settlements have evidence of massive stone building foundations.[63] Alden suggests that these settlers came from Chogha Mish.[64] In the Ram Hormuz plain only Tal-i Ghazir was occupied.

In the Kangavar Valley of northern Luristan there was a dramatic rise in population during Late Uruk (39 sites) followed by a decline to 15 sites when the 'Yanik' culture arrived, only six of them on period VI/V sites.[65]

The Kur River basin, the heartland of historic Anšan, prospered throughout the Early to Middle Banesh (= Susa II-III) periods, supporting 35 sites. The 23 sites which are attributable to particular phases indicate a general increase in settlement from the late fourth to early third millennium accompanied by a process of agglomeration, reaching a peak in Late Middle Banesh (Early Susa III). During that phase Tal-i Malyan, founded at least by Early Banesh (Late Uruk), spread dramatically from 10 to *ca.* 45 hectares, becoming the largest known Proto-Elamite settlement, comparable to the small urban centres around Uruk.[66] Alden attributes this population rise to an influx from Susiana, reflected there in the depopulation of Susa III, but this has been justly challenged.[67] During Late Banesh a decline set in, though no precise figures are available.[68] Tal-i Malyan shrank, though it was still, for some of the period at least, four times larger than in Late Uruk.[69] In the Kaftari

54   Alden 1982: 618; *idem* 1987: 159.
55   Alden *loci cit.* (11 ha.); Nissen 1982: 635; Carter 1984: 119f.; Dittmann 1986: 182f.
56   Alden 1982: 618f.
57   Alden 1982: 617-20, 622.
58   Wright 1987: 147; *cf.* Wright & Johnson 1985: 29.
59   Carter 1984: 120.
60   Wright ed. 1981: 189-95; Wright 1987: 148, Fig. 37, Table 26; Carter 1984: 119f.
61   Wright 1987: 148.
62   Wright ed. 1979: 127; *idem* 1987: 147f., Fig. 36; Alden 1982: 619f. (51.6 ha.); Sajjidi 1979: 93-96.
63   Wright 1987: 147.
64   Alden 1982: 624.
65   Young 1986: 218f.
66   Alden 1982: 620; Sumner 1986: 202. Uruk centres: Adams & Nissen 1972: 18.
67   Sumner 1986: 199.
68   Alden 1982: 620.
69   *Ibid.*: 620, table 2.

period (late third to early second millennium) Tal-i Malyan grew to a new maximum of 150 hectares.[70]

By the early third millennium these developments had given rise to two primary concentrations of population in Sumer and Fars, each connected to smaller satellite centres in the Deh Luran and Izeh plains respectively. Around the same time, survey evidence suggests an increase in transhumance and nomadism in the westernmost ranges of the Zagros mountains. The progressive abandonment of the southern Zagros piedmont and the integration of Khuzistan with the plateau has been interpreted as indicating conflict between Sumer and Proto-Elam but there is no direct evidence.[71]

Lamberg-Karlovsky has suggested that the Late Uruk and Proto-Elamite expansions were the result of earlier dramatic increases in population in Sumer and Susiana leading to crises in agricultural production, which in turn inspired new management technologies and colonisation.[72] However, while such a process is consistent with the evidence from Mesopotamia it is less easily reconciled with the data for Susiana, which, as we have seen, indicate a decline in population already in Late Uruk (Susa II), before the Proto-Elamite expansion.

3. SUMER AND PROTO-ELAM

The great interest generated in the 1960s and 70s by the discovery of Proto-Elamite remains across the Iranian plateau gave rise to an extensive secondary literature which attempts to explain the Proto-Elamite phenomenon in terms of social, economic and even political developments in Sumer and Iran.[73] Especially in the case of anthropologically-oriented American scholars, these accounts have tended to be highly speculative. The difficulty of evaluating reconstructions derived from different 'models' or presuppositions is reflected in the controversy which still surrounds all the key issues raised by Alden and Algaze and their respondents.[74] As the social and economic interpretation has become the major focus of debate, the anthropological or sociological 'theories' which justify one reconstruction rather than another have inevitably assumed greater importance, sometimes at the expense of the primary archaeological data. The danger thus arises that aspects of this evidence will be overlooked, or a particular interpretation taken for granted as the basis for further speculation. References to 'colonists' and 'long-distance trade', and other such hypotheses, are now often the starting point of discussion rather than themselves the object of critical assessment.

From the perspective of the present study there are three key issues. First, there is the question of Sumer's role in the genesis of Proto-Elam. Where are the roots of Proto-Elamite culture to be sought and, more particularly, to what extent is it indebted to Protoliterate Sumer (or perhaps *vice versa*)? Second, what can be gleaned of the political and economic structure of Proto-Elam? Where was its cultural and administrative heartland? Do the Proto-Elamite documents provide any insight into the nature of contemporary administration?

---

[70]   Sumner 1980: 5.
[71]   Wright 1987: 149.
[72]   Lamberg-Karlovsky 1986: 206.
[73]   Alden 1982 with previous literature.
[74]   Alden 1982; Algaze 1989.

Third, what was the scope and nature of relations between Sumer and Proto-Elam? What evidence is there of political contact? or of economic relations? This leads directly to the question of the importance of trade in Proto-Elam, around which much recent work has centred. Is it the case, as some have argued, that Proto-Elam drew its wealth principally from trade with Sumer, exploiting its privileged access to raw materials? What products, if any, did the Proto-Elamites trade? And what effect did their control of these materials, and eventually the passing of Proto-Elam, have on the Sumerian economy? We shall address these issues in turn.

(a) Sumer and the Origins of the 'Proto-Elamite phenomenon'

The origins of Proto-Elamite culture can presently be traced through excavation only in Susiana. At Godin Tepe, Tepe Sialk, Tepe Yahya and Sokhta it appears in an already developed form, evidently introduced from outside, while at Tal-i Malyan the relevant Early Banesh phase is too poorly known to provide any illumination.[75] This last is a particularly serious gap in view of Tal-i Malyan's later importance. Proto-Elamite remains are so far first recorded in the Middle Banesh (Alden's Late Middle phase); but, since this is the only period to have been extensively explored, the argument from silence carries no weight. Regarding the possibility of an earlier stage in the development of Proto-Elamite culture at Tal-i Malyan Alden justly comments:

> Because both ceramic development and important elements of the settlement system show clear continuity throughout the Banesh period, it seems apparent that the entire [Banesh] era is relevant to the Proto-Elamite phenomenon even though tablets are known only from a single phase.[76]

In the Susa II period, during which many of the typical Proto-Elamite 'type fossils' have their origins, the culture of Susiana was thoroughly dominated by Middle-Late Uruk Sumer.[77] Throughout Susiana and Deh Luran all principal aspects of the assemblage, including pottery, glyptic and various administrative devices (sealings, tokens, bullae, tablets), are virtually indistinguishable from those of contemporary Sumer.

While the Uruk-related pottery and glyptic were replaced in the Proto-Elamite period by new highland forms, the legacy of Susa II bureaucracy survived. Indeed, this system of recording and securing commodities, now supplemented by the Proto-Elamite script, became the most characteristic and consistent feature of Proto-Elamite material culture. A key issue in the origins of Proto-Elamite culture therefore lies in the genesis of this accounting system and its relationship to contemporary developments in Sumer.

(i) Sealing.   The practice of sealing doors, tags, jars and other containers by impressing wet clay with a stamp seal (later cylinders) has a long history in Greater

---

[75] Alden 1982: 621. Pottery from surveys provides the principal source of evidence. Alden notes that while much Early Banesh pottery is readily paralleled at Susa Acropole I:17 (1982: 621), Initial Banesh types do not match earlier Susa material (*ibid.*) and lack many typical Late Uruk forms found elsewhere at this time (1982: 622). He therefore regards this as "an *in situ* hybridization of local [Lapui] styles and material introduced from the lowlands" (1982: 621). The ceramics of the Proto-Elamite period at Tal-i Malyan continue in the local tradition which now also appear in quantity at Susa Acropole 1:16 (*ibid.*), probably under highland influence.

[76] Alden 1982: 620.

[77] Amiet 1986: 51-62.

Mesopotamia and Iran. The seals themselves are attested from Neolithic times; rarer sealings indicate their use for bureaucratic purposes by the Halaf period in Mesopotamia and by the late fifth millennium in highland Iran.[78] In Susiana sealings from door knobs, jars, bales and tags first occur in the Susa I period around 4000 BC.[79] Perhaps beginning earlier even than in Sumer,[80]

> Ce procédé ... est ainsi attesté pour la première fois à Suse [period I], où il implique dès avant la naissance de la comptabilité et de l'écriture, l'existence de magasins gérés par une autorité de type administratif.[81]

There is therefore no need to look beyond Susiana itself for the immediate origins of this aspect of Proto-Elamite administration, though ultimately its prevalence there may be attributed to the prior history of close relations with Sumer in the fourth and fifth millennia.

In the third millennium, when Iranian and Mesopotamian glyptic styles diverged, the 'piedmont' cylinders (Fig. 7:15, 21) represent a notable continuing link between the Proto-Elamite and Sumerian realms. Rather than a shared sealing style and practice, this is one of the few instances where it may be plausible to explain the overlapping distribution in terms of highland-lowland trade, the sealings travelling with Iranian goods into the lowlands.[82]

(ii) Bullae and 'Numerical' Tablets.   Recent research into the development of Sumerian and Proto-Elamite bureaucracy has focused on the connection between the earliest writing on tablets on the one hand and previous accounting procedures involving small clay 'tokens' or 'calculi' and envelope bullae in which these were enclosed on the other. At first impressed only with seals (both stamps and cylinders), by the Late Uruk period the bullae were often impressed also with 'plain tokens' or a stylus corresponding in shape and number to the tokens inside.[83] Schmandt-Besserat identifies nineteen signs of which five occur commonly.[84] According to the plausible thesis first advanced by Amiet and since elaborated by Schmandt-Besserat, these token impressions 'represent' the tokens enclosed in the bulla which in turn represent the commodities accounted, each sign probably signifying both a particular type of object and the quantity involved.[85] Since the impressions made the tokens

---

[78] Perkins 1949: 33f. (Halaf); Langsdorff & McCown 1942: 66f., pl. 7:11-19; Voigt & Dyson in press for dates. What is evidently the earliest stratified Mesopotamian cylinder seal yet discovered (a 'drilled style' cylinder) has recently been reported from a late Middle Uruk context at Tell Brak.

[79] Amiet 1972: 24f.; *idem* 1986: 43f. Sealings also occur in Middle Uruk at nearby Tepe Sharafabad (Wright ed. 1981: 277-81, figs 6, 7).

[80] There are isolated stamp seal impressions reported from Uruk Eanna XII and Anu X (Perkins 1949: 138; Amiet 1980: no. 1594). The relative dearth in Sumer compared to Assyria and Susiana may be attributed to the lesser scale of excavation in these periods there.

[81] Amiet 1986: 44.

[82] Pittman n.d. [1].

[83] Schmandt-Besserat 1981: 327; Amiet 1986: 82-87, figs 26-31. X-ray analysis of the Susa bullae has shown that in some cases the token types exactly match the sign types; in other cases the number of token and sign types are the same but not all of the forms; and in others there are more token types than sign types, which perhaps record the total of the enclosed tokens (Amiet 1986: 95; *idem* 1987a; Lieberman 1980).

[84] Schmandt-Besserat 1981: 327, fig. 5.

[85] Amiet 1966; *idem* 1972: 69; *idem* 1986: 82-87; Schmandt-Besserat 1977; 1980; 1981; 1988, with previous literature. There has been considerable debate as to whether the numerical signs represent numbers abstractly conceived, as they do eventually in cuneiform (Vallat 1986: 336f.), or units of some particular commodity in a metrology specific to it (as Amiet 1966; *idem* 1986: 86f.; *idem* 1987a; Vaiman

Figure 10.　Late Uruk bulla and tokens from Susa. Diam. 7.8 cm.

whereby the hollow bulla was transformed into the solid tablet. These at first carried themselves redundant, these were dispensed with in the next stage of development only the five basic 'numerical' signs (and seal impressions) made by impressing the plain tokens or stylus. The same numerals with the same values carry over into the Proto-Elamite and Sumerian writing systems.[86] The invention of these pictographic scripts, inspired by the shapes of the 'complex tokens',[87] forms the final and most significant breakthrough with which the creation of the earliest known writing systems may be considered complete. Thereafter changes affected only the layout of the tablets and the palaeography of the established sign repertories.

Schmandt-Besserat argues that the plain tokens represented staple foodstuffs while the later, more complex tokens represented manufactured products.[88] In support of this distinction she notes that while the plain tokens are typically found inside bullae and were used to make 'numerical' impressions on these bullae and, later, on the numerical tablet, the complex tokens are more often perforated for suspension on a string, were not used for making impressions and are rarely found

---

1972; Friberg 1978-9; *idem* 1984: 85; Nissen 1986: 332; Schmandt-Besserat 1988: 32). Friberg argues compellingly for the latter view, demonstrating that both Proto-Elamite and Proto-Sumerian used a (proto) sexagesimal counting system (1978-9: 15) with five principal signs (Vallat 1986: fig. 1), or rarely a bi-sexagesimal system (*ibid.*: 38; *idem* 1984: 83). Various metrologies, associated with different types of objects (inanimate, people, animals, fields *etc.*) were used concurrently so that the same sign could in different contexts have different numerical or metrological values (*ibid.*: 85; Nissen 1986: 332). A few signs were specific to a particular category or unit of measure. One of the best known systems is the proto-sexagesimal ŠE (grain) metrology used both in Sumer and Proto-Elam (Friberg 1984). A decimal system was used only in Proto-Elam and only for animals (*ibid.*: 85; *idem* 1978-9: 40) and possibly people (*ibid.*: 12, 21). Thus, to the extent that many types of objects were measured in units specific to that type, which determined the reading of the sign, the 'numerical' signs also indicated the commodity concerned. At the same time, however, the proto-sexagesimal system, used for virtually all objects except animals, was, by virtue of its wide application, tantamount to an abstract numerical system.

86　Friberg 1978-9: 15.
87　Schmandt-Besserat 1988.
88　Schmandt-Besserat 1986: 110f. [Susa]; 1988: 4f., 20.

TABLE 2.3

Administrative Documents from Uruk and Proto-Elamite Sites[1]

---

1. Envelope Bullae

Uruk	25	Lenzen 1965: 31ff., pl. 17-19a; Schmandt-Besserat 1988: 9.
Tell Brak	1	D. Oates 1985: 164, pl. XXXa.
Habuba Kabira	3	Strommenger 1973: Abb. 6; *idem* 1977: Abb. 14, 15.
Sheikh Hassan	3	Boese 1986-87: 77, figs 36-39.
Susa	60+	Amiet 1972: 69ff., 84ff.; *idem* 1986: 81-87.
Chogha Mish	?	Kantor 1979: 35; *idem* 1983: 30.
Farukhabad	1	Wright ed. 1981: 156, pl. 16E, fig. 75D.
Tal-i Malyan	6	Pittman 1980: 3, Table 4; Stolper 1985: 3 n. 3 (solid).
Tepe Yahya	1	Schmandt-Besserat 1977: fig. 7.
Shahdad?	1	Hakemi 1972: pl. XXIIA.
Tepe Hissar	2?	Dyson 1987: 659, n. 6.
Dhahran	1?	D.T. Potts 1993b: 180.

2. 'Numerical' Tablets

Uruk	20	Jordan 1932: 29, Taf. 19b; Noldeke *et al.* 1932: 28f., Taf. 14c-h; *idem* 1937: 51, Taf. 51c; Heinrich 1934: 14, Taf. 14b, d, 28c; van Dijk 1960: 50, Taf. 29e; Bottéro 1961: 56; Falkenstein 1963: 2; Lenzen 1964: 23, Taf. 26g, 28c; Nissen 1967: 37f.; *idem* 1968: 40, Taf. 19a; *idem* 1974: 38, Taf. 27k, n; Reade 1992.
Khafajeh	1	Frankfort 1936: 25, fig. 19; Delougaz 1952: 34.
Mari	1	Parrot 1965: 12, fig. 10.
Nineveh	1	Collon & Reade 1983: 33f., fig. 1.
Tell Brak	3	D. Oates 1982: 191, pl. XVc; *idem* 1985: 164, pl. XXXII (with animal drawings).
Habuba Kabira	10	Strommenger 1977: Abb. 11; *idem* 1980: 485; *idem* 1980a: Abb. 56 (top); Schmandt-Besserat 1981: 325.
Jebel Aruda	11	van Driel 1982.
Susa	90	Scheil 1905; *idem* 1923: 10, nos 11, 20, 28, 70, 108, 138, 160, 165, 166, 169, 176, 261, 355, 362, 434, 475; *idem* 1935: nos 4775, 4781; Vallat 1971: 236f.; Le Brun & Vallat 1978: 18-20.
Chogh Mish	5	Kantor 1975: 22f.; *idem* 1976: 25, figs 5, 6.
Tal-i Ghazir	1	Carter 1984: fig. 7:15.
Godin Tepe	42	Weiss & Young 1975: 8, figs 4, 5:1, 5; Schmandt-Besserat 1988: 29.
Tepe Sialk	14	Ghirshman 1938: 65-8, pls XXXI:5, XCIII: S.1628.
Tal-i Malyan	4	Stolper 1976: 89.

3. Proto-Elamite ('Economic') Tablets

Susa	*ca.* 1450	Scheil 1905; *idem* 1923; *idem* 1935; Damerow & Englund 1989: 2, nn. 4, 5.
Tepe Sialk	5	Ghirshman 1934: 115f.; *idem* 1938: 65-68, pls XXXI:1, XCII, XCIII.
Godin Tepe	1	Weiss & Young 1975: 8, fig. 4:2.
Tal-i Malyan	32	Sumner 1976: 106, 108; *idem* 1977: 178; Stolper 1976: 89f.; *idem* 1985.
Tepe Yahya IVC1	27	Damerow & Englund 1989.
Shahr-i Sokhta	1	Tucci ed. 1977: 83, 105, pl. 34; Amiet & Tosi 1978: 24, fig. 16.
Tepe Hissar	1	Tosi & Bulgarelli 1989: 38-40, fig. 6 (and possible blanks fig. 8); *cf.* Damerow & Englund 1989: 2 n. 8.

Notes
1   Totals are calculated from published information in the references cited and therefore provide only minimum estimates. Both complete and fragmentary published tablets are included in the estimates of tablet totals.

---

in bullae. It is these complex tokens, according to Schmandt-Besserat, which were perpetuated in written signs of the Uruk IV script and hence tended to disappear in the Uruk III period as writing superceded the more cumbersome token-bulla system. This otherwise plausible thesis, however, faces the problem that "there are only a few instances where a clear correlation can be made between a token and a later pictographic sign".[89] At Susa, moreover, Schmandt-Besserat recognises that there is no connection between the Proto-Elamite script and the tokens, whose use she regards as a foreign bureaucratic practice imposed by Sumer.[90]

Most of the recent work on this material has been concerned primarily with identifying the stages in the development, now best represented at Susa, and thus defining the conceptual advances and practical processes by which writing came into existence. Material from Susa and Uruk is sometimes freely combined on the assumption that both developments represent aspects of one unified phenomenon. However, since a primary concern of the present study is the question of priority and the direction of influence between early Sumer and Susiana, this evidence must here be considered separately.

In Sumer it is still only at *Uruk* that the emergence of Sumerian writing may be traced through stratigraphically ordered finds representing different script stages.[91] Unfortunately, despite the German expedition's meticulous attention to architectural detail, their excavation and recording techniques, involving virtually no use of sections, left many stratigraphical issues unresolved. The contexts of the finds, including most of the Archaic tablets, are therefore uncertain.[92] This is the case particularly in the Eanna and Anu compounds where most of the tablets were recovered. On the basis of the original (supposedly provisional) stratigraphy, Falkenstein divided the texts into corresponding script stages IV, III and so on, which he further sub-divided on internal palaeographical grounds into IV and IIIa-c. Although these divisions were more typological than stratigraphical, it seems that subsequent discoveries of texts were often used to date their stratigraphical contexts according to Falkenstein's scheme (even using the period III subdivisions which had no stratigraphical basis at all) rather than *vice versa*.[93]

In a review of the stratigraphical evidence relating to the Archaic Uruk texts Nissen concludes that very few contexts are secure. Even in these cases the texts are almost always in rubbish fill deposits (not on floors) so that it is possible only to assign them a *terminus ante quem* from the next architectural phase.[94] As far as may be judged, however, the script development resulting from this redating largely corresponds with that of Falkenstein.[95]

The pre-history of writing is so far poorly represented at Uruk where levels V and below of the Eanna, in which these remains may be expected to lie,[96] have not been extensively explored. Plain tokens appear in level XVII and the first complex ones in level VI,[97] reaching a peak in frequency and diversity in levels VI to IV.[98] They

89   Schmandt-Besserat 1988: 34. Schmandt-Besserat 1988: 30f. lists 12 types, divisible into 31 subtypes, most with Archaic Uruk script parallels. Note the revised parallels for Archaic cloth/garment signs in Szarzynska 1988: 225-30. For general critiques of Schmandt-Besserat's thesis see Le Brun & Vallat 1978, Lieberman 1980 and Michalowski 1990.
90   Schmandt-Besserat 1986: 115f.
91   Falkenstein 1936; Green & Nissen 1987.
92   Strommenger 1980; Finkbeiner 1986.
93   Strommenger 1980; Nissen 1986, 1986b.
94   Nissen 1986: 318-20; Collon 1981-82: 180.
95   Nissen 1986: 320f.
96   Strommenger 1980: 486.
97   Jordan 1931: 47, fig. 41; *idem* 1932: 19. Exceptions are the 'complex' tokens of different types from levels XVII and X.
98   Schmandt-Besserat 1988: 19f.

are still present at Jemdet Nasr[99] as in contemporary Susiana. The first envelope bullae containing tokens and impressed with seals were assigned by the excavators to level IVc but the stratigraphy allows a range of VI to IVa.[100] These represent the postulated first stage in the development towards tablets when envelope bullae were impressed only with seals. The suggested redating of the 'White Temple' to the period of Eanna IV or earlier[101] would make the numerical tablets from there the earliest yet recovered at Uruk. However, in view of the uncertainty which still surrounds all Anu-Eanna correlations, it is best to maintain the conventional starting date of Uruk IVa,[102] the final Late Uruk building phase, as representing the earliest securely stratified tablets.[103] These include both numerical and pictographic texts which, in the 'Red Temple' (probably an administrative building), were found together.[104] Excluding the White Temple texts, the postulated transitional phase when bullae gave way to numerical tablets but pictography had not been invented, is not yet represented at Uruk.

Thus the pictographic texts of Uruk IVa represent the earliest known stage of true writing in Sumer, and Nissen and Powell have argued that, although the script is already standardized, there is unlikely to have been any appreciable prior evolution of the signs.[105] In the next stage, Uruk III (now subdivided typologically by Nissen into 3, 2 and 1), representing the Jemdet Nasr period, the script begins to take its familiar cuneiform aspect and lexical lists appear.[106] Rare grammatical indications now confirm that the language recorded is Sumerian.[107]

The Acropole I excavations provide the first sound basis for tracing the development of writing at *Susa* (Fig. 11),[108] and thus for placing in order the much larger body of poorly stratified material from the earlier excavations. In publishing this material Scheil already distinguished between the purely 'numerical' texts and those which also carry pictographic signs, now often called 'economic' texts.[109] Only these latter can, strictly speaking, be considered Proto-Elamite since the 'numerical' texts, identical to those from Sumer, cannot yet be assigned to a language.[110]

The earliest stratified tablets from Susa occur in Acropole I:18 of Susa II, contemporary with Uruk IV.[111] They bear only numerical signs and one or two cylinder seal impressions. On the same floors were found sealings and spherical envelope bullae, the latter all impressed with one or two cylinder seals and containing tokens. Some bullae, like the tablets, also carry impressions corresponding to the

[99] Mackay 1931: 277f.
[100] Lenzen 1965: 31ff., pls 17-19a; Schmandt-Besserat 1988: 21-23. On the basis of glyptic evidence and Susa-Farukhabad parallels Schmandt-Besserat narrows this to phases VI-V.
[101] Strommenger 1980: 486f.; Heinrich 1982: 63 dates it to IVb or earlier.
[102] This is the date of the texts from the Red Temple, originally dated to Uruk IVb but later reassigned by Lenzen (1950) to IVa. This revision has been universally accepted. Lenzen (1965: 15) later sub-divided IVa into 'IVa' and 'IVa-'.
[103] Nissen (1986: 323) mentions the Anu texts but does not note the possibility that they seem to require an earlier starting date than IVa. Against this possibility it may be noted that the texts in Temple C of period IVa were on a floor, and are thus unlikely to be significantly older than their context (Nissen 1986: 319).
[104] Nissen 1986: 322f.
[105] Nissen 1986: 326; Powell 1981: 419-23; *cf.* Strommenger 1980: 486. This issue is not affected by the probability of an earlier purely numerical phase.
[106] Nissen 1986: 322, 324.
[107] Nissen 1985: 354-57.
[108] Le Brun & Vallat 1978; *idem* 1989; Vallat 1978; *idem* 1986; Schmandt-Besserat 1986.
[109] Scheil 1905, 1923, 1934.
[110] *Cf.* Powell 1981: 207.
[111] Le Brun & Vallat 1982: 633 cite tablets in level 19 but no mention of this is made in later surveys, *e.g.* Vallat 1986: 336.

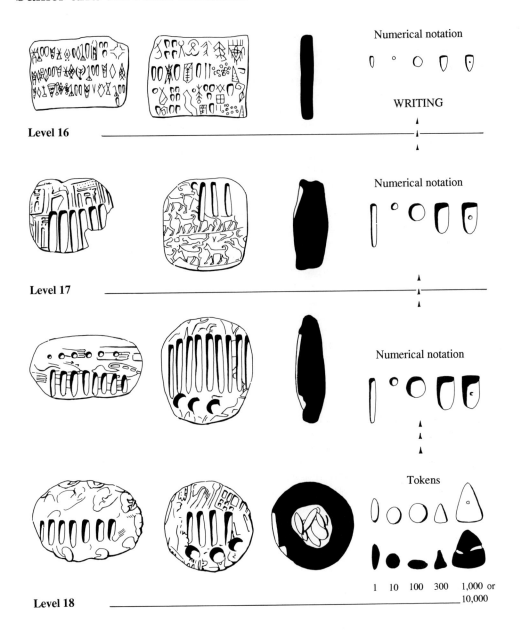

Figure 11. The development of writing at Susa (after Vallat).

tokens inside. Bullae all but disappear in the next level, Acropole I:17, where tablets are still exclusively numerical (but see below for possible exceptions from other contexts). As before, they are all sealed, now often on the sides and reverse as well as on the obverse. In level 16 pictographic tablets appear. Thereafter seal impressions quickly disappear.

The close relationship in the Susa II levels between bullae with token impressions and numerical tablets is important not only as evidence of an important stage in the invention of writing, but also as proof that accounting practices were not introduced to Susa as a *fait accompli*. Indeed the impressed bullae and tablets represent a purely numerical script stage not yet attested in primary contexts at Uruk. The postulated earlier phase, in which only impressed bullae were used, is not yet illustrated by well stratified finds from Susa. But the logic of the development is so compelling that it is plausible to attribute this lacuna to the much reduced exposure of Acropole I levels 19 and below, especially since tokens are present as early as levels 27 to 25. Likewise, for the typologically still earlier phase of envelope bullae with only seal impressions; this is represented at Middle Uruk Farukhabad in the Deh Luran.[112]

The question of priority between Sumer and Susiana must be decided on the basis of the documents themselves since neither the ceramic nor the glyptic typology of the Susa II-Uruk IV assemblages provides a fine enough index of change to establish exact inter-site correlations. Even if it were assured that the earliest known token-impressed bullae from Uruk IV and Susa Acropole I:18 in fact represent the earliest use of these types at each site, it is not possible to say which context is the earlier. Likewise, regarding the numerical texts of Uruk IVa (or earlier?) and Susa Acropole I:18, both are Late Uruk but any closer definition would be tendentious.

As far as one can tell, therefore, up to this point the early stages in the development of writing run parallel in Susa and Uruk. The use of the same repertory of tokens[113] and their impressions for recording commodities – first as three-dimensional representations, then by means of impressions on bullae, and finally on 'numerical' tablets – indicates that both sites participated in a unified process of innovation, or at least were quickly apprized of new developments.

The dissemination of these processes extended beyond Susa throughout the regions under Late Uruk influence. In addition to further examples from sites in Akkad (Khafajeh), Khuzistan (Chogha Mish) and the Ram Hormuz plain (Ghazir), numerical tablets have been recovered at the lowland colonies of Godin Tepe V and Tepe Sialk IV₁ in highland Iran; at Mari on the Middle Euphrates; at Nineveh and Tell Brak in Assyria; and at the Upper Euphrates colonies of Habuba Kabira and Jebel Aruda (see Table 2.3 for statistics and all references). Envelope bullae with token impressions have a similarly wide distribution: to Chogha Mish and Farukhabad in the east; and to Tell Brak, Habuba Kabira and Sheikh Hassan in the north. Importantly, those from Sheikh Hassan, the earliest from a colony site, date to the pre-Uruk IV period. Numerical tablets and bullae appear also in contexts dated to the succeeding Proto-Elamite period at Tepe Yahya (bulla), Shahdad (bulla) and Tal-i Malyan (bullae and tablets). It is noteworthy that while the pictographic Uruk IVa script was used in heartland Sumer the 'colonies' employed only the numerical notation.[114] The smaller scale of economic administration in these settlements evidently did not justify the much greater effort required to acquire proficiency in the infinitely more complicated pictographic script.

(iii) The Direction of Influence and Centre of Power.   The vastly greater scale of urban development in Late Uruk Sumer *vis-à-vis* Susiana leaves little doubt as to

---

[112] Wright ed. 1981: 156, pl. 16E, fig. 75D.
[113] A few rare token types are only represented at Uruk (Amiet 1986: 85f.). On the tokens from Susa and Uruk see generally Schmandt-Besserat 1986 and *idem* 1988.
[114] Likewise, plain but not complex tokens appear at many of these sites (Schmandt-Besserat 1988: 27f.).

where the centre of bureaucratic innovation and development lay.[115] Sumer, particularly the area around Uruk, was clearly at this time (in Adams' phrase) the 'heartland of cities' and thus the region where the need for, and benefits of, a more sophisticated system of administration were greatest. It is in this context that the development of writing should be set. Numeration was, from the outset, an administrative tool, a means of recording and guaranteeing large numbers of transactions. When pictography was introduced it too was used entirely for accounts (85%) and lexical lists (15%);[116] royal inscriptions, literary texts *etc.* do not appear for many centuries, towards the end of the Early Dynastic period. Uruk, the largest administrative centre of its day, is the most likely place for these initial developments to have taken place. As we have seen, each of the early stages – from tokens to token impressions to numerical tablets – was quickly transmitted to Susiana (and elsewhere in the Uruk 'universe') which thus participated directly in the process of innovation and improvement. Complex tokens appear in Late Uruk times in almost identical forms in Sumer, Susiana (Susa, Chogha Mish) and Syria (Habuba Kabira-Qannas).[117] But these peripheral regions probably participated passively, as the recipients, rather than the originators, of new ideas. Susiana has the appearance of a province of 'Greater Sumer', thoroughly dominated by her powerful western neighbour and perhaps already supporting a significant proportion of Sumerian speakers.

Thus the parallel development of record keeping in Late Uruk Sumer and Susiana can be ascribed largely to Sumerian influence on the east rather than *vice versa* and, to this extent, in both areas may be considered aspects of a broadly Sumerian achievement. The inspiration if not always the outward forms of Proto-Elamite bureaucracy lies in the ultimately Sumerian developments of Middle-Late Uruk Susiana.[118]

On the same grounds, it is unlikely that Susa or any other site in Susiana had the necessary human and other resources, or the administrative infrastructure, to sponsor and co-ordinate the series of colonies established in highland Iran in the Susa II period. It is more plausible to suppose that the much larger and more sophisticated administration of Sumer, now the dominant cultural presence in Susiana, was also the motive force behind these settlements, which thus represent the eastern equivalent of the Euphrates colonies in the north-west. The 'merchants of Susa' should perhaps be regarded rather as 'merchants of Sumer', or at least Susians acting as Sumerian agents.[119]

Likewise, the collapse of the eastern Susa II colonies in Iran may be regarded as part of the wider pattern of Late Uruk abandonment at the extremities of Sumerian control. The burning and "hasty abandonment" of Godin Tepe V, along with that of Chogha Mish and Ghazir, parallel the sudden desertion of the Euphrates

---

[115] Nissen 1985a. This gross discrepancy is not affected by the great uncertainy which still surrounds assessments of the area of Susa and other sites in Susiana in the Susa II-III periods (and for Susa I: Weiss 1977: 356f.) due to the extensive overburden of later periods. Although figures assigned to Susa vary by more than 100% (above n. 46), even the maximum estimates for late 4th-mill. Susa (ca. 10-20 ha.) do not bring it above the level of a modest Late Uruk Sumerian village.

[116] Nissen 1986: 326.

[117] Schmandt-Besserat 1986: 112, 115f.

[118] Schmandt-Besserat (1986: 114) reaches similar conclusions. Contrast Amiet (1985a: 38; *idem* 1986: 209) who argues that the "civilisation dite d'Uruk a eu un double berceau: Sumer et Susiane, avec apports réciproques", largely on the basis of iconographical elements which have antecedents only in Iran.

[119] Weiss & Young 1975, *cf.* now Young 1986: 218.

(and Tigris?) sites in the north, and the cessation of direct links with Egypt.[120] However, the withdrawal from Iran did not spell the complete end of lowland influence, for while the colonies cease, traces of lowland culture still appear in the Proto-Elamite colonies that took their place.

(iv) Sumer and the Invention of the Proto-Elamite Script. The Proto-Elamite culture that filled the vacuum thus created had many strong links with its predecessor. There are indeed grounds for considering the Susa II period as an earlier stage of Proto-Elamite culture. In particular, as has been demonstrated, its methods of meticulously administering and recording agricultural activities on various kinds of clay documents derives directly from the practices of Late Uruk Sumer-Susiana.

However, the new and most distinctive feature of Proto-Elamite culture – the like-named script – was a native Iranian invention which is never attested in Sumer. It was devised for writing a non-Sumerian, non-Semitic language, presumably an early form of Elamite. It is still not possible to say where, by whom or in what circumstances this was achieved. The relevant levels (Early Banesh) of Tal-i Malyan are too poorly documented to exclude a highland origin; but it is generally assumed that the Proto-Elamite script was invented in Susiana where (Proto-)Elamites were most directly exposed to the new phenomenon of Sumerian pictographic writing.[121]

There can be no doubt that the inventions of the two scripts are directly connected. Despite their different repertories of ideographic signs, the largely shared numerical signs as well as the temporal and geographical proximity of the two scripts, and their fundamentally similar methods and materials of writing, renders independent development exceedingly unlikely.[122] Stimulus diffusion, if not direct borrowing, provides far the most likely model. The question is which came first.[123]

On presently accepted chronologies Archaic Sumerian is attested marginally earlier than Proto-Elamite. Uruk IVa already used a pictographic script when Susa II had only numerical tablets. The transition from this numerical stage to pictographic Proto-Elamite is not represented in the recent Susa excavations, where there is a stratigraphical break between Acropole I:17, with numerical tablets, and level 16 (= beginning of Susa III), where Proto-Elamite tablets appear with the pictographic script already fully developed. The old excavations provide nothing to fill this gap except perhaps two tablets which are of standard Susa II type in terms of shape, seal impressions and numerical signs, but which each bear also a single pictographic sign.[124] Another single-sign tablet comes from Godin Tepe V and three more from Tepe Sialk IV₁.[125] Le Brun and Vallat suggest that, since the Susa and Godin Tepe single-sign tablets occur in Late Uruk cultural contexts, they should be read as Sumerian rather than Proto-Elamite (they make no mention of the Tepe Sialk tablets).[126] However, an examination of the particular signs concerned suggests that they are Proto-Elamite rather than Sumerian.[127] And it is unlikely that a script newly

[120] Young 1986: 213 (Godin); Amiet 1979: 199 (northern sites). Moorey 1987 argues that Sumerian influence in Egypt, usually dated to the JN period, was restricted essentially to Uruk IV.
[121] Vallat 1986; Sollberger 1984; Stolper 1984: 9.
[122] By contrast, this is still a genuine option in the case of the third early script, hieroglyphic Egyptian (Ray 1986).
[123] Suggestions that the Sumerians adopted their writing system from an earlier non-Sumerian population (Gelb 1960: 262f.) have now been abandoned.
[124] Amiet 1972: nos 474, 604.
[125] Weiss & Young 1975: fig. 4:2 (Godin); Ghirshman 1938: 67; Amiet 1986: 68 (Sialk).
[126] Le Brun & Vallat 1982: 633.
[127] Amiet 1972: no. 604 bears a common Proto-Elamite sign (Scheil 1923: 40 sign no. 480) which occurs on the reverse of other Proto-Elamite tablets alone except for numbers and seal impressions (Scheil 1935: pl.

devised for a non-Sumerian language would be read with Sumerian values. In any case, the first well dated occurrences of substantial Proto-Elamite inscriptions (*i.e.* not just single signs) comparable to those of Uruk IVa are not until the Susa III period, contemporary with Uruk III. While there may have been earlier script stages at Susa during the level 17/16 break, it is simpler to assume that the script was invented in a short space of time, perhaps by a single individual (as has been argued by Nissen and Powell in the case of Sumerian),[128] near the beginning of Susa III.

On present evidence, therefore, Sumerian may be regarded as the older invention which inspired the creation of Proto-Elamite. It was the idea of writing that diffused, not the script itself which is quite different.[129] Subsequent changes in Proto-Elamite during the Susa III period affected only the shape of the tablets, and the number and arrangement of signs.[130]

The invention of Proto-Elamite, probably at Susa, indicates a continuing desire for efficient administration along Sumerian lines, and an eagerness to keep pace with bureaucratic developments in her erstwhile overlord to the west. Whether Sumerians were still directly involved in this process or not, the Proto-Elamite administration remains thoroughly Sumerian in spirit. The Elamites learnt well from the Sumerian occupiers and applied these lessons to their own far-flung administration.

(v) The Later History of Writing in Iran.   It is convenient here to over-reach briefly the chronological limits of the Proto-Elamite period to discuss the later spread of Sumerian cuneiform to Iran in the mid-third millennium. At Susa present chronologies imply a hiatus between the demise of Proto-Elamite in Early Dynastic I/II and the appearance of administrative records in Mesopotamian cuneiform under the Akkadian regime.[131] This apparent gap presents a puzzle and raises the question whether the use of Proto-Elamite may have lasted longer than is presently allowed, more in keeping with Le Breton's original dating of the last tablets to Susa Dd (Early Dynastic III).[132]

Around the time of the foundation of the Ur III dynasty, the Iranian linear Elamite script ('Proto-Elamite B') makes its appearance.[133] Of the nineteen known texts in this script, all but two were found at Susa, many on monuments with Akkadian inscriptions of Puzur-Inšušinak (Figs 12, 34). Whether the new nationalistic Elamite (or 'Awanite'?) script is derived from the earlier Proto-Elamite (A) script is still highly contentious.[134] It too remains undeciphered, Hinz's attempts not having received general acceptance.[135] Linear Elamite seems to have died with Puzur-Inšušinak, unless some similar signs ('potter's marks') on late third millennium

---

VII, no. 44 = Amiet 1972: no. 1021), and just with numbers (Scheil 1935: no. 113). The sign on Amiet 1972: no. 474 is also attested in Proto-Elamite (*cf.* Scheil 1935: sign nos 1140, (?) 838).

[128] Nissen 1986: 326; Powell 1981: 419-23.

[129] Stolper 1984: 8; Vaiman 1972; Sollberger 1984; Damerow & Englund 1989: 7 n. 23. Falkenstein 1936, Merriggi 1971 and Damerow & Englund 1989 for sign lists. Since both are pictographic, there are some basic similarities in the signs representing common objects such as vessels. The Proto-Elamite signs are in general more conventionalized.

[130] Le Brun & Vallat 1978; Vallat 1986.

[131] The latest well dated tablets come from Acropole I:14B (Vallat 1971: 239) and Ville Royale I:18B (Carter 1980: fig. 17:8), which Carter dates to the ED I-II transition. The script shows little palaeographical development and most scholars now date its demise to ED I or II at latest (Alden 1982: 613 n. 3). However, a lower end-date is required by the suggested links with potter's marks of the late 3rd mill. (D.T. Potts 1981a).

[132] Le Breton 1957: 120.

[133] Corpus listed in Hinz 1969; add Hiebert & Lamberg-Karlovsky 1992: fig. 4.

[134] Stolper 1984: 62 n. 24; Vallat 1986; Damerow & Englund 1987: 4f. n. 14.

[135] Hinz 1962.

Figure 12. Clay cone with linear Elamite inscription. Period of Puzur-Inšušinak. Ht. 7.4 cm.

Iranian pottery and southern Turkmenian figurines are related.[136] With the political reintegration of Susa with Sumer under the Ur III dynasty, Sumerian cuneiform documents appear.

In highland Iran there is no evidence of writing after Proto-Elamite until two linear Elamite (B) inscriptions from Shahdad and the Marv Dasht.[137] This script was presumably also used in Anšan (Tal-i Malyan) where, however, there is presently a hiatus in the archaeological record at this point; documents are not attested until Kaftari levels in the early second millennium.[138] Letters were certainly exchanged with Anšan and other highland states under the Ur III dynasty but no evidence of these has come to light in Iran. Neither is there any evidence of cuneiform writing elsewhere on the Iranian plateau in the third millennium.[139] To what extent this reflects a general absence of literacy rather than the paucity of excavation is difficult to judge.

North-west of Sumer there is a similar gap between the Uruk IV 'numerical texts' and the introduction of cuneiform in about Early Dynastic III to write a Semitic language at Ebla. But unlike highland Iran, literacy took firm root there, and a sprinkling of texts at sites such as Tell Brak indicate that the use of cuneiform survived through the remainder of the third millennium and beyond, not to be displaced until the advent of the Aramaeans.

(b) The Proto-Elamite State

At a number of sites (Godin Tepe V, Tepe Sialk IV1, Tepe Yahya IVC2, Sokhta I) there is evidence of an indigenous culture continuing alongside the Proto-Elamite

---

[136] D.T. Potts 1981a; Masson & Sarianidi 1972: 135f.
[137] Hinz 1969: Taf. 2, 4-6; *idem* 1971a.
[138] Stolper 1982: 57 n. 52.
[139] Reiner 1965.

remains which are concentrated in a particular area or compound, usually on the top of the mound.[140] This has generally been taken to indicate the segregation of a small number of intruders in a larger host population. These foreign enclaves, probably ethnically and linguistically distinct from the locals, were apparently established for the purpose of regulating some aspect of the community's life by means of bureaucratic practices which have no local history.

How the 'colonies' were established, whether peacefully for the mutual benefit of colonists and locals alike,[141] or violently for purposes of exploitation, remains unclear. There is positive evidence only at Tepe Sialk where the III7 settlement came to an abrupt end through burning with some loss of life.[142] This need not reflect a general pattern but suggests at least sporadic resistance. There seems often to have been a population vacuum. In Susiana, the Kur basin and the Soghun valley the Proto-Elamite settlements are preceded by long and marked population declines.[143]

The still undeciphered bureaucratic documents which characterise Proto-Elamite sites provide little direct insight into the nature of Proto-Elam.[144] At the very least, however, the implementation and co-ordination of a uniform system of administration over large areas of Iran suggests a powerful and probably centralized politico-economic administration. On the analogy of early Sumer, where similar practices are associated with the beginnings of hierarchical urban society and early 'state' development, Proto-Elam is also generally visualised as an early 'state' society.[145] Although the details of the Sumerian development should not be transposed to Proto-Elam, this provides the most plausible general 'model' for reconstructing the nature of Proto-Elam.[146]

If a considerable degree of centralization seems certain, there has been less agreement as to where that centre lay. Susa has been generally regarded as the focus of Proto-Elam, as it was till recently of historic Elam, a view supported in this case by the fact that only at Susa II can the evolution of tablets and other 'type fossils' of the Proto-Elamites be traced.[147] The suggestion that Tal-i Malyan was from the start the true capital of Proto-Elam[148] cannot be judged until the Early Banesh levels are excavated. Dittmann compromises, suggesting that they functioned as "equal partners" from Early Dynastic I; Amiet likewise suggests twin capitals as in historic Anšan.[149] There can be little doubt, however, that by the Proto-Elamite period proper (= Susa III), the political and administrative heart of Proto-Elam was Tal-i Malyan, then by far the largest Proto-Elamite settlement.[150] It was presumably from there, and not from the now much depopulated settlement of Susa, that Proto-Elamite 'colonies' were sent out across the plateau to Tepe Yahya, Sokhta and Tepe Sialk IV2. Indeed, Susa itself seems now to have become an outpost of highland power, though one assured a special importance due to its key position on the Sumerians' frontier.

---

[140] Weiss & Young 1975; Lamberg-Karlovsky 1977: 37f.; Amiet 1985.
[141] Thus Alden 1982: 621.
[142] Ghirshman 1954: 46f.
[143] Lamberg-Karlovsky 1977: 36f., 38f.; Johnson 1973; Sumner 1986: 199.
[144] Stolper 1984: 8f.
[145] D.T. Potts 1977: 30; Amiet 1979: 196; Alden 1982: 622.
[146] Lamberg-Karlovsky's suggestion (1982: 632) that the Proto-Elamites adopted the trappings of complex, urban life but remained at the level of 'chiefdoms' is hardly a plausible explanation of such a widespread and consistent phenomenon.
[147] D.T. Potts 1977: 30; Lamberg-Karlovsky 1977: 39; *idem* 1982; Young 1986: 221; Amiet 1979: 198-200.
[148] Alden 1982; Stolper 1984: 9.
[149] Dittmann 1986: 193; Amiet 1986: 211.
[150] Stolper 1984: 9.

The principal evidence for the nature of Proto-Elamite economy and society comes from the tablets and sealings. Although the Proto-Elamite script remains undeciphered, the numerical signs which it shares with Archaic Sumerian can be interpreted, and plausible readings of some pictograms have been offered. On this basis it may be suggested that the Proto-Elamite tablets are concerned not with trade, as has often been supposed,[151] but with the administration of local agricultural produce, usually on a relatively small scale.[152] This interpretation is consistent with analyses of the functions of Proto-Elamite sealings which prove to be "wasters of door locking devices and, to a lesser extent, on vessels and other containers", *i.e.* means of regulating and securing local produce.[153] This is not to say there was not trade in Proto-Elam, nor that it was not sometimes recorded in such documents.[154] Such trade, however, was probably just one aspect of the general concern with proper agricultural organisation and security.

(c) Relations between Sumer and Proto-Elam

(i) The Late Uruk period.   The centuries immediately prior to the Proto-Elamite period proper witnessed an unprecedented extension of lowland control into the eastern highlands. Colonies of the Uruk IV culture, perhaps mediated by Susa, were established along the Khorasan Road (Godin Tepe) and on the plateau (Tepe Sialk IV1). As Ghirshman argued in connection with Tepe Sialk, their purpose may have been to secure raw materials by direct control of the source areas, though probably for Sumer rather than Susa.[155] The political dimension of this phenomenon is irretrievably lost, but it is not implausible that an Archaic Sumerian empire along the lines of the later Ur III hegemony in the Zagros mountains should have existed.[156] Any effective control of highland territory – for trade or any other purpose – would have required a network of provincial administrative centres and garrisons. In the Ur III period these were manned by native conscripts under native or Sumerian commanders, closely controlled by the central goverment under the supervision of the sukkalmah Arad(IR)-Nanna (below pp. 137f.). Since no Ur III provincial centre has yet come to light, direct archaeological comparison with the Late Uruk colonies is not possible.[157] In any period, however, such centres might be expected to mirror the administrative practices of the homeland, as do Godin Tepe and Tepe Sialk.

(ii) The Proto-Elamite Period.   Largely on the basis of the Acropole I sounding at Susa, it has become widely accepted that the Proto-Elamite period witnessed the severing of ties with Sumer and the emergence of a vigorously independent Iranian culture whose focus had now shifted from Susa to Tal-i Malyan.[158] Relations between Sumer and Proto-Elam are thus perceived in the context of a radical break which established a lowland-highland dichotomy and thus fixed the geo-political landscape

---

[151] Ghirshman 1938: 67; D.T. Potts 1977: 30; Alden 1982.
[152] Lamberg-Karlovsky 1977: 37; *idem* 1982: 632; *idem* 1986: 208f.; Damerow & Englund 1989.
[153] Ferioli & Fiandra cited by Lamberg-Karlovsky 1982.
[154] Assuming that seals already acted as a form of signature, certifying or guaranteeing the document concerned, Le Brun & Vallat (1978: 37f.) suggest that tablets at Susa with only one seal impression represent the sender's record of the contents of a consignment, and that bullae are records which accompanied such goods in transport. *Cf.* Renger 1977: 75-80 and Schmandt-Besserat 1986: 112, the latter arguing that the bullae were not bills of lading and that the different seals represent different levels of authority.
[155] Ghirshman 1954: 48f.
[156] Contrast Amiet 1979: 198.
[157] Note, however, reports of an Ur III impressed bulla from Dinkha Tepe (Dyson 1969: 18).
[158] *E.g.* Alden 1982.

in the form which was to characterise Mesopotamian-Iranian relations for much of pre-Achaemenid antiquity.

While there may indeed have been a break between these periods at Susa – and there is no doubting the demographic changes which occurred around this time in Susiana and the highlands – there has perhaps been a tendency to assume too readily that the situation at Susa was repeated elsewhere, and thus to exaggerate the wider importance of the transition.

Despite the new predominance of highland pottery, hearth-types and the advent of a local script, there is still, from a typological point of view, considerable evidence of lowland 'presence' or influence in Proto-Elamite Iran. At Susa itself, although the ware changes in Acropole I:16, many unpainted shapes continue from the previous phase.[159] Moreover, the Jemdet Nasr and Early Dynastic I-related painted wares, though never as common as in the Deh Luran, occur in limited quantities at Susa also.[160] Likewise seals and sealings from Acropole I:14B and Ville Royale I:17-18 have good parallels at Khafajeh, Sin Temples IV/V, and the distinctive Riemchen bricks still occur.[161] It is noteworthy that these parallels are principally with the Diyala region.

In the highlands also lowland pottery, especially bevelled-rim bowls and Jemdet Nasr-type polychrome ware, continues to appear. It is reported at Tepe Yahya IVC2 and at Tal-i Malyan, ABC II.[162] At Chogha Maran and other sites in the Mahidasht Jemdet Nasr-Early Dynastic-I-type polychrome pottery has been recovered, though with a local rim form.[163] 'Piedmont'-type seals, known from Jemdet Nasr times in Mesopotamia (*e.g.* Sin Temples IV-V), are also attested at Tepe Yahya, Tal-i Malyan and Sokhta.[164] Numerical tablets, the main lowland link in the Late Uruk period, continue to appear on Proto-Elamite sites also (Table 2.3).

Why, if the Proto-Elamite 'colonies' were exclusively Iranian ventures, do distinctively Sumerian cultural markers continue to appear? To cite an extreme case, why should an eastern outpost of Tal-i Malyan at a site like Tepe Yahya have pottery imported or inspired by types which are at home far to the west of both in Sumer?

Specific answers to these questions are not possible, but some general comments may be offered. Continuing trade with the lowlands may provide part of the answer, especially for seals and sealings. But pottery is another matter; common-wares are unlikely to have been objects of trade (nor are storage jars or bevelled rim bowls likely containers for transporting traded materials), or to have survived in use after their bearers had departed.[165] The evidence is perhaps best explained by

---

[159] See list in Dittmann 1986: 171f. with full references, 192f.

[160] Dittmann 1986: 192f; Carter 1984: 120. Jemdet Nasr-style monochrome ware occurs in Susa levels 16-15B (Le Brun 1971: fig. 64:3-5, 8) and bichrome ware in levels 15A-14B (Le Brun 1971: figs 64:9-12) and Ville Royale I:18B-17 (Carter 1980: fig. 14:15-18; *cf.* Dittmann 1986: Table 2; Amiet 1986: figs 40-42). See also the Jemdet Nasr-style monochrome and polychrome jars found in the excavations of Ghirshman (Stève & Gasche 1971: 148, pl. 29:16-17) and Mecquenem (1943: 18, fig. 15:1, 6, p. 190). This older material is reviewed in Nagel's comprehensive study of Jemdet Nasr and related wares (Nagel 1964) (though his chronology now requires revision). Note especially the scarlet-ware-related 'Proto-Susa-II Keramik'.

[161] Dittmann 1986: 172, n. 15 (Khafajeh parallels); Alden 1987: 158 (Riemchen).

[162] D.T. Potts 1977: 27. Yahya: Bevelled rim bowls, JN-ED II-type 'conical cups/solid-footed chalices', 'JN-type polychrome' jars (Lamberg-Karlovsky 1973: 308, fig. 4::A, B, D; *idem* 1977: 37; D.T. Potts 1977: 28; *idem* in press [a]: Chapter 8, arguing that these types date specifically to JN-ED I; here Fig. 7:18-19). Malyan: Bevelled-rim bowls, 'conical cups', four-lugged jars (Carter 1984: 124; D.T. Potts in press [a]).

[163] Young 1986: 220.

[164] Amiet 1980: 35f.

[165] D.T. Potts (1978: 35) suggests that the four-lugged jars were locally made at each site, but gives no grounds.

viewing the Proto-Elamite settlements as still, to some extent, a co-operative Sumero-Iranian venture, though now dominated more by Tal-i Malyan than Uruk.[166] In any case, the view now prevalent that the Susa III period represented the cutting of links with Sumer and a re-alignment with the highlands oversimplifies the evidence. The difference between the Susa II period, dominated by Uruk, and the Susa III period, dominated by Proto-Elam, seems rather to have been a matter of degree. At times 'Sumerian' ceramics were still imported far into Iran; and essentially highland cylinder seals found their way to Sumer, or were used to seal merchandise which did. To the extent that archaeological evidence can be said to support such speculation, this suggests not a context of confrontation or hostility, but of continuing contact and exchange. Moreover, if the possibility of an Uruk IV 'empire' in Iran may legitimately be raised, some legacy of lowland 'presence' or direct involvement during Proto-Elamite times must also be considered. It cannot be assumed that relations with Proto-Elam were entirely a matter of 'foreign affairs' rather than 'provincial affairs'.

(i) Political Relations with Proto-Elam

In the absence of contemporary historical documents, political and military relations between Sumer and Proto-Elam remain matters of speculation. Hostility between the highlands and lowlands is attested in the earliest historical texts of the late Early Dynastic period and is usually assumed to have been endemic also in earlier times; but, as we have seen, this is questionable. Direct 'political' contact cannot yet be demonstrated. Iranian toponyms do not appear in the Archaic Sumerian texts with the sole and questionable exception of Aratta (above p. 12). The cycle of epics relating to this place may, however, derive ultimately from events of the Proto-Elamite period. Enmerkar is conventionally assigned to Early Dynastic II on the basis of his place in the *Sumerian King List*, but an earlier date may be implied by the reference to the invention of writing in *Enmerkar and the Lord of Aratta*.[167] This poem represents Uruk and Aratta at loggerheads over the supply of precious stones and metals to Uruk for Inanna's shrine; and in *Enmerkar and Lugalbanda* the king of Uruk actually lays siege to Aratta.[168] Yet the fact that such a request could be made, and in the expectation of a favourable response, suggests a background of previous peaceful transactions.

(ii) Economic Relations with Proto-Elam

Economic relations, especially with Sumer, have been the primary focus of recent research on the Proto-Elamites. A number of studies[169] place emphasis on trade as the key factor in the rise and development of Proto-Elam.[170] This view is most thoroughly developed, albeit in very different ways, by Amiet and Alden.

Amiet interprets the domestic bureaucracy of the Susa II period, formally identical to that of the Uruk IV temple administration, as evidence of:

---

[166] *Cf.* D.T. Potts 1977: 30.

[167] *ELA* ll. 503-05 = Cohen 1973: 38, 136f.; Cooper & Heimpel 1983: 82.

[168] Falkowitz 1983: 106f, n. 11; Kramer had previously regarded this action as taking place in Uruk.

[169] Ghirshman 1954: 45-60; Johnson 1973; D.T. Potts 1977; Weiss & Young 1975; Lamberg-Karlovsky 1978; Amiet 1979; *idem* 1986; 91-119; Alden 1982; Algaze 1989.

[170] *Cf.* Lamberg-Karlovsky 1977: 40 who refers to the "merchant madness imposed on the Iranian plateau. The Proto-Elamite expansion is most often interpreted as merchants venturing off in search of new capital in distant areas, exploiting, trading, manufacturing *etc.*" Kohl (1978) presents a similarly trade-oriented view of the succeeding period.

a private management system ... a sort of 'International' of merchants rather than a centralized administration ... Though unable to pass on the Uruk writing system, these merchants will at least have been the indirect media of 'Sumerian' expansion into North Syria and of Susian expansion into Media and further to Godin V and Sialk IV-1.

In the Susa III period Proto-Elam developed "a state administration much more centralized than in previous times" which vigorously exploited the copper and other resources of highland Iran, as had previously Tepe Sialk and Tal-i Iblis. These products were traded through sites like Tepe Yahya which

> might be compared to caravaners' cities, powerful staging posts on trade routes, getting their wealth more from exchange than from local agricultural production. The latter had characterized Susiana during the preceding period and continued to characterize Mesopotamia, which shows how deeply the Proto-Elamite and Mesopotamian worlds differed from each other, though belonging to the same cultural community.[171]

Alden likewise gives primary emphasis to economic factors, claiming that "the rise and fall of Proto-Elamite fortunes in the Middle East could never be understood without a consideration of long-distance trade".[172] Like other investigators, Alden views the Proto-Elamite phenomenon largely as a response to developments in Late Uruk Sumer where the dramatic population growth of the late fourth millennium created unprecedented demand for highland raw materials. To supply this need, the Sumerians established trading outposts along the Upper Tigris and Euphrates, at Tell Brak, and at Godin Tepe V, all stratigically placed to draw on the rich resources of Syro-Anatolia and Iran.[173] Tal-i Malyan at this stage was just one of many remote supply areas and did not merit the effort of colonization. According to Alden, with the collapse of the Uruk IV colonies the highland trade was taken over by the rapidly developing Proto-Elamite culture centred on the Kur basin. "For perhaps a hundred or a hundred and fifty years, the Proto-Elamites controlled overland trade from a seemingly invulnerable position in Fars". Holding a monopoly on the materials which were an increasingly important element of urban life in Sumer, the power and prosperity of Proto-Elam grew. By *ca.* 3000 BC the Kur basin had emerged as "a polity dominating the southern Iranian highlands and with military equivalence to Sumer". Proto-Elam's control of commercial traffic led to a general decrease in the availability of imported materials such as lapis, carnelian and Kerman copper in Jemdet Nasr-Early Dynastic I Sumer. By restricting supply the Proto-Elamites were able to increase demand and thereby command higher prices. In this structure "Susa functioned as a port-of-trade, a weak but independent location where highland resources were exchanged for the products of Sumerian society". Although admitting that some Proto-Elamite 'type-fossils' – tablets, bullae, sealings – may have related to internal controls, Alden views them principally as means of regulating these transfers of goods between highland Iran and Sumer.

Unable to free the Khorasan Road from the 'Yanik' invaders who had overwhelmed northern Luristan and destroyed the lowland colony of Godin Tepe V,

---

[171] Amiet 1979: 199f.

[172] Alden 1982: 628. The following summary and quotes come principally from *ibid.*: 621f., 624f., 637.

[173] Alden (1982: 617) notes the other sites in western highland Iran with some evidence of Uruk-related wares but nowhere suggests that these were colonies. See Young 1986: 219f.

and frustrated by the economic opportunism of the Proto-Elamites, the Sumerians of the Jemdet Nasr period turned to the Gulf. Thus, on Alden's view, began the trade with Bahrain, Oman, coastal Iran and ultimately the Indus which was to supply an increasing share of Sumer's needs in metals, timber, semi-precious stones and many other commodities through the third and early second millennia. Exotic materials like carnelian and lapis thereby became available once more, making possible the lavish consumption evident in Early Dynastic III burials at Ur and Kiš.

Their trade monopoly smashed, Proto-Elam declined. The trading outposts, along with settlements in the Izeh plain,[174] were abandoned; Susa returned once more to the Sumerian orbit; and Tal-i Malyan, now isolated, fell into the regional obscurity of the Late Banesh period.

Alden's thesis is open to serious objections. Most important, his central claim to see evidence of Proto-Elam's monopoly of highland trade in the *reduction* of highland materials in contemporary Sumer is highly implausible. The supposed policy of reducing supply to inflate prices is economic nonsense when taken to this extreme. His own account of its inevitable consequence – the Sumerians turning to the Gulf for alternative supplies – is an admission of its counter-productive, indeed suicidal, character. If ever implemented, it is hardly plausible that such a policy should have been pursued once its deleterious effects became apparent. But it is unlikely that it ever was implemented. If Sumerian trade was at all important to the Proto-Elamite economy, the prosperity of Middle Banesh Tal-i Malyan would suggest that it flourished, and one would expect to see evidence of this in high levels of consumption in Sumer.

It is important to note that the absence of any recognisable concern with trade in the Proto-Elamite texts is not decisive. Evidence from Sargonic Mesopotamia, where foreign trade certainly prospered, provides an instructive parallel:

> Strikingly absent [from Sargonic economic texts] are the very products one might expect to find there if one believed that the role of the trading agent was to acquire goods not locally available in Mesopotamia. One searches in vain for accounts of steatite, chlorite, lapis, or other precious or semi-precious stones ... If the majority of foreign imports such as precious stones were acquired in a way that has left a record in the official and private archives of Mesopotamian urban centres, one must assume that they were either not accountable property, or became accountable property at a point beyond the horizon of these archives.[175]

Similarly, there is no guarantee that any trade which was conducted by the Proto-Elamite colonies will be recorded in its documents; nor, more generally, that the colonies' primary function within the Proto-Elamite economy will be reflected in the administrative remains found there. A Proto-Elamite enclave in a foreign environment may be expected to have brought with it certain aspects of the settlers' native culture, whatever their reasons for being there. It is hardly surprising that they should organize agriculture and other affairs relating to their sustenance and daily life according to standard Proto-Elamite practices. This would apply equally to trade colonies, agricultural colonies (*i.e.* genuine settlements), garrisons or any other form

---

[174] Wright ed. 1979: 128.
[175] Foster 1977: 37f.

of official presence in foreign territories. And some such presence would be a prerequisite of any effective centralized control of the large area covered by the Proto-Elamite settlements.

Some trade between these disparate regions is suggested by the unified bureaucracy and scale of Proto-Elam itself. The Proto-Elamite period was one of pronounced internationalism. The wide distribution of administrative devices and records indicates that people travelled freely and ideas were exchanged across areas of the plateau with widely different resource potentials. With an efficient bureaucracy recording and controlling commodities (of whatever kind) in these regions it would be surprising if it did not also supervise the redistribution of raw materials within the Proto-Elamite realm according to their respective surplusses and defficiences. Thus, although trade was probably not the primary basis of Proto-Elamite prosperity, the bureaucracy which is Proto-Elam's most conspicuous feature provided the ideal administrative structure within which it could flourish.

Moreover, it is clear that something justified the considerable effort and commitment involved in establishing and maintaining outposts across Iran; there must have been some significant benefit to the authorities concerned. Agriculture is hardly the answer. Tal-i Malyan lay in one of the largest, most fertile plains of Iran. In any case, it would have been highly uneconomical to transport bulky agricultural products over large distances to Tal-i Malyan or wherever the administrative centre(s) lay.[176] The acquisition of raw material is the obvious alternative. Metals, stones, timber *etc.* must now have been in high demand among the growing urban population of Proto-Elam, where Tal-i Malyan was approaching 45 hectares and surplus production would have provided the basis for lucrative trade with Sumer.

There was probably little distinction in such circumstances between trade and tribute or taxation, *i.e.* some form of exploitation of foreign regions and populations by a central political authority. Indirect evidence of such exploitation comes from Tal-i Malyan itself where the Middle Banesh operations have yielded evidence of craft activities using a variety of local and exotic raw materials.[177] The latter include beads of Gulf shell (cone shell and dentalium), carnelian and "a few lapis lazuli and turquoise beads and unworked specimens of both minerals", all probably from the east (below Ch. 5). There is also gold, bitumen, and Anatolian obsidian. Copper smelting and/or casting used arsenic-rich Anarak ores. In Kerman also copper was exploited at this time at Iblis and probably also at Shahdad (undated slag) and Tepe Sialk.[178] Simple metal tools are standard on Proto-Elamite sites but otherwise do not supplement the picture from Tal-i Malyan.[179]

More important from the viewpoint of this study, there is also considerable evidence that trade between Iran and Sumer continued under the Proto-Elamites. The dearth of lapis lazuli in Early Dynastic I Sumer[180] is now somewhat alleviated by numerous beads in the revised dating of the 'Jemdet Nasr' Cemetery at Ur (below p. 213f.). Some of this, and other semi-precious stones (carnelian, agate), may have been traded overland through Proto-Elam, as well as along the Gulf. Contrary to Alden's claim that Sumer was forced during the Proto-Elamite period to rely entirely on the Gulf for supplies of copper, analyses of metalwork suggest that some copper

---

[176] Lamberg-Karlovsky 1977: 38.
[177] Sumner 1986: 204.
[178] Iblis – Caldwell ed. 1967: 17-40. **Shahdad** – Haghighi 1977: 23.
[179] The "pins, chisels and wands" reported from Godin V (Young 1986: 213) may have more wideranging parallels.
[180] Herrmann 1968: 37, 53.

from Iran continued to be exchanged westwards. Anarak-Talmessi, the main copper source during Susa I, also probably supplied the Hamrin in Early Dynastic I.[181] Susa II-III likewise drew on the highlands, probably the regions of Bardsir and Kashan, though its arsenic still came from Anarak.[182] Analytical evidence of Omani copper begins in the mid third millennium with the copperwork from the 'Vase à la Cachette', though Archaic texts from Uruk already mention "Dilmun axes" and "Dilmun copper (?)" (from Oman?).[183] The relative prevalence of Iranian vs Gulf copper in these centuries no doubt varied according to price, availability and other economic and political circumstances. The material from third-millennium Sumer is not further divided chronologically by Berthoud, but it is suggested that the pattern roughly follows Susa.[184] Small copper objects appear now in the tombs of the Pusht-i Kuh[185] and these nomads may have played some rôle in the Iranian copper trade with Sumer.

Trade in common stones, particularly for vessels, also continued. Vessels made from hard green-grey-black igneous and metamorphic rocks are most common in Mesopotamia in the Jemdet Nasr to Early Dynastic II periods (below pp. 218f.). The stones used were not available in the Zagros foothills nearest Sumer; they exist only in highland Iran (and Anatolia) which is their most likely source. Since unworked blocks would have been prohibitively weighty, vessels were probably imported in semi-finished or finished form. No production sites, nor even settlements with quantities comparable to Sumer, have yet been found in Iran, but a vessel identical to those in Sumer from Tepe Hissar confirms that such centres existed.[186]

On the other hand, there is very little in the way of specifically Proto-Elamite – as distinct from Iranian – material from Mesopotamia to substantiate the existence of trade. Rare cylinder seal impressions from the Seal Impression Stata at Ur showing animals in human attitudes are clearly Proto-Elamite in inspiration and probably in origin.[187] Dating to the same period are the more common 'piedmont seals' and impressions recovered from Sumer and especially the Diyala. The greatest concentration and variety of such seals is found at Susa (though this may be largely due to that site's greater exposure), where they are a prominent element of Proto-Elamite bureaucracy used for sealing tablets, tags and jars.[188] Other concentrations occur in the Diyala sites (principally cylinders rather than sealings and mostly in temples), in the Hamrin, in Assyria (Nineveh) and into Syria. They are rare at Ur and elsewhere in Sumer.[189] Eastwards seals and/or sealings are found through Fars (Malyan) to Shahr-i Sokhta. Pittman reckons a total of about 580 examples from seventeen sites. This distribution leaves no doubt that the piedmont style was an essentially Iranian phenomenon and that its appearance in Mesopotamia was culturally intrusive. Long thought to reflect the activities of highland-lowland traders operating along the Zagros mountains,[190] the piedmont style should perhaps be linked more specifically with the Proto-Elamites. However, this connection remains speculative and any firmer statement will require further work, in particular to

---

[181] Berthoud *et al.* 1982: 43, Table A; Amiet 1986: 35.
[182] Berthoud & Cleuziou 1983: 243; Berthoud *et al.* 1982: 45.
[183] Amiet 1986: 126 ('Vase à la Cachette'); Englund 1983a: 35; Nissen 1986a: 338.
[184] Berthoud *et al.* 1982: 45, Table A.
[185] Haerinck 1987.
[186] Schmidt 1933: pl. CXXXIX:H391.
[187] Legrain 1936: no. 384.
[188] Amiet 1972; Pittman n.d. [1].
[189] Legrain 1936: *e.g.* no. 161; *idem* 1951: nos 49, 50, 54, 55; Moorey 1979: no. 574.
[190] Most recently Collon (1987: 20-24) suggests a Susa-Syria trade route running along the Zagros piedmont.

establish whether the sealings from Sumer were impressed locally (on doors and other fixtures) or arrived on jars and other sealed goods.

Nor is there any direct evidence concerning the nature of the return trade from Sumer, if such existed. The Uruk-Jemdet Nasr pottery from Iran certainly does not constitute a likely object of exchange and may have been locally produced.[191] 'Invisible' agricultural products, particularly secondary products like textiles, are perhaps most likely. In epic literature Enmerkar sent donkey loads of grain to Aratta in return for lapis. The Old Assyrian caravan trade with Capaddocia, in which garments and tin were sent to Anatolia, is perhaps the best guide to the possible logistics of such exchanges. The exclusively maritime trade with Susa in the later third millennium provides no basis for analogy.[192]

4. SUMER AND THE DEMISE OF PROTO-ELAM

Sumer has often been associated by modern scholars with the demise of Proto-Elam. Alden sees the cause of the fall in Iran's loss of the Sumerian trade to the Gulf. But we have seen reason to doubt that a policy of restricting the flow of goods was ever pursued. In any case, Tal-i Malyan lay in the largest and most fertile plain of the Zagros mountains where agriculture was clearly the primary source of urban growth and prosperity. This wealth supported, rather than derived from, foreign trade, as is confirmed by the fact that Tal-i Malyan expanded more than three-fold (to *ca.* 150-200 ha.) in the Kaftari period,[193] when Sumer's trade was almost exclusively maritime and highland Iran was dominated by the now implacably hostile Elam.

Amiet once suggested that the fall of Proto-Elam be attributed to a devastating attack by Enmebaragesi the king of Kiš who "carried away as spoil the 'weapon' of the land of Elam".[194] It is difficult to know how much credence should be assigned to an anecdote of this kind, but certainly a military cause cannot be excluded. The difficulty of assessing such factors is compounded by chronological uncertainties. The late Proto-Elamite period is poorly represented in the recent Acropole I and Ville Royale I excavations and the end date of the period at Susa remains unclear. Chronology is even more uncertain on the plateau where estimates of the total length of occupation vary greatly from site to site. Although the final Proto-Elamite assemblages largely correspond, it cannot be assumed that the colonies were all abandoned together. Their subsequent histories vary and may reflect a diversity of local circumstances. Susiana returned to the Sumerian orbit. The Izeh plain was abandoned,[195] as were Tepe Sialk and Tepe Yahya, the latter only reoccupied in IVC1 after a gap of some centuries (on D.T. Potts' chronology, below p. 260f.). Tal-i Malyan survived and, to judge by historical references to Anšan, became a major political force, though surveys suggest a reduced population,[196] followed by apparent abandonment at the time of its greatest historical prominence. Shahr-i Sokhta, never fully integrated into the Proto-Elamite world, turned more towards South and Central Asia.

---

[191] D.T. Potts 1978: 35.
[192] M. Lambert 1953: 62-65.
[193] Jacobs 1980: 1.
[194] Amiet 1979: 200.
[195] Wright ed. 1979: 128.
[196] Alden 1982: 620.

More recently, Amiet has suggested that "the Proto-Elamite civilisation collapsed as from a single blow, without any previous sign of decadence, around 2700 BC, apparently the victim of an urbanisation that was excessive for the agricultural and demographic capabilities of its cradle, present Fars, where the city of Anshan was abandoned ...".[197] Other than the collapse itself, however, there is little to suggest that Proto-Elam's urbanisation in heartland Fars was excessive or inherently unsustainable, and the testimony of later Iranian history would suggest that it was not. If the agricultural support system collapsed it must have been for particular reasons and it is in these – whatever they are – that the real explanation resides.

The apparent parallel between the abandonment of the Late Uruk colonies and the collapse of the Proto-Elamite network a few centuries later has suggested to some that the same forces were at work in both. Lamberg-Karlovsky,[198] for example, attributes both to the collapse of the underlying bureaucratic structure, which he argues was adopted by the Proto-Elamites from the Sumerians at Susa (in his view the origin of Proto-Elamite expansion). More particularly, in the case of the Proto-Elamites he argues that a crisis resulted from "upward-spiralling competitive costs and downward marginal returns" in the colonies, *i.e.* that they became more 'expensive' to the core than their fruits justified.[199] This is possible but remains speculative since we have no independent way of measuring these 'costs' and 'returns'.

The decline of the Proto-Elamites did not spell the end of Iranian internationalism. Indeed, while evidence for a unified bureaucratic system ceases, typological parallels in other classes of artefacts increase and evidence of traded goods grows. Susa II pottery, whose floruit should probably be dated to the middle of the third millennium, appears from Susa through Luristan to Jalyan.[200] At the same time chlorite vessels of the *série ancienne*, plain vessels of banded calcite, elaborate copper weapons and tools, and other distinctive objects begin to appear right across the area previously occupied by the Proto-Elamites (excepting, for some categories, Seistan) and beyond to Baluchistan and Central Asia. Some of these goods were traded also to Sumer which continued to rely on the east, increasingly those areas accessible by ship, for raw materials. It is through this pattern of 'échanges inter-iraniens'[201] that the story of economic relations between Sumer and the east may be continued.

First, however, we shall review the documentary evidence relating to diplomatic and military relations between Sumer and Iran which have to this point been matters of speculation. From the Early Dynastic III period onwards cuneiform records allow a basic reconstruction of political events in Mesopotamia and sporadically also her eastern neighbours, which adds a further dimension to highland-lowland relations and provides an historical context for the interpretion of the archaeological evidence of trade.

---

[197] Amiet 1993: 26.
[198] Lamberg-Karlovsky 1986: 197f..
[199] Lamberg-Karlovsky in Damerow & Englund 1989: xi f.
[200] Susa – Stève & Gasche 1971: 90; Amiet 1986: 122. Luristan – Haerinck 1987; Amiet 1986: 129-31. Jalyan – Miroschedji 1974.
[201] Amiet 1986.

Chapter 3

Political and Diplomatic Relations between Sumer and the East

1. SOURCES

The sources for reconstructing political relations between Sumer and the east in the third millennium are of several types which vary considerably in purpose, authorship and historical reliability. The principal categories are:

> (1) Royal inscriptions – mostly Old Babylonian copies – relating the achievements of the kings of Sumer and Akkad;
> (2) Year formulae recording important events under the Akkadian and Ur III kings;
> (3) Rare references to major historical persons, events or situations in contemporary documents (principally administrative texts);
> (4) Akkadian 'historical-literary' compositions describing the exploits of famous kings, especially the dynasty of Sargon;
> (5) Omens preserved in Old Babylonian and later copies mentioning the fates, both favourable and not, of famous kings; and
> (6) Sumerian narrative poems ('literary epics') relating to pre-Sargonic rulers, principally Enmerkar and Lugalbanda of Uruk.[1]

Of these, the first three are generally regarded as broadly 'historical' sources and the latter three as essentially 'literary' works although the distinction is rarely absolute and many compositions fall into an intermediate category reflected more explicitly in the narrative poems' 'historical-literary' label. Indeed, any strict separation between the two concepts would fail to capture the vast bulk of Mesopotamian thinking and writing about the past. There are of course works of pure fiction and some brief records of important events which seem simply to state the facts as far as they go. But most inscriptions are a subtle blend of fact, exaggeration, bombast, cultural prejudice and pure lies, freely mixing the devices and aims we would consider appropriate to the historian with those of the court poet, the political propagandist and the epic storyteller – a mélange which makes the modern historian's task an unusually difficult one.

Royal inscriptions, where available, are the most informative sources for historical reconstruction. As contemporary documents they are the most direct accounts of events which have survived, notwithstanding a considerable degree of propagandistic self-aggrandizement and (in some cases) adulteration through later

---

[1]   Along with these may be classed occasional anecdotal deeds reported in the *SKL*.

editing.[2] Though laconic in the extreme, year formulae of the Akkadian and Ur III periods are also valuable contemporary witnesses of events which are often otherwise unattested – not least because their choice provides a touchstone of contemporary importance. Occasional references in the thousands of archival documents to events such as royal marriages, the provisioning of royal messengers travelling to and from foreign states, and so on provide a wealth of scattered detail but in a form which is again often brief and oblique, depending as it does on an assumed background knowledge which we no longer possess.

The 'historical-literary' compositions,[3] mostly concerning Sargon and Naram-Sin, can occasionally be corroborated by the 'primary' sources (1) to (3) but there remains a degree of exaggeration and elaboration appropriate to their literary purpose. Later editing has often resulted in anachronistic additions, with events of different reigns being telescoped into those of the two great hero-kings Sargon and Naram-Sin. The omens seem often to preserve historical events but their idiom can again be impenetrably metaphorical.[4]

The Sumerian narrative poems bear principally on the proto-historical period of semi-legendary heroes – notably Enmerkar, Lugalbanda and Gilgameš – before contemporary inscriptions are available (approximately equivalent to Early Dynastic I-II in archaeological terms).[5] The commissioning of these tales to writing may have begun by the Early Dynastic III period but probably started in earnest only in Ur III times, and most extant copies date to the Old Babylonian period, some hundreds of years after the events they relate.[6] The question of their historicity,[7] despite considerable discussion, remains highly uncertain; the individuals they treat are, in some cases, almost certainly genuine, and the tales recounted are unlikely all to be pure fabrication. But in the absence of independent corroboration it is notoriously difficult to distinguish any genuine historical elements from their literary overlay, if indeed these were ever entirely separable in the author's mind. Moreover, recent studies have shown that many compositions of apparently 'historical' content (including the *Sumerian King List*)[8] reflect the circumstances and concerns of their own times as much as those of the periods they treat. This has led a number of commentators to disavow the use of 'literary' evidence for historical purposes altogether. While a more critical approach is undoubtedly called for, however, the ancient authors did not concoct stories out of thin air: they were constrained by whatever memory tradition preserved of earlier times and it is legitimate to ask where, if at all, the poems reflect these traditional histories.

The literary idiom of most of the longer and more detailed sources introduces a further barrier. Crucial expressions in royal inscriptions and literary works may be idioms peculiar to the genre or period which do not mean quite what they appear to say, or at least cannot properly be understood in ignorance of nuances which we are no longer in a position to appreciate. Sumerian compositions in particular make

2   Cooper 1983a: 15f.
3   On this genre and its historicity see Grayson 1975: 4-9; Cooper 1983a: 15f. (citing earlier literature); Foster 1990: 43f.
4   See Reiner 1974; Glassner 1983: 10; Starr 1986; *cf.* the sceptical remarks of Cooper 1980.
5   On the definition of this genre see Berlin 1979: 1f. and Kramer in Pritchard 1969: 646 n. 1 ("historiographic literature"). Kramer 1987 reviews categories (4) and (6).
6   Bing 1977: 1-4 for ED dating. Jacobsen (1987: 277, 321) makes the interesting suggestion that the Enmerkar-Lugalbanda cycle was composed in Ur III times as performed entertainment for Iranian envoys at the court of Ur.
7   See *inter alia* Cohen 1973: 1-14; Hallo 1975: 188ff.; Berlin 1983: 24; Michalowski 1986: 134f. ; *idem* 1989: 9; Alster 1990; and note 3.
8   Michalowski 1983a.

extensive use of metaphor, simile, formulaic parallelism and other literary forms of expression which are often difficult to understand literally, and impossible to translate into objective military terms.[9] The "carrying of kingship" from one city to the other in the *Sumerian King List* is transparent enough, but what exactly does it mean, for instance, for Enmebaragesi to have "carried away as spoil the 'weapon' of Elam"?

With the exception of a few longer campaign inscriptions from dedications by Akkadian and Ur III kings, all of the sources available from the third millennium are brief by the standards of later historical annals. The fact of encounter or conquest is usually all we are told, leaving the *casus belli* and secondary details regarding aims, strategy, progress and locale to the realm of speculation.

The distribution of the documentary evidence over the five hundred or so years from (En)mebaragesi to the fall of Ur III is very uneven. This is due both to changing scribal practices and, more directly, to the fortunes of modern discovery. The earliest contacts with the east — or rather, traditions purporting to describe these events — are known only from Sumerian narrative poems and the *Sumerian King List*. Informative royal inscriptions do not begin until Eannatum and become more common under the dynasty of Sargon. Thereafter there is little until the reign of Šu-Sin.[10] Some Old Akkadian year formulae are known[11] but these annual markers become common only in the reign of Šulgi, and even then some years are still unattested. The vast majority of third-millennium administrative texts, which throw sporadic light on foreign concerns, also date to the Ur III empire. Only under these two self-consciously imperialist regimes (and by no means for their entire durations) is there enough information to formulate an overall impression of the scope and intensity of military-political contact. Otherwise a significant proportion of the major military encounters between Mesopotamia and eastern lands are probably completely unattested, or known only from laconic year formulae.

A further obstacle to any historical investigation of Mesopotamian-Iranian relations is the almost total lack of Iranian source material. Only one third-millennium Elamite king, Puzur-Inšušinak, has left accounts of his deeds. Otherwise an Old Babylonian school text listing twelve kings each of Awan and Šimaški, and a poorly understood treaty between Naram-Sin and an Elamite ruler are the only Elamite documents which bear directly on the political history of the period. Being forced to view things almost exclusively through Mesopotamian eyes, we are handicapped by all their biases and deprived of the means to neutralise the distortion and partisanship of the sources that do survive. Moreover, the few relevant Elamite documents all come from Susa on the western fringe of Elam. These do not reflect the state of affairs in the Elamite heartland in Fars. Similarly, the Sumerian and Akkadian inscriptions from Susa, which evidence the city's incorporation into the empires of Agade and Ur, do not provide an appropriate basis for determining the situation further east.

---

9   See *e.g.* Berlin 1979: 28-30.
10   The Utu-hegal inscription (*IRSA*: IIK3a; Römer 1985) may be a later concoction and Gudea's inscriptions contain nothing of direct relevance to military contact except his claim to have conquered and plundered Anšan (Stat. B vii:64-69).
11   Fifty-six years are accounted for out of a total of 181, most of these belonging to Naram-Sin (14) and Šarkališarri (17) (*AKI*: 49).

2. THE EARLY DYNASTIC PERIOD

The beginnings of political relations between the peoples of Mesopotamia and their eastern neighbours no doubt extend back far beyond the Early Dynastic II/III period, the point at which the first contemporary 'historical' inscriptions begin and to which later quasi-historical works such as the *Sumerian King List* seem to relate. At present, however, this background remains largely shrouded from view. For while aspects of prehistoric foreign exchange have been much illuminated by archaeological research in Mesopotamia and neighbouring regions, and features of the local economy from the mid-fourth millennium on are gradually yielding to detailed examination of the Archaic account texts from Uruk, when it comes to the specifics of political relations *strictu sensu* before the mid-third millennium we have only the testimony of the Sumerian narrative poems to go by. But these are literature not history and attempts to read them as such have been increasingly discredited. The hero-kings of Uruk – Enmerkar, Lagalbanda and Gilgameš – are often associated with purely mythical beings (the Anzu-bird, Humbaba) and may themselves be really fictional, or so heroised as to be virtually so – indeed, later tradition often regarded them as divine. Likewise, Aratta and other locales are portrayed in such 'fairy-tale' terms that some commentators are inclined to view them as unreal.[12] The best one can hope (and this is still little more than wishful thinking) is that the stories told by the Sumerian bards reflect the *sorts* of concerns, situations and events that occurred in proto-historical times. Here again there may be exceptions. Events such as Enmerkar's seige of Aratta and the caravan trade between Uruk and Aratta may have had no precedents in actual events of the times. Perhaps indeed it was usual for such stories to be woven around deeds which were in a practical sense 'inconceivable' in their own day, and thus more intrinsically heroic.

Once all these uncertainties are acknowledged it is difficult indeed to see how the Sumerian epic poems can be critically controlled as historical sources. Yet to ignore them altogether would be to adopt an extreme judgement which cannot yet be proven. Consequently, it may be useful to summarise briefly what the Sumerian epics relate about early relations beween Mesopotamia and the east, leaving open the question of which (if any) episodes are to be regarded as having some historical basis. So far there is nothing in the contemporary archaeological or historical record to corroborate the particular episodes related in any of these compositions; but then neither perhaps should we expect there to be.

Four poems are known – *Enmerkar and the Lord of Aratta, Enmerkar and Lugalbanda* (also called the *Lugalbanda Epic*), *Lugalbanda in Hurrumkurra* (the "mountain cave") and *Enmerkar and Ensuhkešdanna*[13] – which seem to form a related cycle of stories, although the narrative sequence and many matters of detail remain uncertain. The general context for all poems is an 'intellectual' and economic rivalry between the rulers of Uruk and Aratta for the favours of Inanna. Often the tales involve messengers being dispatched between the two cities[14] and at least once Enmerkar himself travels to Aratta.[15] In *Enmerkar and the Lord of Aratta*, after a contest of wits, Arattan lapis lazuli and other precious materials are sent by caravan

---

[12]　Above p. 13 n. 15.
[13]　Above p. 13 n. 12.
[14]　The prominence of envoys and message sending is the basis of Jacobsen's suggestion (above note 8) that the poems were composed in Ur III times as entertainment for Iranian envoys while in Sumer.
[15]　*ELA*: 595ff.

to Uruk in return for Sumerian grain. Jacobsen has emphasised the exceptional circumstances in which this exchange is set (famine in Aratta), further undermining earlier interpretations which saw in it a formulaic illustration of regularised highland-lowland caravan trade in Early Dynastic times.[16] Hostilities eventually escallate to a point where an Urukian army lays seige to Aratta.[17] The focus of both stories remains however on Lugalbanda – his illness, subsequent wanderings, encounter with the Anzu-bird and journey as messenger from Aratta to Uruk and back again – not on the seige, about which we are told only that Enmerkar is unable to take the city and, as the weather worsens, sends Lugalbanda back to Uruk to seek Inanna's blessing (which she does not give) to decamp. The end of the story, presumably relating the eventual surrender of Aratta, is lost.

While none of the hero-kings of Uruk is mentioned outside literary sources, the penultimate ruler of Kiš I[18] – (En)mebaragesi – is attested in contemporary inscriptions and the conquest of Elam attributed to him in the *Sumerian King List* therefore represents the earliest military encounter between Mesopotamia and the east involving an historically attested individual.[19] The event is noted in the form of an epithet: "he who carried away as spoil the 'weapon' of the land of Elam".[20] No further details are given, but the choice of words – if these reflect a contemporary account – suggests only a swift, devastating razzia. According to the *Sumerian King List*, kingship passed from Kiš I to Eanna (Uruk) I, the dynasty of Enmerkar and Lugalbanda. The statement that the founder of this dynasty, Meskiaggašer, "went (daily) into the (western) sea and came forth (again) toward the (sunrise) mountains" has been thought to imply some activity in the highlands of Elam,[21] but this expression is susceptible to other interpretations.[22]

An event of greater importance, though again there is only the testimony of the *Sumerian King List*, is the transfer of kingship from Ur I to the Elamite city of Awan, tentatively located in Susiana or the neighbouring highlands.[23] Of the three royal names listed under this dynasty, only the first syllable of the last, *Ku-u[l...]*, survives.[24] He is assigned thirty-six years and the dynasty as a whole a no doubt exaggerated 356 years. As yet, there are no contemporary inscriptions which confirm the sovereignty of this foreign power over all or part of Sumer-Akkad, but it is unlikely that Mesopotamian historiography would have perpetuated the memory of a humiliating incident which had not some basis in fact. In any case, this is the first time the *Sumerian King List* reports a foreign invasion of Mesopotamian soil.

---

16 Jacobsen 1987:275f.; *cf.* Kohl 1975; *idem* 1978.
17 *EL*; *LH*; Falkowitz 1983: 106f. n. 11.
18 For convenience, numbering of dynasties follows Jacobsen 1939. This is not meant to prejudice the many cases where different traditions preserve alternative sequences. All such points of detail, and indeed the general historicity of the composition, remain open.
19 For contemporary inscriptions on stone vessels see Edzard 1959=*SARI 1*: Ki 1. Although there is yet no contemporary confirmation of (En)mebaragesi's Elamite campaign it is perhaps significant that one inscription comes from east of the Tigris (Tutub); *cf.* Charvát 1976: 348.
20 *SKL* ii:36f.; Oppenheim in Pritchard 1969: 265. The verb *gúr* can mean "carry away as spoil" (Jacobsen 1939: 84 n. 96) or "subjugate" (Thomsen 1984: 302f.). *Cf.* A. Shaffer 1981: 311; "the one who crushed the land of Elam together with its armed might".
21 *SKL* iii:5f.; Oppenheim *loc. cit. Cf.* Cameron 1936: 22f.; Kammenhuber 1976: 246 n. 182.
22 Perhaps a metaphor of the passage of the sun; Utu is listed as Meskiaggašer's father (Jacobsen 1939: 86 n. 114; Gadd 1971: 110). *Cf.* Berossos' description of Oannes coming out of the sea and returning by night.
23 *SKL* iv:5-16. For location see *RGTC 1*: 21 (Susiana) and Schacht 1987: 175f.; Stolper 1987: 113f. (highlands).
24 *SKL* iv:13; Edzard 1980-83: 83; Hinz 1971: 647 reconstructs "Kurissak".

The third ruler of the Dynasty of Awan fell to a king of Kiš, the founder of the second dynasty of that city, whose name is incompletely preserved as *Su*-[...].[25] According to the *Sumerian King List*, kingship was next carried to Hamazi, perhaps located in the mountains east of Kirkuk and therefore often assumed to be in a loose sense Elamite.[26] The sole king of this dynasty, however, bears the Akkadian name Hadaniš (possibly a contraction from **hataniš-qabi* "he [a god] promises to protect").[27] Somewhat surprisingly, Hadaniš reappears in the god list AN:*anum* described, along with the preceding entry *lumma* (the battle name or 'Tidnum name' of Eannatum),[28] as a ghost of the Ekur in Nippur. If, as this suggests, Hadaniš had erected a statue of himself in the Ekur and provided for offerings to be made, he must once have possessed the city and to this extent the tradition preserved in the *Sumerian King List* stands confirmed.

Scattered contemporary inscriptions dating approximately to the period covered by these sections of the *Sumerian King List* confirm the general pattern of intermittent warfare and hostility, even if the particular incidents and individuals concerned cannot be placed within the artificial framework of that composition. A vase from Nippur is dedicated by a "[son of (?) P]uzuzu, the conqueror (TÙN.ŠÈ) of Hamazi".[29] An Ur III copy of another dedication inscription from Nippur relates that a certain "Enna-il, son of A-anzu, who vanquished Elam, dedicated (this)".[30] Although Enna-il, like Puzuzu, is not mentioned in the *Sumerian King List*, a fragmentary inscribed statuette from the same site confirms his historicity and accords him the title "King of Kiš". On palaeographic and onomastic grounds Goetze places Eanna-il between Mesalim and Ur I, *i.e.* approximately the time of the Fara tablets .[31]

---

[25] *SKL* iv:20; Edzard 1980-83: 84.
[26] *SKL* iv:36-43. For location see *RGTC 1*: 70.
[27] Jacobsen 1939: 98 n. 168.
[28] Poebel 1914: 166; *IRSA*: IC5b n. 2.
[29] *AKI*: VP 11. This fragment was till recently thought to join another from the same site bearing the name 'Uhub', who was therefore erroneously credited with this conquest of Sumer's erstwhile overlord (Cooper 1984: 92f.). Both vessel fragments – of visually identical stone type and profile – may well be from the same vase, this having received the two inscriptions at different times.
[30] Goetze 1961: 107ff., figs 2, 3; *SARI 1*: Ki 7.
[31] Goetze 1961: 107f., fig. 2. Excluded from our account at this point is Lugalannemundu, sole ruler of the dynasty of Adab, which the *SKL* places after the poorly-known dynasties of Uruk II and Ur II (*SKL* v:15-21). Three OB copies of a building inscription of this king (Poebel 1909: 123 no. 130, pl. 57; *idem* 1914a: no. 75; CBS 342 [unpubl.]; edn. by Güterbock 1934: 40-46; *cf.* Civil 1979; Yang 1989: 131-36) are prefaced by an account of a supposed revolt against the king by thirteen ensis of foreign lands, including Elam, Marhaši and Gutium, most of whom nevertheless bear Semitic (Akkadian or Amorite) names. A phrase reminiscent of *The Curse of Agade* says how Lugalannemundu "returned Marhaši to the (tax?, work?) register" and "established tribute among the countries" (Yang 1989: 133; *cf. CA*: 20). Lugalannemundu's titles at the beginning of the text would also have him ruling "the four quarters". After defeating the coalition and seizing Gutium, Subir and other regions (the text is damaged), the sukkalmahs of eight conquered lands – the Cedar Mountain, Elam, Marhaši, Gutium, Subir, Amurrum, Sutium (mardu sutium[ki]; *cf.* Yang *ibid.*) and Eanna (*i.e.* Uruk) – offer sacrifices at the dedication of the king's new temple.

The OB date of the three known copies of this text and its apparent anachronisms – early references to Marhaši, Amurru, Sutium and Gutium; use of the titles "king of the four quarters" and "sukkalmah" – have led most commentators to regard it as a late literary creation of little or no historical value (originally Güterbock 1934: 46f. with further arguments in Falkenstein 1951: 18; followed by Kupper 1957: 83; Edzard 1957: 32; Civil 1979; Steinkeller 1982: 255 n. 71; Cooper 1983a: 17; Michalowski 1986: 143; Yang 1989: 134; Jacobsen 1939: 102 n. 183 is cautiously agnostic; Kramer 1963: 51 alone was inclined to accept it as "quite genuine and convincing"). Without pursuing the matter further, it may be remarked that, if the text should prove to be based on a genuine tradition, the extent of Sumerian control over the east in the mid-3rd mill. would be much expanded, and the history of Mesopotamian imperialism would have to start here rather than with Sargon or Lugalzagesi.

Figure 13. Battle scene from "Vulture Stele" of Eannatum. Girsu, Early Dynastic III. Limestone.

The most detailed account of Sumerian military conflict with Iran comes from the contemporary inscriptions of a ruler whose dynasty is not included in the *Sumerian King List*,[32] and whose exploits were not, as far as is known, preserved in other historiographic literature. How many similar records have not been so luckily recovered can only be guessed; but we may be certain that a very different picture would emerge were more major Sumerian cities as extensively excavated as Girsu.

The ruler concerned is Eannatum, third ensi of the dynasty established by Ur-Nanše.[33] Six texts, some preserved in many copies, record Eannatum's victories over various eastern towns and states.[34] In many of these he adopts the epithet "he who subjugates (foreign) lands (kur-gú-gar-gar) for Ningirsu".[35] The differentiation of campaigns and incidents in some of the inscriptions provides a rough basis for determining the sequence of events, but a detailed chronology of Eannatum's reign is not possible[36] and there is reason to suspect that some of his eastern exploits may not yet be attested.[37] These limitations notwithstanding, Eannatum provides a

---

32 For a possible explanation of this omission see Michalowski 1983: 242.
33 Eannatum's relative date is fixed by the fact that his second successor, Enmetena, established a treaty with Lugalkinišedudu (*SARI 1*: La 5.3). This king's name is reconstructed by Jacobsen (1939: 100, 171ff.) in Dynasties Uruk II and Ur II but the traces are inconclusive (*cf.* Kramer 1963: 326; Gadd 1971: 998; Edzard 1980-83: 83 [not listed]).
34 *SARI 1*: La 3.1, 3.5-3.9.
35 Also in *SARI 1*: La 3.2, 3.4, 3.10, 3.14.
36 For attempts see Jacobsen 1970: 390-393; Poebel 1914: 159-169; M. Lambert 1952: 71-77; Hallo 1957: 40-42.
37 Eannatum's conquest of Susa is mentioned only in the Stele of the Vultures (*SARI 1*: La 3.1) which may therefore have been the most complete source; 44 lines of the section listing Eannatum's conquests are

unique illustration of the hegemony a powerful and ambitious Sumerian ruler might attempt to establish in the east.

The fullest account is inscribed on two river stones which recount all of the king's major achievements – building and canal constructions as well as military exploits – seemingly in chronological order.[38] They were presumably inscribed at a late stage of Eannatum's reign and record all his known conquests except the city of Susa. The first section tells how the king vanquished (TÙN.ŠÈ bi-sè) Elam, the ensi of Urua, Umma, Uruk, Ur and Kiutu, laid waste (mu-hul) Uruaz and Mišime (Pašime), and destroyed (mu-ha-lam) A-DÙ-a (=Arua?). The theatre of these operations seems to be Sumer and the lands immediately to the east and south-east. It is unlikely that the battles all took place in a single campaign, but there is now no basis for establishing a sequence unless one accepts the order as given.

The text then relates how Zuzu, the king of Akšak in northern Akkad,[39] "rose up" and was subdued. This was evidently a separate action, though whether it saw Eannatum venturing north into Akkad or was again fought in Sumer is not clear. After mention of some constructions, Eannatum's accession from the ensiship of Lagaš to the kingship of Kiš is noted. This may indicate more than the nominal sovereignty over that city which this title often conveys, since the next section relates how first Elam and then Kiš rose against Eannatum. The Elamites were driven back to their land, as were the warriors of Akšak, presumably acting in collusion with Kiš.[40]

The passage which follows is problematic. Eannatum, described for the first time as "he who subjugates the (foreign) lands (for) Ningirsu", is said to have "vanquished Elam, Subir (and) Urua at the A-suhur (canal)" and to have "vanquished Kiš, Akšak (and) Mari at the Anta-sura (canal) of Ningirsu". Is this a claim to further conquests or a different version of previous battles, perhaps a summary indication of the range of his military achievements?[41] The second interpretation is supported by the use of the general regional terms "Elam" and "Subir", which define the extent of his eastern and north(-eastern?) fronts respectively, and the circumstantial detail that the defeat of Akšak (and Kiš and Mari) is, as in the earlier account of Akšak's initial revolt, said to have proceeded from the Anta-sura canal.[42] Had further revolts occasioned a second major round of campaigns in the east (Elam), north (Subir) and north-west (Kiš, Mari), one would expect this to have been given greater emphasis.

On the basis of this evidence at least three campaigns, or perhaps series of campaigns, may be reconstructed. The first saw the conquest of Umma, Uruk and Ur in Sumer,[43] and the Elamite borderlands of Susa,[44] Urua, Arua, Uruaz, Kiutu and

---

now lost, of which only five and a half are reconstructable. *Cf.* M. Lambert and Hallo (above note 36) who, for different reasons, date the stele early in Eannatum's reign.

[38] *SARI 1*: La 3.5.

[39] For location see *RGTC 1*: s.v.; Frayne (in press [a]: *LGN* 99) suggests Tell Sinker on the ancient course of the Tigris north-west of Baghdad.

[40] Since Kiš revolts one expects this city to be repulsed (as in the parallel case of Elam) yet the text has here Akšak.

[41] Maeda 1981: 10f. (further conquests); M. Lambert 1952: 71 (same events; arguing that everything after the battle with Akšak is repetition); *cf.* Michalowski 1986: 136.

[42] The account in *SARI 1*: La 3.1 may be interpreted similarly, though here the order is reversed: first are listed the regions subjugated (Elam and Subir), then the cities involved. Urua may have been repeated because it lay outside these limits or because of its special importance; note the unusual description of the city's ensi marching before his "emblem".

[43] Other sources show that Eannatum also conquered Šuruppak, Nippur (where his 'ghost' was later venerated) and probably Adab where a stamped brick has been found; *cf.* Charvát 1974: 164; Curchin 1977.

[44] Susa is included on the testimony of *SARI 1*: La 3.1.

Mišime to the east and south-east. Second came the uprising and conquest of Akšak in Akkad (perhaps also fought in Sumer); third and last, the unsuccessful uprisings of Elam, Kiš and Akšak. If a pattern may be divined in this, the first stage seems to represent the establishment of Eannatum's power base at home and the assertion of his dominance over Sumer's traditional enemy to the east. There is no suggestion that the king's opponents instigated these confrontations; he is represented rather as the agressive conquering hero. Quite the opposite is the case in the second and third phases. Here it is stated that the enemy attacked Eannatum and was defeated. Having established a broad hegemony, and probably the status of supreme national leader ('King of Kiš'), Eannatum seems to have been faced with the inevitable consequences of peripheral dissent and secession, making himself the natural target of any highland power with pretentions to conquest.

Continuing uncertainty regarding key geographical terms precludes any definitive assessment of the extent of Eannatum's penetration into the mountains. The cities which can be more or less precisely located are those within range of frequent contact with Sumer on the border of the alluvial lowlands (Susa) or up river (Mari). That 'Elam' already referred primarily to a highland entity is clear from its epithet "the lofty mountain", hur-sag-u$_6$-ga and (with Subir) "mountain lands of timber and treasure".[45] Although no campaign description is sufficiently detailed to provide a picture of the terrain through which Eannatum ventured, there can be little doubt that some at least of the places cited in the first section of the text lie among the mountains of Luristan/Fars. Since Anšan is not mentioned one may be sure he did not venture that far. The conspicuous absence of Awan, another city one might expect to appear if Eannatum had had any basis for claiming its defeat, is less easy to evaluate since its location remains uncertain.

Eannatum's successors were preoccupied with more local conflicts and none followed up their ancestor's eastern successes. Extant evidence contains only scattered indications of continuing contact and hostility. The dedication inscription on the bitumen/bituminous stone plaque of Dudu, sanga of Ningirsu under Enmetena, says that he "had (this material) brought down from Urua (URUxA.A^{ki})[46] and had it made into a wall-plaque(?)[47] for him" (Fig. 14).[48] Bituminous stone abounds in Khuzistan and was commonly worked at Susa (see below p. 191). Dudu appears to have acquired the material by purchase rather than force since nothing is said of booty, in keeping with the close economic relations this city enjoyed with Sumer, especially Lagaš, during Early Dynastic III.[49] Whether Urua was still under Sumerian (Lagašite?) control is doubtful; Sargon had to reconquer it a century later (see below).

A letter from another sanga, Luenna, reports to Enentarzi of Lagaš that he has intercepted a group of six hundred Elamites carrying booty from Lagaš to Elam and has been able to capture 540 of them.[50] The Elamite leader is not named and it is indeed not clear from the report whether the attack was a royally sponsored campaign or an opportunistic raid by highland bandits. It is also curious that Luenna was able to overpower troops who had successfully pillaged Lagaš. Was the

---

45 *SARI 1*: La 3.5, La 3.1.
46 *Cf.* Steinkeller 1982: 244 n. 26.
47 ŠITÁ.ÙR literally "mace-beam" or "mace-support". *ABWI*: 131 n. 2 prefers "Weihplatte (?)" on the basis of the apparent self-reference of this text. *Cf.* Thureau-Dangin 1907: 34f., i, n, h; Hansen 1963: 151ff.
48 *SARI 1*: La 5.28.
49 Steinkeller 1982: 245 nn. 27, 28; M. Lambert 1981.
50 Thureau-Dangin 1907; Kramer 1963: 331.

Figure 14.   Votive plaque of Dudu. Girsu, Early Dynastic III. Bitumen/bituminous stone. 25 x 22 cm.

ensi perhaps away at the time, or was the city for some other reason inadequately defended? Sorties of this type were no doubt much more frequent than the survival of this isolated incident suggests. Their primary object seems to have been plunder, as were those of the better-attested Sumerian reprisals detailed above. The goods recovered by Luenna provide an indication of their object: five silver vessels (?), five royal garments and fifteen hides of "fold-sheep". This is surprisingly little. Perhaps the bulk of the loot was lost with the Elamites who escaped.

A stone macehead, reportedly from 'Luristan', bearing a Sumerian inscription may reflect Sumerian military or economic involvement with this region but no more precise significance can be ascribed to it.[51]

---

[51]   Amiet 1970; *idem* 1976: 7.

3. THE AKKADIAN PERIOD

Lugalzagesi, perhaps the greatest of all early Sumerian conquerors, has left no sure indication of any eastern military expeditions. He regularly claims lordship over "all foreign lands"[52] but when he does mention particular places they are always in Mesopotamia proper, never in Elam. Judging by the assertion that "from the Lower Sea (by) the Tigris and Euphrates to the Upper Sea he made straight its road", a primary concern was to keep open the lines of communication with the north-west.[53] Perhaps, also, the Elamites avoided confrontation with so powerful an enemy. In any case, it was with a Mesopotamian leader of a new and different kind, the first great Semitic empire-builder, that supremacy was next to be decided by force of arms. The Elamites were probably in no position to appreciate the change in the cultural complexion of their western neighbour that Sargon's rise to power represented, but they can not long have been left in doubt that the military threat from that quarter was vastly stronger and more sophisticated than ever before.

A new era in Mesopotamian-Elamite relations had begun. The energetic kings of Agade campaigned further afield than their Sumerian predecessors, encountering many new peoples and laying waste to foreign lands which had never before suffered the onslaught of a Mesopotamian army. Numerous cities were ravaged and large amounts of booty taken. For the first time we see evidence of some attempt to consolidate control of conquered territories. Sargon explicitly states that he appointed Akkadian "citizens" (DUMU-DUMU *Agade*[ki]) to governorships in the regions he ruled,[54] which can therefore be considered true provinces. Under his successors there is some evidence of appointed governors being moved around from city to city and of offices being passed down from father to son,[55] features that later became typical of the Ur III adminstration. Talk of "empire" begins now to have some validity.[56]

As to the scale and course of these campaigns we are left little less ignorant than before. Omens provide some colourful, if unreliable, circumstantial detail, but the royal inscriptions are concerned to inform us only of the outcome, and even this is rarely free from hyperbole. True campaign narratives in the manner of the Assyrians are still a long way off. We are told next to nothing of the motives or occasion for expeditions, and left guessing about the most intriguing issue of all – how much the growth of Akkadian imperialism depended simply on the momentum of success and how much on planning and a 'grand design'.

(a) Sargon

The imperialist ambitions of the new master of Mesopotamia inevitably brought him into conflict with the highland powers of Iran. It is unlikely that Sargon inherited from his Sumerian predecessor any legacy of Mesopotamian control over the east; had Elamite lands paid obeisance to Lugalzagesi they would no doubt have

---

52   *SARI 1*: Um 7.1; A. Westenholz 1979: 120 n. 9.
53   *SARI 1*: Um 7.1.
54   Sargon C1:80-86; A. Westenholz 1979: 121 n. 20. There must have been cases where defeated enemies were allowed to retain their dominions on an oath of fealty, since Sidgau, the šakkanakku of Parahšum humiliated by Sargon, reappears as an opponent of Rimuš. Likewise Meskiaga, ensi of Adab under Lagalzagesi, was defeated by Rimuš, but may have been reinstated in Umma (A. Westenholz 1979: 121 n. 16).
55   Kutscher 1989: 38.
56   *Cf.*, however, the reservations of Garelli 1980: 29ff.

considered themselves freed when the king of Uruk was marched in a yoke through the gate of Enlil.[57]

Sargon probably turned to the east fairly early in his long reign,[58] before the series of western conquests which delivered him "Mari, Yarmuti and Ebla as far as the Cedar Forest (Amanus Mts?) and the Silver Mountain (Keban region?)".[59] Year formulae tell of his vanquishing the border town Urua, a target earlier of Eannatum, and going to Simurrum.[60] The Urua expedition probably formed the prelude to the major highland action commemorated in another year name and an omen claiming the conquest of Elam itself.[61] Two Old Babylonian copies of statue or stele inscriptions provide more details of the peoples and cities involved in these offensives from which Sargon took the title "conqueror of Elam and Parahšum".[62] The rulers of these two highland powers are prominent amongst the enemy: Sanamsimut, variously the ensi and šakkanakku of Elam; Luhišan, son of Hisibrasini, King of Elam;[63] Ulul and Sidgau, both šakkanakkus of Parahšum; Dagu, brother of the King (unnamed) of Parahšum; and Kumdupum, the "Judge" (*dayyanum*) of Parahšum. Also listed are a [...]suhru, ensi of Šerihum (coastal Fars?) and the ensis of two lesser known places, Zina of Huzi[...] and Hidarida[...] of Gunilaha.[64]

One of the inscriptions also lists eight cities from which Sargon took booty: Urua, Šaliamu, Kardede, Heni, Bunban, Sabum, Awan and Susa.[65] As Steinkeller has noted , at least five of these places are certainly or probably located in the general region of Susiana, which is therefore the most likely area of engagement.[66] If

---

[57] Sargon C1:21-30.
[58] Such is the general consensus based on what seems the logical progression (but for a different view *cf.* Gadd 1971: 420, 432; Hinz 1971: 648) thought there is little basis for establishing the order of events. The conquest of Elam must post-date that of Nippur where it appears in a date formula (A. Westenholz 1984: 78 n. 10). On the other hand, the inscriptions Sargon C1 and C4, recording the king's conquest of Uruk, Ur, E-ninnar, Lagaš and Umma, remark that "Mari and Elam are standing (in obedience) before Sargon" (C1:87-94; C4:92-99). This expression, as generally understood, implies that Elam had already been conquered at the time of the events described (Lewis 1980: 126 gives no justification for his claim that it records the subjugation of these places). One cannot be sure, however, at what point in Sargon's reign the text was written; and since a late composition might make allusion to events which took place after the main action, this passage cannot be considered decisive. On the length of Sargon's reign (probably 37 years, rather than the 56 years cited in the *SKL*) see Foster 1982: 153f.
[59] Sargon C2:24-35.
[60] D-2-3, D-1.
[61] D-4; King 1907: 25f. § 1; Starr 1986: 635 ll. 1-3.
[62] Sargon C7, C13. There were certainly many campaigns – not the two imagined by Hinz 1971: 648 and Cameron 1936: 28 – as the existence of at least three year names and the 34 battles of Sargon C2:4 makes clear. See also above note 58. For Parahšum, *cf.* the claim of the *Curse of Agade*: 20f. that under Sargon Marhaši was "put back on the (tribute?) rolls"; and for Elam note Sargon C1 and C4, quoted above (note 58) and Sargon's Susa stele (below note 68).
[63] Hisibrasini very probably corresponds to Hišepratep, 9th king of the Dynasty of Awan (König 1965: 1). Hinz (1971: 647) takes Luhišan (rather than Hisibrasini) to be designated "king" in these passages (Sargon C7: Beischrift (e); Sargon C13: Beischrift (g)) and therefore manufactures a second Hisibrasini, a son of his supposed "king Luhišan", to accommodate the unambiguous reference to "Hisibrasini, King of Elam" at Sargon C13: Beischrift (j) (*cf.* Stolper 1997: 113). On this account the Hisibrasini, father of Luhišan, attested in Sargon's inscription must have been omitted by the Susian scribe from the Awan king list. There is, however, a more straightforward interpretation of the text which does not require such revisionism: Hisibrasini is King of Elam in all passages cited; his son, Luhišan, is never given a title and probably never attained any. In particular, he is not the ruler of that name but his grandson (or nephew). Taken, as the text says, to Agade, he is never heard of again. Although not mentioned in the narrative as being involved in the campaign, Hisibrasini, king of Elam, is listed with the other conquered rulers in text Sargon C13: Beischrift (j). It is likely, therefore, that he too was captured. The conquest of Parahšum is also mentioned in an omen (Lewis 1980: 139 no. 28; *cf.* also nos 2, 4, 17).
[64] Sargon C7: Beischr. m-n; C13: Beischr. d. For location of Šerihum see Steinkeller 1982: 256, n. 74.
[65] Sargon C7: Beischr. c, f, g, k, l, o, p, s.
[66] Steinkeller 1982: 256.

Figure 15. Stele of Sargon. Susa. Diorite. Ht. 91 cm.

this is correct, these were not highland actions; the Parahšians, and probably others too, were fighting as allies in lowland Elam. This may explain the otherwise surprising lack of correlation between the cities looted and the geographical names which occur in the foreign rulers' titles; one would normally expect at least some of these commanders to have fallen protecting the cities that were subsequently pillaged.

It was noted earlier that inscriptions dealing with Sargon's Mesopotamian conquests record his installation of Akkadians as governors of conquered territories.[67] None of the texts relating to his eastern conquests makes this claim, and it is indeed unlikely that the same policy was employed there to anything like the same extent. One possible exception is Susa, where governors from at least the time of Maništušu paid obeisance to the kings of Agade.[68] These may well have been royal appointees (see below).

---

[67]   It is probably this policy which is remembered in the late chronicle and omen collections which report his stationing court officials at intervals of 5 double-hours (*ABC*: 153 line 7; Starr 1986: 635 ll. 28f.).

[68]   Note also Sargon's stela from Susa (Fig. 15; Amiet 1976a: no. 1; Sargon 1). It is uncertain whether this was set up in Susa by Sargon or was later taken there as booty by Šutruk-Nahunte.

If Sargon's own inscriptions do not suggest that he ventured very far east, later tradition is quite another matter. Chronicles, epics, legends, omens and other 'historical-literary' compositions extol at length the mighty deeds of this great and glorious king, attributing to him a far-flung series of conquests from Anatolia (Purushanda) and the Upper Sea in the west to Parahšum, Magan and Meluhha in the east.[69] Through these works Sargon came to epitomise the great warrior king, the central reference point for all later conquerors who would emulate his deeds in pursuit of fame and immortality.[70]

It has long been acknowledged that these stories are exaggerated and involve anachronistic attributions to Sargon of deeds of later Akkadian kings, with whom his hegemony was assumed to be comparable, or even his later namesakes, who attempted by association to inflate their own prestige.[71] The testimony of these stories certainly cannot be considered historical as it stands. The issue is whether any of them incorporate historical elements and, if so, how this might be identified. Despite much discussion, no general agreement on these issues has been reached.[72]

(b) Rimuš

First-millennium literary texts and omen collections tell of revolts against Sargon by "the elders of the land".[73] Doubtful as these late compositions may be, there is evidence that Sargon's successor Rimuš was faced at some stage in his nine-year reign with widespread resistance to Akkadian rule. The Old Babylonian copies of his inscriptions from Nippur are largely preoccupied with campaigns against the recalcitrant governors of Sumer (Ur, Umma, KI.AN, Lagaš, Adab, Zabalam and Girsu) and Akkad (Kazallu).[74]

Rimuš also led a major expedition to the east against Elam, Parahšum and Zahara, which is reported in Old Babylonian copies of contemporary inscriptions.[75]

---

[69]   Reviewed in J. Westenholz 1983: 328-30; Lewis 1980: 130-34; Glassner 1987.
[70]   Finkelstein 1963: 466.
[71]   Grayson 1974-77: 57; D. Potts 1982: 287f.; J. Westenholz 1983: 328.
[72]   One document of particular interest is the *Sargon Geography* (Grayson 1974-77). Though clearly edited in the 1st mill., this composition seems to have been based on earlier texts, at least one of which must have included a list of place names (*ibid.*: 57). (Frayne [pers. comm.] suggests that some of the toponyms in the *Sargon Geography* may be identified with places in the ED III *LGN* [*e.g.* Lulubum/Luluban, Ebla/Abla, Arameans/Arim(an)] all of which he places east of the Tigris, supporting the suggestion that the author(s) of the *Sargon Geography* had access to an early source, perhaps a Sargonic 'cadastre' like Sollberger 1965: no. 14). The vast realm assigned by implication to Sargon stretches from the Upper Sea (Mediterranean) eastwards to Anšan (here cited as the limit of Subartu), including also Dêr (Badra), Lulubum, Gutium and Niqqu (Grayson 1974-77: ll. 3, 12, 15-17). There follows a list of the distances of various lands, presumably places he was supposed to have conquered (there is some overlap with the preeceeding list), beginning with "Meluhha and Magan, the borders of which Sargon, king of the universe, when he conquered (all) lands covered by the sky, defined and the *magnitudes* of which he measured" (*ibid.*: ll. 30-32). The text then lists other eastern lands which he "measured", including Marhaši, Tukriš, Elam, Lulubum, Anzan (Anšan), "Dilmun and Maganna (=Magan), the lands across the Lower Sea, and the lands from east to west which Sargon ... conquered thrice" (*ibid.*: ll. 33-35, 39-43). The clearly propagandistic character of the composition makes it unwise to acredit Sargon with control over any of these regions except where there is contemporary corroboration.
[73]   Literary texts: *ABC*: Chron. 19:52 (add now al-Rawi 1990), Chron. 20:A20-23. Omens: King 1907: 33f. (§ix: 31-34), 36 (§xi: 5-8), 43f. (§xi: 1-7); Starr 1986: 636 ll. 37f.
[74]   Sumer: Rimuš C1, C2, C4, C5. Akkad: Rimuš C1, C3. *Cf.* also the Ur III copy of a dedication inscription (Goetze 1968: 54) which records Rimuš depositing booty after the defeat of Girsu. Foster 1985 argues that the destruction of Lagaš is also the subject of the Tello victory stele.
[75]   Rimuš C6, C8, C10.

One of these cites also ⸢Gu⸣pin[76] and [Me]luhha among the king's opponents.[77] Should the inclusion of Meluhha prove genuine – and the Old Babylonian copyists were by and large highly faithful to the originals – this would greatly expand the horizon of direct Sargonic contact, even if the Meluhhan army was fighting far from home. However, since there is no other evidence of military contact with these regions or their armies in contemporary Rimuš inscriptions, nor in other Old Babylonian or later copies, their inclusion here must be treated with caution.

Some of the spoils from these campaigns, appropriately inscribed as dedications to the gods, have been recovered in excavations in Mesopotamia. Those that have survived are stone vases and maceheads (below p. 227; Fig. 41:2-3).[78] The fullest text reads: "To Enlil (var.: Sin), Rimuš, King of Kiš, when he had conquered Elam and Parahšum, from the booty of Elam dedicated (this)" (Table 6.1, Inscr. A). Examples of these dedications have been found not only in Sumer but also at Tutub and far to the north-west at Tell Brak.

More details of the battles in which this booty was taken are provided by the Old Babylonian inscriptions.[79] The reference towards the end of one text to the third year of Rimuš's kingship may provide a clue to the date of these events,[80] but otherwise nothing in his inscriptions provides a basis for establishing even the relative order of the Sumerian and Elamite campaigns, since they are always treated separately.

The coalition opposing Rimuš comprised not only Elam and Parahšum, lands mentioned in the dedication inscriptions and familiar as Sargon's antagonists, but also Zahara. The armies of Elam and Parahšum were led by their kings, Emahsini(?)[81] and Abalgamaš respectively, supported by Sidgau, šakkanakku of Parahšum (no doubt the man of the same name and title defeated by Sargon some years before), and Sargabi, šakkanakku of Zahara.

The most detailed version (C6) first states that Rimuš defeated Abalgamaš king of Parahšum, and then relates details of a victory over Zahara and Elam (and in C10 Gupin and Meluhha) when these forces "assembled for battle in the midst of Parahšum".[82] At this point, as elsewhere, it is not clear whether the text is presenting a more detailed account of the same incident (as apparently Gadd) or a second confrontation (as Steinkeller).[83] In any case, we are again told that Rimuš prevailed, killing 16,212 warriors and capturing another 4,216, including Emahsini, Sidgau and Sargapi. The apprehension of these highland leaders is specifically located "between Awan and Susa at the Middle (*qab-lí-tim*) River".[84] Finally it is stated that Rimuš conquered the cities of Elam, tore down their walls and "tore out the roots of Parahšum from the land of Elam".[85] With this victory, the text continues, "Rimuš,

---

[76]   Gupin is a distant eastern land which is mentioned also by Gudea as a source of *halub*-wood (Stat. B vi:45; Stat. D iv:9) and in OB lexical lists (refs. cited *RGTC 1*: s.v. Gubi(n)). Its association in these contexts with Magan and Meluhha suggests a location on or near the Gulf (*ibid.*; Leemans 1960: 12, n. 1).

[77]   Rimuš C10:10f.; Oelsner 1989: 403.

[78]   T.F. Potts 1989. *Cf.* the "diorite, duh-ši(-a)-stone and (other) stones (or stone objects)" which Rimuš brought back as booty from Parahšum for the temple of Gula (C10:41-45).

[79]   Rimuš C6, C8, C10.

[80]   Rimuš C6:75-80; *cf.* Gadd 1971: 434.

[81]   Collation shows this reading to be uncertain.

[82]   Rimuš C6:1-18; C10:1-18.

[83]   Gadd 1971: 436f.; Steinkeller 1982: 256.

[84]   Rimuš C6:43-48; *cf.* Michalowski 1980: 238.

[85]   *Cf.* Stolper 1984: 12: "tore the foundation of Barahši from among the people of Elam". Steinkeller (1982: 257) takes the expression to imply that Parahšum previously held sway over Elam.

King of Kiš, ruled [or: became lord over] Elam".[86] A total of 9,626 enemy are reckoned fallen and captured.[87] A colophon closes by recalling the booty of metals and slaves which Rimuš dedicated to Enlil from the spoils.[88] The full text reads:

> Rimuš, king of Kiš, conquered Abalgamaš, ⌈king⌉ of Parahšum, in battle. And Zahara and Elam (and ⌈Gu⌉pin (?) and [Me]luhha) assembled for battle in the midst of Parahšum; and he conquered (them); and he felled 16,212 men, and captured 4,216 prisoners. And he captured Emahsini (?), king of Elam, and he captured all ... (of) Elam; and he captured Sidgau, the šakkanakku of Parahšum; and he captured Sargapi, the šakkanakku of Zahara, between Awan and Susa, at the Middle River/Canal.[89] And in the area of the city *he heaped up a tumulus over them.*[90] And he vanquished the cities of Elam and destroyed their walls. And the roots of ⌈Parahšum⌉ [he tore out of the land of Elam. (Thus) Rimuš, king of Kiš], ruled over [Elam]. Enlil (to Rimuš) showed (the way), in the third year, in which Enlil gave him the kingship. In total: 9,626 men, including (those) felled and prisoners. (By) Šamaš and Aba, I sware, (these are) no lies; it is true! ...

> (various curses *etc.*; then follows a colophon:)

> ... When he had conquered Elam and Parahšum, he brought back 30 minas of gold, 3,600 minas of copper, 360 (or 6) male and female slaves, and dedicated them to Enlil.[91]

The general locale and nature of Rimuš's eastern expedition(s) bear close comparison with those of Sargon. Motive is again left unspecified, unless the enumeration of booty be taken as indicative. Although the eastern wars are recounted in much the same terms as those against rebellious Sumerian cities, this need not imply that the reassertion of direct Akkadian sovereignty was the basis of both. The official rhetoric of 'conquest' and 'destruction' evidently served both for the suppression of rebellion and for unprovoked imperialism.

How far Rimuš is judged to have penetrated the highlands depends on the location of Parahšum, where the decisive encounter took place. A location in Kerman[92] would perhaps make more credible the inclusion of forces from Meluhha and Gupin among the highland allies in one account of the battle, but the option of a more western location remains open. The inclusion of Zaharans, another highland people, is no real help in this, since they may have come to the aid of the Elamites and Parahsians without their own land(s) being invaded, just as many ensis rallied round Hisibrasini of Elam, although their cities were not looted when the defence failed, and were perhaps never directly threatened. Nowhere is it stated that Rimuš "ruled over" Zahara or Parahšum.

---

[86]   Rimuš C6:55-72; C10:36-48; *cf.* Steinkeller 1982: 257.
[87]   That this figure does not agree with the one stated earlier confirms that the campaign involved more than one major battle, the second perhaps in Susiana where the leaders were captured.
[88]   Rimuš C6:138-47. See above note 78. Foster also draws attention to the "Elamites with their necks in stocks" in a mu-iti text he dates to the reign of Rimuš (Foster 1982: 16).
[89]   See above p. 28, n. 179.
[90]   Much of this sentence is restored and therefore uncertain.
[91]   Rimuš C6.
[92]   As Steinkeller 1982.

(c) Maništušu

Maništušu was not widely celebrated in Mesopotamian historiography and few historical records – either original inscriptions or later copies – survive to elucidate his fifteen-year reign.[93] Of the documents that do purport to describe his career the most informative for Maništušu's eastern expeditions, the 'Cruciform Monument', is a pious fraud concocted by Neo-Babylonian partisans of Šamaš at Sippar, albeit perhaps based on original sources.[94] One must therefore be sceptical of its claim, perhaps stemming from confusion with Rimuš, that "the countries, all of them, which Sargon, my father, had bequeathed me, like enemies rebelled against me". The two brothers are often confused in late compositions and the order of their succession in these works varies.[95]

Since nothing is heard of Elam under Maništušu it may be assumed that the authority established by Rimuš's ruthless devastation was maintained. This is confirmed, at least as regards Susa, by the bust dedicated to the Elamite deity Naruti for Maništušu by "Išpum, his servant", known from seal impressions as the ensi of Elam (Fig. 16); and also by the discovery at Susa of four fragmentary statues of the king, some bearing Maništušu's standard inscription.[96] Rimuš and Maništušu probably continued Sargon's practice of appointing Akkadian governors, and this Išpum was very likely one such deputy.[97]

Despite his relative obscurity, Maništušu was not militarily or politically ineffective. Inscriptions indicate that he held Aššur and tell of his building a temple of Ištar in Nineveh.[98] A bronze bowl inscribed "Maništušu, King of Kiš" is said to have come from Qamishli on the Upper Habur.[99]

Maništušu's chief eastern venture seems to have been an expedition against Anšan and Šerihum which is reported most fully in the 'Cruciform Monument' and in less detail in an Old Babylonian copy, which faithfully reproduces in part or whole Maništušu's original standard inscription and can thus be regarded as genuine.[100] According to the 'Cruciform Monument', the occasion of this expedition was the alleged general revolt. Maništušu divided his troops in two, conquered Anšan and Šerihum and captured the king of these lands along with his "gifts and presents".[101] One variant of the 'Cruciform Monument' substitutes "the city of Meluhha" for "Šerihum" in both occurrences in this passage, but this can not be trusted in such a late source.[102] Further suspicion is aroused by there being just one king for Anšan and the city of Meluhha.

The Old Babylonian copy Man. C1, and for some passages the original text Man. 1, go on to describe how Maništušu continued the campaign in ships. The text is unfortunately obscured by lacunae and philological uncertainties:

[93] Regarding the length of reign see Steinkeller 1989: 334.
[94] Sollberger 1967-68: 50-53; Powell 1991.
[95] Each generally claims to be the successor of their illustrious father Sargon. The order of the *SKL*, which places the younger brother Rimuš first, is probably to be preferred (Gadd 1971: 434).
[96] Scheil 1908: 1-3, pl. 1; Man. B2; *cf.* seal S-4. Strommenger 1989: 336 = Amiet 1976a: nos 11-14; standard inscription Man. 1. The flat faces of the inscribed pieces suggest bases rather than a "statue" (Gelb 1961: 197), as Scheil evidently realised since he omitted this word in the republication (Scheil 1913: 1). It is possible that the statues are part of the booty brought back to Susa by Šutruk-Nahunte.
[97] M. Lambert 1979: 17 n. 18; *cf.* Kammenhuber 1976: 225.
[98] Man. B1, Fragment 1; *ARI 1*: 23 no. 4.
[99] Nagel 1970: 195.
[100] Man. C1, Man. 1.
[101] ll. 29-58.
[102] Sollberger 1967-68: 63.

Figure 16.   Statue of Išpum, ensi of Elam, with dedication to Naruti (Narundi). Susa, period of Maništušu. Calcite/ gypsum. Ht. 31 cm.

Maništušu, king of Kiš – when he had conquered Anšan and Šerihum crossed[103] the Lower Sea in GIŠ.LA-*e* boats. The towns across the sea, thirty-two altogether, united for battle. But he beseiged (them) and conquered their cities (and) defeated their rulers. And he tore out (the land) from the .... R[iver] to the silver/precious metal (KÙ) mines. The mountains across the Lower Sea – he mined their black stones and loaded them onto ships and anchored at the quay of Agade. (From this stone) he made his statue and dedicated (it) to Enlil.[104]

Unfortunately, no geographical names are supplied in this passage, which represents the earliest well-documented Mesopotamian maritime expedition.[105] Much

---

[103] Reading *u-ša*-ŠI-*ir* with Kienast as *ušabir*, causative of *eberu* "to cross", taking the ŠI as a miscopy by the OB scribe of an original *bi* (*AKI*: 77, comm. to ll. 9-12). For alternative readings see below.
[104] Man. 1; Man. C1:1-46. *Cf.* discussion of this passage by Glassner 1989: 185f.
[105] Excluding the doubtful claim in late omen collections that Sargon "crossed the sea in the west" (*i.e.* Mediterranean) and conquered the foreign lands (King 1907: no. 3:24; Starr 1986: 635 ll. 24-26). In *ABC*: Chron. 20:A3 Sargon is said to have crossed the sea in the east.

depends on the verb here read *ušabir*, "crossed".[106] "Crossing" the Persian Gulf from a starting point in Iran (Anšan and Šerihum), Maništušu's destination can only have been on the Arabian littoral[107] and on this basis is usually identified with Oman, *i.e.* Magan, where Naram-Sin and Gudea also mined dark stones.[108] However, the verb can also be read *ušašir*, "readied", thus not necessarily implying a crossing of the sea at all and allowing a location in Iran.[109] (The description of the thirty-two cities as lying "across the sea" would not exclude such an interpretation since this expression is sometimes used to refer to Iran).[110] The materials brought back by Maništušu offer further clues. The "black stone" which the king mined near the site of his victory, shown by analysis to be olivine-gabbro,[111] occurs on both sides of the Gulf. More helpful may be the reference to mines of KÙ-metal, *i.e.* "precious metal" or, more specifically, "silver", which occurs widely in Iran[112] but has not been reported in recent geological surveys of Oman. Here too, however, caution is necessary since a number of nineteenth-century explorers refer to lead and/or silver production in Oman.[113] Thus the possibility that Maništušu preceded Naram-Sin to Magan (Oman) cannot be excluded.

The appearance of Iplum, the son of Ilšurabi, the ensi of Pašime as a witness on the Obelisk of Maništušu[114] raises the possibility that control over that region (probably within or adjacent to Susiana) was established already under Maništušu. More secure evidence of Akkadian rule appears under his successor, to whom we now turn.

(d) Naram-Sin

In the reign of Maništušu's son Naram-Sin the Akkadian empire reached its apogee. Like his grandfather Sargon, Naram-Sin looms large in the historical-literary tradition and not a few of his famous deeds have to do with campaigns in the now familiar extremes of imperial control stretching in a mountainous arc from Upper Syria around Upper Mesopotamia and along the Zagros to south-central Iran.

An unfortunate corollary of Naram-Sin's later celebrity, which greatly compounds the difficulties of historical reconstruction, is the heightened tendency to conflate historical fact with epic fiction. Although a greater number of Naram-Sin's original inscriptions survive than of any other Sargonic king, with a few notable exceptions they are relatively uninformative regarding foreign affairs. And since he is not well represented among the Old Babylonian copies from Nippur (the principal source for earlier kings) a more complete picture of Naram-Sin's activities can only be

---

[106] Above note 103.
[107] Gadd 1971: 438ff.
[108] *E.g.* Heimpel 1982: 67; below pp. 113, 188 n. 105.
[109] Heimpel 1982: 66 n. 13; *cf.* Glassner 1989: 185f.
[110] Glassner 1989: 186. It is noteworthy also that Sennacherib "crossed" the Lower sea in his campaign against Elam (Luckenbill 1924: 38f ll. 32-53; 73ff. ll. 48-106; 77f. ll. 25-32; 86f. ll. 19-26; Hansman 1973: 558).
[111] Heimpel 1982: 65; *idem* 1987: 69.
[112] Moorey 1985: 111.
[113] Wellsted 1838: I 315 (lead and silver); Germain 1868: 342 (lead); Keun de Hoogerwoerd 1889: 203 (silver mine) (reviewed in D. Potts 1990: 113-19). *Cf.* Howard-Carter 1987: 80 who cites possible Omani sources of lead/silver and the [non-argentiferous?] lead in Oman cited by Tosi 1975: 202. Heimpel suggests that KÙ be read in this passage as a generic term for base metal, thus allowing identification with the extensive copper deposits of Oman (1982: 67 n. 21). Other evidence, however, suggests that it means specifically "silver" (Waetzoldt 1981: 367 n. 23) or, when used as a generic term, "precious metal" (Pettinato 1972: 80f.; Glassner 1987: 23 n. 134; *idem*: 1989: 186).
[114] Scheil 1900: 16 A xiv:14-17.

derived from later historical-literary works which record battles with various coalitions of local and foreign peoples. These will be considered after a review of the primary 'historical' sources.

The order of events within Naram-Sin's fifty-six-year reign[115] is still uncertain, although his adoption of divine status (reflected in the use of the divine determinative in inscriptions) may provide a pivot for distinguishing early from late. On this assumption it has been suggested that the suppression of the 'Great Revolt' and the campaign against Magan belong early in his reign (before deification), while all his other major conquests (Subartum, Simurrum, Lulubum, Armanum and Ebla) come later.[116]

Like his predecessors, Naram-Sin claimed dominion over the highlands to the north-west. He boasts of ruling all Subartu as far as the Cedar Forest where, according to other texts, Armanum (=Aleppo?) and Ebla were conquered.[117] Year names state that he reached the headwaters of the Tigris and Euphrates rivers and defeated a place called Senaminda,[118] and that he conquered Maridaban, probably to be identified with Mardaman.[119] An Old Babylonian copy of a royal inscription describes how he "conquered from the 'face' (*i.e.* hither side?) of the Euphrates River to Basar, mountain of the land of the Amorites", taking in the cities of Simanum ("Asimanum"),[120] Apišal? (*RÉC* 349), Sisil and Habšat.[121] A year date records "the year Naram-Sin was victorious in a campaign against Subir in Azuhinum"[122] and captured its ruler with the Hurrian name Dahiš-atal(i) (or: Tiš-atal).[123] In an

---

[115] See Foster 1982: 152ff. for the argument for this length, versus the shorter reign (37 years) suggested by Jacobsen to accommodate the dynastic totals in the *SKL*.

[116] Kutscher 1989: 17-19; *cf.* Foster 1990: 42. A further refinement of this chronology is suggested by Frayne in his forthcoming RIM edition of the OAkk royal inscriptions. Frayne places in sequence: (1) suppression of the ABxŠUŠ revolt (Foster 1990) and adoption of "king of the four quarters"; (2) conquest of Magan; (3) suppression of the 'Great Revolt', adoption of "victor of nine battles in one year" and adoption of divine status; (4) reversion to "king of the four quarters". Certain anomalies however urge caution: some accounts of the conquest of Magan use the divine determinative while others do not; and the principal inscriptions describing or alluding to the 'Great Revolt' (NS 1; NS C1) do not yet use the divine determinative.

[117] NS 11; C3:1-6; C5:11-20; D-7. Armanum reappears in historical-literary texts (see below). A new year name attributed to Naram-Sin by Westenholz adds further to his exploits in the west: "[the year when Naram-Si]n [con]quered [...]-at and [Abul]-lat [and personally (?)] felled [ced]ars in [Mt A]manus/[Mt Le]banon ([[KUR a]m?-na-an)" (A. Westenholz 1987a: no. 16, p. 41). Also possibly relevant in this connection is the royal inscription edited by Foster 1990 which refers to Naram-Sin's conquest of a place written *RÉC 349* (=ABxŠUŠ? [Deimel]). Foster (1990: 40-43) suggests that this should perhaps be read "Apišal", a place whose conquest by Naram-Sin is much celebrated in later tradition. There seem to have been two 3rd-mill. Apišal's, one near Umma the other in northern Syria (Glassner 1983:10; Foster 1990: 41). There is no compelling evidence as to which was the one ruled by Riš-Adad and conquered by Naram-Sin, though ABxŠUŠ's allies are Sumerian and Amorite cities. The two may have been confused in later tradition.

[118] D-14. Some "slaves of Šenaminda" mentioned in an OAkk ledger tablet are also probably from this campaign (Foster 1982a: 15 no. iv).

[119] D-9; for location see Edzard 1989: 357. *Cf.* "Duhsusu, king of Mardaman" in *The Great Revolt* (Grayson & Sollberger 1976: 112 l. 34). Also in this general region, perhaps on the road from Aššur to Kaniš (*RGTC 1*: 156; *RGTC 3*: 232f.), was Talhatum whither Naram-Sin "went" at some point (NS C3:18-21).

[120] In this connection it is interesting to note that people of Simanum receive foodstuffs at OAkk Susa (Foster in press). The Hurrian city of Simanum seems to have been located in the mountainous region to the north of Mardin (*RGTC 3*: 165f.).

[121] Foster 1990: 32 (pericopes 1-4), 36.

[122] There were probably two sites of this name located in the Upper Habur/Sinjar and near Nuzi (perhaps Gök Tepe on the Lower Zab?) (Michalowski 1986a: 10f.; Frayne in press [a]: LGN 13). The trans-Tigridian Azuhinum seems the more likely candidate in this context (Fadhil 1983: 72; Wilhelm 1989: 8).

[123] D-13. On this basis Michalowski identifies Naram-Sin as the author of another Sargonic royal inscription describing a ruler "who shattered the might (giš.tukul) of Subir" (Fragment C5; Michalowski 1986: 136f.; *idem* 1986a), and of a fragmentary list of 49 cities, including Azuhinum, probably deriving from the same

inscription later plagiarised by Šarkališarri, Naram-Sin asserts formulaically that he "conquered all the peoples and mountain lands from across the Lower Sea to the Upper Sea".[124]

Naram-Sin's presence in the north and north-west is confirmed by discoveries of inscribed monuments at Bassetki and Pir Hussein.[125] Destruction levels at Mari and Ebla (and possibly Tell Brak) are attributed by some to him.[126] Naram-Sin's interest in maintaining control of these regions and their routes of supply is confirmed by the construction of a fortified palace at Tell Brak.[127]

In the east Naram-Sin claims sovereignty over "all Elam as far as Parahšum".[128] No wars with Elam are recorded but the inscriptions on a group of stone maceheads from 'Luristan' dedicated for the life of Naram-Sin include Elam in his epithet "conqueror of Armanum and Ebla and Elam" instead of the standard "... Armanum and Ebla".[129] This may simply be flattery by the dedicant, Karšum, whose kingdom of Niqum probably lay within greater Elam.[130] But a military action of some kind against this region cannot be excluded.[131] This would explain the inclusion of Elam among the rebel lands in 'Text L' (below p. 115) and would provide an

---

124 text (Fragment C6). Interestingly, many of the geographical names in this latter text are Hurrian, making it the earliest attested Hurrian toponymy (Michalowski 1986a). Kienast (*AKI*: 284f.) leaves the attribution of these inscriptions open.

124 NS 2:16-29; ŠkŠ C1:15-28 (NB). The royal name in NS 2 is virtually entirely lost and should perhaps rather be reconstructed as "Šarkališarri" – as is preserved in the NB copy ŠkŠ C1 – thus making this an inscription of Naram-Sin's successor. This attribution is supported by the fact that the royal name is followed by the epithet "mighty (one), king of Agade" (*dannum šar Agade^ki*) (this occurrence of *šar Agade* seems to have been omitted in the standard compilations [Hallo 1957: 67; Seux 1967; Hirsch 1963: 17, 18 4 β] although correctly read already by Weidner 1931-32: 280 [to which Hirsch refers]; the signs [see Thompson *et al.* 1929: pl. XLIII:47] allow for no other restoration), an epithet which is standard for Šarkališarri (Hirsch 1963: 28) but is attested otherwise only once in Naram-Sin's original inscriptions (NS 1). (Elsewhere Naram-Sin is either "mighty (one)" *or* "king of Agade"; the OB "copies" in which he appears as the "mighty (one), king of Agade and the four quarters" (NS C7, C11, C14) are probably later conflations of two separate titles, as can be demonstrated in the case of C1:475ff. [see now Foster 1990: 31, 33] where each redaction has only one or the other.) Furthermore, in all of Naram-Sin's contemporary inscriptions the epithet *dannum* immediately follows the king's name, together occupying one case only, while there is room in the present text for two cases. (The reconstruction of Frayne, followed by Kienast, which leaves the first case empty is implausible.) Moreover, the few preserved traces do not easily fit "Naram-Sin" (as restored by Kienast, seeing traces of [E]N) but accord well with the *lil* which concludes Šarkališarri's epithet "beloved son of Enlil", which typically occurs between his name and *dannum* (e.g. ŠkŠ 2), thus occupying both cases. Nevertheless, the OAkk Šarkališarri texts (C1 and 'NS'2) must be works of plagiarism based on (an) inscription(s) of Naram-Sin since (as all editors have commented) the deeds recounted – suppression of a widespread rebellion, reaching the headwaters of the Tigris and Euphrates, cutting cedars in the Amanus – are all elsewhere attributed to him. (Might Šarkališarri have led these campaigns as crown prince?) An original Naram-Sin text (or group of texts) must therefore be postulated and whatever historical value the extant inscriptions have thus relates to the time of Naram-Sin rather than his successor.

125 NS 1, NS 5; Amiet 1976a: fig. 21.

126 J. Oates 1985 (Brak). Note however that the year date recording the destruction of Mari (D-5) is probably better attributed to Sargon.

127 Mallowan 1947: 63-68.

128 NS C3: 4-10. *Cf.* the late omen recording Naram-Sin "going" to Parahšum (Glassner 1985: 124).

129 NS B7.

130 *Cf.* Frayne (in press [a]) who suggests a location on the upper Alwand (Diyala) between Me-Turran (Tell Haddad) and Karahar (near Sarpol i-Zohab), possibly at modern Khanaqin midway between the two.

131 Other possible evidence for a campaign in the Hamrin-Diyala region includes: an unattributed year name recording victory over the "mountain (lands) in Hašimar" (D-44), which also possibly lay near Niqqum (*RGTC 5*: s.v.) (might the [B]ibi defeated in this campaign be the Baba of Simurrum whose defeat is celebrated in Naram-Sin's year name D-12?); the myth *Inanna and Ebih* describing the defeat of Mt Ebih; and a Hittite literary text which includes Niqqum among Naram-Sin's opponents (below p. 116). On this basis Frayne dates Naram-Sin's conquests of Simurrum, Hašimar, Niqqum and Arame all to the same (series of) campaign(s).

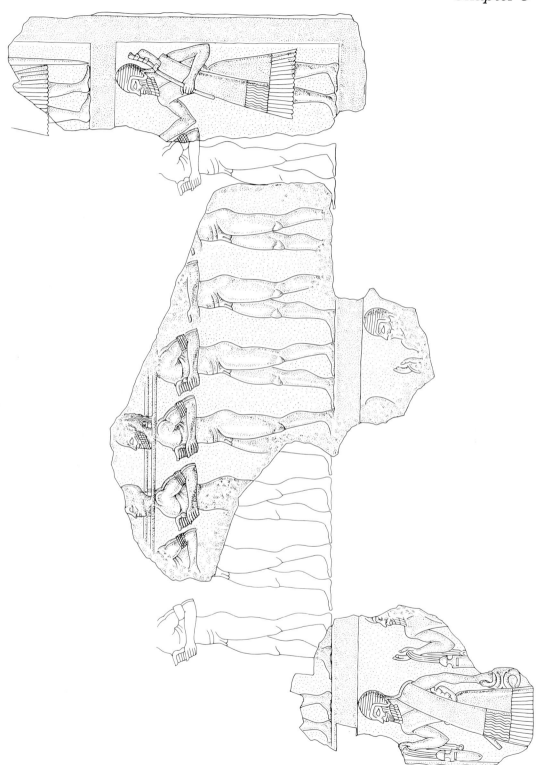

Figure 17.   Sargonic relief showing prisoners of war and booty. From near Nasriyeh(?). Pale green calcite(?). Ht. 21 cm. (main fragment).

immediate context for the Naram-Sin 'treaty' from Susa.[132] Written in the Elamite language but using the Akkadian script, much of this latter document remains obscure; but the twice-repeated phrase "the enemy of Naram-Sin is also my enemy; the friend (?) of Naram-Sin is also my friend (?)" is clearly intended to ensure the co-signatory's submission by forestalling any hostile action. Moreover, the absence of a reciprocal promise indicates Naram-Sin's precedence in the relationship. Since the treaty was found at Susa it is sometimes assumed to have been struck with a prince of that city, but there is no evidence for this in the text as presently understood. Neither Susa nor any other Elamite city, nor even Elam itself, seems to be mentioned.[133] The fact that Susa's tutelary goddess Inšušinak appears in only sixth place in the introductory list of deities – after Pinikir, Hupan (both Elamite), Ilaba (the god of Agade), Zit and Nahiti (=Nahunti) – reinforces this doubt.[134] The name of the second party seems to have occurred, if at all, in only one place where the traces are consistent with either *hi-t[a-a]* or *hi-i[t][...?]*.[135] The first of these certainly, and perhaps also the second, would allow identification with Hita, eleventh king of the Dynasty of Awan in the Susa king list.[136] If, as seems likely, Susa was already an Akkadian province (see below) the treaty is unlikely to have been with a ruler of that city (unless to cement an earlier agreement) but rather with someone previously beyond direct Akkadian control who, as the text proves, used Elamite as his official (and native?) language.

There is evidence to suggest that Susiana was indeed governed directly by Akkadians by the time of Naram-Sin.[137] The tenure of Epirmupi as "ensi of Susa" and "military governor (GÌR.NITÁ) of the land of Elam"[138] is most plausibly dated to this reign (or slightly later) since cylinder seal inscriptions qualify him as *dannum* "the mighty one", an epithet first used in Mesopotamia by Naram-Sin.[139] Such a chronology is corroborated by the style of Epirmupi's seals.[140] The similarly titled Ilišmani[141] may also have ruled Susa under Naram-Sin.[142] A Tello messenger text records him, described as ensi of Susa, together with five other Susian officials (two couriers, one scribe and two "men (lú) of Susa"), receiving rations when passing through Girsu.[143] Many similar journeys within southern Mesopotamia are recorded for Mesag, ensi of the province of Umma-Girsu under Šarkališarri, and Ilišmani's

---

132 Scheil 1911: 1-11; Hinz 1967; Kammenhuber 1976: 172-213.
133 M. Lambert 1979: 28 n. 66 (not Susa); but note that, *pace* Lambert, since no other Elamite city is mentioned, the absence of Susa's name in particular is not an argument against this city being the second party. Regarding Elam, for Hinz's *ha-da[m-tl]* (*i.e.* "Elam") (iii:3) König 1965 reads *ha-rak-[...]*. However, the language of the document puts beyond question that the treaty was with some Elamite power.
134 M. Lambert 1979: 28; Vallat 1980: 5, suggesting that the otherwise unattested deities are Awanite.
135 vi:22. Cameron 1936: 34, Hinz 1971: 651 and Gadd 1971: 444 read *hita*; Scheil 1911: 7, Hinz 1967: 92 and König 1965: 32 read *hit...*
136 Perhaps the same as the king *hi-i-dam* of the Hurrian King List from Hattuša (Kammenhuber 1976: 167). *Cf.* Stolper 1987: 114.
137 As suggested already by Cameron (1936: 34, 36) and argued compellingly by M. Lambert (1979). Stolper (1984: 14) takes a different view on the basis of the Susa treaty.
138 M. Lambert 1979: 15.
139 Hallo 1957: 65. This epithet would not usually be taken by a loyal governor and may indicate that Epirmupi became independent of Agade. The supposed mention of Epirmupi in a Rimuš inscription is to be read Ašarmupi (Foster 1982: 48f.).
140 Boehmer 1967: 305f.
141 Elam 1. The name is perhaps to be read Ili-išmani, for which see *MAD 3*: 275.
142 However, there is no good evidence for dating Ilišmani after Epirmupi, as M. Lambert argues (1979: 15f.); see below note 204.
143 M. Lambert 1979: 13f.

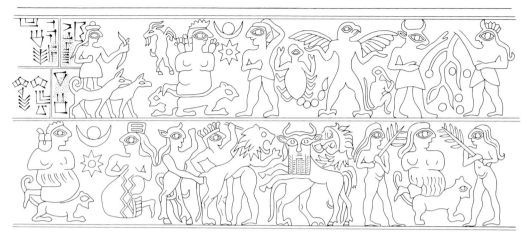

Figure 18. Door seal impression in Iranian-Mesopotamian style from Susa. Late Early Dynastic period.

appearance in such a context makes it highly likely that he too was a "citizen of Agade" owing his position directly to the king.[144]

A handful of inscribed cylinder seals are the only evidence for the use of Sumerian writing at Susa in the Early Dynastic period (Fig. 18).[145] Not a single administrative tablet in Sumerian (or Elamite) has been recovered there despite the abundance of mid-third-millennium administrative archives in Sumer. It can, then, only be as a direct result of the incorporation of Susiana into the Akkadian empire that economic texts written in Akkadian cuneiform now make their appearance.[146] Among them are accounts of a Sumerian (Ummaite) merchant colony residing at Susa together with a garrison and 'grand household' of Mesopotamian type.[147] This occupation provides some illustration of the broadening of economic horizons that must have accompanied the new regime. With the opening up of the empire into lowland Iran and the added security this entailed, south-eastern Sumer witnessed a period of exceptional economic growth becoming one of the richest provinces of the empire.[148]

The recovery at Susa itself of a group of monuments inscribed by and for Naram-Sin may be further evidence of his authority over the provincial capital, if they are not, like his stele, booty brought back to Susa by Šutruk-Nahunte:[149] a statue base celebrating the king's conquest of Magan (see below); a stone vase (Table 6.3: B1a) probably from the booty of that country; and a statue dedicated for the life of

---

144 M. Lambert 1979: 19. The [king] of Elam, Autalumman, attested in the Hurrian king list (Kammenhuber 1976: 167), sometimes dated to this period (Stolper 1984: 15), is not otherwise attested and cannot yet be given a place in this reconstruction.

145 Delaporte 1920: pl. 45:11, 12 (S.462=Fig. 18 here); Amiet 1972: nos 1464 (?), 1466, 1467; Amiet 1966a: fig. 156.

146 Scheil 1913: 61-130.

147 Foster 1977: 39; *idem* 1982: 7; *idem* in press; *cf.* M. Lambert 1979: 20 n. 32.

148 Foster 1977: 39; M. Lambert 1979: 19f. This area's richness is evidenced in, *e.g.*, transfers of large numbers of livestock; see the texts cited by M. Lambert 1979: 19 n. 31.

149 It is notable that none bear secondary inscriptions.

Figure 19.   Detail from stele of Naram-Sin. Susa. Pink sandstone. Ht. 2.0 m.

Naram-Sin to ᵈNIN.KIŠ.UNU (= Erra?)[150] by ⌈Šuaš⌉-takal, the scribe, the majordomo (ŠABRA É)".[151]

Naram-Sin's most famous monument, the stele set up in Sippar and later taken by Šutruk-Nahunte to Susa, commemorates an expedition, probably one of many, to the central Zagros highlands (Fig. 19).[152] The enemy was no doubt a coalition of forces, but the names are now lost in a break of about nine lines between Naram-Sin's epithet *dannum* "the mighty one" and a sentence stating that "[PNs/GNs?] Sidur-[...] ... assembled in the mountains of Lulubum (and) the battle ... (rest lost)".[153] Although the identity of the opposition forces cannot now be more than speculation, likely candidates include the Lulubi in whose territory the battle was

---

150 Reading suggested by Steinkeller 1987: 164 n. 18a. Others have suggested that this otherwise unattested deity is Elamite.

151 NS B2; Amiet 1976a: no. 28. The inscribed brick of "Naram-Sin" from Susa cited by Stolper 1984: 14, n. 71 is of Šu-Sin (*NBWI II*: ŠS1).

152 NS 4; Amiet 1976a: no. 27. *Cf.* the claim in the Nineveh OAkk text NS 2 (above note 124) that "from beyond the Lower Sea all the way to the Upper Sea, the peoples and mountains in their totality he [the king] smote for Enlil".

153 The reading of this passage (here following Kienast *AKI*: 91) is highly problematical and none of the suggested interpretations is entirely satisfactory. Others have read *ša-dú-i* as a PN, yielding: "... A-[...] [of] Sidur[...], Šatuni of Lulubum assembled, a battle ..." (Amiet 1976a: 128 no. 27; *RGTC 1*: 111, 142). Frayne (pers. comm.) reads: "Sidur-[...] (and) the highlanders of Lullubum assembled together."

fought, and perhaps also the Guti, Naram-Sin's nemesis in later tradition. The Lulubi reappear among Naram-Sin's opponents in some literary texts ('Text L' and the Hittite Naram-Sin text; see below); and themselves suffer the onslaught of the Guti in *The Cuthaean Legend of Naram-Sin*.[154]

If the rock relief at Darband-i Gawr, whose composition parallels closely that of the Susa stele, celebrates the same victory as that work, the location of the engagement (and of Lulubum?) would be broadly fixed. However, since some aspects of the representation – particularly the conqueror's headdress – are best matched in the Ur III period, its attribution to Akkadian times can no longer be considered likely.[155] Likewise with the relief of Anubanini,[156] whose sons lead the Umman Manda against Naram-Sin in *The Cuthaean Legend* (though not there called Lulubians), the inscription cannot be earlier than the second millennium. Similar doubts surround other reliefs, mostly uninscribed, previously assigned by some scholars to the Akkadian period at Darband-i Ramgan and Sarpol-i Zohab.[157]

An action against Simurrum[158] at some stage of Naram-Sin's reign is proved by two date formulae, one recording his going to Simurrum, as had Sargon before him; the other, attested on documents from Tutub, his defeat of "Simurrum in Kiraseniwe" and the capture of its ensi Baba, along with Dubul(?), ensi of Arame.[159] Simurrum also appears among the rebels in *The Great Revolt*.

Inscribed objects in Iranian collections said to come from 'Luristan' may reflect Akkadian control of the eastern highlands. A copper bowl is inscribed "Naram-Sin, King of the four quarters"; and an epsilon-type axehead also carries his inscription.[160] A copper macehead and a group of six stone maceheads were dedicated in the name of Naram-Sin by Karšum, ensi of Niqum, who describes himself as "your/his [Naram-Sin's] servant".[161] Although Niqum, probably situated in the central Zagros,[162] is not mentioned in any of Naram-Sin's annals, memory of its association with the king may be preserved in the listing of a place called Niqqi[...] in the Hittite Naram-Sin text.[163]

To the south-east, Naram-Sin conquered Magan, an operation which represents the only reliably documented military expedition to this region by a third-millennium ruler. A contemporary account is partly preserved at the bottom of a statue from Susa:

> Naram-Sin, the mighty, king of the four quarters, victor of nine battles in one year. After he had won those battles he brought their three kings in fetters before Enlil ...

> (lacuna of at least 9 lines)

---

[154] Gurney 1955.

[155] Börker-Klähn 1982: 137 no. 29. The inscription also supports an Ur III-OB date (Hallo 1957: 97f.; Edzard 1973: 75). *Cf.* Klengel 1988: 165 who still cites these as Sargonic monuments.

[156] *Ibid.*: 138 no. 31; *AKI*: Varia 6.

[157] *Ibid.*: 140 N34 (Darband-i Ramgan); *ibid.*: 138-40 nos 30 (=*AKI*: Varia 7), 32, 34 (Sarpol-i Zohab).

[158] For location see al-Fouadi 1978 (Lower Zab); previously *RGTC 2*: s.v. (between Lower Zab and Diyala). Weidner placed it where the 'Adaim River cuts through the Hamrin and thus still Frayne (pers. comm.).

[159] D-11 (*cf.* Sargon D-1); D-12. Frayne (in press [a]) suggests a location for Arame on the Diyala downstream of the Hamrin and that this Baba may be the [B]ibi mentioned in a year date (D-44) celebrating the conquest of "the mountain (land) of Hašimar".

[160] Dossin 1962: no. 28; NS 14, text E (bowl); Calmeyer 1969: 30 (axehead).

[161] Dossin 1962: no. 15; NS B6 (copper); M. Lambert 1968; NS B7 (stone).

[162] See above note 130.

[163] Güterbock 1938: 68, l. 14′.

> ... He subjugated Magan, and captured Maniu[m] (?), the lord (EN) of Magan. He quarried blocks of diorite in their mountains, and transported (them) to Agade, his city, and made his statue (and) dedicated it to [....][164]

An Old Babylonian copy of another contemporary inscription adds that Naram-Sin "crossed the sea ... and smote Magan in the midst of the sea[165] and washed his weapons in the Lower Sea".[166] Stone vessels taken on this campaign and dedicated by Naram-Sin "from the booty of Magan" have been recovered in excavation, one from Susa, one from Ur and two from unrecorded provenances in Mesopotamia (Table 6.3: Inscr. A; Fig. 41:1, 4).[167] This conquest – clearly regarded as one of his greatest victories – is also recorded in the *Chronicle of Early Kings*, which relates that Naram-Sin "marched to Magan and captured Mannum [=Manium], the mighty one, king of Magan".[168] The Neo-Babylonian omen collection adds that Naram-Sin "seized" Magan;[169] and Mannu [=Manium], king of Magan, appears in *The Great Revolt*.

Naram-Sin's Magan campaign, following upon Maništušu's defeat of thirty-two cities on the "other side" of the Lower Sea, must have established the Akkadians as the dominant maritime power in the Gulf. Outside literary accounts, there is no evidence that any other third-millennium Mesopotamian ruler could lay claim to this region; and, indeed, it must be questioned whether Naram-Sin was able, or even attempted, to establish effective control, or merely asserted his dominance, plundered and withdrew.

Various *historical-literary compositions* concerning Naram-Sin have been mentioned in the preceding discussion where they complement historical evidence. Much of what these texts relate – mostly concerning revolts or invasions of foreign hoards – is not corroborated elsewhere, and their reliability therefore remains unproven. Apparent anachronisms have led a number of scholars to reject them as a legitimate source of historical study.[170] However, despite the likelihood of literary embellishment and interpolation, their testimony should not be entirely dismissed, especially since the tendency of new evidence has been to confirm them in regard to general historical circumstances and occasionally in points of detail, notably the recent publication of an Old Akkadian version of the Mesopotamian 'Great Revolt'.[171] Although there is yet no contemporary confirmation for many of the places and peoples mentioned in the accounts of foreign uprisings, neither are there compelling reasons to regard them all as fictional.[172] While the structure and content of literary works was often

---

[164] Amiet 1976a: no. 29=NS 3:1-48; NS A1:1-18 *Cf.* previously Heimpel 1987: 75 no. 16; A. Westenholz *apud* D. Potts 1986b: 275f.; Glassner 1987: 15; *idem* 1989: 184f.

[165] Foster (1990: 38, x[25]) takes this description to apply not to the location of Magan but to the battle, which he thus envisages as a naval encounter.

[166] Foster 1990: 33, pericope 10.

[167] NS 13. Note also the copy of a longer dedication inscription on a bowl mentioning the Magan campaign (Foster 1990). The OB copy Michalowski 1980: 241 col. vii is a dedication inscription also possibly from booty of this kind.

[168] *ABC*: Chron. 20:A27. Alternatively *dannum* may be read as part of the royal name: Mannumdannum.

[169] King 1907: no. 3 rev. 16-18; Starr 1986: 637 ll. 16-18; Glassner 1983: 4-6.

[170] Güterbock 1934; Grayson & Sollberger 1976: 108-11; Cooper 1983a: 15f., 31.

[171] NS C1.

[172] *Cf.* Smith 1928: 94-96. Of those often cited, Kaneš does not appear in Assyrian documents until the period of the *karum*, but the city itself dates back through the Early Bronze Age (Orthmann 1976-80: 378-80) and there is no reason why this should not be mentioned here; Amurru (MAR.TU) appears already in Fara, Ebla and Sargonic texts as a geographical name and as a descriptive term (*RGTC 1*: 14,

constrained by considerations other than historical fidelity, provided appropriate critical standards are applied it is legitimate to consider, if not always to accept, their evidence.[173]

Four compositions concerning hostile coalitions of foreign forces and/or barbarian hordes are known:[174] *The Great Revolt*, 'Text L' (perhaps part of the same composition), the 'Hittite Naram-Sin text' and *The Cuthaean Legend of Naram-Sin*. While there is some overlap, the rebels are largely different in each case. It is unlikely that each preserves the memory of a different encounter; more probably, later editing and interpolation have generated garbled versions of the same event or events in different guises, further distorted by confusion or conflation with other events in the reign of Naram-Sin and other Sargonic (and even later?) rulers.[175] In all cases where an outcome is preserved Naram-Sin eventually wins through, though sometimes after serious set-backs, and a favourable conclusion was probably reached also in the lost endings of *The Great Revolt* and 'Text L'.[176]

The most informative and probably the most reliable of these is *The Great Revolt*, a composition preserved in Old Babylonian copies which describes a revolt against Naram-Sin led by Iphur-Kiši of Kiš.[177] Along with Kiš, the beginning of the text states that the northern Babylonian cities of Kutha, Tiwa (*Ti*-PI), Wurumu, Kazallu, Giritab, Api(w)ak, Ibrat, Dilbat, Uruk (the only southern Babylonian city) and Sippar also rebelled. The historicity of this local uprising is confirmed by a more detailed account in an Old Babylonian copy of a contemporary royal inscription.[178] The two principal *dramatis personae*, Iphur-Kiši of Kiš and Lugalane of Uruk, also turn up in an Old Akkadian royal 'praise hymn' (?) from Ešnunna.[179]

It is probably the suppression of this unrest to which allusion is made in the Bassetki statue inscription when it refers to the time "when the four quarters together rebelled against him"[180] and in Naram-Sin's oft-repeated claim to have fought nine battles in one year, for a fragmentary passage of *The Great Revolt* claims that Agade raised precisely this many expeditions against the rebels.[181] It was

116; Archi 1985 with bibliography); likewise Hatti, the pre-Hittite name for central Anatolia, need not be anachronistic.
[173] *Cf.* Cooper 1983a: 16.
[174] Grayson & Sollberger 1976; Güterbock 1938: 68-71; Gurney 1955. For further bibliography of these and other historiographic Naram-Sin literature see Cooper 1983a: 16 with notes. A further fragment of the Mari copy of *The Great Revolt* (Text M) is to be published by D. Charpin. Van Dijk 1971: no. 42 may represent a fifth composition; this text has not been edited and will not be considered here. J. Westenholz 1983: 330 n. 25 considers it and 'Text L' versions of *The Great Revolt*.
[175] Cooper 1983a: 10; Foster 1990: 42f. Frayne (1992: 634) makes the interesting suggestion that the Umman Manda of *The Cuthaean Legend* are to be related to the Manda (PN) who, according to an OB letter, "entered" Niqq[um], Ha⌈man⌉ and Dadl[a-] in the region north-east of Ešnunna (Whiting 1987a: no. 2).
[176] Cooper 1983a: 17.
[177] Grayson & Sollberger 1976.
[178] NS C1; possibly also NS C2 (see now additions in Foster 1990). See the reconstruction of events based on the literary and historical sources in Kutscher 1989: 16f. NS C1 goes on to describe a revolt by a southern Babylonian coalition led by Amar-girid (see NS C1 for this reading of PN) of Uruk.
[179] A. Westenholz 1974-77: 96f.; Jacobsen 1978-79: 2f.; *cf.* Foster 1990: 44 n. 14. On the other hand, it should be noted that Naram-Sin's contemporary inscription (NS C1) has Amar-girid in place of Lugalanne as the rebellious ruler of Uruk (was Lugalanne perhaps a throne name?). Other possible inconsistencies between the rulers cited in *The Great Revolt* and contemporary sources are the rulers of Simurrum (Pittumatal vs. Baba [*MAD 1*: nos 217, 220]) and Nippur (Amar-Enlila vs. Lugal-[...] [NS C1:315, collation Frayne]), although these variations may rather derive from the fact that the texts describe events at different points in Naram-Sin's reign.
[180] NS 1; NS 2:10ff. (above note 124) Foster 1990: 33 pericopes 8, 9; NS C1:411ff.
[181] NS 1; 3; A1; C9; Foster 1990: 39f.; *cf.* Grayson & Sollberger 1976: M rev. 3'-4'; Jacobsen 1978-79: 11 (translat.). The OB Naram-Sin text van Dijk 1971: no. 42, perhaps deriving from an original inscription

probably in the wake of these victories (though after the commissioning of NS 1 and NS C1) that Naram-Sin adopted divine status.

Having described Iphur-Kiši's election to kingship by the confederates, *The Great Revolt* goes on to describe a revolt of foreign lands against Naram-Sin, indicating a much broader insurrection than the royal inscriptions. The text lists a number of foreign and two additional Babylonian "kings", plus Uruk again, representing the following cities and regions: Simurrum, Namar, Apišal, Mari, Marhaši, Mardaman, Magan, Uruk, Umma and Nippur. (Interestingly, Elam is not mentioned in the preserved text.) There the tablet breaks off, before stating what the kings of these places did, but the context suggests that they too joined the secessionist cause and were eventually defeated by Naram-Sin. As detailed above, there is independent evidence for conquests by Naram-Sin of a number of the places listed: Simurrum, Apišal, Mari (?), Mardaman ("Maridaban"), Magan, Uruk and Nippur. Unfortunately, the royal inscription which preserves an account of the Babylonian revolt breaks off without any mention of a foreign uprising; whether such was originally related in the lost part of the tablet cannot now be determined.

Another Old Babylonian text which Grayson and Sollberger call Text L (London) and regard as a later section of *The Great Revolt*, may be a separate composition.[182] Of the eighteen kingdoms whose names are preserved in the text, only Marhaši occurs in *The Great Revolt*. The chief opponent is Gula-AN, king of Gutium. Along with him are listed (names only partly preserved) the kings of Kakmum, Lulubum (Lullum), Hahhu[183] and Turukkum; the "men" (lú) of Kanišum (=Kaneš-Kültepe), Amurru, Dêr, Ararru; the Kassite; the "men" of Meluhha and Šuruppak (error for Aratta?);[184] and the kings of Marhaši, the totality of Elam, GIŠ.GI-land, 'Fifty'-land, Armanum and Hana[...].[185] The fragmentary end of the text relates Naram-Sin's initial victory and then defeat at the hands of the Guti.[186] The final outcome is lost but other coalition stories suggest that Naram-Sin eventually won through.[187] Since the beginning of the text is also missing it is impossible to be sure whether the alliance was portrayed as constituting a rebellion of subjects or a hostile coalition of independent powers. The fact that only Marhaši occurs in the present list and *The Great Revolt*, and that its king ([...]-en) does not seem to be the one mentioned there (Hupšumkipi), may suggest that these are supposed to be accounts of different events. The anachronistic inclusion of "the Kassite", Kanišum and Amurrum suggests in any case that some interpolation has occurred.[188]

The remaining entries in the list do not add much to what is known from other sources of Naram-Sin's empire. The evidence relating to Lulubum, Marhaši, Armanum and Elam has been cited above. Dêr, near the highland border at modern Badra, is well within these limits. The "man of Meluhha" is less easy to evaluate; though not impossible in a highland coalition, there is no other evidence for military contact with Meluhhans under Naram-Sin (though there is evidence relating to

---

(Cooper 1983a: 16), likewise reports Naram-Sin's final victory over a rebel coalition after the same number of engagements. *Cf.* Foster 1990: 42 who relates these phrases not to the 'Great Revolt' but to the *RÉC 349* and Magan campaigns.

[182] *Cf.* Cooper 1983a: 16.

[183] On the Aššur – Kaneš road (*RGTC 1*: s.v.).

[184] Thus Grayson & Sollberger 1976: 126 comm. to L i:13´, followed by Vallat 1985: 54.

[185] Text L i:2´-21´.

[186] ii:14´ff. The victory is also over "Mengi, king of Nagu" (or the PN "Mengišarnagu"?; see commentary to Text L i:12f.).

[187] Cooper 1983a: 17.

[188] Grayson & Sollberger 1976: 108.

Rimuš; see above p. 101). The question of the remaining places, mostly unlocated or only vaguely localisable, must be left open until independent testimony of their involvement appears.

A Hittite text from Hattuša bears a list of seventeen kings, of whose kingdoms thirteen names are legible, who united against Naram-Sin.[189] They are defeated by the king who then prevails also against the Hurrians. The rebels comprise: GÚ.ŠU.A, Pakki..., Lulubum, ..., Hatti, Kaneš, ..., Amurru, Paraši (= Parahšum/Marhaši), ..., Armanu, the Cedar Mountain, ..., Larak, Niqq..., Turki and Kuršaura. Para[h]šum (*i.e.* Marhaši) is the only place which also occurs in *The Great Revolt*, but the text shares five or six places with 'Text L': Lulubum, Kaneš, Amurru, Parahšum, Armanum (? and Turukkum = Turki) and so may stem from the same tradition.[190] Niqqi... of line 14´ is almost certainly the Niqum whose ensi, Karšum, dedicated maceheads for Naram-Sin (see above). It does not appear associated with Naram-Sin in any other literature but is listed among Sargon's dominions in *The Sargon Geography*.[191] Kuršaura may derive from Gursar, referred to in an Early Dynastic text from Susa.[192] Thus, with the exception of Hatti, the places in this text that can be located are on the whole consistent with what is known from other sources of the field of Naram-Sin's campaigns.

What should be our conclusion as regards the historicity of a great foreign revolt? The newly published Old Akkadian account of the 'Great Revolt' makes no mention in the preserved sections of any foreign uprising and the nearest other contemporary sources come is in vague references to a time "when the four quarters together revolted against him". We do have contemporary evidence that Naram-Sin conquered some of the places which, according to the literary sources, participated in the foreign uprising. But these are represented as 'normal' conquests, not as operations to suppress a revolt. This raises the crucial – and so far unanswerable – question: are these conquests nonetheless to be understood as accounts of the suppression of the revolt (in which case we do not have accounts of the original conquests of these places, some perhaps inherited from Maništušu)?; or as records of the conquest of places which later revolted (in which case we have no contemporary accounts of their reconquests)?;[193] or was there in fact no great revolt of foreign lands but only a series of individual conquests which later traditon conflated with the genuine memory of a revolt of local Mesopotamian cities to yield a bogus foreign revolt?[194] The last alternative seems at present the most likely.

(e) Šarkališarri

The inscriptions of Naram-Sin's successor Šarkališarri indicate increasing pressure from highland peoples at both extremes of the empire, presaging the

---

[189] Güterbock 1938: 68-71.

[190] The first five places are listed in this order in both texts (though differently separated by other places); Lulubum occurs third and Kaneš sixth in both; and the king of Armanum, Madakina, seems to be the same in both (as is perhaps that of Lulubum). On the other hand, it should be noted that Turki and Turukkum, if these denote the same place, appear out of order, though their kings may be identical; and that the preserved traces of the names of the kings of Kaneš, Amurru and Marhaši in 'Text L' seem to be different from those here.

[191] Grayson 1974-77: 16.

[192] Sollberger 1971: 700; *RGTC 1*: 65.

[193] This option is not available to those who use Naram-Sin's adoption of divine status to date the events of his reign, for in that scheme all of these conquests (except Magan) come after the 'Great Revolt'; see above p. 106.

[194] *Cf.* Foster 1990: 42f., who seems to vacillate between the latter two options.

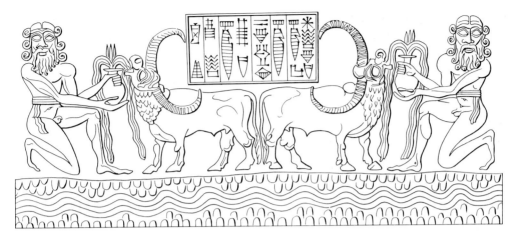

Figure 20.   Cylinder seal of Ibni-šarrum, scribe of Šarkališarri. Jasper. Ht. 4.0 cm.

disintegration of imperial control which was soon to set in. On the western front the Amorites of Mount Basar=Jebel Bishri,[195] whose conquest Naram-Sin had claimed,[196] now reappear and were evidently posing some threat to the security of that region. But it was from the east that the more immediate danger stemmed. Dedication inscriptions to Šarkališarri on metal bowls from Luristan and on a stone bowl allegedly from Tutub, but inscribed by a priest of Niqum, show that he was able for a while at least to command loyalty from the provinces in the nearby eastern highlands.[197] At the same time, however, a year name records a campaign against the Guti and the capture of their king (A)šarlag,[198] indicating that the depredations of these fierce highlanders on the farmers of the plain had begun. The seriousness of the Gutian raids under Šarkališarri is illustrated by a letter from an Iškun-Dagan instructing the local governor to establish watch stations and laying down conditions on reparations for lost livestock.[199]

As yet, however, the Guti did not have the power to force a split between Akkad and Sumer[200] or her chief eastern province centred on Susa. Šarkališarri probably ascended the throne with Susiana intact. During the course of his tenure there are signs of weakening and by his death lowland Elam may have seceded from the failing empire entirely. The difficulty, as before, is with the relative ordering of events. Very different reconstructions are possible depending on how the scattered incidents and connections are interpreted and arranged. Two key issues are: (1) the date of Ilišmani, ensi of Susa and viceroy (GÌR.NITÁ) of Elam, who was apparently still answerable to the king of Agade, at least for part of his career; and (2) the

[195] *RGTC 1*: 26; *cf.* Michalowski 1976: 103f.

[196] Foster 1990.

[197] ŠkŠ B3; B4 (metal bowls); ŠkŠ B1 (stone bowl [*AKI*: 117]; note that Hirsch 1963: 29 and Feigin 1939 call this a macehead).

[198] D-27; *cf.* D-42, which Hirsch 1963: 29 attributes to Šarkališarri.

[199] Smith 1932: 295-301; Oppenheim 1967: 71f. no. 2; with corrections by Foster 1990a.

[200] Evidence of Akkadian control of Sumer comes from loyal inscriptions of Lugalušumgal, ensi of Lagaš (dedication seal *RTC* 162), and economic texts from his reign dated by imperial Akkadian formulae. One possibly local formula may indicate the severing of ties after Šarkališarri's death (Sollberger 1954-56: 31).

interpretation of two year formulae of Šarkališarri recording the defeat of Elam and Zahara on Mesopotamian soil near Akšak.[201]

Ilišmani is known from two texts, an inscribed shaft-hole axe-head from Susa and a Lagaš messenger text where he and his retinue receive provisions, as were due to Akkadian officials.[202] His Akkadian name suggests that Ilišmani, like the other known ensis of Susa, was an Akkadian appointee, and that Susa was in his time still under Akkadian rule.[203] However, there is no firm evidence for the dating of his tenure of this office *vis-à-vis* Epirmupi,[204] and thus whether he was a contemporary of Naram-Sin or of Šarkališarri. Only two ensis of Susa are known for the entire Sargonic period: Epirmupi and Ilišmani.[205] Neither is explicitly synchronized with an Akkadian king in their inscriptions. There are good circumstantial grounds for correlating Epirmupi with Naram-Sin;[206] but it is unlikely that he accounts for all of this king's long reign of fifty-six (in one reconstruction thirty-seven) years. Ilišmani also may easily be accommodated within this stretch, rather than under Šarkališarri.[207] It remains to be seen, therefore, whether Akkadian suzerainty continued to be exercised over Susa under Šarkališarri.

These doubts might seem to be confirmed by the second datum, a year date of Šarkališarri recording a battle against Elam and Zahara (the same coalition confronted by Rimuš), but this also is an uncertain guide. The encounter is specifically located near Akšak in northern Akkad.[208] This makes little sense as an attempt to suppress rebellion in Susiana; the king's opponents must have been highlanders – Elamites in the true sense of the term – from somewhere in the Zagros mountains or beyond. This conflict therefore leaves unsettled the question of the king's authority over Susa. It is unlikely that Šarkališarri had substantial direct dealings with more distant eastern lands. Akkadian control over states such as Anšan, Marhaši and Magan – perhaps only nominal to begin with – seems by now to have entirely dissolved.[209]

After the reign of Šarkališarri evidence of diplomatic or military activity between erstwhile vassal and suzerain dries up as the Akkadian imperial structure begins to crumble and Elam enters a period of historical obscurity from which it does

---

[201] D-25-26; Hallo 1971: 709.

[202] M. Lambert 1979: 11-14.

[203] *Ibid.*: 22f.

[204] M. Lambert, following Boehmer (1967), dates Epirmupi to the reign of Naram-Sin and Ilišmani immediately after, thus placing the latter in the range late Naram-Sin to Šarkališarri. His argument for this order rests on the fact that 'Susa' in Epirmupi's title is written in the Early Dynastic syllabic form šu-šin[ki] while the same title as used by Ilišmani employs the henceforth canonical logographic writing MÙŠ.ERIN[ki] (M. Lambert 1979: 15 ff.). But Lambert himself undermines this criterion when he goes on to observe that: "Quand un Mésopotamien, ou un Susien de culture mésopotamienne, écrit le nom de Suse, il emploie un idéogramme. Lorsque un Elamite écrit le nom de Suse il emploie la graphie phonétique." (M. Lambert 1979: 16 n. 15). If the variation is regional as well as chronological it cannot be a reliable indicator of date here since the Epirmupi text is Susian and the Ilišmani text Lagašite.

[205] There are also references to "ensis" of Susa whose names are not given: *ITT 2*: 4 560; 5; *RTC* 143 rev. 8'. It is unclear whether "ensis of Elam" should also be counted here. The two dated holders of this title belong to the reigns of Sargon (Sanamsimut: Sargon C7, C13) and Maništušu (Ešpum; S-4). It is interesting that the two titles seem to be chronologically exclusive, as if the ensi of Elam were superseded by the ensi of Susa. Puzur-Inšušinak's tenure as ensi of Susa has recently been redated to the early Ur III period (Wilcke 1987: 110).

[206] Boehmer 1967: 305f.; M. Lambert 1979: 16f, n. 19; Foster 1982: 48f.

[207] As M. Lambert 1979: 22f.

[208] *RGTC 1*: 10; *RGTC 2*: 6f.

[209] A possible qualification to this picture is the reference in a Nippur text to a "prince" (dumu lugal) receiving onions "when he went to Marhaši" (A. Westenholz 1987a: no. 133). Westenholz suggests that this was Šarkališarri as crown prince or his son and that the trip was to effect "the prince's wedding" (to a Marhašian princess?) referred to in another text (*ibid.*: no. 154).

not emerge until Puzur-Inšušinak. The agents of Akkad's malaise, and perhaps also of lowland Elam's temporary decline, were the fierce Zagros highlanders who would eventually bring Agade itself to the point of destruction – the Guti.

4. THE FALL OF AGADE AND THE GUTIAN INVASION

During the reign of Šarkališarri, if not his predecessor Naram-Sin, the Akkadian empire fell victim to barbarian invaders from the eastern highlands.[210] Contemporary documents do not, of course, report events in these terms but the collapse of Agade features prominently in later literary tradition where the intruders are identified as Gutians and their influx is dated to the reign of Naram-Sin.[211] The sparse detail that the accounts of Gutian and other barbarian invasions provide cannot be trusted, and it is impossible now to say even in general terms how the end came – whether by a process of gradual attrition, a lightning strike or whatever. Other foreign groups besides the Gutians – perhaps even the Sumerians[212] – may have been involved. The Elamites were always ready to exploit their western neighbour's weaknesses – as were probably the Hurrians, Lulubians, and other highland peoples who had fought the Akkadians or suffered their rule.[213] It is also possible that some of the stories about coalitions of foreign kings rebelling against Naram-Sin have transposed events that belong to this collapse.

Whatever the truth of these matters, the eventual effect of the invasion was devastating. Akkadian control over the Sumerian south was lost; where they turn up, inscriptions now show local Sumerians – of whom Gudea is the best known – holding the reigns of power. The almost total dearth of documentation from the more distant provinces suggests, as would be expected, that all of these also fell away from central control. Lowland Elam may already have been lost in a local revolt under Šarkališarri (see above); if not, it certainly was now, along with Niqum, and any other dependent principalities along the westernmost highlands through to Aššur, the Habur and Anatolia.[214] There is no inscriptional or archaeological evidence that any form of centralized rule, by Gutians or others, replaced the Akkadian hegemony in these regions, and it must at present be assumed that they reverted to local rule.

The Gutian dynasty itself remains a very shadowy entity mentioned only in a handful of contemporary Sumerian and Akkadian inscriptions.[215] The principal source remains the *Sumerian King List* which reckons twenty-one or twenty-three kings,[216] whom Hallo assigns a period of no more than fourty or fifty years between the end of Šarkališarri and Ur-Nammu.[217] Their names, at first Gutian(ised), become more Akkadian towards the end. According to Utu-hegal they "carried off the kingship of Sumer to the highlands" but it is unclear what this metaphor meant in

---

[210] Later literature (*ABC*: Chron. 19 [add now new copy al-Rawi 1990]; 'Text L', *The Curse of Agade*) ascribes the invasion to the reign of Naram-sin but contemporary evidence begins only with his successor (cf. Speiser 1952: 98). The entry of the *SKL* (vii:1-7) after Šarkališarri, "who was king?; who was not king?", is often understood to reflect this invasion, though the Gutian Dynasty is not listed till later.

[211] *CA*; *ABC*: Chron. 19:53ff.; Text L.

[212] Cf. van Dijk 1969: 206.

[213] Speiser 1952: 98f.; Lewy 1971: 740.

[214] Hallo 1971: 710.

[215] Hallo 1971: 711f.; *AKI*: Gutium 1, C1-C3.

[216] Jacobsen (1939: 117 n. 285, 120 n. 308; cf. *AKI*: 293) lists 21 rulers including the "king without a name". Edzard 1980-83: 82f. reckons the same number without this king, inserting a 5th king (who he does not list) between Šulme/Iarlagaš (his no. 4) and Elulumeš (his no. 6).

[217] Hallo 1971: 714.

real terms and very little can now be established of the Gutian dynasty's relations
with the petty dynasts who succeeded the king of Agade outside heartland Akkad.
Inscriptions from Umma dated by reference to the reigning Gutian king[218] suggest
that the Ummaites were his vassals, though other interpretations are possible.[219]

The fate of Akkad itself remains unclear. Much again depends on intractable
questions of dating. In essence, an early invasion (late in the reign of Naram-Sin)[220]
cannot plausibly be coupled with an effective Gutian conquest, since Šarkališarri
continued to oppose them (not without success, if his inscriptions can be believed)
and retained at least nominal control of some of Naram-Sin's empire. The letter of
Iškun-Dagan, probably dating to the reign of Naram-Sin, portrays them still outside
the law – an imminent danger certainly, and likely at any time to descend on the
vulnerable farms of the lowlands but not, it seems, as an occupying force, and
certainly not in control of Agade. An invasion late in Šarkališarri's reign[221] could have
been more serious, for by this point evidence of continuing Akkadian rule beyond
heartland Akkad virtually ceases. Neither the *Sumerian King List* nor contemporary
documents, however, suggests that the Akkadian royal line was yet brought to an
end. Akkadians still occupied the throne of Agade,[222] the tendentious *Curse of Agade*
being the only source to state that the capital was taken.[223] Documents dated by the
last kings of Agade, Dudu and Šu-Durul,[224] indicate that they continued to rule the
region of Akkad proper from approximately Agade north to Ešnunna;[225] and
inscribed metalwork of Elulu ("Eluldan") and Šu-Durul from 'Luristan' may indicate
some continuing influence in the Zagros.[226] The epithets of the later Akkadian rulers
accurately reflect this state of affairs, dropping the more extravagant imperialist
affectations for the modest "mighty king of Agade".[227]

In the south too the existing political and social structure was evidently not
entirely erradicated, for the rulers attested by local documents are still Sumerians,
though two from Umma date their inscriptions by reference to Gutian kings.[228] The
IVth and Vth Dynasties of Uruk (placed immediately before and after the Guti in the
Sumerian King List), and the ensis of Lagaš from Lugalušumgal on (including the
famous dynasty of Ur-Bau) were able to reassert themselves in the period following
the Gutian invasion, thus laying the basis for the Sumerian 'renaissance' under Ur.

Against this evidence must be weighed the fact that the fourteenth Gutian
king, La-arab, dedicated a macehead in Akkadian adopting the titles of Naram-Sin
and invoking "the gods of Gutium, Ištar and Sin";[229] and that Erridupizir, a self-
styled "King of Gutium" not mentioned in the *Sumerian King List*, likewise adapts
Naram-Sin's titles as "the mighty one, king of Gutium and the four quarters" in the
inscriptions on three statues set up by the king in the Ekur at Nippur.[230] In these

[218] Note also the seal of Elulu (Moortgat 1940: no. 186) which acknowledges a Siaum as king.
[219] Hallo 1971: 712.
[220] As Speiser 1952: 98; Hinz 1972: 77.
[221] As Gadd 1971: 456.
[222] Unless the Elulu of the *SKL* is the Gutian Eluleš, as Jacobsen 1939: 207 suggests.
[223] *Cf.* Cooper 1983a: 10 f.
[224] Gelb 1961: 209; Hallo 1971: 710; Grégoire 1981: no. 31.
[225] It is unclear what, if any, credence should be given the problematic mu-iti text which refers to the time
"when Dudu (?) destroyed Umma together with El[am]" (or: "when Umma together with El[am] was
destroyed" [by an unspecified agent]) (Wilcke 1974-77: 84f, comm. to ll. 6-10).
[226] Eluldan 1; Šu-Durul 1.
[227] Hallo 1957: 67 n. 12.
[228] Hallo 1971: 712.
[229] Gutium 1: 20-23; Hallo 1971: 711f.
[230] Gutium C1-C3; in C1: 89-92 he cites the patron gods of Agade, Inanna and Ilaba, along with Šamaš.

inscriptions, preserved in Old Babylonian copies, Erridupizir describes suppressing uprisings in Madga,[231] Simurrum, Urbilum and Lulubum, invoking standard Akkadian curses and deities.[232] Some at least of the Gutian kings were therefore in a position to adopt the trappings and act as would a true Akkadian monarch, and were treated as such for diplomatic purposes by native city governors. Moreover, if the testimony of the *Lament Over Sumer and Ur* can be trusted, the Guti may have established a firm presence in the Keš-Adab region which lasted into the succeeding Ur III period. The Guti, we are there told, "made his lair [in Keš and Adab], it became a rebellious land; the Gutians bred there, issued their seed".[233] From the inscription of Erridupizir it seems that they also established some degree of control over the peoples bordering their mountain homeland.

On balance, it seems likely that the Gutian invasion was not a pervasive political occupation; the conquerors did not succeed in destroying the native dynasty, nor (*pace* the *Curse of Agade*) did they take the capital. Outside the Keš-Adab region, the evidence suggests rather the familiar pattern of swift, mobile marauders preying on a richer sedentary population. Such opportunists are notoriously reluctant to settle. It is hardly surprising, therefore, that the Guti had no discernible impact on Sumero-Akkadian culture: there is no recorded Gutian literature, no recognisable Gutian art, no influx of Gutian personal names[234] and only a handful of extant contemporary royal inscription (La-arab and Erridupizir) – and even these are written in Akkadian.

What then did the conquest mean to life in Mesopotamia? In the short term it must have meant chaos and hardship for those who survived: "The criminal manned the watch / The brigand occupied the highways ... The great agricultural tracts produced no grain / The inundated tracts produced no fish / The irrigated orchards produced neither syrup nor wine ... People were flailing at themselves from hunger".[235] This is poetry not history, but it is consistent with contemporary documents as far as they go. The inscription of Lugalanatuma of Umma, recording his rebuilding of the E-gidri during the reign of Sium, says that thirty-five years had passed since the destruction of the city.[236]

In the longer term, the Gutian invasion spelt the end of centralized imperial administration and its replacement by numerous local authorities. It is a sign of the times that the independent ensis of the south now dated events by local calendars, or by the kings of Gutium, instead of the imperial Akkadian calendar.[237] What it apparently did not mean was pervasive foreign domination in the manner of the Akkadian empire itself.

---

[231] Gutium C1. Magda was located to the east of Sumer, though not necessarily near Kimaš (as *RGTC 1*: 113; *RGTC 2*: 113) since the text on which that association was based has been collated as "Elam" not "Magda" (Edzard & Röllig 1976-80: 593).

[232] Gutium C2, C3; Kutscher 1989: 66 comm. to vii:2´-8´.

[233] Michalowski 1989: 45, ll. 143-46; *cf.* Sjöberg *et al.* 1969: 162. Late OAkk texts from Adab confirm the troubled nature of these times and the presence of Gutians, one referring to the messenger of an ensi having been killed (Yang 1989: 127); another to a Gutian general (GÌR.NITÁ gu-ti-um) travelling from Adab to Uruk (*ibid.*: 135); and another to "the conveyors (?) of the Gutian(s)" (*ibid.*: 333; Steinkeller 1980: 7).

[234] However, see Hallo 1971: 712 on a few names similar to Sium, the penultimate Gutian king, in Diyala and Nuzi texts.

[235] *CA*: 166ff., trans. Cooper 1983a.

[236] *IRSA*: IID4a. Frayne (pers. comm.) suggests that the destruction concerned was rather that alluded to in the enigmatic text published by Wilcke 1974-77: 84 (above note 225). The grammar of that passage, however, is ambiguous and may not in fact intend to link Dudu with the destruction.

[237] Jacobsen 1939: 204 f.; Gadd 1971: 458; *cf.* Foster 1982: 7.

5. GUDEA

Historical evidence concerning political relations between Sumer and Iran begins again in the inscriptions of Gudea of Lagaš, whose rule probably extended from the late Gutian period into the reign of Ur-Nammu.[238] In an inscription celebrating the rebuilding of the E-Ninnu, Gudea states that he "smote the city/state (uru) of Anšan (in/of/and)[239] Elam; into the E-Ninnu he brought its booty for him [*i.e.* Ningirsu]".[240] The ensi of Lagaš may have been fighting as an ally of Ur-Nammu, who reports a victory over Elam/Anšan in a number of inscriptions.[241] If so, it would make all the more surprising that Gudea's many inscriptions make no reference to Ur-Nammu or other Ur III kings, a fact long regarded as grounds for dating him to the preceding Gutian period.[242]

Gudea details at length the sources of exotic materials employed in the construction of his great temple the E-Ninu. Among these foreign lands are listed the "Elamites of Elam and the Susians of Susiana", whose riches were perhaps elicited in the wake of the Sumerian conquest.[243]

6. PUZUR-INŠUŠINAK

Only once during the third millennium, around the beginning of the Ur III Dynasty, do contemporary inscriptions provide a picture of events from the Elamite perspective, more particularly from Susa. This is during the reign of Puzur-Inšušinak,[244] listed in the Susa king list as the twelfth and last "King of Awan". The king's reign, long thought to have fallen in the Akkadian period, has recently been more securely correlated with Ur-Nammu.[245] His accession marked the start of a patriotic revival, manifested above all in the use of a native 'linear Elamite' script (above pp. 75f.) alongside cuneiform, the legacy of Akkadian rule.

Like the Akkadian governors who preceded him, Puzur-Inšušinak took the titles "ensi of Susa" and "viceroy (GÌR.NITÁ) of Elam". But in two Akkadian inscriptions he calls himself "King of Awan (ZA-*wa-an*)" and adopts the Akkadian epithet *dannum* "mighty one".[246] Furthermore, one of these texts mentions "the year

---

[238] Steinkeller 1988a.
[239] The preposition relating Anšan and Elam – "in" (Steinkeller) or "and" (Steible) – is not explicit and thus leaves a crucial aspect of this inscription ambiguous.
[240] Statue B vi:64-69; *NBWI I*: 168; *NBWI II*: 27 n. 78; trans. after Steinkeller 1988a: 52.
[241] Steinkeller 1988a: 52f.; below p. 127.
[242] Sollberger 1954-56: 32.
[243] Cyl. A xv:6-7.
[244] "Puzur-" is the Akkadian version of the name; the Elamite has been reconstructed as "Kutik-".
[245] Wilcke 1987: 110. *Cf.* earlier datings based on general historical considerations (Boehmer, Lambert) and/or art-historical analysis of his monuments (Boehmer, Amiet): Boehmer 1966, Hinz 1972: 77f. (Naram-Sin to Šarkališarri); M. Lambert 1979: 16f. (immediately post-Šarkališarri); Amiet *apud* M. Lambert 1979: 24 (final or post-Akkadian); Stolper 1984: 15 (Šarkališarri or later).
[246] Elam 7:4f.; Elam 8:3-5; André & Salvini 1989: 65, ll. 3-5, 69f. A *cursus honorum* is sometimes reconstructed on the basis of these titles: first ensi of Susa, then also viceroy of Elam, and finally King of Awan (Hinz 1971: 652; Miroschedji 1980: 133 n. 28; André & Salvini 1989: 67-71; Vallat 1980: 5; for a different view see M. Lambert 1979: 15, n. 10). However, there is reason for caution: (1) In the text where Puzur-Inšušinak relates his conquests (Elam 2; see below) he is just "ensi of Susa and viceroy of Elam". (2) In texts which are accompanied by linear Elamite inscriptions, and may therefore be presumed to date to the period of greatest independence, he is just "ensi of Susa" (Elam 10), sometimes also "viceroy of Elam" (Elam 4), but never "king of Awan". This occurs only on two inscriptions on stone steps (Elam 8; see now André & Salvini 1989: 65, ll. 3-5). Corroborating these doubts, Vallat has recently suggested an

in which Inšušinak looked (graciously) upon him, and gave him dominion over the four quarters".[247] This is a clear allusion to the Akkadian epithet "king of the four quarters", adopted only by rulers with pretentions to 'world' domination. More details of his military exploits are provided by a lengthy statue inscription which lists the places conquered in suppressing a revolt of Kimaš and the land of Hurtum, both usually sought between the Hamrin and the Lower Zab.[248] More than seventy places were conquered, most of which are not otherwise attested and may be assumed to be minor settlements of the central western Zagros.[249] However, Huh(u)nuri, elsewhere called "the lock of Elam/Anšan", (and perhaps also Hupsana) extends the field of operations into Susiana.[250]

Puzur-Inšušinak's conquests also established supremacy over Šimaški, soon to achieve prominence as the seat of the preeminent Elamite dynasty. The king of Šimaški is said to have "grasped his [Puzur-Inšušinak's] feet" in submission.[251] This raises the possibility that Puzur-Inšušinak established some form of highland hegemony east of Susa, the site at which all of his extant inscriptions have been found. Anšan, on the other hand, is conspicuously absent from this account and was presumably ruled separately. Nor is there any reference to places in Mesopotamia, which might be taken to imply that Puzur-Inšušinak's direct dominion did not at this time extend westwards beyond the traditionally Elamite territory of lowland Susiana. An Ur-Nammu inscription, however, describes a battle involving Puzur-Inšušinak "in the land of the mountain of Elam," and then lists the Mesopotamian towns "Awal, Kismar, Maškanšarrum, the land of Ešnunna, the land of Tutub, the land of Zimudar, the land of Akkad, ...".[252] The context is broken but seems to suggest that these places had been ruled by Puzur-Inšušinak before their liberation by Ur-Nammu (below p. 127).[253] An inscription of Puzur-Inšušinak to the Diyala deity Belit-Terraban confirms his interest in this region.[254]

The texts do not state whether Puzur-Inšušinak was captured and removed from power by Ur-Nammu or allowed to rule on over a diminished territory as a Sumerian vassal. It is perhaps significant that there is no definite archaeological evidence of Ur III building or control at Susa until the reign of Šulgi (see below).

---

opposite scheme according to which énsi and GÌR.NITÁ were superior in the local titulature to "king", the latter title being adopted first and the others only later (Vallat 1990: 121).

[247] Elam 8:7-13.

[248] Elam 2.; for locations see *RGTC 2*: 81, 101; above p. 24.

[249] The Gu-UD of line 46 is perhaps to be read "Gutium" (Hallo 1971: 709).

[250] ll. 61, 18. On the location of Hupšan see Hinz 1972: 78; Amiet 1986: 26 (Deh-i Now); *RGTC 1*: 74 (in Elam). On Huhunuri see *RGTC 1*: 73 (Qal-i Toll, 20 km south of Malamir); Hansman 1972: 117-19 (Tang-i Has gorge, Fahliyun plain); Duchene 1986 (Arrajan near Behbehan).

[251] Elam 2:104-09.

[252] Wilcke 1987: 110f.

[253] On the basis of stylistic links with Akkadian statuary from the reign of Maništušu, Strommenger (1959: 36ff.) regards some of Puzur-Inšušinak's statues (*e.g.* Amiet 1976a: no. 35) as Babylonian booty. Such stylistic judgements, however, are contentious (*ibid.*: 37f.) especially since there is no adequate basis for saying what a local Susian piece would look like. Moreover, all of Puzur-Inšušinak's sculptures are in local light-coloured stones whereas those of the Akkadians tended to be in harder dark stones (Fig. 35; see below p. 190).

[254] *IRSA*: IIG2d; Elam 5-6.

7. Utu-hegal and the Expulsion of the Guti

Literary tradition unanimously attributes the expulsion of the Guti to Utu-hegal of Uruk. According to the king's account,[255] Tirigan, the last Gutian king, fled from the king's forces but was captured and handed over by the inhabitants of Dubrum (near Umma). Whether such details can be believed, it is clear that the remaining occupation was ousted by force of arms. This liberation was doubtless accompanied by patriotic rejoicing, since the Guti were regarded as bestial, barbaric and untutored in a way others of the Sumerians' traditional enemies were not.[256]

The Guti remained a thorn in the Sumerians' side under the kingdom of Ur when, according to royal inscriptions and praise hymns, Ur-Nammu (and perhaps Šulgi) were forced to wage war against them.[257] Never again, however, are they recorded as occupying Mesopotamian territory.

8. The Third Dynasty of Ur

During the last century of the third millennium native control of Babylonia was reestablished and consolidated under the leadership of the Third Dynasty of Ur. But beyond the Babylonian lowlands lay many peoples still openly or potentially hostile to the cities of Mesopotamia, and the Sumerian renaissance predictably saw the reappearance of an aggressive foreign policy. As in the case of the Akkadians, this need not imply wilful 'imperialism', for inaction in such circumstances would have been suicidal and was no real option.[258] The Guti were still a vivid memory and a firm military posture around the periphery of the Sumerian domain no doubt seemed a fundamental prerequisite of territorial security.

The hegemony of Ur came to involve direct rule of extensive territories beyond the Mesopotamian plain and an elaborate provincial system of regulation and security, which is copiously documented in contemporary archives.[259] A change in the main orientation of foreign intervention is apparent: except for the final desperate actions against the Amorites, less military activity was directed to the north-west where the Akkadians had been so active. Instead the Hurrian-dominated Zagros Mountains to the east and north-east were evidently now the focus of political expansion and unrest.

Direct evidence of Neo-Sumerian imperialism begins mid-way through the reign of Šulgi when year formulae, many recording military expeditions, were re-introduced. More discursive accounts of these campaigns in royal inscriptions are rare and concentrate towards the end of the dynasty.[260] Much other evidence is

---

[255] *IRSA*: IIK3a; Römer 1985. The authenticity of this composition, often regarded as doubtful (Römer 1985: 274f.), has been strengthened by the publication of a new tablet where it appears along with other authentic inscriptions of the king (Michalowski 1984: 124). See also *ABC*: Chron. 19:58-61.

[256] Cooper 1983a: 30f.; above pp. 24f.

[257] Michalowski 1976: 78; Civil 1985: 28f. col. iii´-iv´ (Ur-Nammu); Klein 1981: ll. 229f., 345f. (Šulgi D). Since no campaign against the Guti is recorded in Šulgi's known year names it has been suggested that this campaign, if it occurred at all, was waged against other eastern highlanders for whom "Gutians" was a convenient, though not necessarily accurate, designation (Klein 1981: 59f.).

[258] *Cf.* Larsen 1979: 79f., 92.

[259] *Ibid.*: 96; Steinkeller 1987.

[260] For royal inscriptions see Kärki 1986, (earlier listing by Hallo 1962), some also in *NBWI* (buildings and dedication inscriptions) and *AKI* (OAkk inscriptions). Add Civil 1985; Kutscher 1989: BT4 i-vi.

circumstantial and to various degrees questionable: the issuing of provisions to messengers on diplomatic missions ('messenger texts'); references to tribute (gún) and booty (nam-ra-ak); "Elamites" (NIM) or workers (erén), specified as coming from a certain place, under the supervision of Sumerian officers; references to foreign ensis or other officials in contexts which suggest their subservience to Ur; and so on. Before describing the pattern of Sumerian sovereignty that this evidence suggests it is relevant briefly to review its nature and limitations:

(1)   *Claims of conquest in royal inscriptions and year formulae.*[261] Claims to have "conquered" or "destroyed" a place may (in some cases) indicate raids rather than thorough conquests and need not have been followed by annexation. Indeed the evidence for repeated campaigns against certain places (*e.g.* Simurrum, Simanum, Karahar) belies the ineffectiveness of these actions. Since year formulae recording foreign conquests do not begin until mid-way through the reign of Šulgi earlier military activity is poorly attested.

(2)   *Claims to have taken booty.* Similar considerations apply.

(3)   *'Messenger texts'.*[262] These documents from Girsu and Umma record the issuing of rations to 'messengers' and various other functionaries[263] whose official business took them beyond the borders of Babylonia. Extant texts span the years from Šulgi 32 to Ibbi-Sin 2.[264] In the Girsu texts they are often qualified as coming from or going to a place in Susiana or the eastern highlands.[265] Such expeditions were overland but there are also rare references to messengers travelling by boat.[266] Many are described as the "messenger of PN, ensi/man of GN (foreign state)". Foreign officials of these and other types are listed also, sometimes even the "man" (*i.e.* ruler) or ensi himself.[267] Other texts cite the sukkal-lugal, dumu-lugal, and dumu-SAL-lugal.[268] Such references serve to prove diplomatic contact with the places mentioned, but since Ur III titulature is often ambiguous between independent potentates and Sumerian appointees, the dispatch and arrival of officials to and from rulers of foreign lands does not necessarily reflect the extent of direct Sumerian control (as is assumed by Jones *et al.*).[269] Delegates from friendly independent states, or even all foreign delegates, may have been assured safe passage and provisions. Officials coming from Anšan, Marhaši, Dilmun and even Magan are listed yet these places were almost certainly independent.[270] Frequency of reference may be thought to provide some basis for distinction, and in a large enough sample it might;[271] but, for the present, caution is counselled by the fact that Anšan, though not under Sumerian control, is among the most commonly cited places. Since the texts come exclusively from archives at Girsu and Umma, staging posts on the journey to the

---

[261] For full list of year formulae see Sigrist & Gomi 1991.

[262] See generally Jones *et al.* 1961: 280-310; McNeil 1971; Sigrist 1986; *idem* 1990.

[263] See the discussions of titles and functions in McNeil 1971: 23-31; Jones *et al.* 1961: 287, 290, 295f. McNeil is sceptical that these were all messengers.

[264] McNeil 1971: 31f.

[265] *Cf.* the list of destinations in Girsu texts in Fish 1954: 81-88.

[266] Sigrist 1986: 58f.

[267] *E.g.* the "man" of Marhaši (Steinkeller 1982: 261 n. 95) and the ensis of Susa and Sabum (Sigrist 1986: 54f.).

[268] Jones *et al.* 1961: 292f., 295; McNeil 1971: 62 n. 128.

[269] Jones *et al.* 1961: 302.

[270] Fish 1954 s.v.; *RGTC 2*: s.v.; Leemans 1960: 140; Spar 1987: no. 17.

[271] In 1961 texts recording only 10% of the days covered by the archives had been published (Jones *et al.* 1961: 284; *cf.* McNeil 1971: 35).

east and south-east, messengers travelling to and from the north(-west) will be under-represented.

(4)   'Elamites' (NIM). Many messenger texts record the assignment of poor rations to bands of people qualified as "NIM of GN", literally "Elamites" or "highlanders" from places in the east and north-east.[272] Many of these states owed loyalty to Ur by right of conquest, and their NIM were probably conscript troops or mercenaries. Some, however, may have been captured in expeditions which did not lead to annexation, and others were perhaps corvée labourers (below p. 138).

(5)   *Deliveries of animals and other goods as taxes and loyal offerings.* Friendly independent states as well as provinces can sometimes be shown to have supplied animals or other offerings as proof of goodwill and to stave off the threat of appropriation.

(6)   *Diplomatic marriages.*[273] Marriages between members of the Sumerian royal family and foreign rulers are a conspicuous aspect of Neo-Sumerian foreign policy. Though attested in earlier times, it was only in this period that they were regularly employed as a means of fostering or cementing amicable relations with foreign powers. As applied, however, the practice again bridges the key distinction between independent rulers and subject governors. Daughters could be married off to Sumerian governors at home as well as to foreign potentates who, so far from being loyal vassals, were sometimes the objects of military campaigns.[274] Šulgi, for example, attacked Anšan only four years after sending his daughter there to wed.

(7)   *The 'Royal Correspondence of Ur'.*[275] These letters, purportedly to and from the kings of Ur, very probably have an historical basis. However, their incorporation into the body of Sumerian literature inevitably introduces the possibility of later editing and interpolation, seriously compromising their usefulness as historical sources.

(8)   *Inscriptions, sculptured reliefs and other monuments of eastern rulers employing Mesopotamian language and literary or artistic styles.* Lowland artistic and literary motifs were adopted by a number of Zagros rulers of the Ur III to Old Babylonian periods.[276] Although such monuments evidence the dissemination of Mesopotamian culture, they are not a reliable gauge of political alignment. Indeed, some of the rulers represented seem on the contrary to have been among the fiercest enemies of Sumer and Akkad. Moreover, such monuments were sometimes usurped and reinscribed by later rulers, making dating and attribution problematic.

Each line of evidence has its shortcomings and none can in isolation be regarded as decisive proof of Sumerian rule. Where their testimony is complementary, however, the presumption of Sumerian control is a reasonable working hypothesis. We turn now to a more detailed consideration of the four key areas in the foreign relations of Ur: Susiana and lowland Elam; Anšan and highland Elam; the 'Hurrian frontier'; and the 'Amorite frontier'.

(a) Susiana and Lowland Elam

Susa may have returned to Mesopotamian control under Ur-Nammu in the aftermath of his victory over Puzur-Inšušinak (see above), but it is only under Šulgi

---

[272] Jones *et al.* 1961: 228.
[273] Listed by Sigrist & Butz 1986: 27, n. 4; previously Röllig 1975.
[274] Stolper 1982: 53, n. 37.
[275] See generally Michalowski 1976; *idem* 1983; and a forthcoming major study by the same author, *The Royal Correspondence of Ur.*
[276] *E.g.* Börker-Klähn 1982: 138ff., nos 30-32, 34, N34; al-Fouadi 1978.

that historical and archaeological evidence from the site confirms its incorporation into the burgeoning empire of Ur.[277] By the end of Šulgi's reign there is also evidence of control over Adamdun in southern Susiana,[278] and an archival text shows that the king had married one of his daughters to the "ruler (lú) of Pašime" on the coast of the Gulf. This region too was soon bought under direct Sumerian rule, either by Amar-Suen or Šu-Sin. The conquest of Pašime's near (northern?) neighbour Huhnuri, commemorated by Amar-Suen in his seventh year name, may mark the beginning of a concerted drive to the south-east.[279]

Once conquered, Susa and the surrounding lowland territories were thoroughly integrated into the Ur III imperial administration and remained under direct Sumerian control until the disintegration of the empire early in the reign of Ibbi-Sin.[280] Sumerian civil and military governors (ensis and šagins) organised affairs under the direction of the central government. As in Babylonia, they seem to have functioned as instruments of royal policy, answerable to the king and unable to exercise real independence in matters of any importance. Susian officials frequently travelled to the capital, presumably to report on developments in the east. Governors could be transferred from post to post. In this way, for a brief half-century, the natural geographical unity of Susiana and Sumer again found political expression in a centralised Mesopotamian leadership, as it had previously under the rulers of Akkad.

(b) Anšan and Highland Elam

A recently discovered Ur-Nammu inscription from Isin describes a campaign in which the king engaged an army of Elamites under Puzur-Inšušinak and liberated various regions of northern Babylonia and the Trans-Tigris.

> ... I, ⌜Ur-Nammu⌝, the mighty, king of Sumer and Akkad, dedicated (this) for my (text: his) life. At that time, Enlil brought to the Elamites ... In the territory of the land of Elam (they) went to battle with each other. Their king, Puzur-Inšušinak, ... (verb lost) Awal, Kismar, Maškanšarrum, the land of

---

[277] Šulgi was remembered as a conqueror of Susa in later literature (Borger 1971: iii:20´ff.) and has left evidence of building activity on the site (below note 280). Hinz 1971: 655 dated the event to Š28, but M. Lambert 1979: 30 notes the significance of a macehead from Susa dedicated to the undeified Šulgi (Scheil 1913: 22), which should belong early in his reign and thus supports an Ur-Nammu conquest (Hallo 1957: 60). The gún, 'tribute/tax' of Susa is mentioned in a text dated to Š46 (Michalowski 1978: 48).

[278] *RGTC 1*: 5. Deliveries of sheep from Adamdun to Sumer in Š44 and after (Michalowski 1978: 42).

[279] Steinkeller 1982: 241-43 nn. 16-18.

[280] Evidence of Ur III building activity at Susa is provided by inscribed bricks and foundation inscriptions: *NBWI II*: Šulgi 6, 12, Amar-Suen 16, Šu-Sin 1 (add Vallat 1980a: 135), 2; *cf.* also the loyal inscriptions *NBWI II*: Šulgi 40, 43. An ensi of Susa, Urkium, perhaps a Sumerian appointee (Hinz 1971: 655), is known already in Š34 (*RTC* 329: 3; *RGTC 2*: 190); one of Adamdun in Š43 (Goetze 1963: 16; Michalowski 1978: 38ff.); and a military governor (šagin) of Pašime (Arad-Nanna) by the reign of Šu-Sin (*IRSA*: IIIB5a). Zariqum, ensi of Susa from AS4 to ŠS4, was certainly a Sumerian appointee who had served previously (Š47 to AS5) as governor of Aššur (Hallo 1956; dates adjusted after Kutscher 1979) and perhaps also before that at Susa (in Š40; Kutscher 1979). The military governor Šamši-illat, who accompanied Zariqum to Susa in Š40, may have been responsible for the protection of Susa at that time. The provincial administration's workings at Susa are well attested by Sumerian documents (beginning in the reign of Amar-Suen), the oldest texts (other than rare seal inscriptions) in this language known from the site (Scheil 1908: nos 125, 126; *idem* 1939: nos 424, 454, 467; *cf.* Stève *et al.* 1980: 87, 133). Tablets dated by imperial formulae cease in IS3 (Jacobsen 1953: 38) which provides a probable marker for the province's secession. On the sequence of revolt see Wilcke 1960; Sollberger 1976: 2; Michalowski 1976: 87f.

> Ešnunna, the land of Tutub, the land of Zimudar, the land of Akkad, the
> peo[ple ...].[281]

Although the text breaks off, the context suggests that these regions had previously
fallen under Elamite control[282] and were now nominally 'liberated' by Ur-Nammu
(though it is questionable whether he actually campaigned this far north).[283] All
except Agade are to the north of Babylonia in the region of the Diyala, Jebel Hamrin
and Tikrit.[284] The inclusion of the "land of Akkad" is more surprising, especially if, as
Wilcke suggests, that area extended further south than is generally realised.[285]

This interpretation of the Isin text is supported by a recently published
fragment of the 'Ur-Nammu' law code which also describes a conflict with Elam.
Whether this code was promulgated by Ur-Nammu or by Šulgi (with the prologue
providing a flash-back to events in his father's reign) is still disputed.[286] However, the
fact that a conflict with Elam is recorded also in the Isin tablet and other Ur-Nammu
texts (see below) makes it very probable that at least this part of the text describes
events in the reign of Ur-Nammu.[287]

The passage relates:

> at that time Akšak (?), Mar(a)da, Girkal (?), Kazallu, and their settlements,
> (and) Uṣarum, (and) whatsoever had been enslaved by Anšan, through the
> strength of Nanna, my lord, I established their freedom.[288]

Here it is explicitly stated that Anšan had exercised control over Mesopotamian
territory until some point in Ur-Nammu's (or Šulgi's) reign. None of the places – all in
northern Babylonia – corresponds to those specified by name in the Isin tablet, but
could be covered by the latter's blanket "land of Akkad".[289] The same events again
may be related in another fragmentary inscription of Ur-Nammu,[290] which describes
a conflict when "all the ensis of Elam, like birds stealing eggs together, committed
murder against him".[291] However, the text (here increasingly damaged) goes on to
relate a war with the Guti under Gutarla so perhaps "Elam" (NIM) is intended here in
the generic sense of "highland(ers)".[292]

Ur-Nammu's son Šulgi evidently maintained the offensive, taking the war into
Iran. In years 5 and 19 he restored and fortified the Elamite border town of Dêr, near
modern Badra,[293] though he later (Š21) claims its destruction. In year 30 Šulgi sent a

---

[281] Wilcke 1987: 109ff.
[282] As does also Puzur-Inšušinak's dedication inscription to the Diyala deity Belit-Terraban (*IRSA*: IIG2d).
[283] The Cadastre of Ur-Nammu (Kraus 1955) mentions several places in the north of Babylonia (*e.g.* Kazallu, Apiak, Kiš, Marad), but the new text is the only source which suggests that he gained control of that region (*ibid.*: 55ff.). No contemporary inscriptions of the king have been recovered from there.
[284] Steinkeller 1981: 164f.; *RGTC 1, 2*: s.v.; Wilcke 1987: 110.
[285] Wilcke 1987: 110f. Alternatively, this may be a second, Trans-Tigridian Agade.
[286] Yıldız 1981; Kramer 1983; Steinkeller 1987: 19f. n. 1; *cf.* Michalowski & Walker 1989; Geller 1992: 145f.
[287] Steinkeller 1987: 20 n. 1 addendum; *idem* 1988a: 52.
[288] Translation after Steinkeller 1987: 19 n. 1; Yıldız 1981: 93; Michalowski 1986: 140f. n. 22.
[289] Wilcke 1987: 110f.
[290] Only traces of the royal name are preserved, so the attribution to Ur-Nammu is not certain (Civil 1985: 27).
[291] Civil 1985: 28, col. ii :7´-9´; *ibid.*: 30.
[292] A third fragmentary inscription mentioning events near the Taban river and stating that the king (Ur-Nammu?) "conquered the cities and ruled (them)" (Frag. C7; Frayne 1992: 631f.) may also relate to the conquest of this area.
[293] Michalowski 1976: 78.

daughter to marry the ruler of Anšan;[294] but this *prima facie* act of goodwill evidently failed, or perhaps it was only ever a ploy, for four years later he led an army against his son-in-law. The destruction of Anšan was commemorated for three years (Š34-36) and some archival texts have been plausibly interpreted as lists of booty from this victory.[295] One text records the objects of precious metals, stones, garments, copper, bronze *etc.* deposited in temples as "treasure (gi_{16}-sa) of Elam" and is dated to the year of the defeat of Anšan. Davidović argues that two further texts, dated two years later, listing similar goods which are described by a word (nì-ga) also translated as "treasure", are likewise from this campaign.[296]

Such exploits were apparently beyond Šulgi's successors and no further expeditions against the highland capital are recorded. Unable and probably unwilling to bring Anšan within the orbit of the Neo-Sumerian empire, relations between Ur and the highland capital were henceforth restricted to diplomatic exchanges. The lines of communication were kept open, messengers from Anšan frequenting the court at Ur and *vice versa*,[297] but supremacy seems not to have been conceded by either side and a stable *modus vivendi* was never achieved. Only a few isolated instances are preserved in what must have been a perennially fluid and unpredictable relationship. Both Amar-Suen (AS7) and Ibbi-Sin (IS9) claim the conquest of Huhnuri, which the latter describes as "the bolt/lock of the land of Anšan (var.: Elam)".[298] Like Šulgi, Šu-Sin probably sent a daughter to marry the ensi of Anšan,[299] though whether at this point this should be interpreted as a sign of strength or weakness is unclear.

There is relatively little evidence of military action against other highland regions of Elam and its neighbours with the notable exception of Šimaški. A Lagaš text dated near the end of Šulgi's reign (Š46) referring to "the donated slaves of Guriname"[300] – almost certainly the like-named first king of Šimaški – suggests that this nascent 'Elamite' state was not yet openly hostile.[301] The situation was evidently different by the reign of Šu-Sin, however, who led a major expedition against the six "lands of Šimaški". The prominence accorded this campaign in Šu-Sin's inscriptions[302] leaves no doubt but that it was regarded as a highly significant victory, and the destruction of Šimaški's principal region Zabšali was duly commemorated in the king's seventh year formula.

The most informative sources are two dedication inscriptions preserved on a single Old Babylonian tablet from Nippur. Whether these represent different accounts of one campaign or two different campaigns (and if so which came first) is not certain: the geographical names are the same, and both relate at the end how the king made a gold statue of himself from the booty taken and dedicated it to Enlil at Nippur; but the accounts differ in the name of the ensi/king of Zabšali.[303]

---

[294] Röllig 1975: 283.
[295] Pettinato 1982; Davidović 1984, texts B and C.
[296] Davidović's Text D, dated to AS3, records "treasure" (gi_{16}-sa) of different types of objects, probably representing booty taken in a later campaign, perhaps against Urbilum which Amar-Suen defeated the year before, or from the Amorites whose "booty" is mentioned in a list dated AS2 (Michalowski 1976: 81f.).
[297] Fish 1954: s.v. Anšan.
[298] Sollberger 1976: 5f. Above note 250.
[299] Michalowski 1975: 716, n. 8; Sigrist & Butz 1986: 27.
[300] Steinkeller 1988: 201f.
[301] Note also the text dated ŠS6 recording messengers from *inter alia* Girname (Kirname) (Stolper 1982: 49).
[302] Kärki 1986: ŠS20a, ŠS21; Kutscher 1989: BT4 i-vi, viii-xii:12 [=Ur C2] + Oelsner 1989: 407f. Note also the parallel inscriptions on dedications to Ninlil (in OB cursive script) (Edzard 1959-60: Inschr. B; Sjöberg 1972: 70-73).
[303] *Cf.* Kutscher 1989: 98-101, arguing for two campaigns.

The first inscription,[304] written in Sumerian, relates how "Šimaški (LÚ.SU^{ki}), (which comprises?) the lands of Zabšali, rose like locusts from the borders of Anšan up to the Upper (Caspian?) Sea".[305] The text then list Nibulmat, [...]m, Sigriš, Alumidatim, Garta, Azahar, Bulma, Nušušmar, Nušganelum, Zizirtum, Arahir, Šatilu, Tirmium and [...], places known from other inscriptions as "lands of Šimaški/Zabšali" (see below). Šu-Sin describes how, after defeating the enemy forces, he "captured their lords and kings as bound (prisoners), ... turned their firmly established cities and countryside into mounds (and) razed their walls". Bulma (of unknown location) seems to have been singled out for special punishment: "Bulma, the land of Šimaški, its people, male, female, life-breathing, having a name, he [killed] with weapons". A label identifying "Ziringu, ensi of the land of Zabšali" on the monument is annotated by the Old Babylonian scribe as "an inscription of Ziringu, the bound/captured king (lugal heš₅)".

In the second inscription,[306] a much briefer text written in Akkadian, the ensi of Zabšali is given as Indasu. The text states that Šu-Sin destroyed the six lands of Šimaški, here specified as Zabšali, Sigriš, Nibulmat, Alumidatum, Garta and Šatilu. More geographical names follow, no doubt of places that were also destroyed, but the text breaks off.[307] After describing the dedication of the gold statue, the labels of the figures represented on the monument are listed, including: "Indasu, ensi of Zabšali", described by the copyist as "the bound/captured king".[308] Ten other Iranian ensis of Šimaškian (?) lands are likewise described as "prisoners", suggesting that they too were taken alive.[309]

Large quantities of gold and other booty were taken from Zabšali and Šimaški and dedicated to the temples of Sumer.[310] Having "blinded the young men whom he reached in their cities", Šu-Sin enslaved the men and women and dedicated them, together with large numbers of livestock and donkeys, to the temples of Enlil and Ninlil. Gold, silver, copper, tin, bronze and artefacts "he loaded on pack donkeys ... he made them eternal in the temple of Enlil, the temple of Ninlil and the temples of the great gods". Finally the king "fashioned the gold of the lands of Šimaški (LÚ.SU^{ki}) that he had taken as booty into a statue of himself and dedicated it to Enlil, his king, for his life". In another inscription referring to his Šimaškian campaign Šu-Sin also notes a he-goat which he took as the "tribute" (gú-un) of Anšan.[311]

Did Šu-Sin attempt to rule Šimaški? The campaign inscriptions make no such claim yet Šu-sin's sukkalmah Arad-Nanna lists Šimaški (LÚ.SU^{ki}) among the regions

---

[304] Kärki 1986: ŠS20a; Kutscher 1989: BT4:i-vi.

[305] Kutscher 1989: BT4 ii:14-20.

[306] Kutscher 1989: BT4 viii-xii:12 [=Ur C2] + Oelsner 1989: 407f.

[307] Azahar, Bulma, Nušušmar, [N]ušg[an]e[l]um, [Z]izir[t]um, [A]rahir, [...] (Ur C2:23-25 + Oelsner 1989: 407); unlike the previous six, these are not described as "land of GN", but just "GN" (perhaps cities?). However, in the first inscription (BT4 ii:21-33) these places occur (in the same order) mid-way through a list headed "Šimaški (LÚ.SU^{ki}), lands of Zabšali", which includes also those here called the "six lands of Šimaški", suggesting that they too were in some sense regarded as Šimaškian territories.

[308] Ur C2: R09:33-R10:12.

[309] Titi, ensi of Nušušmar, Samri ensi of [...], Nu[...]li ensi of Alumidatum, Bunirni ensi of [S]igriš, Barihiza ensi of Arahir, Waburtum ensi of [Lu²]lubum – "six prisoners (lú šu-du₈-a-me-eš)"; Nenibzu ensi of Zizirtum, Tirubiu ensi of Nušganelum, [...]amti ensi of Garta, Dungat ensi of Ni[bul]ma[t] – "[four priso]ners". The names seem not to be Hurrian or Elamite and so far cannot be categorised (except for a few possibly Semitic: PN Waburtum, GN *Alu-middatum).

[310] Kärki 1986: ŠS20a:Inscr. 1; *IRSA*: IIIA4e-g; Kutscher 1989: BT4; Ur C2:48-57.

[311] Kärki 1986: ŠS21 i:19'f.=*IRSA*: IIIA4g. The text refers to making a statue of this animal (Michalowski 1975: 43 seems to interpret this as saying that the statue itself was taken but the text states that Šu-Sin fashioned it). It is doubtful that the episode indicates any real submission on the part of Anšan, and questionable even whether any official tribute was handed over. A single goat can hardly have constituted such, and one should probably interpret it as a "diplomatic gift" (*cf.* Steinkeller 1982: 253, n. 60).

under his generalship.[312] While not conclusive this at least raises the possibility that Šu-Sin's campaigns were more than just raids and that Šimaški fell for a while under Sumerian rule. Seven years later (IS5) Šu-Sin's successor Ibbi-Sin married a daughter to the ruler of Zabšali, probably to stave off hostility at a time when the empire was already beginning to disintegrate. [313]

Of Marhaši we hear only that Šulgi's daughter was elevated to the 'queenship' of that land (Š18) and that Ibbi-Sin received a "speckled Meluhhan dog/leopard (ur)" as the "tribute (gún^{un})" of Marhaši.[314] As in the case of the he-goat taken by Šu-Sin as the "tribute" of Anšan in his Šimaškian campaign, this is probably to be understood as a diplomatic gift and need not imply effective sovereignty.[315] Such diplomacy apparently succeeded in averting the more direct military confrontations which had characterised relations with Marhaši under the Akkadians.

Many other highland towns and regions of greater Elam, which are not recorded as the objects of military actions, may be plausibly included within the empire of Ur on the basis of administrative texts recording their "tribute/tax" (in basic foodstuffs) and their local rulers, many with Sumerian names, who seem to receive instructions from Ur. This evidence is considered below (p. 139).

(c) The 'Hurrian Frontier'

The military expeditions of the Ur III kings were directed principally against what Hallo has called the 'Hurrian frontier' stretching in an arc along the Zagros Mountains from south of the Diyala to the upper Habur basin.[316] These campaigns feature prominently in the royal correspondence and account for a large proportion of the year formulae from mid-way through the reign of Šulgi[317] to the collapse of the empire under Ibbi-Sin, a span of something less than fifty years, indicating the crucial importance of this region in the foreign affairs of the empire.

Of the places cited as objects of expeditions, Simurrum (on the Lower Zab?) comes in for repeated attack when this area was first being subdued by Šulgi[318] and once again when the empire was disintegrating under Ibbi-Sin. Kar(a)har is prominent under Šulgi but then disappears. Šašrum and Urbilum[319] are each mentioned once under Šulgi and again under Amar-Suen, while Harši, Lulubum, Kimaš, and Hu(m)urti each feature twice in Šulgi's year names,[320] in some cases in successive years.

---

312 Kärki 1986: ŠS13:25=*IRSA*: IIIB5a.
313 Röllig 1975: 283.
314 Kärki 1986: IS12:9-18. Sollberger 1976: 2 suggests that this was taken on the campaign against Simurrum in year 3.
315 Steinkeller 1982: 253, n. 60.
316 Hallo 1978. See Michalowski 1986: 138f., 146f. for the Ur III distribution of Hurrian names, much expanding the list in Gelb 1944. They now extend from the Upper Diyala region (Šetirša, Šuruthum, Simurrum etc.) to the northern Zagros (Urbilum, Simanum) and possibly Ebla. For Simurrum see also Whiting 1987: 30.
317 Š24 records the first foreign conquest (Karahar). The scarcity of year formulae or other historical evidence for the reign of Ur-Nammu precludes any judgement as to whether these expeditions had begun earlier.
318 The year formula for Š44 reports the "ninth" conquest of Simurrum, and it is again destroyed the following year. The newly published inscription of the "Gutian" king Erridupizir relates that a "Kanišba, king of Simurrum, instigated the people of Simurrum and Lulubum to rebel" (Kutscher 1989: BT2+3 viii:8´-15´) but was crushed by Erridupizir.
319 Nirišuha, ensi of Urbilum, also took part in the rebellion against Erridupizir (see previous note).
320 Lulubum perhaps three times (Edzard 1959-60: 2). Note also the possible inclusion of Lulubum among the Šimaškian enemies of Šu-Sin in Ur C2: Beischrift (h).

The locations of these places are in varying degrees uncertain but their broad placement and relative proximity to Sumer are reasonably secure.[321] Šulgi's campaigns, which Hallo groups into three 'Hurrian wars',[322] were conducted nearest Sumer at the southern extreme of the frontier, between the Upper Diyala (Lulubum) and Urbilum (Arbela). The first two wars (Š24-27 and Š31-33) focused almost entirely on Karahar and Simurrum; and even the third war does not seem to have been pursued beyond the Upper Zab, though this did not prevent him adopting the Akkadian title "king of the four quarters".[323] After the second war Šulgi built "the wall of the unincorporated territories (ma-da)" (Š37)[324] whose line marked the effective limit of Sumerian control. As rebuilt by Šu-Sin, this ran from the Abgal canal of the westernmost Euphrates to the Tigris and Zimudar in the Diyala.[325]

The third Hurrian war (Š42-48) saw Šulgi broadening the offensive to include Šašrum (Š42), Urbilum (Š45), Lulubum (Š44, 45), and Kimaš, Humurti and "their lands" (Š46, 48).[326] Operations were also necessary against the familiar territories of Simurrum (Š44, 45) – which was by now incorporated as a province[327] – Karahar (Š45) and Harši (Š48). A number of texts record the booty taken in these campaigns and include also booty of Šimaški (LÚ.SU(.A)) and the Amorites (Mardu).[328]

Aššur was governed by a Sumerian appointee at least from Š47, and control was maintained by Šulgi's successors,[329] suggesting that the Middle Tigris was now firmly incorporated into the empire.[330] The southern end of the Hurrian frontier seems to have been quiet, and in Amar-Suen's reign military activity concentrated instead on the more distant outposts around or beyond the Lesser Zab, notably Urbilum (AS2) and Šašrum and Šurudhum (AS6), the latter pair "for the second time". Diplomatic contacts were maintained with Simanum in the far north-west[331] and the marriage of Šu-Sin's daughter to one of the sons of its Hurrian ruler had probably now taken place.[332] Relations soured, however, in the reign of Šu-Sin who relates that Simanum, along with Habura (in the upper Habur?), rebelled, expelling

---

[321] Above pp. 21-24.

[322] Hallo 1978: appendix II.

[323] *Cf.* also the OB "omen of Šulgi who subdued the four regions" (Goetze 1963: 14 n. 37). This tradition is reflected in the Weidner Chronicle's statement that Marduk gave Šulgi "sovereignty over all lands" (*ABC*: Chron. 19:63).

[324] See also letters U.6, U.10, U.11. References to the royal correspondence follow Michalowski 1976.

[325] U.17:6-11; Michalowski 1976: 113ff.; *cf. RGTC 2*: end map 2.

[326] Other evidence of the conquest of Kimaš (here coupled with Hurtum) includes a stamped brick from Susa (Ur 5: 8-9; Kärki 1986: Š71) and an unpublished text mentioning the capture of the ensi of Kimaš (Hallo 1978: 77 n. 68).

[327] maš-da-ri-a offerings from Simurrum are recorded as early as Š40 (Hallo 1978: 77). An ensi of Simurrum, Šilluš-Dagan, was installed already by Š42 (*ibid.*: 77f.) and is often mentioned in Drehem texts thereafter till IS1 (Goetze 1963: 13f.). These data suggest an annexation earlier than the Š44 campaign. Šulgi's previous capture of the Hurrian ensi of Simurrum, Tabban-darah, probably in Š32 (Hallo 1978: 74), is related in three OB omens (Goetze 1947: 259f. nos 25-27). Thereafter, he and his family appear in a number of Drehem texts (Hallo 1978: 74f.). Under Šu-Sin he is still called "the man of Simurrum" and must, therefore, have remained active after his deposition, perhaps even retaining some connection with Simurrum. Later literary and omen texts which may allude to the capture of Tabban-darah are noted by Hallo 1978: 75f. An "Idi-Sin, mighty king of Simurrum" and his son Zabazuna appear in an Ur III or OB monumental inscription from the Raniyah plain on the Lower Zab (al Fouadi 1978).

[328] Michalowski 1976: 81f.; *idem* 1978; Lieberman 1968-69: 53-62; Gelb 1973: 74-77.

[329] Hallo 1956; Kutscher 1979 for adjusted dates.

[330] *Cf.* Michalowski 1976: 116.

[331] Simanum is tentatively located between the Upper Tigris and the Upper Habur (Hallo 1978: 83 [map]; Civil 1967: 36).

[332] The details are related in Šu-Sin's historical inscriptions (Kärki 1986: ŠS20b i-v; previously Civil 1967: 29-31). Michalowski (1975) argues that the marriage occurred late in the reign of Šulgi. Certainly it preceded ŠS3 when this invasion is recorded in the year formula.

his daughter and the governor Pušam.[333] The king attacked and reduced the city, reinstating his daughter and probably the loyal governor.[334] He also took the interesting precaution of forcibly resettling the people of Simanum "on the frontier of Nippur".[335]

Šu-Sin's Simanum-Habura expedition represents the furthest recorded extension of Sumerian military intervention into Hurrian territory.[336] Almost from the beginning of Ibbi-Sin's reign (IS3), the frontier had retreated to Simurrum, and all pretence of Sumerian control over the more distant Hurrian centres must swiftly have been dispelled.

(d) The Amorite Frontier and the Collapse of Ur

Friendly diplomatic relation involving royal marriages, exchanges of envoys and diplomatic gifts were maintained with the sedentary Semites of the north-west such as Mari and Ebla. The nomadic Amorites, however, were a very different matter. Šulgi's chief minister Arad-mu (see below) reports in a letter to the king that the Amorites had been defeated and turned back to the mountains.[337] But their incursions continued to escallate. Šulgi's year 37 was named for the building of "the wall of the (unincorporated) territories (bàd ma-da)".[338] This was completed by Šu-Sin,[339] and its new name – "the wall of the Amorites for keeping Tidnum at bay (bàd mar-tu mu-ri-iq ti-id-ni-im)" – now indicates clearly the nature of the threat it was designed to avert: not the Hurrians but the Amorites, whose growing pressure is reflected also in the royal correspondence.[340] A letter from the governor Šarrumbani to Šu-Sin is explicit:

---

333 Note also Šu-Sin's Šimaški/Zabšali text BT4 v:1-18 (Kutscher 1989: 90f.) which refers in a damaged context to Ha[bura] and [Mar]daman and the mining(?) of silver and gold.

334 Kärki 1986: ŠS20a=*IRSA*: IIIA4e-f. This is the interpretation of Michalowski 1975, followed by Hallo 1978: 79; M. Lambert's (1979: 34 n. 104) interpretation of the text as stating that his daughter was installed in the new city near Nippur is less plausible.

335 Kärki 1986: ŠS20b v:3; *cf.* Civil 1967: 36, comm. to ll. 36ff.

336 The question of control over Subir/Subartu, apparently a general designation for nothern Mesopotamia at this time, remains unclear. There are no explicit Ur III references to its conquest or control, as there are for Akkadian times (Michalowski 1986: 135ff.). Hallo argues that Šulgi's adoption of the title "king of the four quarters" assumes control of Subir and mar-dú (=Amurru). More suggestive are some passages in the royal correspondence from the sukkalmah Arad-mu to Šulgi: "You have instructed me to take the road to Subir to put in order the taxes (gú-un) of the unincorporated territories (ma-da)" (Michalowski 1976: 136ff.). See also letter U.4 quoted in main text below; and U.21: 35 (Michalowski 1976: 142) reporting that Išbi-Erra has captured Zinnum the ensi of Subir. Furthermore, if Hallo's restorations of 2nd and 1st mill. literary and omen texts about Šulgi are correct (Hallo 1978: 75f.), Simurrum and Kimaš fell within the territory covered by Subir in the usage of those times. "Subir on the borders of the Upper Sea (*i.e.* Lake Urmia?)" appears in a Šu-Sin inscription (Kärki 1986: ŠS20b Rs i´:9´ = Civil 1967: 37 ll. 5´-11´) in a list of far-flung places (including also Ebla, Urkiš and Magan) apparently beyond his control but perhaps honouring him on some occasion (Michalowski 1986: 141). In view of the generally propagandistic nature of these sources and the Ur III kings' general lack of interest in the far north, it may on balance be considered unlikely that they ever conquered or controlled Subir.

337 Letter U.6.

338 In the royal correspondence Puzur-Šulgi/Numušda calls it "the wall facing the highland" (U.9, U.10, U.11; Michalowski 1976: 84; *cf. RGTC 2*: 23f. which takes this as a place name).

339 ŠS4; *IRSA*: IIIA4f.

340 However, there is evidence that to some extent the Amorites and Hurrians threatened from the same direction. A letter from Šarrum-bani states: "... the Amorites were camped in the mountain(s). Simurrum had come to their aid. (Therefore) I proceeded to (the area) 'between' the mountain range(s) of Ebih [Jebel Hamrin] in order to do battle" (U.17:14-16; Michalowski 1976: 229). "Booty of the Amorites" is recorded in years named for the defeat of places whose rulers have Hurrian names. *Cf.* Michalowski 1976: 103-09, who argues that the chief "land of the Amorites" was north-east of Babylonia, not to the north-west (Jebel Bishri) as is generally believed.

> You have instructed me to build the wall to cut off their [the Amorites'] path (so that) they may not overwhelm the field(s) by a breach between the Tigris and Euphrates.[341]

Under Ibbi-Sin this pressure increased dramatically and the imperial defenses eventually proved unable to stem the tide. The deteriorating economic and political situation can be traced in contemporary economic texts (which show barley trading at up to sixty times its usual price) as well as the royal correspondence.[342] A letter from Išbi-Erra to Ibbi-Sin relates: "And now all of the Amorites have entered into the land. One by one they have seized all the fortifications. Because of the Amorites I have been unable to thresh the grain. They are too strong for me, I am trapped."[343] Judging by the cessation of imperial year names, Ešnunna fell away from the control of Ur in the king's second year, Puzriš-Dagan in year three, Umma in year five or six, Lagaš in year six (depriving the king of his powerful sukkalmah Arad-Nanna/Mu), and Isin and Nippur in year eight. Against this background the king's seventeenth year name, ostentatiously celebrating the obeisance of "the Amorites, the strength of the south wind, who from old had not known cities", is probably to be seen as an attempt to achieve by propaganda what he had been unable to achieve on the battlefield.

The loss of Isin in IS8 stemmed from the effective desertion of Šu-Sin's general Išbi-Erra, with whom the king was increasingly forced to divide his kingdom during the latter two-thirds of his reign. The letter from Išbi-Erra quoted above and another from "Šulgi" (originally Ibbi-Sin) to Išbi-Erra provide the background to their split.[344] Ibbi-Sin had evidently been driven by the Amorite threat to consider some kind of alliance with "the Elamites".[345] Išbi-Erra, away from Ur on a grain procuring mission, warns the king against any such compromise, urging him instead to trust in him (Išbi-Erra) for which purpose he asks to be placed in charge of Nippur and Isin. Ibbi-Sin's reply is sharp, but the king desperately needed the grain now controlled by Išbi-Erra and had no option but to agree. Išbi-Erra duly took charge of Nippur and Isin, henceforth adopting his own year dates (IE1 = IS8).[346] A letter from Puzur-Numušda, ensi of Kazallu, to Ibbi-Sin recounts Išbi-Erra's subsequent conquests.[347] In his reply the king hopes against hope that one enemy will prove his salvation against the other: "Now Enlil has stirred up the Amorites from out of the land; they will strike down the Elamites and capture Išbi-Erra".[348]

In the context of such turmoil at home it is not surprising that the Ur's eastern domains soon began to fall away. The provinces of the periphery had stopped contributing taxes already in the last year of Šu-Sin and receipts cease completely in IS2, leading to the collapse of the redistributive (bala) system by the king's fifth year, when the officialdom of the collecting centres was disbanded and evacuated to Ur. Expeditions to Simurrum in IS3 and Huhnuri in IS9 were acts of desperation at a

---

[341] U.17:6-8.

[342] Jacobsen 1953; Hallo 1960; Gomi 1984.

[343] Michalowski 1976: U.19:7-12 = Sollberger 1976: 7 no. 2.

[344] Sollberger 1976: letters 1, 2; Michalowski 1976: 88, 249, U.19:24-28. Jacobsen 1953: 41 and van de Mieroop 1987a: 126 date this correspondence to IS6.

[345] This is perhaps the background to the marriage of Ibbi-Sin's daughter to the ruler of Zabšali in IS5 (above p. 131).

[346] Sollberger *loc. cit.*: letter 3. Year dates of Ibbi-Sin follow Sigrist & Gomi 1991; those of Išbi-Erra follow van de Mieroop 1987a: 125f., followed by Sigrist 1988, superceding Kienast 1965.

[347] Sollberger 1976: 7 no. 4.

[348] Sollberger 1976: 7 no. 5; Kramer 1963: 334f. no. 6.

time when the empire was already a dead letter. Susa seceded in, or soon after, Ibbi-Sin's third year and it is unlikely that the king ever regained effective control during his remaining twenty-one years of reign. Messenger texts cease in the same year.[349] Despite the allusion to a possible Elamite alliance in the royal correspondence, contemporary documents record only the escallation of hostilities. Year IS14 was named for the defeat of Susa, Adamdun and Awan and the capture of their leader(s) "in a single day". Successful or not – and such claims are especially suspect in times of strife – the necessity for action of this kind belies the imminent collapse of Sumerian suzerainty over Susiana. Nearer the end even the year names indicate impending doom. IS22 states how "a hurricane decreed by the gods had overwhelmed the borders of the universe" and the following year that "the 'stupid monkey' in the foreign lands (kur) struck against Ibbi-Sin".

Tradition ascribed the final downfall of Ur in IS24 to a combined attack of her former vassals the Elamites and Šimaškians (LÚ.SU.A) (sometimes also the peoples of Gutium, Tidnum and Subir),[350] who captured the hapless Ibbi-Sin and (as an astronomical omen has it) took him "in chains to Anšan weeping". The praise-hymn to Išbi-Erra identifies the leader of the Elamite invasion as Kindattu, sixth of the Šimaškian rulers in the Susa king list.[351] An eclipse of the moon was said to have portended Nanna's abandonment of his earthly representative and Ibbi-Sin became in Mesopotamian literature the architypical ill-fated king whose own land rebelled against him and was carried off in captivity to a foreign land.[352]

The Elamites did not overthrow Išbi-Erra, however, who since installing himself as king of Isin had been waging his own war against the enemy on both fronts.[353] Mixing warfare with diplomacy Išbi-Erra had conquered the "city of the Amorites" in year IE8 (=IS15) and wed his daughter to the son of an Elamite sukkal in year 15 (IS22).[354] This did not mark a lasting alliance, however, for the very same month another text records gifts from the Amorites "when Elam was smitten".[355] It is no doubt this victory which was celebrated in the next year name (IE16) which reports the smiting of "the armies of Šimaški (LÚ.SU.A^{ki}) and Elam (var.: Elam and Šimaški)." Interestingly, this supposed victory occurred only a year before these states invaded Sumer and carried off Ibbi-Sin. The occupiers evidently maintained a lowland presence and it was not for another ten years (IE26) that Išbi-Erra was able to boast the defeat of the Elamite garrison stationed in Ur itself,[356] presumably their

---

[349] Jones *et al.* 1961: 302.

[350] *LSU* (Michalowski 1989): Šimaškians and Elamites (ll. 33-35, comm. to l. 33), Elam (ll. 166, 172, 261, 401), Gutium (ll. 75, 146, 230), Elam and Tidnum (ll. 256f.), Tidnum, Gutium and Anšan (ll. 488-91); *Lament for Eridu* (Green 1978): Šimaški and Elam (iv:10); *Lament for Ur* (Kramer in Pritchard 1969: 455-63 [for "Subarians" read "Šimaškians"]; Jacobsen 1987: 447-74): Šimaškians and Elamites (l. 244) ; *Lament for Uruk* (Green 1984a): Gutium and Subir (iv:20-22); *Lament for Nippur* (Kramer 1991): Tidnumites (?) (l. 235).

[351] van Dijk 1978; Michalowski 1989: 7 n. 42.

[352] Jacobsen 1953: 38f. n. 18.

[353] On the basis of references to messengers from "Kindadu" and "Ida[du]" to Išbi-Erra in IE19 (two years after the fall of Ur) (Stolper 1982: 47f.) and references in IE14 to leather bags in which to put sealed documents and letters from Anšan (Frayne 1982: 27), it is sometimes suggested that Kindatu tried to draw Išbi-Erra into an alliance before his attack on Ibbi-Sin (*e.g.* Steinkeller in press [b]). However, since we do not know the contents of this correspondence, and since it bridges Išbi-Erra's war against Šimaški and Elam in IE16 and the sack of Ur the year after, this remains questionable.

[354] Röllig 1975: 283; but *cf.* van de Mieroop 1987: 109 n. 24.

[355] *BIN* IX: 152; *cf.* 124; Frayne 1982: 27. Does this imply that Išbi-Erra had made some form of alliance with the Amorites (as Steinkeller in press [b])?

[356] Išbi-Erra "brought down by his mighty weapon the Elamite who was dwelling in the midst of Ur." Note also IE31, "the year when Ur was made safe in its dwelling place".

final stronghold.[357] Meanwhile, year formulae recording the construction of "fortifications" (bàd) (IE12, 14, 17, 19) are symptoms of continuing internal insecurity.[358]

As the royal correspondence confirms, Amorite pressure from the north-west contributed greatly to Ur's critically weakened condition, and it was they who ultimately benefitted most from her demise.[359] Although overshadowed by Mesopotamia's eastern enemies in the Sumerian literary tradition which grew up around these events, the Amorites had long been posing a menace to the northern and western marches of Sumerian territory, and, as the onomastics of the early second millennium confirm, now moved into the Mesopotamian lowlands in increasing numbers, submerging the last great floruit of Sumerian civilisation.

(e) The Imperial Administration

The meticulous record-keeping of the Ur III bureaucracy, as reorganised by Šulgi,[360] provides a wealth of information on the extent and nature of the Neo-Sumerian empire. Aspects of day-to-day administration are abundantly illustrated by tens of thousands of texts from Ur, Drehem (Puzriš-Dagan), Umma and other provincial centres. Yet even this greatly improved data base has serious limitations from the historical point of view. The sample is heavily biased by the accidents of discovery and the concerns of the texts that are preserved are narrowly focused on immediate practical matters. They provide abundant circumstantial detail relating to particular events in the careers of imperial officials, for example, but rarely do they indicate the scope of their responsibilities. We know the dates and itineraries of many messengers passing between Ur and foreign cities in the east, but the contents of their messages are never vouchsafed. Nor do the texts indicate the status of the corresponding city – free or subject vassal – a problem compounded by the Sumerian practice of referring to both independent foreign rulers and Sumerian governors as ensis. Many basic questions about the general features of the imperial administration thus remain unanswerable, buried beneath a wealth of interesting but highly specific detail.

The provinces of the Ur III empire, concentrated along its eastern and north-eastern periphery, were ruled by "generals" (šagins), rarely "governors" (ensis),[361] supported by a staff of officers and troops.[362] The responsibility of the chief provincial administrator, whether general or governor, seem to have been much the same:[363] to maintain the security of the region against invasion or insurrection and to collect

---

[357] That Kindatu still ruled at this time – and was not killed in the invasion of Sumer (as van Dijk 1978: 205) – is suggested by an allusion to Kindatu withdrawing from Ur in the Išbi-Erra praise hymn (Frayne 1982: 29) and the fact that a few years earlier (IE19) the king received messengers from "Kindadu" and "Ida[du]", almost certainly the "Šimaškian" kings of these names (Stolper 1982: 47f.).
[358] Aside from "the great wall of Isin" of IE12, these walls are not given geographical designations.
[359] For suggestions that the Hurrians and others may have played a part in the collapse of Ur see Speiser 1952; Hallo 1978: 77f.
[360] Steinkeller 1987.
[361] Of the places probably controlled by Ur, ensis are recorded for Adamdun, Aššur, Elam (*i.e.* Susa), Gutebum (=Gutium), Hamazi, Harši, Hu-urti, Karahar, Kimaš, Lulubum, Mišime, Sabum, Sigriš, Simanum, Zimudar, Simurrum, Susa and Urua. Places probably beyond Ur's control also recorded as having ensis include Anšan, Zabšali, Marhaši, and Subir (*RGTC 2*: s.v.; Owen 1981: 267-69).
[362] Typically the nu-banda, 'captain', ugula-geš-da, 'officer in charge of sixty men', érin GN, 'troops of GN'. Jones *et al.* 1961: 301 suggest that the lú giš-ku (gu-la), 'armed men' and various types of sukkal were also concerned with military security.
[363] This contrasts with usual practice in the 'core' territories where civil and military responsibility was divided beween these offices (Steinkeller 1987: 24f.; Michalowski 1987: 58f.), usually held by men of very different backgrounds.

taxes (see below).[364] Provincial generals, like those in Sumer itself, usually bear non-Sumerian names, most often Akkadian, sometimes Elamite, Hurrian or Amorite.[365] The direct administration of the empire thus fell largely to *novi homines* who owed their positions directly to the king, with whom they were often connected by blood or marriage.[366] The careers of the provincial generals that can be reconstructed in outline from archival documents show that they did not necessarily hold their posts indefinitely but could be moved around much like career diplomats today.[367] As in Sumer, some positions tended to become hereditary.[368]

Although all the kings of Ur were actively involved in affairs with the east, particularly when military intervention became necessary, effective administration inevitably meant delegation. From late in the reign of Šulgi or early in that of Amar-Suen until the disintegration of the empire under Ibbi-Sin, the routine administration of the highland states and general reponsibility for the security of the eastern front seems to have lain principally with one man called variously Arad(IR)-Nanna or Arad-mu.[369] He inherited the prestigious post of sukkalmah,[370] which, at least during his tenure, seems to have represented the highest political office in the imperial administration, inferior only to that of the king, to whom he was in any case related by marriage.[371] Arad-mu had authority over other provincial generals and himself laid claim to an unrivalled field of command. In an inscription dating to the reign of Šu-Sin, he claims direct responsibility, either as general or governor, for twelve provinces stretching from Urbilum (Arbela) to Pašime (on the Gulf), including also Sabum, Hamazi, Gutium, Karahar and Šimaški (LÚ.SU.A).[372] A royal letter to Šulgi suggests equally broad responsibilities:

> O my king, you have given me instructions about everything from the sea of
> the country of Dilmun to (var: from) the bitter waters at the slopes (gaba) of
> the mountain (kur) of the Amorites (mar-du), to (var: from) the border (da?) of

---

[364] It is perhaps significant, however, that "governors" occur only in the inner periphery, away from the battle-front.

[365] Goetze 1963: *passim*; Steinkeller 1987: 25.

[366] Even ensis, who in Sumer are almost always Sumerian, could in the provinces be foreigners. Note, *e.g.*, Hulibar, ensi of Duduli, and Šelibum, ensi of Sabum, who are qualified as NIM, "Elamites". On the other hand, Uba-a, the ensi of Adamdun was a Sumerian whose brother acted as gir-official at Drehem (Michalowski 1978: 41f.; Goetze 1963: 16). For blood and marriage links to the royal family see Michalowski 1987: 58f.

[367] Zariqum was ensi at Aššur and Susa (Hallo 1956; Kutscher 1979); Kallamu seems to have been shifted from Kazallu to Ešnunna (Goetze 1963: 27); and Šarrumbani was replaced by Babati as overseer of the *Muriq Tidnim* (Michalowski 1976: 51f., letter U.18).

[368] *E.g.* Iribum and his son Ahuni of Abibana; and Hašibatal and his son Puzur-Šulgi of Arraphum (Steinkeller 1987: 39, n. 63). For the passing of offices from father to son see Hallo 1972; Parr 1974; McGuiness 1982.

[369] Goetze 1963: 9-11; Sollberger 1954-56: 36-38; M. Lambert 1979: 36f.; Michalowski 1976: U1-8 (royal correspondence). The identity is based on parallel titles in corresponding years: both were sukkalmah in AS3, AS8 and ŠS1 and ensi of Girsu in AS8 and ŠS1 (Goetze 1963: 9, Sollberger 1954-56: 37; Hallo 1957: 115). Arad-Nanna/mu's responsibility for the eastern provinces, certain under Šu-Sin (see below), dates back to Šulgi according to the royal correspondence (letter U4: 4ff. quoted below).

[370] Arad-Nanna was sukkal from at least Š42 and sukkalmah by AS3. His father and grandfather also took the latter title (Jacobsen 1953: 37 n. 8) though there is no evidence that they had any particular responsibility for the eastern empire. In turn, Arad-Nanna may have appointed members of his family as subordinates. There seems only to have been one sukkalmah at a time – assuming the "Irgu", who was sukkalmah in ŠS1, is also to be read "Arad-mu" (*cf.* Sollberger 1954-56: 37). The title is variously translated as "grand regent" (Stolper 1984: 18), "prime minister" (Sollberger 1954-56: 37), "grand vizier" (Jones *et al.* 1961: 301) or "chancellor" (Steinkeller 1987: 25). See generally Scharaschenidze 1976.

[371] Michalowski 1987: 58 n. 15.

[372] Kärki 1986: ŠS13 = *IRSA*: IIIB5a. He is ensi of Sabum, the lands of Gutebum (=Gutium), Hamazi and Karahar; and šagin of Pašime, Urbilum, Nihi, Šimaški (LÚ.SU^{ki}) and the lands of Kardak.

Simurrum (in/of) Subir... Watches have been established over their fortifications, their troops have submitted.[373]

Unfortunately, no inscriptions relate any significant events of his stewardship[374] though he may be presumed to have played a part in the campaigns against Šašrum (AS6), Bitum-rabium, Iabrum and Huhunuri (AS7), Simanum (ŠS3) and Zabšali (ŠS7) which took place during the tenure of his office. Little light is thrown on the mechanism of his administration though it did involve active presence in the provinces[375] and he sometimes appears directing the movements of NIM in the highlands.[376] He claims the governorship of Girsu[377] and Lagaš[378] and this city probably acted as his base of operations, as it did for much commercial activity between Sumer and the east from Early Dynastic times.[379]

The security and loyalty of the eastern provinces must have been safeguarded by arms. Šulgi instituted a standing army of Sumerian conscripts by his twentieth year[380] but these troops did not garrison the provinces. Evidence for such a system has been sought instead in the archival references to groups of NIM, literally "Elamites", "highlanders" or "foreigners", interpreted in these contexts as provincial conscript troops[381] though they may also have served corvée labour.[382] Their origin is usually further specified by a geographical name, occasionally by reference to the chief officer of their city.[383] These places, when localisable, lie in the Elamite and Hurrian lands to the east and north-east of Sumer.[384] The NIM appear to be conscripts from regions conquered by Ur;[385] places cited as sources of NIM appear among cities and regions whose conquest by the king is related in date formulae (*e.g.* Anšan, Karahar, Simurrum, Kimaš, Harši, Urbilum), although the incidence of NIM from a particular place does not seem to increase in the wake of a campaign against it.[386] NIM-troops are noted in archival documents mainly when travelling between places in the highlands. Only rarely are they posted in Sumer.[387] Nor do they seem to have guarded their own homelands; the general policy may indeed have been quite

---

[373] U4:3-13. Translation after Hallo 1978: 78, 81 [11] and Michalowski 1976: 170; *idem* 1986: 142.
[374] Like other generals, he was responsible for deliveries of taxes and heads the list of receipts as ugula or maškim (Goetze 1953: 114; *idem* 1963: 5, 9). He also presided in the local court (Jones *et al.* 1961: 301).
[375] In letter U.14 Arad-mu travels from Zimudar to Simurrum (Michalowski 1976: 218).
[376] Jones *et al.* 1961: 301.
[377] From at least AS8 (Sollberger 1954-56: 37 with additions in Goetze 1963: 9, n.9).
[378] Kärki 1986: ŠS13 = *IRSA*: IIIB5a.
[379] M. Lambert 1981.
[380] Steinkeller 1987: 20 n. 5.
[381] See Jones *et al.* 1961: 299f. The term is often read "mercenary" or with some other semi-professional connotation (*e.g.* Goetze 1953b: 116 n. 7; *cf.* Leemans 1960: 175 n. 4 for the OB period) but this has been questioned (Fish 1955: 1, 12f.; Stolper 1984: 70 n. 110). NIM served also as labourers (guruš) (Fish 1955: 13; Salonen 1968: 166f.; McNeil 1971: 69-72) but their usual function seems to have been military; *cf.* the Marhašian NIM described as "guardsmen" (aga-ús) (Steinkeller 1982: 262 n. 97).
[382] McNeil 1971: 69-72.
[383] Fish 1955: 2-12; *RGTC 2*: 311; Jones *et al.* 1961: 300.
[384] Places cited include Anšan, Duduli, Gisa, Harši, Huhnuri, Humurti, Hurtum, Kimaš, Marhaši, Pašime, Sabum, Simurrum, Šašrum, Sigriš and Šimaški. See, *e.g.*, *RGTC 2*: s.v.; Sigrist 1990: *passim*.
[385] They are sometimes described as nam-ra-ak, "booty", dab-ba, "seized", and possibly as ir, "slaves" (McNeil 1971: 67f.; Fish 1955: 12f.).
[386] Jones *et al.* 1961: 300.
[387] McNeil 1971: 71 n. 164. The group of Marhašian NIM stationed in Sumer (Steinkeller 1982: 261f. n. 97) is a rare exception, and the details are in any case uncertain. They are said to be "guardsmen of the man of Marhaši", *i.e.* a foreign expedition in Sumer, and they go to Marhaši. Yet in Sumer they are placed under a Sumerian general, Abuni, who elsewhere takes charge of érin from Ešnunna, Arami and BI-dadun (Goetze 1963: 13).

the reverse. They received very low rations and sometimes fled their posts.[388] NIM from Susa, Awan and Adamdun are very rare or unattested;[389] as lowland centres their inhabitants probably did not fall under this rubric.[390]

Evidence for a system of provincial tax or tribute is also sporadic. Administrative texts list taxes called the máš-da-ri-a, šu-gíd and gún ma-da[391] paid by personnel in the provinces to the imperial storehouses in Sumer (including Drehem), from where they were redistributed as bala throughout Sumer.[392] Contributions of all three types were usually of livestock (cattle and sheep/goat), though silver is once recorded as the máš-da-ri-a offering of Urua,[393] and Ebla and Zimudar contributed wooden objects and wine respectively.[394]

Of these taxes the best known is the gún ma-da, the "provincial tax" which is recorded in over a hundred account texts from Drehem[395] dating from Š43 to IS2. It was paid annually, between September and December, by military personnel stationed in foreign (*i.e.* non-Babylonian) provinces.[396] All troops from the general down to provincial conscripts (érin) contributed to the provincial tax, the amount decreasing with rank. Steinkeller argues that it was raised by each man from land assigned to him by the crown and collected by the general, who had overall responsibilty for seeing that the region's quota was met.[397] Arad-mu reports to Šulgi on his expedition to Subir "for the purpose of putting in order the taxes on the unincorporated territories".[398] The amounts involved can be quite substantial: a text registering the tax of Adamdun lists 7,200 oxen, 1,331 sheep, 62 he-goats and 225 dead cattle.[399] Tax deliveries are high under Šulgi and Amar-Suen and decline with the empire's fortunes under Šu-Sin and Ibbi-Sin.[400] As part of the redistribution system other commodities, usually cereals, were sent from Sumer to some peripheral states (*e.g.* Susa, Adamdun).[401]

On the assumption that territorial taxes would only be paid by regions under direct Sumerian control,[402] Steinkeller uses them to plot the extent of the Neo-Sumerian 'periphery', *i.e.* the conquered territories which had been incorporated into the Ur III state.[403] Provincial tax is recorded from ninety places all of which, when localisable, lie in the eastern borderlands and mountains stretching from Aššur and Urbilum (Arbela) in the north to Susa, Adamdun, Urua, Sabum and Pašime in the south. Places in between include Ešnunna, Arraphum, Hamazi, Harši, Hurti,

---

[388] Jones *et al.* 1961: 286-88.
[389] *RGTC 2*: 176.
[390] *Cf.* Stolper 1984: 18; Fish 1955: 1.
[391] Steinkeller 1987: 30-37, 40.
[392] Steinkeller 1987: 27-29, revising Hallo's 1960 interpretation of the bala system. The following account is much indebted to Steinkeller, who revises substantially the conclusions reached in Michalowski 1978. For the translation of the term see Michalowski 1978: 35 who prefers "impost/tribute of the unincorporated territories" to Hallo's "territorial tribute".
[393] Steinkeller 1987: 40, n. 67; Michalowski 1978: 48 lists this as gún.
[394] Michalowski 1978: 48.
[395] Steinkeller 1987: 30; this figure includes many texts which are labelled just gún (of a particular GN) or not specified as tax at all. The term gún ma-da was only used from ŠS3 (*ibid.*: 31).
[396] Perhaps as far south as Pašime on the Gulf which was conquered under Amar-Suen or Šu-Sin (Steinkeller 1982: 241f.).
[397] Steinkeller 1987: 31ff.
[398] Michalowski 1983: 53.
[399] Michalowski 1978: 39.
[400] Steinkeller 1987: 36.
[401] *Ibid.*: 40f., n. 68.
[402] This excludes other uses of the term gún by which it may refer to taxes on Sumerian cities (Michalowski 1978: 35).
[403] Steinkeller 1987: 36f., Fig. 6.

Kakmum, Lululu/Lulubu, Simurrum, Tutul and Zimudar.[404] Following Michalowski, Steinkeller plausibly interprets this system of provinces as constituting a 'buffer zone' between the Sumerian 'core' of the empire and the network of independent or semi-independent states of the highlands, which are sometimes connected to Ur by marriage or other ties but do not pay "provincial tax" and did not become part of the Ur III state.[405] These latter include Anšan, Huhnuri, Marhaši, Šimaški, Zabšali in the east; Nineveh and Simanum in the north; and Ebla, Mardaman, Mari and Urkiš in the north-west.

The provincial tax also provides a basis for estimating the size of the provincial armies. Steinkeller reckons the total number of troops in the province centred on Abibana (in the Diyala region) at 2,400.[406]

Provincial tax was levied on imperial officers and conscript troops, and was to be met by wealth derived from crown land; it was not a means of extracting wealth from the province itself or the bulk of its native inhabitants. This must have been done – if it was done – by means of a separate tribute, or by trade. It is not surprising, then, that precious stones, metals and other highland raw materials are entirely absent from the tax records. It serves also to reinforce the point that the chief economic importance of the temperate highland zone to the Sumerians was its livestock.

Besides administrative records, two canonical texts refer to tribute or tax (gún): a "speckled dog (ur) of Meluhha" was offerred to Ibbi-Sin as the gún of [Marh]aši, and a he-goat is recorded as the gún of Anšan taken by Su-Sin in his campaign against Šimaški.[407] Both items are of such insignificant economic value (the former surely was valued for its exoticism) that the term must be understood here to mean "diplomatic gift".[408]

The 'messenger texts' provide a guide to Ur's diplomatic horizon though not necessarily to the extent of her hegemony.[409] Susiana is predictably well represented. Susa receives the greatest number of citations and Adamdun is also well attested. Awan, however, is conspicuously absent,[410] perhaps reflecting its diminished political status. Still within the lowlands and the immediately neighbouring hills, there are regular references to messengers of Guabba (on the shore of the Gulf) and Sabum, and fewer to Urua and Huhnuri. Of the places which probably lay further into the highlands, Kimaš and Šimaški are cited quite frequently, Marhaši rarely. (The general term "Elam" does not occur; a specific destination was always nominated.) Far the most commonly mentioned highland messengers, however, are from Anšan. Interestingly, records of messengers coming *to* Sumer *from* Anšan far out-number those travelling the other way. This may reflect not only Anšan's political importance *per se* but also its strategic position from where developments in neighbouring regions could be monitored. There are exceptional references to messengers from Dilmun.[411]

---

[404] Full list in Steinkeller 1987: 36f., nn. 56, 57 (Pašime).

[405] However, some were 'conquered' according to year formulae and other inscriptions, *e.g.* Anšan, Simanum, Huhnuri, Šimaški, Mardaman, Zabšali; and others were recorded as being ruled by (appointed?) ensis.

[406] Steinkeller 1987: 39.; for location see *RGTC 2*: s.v.

[407] Kärki 1986: IS12:9-18, ŠS21 i:1´-15´.

[408] Michalowski 1978: 35, 46; Steinkeller 1982: 253 n. 60.

[409] Fish 1954; *idem* 1955; Jones *et al.* 1961: 280-310.

[410] None listed in Fish 1954 or *RGTC 2*.

[411] Leemans 1960: 140; Snell 1977: 47 (lú girím), *RTC* 337) and Magan (Fish 1954: s.v.; Foster 1977: 39 n. 106 (OAkk); *idem* in press (OAkk Susa).

9. CONCLUSIONS

The keynote of early relations between Mesopotamia and Iran is hostility. Wars with the peoples of Susa and the eastern highlands are recorded in the earliest historical inscriptions and continue to feature prominently throughout the third millennium and beyond. Court diplomacy, treaties, royal marriages and other attempts to establish a more amicable and stable relationship invariably dissolved into renewed fighting, in which the highland states, particularly Elam, Marhaši and Šimaški, proved themselves formidable opponents. Their rulers clearly had imperial ambitions of their own, and even the biased picture presented by the lowland sources indicates that fortunes vacillated. Kings of Sumer and Akkad might 'conquer' Anšan; but there were times also when Anšan 'enslaved' parts of Sumer.

Equally dangerous, because more mobile, were the uncivilized semi-nomads and transhumant highlanders of the uplands – especially the Guti and Lulubi of the Zagros, and the Amorites of the north-west – who would readily seize the opportunity to sweep down from the mountains or steppes, plunder the rich settlements of the plains, and retreat. Such invasions were largely responsible for bringing down both Agade and Ur, the two great empires of the third millennium.

Lowland Susiana, although geographically linked to Sumer, maintained friendly relations only as long as Mesopotamia was sufficiently powerful to keep the highland Elamites at bay. Otherwise an Iranian culture with local roots took hold, notably in the Proto-Elamite period and under Puzur-Inšušinak. The numerous 'conquests' of the city attested by third-millennium sources are a measure of the strength of this highland connection. Only during the two periods of 'empire' (three if the Late Uruk period may be counted), and perhaps under exceptional Sumerian rulers like Eannatum, did Mesopotamia have the military and political resources to establish secure control of Susa. For these periods at least, Susiana became effectively a political and cultural extension of Mesopotamia.

At the root of the perennial enmity between lowlands and highlands was a great ethnic, linguistic and cultural divide which separated the Mesopotamian lowlands on the one hand from the eastern highlands on the other. Whereas the former were inhabited by Sumerians and Semites, the latter supported a multitude of non-Sumerian, non-Semitic peoples who worshipped different gods and, except in a handful of large urban centres, had an altogether different lifestyle and mode of subsistence. In other circumstances this might have formed the basis of a mutually profitable co-existence but, as it was, imperialism and opportunism on both sides repeatedly brought them into conflict. Each region was in its own way extremely rich; and the temptation for powerful regimes to benefit from their neighbours' wealth by plunder, tribute and occupation, exaccerbated at times by outside pressure, periodically proved too great to resist.

Judgement on the crucial issues of how far eastwards Mesopotamian armies reached, and which territories may have been annexed, are seriously hindered by two basic uncertainties. First, nearly all the key geographical regions are still to varying degrees unlocated. Secondly, it is not always clear (especially when dealing with edited accounts of earlier events) how seriously claims of 'conquest' should be taken or how they should be interpreted. The expansion of the geographical horizon caused by the relocation of Anšan in Fars has reinforced the already sceptical attitude of many scholars towards Mesopotamian claims to have conquered this and other eastern lands. But this should perhaps be resisted. A third-millennium

Mesopotamian empire, or network of satellites, in Iran is by no means logistically impossible.[412] Although definitive evidence is lacking the question should for the present be left open.

As far as may be judged, direct military penetration of highland Iran (and Syria) seems to have been greatest under the Akkadians. Their kings certainly campaigned as far east as Anšan (Fars), Zahara, Šerihum and Marhaši, as well as across the Gulf to Magan (Oman). The Ur III kings, on the other hand, were more concerned with the Hurrian and Amorite frontiers to the north/north-east and north-west respectively, recording only isolated expeditions to Anšan and Šimaški. But the regions they did annex, mainly in the Zagros mountains, were more thoroughly integrated and controlled through an elaborate provincial administration. There is no comparable evidence concerning direct Akkadian rule in the east, where the armies of Akkad may often have plundered and withdrawn. But something comparable to the Ur III system should perhaps be envisaged for those regions which were retained under Akkadian control, as can be documented archaeologically more fully at Tell Brak and other sites in Syria.

Highland-lowland animosity was offset to some extent by more friendly economic contacts. Again the strongest links attested by existing textual evidence are with Susa. Some livestock and slaves also came into Sumer as tax/tribute (and rarely by trade) from the Iranian highlands. This picture is complemented by archaeological evidence regarding less perishable commodities, both raw materials (stones, metals) and finished artefacts, which will be examined in detail in the following chapters. At the end of this study we shall return to the important question of how far the two factors were linked, *i.e.* to what extent economic motives may have lain behind Mesopotamian military expansion.

---

[412] The much larger Achaemenid empire provides a useful point of comparison. The only significant development in transport between the 3rd mill. and Achaemenid times was the advent of the camel as the principal pack animal (contrast Larsen 1979: 93). This speeded up transport over flat ground and opened the more arid thoroughfares to traffic; but equids would still have been the natural beast of burden for supplying an army operating in the heavily populated temperate areas where the main targets of military action lay.

Chapter 4

Metals and Metalwork

In shifting from military and political relations to matters of trade and exchange the nature of the evidence which has been preserved and the level of focus which it provides change significantly. Instead of named individuals more or less precisely fixable in space and time we have to deal with largely nameless persons whose deeds are traceable only when they reach a scale and regularity that impacts the limited and highly selective archaeological record. The nature of the information that can be extracted is consequently very different. Historical texts tend to dwell on the extraordinary – the first expedition to some distant place, the construction of a temple "without rival" – and pass over the commonplace. The archaeological record does exactly the reverse, presenting a cross-section of everyday life with only occasional glimpses of the rare and exceptional. This applies equally to domestic remains and to the more imposing religious and administrative complexes on which archaeologists have tended to concentrate. Rather than particular events of any significance it is long-term, large-scale developments in the types of materials used and artefacts made that emerge most clearly from excavation. In charting the shifting pattern of Mesopotamia's economic relations with the east it is of primary relevance when such changes first occurred, but typically all that can be determined is the point at which the new pattern is widespread enough to manifest itself in the sparse and irregular archaeological record.

This raises another point of contrast: incomplete as the historical evidence may be, the practice of commemorating great deeds in canonical literature and of faithfully copying royal inscriptions many generations after the events they relate has meant that some memory of the seminal historical events of the later third millennium, however tendentious, has often been preserved. By contrast, since only a tiny proportion of the extant archaeological sites of Mesopotamia and Iran have been excavated, there can be no such confidence when it comes to questions of archaeological particulars. The difficulty is particularly acute with regard to the material culture of the social and political élites. Temples and palaces were inevitably stripped bare in the wake of local or international power struggles and the 'Royal Tombs' of Ur so far stand virtually alone as testimony to the oppulence of royal court (or temple) life at this time. For this reason they feature prominently in the discussion of metals and stones that follows, but it should be recognised that this uniqueness is itself an obstacle to broader generalisation and may serve as a reminder of how different a picture might have been painted had similarly rich discoveries been made elsewhere in southern Mesopotamia.

1. THE SOURCES OF SUMERIAN METALS

The exploitation of metals in Mesopotamia, initially restricted essentially to small personal ornaments, increased substantially with the growth of urban societies in the late fourth millennium. A wide range of prestige objects is attested already in Late Uruk times, heavy tools and weapons becoming prominent in the later third millennium. To meet the demand for raw materials which the increasing use of metal tools created – principally copper and alloying materials, as well as lead, silver and gold for luxury items – Sumer was entirely dependent on external supplies, and the quest for metals played a significant role in stimulating foreign contacts during this period.

Many potential sources lay in the surrounding highland zones of Anatolia, Iran and across the Gulf in Oman. Of these, Iran offered the nearest and greatest variety of metals, but procurement also presented particular problems. Gold, silver, copper, arsenical copper (and perhaps tin) were all available on the Iranian plateau and were worked there from an early date, as excavations at Ghabristan and Tal-i Iblis have demonstrated.[1] However, two factors rendered access problematic. First, the intervening Zagros mountains presented a formidable obstacle to bulk transport. The copper reserves of Oman and the metals traded by the Meluhhans, on the other hand, were readily accessible by boat. Thus, in the second millennium, Maganite copper was cheaper even than supplies from Anatolia. Secondly, the highland kingdoms of the plateau, where the minerals lay, were never brought under lasting Mesopotamian control. Regular supplies from these regions must generally have been contingent on the neutrality, if not co-operation, of the highland states in which they were mined and through which they were transported. The economic self-interest of the Elamites and other highlanders must often have been sorely tested in the atmosphere of mutual hostility which characterised Mesopotamian-Iranian relations during the later third millennium. It is not inconceivable that economic sanctions, including the blocking of metal supplies, would have been invoked during periods of stress – a practice which would have discouraged the Mesopotamians from relying exclusively on these supplies.[2] A policy of exploiting the resources of regions which could be politically controlled may be reflected in Akkadian royal inscriptions that refer to "the silver mountain" (probably the Keban silver mines in the Taurus mountains), "the Cedar forest" (the Amanus or Lebanon) and "the copper mountain" of Magan (Oman), all regions which were claimed to have been conquered by kings of Agade. No such epithets are applied to places in Iran except in literary texts and in Gudea's reference to Kimaš as "the copper mountain" (see below).[3]

In tracing the sources of Sumerian metals geological data may be combined with recent source-provenance analyses and contemporary textual evidence. All have their difficulties. Geological knowledge is still very uneven and often unreliable, especially concerning the small deposits which might have been exploited in antiquity. Analyses must be used with extreme caution; older methods have since proved fallacious and a much larger corpus of reliable tests is required before

---

[1]   Majidzadeh 1979, Caldwell ed. 1967.

[2]   *Cf.* Alden's suggestion (1982: 628), questioned above, that the Proto-Elamites' monopoly over highland resources allowed them to restrict supplies to the lowlands, forcing the Mesopotamians to find alternative supply routes.

[3]   Note also Aratta "the lapis lazuli mountain" in Sumerian literature, above p. 13, below pp. 211f.

categorical statements will be possible.[4] Whether based on trace elements, lead isotopes or whatever, all metalwork source-provenance 'fingerprinting' encounters the pervasive problem of chemical change and blending through refinement, alloying and remelting, a barrier which some regard as insuperable.[5] Textual evidence is hardly more precise since the crucial distinctions between source zones, transit stations and depôts are rarely made explicit. Metals being a primary form of hoarded wealth, they could be obtained from many more places than their zones of primary production.

(a) Copper

Copper ores are widespread in the Near East and many sources were exploited in antiquity (Fig. 21).[6] North of Sumer, substantial deposits are known in central and eastern Anatolia, principally at Ergani Maden, and in the Caucasus and Azerbaijan. To the east, the Iranian plateau also offered large ore reserves as well as native copper.[7] An important series of deposits runs along the western fringe of the central deserts, the richest around Anarak-Talmessi and Veshnoveh. Further afield, copper supplies were available through Baluchistan, Pakistan and Afghanistan to India, and in Central Asia.[8] South-east of Sumer extensive ore deposits were accessible by boat in Oman.[9] Large deposits west of Sumer occur in southern Palestine (Wadis Arabah and Feinan)[10] and in Egypt. The question of which ores were exploited – oxides, hydroxycarbonates, sulphides or sulphates – and in which order remains unclear.[11]

There is evidence of third-millennium mining and smelting in many of these regions, including two of the largest deposits – Anarak-Veshnoveh and Oman.[12] On the basis of slag and other smelting evidence, Hauptmann estimates the total late third millennium (Umm an-Nar) copper production of Oman at 2,000-4,000 tons.[13] Tepe Hissar seems also to have been a major copper smelting centre in the later third millennium (periods II-III).[14] Indirect evidence for the exploitation of local sources elsewhere in Iran, beginning in the fifth millennium, comes from copper-working installations (some for melting and casting native copper rather than smelting)[15] at Tal-i Iblis, Tepe Ghabristan, late fourth to third-millennium (?) Shahdad, Banesh-period Malyan and Shahr-i Sokhta II, phase 7.[16] Ancient smelting at Ergani has not

---

4   Far the best served site at present is Susa, thanks to the recent comprehensive investigation of the Louvre's holdings (Berthoud *et al.* 1982; Malfoy & Menu 1987).

5   Berthoud *et al.* 1982; Weisgerber & Hauptmann 1988 (trace element analysis); Yener *et al.* 1991 (lead isotope analysis). The most prominent sceptic is Muhly, who writes: "Although still not widely appreciated, it has long been recognised that the various processes of smelting, remelting, refining, mixing, and even alloying so altered the basic chemical composition of every ancient artifact that attempts to establish provenance [of source metals] on the basis of chemical composition are doomed to failure" (Muhly 1988: 7).

6   Reviews in Muhly 1973: Ch. II; Moorey 1985: 9-14.

7   Muhly 1973: 232-4; Harrison 1968: 501-05; Berthoud *et al.* 1982.

8   Muhly 1973: 220-39; Ratnagar 1981: 88f.; Agrawala 1984; Agrawal 1984: 166.

9   Weisgerber 1981; Hauptmann 1985.

10   Hauptmann *et al.* 1985; Weisgerber & Hauptmann 1988.

11   Rapp 1988: 25f.

12   Holzer & Momenzadeh 1971 (Anarak-Veshnoveh); Weisgerber 1981; Hauptmann 1985: 95, 116f.; D.T. Potts 1990: 119-25 (Oman).

13   Hauptmann 1985: 109.

14   Pigott *et al.* 1982; Pigott 1989.

15   *Cf.* Muhly 1988: 7, arguing that the 5th mill. Ghabristan and Iblis installations probably represent only melting, not smelting.

16   Iblis: Caldwell & Shahmirzadi 1966; Muhly 1980-83: 352. Ghabristan: Majedzadeh 1979; Muhly *loc. cit.* Shahdad: Vatandoost-Haghighi 1977: 36-42. Malyan: Amiet 1986: 108; Sumner 1986: 204. Sokhta: Hauptmann & Weisgerber 1980: 120; Tosi 1984: 34-50. For a review of these and other Near Eastern copperworking sites see Yener & Vandiver 1993: 237. Ratnagar (1981: 88) also mentions evidence from south-eastern Iran.

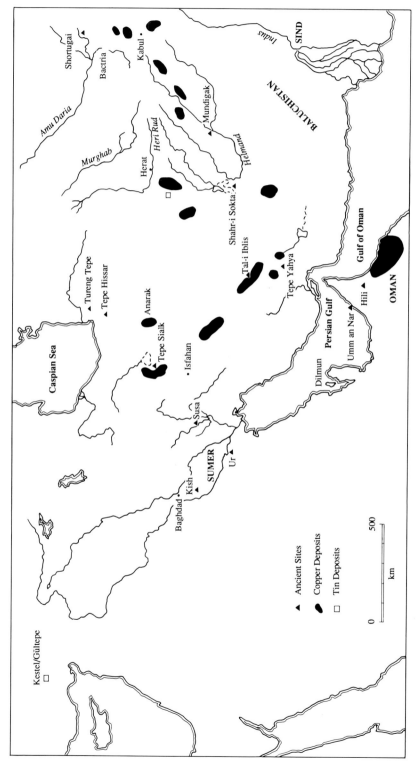

Figure 21.   Map showing major sources of copper and tin (after Berthoud et al. 1982: 41).

been dated,[17] though there can be no doubt that Anatolian copper was worked from very early times. The unparalleled scale of copper use at Susa I (late fifth millennium) implies smelting, not just melting.[18] Recent reports of copperworking installations in the Agdam region of Transcaucasia raise the prospect of early exploitation in this region also.[19] Ancient smelting sites in the rich Khedri belt of northern Rajasthan suggest that this area was a major source of Harappan copper.[20] No third-millennium copper workshop has yet been discovered in Mesopotamia and no workmen's tools till *ca.* 2200 BC,[21] though there can be no doubt that it was widely worked. Most of the copper used in Sumer was probably introduced already smelted as ingots, though some ore earlier travelled as far as Yarim Tepe in northern Iraq.

Much progress has been made in tracing patterns of copper exploitation and trade in recent years by the development of sophisticated source provenance analysis based on trace element 'finger-printing', especially the comprehensive programmes of analysis undertaken on the Near Eastern copper(-alloy) holdings of the Louvre, and a CNRS (RCP 442) investigation of the fourth-third millennium metals trade.[22] These programmes have provided a wealth of new evidence which will be drawn upon heavily in the following discussion. It should be noted, however, that aspects of the analyses and the methodology employed have recently been questioned,[23] and conclusions drawn from this evidence must therefore be regarded as tentative.

Numerous analyses indicate that the ores of Anarak-Talmessi characterised by significant levels of arsenic were widely used in highland Iran, notably at Tepe Yahya VA,[24] Banesh-period Malyan, Tepe Giyan and possibly Tepe Sialk and Tepe Hissar.[25] Less predictably, these inland reserves were exploited also in the lowlands at Susa I (Late Ubaid–Early Uruk period) and in the settlements of the Early Dynastic I Hamrin.[26] During the Uruk period Susa may still have obtained some copper from Talmessi, but most of the now more heterogeneous Susa II-IIIA material (bridging the Uruk–Jemdet Nasr periods) relates to sources in the valleys of Bardsir or Sheikh Ali in Kashan, although the correlation here is said to be less clear.[27] It is notable that the early sources attested by analytical data (see below for textual evidence), are all Iranian, despite the difficulty of overland transport.

Although Sumerian metalwork dating from before Early Dynastic III[28] has so far not been subjected to the same methods of analysis, Susa, whose pattern of exploitation largely corresponds to that of Sumer in the latter half of the millennium, may perhaps be taken as a rough guide. Iranian copper could have arrived in Sumer via Susa itself or along the Diyala.

---

17 de Jesus 1980: 22.
18 Muhly 1988: 8.
19 Kohl in Algaze 1989: 593f.
20 Agrawala 1984.
21 Moorey 1985: 36-9; *idem* 1988: 29. See Davey 1988 for the OB evidence.
22 Above note 4. Earlier source provenance studies have since been shown to be in varying degrees unsound (Muhly 1980-83: 358; Ratnagar 1981: 89-91; Moorey 1985: 12-14).
23 Seeliger 1986: 643 n. 74; Hauptmann *et al.* 1988: 34, 42, fig. 4.9.
24 In periods IVC-B Yahya seems to have derived copper from closer sources at Sheikh Ali (Berthoud & Cleuziou 1983: 243).
25 Berthoud *et al.* 1982: 45; Sumner 1986: 204; Amiet 1986: 58; Wertime 1964: 1264; Pigott *et al.* 1982: 231. Hauptmann & Weisgerber 1980: 120 argue that Sialk obtained its copper not from Anarak-Talmessi but from Veshnoveh, where a Sialk IV-style pot has been found in association with an ancient mine (Holzer & Momenzadeh 1971).
26 Berthoud *et al.* 1982: 43; Amiet 1986: 35.
27 Amiet 1986: 58; Malfoy & Menu 1987: 364; Berthoud & Cleuziou 1983: 243.
28 Moorey 1985: 51-68; Muhly 1980-83: 355.

TABLE 4.1

Origins of Third-Millennium Copper (urudu/*erû*) According to Cuneiform Sources[1]

Economic Texts

Dilmun	*Archaic Uruk (?)*: Englund 1983a: 35[2]
	ED III: Heimpel 1987: 70ff. nos 2-4 (latter a-EN-da); Bauer 1972: nos 188, 191 (both a-EN-da); *RTC*: no. 25; Hruška 1983: 83-85; Alster 1983: 49. *Cf.* also for *OAkk* and *Ur III* periods (return trade unspecified): Englund 1983: 87; Heimpel 1987: no. 49
Magan	*OAkk*: Heimpel 1987: nos 19, 20
	Ur III: Oppenheim 1954; *UET III*: 1666 (=Leemans 1960: 20 no. 3); Heimpel 1987: nos 43, 46, ?47; Röllig 1983: 346. *Cf.* also for *Ur III* (return trade unspecified): Heimpel 1987: no. 48
Meluhha	*Ur III*: *UET III*: no. 368 (*cf.* Leemans 1960: 161)

Royal Inscriptions

Kimaš (mines)	*Gudea*: Stat. B vi:21-23 (Abullat) (*NBWI*: I 166); Cyl. A xvi:15 (Pettinato 1972: 144; Jacobsen 1987: 408)
Dilmun/Magan?	*Gudea*: Cyl. A xv:11ff. (Pettinato 1972: 145); *cf.* Röllig 1983: 346; Englund 1983: 88f. n. 6
Meluhha	*Gudea*: Cyl. B xiv:13 (Pettinato 1972: 146)

Literary and Lexical Texts

Dilmun	*Archaic Uruk*: Englund 1983a: 35 ("Dilmun axe"); Nissen 1986a: 338; D.T. Potts 1990: 86 n. 111
	H*h* xi:339f. (Pettinato 1972: 152); Pettinato 1983: 77f. (Ebla)
Magan	H*h* xi:341, xxii:23´ (Pettinato 1972: 152, 154); *lipšur* 34 (*ibid.*: 156); *EN* BII: 8f. (Attinger 1984: 13)
Meluhha	H*h* xi:342 (Pettinato 1972: 152)
Aratta?	*ELA* 17f. (S. Cohen 1973; *cf.* Röllig 1983: 346)
?	Hymn to Ninurta (M. Cohen 1975: 31, ll. 144f.)

Notes
1 For the early 2nd mill. see also *UET* V: 292, 367, 526, 546, 678, 796 (Leemans 1960: 24-39; Heimpel 1987: 83-86 nos 56, 58, 59, 61-63).
2 W.14731bb mentions urudu.urudu.si dilmun in a broken context. Whether this refers to copper or a copper object, and whether from Dilmun or of Dilmun type, is unclear.

A shift in the pattern of Susian-Sumerian copper exploitation seems to have occurred around the second quarter of the third millennium. Artefacts from Susa IVA2-V, the earliest well dated material being the Early Dynastic IIIB *Vase à la Cachette* (Fig. 22), no longer match the ores of Iran but rather those of Oman, which are characterised by higher levels of nickel and iron.[29] The same trace element patterns appear in contemporary artefacts from Sumer; according to Cleuziou Omani copper is attested there from at least Early Dynastic II and is predominant by Early Dynastic III (the 'Royal Cemetery' at Ur).[30] Recent surveys and excavation have confirmed that the smelting of copper ores took place in Oman by the late third

---

29 Amiet 1986: 126; Berthoud & Cleuziou 1983; Malfoy & Menu 1987: 364f. Early attributions of Sumerian copper to Oman on the basis of high nickel contents alone (Peake 1928) subsequently proved unjustified but recent analyses of Omani ores, ingots and (from Maysar) artefacts confirm consistent, relatively high nickel levels in the Umm an-Nar period and higher average contents in the 2nd mill. (Hauptmann *et al.* 1988: 41-46).
30 Cleuziou 1986: 145; *cf.* Moorey 1985: 12, 14.

Figure 22. '*Vase à la Cachette*' *and selected contents from Susa. Early Dynastic III.*

millennium and likely earlier.[31] Bun-shaped ingots of the type found in Oman have been recovered from Tell Khuera and Mesopotamia in the west to Lothal in Gujarat.[32]

This analytical evidence is complemented by references to sources of copper in third-millennium cuneiform documents and later collections deriving from that period (Table 4.1). Most prominent in the economic, lexical and literary texts of the Akkadian to Ur III periods is the copper of Magan (Oman), clearly the most important Sumerian source at that time.[33] Along with its Gulf partners Dilmun and Meluhha, Magan accounts for virtually all contemporary references to the sources of Sumerian copper.[34] Sargonic texts mention a type of copper called "a-EN-da copper", in some instances specified as coming from Dilmun.[35] Early Dynastic III shipments of Dilmunite/Maganite copper record quantities up to about 100 kilograms (234 mina) at a time. Regarding Dilmun and Meluhha, the former, if correctly identified with Bahrain, was only an entrepôt which must have derived its copper from Magan; and

---

[31] Weisgerber 1981; *idem* 1987; Hauptmann 1985; Cleuziou 1986: 146; D.T. Potts 1986a: 133; *idem* 1990: 119-25; Hauptmann *et al.* 1988: 35f.
[32] Hauptmann *et al.* 1988: 41, fig. 4.6 (Oman); Weisgerber 1984: 198.
[33] This starting date for the use of Magan copper can probably be pushed back to ED III and even to the Archaic period since the copper of Dilmun, cited in those times, almost certainly came from Magan (Cleuziou 1986: 153).
[34] Significantly, these are the only sources cited in H*h*; see Table 4.1.
[35] Waetzoldt & Bachmann 1984: 6, n. 23.

while Meluhha certainly supplied some copper, probably from Rajasthan,[36] in the time of Gudea and after, it was better known for other commodities.[37] Occuring in lexical lists at Ebla, "Dilmun copper" and a "Dilmun shekel" (GIN.DILMUN) need not imply that these materials travelled as far west as Syria.[38] However, the still earlier references to "Dilmun copper" (?) (urudu-urudu.si dilmun) in an Archaic Uruk administrative text and to "Dilmun axes" (dilmun tùn) in the Archaic metals list from Uruk III indicate that Dilmun (*i.e.* originally Magan) was already supplying copper(work) to Sumer in the later fourth millennium, when analyses point rather to Iran.[39] The pattern of exploitation was evidently already quite complex, supplies being drawn from various regions at the same time.

The preeminence of Omani (Maganite) copper in the late third millennium was probably due in large part to the greater ease of transport by sea- or river-craft as opposed to equid caravans. Political factors, including the collapse of Proto-Elam, may also have played a part, but direct evidence is lacking.

There is yet no documentary support for the analytically attested pre-Early Dynastic III copper trade with Iran except for a vague allusion to the copper of the "mountains" in *Enmerkar and the Lord of Aratta*. When texts become more common, trade was already oriented towards Oman (Magan) and it is therefore not surprising that Iran is mentioned only once, in the later third millennium: Gudea refers to "mining" (ba-al)[40] copper at Abullat (KÁ.GAL-at^{ki}) in "the mountain of Kimaš", which he elsewhere calls "the copper mountain". If Abullat was really a mining area and not just an entrepôt it might be identified with the reserves near Amadiyeh in the Tiyari mountains.[41] However, historical evidence for Kimaš's proximity to Elam,[42] now understood as a principally highland entity, broadens the scope considerably and brings into consideration the large mines of the interior.

There is no third-millennium textual or analytical evidence for copper from Anatolia. Indeed the name of the Ergani mine area, extensively exploited by the Anatolians in the early second millennium, remains unknown.[43] This is hardly surprising for the late third millennium, when abundant supplies were accessible by sea in Oman, but the same cannot be said of earlier times when copper was being imported to Susa and the Hamrin from inner Iran. Ergani should have been more accessible since copper from there could be sent most of the way by boat or raft. It has been plausibly suggested that the Akkadian kings' campaigns in the north-west, and Naram-Sin's palace at Tell Brak, were designed to secure the trade routes to these mines. Even in the Old Assyrian period, however, though copper of various Anatolian places is mentioned,[44] there is very little evidence of copper trade with Mesopotamia. One letter from Der (near Sippar) indicates that some Anatolian copper

---

[36] The discovery of smelting sites in the copper-rich Khedri belt and artefact analyses confirm that the Indus exploited the copper of Rajasthan (Allchin & Allchin 1982: 186, 193, 253; Agrawala 1984; Agrawal 1984: 166). They may also have imported copper from Oman and Baluchistan (Allchin & Allchin 1982: 186; Lamberg-Karlovsky 1967: 151).

[37] Ratnagar 1981: 68-71.

[38] *Cf.* Michalowski 1990a, who argues that DILMUN in this expression is just an Eblaite writing for 'shekel' (*šaqil̮um*)), with no connection to the toponym.

[39] *Cf.* Glassner and Michalowski (above p. 35 n. 224), who argue that Archaic Dilmun is not Bahrain but a local Mesopotamian toponym.

[40] On the reading of ba-al here see *NBWI*: II 23 n. 60 and Behrens & Steible 1983: s.v. ba-al (1) and (2).

[41] *Cf.* Muhly 1973: 232. This would accord with the traditional location of Kimaš between the Hamrin and the Lower Zab (*RGTC 1*: 89). Falkenstein's suggestion of Ergani (1966: I, 50 n. 8) is less tenable.

[42] Edzard & Röllig 1976-80: 593.

[43] Röllig 1983: 346; Lewy 1971: 758 suggests Harana.

[44] Röllig 1983: 346.

reached Aššur, but there is no proof of movement further south.[45] One reason may be the southern bias of the extant documents (all from Girsu, Umma and Ur) and in particular the lack of texts from Agade, where most imperially organised trade would presumably have been recorded.

Lead isotope analyses may eventually provide an alternative basis for plotting the trade routes but only preliminary results are yet available.[46] A handful of tested copper objects from third-millennium Mesopotamia fall within the groups Yener defines as Anatolian.[47] Should this be confirmed it will represent the first solid analytical evidence for the use of Anatolian copper at this date in the south.

(b) Arsenical copper

Arsenic occurs as an independent ore body, rarely as a native metal and as a natural component of some copper ores in Anatolia and Iran. It seems not to have been extracted in pure form in the period concerning us and was not itself an object of trade. However, arsenic-rich ore or arsenic-rich smelted copper was widely exploited for alloying with copper.[48]

The first arsenic-copper alloys were doubtless produced unintentionally by smelting arsenical copper ores.[49] By the late fourth millennium, however, the advantages of the alloy were recognised and some means of producing arsenic-rich coppers, though of very variable proportions, was regularly employed. The precise means by which this was achieved is uncertain; it may not have involved alloying in a direct sense.[50] The lack of tin in high arsenic coppers at Early Dynastic III Ur shows at least that the two additives could be controlled independently.[51] It is perhaps significant that arsenic tends to occur in slags at urban sites, not at mining centres.

Whatever the method, numerous analyses attest that copper and arsenical copper remained the staple of the Sumerian and western Iranian base metal industries even after the introduction of tin-bronze in the second quarter of the third millennium.[52] Plotting the distribution of arsenic contents above 3%,[53] it becomes clear that arsenical copper was supplied on a regular basis to Mesopotamia, whence it reached Habuba Kabira,[54] and to northern Iran (Tepe Hissar),[55] western Iran (Susa II-IV and Tepe Sialk), Afghanistan (Mundigak and Shortugai), the Indus valley[56] and possibly Oman (see below). In south-central and eastern Iran the situation seems to have been more complex, arsenic being virtually absent at some sites (Tepe Yahya, Shahr-i Sokhta)[57] and present at others (Shahdad, Khurab, Khinaman).[58]

---

[45] Muhly 1973: 206-8; Larsen 1976: 77f.
[46] Yener *et al.* 1991.
[47] Below note 163.
[48] Moorey 1985: 4, 15f.
[49] Muhly 1985: 278. Arsenic-rich minerals can look like copper and tin, and could easily be mistaken for either (Charles 1980: 168, 172f.). Note, *e.g.*, the awl with 0.8% As at Cayönü (Muhly 1980-83: 350).
[50] Charles 1980: 168f.; Moorey 1985: 16.
[51] Moorey 1985: 17; Tallon 1987: 362.
[52] Muhly 1980-83: 355.
[53] Berthoud *et al.* 1982: 43ff.
[54] Muhly 1980-83: 354.
[55] Pigott *et al.* 1982: 230f., Table 3. Of 198 analyses all but 13 had arsenic of up to 5% with a mean of 1.32%. The mean increases from period I to period II/III, suggesting preferential use of arsenical ores. Slag and other debris indicates that smelting was done on the spot. See also the analyses of Hissar objects in Dayton 1978: 150, 151 fig. 86: As contents of 1.13, 2.5, 3.40, 0.61 and 4.00%.
[56] About 8% of metalwork from Indus sites is arsenical copper with between 1%-7% As (Agrawal 1971: 168; *idem* 1984: 163; *idem* 1985: 151; Ratnagar 1981: 83f.; Muhly 1973: 236f.).
[57] Berthoud *et al.* 1982: 43, 47 Table B, 51. However, Berthoud *et al.* (1982: 43, 45) concede that arsenic may have been added to some objects from Yahya, as implied by Curtis 1988: 120. The small proportions

At Susa (and to a lesser extent Mesopotamia) it is possible to follow variations in use more closely through the recent Louvre analyses.[59] Significant arsenic contents in the Susa I period (average 0.67%) are attributable to the use of Anarak ores rather than intentional alloying.[60] In the final Late Uruk to Early Dynastic I periods (Susa II/Susa IIIA), however, a higher average of 3.13% (accompanied by unusually high lead contents) indicates a period of experimentation which represents the transition to intentional alloying. Contemporary Sumerian and Akkadian (Hamrin) copper presents a similar, if less well documented, picture of arsenical coppers (above 1% As) and only traces of tin,[61] suggesting a similar reliance on Anarak copper at least down to Early Dynastic I. In Early Dynastic III and Akkadian times (Susa IVA1-IVB) – the highpoint of arsenic use at Susa – a greater clustering of arsenic contents between 1% and 3% (average 1.76%)[62] indicates that alloying technology was now well established and successfully controlled. Arsenic contents drop off to an average of 1.2%[63] in the Ur III to Isin-Larsa periods (Susa V) as the use of tin-bronze gains ground. Somewhat surprisingly, there is no clear correlation at Susa between type of object and arsenic content[64] – as would be expected if the arsenic was being added primarily for its hardening qualities and as begins to appear in tin-bronzes at the end of the millennium.

The lack of a recognised word for arsenic in third millennium texts,[65] forces the search for sources to rely entirely on modern geological information. The major Near Eastern deposits of arsenic (and arsenical copper) ores are the Talmessi and Meskani mines near Anarak.[66] Copper from these regions typically contain about 1-2% arsenic, and recent studies are surely right in taking this as the origin of the arsenical copper used at Susa, Tepe Sialk, Tepe Hissar, Shahdad, Khinaman and (rarely) Tepe Yahya.[67] Arsenic-rich ores are also reported in Armenia and these, rather than Anarak, may account for the early arsenical coppers of Syro-Anatolia.[68] Further east, arsenical ores are said to occur in copper-rich Rajasthan.[69] In the later third millennium, when much copper was coming along the Gulf from Oman, Sumer

of As at Malyan (Pigott 1980: 107) are probably natural alloys from the use of Ararak copper ores (Sumner 1986: 204).

[58] Curtis 1988: 118-20; Cowell *apud* Curtis 1988: 122.
[59] Berthoud *et al.* 1982: 46; Malfoy & Menu 1987: 356-60.
[60] Malfoy & Menu 1987: 357, 364.
[61] Moorey *et al.* 1972; Craddock 1984; Berthoud *et al.* 1982: 47 Table B. A significant proportion of the ED I copper from the Hamrin has 1%-3% As and somewhat less has over 3% As (Berthoud *et al.* 1982: 47).
[62] Weighted average for the whole period as reported in Malfoy & Menu 1987: Table A. Total sample size 295.
[63] Weighted average on total sample of 232. The average for 20 samples from the Ur III (Susa VA) period alone is much lower: 0.6% (*ibid.*).
[64] Malfoy & Menu 1987: 358 Table C, 360.
[65] Berthoud *et al.* 1982: 42, 45; Moorey 1985: 1 (not sù-gan), 16 (not *annaku*). But for sù-gan see now Waetzoldt & Bachmann 1984: 8-10, 13f., 18, where it is clear that sù-gan is a valuable material and an additive, so perhaps arsenic or antimony (the latter now attested by a cast tube of 99.7% antimony from 3rd-mill. Leilan in Syria [Moorey pers. comm.]). The word for arsenic, if there was one, may be among the many metal terms which had fallen out of use before the Ur III period. Note also the OAkk term urudu zabar "copper-bronze", which seems to refer to a copper alloy of some kind (not necessarily tin) (Limet 1972a: 10).
[66] Heskell & Lamberg-Karlovsky 1980: 258f.; Malfoy & Menu 1987: 357. A third Iranian source of arsenical copper is Taknar, 300 km east of Tepe Hissar (Bazin & Hübner 1969: pl. XVIII no. 123); but to what extent this may have been exploited in the 3rd mill. is unclear (Pigott *et al.* 1982: 232).
[67] Heskell & Lamberg-Karlovsky 1980: 259; Pigott *et al.* 1982: 231; Berthoud *et al.* 1982: 43-45; Malfoy & Menu 1987: 357; Curtis 1989: 118, 120, 122.
[68] Muhly 1976: 90. Ratnagar (1981: 84) also reports arsenical ores at Takht-i Suleiman in southern Kurdistan but these are not mentioned in the CNRS report (Berthoud *et al.* 1982).
[69] Agrawal 1984: 165.

must also have maintained connections with one or other of these highland regions for their supplies of arsenic-rich additives.[70]

The situation in Oman is currently unclear. The arsenic contents in sampled ores are low, as are those of Hafit period slags, ingots and artefacts.[71] On the other hand, Umm an-Nar period ingots, raw copper and especially artefacts show substantially higher arsenic levels.[72] These and similar discrepancies at Timna in Sinai and at Shahr-i Sokhta may be explained by the fact that some refining processes cause a significant enrichment of certain minerals in the copper, including arsenic and nickel.[73] Alternatively, Hauptmann suggests that Omani metalsmiths may have drawn upon localised arsenic-rich mineralizations, *e.g.* in the Wadi Samad area, which were subsequently worked out.[74] Whatever the precise explanation, the existence of arsenical coppers in Oman raises the possibility that at least some of Sumer's (low) arsenical coppers are from that region rather than inner Iran.

(c) Tin

Along with arsenic, tin was the principal material alloyed with copper in third-millennium Mesopotamia. Near Eastern copper ores have varying natural tin contents of up to about 0.05%, not enough to have an appreciable effect on the qualities of the smelted metal.[75] The addition of anywhere between 3% and 15% tin yields a significantly harder product[76] and achieves a more gold-like colour, while lesser quantities (down to *ca.* 0.05 %) lower the melting point, act as a flux and facilitate casting, especially important for *cire perdue* work.[77] The similar effects of tin and arsenic are cumulative, so that both could be used together.[78] Metallic tin was occasionally used as a solder, for plating copper bowls and for making small objects of pure tin.[79]

Already in the Early Dynastic I period, texts from Ur distinguish between tin bronze (zabar)[80] and copper (urudu).[81] Metallic tin (AN.NA) first appears in the Early Dynastic II/III Fara texts.[82] Recipes from that period and later for making bronze specify proportions of 6:1 copper to tin (*i.e.* 14% tin), indicating that the refined metal was being used in alloying.[83] In earlier periods tin may have been added as cassiterite ore.[84]

---

70   Berthoud *et al.* 1982: 45.
71   Ore analyses show As averaging 0.01%-0.40% (Berthoud *et al.* 1982: 42f.; Hauptmann 1985: 79, Table 19).
72   Averages as follows: 16 ingots - 0.42%; 6 raw copper frags. - 0.62%; 7 artefacts - 0.94% (Hauptmann *et al.* 1988: 41-46; *cf.* Hauptmann 1985: 81, Table 21). Berthoud *et al.* 1982: 45 report artefacts with up to 7% As.
73   Hauptmann *et al.* 1988: 43, 46.
74   Hauptmann 1985: 83; *idem* 1987: 212; Hauptmann *et al.* 1988: 46.
75   Malfoy & Menu 1987: 361.
76   See Moorey 1985: 17f. and Malfoy & Menu 1987: 361 on the minimum tin content attributable to intentional alloying.
77   Berthoud *et al.* 1982: 48f., 50; Malfoy & Menu 1987: 361.
78   This was clearly done at Susa where tin contents of 0.05-1% are often found together with arsenic contents of over 1% while true bronzes of over 5% tin usually have less than 1% arsenic (Malfoy & Menu 1987: 361).
79   Craddock 1984 (solder); Moorey 1985: 127 (plating); Limet 1960: 52; Muhly 1985: 279, n. 29 (tin objects).
80   That this word could also mean "mirror" (Steinkeller 1987) suggests an appreciation of its ability to create a more reflective surface.
81   Limet 1960: 52.
82   *Ibid.*: 66, 254.
83   *Ibid.*: 67-73, 121-24 (Ur III); Moorey 1985: 18f.; Muhly 1985: 280f. (Ebla). These texts also specify tin contents of 5:1 (17%), 7:1 (12.5%) and 9:1 (10%), the lower proportions corresponding to the majority of

Analytical data substantiates and supplements this evidence. Excluding an anomalous 5.62% tin-bronze at Gawra VII,[85] tin-bronze is not attested by analyses as a consistent feature of Mesopotamian and Susian metallurgy until Early Dynastic III, by which time the techniques of copper alloying seem to have been standardized throughout Sumer-Akkad and Susiana.[86] These regions, and to a lesser extent Luristan,[87] seem to have maintained an almost exclusive monopoly on the casting of tin bronzes until the end of the millennium.[88] Tin contents of any significance (above 1 or 2%) are conspicuous by their absence at sites in highland Iran and Afghanistan even along the Khorasan road (*e.g.* Tepe Hissar), the natural route of overland supply to Mesopotamia from northern Iran and Central Asia.[89] Likewise in the Gulf, substantial levels of tin are very rare in Oman (although even low tin contents are probably the result of foreign tin-bearing elements) and virtually unattested on Bahrain and Umm an-Nar islands.[90] Tin was rarely used in southern Turkmenia before the Namazga V period.[91]

---

excavated artefacts. At Susa, *e.g.*, more than 60% of the objects tested had tin contents of below 9% (Malfoy & Menu 1987: 362).

[84] Moorey 1985: 128; Berthoud *et al.* 1982: 45, 49.

[85] Speiser 1935: 102; Moorey 1985: 20. This analysis cannot be confirmed since the object is now lost. Bronzes seem to appear somewhat earlier in Syria (early 3rd mill. Judeideh; Muhly 1980-83: 354) and Anatolia (see below). Previous reports of occasional tin-bronzes at Susa I (axe 2.3% Sn; Stech *et al.* 1986: 43) and Susa II (Berthoud *et al.* 1982: 47, Table C) are implied to be erroneous by the more recent report of the systematic analyses (Malfoy & Menu 1987: 360-62, Table D).

[86] Berthoud *et al.* 1982: 47; Malfoy & Menu 1987: 361, 368f. Mesopotamian analyses collected in Moorey 1985: 51-68. Add now Malfoy & Menu 1987: 364, 371 (Tello); Muscarella 1988: nos 435, 464-67, 494-95, 508.

[87] The 3rd-mill. 'Luristan bronze' industry is usually regarded as being based on arsenical copper (Amiet 1976: 23; *idem* 1986: 131; Moorey 1981: 16; *idem* 1982: 87). The published analyses, however, indicate that tin-bronze was employed there as commonly as in Sumer-Susiana, especially from the Akkadian period on (*cf.* Vanden Berghe 1968: 56; Malfoy & Menu 1987: 362). In two major collections which have been systematically tested (Moorey 1971a; Amiet 1976), between a quarter and a third of the 3rd-mill. types have tin contents of 2% and over (Moorey 1971a: nos 2 (3.6%), 3 (9.3%), 4 (6.1%), 5 (10.3%), 6 (5.3%), 7 (11.7%), 8 (2.1%), 9 (8.9%), 12 (13.0%), 13 (8.4%), 29 (8.3%), 31 (12.2%), 33 (9.9%), 34 (13.1%); Amiet 1976: nos 11 (7.5%), 12 (10.5%), 13 (16.2%), 17 (7.7%), 18 (7.0%)). Note also an inscribed Luristan-type adze with 17.8% Sn (André-Leichnam & Tallon 1985) and the Susa hammer inscribed by Šulgi which is 7% Sn (Tallon 1987: no. 195; *cf.* Amiet 1976: 24, "20%"). Also relevant are the dozen or so analyses from Godin III (ED III - early 2nd mill.) which typically reveal about 9% Sn (Young, pers. comm.). Amiet 1976: 23 notes the increase in tin use in the Akkadian period, though the supposed decrease at Ur is spurious.

[88] Berthoud *et al.* 1982: 51.

[89] Heskel & Lamberg-Karlovsky 1980: 250, 260; Pigott 1980: 105, 107; Berthoud *et al.* 1982: Table C; Moorey 1982: 87f.; Stech *et al.* 1986: 43; Tallon 1987: 335; Dyson 1987: 653, n. 4; Beyer 1989: 118. Among the rare significant tin contents (>1%) reported from highland Iran (*cf.* previously Moorey 1982: 87f.) and Afghanistan are: *Iran –* Tepe Hissar, of 203 objects tested only 2 had above 1% Sn (Pigott 1989: 29-32), Period II/III: belt hook 4.1%, spearhead 3.6%; Tepe Yahya, IVB: 8%, IVA: many articles 2-3% (Pigott 1980: 105; Heskel *et al.* 1980); Tepe Sialk: "bronze" in period V, and possibly IV, needle in III6 (Muhly 1973: 232; Stech *et al.* 1986: 43; Ghirshman 1938: 206); Tal-i Malyan, Kaftari period: 3 "tin bronzes" (Pigott 1980: 107); Khinaman: axe 2.5%, dagger 8.1% (Curtis 1988: 104, 106). *Afghanistan –* Gar-i-Mar, Chalcolithic: 1 object *ca.* 7% (F. Shaffer 1978: 89); Mundigak, Period I5: one "low tin bronze" (Casal 1961: 247; F. Shaffer 1978: 141ff.), Period III6: shaft-hole axes and adze *ca.* 5%, other objects *ca.* 1% (*ibid.*; Berthoud *et al.* 1982: 50), Period IV: pins etc. *ca.* 1.5%; 'Snake Cave' artefacts (F. Shaffer 1978: 89, 115, 144).

[90] Reported bronzes include: Hili A, late 3rd mill. – dagger 6% Sn (Cleuziou 1989a: 74); copper residue from a furnace at Hili 8, Phase IIf (late 3rd mill.) had *ca.* 0.5% tin (Hauptmann 1987: 214-17; Cleuziou 1989a: 74). Umm an-Nar – no tin among analyses of 10 grave goods (Frifelt 1991: 99f.); late 3rd mill.: 0.11%, 0.26% and three others between 0.05-1.0% Sn (Berthoud *et al.* 1982: 47f. 50). Bahrain – no tin among 30 analyses dating 2300-1700 BC (Muhly 1980-83: 360; *cf.* previously McKerrell 1978: 21; Berthoud *et al.* 1982: 50). Even the low percentages may reflect alloying since the copper of Oman has a very low natural tin content (*ibid.*: 48).

[91] Stech *et al.* 1986: 44.

The detailed information from Susa may again be used to complement the more meagre Mesopotamian evidence. Average tin contents up to the Early Dynastic IIIA period (Susa IVA1) of below 0.015% reflect natural ore contents. It is only in Early Dynastic IIIB (Susa IVA2) – notably in the *Vase à la Cachette* [92] – that significant tin contents appear. These are still overwhelmingly (93%) below 5% tin, thus added as flux rather than hardener. Definite bronzes of over 5% tin remain relatively rare in the Akkadian (Susa IVB) period (3% of tested objects) and Ur III (Susa VA) times (10% of sample). The clear emergence of tin-bronze technology as a regular feature of Susian metallurgy does not occur until the succeeding Isin-Larsa (Susa VB) period, when 48% of tested objects fall above the 5% threshold.[93]

Third-millennium texts often associate tin (AN.NA, *annaku*)[94] with lapis lazuli and carnelian, and indicate that, like these stones, it came from the east (Table 4.2). The epic poem *Enmerkar and Lugalbanda* says of Aratta that "its soil is (the colour of?) tin-stone (im-an-na)". Magan is said to have tin (and copper) in a hymn to Ninurta, and "Dilmun tin" is mentioned at Ebla, where there are recipes for making 10% tin-bronzes.[95] The original point of trans-shipment of the Gulf supplies may be more accurately indicated by Gudea who claims to have brought tin from Meluhha. An Early Dynastic III administrative text records the assignment (for trade?) of one mina of tin to the ensi of Urua, an eastern border town, and five minas of tin are mentioned among the records of Ummaite merchants residing at Susa in Akkadian times, though where it was traded to or from is unclear.[96] The description of various places as "tin mountains" in the *lipšur* litanies and HAR-RA:*habullu* is of little help while their locations remain unknown. Tin was taken as booty from Zabšali-Šimaški by Šu-Sin and probably also from Anšan by Šulgi. It continued to be supplied to Mesopotamia from the east in the early second millennium, both Susa and Šušarra (Shemsharra) apparently serving as points of entry into the lowlands;[97] but western sources (Cornwall, Etruria and (?) Spain) were perhaps then beginning to be drawn upon, especially for the Levant.[98] These alternatives became increasingly important in the later second and first millennia.

---

[92] Of 42 copper objects in this hoard 4 have tin contents above 7%, 2 have 2% and 36 are of copper/arsenical copper (Malfoy & Menu 1987: 361, Table D, 368f.; Tallon 1987: 333).

[93] Malfoy & Menu 1987: Table D. In the Susa VB period there is also the first clear evidence of the preferential use of tin-bronze for certain kinds of objects, *viz.* weapons and hard-wearing utensils (Malfoy & Menu 1987: 362, Table E).

[94] In later periods there is some evidence, including surprisingly low prices, to suggest that AN.NA/*annaku* may have denoted 'lead', and the possibility of some equivocation in earlier periods cannot be excluded (Landsberger 1965; Muhly *et al.* 1973; Powell 1990: 87). Exceptionally kù-an-na may also denote iron (Muhly 1973: 440 n. 341). In one passage kù may mean 'tin' (Heimpel 1982: 67 n. 21).

[95] Muhly 1985: 280f.

[96] Lambert 1953: 65 (Nik. 310) (Urua); Foster in press; Scheil 1913: no. 35 (Susa).

[97] For tin trade in the OAss and OB periods see Larsen 1976: 87-9; *idem* 1982: 40; Leemans 1960: 123f.; Muhly 1973: 292ff. In the OAss Cappadocian trade, tin supplied to Aššur from the east was sent north-west to Kaneš. In the OB period also, tin was traded from east to west, the cities of Susa, Der, Ešnunna, Sippar and Larsa acting as transit stations, though the precise route, and often the direction of travel, is uncertain (Leemans 1968: 201-14; Malamat 1970; Dossin 1970). From Mari tin was sent on to Syro-Palestine and perhaps Crete (Muhly 1973: 292ff; Dossin 1970). Especially important is the reference to tin sent to Mari from "Šelarpak", identified as Siwe-palar-huppak, king of Anšan (Dossin 1970: 97). Some eastern tin also entered Mesopotamia via Šušarra (Shemshara) (Laessøe 1959).

[98] Berthoud *et al.* 1982: 50.

TABLE 4.2

Origins of Third-Millennium Tin (an-na/*annaku*) According to Cuneiform Sources[1]

Literary Texts

Aratta	*EL* 415
Near Aratta?	*ELA* 17-19
Magan[2]	Hymn to Ninurta (M. Cohen 1975: 28 l. 144)
Mines beyond Ebih (Hamrin)	*Innana and Ebih* (Muhly 1973: 288, n. 341)[3]
Unspecified	*The Curse of Agade* 27
?	Hymn to Ninurta (M. Cohen 1975: 31, ll. 144f.)[4]

Lexical Texts[5]

Zaršur	H*h* XXII:25´ (Leemans 1960: 7, l. 25)
[Za]rha	*lipšur*.23 (*ibid.*: 8, l. 23)
BAR-gungunnu	*lipšur*.24; H*h* XXII:26´ (*ibid.*: l. 24)
Dilmun	*MEE 1*: 1298 Rs. xi:6-7; Pettinato 1983: 77; Waetzoldt 1981: 365-67 (Ebla)

Royal Inscriptions

Meluhha	*Gudea*: Cyl. B xiv:13 (Landsberger 1966: vol. I, 48; Pettinato 1972: 82)[6]
Šimaški/Zabšali (booty)	*Šu-Sin*: Kutscher 1989: BT4 v:9-13 (=*IRSA*: IIIA4e), Kärki 1986: Šu-Sin 20a
Unspecified	*Gudea*: Cyl. A xvi:28 (Pettinato 1972: 144)

Administrative Texts

Anšan? (booty)	*Šulgi* (Davidović 1984: 186f., 200)
Dilmun?	*Ur III*: *UET III*: no. 368 (Leemans 1960: 161)

Notes

1   *Cf.* previous reviews in Pettinato 1972: 82; Muhly 1973: 288-90, 306f.; Moorey 1985: 128-132; Howard-Carter 1987: 75f.
2   Name restored.
3   kù-an-na: Heimpel (1982: 67 n. 2) suggests that this may be iron rather than tin.
4   *Pace* Pettinato 1972: 82 (followed by Muhly 1973: 309) *EWO* 232 (Kramer & Maier 1989: 46) does not cite Meluhha as a *source* of tin.
5   Each except Dilmun described as a "tin mountain" (kur an-na).
6   Pettinato apparently takes the "from Meluhha" to apply only to the carnelian and thus regards the source of this tin as unspecified.

Correlating the testimony of these documents with the evidence of modern geological reconnaissance has proved much more difficult, and the origin of Near Eastern tin remains one of the outstanding problems of ancient metallurgy (Fig. 21). As Muhly's recent statement puts it, "the problem has always been that there are no nearby sources of tin that could have supplied the major bronze industries of the eastern Mediterranean [and Near East]".[99] Tin exists as ore veins in granite and as eroded placer deposits in streams. Vein mining is very difficult and virtually all ancient tin was probably derived from alluvial deposits. Claims regarding the existence of tin deposits of both kinds in the Near East, both east and west of Mesopotamia, have often been made.[100] Many of these regions can be excluded on geological grounds but much scope for uncertainty remains.

---

99   Muhly *et al.* 1991: 209.
100   Reviewed in Forbes 1972: 140ff. (now largely outdated); Muhly 1973: 248-61; Muhly *et al.* 1991: 209f.; Franklin *et al.* 1978: *passim*; de Jesus 1980: 53ff.; Berthoud *et al.* 1982: 49.

To the east, some areas of modern Iran are geologically suitable for the occurrence of tin and a number of reports of stanniferous ores have been made but subsequent reconnaissance has thrown many of these into doubt and the existence of any usable deposits remains unconfirmed.[101] Scepticism regarding Iranian tin continues[102] but in the present state of uncertainty it would be hasty to assume that these reports are all entirely baseless.

For confirmed deposits, however, it is necessary to look further east to Afghanistan where tin deposits have recently been discovered south of Herat.[103] These include deposits of stannite at Misgaran and alluvial cassiterite in the Sarkar valley.[104] The Misgaran tin deposits give way to copper ores with traces of "protohistorical" workings.[105] This Afghan tin source probably represents the tin of Drangiana (modern Seistan) mentioned by Strabo (XV, ii: 10). Other tin sources are reported in eastern Afghanistan.[106] At a similar distance from Sumer, tin has long been known to exist in the Zeravshan Valley of Uzbekistan. This Central Asian supply seems to have been exploited locally from the late third millennium when bronze appears in Turkmenia (Namazga V).[107] Further afield there is tin in Pakistan and India, including Gujarat, but no evidence for its use at this date.[108] The possibility of tin trade with Thailand has largely been abandoned since the discovery of the Afghan sources.[109]

The possibility of alternative supplies of tin north and north-west of Sumer remains problematic. Forbes followed by Muhly cites reports of tin around Mt Sahand in Azerbaijan and further north along the Kura river between Baku and Tiflis in Caucasia.[110] However, Muhly later questions the existence of any tin in Iran and likewise concludes from more recent geological reports that "It can now be stated with some confidence that there is no tin in the Caucasus".[111] But tin (cassiterite) has been recovered from Middle Bronze Age Metsamor on the southern side of the Armenian massif, and a geological report is said to have confirmed the presence of nearby tin deposits at the foot of Mt Aragats.[112]

The possibility that some tin was mined somewhere in Anatolia, at least for local use, has been suggested on the basis of a series of early tin bronzes noted from the north-eastern Aegean (Troy, Poliochni, Thermi) as well as western (Kusura), south-eastern (Judeideh, Tarsus) and central Anatolia (Horoztepe, Alaca Hüyük,

---

[101] Forbes 1964; revised ed. 1972: 140ff. reviewing a variety of supposed sources across the Iranian platau in Kerman (Karadagh, Kuh-i Benan and Bam), Meshed, the southern slopes of the eastern Elburz (near Damghan, Shahrud and Asterabad) and Mt Sahand (Azerbaijan). This picture was initially largely accepted by Muhly (1973: 260f.) (omiting sources in the Kerman regions of Kara Dagh, Kuh-i Benam and Bam) and was still quoted by Ratnagar (1981: 92f.). Muhly later implied that all of these sources are questionable, at the same time noting a report of alluvial and vein tin ore near the Shah Kuh in the Dasht-i Lut (Muhy 1976: 97f.; cf. Ratnagar 1981: 93). More recently he seems to suspect even this (Muhly 1980: 30f.; *idem* 1985).

[102] Moorey 1985: 131; Malfoy & Menu 1987: 360f.

[103] Cleuziou & Berthoud 1982: 24ff.; Berthoud *et al.* 1982: 49f.; Stech *et al.* 1986: 44-46; Muhly *et al.* 1991: 210.

[104] Tallon 1987: 334f.

[105] Berthoud *et al.* 1982: 49.

[106] Moorey 1985: 131.

[107] Masson *et al.* 1972: 128; Terekhova 1981: 319.

[108] Agrawal 1984: 165; Moorey 1985: 132.

[109] Muhly 1980: 31f.

[110] Forber 1972: 141; Muhly 1973: 261.

[111] Muhly 1976: 98.

[112] Crawford 1974: 243; Moorey 1985: 131.

Ahlalatlibel).[113] De Jesus notes that many of the earliest pieces are from coastal sites (Troy, Thermi, Mersin, the Amuq and Poliochni), perhaps suggesting a sea-borne distribution network.[114]

The Troy II/III date usually assigned to these precocious bronzes would place them in the late fourth and early third millennia, earlier than the sustained appearance of bronze in southern Mesopotamia. More recent assessments, however, place the beginnings of Anatolian bronze in the Troy IIg/Poliochni-*Giallo*/Early Bronze III horizon at the end of the third millennium, *i.e.* later than in Sumer.[115] While this later dating seems presently the more acceptable, to the extent that the question of chronological priority remains open so too does the possibility of tin being exported from Anatolia to Sumer.

It is perhaps significant that the first substantial use of tin and gold – both alluvial minerals – in Anatolia occurs at about the same time (Troy II, Poliochni-*Giallo*, Alaca Hüyük). Furthermore, recent analyses of copper-based material from Troy IIg and Poliochni-*Giallo* suggest that the appearance of these metals was accompanied by the occurrence of radically different lead isotope profiles, indicating the use of much older (Precambrian), non-Anatolian ores.[116] Such ores are known to exist in Central Asia, and it would be tempting to link the 'exotic' lead with Afghan tin were it not for the fact that the lead also appears in non-bronze artefacts. This leads Muhly to conclude that the 'exotic' lead comes from the copper ore, which he suggests began then to be imported from some eastern (Central Asian?) region, along with the new metals tin and gold and their associated technologies, positing a trade route across the Black Sea. As regards the tin itself, however, these analyses provide no basis for deeming the ores local or foreign; nor is the association with 'exotic' copper compelling, since it is unclear why copper-rich Anatolia should have drawn on such a remote source. Moreover, as regards the third millennium, it must be emphasised that the existing documentary evidence gives no grounds for believing that any northern sources were exploited in Mesopotamia. Indeed, if the pattern of trade in the early second millennium is any reflection of earlier practice, the direction of supply was precisely the reverse, tin being traded from Babylonia through Assyria to Cappadocia.

Geological evidence also is equivocal. The presence of various forms of tin in Anatolia has often been asserted but proof remains elusive.[117] Recent claims centre on five areas, three of them in the north-west (the Sakarya basin; nearby Bilecik; and the Handere Valley near Bursa) and two in the Taurus mountains near Sulucadere and at Kestel, the latter in close proximity to sites (some third millennium) where smelting was undertaken.[118] De Jesus also notes the relatively high tin contents (0.27%) recorded in native copper at Ergani and in ancient slag samples from Bakir

---

[113] Muhly 1976: 100; *idem* 1985: 283f.; *idem* 1993: 240f.; de Jesus 1980: 58f., 124ff.; Yakar 1984: 72; Stech *et al.* 1986: 52-55; Yener & Goodway 1992: 84f.; Yener & Vandiver 1993: 208f. In support of an Anatolian tin source it has also been pointed out that places in these regions (viz. the Nairi Lands and various Neo-Hittite city-states) feature as major sources of tin (often booty) in the second and first mill. (Leemans 1968: 209; Moorey 1985: 129f.; *contra* Muhly 1985: 284f.). A nearby source such as this would also account for the depreciation in tin prices in the late second mill. (Moorey 1985: 130).

[114] de Jesus 1980: 58; *cf.* Muhly 1985: 284.

[115] Muhly *et al.* 1991: 215f.

[116] Muhly *et al.* 1991: 216-19.

[117] Regions cited include those around Eskişehir, Tilek (north of Ergani), Kastamuni (in the Akdagh), the Sakarya river, Bilecik (four deposits), Balikesir and Manisa. See Forbes 1972: 140; Muhly 1973: 257; *idem* 1976: 100; Muhly & Wertime 1973: 119; Pernicka *et al.* 1992.

[118] de Jesus 1980: 55f., Map 20 (north-west); Yakar 1984: 80; Yener 1986: 472; Yener & Özbal 1987; Yener *et al.* 1989; Yener & Vandiver 1993: 213; Willies 1990 (Taurus).

Çay.[119] Potentially the most compelling evidence are the analyses of slag on twenty-four crucible fragments from the third-millennium smelting site of Göltepe near Kestel, of which twenty-one have tin oxide contents enriched to an average 20-30 wt %, some over 90 wt %. Yener believes the ore was smelted to create tin ingots.[120] The ores presumably came from the adjacent Kestel mine, where worked-out veins bearing up to 1.5% tin as well as iron have been identified by Yener, and cassiterite has been panned in the stream at the base of the site.[121] However, while the evidence for an Anatolian tin source is accumulating, its interpretation remains controvercial.[122] A key issue in any resolution of the current debate will be the determination of the original concentrations of tin mineralization in the potential sources cited, and in particular the question whether they could have been exploited using Bronze Age technology to yield tin suitable for alloying.

Looking beyond Turkey, the possibility of Bohemian tin entering the Near East, particularly Anatolia, cannot be excluded but remains unproven.[123] The deposits are alluvial and were exploited very early in the local Early Bronze Age. To the south-west of Mesopotamia, there is alluvial tin in the Egyptian eastern desert but it seems not to have been exploited on a significant scale in the third millennium.[124] In the western Mediterranean, tin occurs in France, Spain, Portugal, Italy and Cornwall, but this seems not to have reached the Near East in significant quantities.[125]

As the evidence stands, therefore, the possibility of tin reaching Mesopotamia in the third millennium from Iran, Uzbekistan or Bohemia cannot be excluded but Afghanistan and Anatolia are the most likely sources. With regard to the Afghan source, the primarily Mesopotamian-oriented distribution pattern of tin-bronzes during this period, and in particular their scarcity in highland Iran, implies either that the tin trade was so effectively controlled by, or directed towards, the Mesopotamian consumers that virtually no 'drain off' occurred en route across Iran;[126] or that the trade did not pass through these regions at all but rather south from Afghanistan through territory controlled by the cities of the Indus Valley and thence by sea up the Gulf. A sea-route is supported by the fact that tin was used in considerable quantities by the Harappan metalsmiths but not in the pre- or post-Harappan periods.[127] It would also account for the tradition of Meluhhan (and Dilmunite and Maganite) tin, its association with lapis lazuli and carnelian (likewise brought from Meluhha) and for the presence of tin-bronze in Oman and ceramic parallels between Umm an-Nar and the Indo-Iranian borderlands (Sokhta, Bampur).[128]

---

[119] de Jesus 1980: 55f.
[120] Yener & Goodman 1992; Yener & Vandiver 1993: 234; *idem* 1993a: 257.
[121] Yener *et al.* 1989; Yener *et al.* 1989a; Yener & Goodway 1992; Willies 1990; Yener & Vandiver 1993: 215.
[122] Muhly 1993; Muhly *et al.* 1991; Hall & Steadman 1991; Pernicka *et al.* 1992; *cf.* Yener & Goodway 1992; Willies 1992. Muhly *et al.* 1991: 212-15, Hall & Steadman 1991 and Pernicka *et al.* 1992 maintain that silver and gold, rather than tin, were mined at Kestel and Sulucadere. The presence of simple iron artefacts at mid-3rd mill. Göltepe, along with iron contents of around 17% on one crucible fragment, also raise the possibility that the Taurus miners were somehow processing iron.
[123] Moorey 1985: 132; Muhly 1985: 288f.
[124] Muhly 1976: 102-4; Muhly *et al.* 1991: 210f.
[125] *Ibid.*: 209f.
[126] Moorey 1982b: 88; Berthoud *et al.* 1982: 51; Stech *et al.* 1986: 43, 48.
[127] Ratnagar 1981: 83; Muhly 1973: 236; Agrawal 1984: 164. Of the 210 analyses reported by Agrawal (1984: 164), 33% are tin bronzes (> *ca.* 2%), and 20% of the 177 from Mohenjo-daro contain between 8% and 12% tin.
[128] D.T. Potts 1990: 125.

(d) Lead and Silver

Lead was smelted from a very early date to make a wide variety of objects, and for alloying with copper, for which it facilitates casting and yields a more silvery colour.[129] It is present in contents of up to 1% in Iranian copper ores but only as traces in Omani ores.[130] High lead coppers are conspicuous in the final Late Uruk to Early Dynastic I periods at Susa (average 3.27% for late Susa II-IIIA) and in Late Uruk Sumer,[131] probably the outcome of general experimentation with various alloys in a situation where copper and lead smiths worked closely together. The use of metallic lead for making objects, particularly vessels, is also common at this time, reaching a peak in the early Early Dynastic period.[132] Thereafter, lead objects, as well as high-lead coppers, are less common[133] except in Luristan[134] and at Tepe Hissar.[135] This analytical data is confirmed by the Ur III recipes in which lead is mentioned only once, apparently to give colour to part of a statue.[136] In contrast to Sumer, lead is practically absent from Early Dynastic I copper in the Hamrin; likewise in Oman which has no close sources.[137] A few highly leaded coppers are reported from Mundigak and Shortugai.[138] Third-millennium lead (and copper) smelting installations, perhaps used for obtaining silver, have been excavated at Tepe Hissar and Tal-i Malyan.[139]

Artefacts of silver appear widely from the fourth millennium in Mesopotamia, Iran and elsewhere in the Near East.[140] Silver was regarded as a valuable metal, reserved primarily for ornaments and luxury items (Fig. 23). From the Akkadian period on it served also as the principal standard of exchange. Since silver seems to have been obtained chiefly by cupellation from argentiferous lead ores,[141] their sources may be discussed together.

Sources of lead-silver are widespread in the Near East.[142] Of the numerous Anatolian ore deposits the richest is Bulgar Maden in the Taurus.[143] In Iran argentiferous silver has been reported from Azerbaijan, the Miyana-Zanjan and Sava-Qazvin-Teheran regions, Khurasan, the Isfahan-Kashan and Anarak-Yazd regions, and Kerman.[144] Lead deposits are widespread around the periphery of the central

---

[129] See review in Moorey 1985: 121-126.
[130] Malfoy & Menu 1987: 362.
[131] Moorey 1985: 24; Malfoy & Menu 1987: 362f., Tables F, G.
[132] Lead vessels are common in the 'Jemdet Nasr' Cemetery at Ur (Woolley 1955), the Khafajeh graves (Delougaz 1967) and at Susa (Amiet 1986: 59, 96).
[133] Berthoud *et al.* 1982: 47. Use of lead revives somewhat at Susa in the Isin-Larsa period (Susa VB) (Malfoy & Menu 1987: 364).
[134] The use of lead continues in Luristan through the 3rd mill. (average 2.3%), with the highest average contents in the ED IIIB (4.1%) and Akkadian (4.5%) periods, ceasing in the late 3rd mill. (Susa V) (Malfoy & Menu 1987: 364). Lead use seems to be associated particularly with arsenical copper rather than tin bronze.
[135] Lead occurs in significant traces throughout Hissar I-III (mean 0.73%), the highest levels occurring in period II/III where 16 objects had betwen 4% and 5% Pb (Pigott *et al.* 1982: 230, Table 4). Pigott suggests that it was deliberately added to facilitate casting (*ibid.*).
[136] Limet 1960: 23f.
[137] Berthoud *et al.* 1982: 51; but note lead ores, smelting and leaded coppers (Umm an-Nar grave goods) in Oman cited by Tosi 1975: 202.
[138] Berthoud *et al.* 1982: 43.
[139] Pigott 1980: 105; Stech *et al.* 1986: 49.
[140] Moorey 1985: 14f. (Mesopotamia); Stech *et al.* 1986: 49 (Iran).
[141] Moorey 1985: 108.
[142] Moorey 1985: 110-113.
[143] de Jesus 1980: 64; Yener 1986; Muhly *et al.* 1991: 212f.
[144] Moorey 1985: 111.

Figure 23.   Bull holding spouted vessel. From (?)Iran. Silver. Proto-Elamite period. Ht. 16.3 cm.

deserts, especially in the region of Anarak. Analyses of slag from Tepe Hissar suggest that lead was smelted at that site along with copper.[145] Further afield, silver occurs in Afghanistan and India.[146] It was widely used in the Indus in the Harappan period, perhaps partly obtained by trade with Sumer.[147]

The lead-silver ores of southern Anatolia were exploited locally from prehistoric times and probably supported the extensive consumption at Byblos in the fourth millennium.[148] Textual evidence indicates that these regions supplied Mesopotamia from at least the early second millennium. Although there is no direct documentary

[145] Pigott *et al.* 1982: 227.
[146] Agrawal 1984: 165.
[147] Ratnagar 1981: 140ff.
[148] Yener 1986; Prag 1978.

TABLE 4.3

Origins of Third-Millennium Silver (kù-babbar/*kaspum*) According to Cuneiform Sources[1]

Literary Texts

Near Aratta?	*ELA* 18f., 39
Dilmun	Hymn to Ninurta (M. Cohen 1975: 31, 149f.)
Meluhha	*EWO* 128-30 (Kramer & Maier 1989: 43)
'the 15 cities'	Hymn to Ninurta (M. Cohen 1975: 31, 142ff.)

Lexical Texts

Zaršu	*lipšur* 20 (Pettinato 1972: 155)
Hašbar	H*h* xxii:16´ (*ibid.*: 154)
Ianakita	H*h* xxii:17´ (*ibid.*)
Kusu (= Kush?)	H*h* xxii:18´ (*ibid.*)

Royal Inscriptions

"silver mountain" (= Keban?)	*Sargon*: C2:34f.
Unspecified	*Gudea*: Cyl. A xvi:18f. (Pettinato 1972: 144)
Near [Mar]daman & Ha[bura] (mines?)	*Šu-Sin*: (Kutscher 1989: BT4 vi:1-18, pp. 90ff.)
Šimaški (booty)	*Šu-Sin*: (Kutscher 1989: BT4 v:5-8)

Administrative/Economic Texts

Dêr	ED III (Lambert 1953: 61 [*DP* 513])
Elam (Susa)	ED III (Lambert 1953: 63 [*Nik.* 292])
Urua (tribute/tax)	Šu-Sin, year 7 (Michalowski 1978: 48)

Sources of kù [2] *and* kù-^{na_4}za-gìn[3]

"other side" of "Lower Sea" (kù mines)	*Maništušu*: C1:29
Elam and Marhaši (booty)	*EWO* 242, 246 (Kramer & Maier 1989: 47)
Aratta	*ELA* 482f., 620 (Jacobsen 1987: 310, 318)
Meluhha	*EWO* 231 (Kramer & Maier 1989: 46)

Notes
1   *Cf.* previously Pettinato 1972; Moorey 1985: 110f.
2   "Silver" (Waetzoldt 1981: 367 n. 23) or, more generally, "precious metal" (Pettinato 1972: 80).
3   Variously translated as "silver and lapis lazuli", "bright lapis lazuli", "pure lapis lazuli" and "precious metals and stones" (Pettinato 1972: 80; S. Cohen 1973: 286; Klein 1981: ll. 348-50).

or analytical evidence for the source of Sumer's third-millennium lead, it would be natural to assume that Anatolia already played a major rôle.[149]

However, textual evidence (Table 4.3) suggests that Sumerian silver (Sumerian kù, kù babbar, Akkadian *kaspum*) came largely from the east; and if, as is generally assumed, it had been extracted from lead, the same should apply to that metal also. Interpretation of the cuneiform sources is obscured by silver's widespread use as a medium of exchange. In Early Dynastic III various goods were exchanged for silver in the river trade with Elam (*i.e.* Susa?) and in (caravan?) trade with Dêr (Badra), and

---

[149]   As Yakar 1984: 72f.

was used to buy copper in Dilmun.[150] Literary sources mention eastern silver from near Aratta (and possibly Elam and Marhaši) in Iran, and from Dilmun and Meluhha along the Gulf, the latter perhaps deriving ultimately from Afghanistan.[151] Maništušu describes crossing (?) from Anšan to the towns "across the (Lower) Sea" and conquering as far as the "KÙ-metal mines (*hu-rí* KÙ)". The sign KÙ generally means "silver", or more generally "precious metal".[152] It has been translated with both meanings here.[153] Silver ores are widespread in Iran and are mentioned by nineteenth-century travellers in Oman,[154] but have not been reported there in more recent surveys. Heimpel has argued that KÙ may be intended here as a generic term for "metal", thus allowing identification with the copper mines of Oman, but the evidence for such a reading is not compelling.[155]

Gudea does not name the mountain source of his silver, but mentions Kimaš just before, suggesting that, like the other materials he acquired, it came from the east.[156] An Ur III text dated to Šu-Sin year 7 lists silver as the 'tribute' of Urua, an Elamite border town. Litanies and lexical texts supply further names of silver sources, again presumably eastern, but none of them can be located (unless Kusu be Kush [*i.e.* Nubia]).[157] Some silver was still traded up the Gulf in the second millennium[158] but the primary source by then was Anatolia. In the Cappadocian trade of Old Assyrian times silver was the staple commodity exchanged for Mesopotamian textiles and tin.

Earlier documentary evidence of silver from the north and north-west is sparser, and the extent of Mesopotamian exploitation in the third millennium remains uncertain.[159] Sargon's campaigns to the north-west extended to the "silver (KÙ) mountain", usually identified with the Taurus, probably the Keban mines on the Upper Euphrates.[160] His use of this and other similar epithets has often been taken to imply an economic motive for the western conquests, but while this remains an attractive hypothesis it must be admitted that there is as yet no other textual evidence of silver trade with the north-west at this time.

Lead isotope characterisation gives promise of identifying the lead and lead-bearing silvers used for individual artefacts.[161] Analyses indicate a similar (so far unidentified) source for the lead in copper objects from Gubba VIIa (Early Dynastic I) and from Ur.[162] A broad programme of analyses currently in progress by Yener has tentatively characterised a number of Anatolian and Greek silver sources. Objects attributed to Taurus sources include a handful of third millennium silver (and two

---

[150] M. Lambert 1953: 63 (DP 518). Leemans 1960: 117 deduces from the fact that silver was used to buy Maganite copper that it cannot have come from overseas, but this fails to take adequate account of silver's role as currency.
[151] Stech *et al.* 1986: 49f.
[152] Waetzoldt 1981: 367 n. 23; Pettinato 1972: 80.
[153] Man. 1: 29; Pettinato 1972: 59.
[154] Moorey 1985: 111. Above p. 105 n. 113.
[155] Heimpel 1982: 67.
[156] Leemans 1960: 117; Limet 1960: 94f.
[157] Moorey 1985: 110.
[158] Oppenheim 1954; *cf.* Leemans 1960: 130ff.
[159] Yakar 1984: 80.
[160] Sargon C2:34f. For location see Gadd 1971: 425f.; *cf.* Shalmaneser III who uses this epithet of the Taurus ("Tunni") mountains (Luckenbill 1926-7: I 246).
[161] Moorey 1985: 112f.; Yener *et al.* 1991.
[162] Fujii *et al.* 1981: 216-18; *cf.* Moorey 1985: 113.

copper) artefacts from Mesopotamia, providing possible confirmation of the tradition of northern tin.[163]

(e) Gold

More than any other metal, the exploitation of gold is likely to be vastly under-represented by the evidence of archaeological discoveries. Although widely distributed in nature, the relatively small quantities in which gold occurs, along with its attractive colour and unique incorruptibility, made it a universal synonym for wealth and luxury, and assured its status as the most valuable of all metals. As such, its use was restricted largely to personal ornaments and conspicuous displays of wealth in temples, palaces and other prestigious institutions. Damaged artefacts were scrupulously recycled and the burial of gold with the dead, which thereby removed it from circulation, was a mark of particular wealth and status. The finds from the rare gold-rich burials that have been found intact, notably the 'Royal Tombs' at Ur, provide a valuable insight into the true range and quality of third-millennium Mesopotamian goldwork. Otherwise there is very little gold from this period and less still from earlier times, most of the finds deriving from a few tombs at Gawra XI-X.[164] When combined with the often elaborate descriptions of gold objects in third-millennium texts, however, it is clear that gold was worked in considerable quantities.[165]

The possible sources of supply are numerous and widespread. Though no gold occurs in Mesopotamia itself, placer and vein deposits surround it on all sides across much of the rest of the Near East. The most abundant supplies are in Egypt and Nubia[166] but, having rejected the identification of third-millennium 'Magan' and 'Meluhha' with these regions, there is no evidence that any of this was yet exported. Closer to Mesopotamia, gold occurs in primary and secondary deposits in Anatolia, especially in the west and south-west of the plateau and probably also in the Taurus.[167] In Iran gold occurs in the regions of Hamadan, Anarak, Isfahan, Kerman, Zanjan, Damghan and Meshed-Nishapur.[168] It is noteworthy that many of these sources are in the north of the country along the Great Khorasan Road. Gold could easily have been transported to Akkad this way. Further east, gold is attested in Turkmenia and in Afghanistan where it occurs in placer deposits with tin.[169] Like the latter, Afghan gold may have been among the cargoes traded to Sumer as the "gold of Meluhha". Classical authors mention the abundant gold of India, and this too was probably exploited already by the Harappans, notably the Kolar and Hatti mines of Karnataka and various alluvial placer deposits.[170] South of Sumer there is gold in southern and western Arabia, later famous as the gold of Ophir.[171] From Sumer this would involve a long sea voyage.

---

[163] Yener *et al.* 1991: 559-66. Taurus 1B Group: silver rings from Gudea-period Girsu. Taurus 1B or Eastern Troad Group: Ur III copper pendant from Aššur. Taurus 2A Group: Ur III-OAss silver bracelet from Aššur; ED silver coil from Khafajeh; ED silver cups from Ur Royal Tomb PG800. Ore samples from Esendemirtepe were found to have a close correlation with many 3rd mill. objects from Syro-Mesopotamia, including 3 items from Khafajeh (a silver ring frag., a silver lump and a copper statuette of a priest).
[164] Reviewed in Maxwell-Hyslop 1971: 1-37, 64-76; Moorey 1985: 76-81.
[165] Limet 1960: 190-236 *passim.*
[166] Lucas 1962: 224-228.
[167] de Jesus 1980: 82-84; Muhly *et al.* 1991: 212.
[168] Maxwell-Hyslop 1977: 85; Ratnagar 1981: 107; Allan 1979: 3ff.; Moorey 1985: 111-114.
[169] Moorey 1985: 74.
[170] Agrawal 1984: 165; *cf.* Ratnagar 1981: 106f.
[171] I Chronicles 29: 4; I Kings 10; Job 22: 24.

TABLE 4.4

Origins of Third-Millennium Gold (KÙ.GI=guškin/ *huraṣu*) According to Cuneiform
Sources

Literary Texts

Aratta	*ELA* 39, 124, 618f. (Jacobsen 1987: 282, 288, 318)
(H)arali	*EN* BII:1 (Attinger 1984: 13; Kramer 1963: 279); Hymn to
(via Tukriš)	Ninurta (M. Cohen 1975: 31, ll. 136f.); Hymn to Inanna (Sjöberg 1988: 169, ii 4)
Meluhha	*EWO* 128 (Kramer & Maier 1989: 43)[1]
Unspecified	*ELA* 18; *The Curse of Agade* 25 (Cooper 1983a: 51)

Lexical Texts[2]

(H)arali	H*h* xii:253 (Pettinato 1972: 79 n. 235), xxii:19´ (*ibid.*: 154); *lipšur* 21 (*ibid.*: 155); *Diri* VIA: 13´ (*ibid.*: 156)
Hublul	H*h* xxii:20´ (*ibid.*: 154); *lipšur* 22 (Hubu) (*ibid.*: 155); *Diri* VIA: 14´ (K[A]B-u$_5$) (*ibid.*: 156)
Zaršašum	H*h* xxii:21´ (*ibid.*: 154)

Economic and Administrative Texts

Dilmun ?	*Ur III: UET III*: 345 (Leemans 1960: 18); *UET V*: 526 (*ibid.*: 24f.) (Oppenheim 1954: 7; Leemans 1960: 18, 120f.)
Magan ?	*Ur III: UET* III: 299 (Leemans 1960: 89; Heimpel 1987: 79 no. 38)

Royal Inscriptions

Elam, Parahšum (booty)	*Rimuš*: C6:138f.
Mt Hahhum	*Gudea*: Stat. B, vi: 33-35[3] (*NBWI*: I 166)
Meluhha	*Gudea*: Stat. B, vi: 38-42[3] (*ibid.*: 166ff.); Cyl. A xvi: 19f. (Pettinato 1972: 146)[4]
Šimaški (booty)	*Šu-Sin*: Kutscher 1989: BT4 v:5-8, vi:19-33 (=*IRSA*: IIIA4e, Kärki 1986: Šu-Sin 20a)
	Šu-Sin: AK: Ur C2:48-57=Kutscher 1989: BT4 ix:12-20 *(IRSA*: IIIA4f)
[Mar]daman & Ha[bura] (mines?)	*Šu-Sin*: Kutscher 1989: BT4 vi:1-18, pp. 90f. ("Coll. A")
Susa, Adamdun & Awan (booty)	*Ibbi-Sin*: Kärki 1986: Ibbi-Sin 9, 10 (=*IRSA*: IIIA5b, IIIA5c)

Notes
1   It is unclear whether the Meluhhan origin attributed to the magilum-boat is intended to apply also to its gold and silver cargo.
2   Each described as a "gold land/mountain" (kur guškin).
3   "Gold-rich earth" (kù-sig$_{17}$ sahar-bar); on this expression see *NBWI*: II 24 n. 64.
4   Pettinato takes "Meluhha" to apply only to the last mentioned commodity, carnelian.

As in the case of copper, the profusion of possible sources of gold shifts the
burden of demonstration onto the textual evidence (Table 4.4), which can now be
supplemented by scientific attempts to fingerprint particular source areas.

In *Enmerkar and the Lord of Aratta* gold (and lapis lazuli) forms the basis of
the highland kingdom's prodigious wealth. Other literary works refer to gold (Sum.
KÙ.GI/guškin, Akk. *huraṣu*) brought via Tukris from (H)arali/u, which Vallat
identifies with the mines of Jiroft in Kerman, and from Meluhha, which presumably
derived from Afghanistan and/or India.[172] Lexical collections confirm the connection
with (H)arali/u and add Hublul and Zaršašum. Gudea corroborates Meluhha as a
source of "gold-rich earth" (kù-sig $_{17}$ sahar-gar), which he also brings from Hahum.

---

172 Vallat 1985: 54.

Economic texts from the reign of Šu-Sin suggest that some gold still came up the Gulf at that time; its likely immediate source – Dilmun – was only a clearing house for supplies originating further east (probably still Meluhha). Of the Akkadian kings, only Rimuš refers to plundering gold; he took 30 minas from Elam and Parahšum. Gudea had gold brought from Mt Hah(h)um and Meluhha. Šu-Sin dedicated a statue to Enlil made from gold taken as booty in campaigns against Zabšali and other lands of Šimaški. Šu-Sin's successor Ibbi-Sin likewise dedicated gold taken in his victory over Susa, Adamdun and the land of Awan after having it fashioned into an elaborate vase. As records of booty, these reports need imply no more about ultimate sources of supply than their subsequent consignment by the Sumerians kings to temple repositories in Sumer. A better indication in this regard is an earlier section of one Šu-Sin text (unfortunately badly damaged) in which the king prepares (ba-ni-zi) something (tools?) at the border (zà-ba) of [Mar]daman and Ha[bura] "in order to dig (ba-al) for gold (and) silver." If correctly understood the verb indicates mining rather than panning for alluvial gold – in any case some form of primary procurement.[173]

The emphasis of this evidence is eastern. Besides the familiar eastern lands of Aratta, Elam, Parahšum/Marhaši, Susa-Adamdun-Awan, Dilmun and Meluhha, both Zabšali-Šimaški and Harali may be placed broadly in Iran (above p. 33).[174] Such is also the most likely general context for the otherwise unknown places Hublul/Huba/KAB-u and Zaršašum. North-western sources, however, are also represented. Hahum, mentioned by Gudea, if the same as the place cited in the Cappadocian texts, lay on the road to from Aššur to Kaneš. Suggested locations are between Diyarbakir and Elazig, the Elbistan plain and the site of Lidar Hüyük near Samsat.[175] The site where Šu-Sin prepared for mining gold and silver seems to be located by the text in northernmost Mesopotamia, in the region of [Mar]daman (probably modern Mardin)[176] and Ha[bura] (somewhere in the modern Habur). This is hardly the area in which one expects a campaign against Šimaški, however, and it is well to recall that both toponyms are partly restored. Moreover, it is not entirely clear from the damaged text whether these toponyms relate to the site of mining (as Edzard) or to the origin of the prisoners put to work in the mines (as Kutscher, who locates the mines in Šimaški).

Cuneiform documents of the second millennium and later add little to this picture of the range of potential sources, but suggest a shift in primary dependence to the north. In general, gold is mentioned less often in connection with the east (though some may have continued to come from Dilmun in the early second millennium) and more often in connection with Syro-Anatolia.[177] As records of temple or palace holdings, most of these references are unreliable guides to source areas. Egypt became a major supplier to Babylonia in the fourteenth century.

Scientific source provenance analysis has yet to yield any more positive answers. Young's suggestion that the Pactolus valley be identified as a major source of Sumerian gold through the presence of platinum-group elements has since been discredited. Various combinations of these metals occur also in the goldfields of eastern Turkey, Zanjan and Damghan in Iran, and perhaps elsewhere.[178] South-eastern Turkey and Damghan, situated on well-established overland trade routes

---

[173] See commentaries by Edzard 1959-60: 16 and Kutscher 1989: 90f.
[174] Pettinato 1972: 111.
[175] *RGTC 3*: 85f.; Limet 1960: 93 n.4 (Diyarbakir/Elazig); Garelli 1963: 109 (Elbistan); Liverani 1988 (Lidar).
[176] Goetze 1953b: 20 n. 55; *RGTC 2*: 118.
[177] Leemans 1960: 120f.; Moorey 1985: 73f.
[178] Young 1972; *cf.* Ogden 1977; Maxwell-Hyslop 1977: 84f.; Meeks & Tite 1980.

with Sumer, are perhaps the more likely sources of supply. Platinum-group inclusions are a regular feature of the gold used in Mesopotamia throughout the third and early second millennia and in the Achaemenid period, but not during the second millennium in the eastern Mediterranean (Palestine, coastal Turkey [Alalakh], Cyprus, the Aegean). This gross distinction at least suggests that the Sumerians drew upon supplies other than those most easily accessible to the these western regions, in particular Egypt.

(f) Conclusions

To the extent that it can be reconstructed from artefacts and the few known industrial sites, third-millennium metallurgical technology seems to have been largely consistent throughout Mesopotamia, Iran, the Indus Valley and Central Asia.[179] All industries were based on copper and its alloys for utilitarian types, and gold and silver for luxury items. What variation there is from region to region seems to have depended principally on the affordable availability of alloying materials – chiefly arsenic, tin and lead – rather than differences in technological expertise. Arsenical copper, much of it drawn from the large reserves at Anarak, represented the staple alloy throughout most of the Near East, excepting only central and eastern Iran, where unalloyed copper prevails. This may be due as much to the overwhelming importance of the arsenic-rich Anarak ores as to any intentional alloying preferences. But certainly in the latter half of the millennium copper was being consciously alloyed with arsenic, lead and tin.

An apparent exception to this general uniformity is the increasing use of tin-bronze in the latter half of the third millennium in Mesopotamia, Susiana and Luristan, but not in central or eastern Iran. This again probably reflects differential ease of access, especially if the tin came from Afghanistan along the Gulf, rather than overland.[180]

With the exception of Mesopotamia-Susiana, all of the major copper-using cultures had fairly ready access to the necessary ores. The sequence of copper deposits running down the Kerman Range supplied Tepe Sialk, Tal-i Iblis, Tal-i Malyan, Shahdad and (sometimes) Tepe Yahya. Shahr-i Sokhta exploited a closer source at Chehel Kureh, characterised by high levels of zinc.[181] Bactria could draw on the large reserves in Afghanistan, while the settlements of Oman had abundant local reserves which they exploited for trade with Sumer and possibly also the Indus.

As a primary form of stored wealth metals often travelled as plunder, taxes and tribute, as well as by trade. In all periods the pattern of commercial and other exchange was no doubt complex, different sources being drawn upon according to fluctuations in price and availability. These in turn would have depended on a multiplicity of factors, including political conditions and social and technological developments in the source zones and intermediaries. References to Dilmun copper at Archaic Uruk, long before Omani copper has been recognised analytically, warn against drawing generalisations from limited data.

In the latter half of the third millennium the Sumerian metals trade was oriented principally to the east, mostly by ship along the Gulf. In earlier centuries, for which contemporary documents are less informative, Sumer may have drawn more on the land-locked supplies of highland Iran and Syro-Anatolia. Copper, perhaps

---

[179] Heskell *et al.* 1980: 258, 260.
[180] *Cf.* Berthoud *et al.* 1982: 52, who regard this as a Mesopotamian innovation which was not diffused back to Iran.
[181] Berthoud *et al.* 1982: 51.

originally acquired from Anarak or Ergani, came overwhelmingly from Oman (Magan) from the Early Dynastic III period on. Gold and tin, obtained largely from Meluhha, originated further afield, probably in Afghanistan. This presents an interesting parallel with lapis, which was available in the same regions and was also traded by the Meluhhans (below p. 212). Only arsenical copper may have been restricted to source areas which could not have been distributed by Gulf shipping, *viz.* Anarak and Armenia (though not the possible Afghan sources), and this does not allow for the possibility that Omani metalurgists were able to enhance the concentration of arsenic during refining. Some silver too probably came south by caravan or boat from the Taurus, as well as from the eastern sources mentioned in cuneiform texts.

The extent to which the metal-rich north and north-west constituted major alternative sources for copper, tin and gold remains a major problem. Geographical logic suggests that these regions should have been exploited, but contemporary documents are strikingly devoid of evidence for their use. Efficient trade with these lands may have been contingent on political control which is documented only in the Akkadian period (*cf. The King of Battle* where Sargon comes to the aid of the merchants of Purušhanda). The southern emphasis of the third-millennium archives from which present information derives no doubt introduces some bias; texts from Agade might reveal a very different picture.

There is strikingly little evidence in non-literary sources of overland trade in metals with Iran. Gudea's copper from Kimaš (Abullat) is exceptional. Dêr lay on an important road to the east, yet "nowhere ... is there evidence that metals were imported into southern Mesopotamia by this route".[182] Suggestions that the transhumant copper-using nomads of Luristan were middlemen in an Iranian-Sumerian trade, or that they were themselves specialist metallurgists, remain conjectural.[183]

2. TRADE IN FINISHED METALWORK

Unlike Sumer, where metalwork was in general only sparingly deposited in graves, third-millennium burials in highland Iran and Bactria were often lavishly equipped with tools, weapons, vessels, ornaments and other metal goods manufactured from the abundant local copper ores.[184] Due to the unscientific manner of excavation of the material from Luristan and Bactria,[185] and incomplete publication of the finds from Shahdad, the archaeological context and dating of most of this material remain matters of great uncertainty.[186] Discoveries in recent years, however, leave no doubt as to the range of the highland corpus and the scale of production.

---

[182] Leemans 1960: 174. The silver brought back from Dêr in one ED III text (Lambert 1953: 61, DP 513; *cf.* Leemans 1960: 116) was currency rather than itself the object of trade.

[183] Amiet 1986: 129-32, 157.

[184] Only Luristan has so far failed to produce evidence of copper deposits. For evidence of metalworking at Sapalli Tepe and elsewhere in northern Bactria, in levels dated by Kohl to the centuries around 2000 BC, see Kohl 1984: 155 and Maxwell-Hyslop 1987: 18f.

[185] 'Luristan' and 'Bactria' are used in this study to refer to the regions whence derive the unprovenanced objects conventionally assigned to those regions. Both should be treated with caution.

[186] Great advances in the dating of the 'Luristan bronzes' have been made by the excavations of Vanden Berghe, whose latest chronological conclusions are outlined in Vanden Berghe & Haerinck 1984 and Haerinck 1987; *cf.* the lower chronology suggested previously in Vanden Berghe 1972; *idem* 1982. See now also Schmidt *et al.* 1989: 179ff., 133f., 485f.

Figure 24. Decorated copper/bronze axe from Susa. Bactrian(?). Late third to early second millennium. Ht. 7.6 cm.

Much of the metalwork from Sumer and the highlands, especially from controlled excavations, consists of simple utilitarian types (knives, daggers, axes, adzes, hoes, tools, pins etc.) whose forms are closely related to function, and display little regional variation (Fig. 22). It is in the more complex, especially the decorated, forms that regional styles may be distinguished and patterns of influence and exchange plotted. Looking eastwards, far the closest relations of the Sumerian metal industry were with her immediate neighbours, Susiana and Luristan, where shaft-hole tools/weapons, vessels and other more distinctive forms may be closely matched, especially from Early Dynastic III on.

The more elaborate versions of these types, however, are restricted essentially to the highlands (Luristan, Kerman/Lut, Bactria) and do not occur in Sumer. Particularly characteristic of the highlands in the later third millennium (and again in Iron Age Luristan) was a predilection for zoomorphic relief decoration, especially on the butts of shaft-hole weapons. Two well attested series are axes from Luristan and further east, with animals in high relief set along the butt, and Bactrian hammers and axes with an animal protome projecting from the butt.[187]

During the later third millennium, the wide-ranging network of inter-Iranian exchange documented by Amiet distributed such metalwork, along with objects of stone and no doubt many perishable materials, across large tracts of Greater Iran.[188] Various plain and decorated axes, 'hammers', mirrors, compartmented seals (Fig. 30) and other distinctive metal types recently unearthed in large quantities by tomb

---

[187] Axes with animals along butt – Amiet 1986: nos 18-20; Moorey 1971: no. 10; de Waele 1982: no. 6; Moorey *et al.* 1981: nos 1, 16. Animal protome axes/hammers – Amiet 1986: figs 169-71; Pittman 1984: fig. 32. The penchant for zoomorphic decoration, which soon became the leitmotiv of Luristan metalwork, seems to have begun in the ED III period, and became more popular in Akkadian and Ur III times. On the chronology of this phenomenon see most recently Amiet 1986: 130f., 155f.

[188] Amiet 1986.

Figure 25.   Seal impression of Kuk-Simut, chancellor of Idadu II, ensi of Elam, showing Idadu presenting Kuk-Simut with a Bactrian-style(?) axe with splaying blade and butt curls. 20th century BC.

robbers in Bactria occur in identical forms far to the south in Baluchistan (notably Sibri/Mehrgarh), and south-west across the plateau at Shahdad.[189] The shaft-hole weapons are characterised particularly by the free use of zoomorphic decoration and by distinctive wing-like or curled streams projecting from the butts of axes and 'hammers' (Figs 24, 26-29). Most of these types (excepting mirrors), along with plainer Lut/Kerman-type axes, appear also at Susa, where they were till recently classed with the 'Luristan bronzes'.[190] Judging by present finds, it was much rarer for types characteristic of Luristan to move eastwards.[191]

   Distinguishing genuine objects of trade from shared types is not always possible. At Susa, for example, it is not clear whether the 'hammers' and axes (*e.g.*

---

[189] Sibri/Mehrgarh – Santoni 1984: fig. 8.1. Baluchistan – Stein 1931: pls XIV, XXXII; *idem* 1937: pl. XVIII; Curtis 1988. Shahdad – Hakemi 1972: pls XX-XXI; Hiebert & Lamberg-Karlovsky 1992: pls II-III; Hakemi & Sajjidi n.d.: fig. 2. On the definition of the Bactrian corpus see Pottier 1984: *passim*; Amiet 1986: 196-98; Sarianidi 1988: 166-218; Maxwell-Hyslop 1987: 19 (pins). It has been suggested that compartmented copper seals from Shahdad and Bactria were made from the same mould (Kohl 1987: 21; Sarianidi 1977: 94 fig. 48:2=Hakemi 1972: pl. XXIB).

[190] The principal Iranian/Bactrian imports and local imitations/adaptations are: 'Hammers' – Tallon 1987: nos 189-96, Figs 13, 14; Mecquenem 1934: fig. 58:2,3,5. Axes – Tallon 1987: 95f. nos 72, 73 [Kerman/Lut type], p. 90f., fig. 6 [Kerman/Lut or Bactrian type]. Miniature vessel on openwork support – *ibid.*: no. 806. Gold eagle pendant – *ibid.*: no. 1163. Compartmented seals – *ibid.*: nos 1249-50. Pins with decorated heads – *ibid.*: nos 967-93; *cf.* Sarianidi 1986: 177-80 (figures). Cosmetic applicator – Tallon 1987: no. 1066. *Cf.* Tallon 1987: 341 and *passim* for Bactrian and highland Iranian parallels. The dating of these types, all from old excavations, remains uncertain. Aside from the pins, which begin in the Late Uruk period, stratigraphical datings (all very approximate) range from Akkadian times (Mecquenem's "XXVe" century) through the Ur III period ("XXIIIe" century) and into the early 2nd mill. (Tallon 1987: nos 72, 191, 195, 196, Figs 6, 13, 14; *cf.* fig. 5). More reliable is a radiocarbon dating of wood from a Bactrian shaft-hole 'winged' axe which has given a corrected date of 2080 BC ± 110 (Maxwell-Hyslop 1987: 21). On the dating of the 'Bactrian' axes see further Maxwell-Hyslop 1987: 20f.

[191] One likely example is the Luristan-type tubular macehead/cudgel found at Shahdad (Hakemi 1972: pl. XXII).

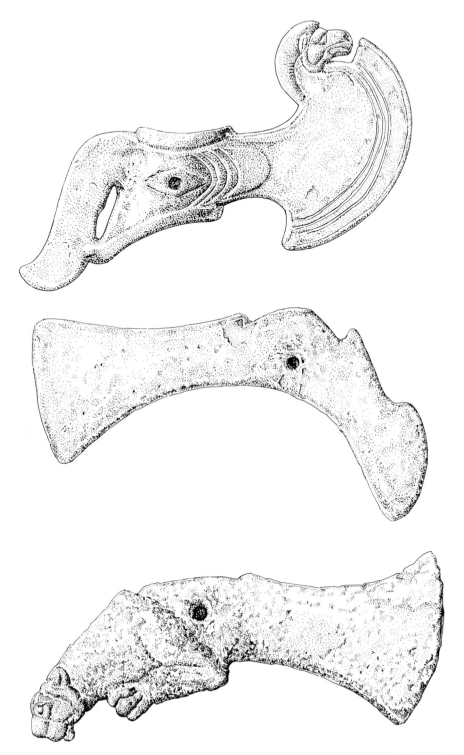

Figure 26. Bactrian(?) axes. (1) Arsenical copper. Lth. 15.0 cm. (2) Copper/bronze. (3) Copper. Lth. 12.2 cm. Late third to early second millennium.

Fig. 24; *cf.* Figs 25, 26:1) with 'winged' butts and/or zoomorphic decoration are imports from Kerman/Bactria or local adaptations of foreign types (though such sharing too presupposes a previous familiarity through long-distance movement).[192] Even when trade seems likely, the direction of movement often remains open to question, with the result that a number of types are variously described as Iranian (Kerman/Lut/'trans-Elamite' types) and Bactrian.[193] Fortunately, for present purposes, such uncertainties do not obscure the clear indications of an active and widespread exchange network stretching the entire breadth of the Iranian plateau from Bactria through south-east and south-central Iran as far as Susa.

In striking contrast to the wide circulation of metalwork within greater Iran, there is very little evidence of exchange between these highland regions and Mesopotamia.[194] From Late Uruk times, a number of types in the Sumerian repertory were shared also by Susa and Luristan, indicating the free transmission of ideas between these close neighbours.[195] But while the Sumerian (and most of the Susian) examples are consistently plain, the same or similar forms in Luristan were regularly decorated – a sure sign that demand in each region was met by local production. There are only a handful of elaborate pieces from Sumer which may plausibly be regarded as imports from Luristan, and a proportion of these probably arrived as plunder rather than by trade (see below).[196]

Links with the Iranian plateau are more tenuous still, there being no close analogues for any but the most simple utilitarian Sumerian forms. Types distinctive of these more distant regions are likewise virtually absent from Mesopotamia, plausible imports being restricted to a compartmented stamp seal recovered from

---

[192] See Tallon 1987: 341 for a minimal list of foreign metalwork at Susa, taking nos 72-73 and 806 as Iranian, and nos 192 (here Fig. 24), 1249-50, 1066 and 1163 as Bactrian.

[193] *Cf.* Amiet 1987b: 176, arguing that not all of the Shahdad metalwork with Bactrian parallels was necessarily made there. Amiet sees Elamite influence in the development of elaborate (horse-headed *etc.*) axes in Bactria, although no Elamite imports have yet been found there (Amiet 1986b: 16).

[194] *Cf.* the same by-pass phenomenon in the distribution of other types, such as double spiral-headed pins, which seem to have originated in 4th-mill. Central Asia (Khlopin & Khlopina 1989) and spread to the Caucasus, Anatolia and Syria but avoided Mesopotamia (Huot 1969: 85 [map]).

[195] Distinctive types common to Mesopotamia, Susa and Luristan (the latter attributions to be treated with caution) include shaft-hole axes (Tallon 1987: nos 1-20, 31, 39-42, 92-94) and adzes (*ibid.*: nos 533-48, 549-52), 'Naram-Sin'-type axes (*ibid.*: 81, fig. 3), spike-butted pick-axes, some with a rolled blade (*ibid.*: 79f., fig. 2), ε-axes (*ibid.*: nos 95-97), swollen-butt axes (early 2nd mill; *ibid.*: no. 45), 'Puzur-Inšušinak'-type spearheads (*ibid.*: nos 205-07), 'laurel-leaf' daggers (*ibid.*: nos 119-29, 138-41, 147-59, 161-71, 178-79), footed cylindrical bowls (*ibid.*: no. 756, fig. 20) and spouted bowls (*ibid.*: 780-83, pp. 216f. Type F, fig. 24). Tallon cites Mesopotamian and other parallels for all types (*cf.* Calmeyer 1969: Groups 2, 4-6, 9, 11, 13, 16, 20). Numerous further parallels from Mesopotamia, Luristan and elsewhere in more simple tools/weapons, vessels, utensils and ornaments (Tallon 1987: *passim*) confirm the general community of traditions extending back to Ubaid times (*ibid.*: nos 71, 75), even if some may be attributed to functional convergence. Stratigraphical dates assigned by the excavators to the Susian pieces with Mesopotamian and Luristan parallels range from the 'XXVIIIe' (Mecquenem 1934: 216, fig. 60:19-20) and 'XXVe' centuries (Tallon 1987: nos 72, 196, fig. 6 [with p. 90], fig. 14 [with p. 135]) to the 'XXIIIe' cent. (*ibid.*: no. 191) and Šulgi (*ibid.*: no. 195). Mesopotamian parallels concentrate in ED III and after.

[196] Likely 'imports' include a decorated tubular 'macehead' from Girsu (Cros 1910-14: 65, 77; *cf.* Moorey 1971a: nos 95-96; *idem* 1974: no. 19; Tallon 1987: nos 185-87), a shaft-hole axe with ibexes on the shaft from an OB context at Tell edh-Diba'i (al Gailani 1965: pl. 9) and an Addahušu-type axe from Tell Yelkhi in the Hamrin (Quarantelli ed. 1985: 316 no. 122). There is very little typologically Sumerian metalwork from 'Luristan' to indicate movement in the other direction, and none of the handful of types attested (*e.g.* decorated rein rings: Calmeyer 1969: Group 1) have assured provenances, making their presence outside Mesopotamia questionable. The findspots of the supposedly 'Luristan' sheet-metal vessels with dedication inscriptions to Akkadian and Ur III kings (*ibid.*: 38, Group 12; Nagel 1970) are likewise problematical (*cf.* Amiet 1986: 155f. who accepts their Iranian provenances but regards them as locally made).

Figure 27. Silver axe, partially gilded, from Bactria(?). Late third to early second millennium. Max. l. 15 cm.

Figure 28. Ceremonial hammer/standard from Bactria(?) in the form of a recumbent boar. Silver with gold rivets. Ht. 8.0 cm.

Figure 29. Bronze hammer with inscription of Šulgi, from Susa. Ht. 12.3 cm.

Mari, a shaft-hole axe from Ur which is best paralleled in the Kerman/Lut region, and possibly a few other items.[197]

Nor is there clear evidence of movement in the opposite direction east of Luristan, with the possible exception of some earrings of Sumerian type and a group of 'harpe-swords' of Near Eastern type, both reported from Bactria.[198]

This pattern of exchange indicates a pervasive rift between Mesopotamia and Iran. For much of the later third millennium, while Susa fell under Mesopotamian control, there can have been no political barrier to the movement of highland metal goods further west; the explanation must rather be cultural or economic. Perhaps the appeal of the more elaborate Iranian metalwork depended on an appreciation of its complex and original highland iconography which the Mesopotamians lacked. But this can hardly have been the principal factor, since they were apparently willing on

---

[197] Stamp seal: Amiet 1986: 199; Beyer 1989. This piece perhaps reflects a more northern channel of contact which bypassed Sumer; *cf.* a number of metal types known from northern Mesopotamia and western Iran but not attested in Sumer (below note 202). Axe: Woolley 1934: pl. 223, Type A11, U.15314 (not listed in the catalogue); *cf.* Amiet 1986: fig. 119; Tallon 1987: 95, no. 72, with parallels. Other possible imports include pins topped by a clenched fist or a bull's head from Ur (Woolley 1934: pl. 231:U.8014, 13034) which are closely matched by pieces from Bactria (Sarianidi 1979: fig. 2:9, 11, 12; *idem* 1986: pl. 70) and Susa (Tallon 1987: nos 984-86); it is not clear where these were produced. More dubious imports are the ED IIIA spiked macehead/cudgel from Ur (Woolley 1934: pl. 224:U.9137), which finds general analogues at Susa (Tallon 1987: fig. 12, no. 184; Carter 1980: fig. 22b) and in Luristan (Calmeyer 1969: Gr. 7; Moorey 1971a: nos 95-97; *idem* 1974: nos 18-19; Tallon 1987: 130) and Bactria (Pottier 1984: no. 41); spearheads with a distinctive waist between the tang and blade, known from Mesopotamia (De Maigret 1976: fig. 9, especially no. 3 from Aššur) and Bactria (Pottier 1984: 12f., no. 6); and a decorated gold vessel, probably from north-eastern Iran, said to have been recovered from the Euphrates (Bellelli 1989).

[198] Earrings: Amiet 1977: fig. 18:18; *cf.* Maxwell-Hyslop 1971: 84, pls 58, 59, Amiet 1966a: fig. 193C; Maxwell-Hyslop 1987: 22. 'Harpe-swords': Pottier 1984: nos 23-26; *cf.* Cros 1910-14: 129, pl. VII; Collon 1986: 28f., 52. Note also the headed pins (previous note).

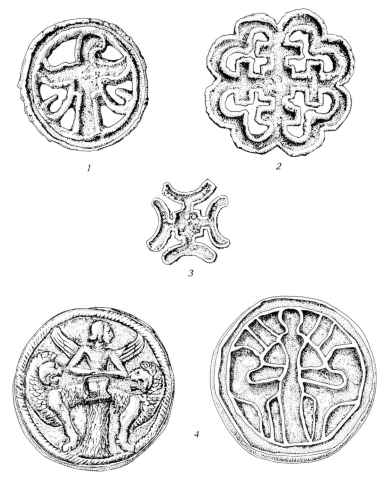

Figure 30.   Compartmented stamp seals from Bactria. Copper (1-3) and gold (4). Late third to early second millennium.

occasion to reinterpret foreign stonework in local terms.[199] Considerations of economy probably played a more decisive rôle. In particular, it may be suggested that the direction and intensity of exchange in finished metalwork was largely determined by the economically primary trade in raw materials. That this was the case in highland Iran is suggested by the fact that Bactria and Kerman/Lut, which seem to have been among the principal exporters of finished metalwork, also possess some of the largest copper reserves.[200] And since trade in metals (as in all materials) within highland Iran had to be conducted over land, finished products casually exchanged in the wake of this movement also became widely distributed. Old cultural and historical connections were probably responsible for the circuit extending outside this

---

[199] Note the *série ancienne* vessels from Nippur with a feline-serpent combat scene inscribed "Inanna and the serpent", and the (Iranian?) basalt vase with a vegetation goddess inscribed by Enmetena (Orthmann *et al.* 1975: pl. 87a).

[200] Since no major burial grounds with substantial metal offerings have yet been excavated near Anarak, it is not clear whether that region too was the origin of some of the widely circulated types.

range to the edge of the lowlands at Susa. But there it stopped. Once Sumer had access to Omani copper by sea-borne trade along the Gulf – an exchange which had clearly begun by Early Dynastic III and probably as early as Uruk IV/III – copper supplied by overland trade from Iran would not have been economically competitive. And where there was no raw copper trade there was no regularised structure of exchange for the movement of finished products.[201]

   This negative conclusion should not be allowed to stand, however, without a note of caution. The surviving corpus of Sumerian metalwork upon which the scale of exchange with highland Iran must be judged may be seriously unrepresentative. Owing to the Sumerians' reluctance to dispose of large quantities of metalwork in any but the most high-ranking burials, and, more particularly, to the practice of melting down old or broken objects, the vast bulk of the evidence has been irretrievably lost.[202] In these circumstances, it may now be possible to estimate the true extent of highland-lowland exchange only from documentary evidence. At present, the scarcity of references to foreign metalwork in third-millennium texts[203] tends to support the sceptical conclusions reached above. There are, however, references to large quantities of metal taken as booty by Akkadian and Ur III kings on campaigns in the east. Although often accounted simply by weight,[204] this booty consisted largely of finished artefacts which were assigned in that state to temples by Šulgi and Amar-Suen.[205] Much was no doubt subsequently melted down, but some of the more elaborate objects were probably retained and 'used' intact.[206] Šulgi had a typologically Bactrian hammer (with lock-like curls on the butt and birds' heads rising from the top) inscribed for a loyal subject at Susa (Fig. 29).[207] The Susa sealing of a twentieth-century chancellor, Kuk-Simut, shows him receiving a Bactrian-style axe from the Susian ensi Idadu II (Fig. 25). The significance of such presentation pieces clearly derived largely from their status as exotic items. Might Šulgi and other rulers have presented similar pieces to royal favorites in the cities of Sumer? Craftsmen too were considered booty, as is clear from *Enmerkar and Lugalbanda* where Enmerkar takes the metalsmiths of Aratta together with their tools of trade back to Sumer.[208]

---

[201] Even where there was a trade in metals the logistics of transport favoured ingots rather than finished products, which were less managable and more prone to damage *en route*. Moreover, unlike stone blocks, much of which would be wasted in production, all of a metal ingot could be used.

[202] Indications of the paucity of the surviving evidence are that many metal types are attested in Sumer by only a single example from Ur (the spiked cudgel, spike-butt pick-axe, 'anchor' axe, Puzer-Inšušinak spearhead, cylindrical goblet, Kerman/Lut-type axe and fist-headed pin; Calmeyer 1969: Groups 4, 9, 13, 16, 73 and refs above, notes 196, 197); that others are known there only through illustrations ('Naram-Sin-axe' and 'Naram-Sin-macehead'; *ibid.*: Groups 10, 11); while others still are attested both to the north and east of Babylonia but have not yet been recovered in Sumer itself in any medium (crest-butt pick-axe and shaft-hole axe with cut-away blade; *ibid.*: Groups 15, 19).

[203] Metal objects from Ur III texts are listed by Limet 1960: 190-236. References to foreign metalwork in literary and lexical texts (a total of three) are collected in Pettinato 1972: 83. Note also the bronze sà-hum from Magan (Luckenbill 1930: 103:4; Limet 1972a: 14), the 'Dilmun axes' in the Archaic metals list from Uruk (Nissen 1986a: 338; Englund 1983a: 35), and the bronze model 'Dilmun-ships' brought by merchants to ED III Lagaš (*VS 14*: 13; *DP.* 69, 70; *cf.* Bauer 1972: 460f.).

[204] *E.g.* Rimuš C6:138-41, recording 30 minas of gold and 3600 minas of copper.

[205] Pettinato 1982: 61-64; Davidović 1984: 200-03.

[206] *Cf.* the elaborate Bactrian-type axe from a Middle Elamite burrial (the so-called *dépot de fondation*) cut into the Temple of Inšušinak at Susa, here Fig. 24 (Tallon 1987: no. 192).

[207] Tallon 1987: no. 195.

[208] Wilcke 1969: ll. 409f.

Chapter 5

Stones and Stonework

1. The Origins and Exploitation of 'Common' Stones

(a) Sumer

Southern Mesopotamia's proverbial dearth of raw materials, though valid for many other commodities, is frequently overstated as regards 'common' stones.[1] The variety and quality is limited but some stone is readily available in Sumer. In the south, limestone-gypsum and sandstone outcrops occur on the Euphrates west of Uruk at Samawwa and el-Khidr, and into the desert at Umayyad.[2] These are almost certainly the sources of the considerable amounts of building stone used at Protoliterate Uruk. Eridu is "a *cul-de-sac* surrounded on three sides by bedrock outcrops".[3] Even more extensive supplies of limestone, gypsum, calcite, sandstone, marl, breccia and bituminous stone are accessible by boat along the eroded banks of the Tigris and Euphrates rivers from Syro-Anatolia downstream to the latitude of Baghdad.[4] Some of this material is washed down the rivers, especially the swift-flowing Tigris and its affluents, during the annual floods. The use of such boulders, rather than mined blocks, is suggested by the dumpy proportions of much Sumerian light-coloured stone statuary and especially by the smooth, rounded surfaces of the unworked areas.[5] These are features also of door sockets and later kudurrus. The great advantage of the local sources was their accessibility by boat, which allowed large-scale exploitation and the use of sizeable blocks.

It remains true, however, that a significant proportion of the 'common' stones used in Sumer – including most of the dark stones and the finer, more decorative light stones – had to be imported. The principal source areas, as for metals, were the highlands enclosing Mesopotamia from Syro-Anatolia in the north-west to Fars in the south-east, as well as the mountains of Oman across the Gulf. Many of the stones used most commonly in Sumer occur widely in these regions, especially the Amanus/Taurus-Zagros arc, from where they were probably obtained down to at least the middle of the third millennium.[6] The small number of potential sources which made possible the tracking of the origins of Neolithic obsidian and Bronze Age lapis lazuli do not obtain for any of these 'common' stones.

Limestone and its secondary calcite and gypsum formations, along with sandstone, shale and other sedimentary rocks, constitute the principal rock types in the 'zone of normal folding', *i.e.* the westernmost ranges of the southern Zagros, from Luristan south-east to Fars.[7] These stones continue into the next zone east, the

---

[1]   *E.g.* Schüller 1963; Heinz 1989: 206f.
[2]   Williams 1981: 311; Boehmer 1984.
[3]   Wright 1981: 300; *cf.* Woolley 1955: 31.
[4]   Ainsworth 1838: 49-92, esp. 89, end plate 3.
[5]   *Cf.* Woolley 1961: 69.
[6]   Schüller 1963.
[7]   Williams 1981: 312; Harrison 1968: 166f.

'complex belt', in which Harrison notes that the crags of Behistun on the Khorasan road are formed of "calcite-veined and crushed crataceous limestones ... stacked as a pile of recumbent synclines".[8] In addition to these materials, the 'complex belt' contains a variety of harder, darker metamorphic and igneous rocks such as marble, quartz, granite, schist and serpentine.[9] Steatite/chlorite is widely available in the 'crushed zone' extending almost the full length of the Zagros, with a large outcrop south of Sanandaj, through Fars and Kerman to Zahedan and at Taknar, 300 km east of Tepe Hissar.[10] Farther east again, in the 'volcanic belt' stretching from Azerbaijan south-east to the border of Baluchistan, intrusive eruptive rocks (*e.g.* granite, gabbro, diorite, quartz porphery, dolerite and basalt) become readily available.[11] Calcium-based stones also continue across the Iranian plateau and into Arabia.[12] In the mountains of Makran and Oman these are accompanied by steatite/chlorite as well as diorites and olivine-gabbros.[13] Steatite/chlorite extends also into Baluchistan and Arabia.[14]

The 'common' stones employed in the alluvium in the third millennium fall broadly into four categories:

> (1)   calcareous sedimentary and altered sedimentary rocks (limestone and marble) and secondary mineral formations (calcite and gypsum);[15]
>
> (2)   other sedimentary rocks and metamorphic derivatives (*e.g.* sandstone, shale, schist, slate, dolomite, conglomerate);
>
> (3)   igneous and altered igneous rocks of an opaque green-grey-brown-black colour (*e.g.* diorite, dolerite, basalt, granite); and
>
> (4)   soft, dark, green-grey secondary minerals occurring in metamorphic rocks (*e.g.* steatite, chlorite, serpentine).

To a limited extent, these categories correspond to the non-technical groupings employed in most archaeological reports, *e.g.* soft, light stones (1 and most of 2), soft, dark stones (4 and some of 2) and hard, dark stones (3).

Scientific analysis of the 'common' stones exploited in the Near East has not yet been able to provide reliable criteria for source provenance identification. Although mineralogical 'fingerprinting' (notably of metals) has been greatly refined in recent years, common stones offer relatively poor prospects for meaningful regional characterisation due to the sheer multiplicity of sources and their intra-site mineralogical variabilty. A start has been made in defining the 'fingerprints' of steatite/chlorite sources in Iran and Arabia and of limestone outcrops near Uruk,[16]

---

[8]   Harrison 1968: 162.
[9]   *Ibid.*: 159-63; Morgan 1900: 35.
[10]   Kohl 1975: 30; *idem* 1977: 113; Pigott *et al.* 1982: 231.
[11]   Harrison 1968: 156; Schüller 1963.
[12]   Beale 1973: 136.
[13]   Vallat 1985: 52; Kohl 1975; *idem* 1977: 113; Heimpel 1982; Hauptmann 1985: 17, 22f.; Abb. 5, 6.
[14]   Asthana 1984; Zarins 1978: 67.
[15]   On the definition of the terms 'calcite' and 'gypsum', whose non-technical usage varies considerably, see *e.g.* Webster & Anderson 1983: 293-95, 297-99. Calcite properly so called is crystaline calcium carbonate, a variety of 'marble'. It is also known as 'marble onyx' and, in antiquity, 'alabaster'. Calcite can be variously coloured and banded (commonly yellow, green or brown with veins of red, brown, ochre or grey), and may be translucent or opaque. A dimorphous variety of calcite is called aragonite (a term much used in French publications), which can also be green or grey. Confusingly, in English 'aragonite' is sometimes used to refer to shell (*e.g.* Collon 1982: 13). Gypsum is hydrous calcium sulphate. The pure form is white but it is often tinted yellow, brown or grey and can have ferric orange or brown veins. This is what is today called 'alabaster'. It usually survives in archaeological contexts less well than calcite.
[16]   Kohl *et al.* 1979 (steatite); Boehmer 1984 (limestone).

but much more analytical data from potential sources and artefacts is required (and perhaps also new characterization techniques) before definitive attributions will be possible. Added to this is the problem that much of the relevant territory remains geologically very poorly explored, especially as regards the small outcrops which could have been used by village craftsmen. At present, any choice between the known geological options must be based on considerations of proximity, stylistic and typological connections of the finished stonework, and, where available, on textual evidence.

Documents refer to various kinds of Sumerian stoneworkers – the zadim, bur-gul and GAL.ZADIM – already in the Archaic and Early Dynastic professions lists.[17] The term for lapidary, zadim, appears again in the Fara texts and one such craftsman made a bowl for dedication at Girsu.[18] According to the *Sumerian King List* the last Early Dynastic king of Kiš was a stoneworker (zadim).[19] A Sumerian cult song relates: "my (house whose) stonecutter (bur-gul) used to carve bowls, my (house whose) lapidary (za-gin-dím-e, lit: "maker of lapis lazuli") used to make jewellery".[20] Sumerian distinguished between the 'stonecutter/seal engraver' (bur-gul) and the 'lapidary' (zadim), whose names probably reflect their original roles as makers of bowls (bur) and lapis ornaments (za-gin) respectively.[21] After the Ur III period zadim is replaced as the standard term for lapidary by Akkadian *kabšarru* (from Sumerian gáb-sar),[22] the jeweller working with semi-precious stones, and *purkullu*, the seal engraver. An interesting Ur III text from Ur provides further detail on late third millennium practices, listing the materials and products of a lapidary workshop.[23]

Throughout the third millennium the vast majority of Sumerian stonework is in the light-coloured sedimentary-metamorphic rocks and their derivates (1 above) which lay closest to hand in the outcrops of western Sumer and along the rivers upstream from Baghdad.[24] Rarely these stones were brought in from further upstream in Syria, as did Gudea,[25] and perhaps also from the nearest chains of the Zagros mountains. The reliance on light-coloured stones is particularly noticeable in the case of Late Uruk to Early Dynastic figurative stonework which can be identified as Sumerian workmanship on stylistic and iconographical grounds. Late Uruk and Jemdet Nasr vases with relief decoration (especially animal-files),[26] sculpture,[27] amulets[28] and cylinder seals[29] are overwhelmingly carved from light calcareous

---

17 *MSL XII*.
18 Loding 1981: 6 (Fara); de Genouillac 1936: pl. 85 (Girsu).
19 *SKL*: vi:19.
20 *PSD B*: 184 bur A, biling. 1.
21 Note also the [al]an-dím-dím, perhaps a statue maker, in Proto-Lu (*MSL XII*: 57 l. 680). Other Sumerian lexical texts mention the alamgu, who is equated with the *purkullu*.
22 *MSL XII*: 34 l. 45.
23 *UET III*: 1498.
24 This is represented dramatically in Meyer's (1981) histogrammes showing the frequencies of stone types for the ED-OB periods at Nippur, Ešnunna and Tutub.
25 Stat. B, vi:3-8, 13-20.
26 *E.g.* Heinrich 1936: Taf. 2, 22f.; Woolley 1955: pl. 31. Rare exceptions in other materials include two vessels from Ur: one of 'steatite' found in a Persian house (Woolley 1955: pl. 35:U.18118); and an animal relief vase of grey-green (altered volcanic?) stone (Smith 1936: 116f., pl. XXXIa).
27 Heinrich 1936: Taf. 7a; Amiet 1980a: figs 248-50. A recent series of analyses of 17 'Sumerian' statues/statuettes in the British Museum broke down as follows: gypsum 13, calcite 1, ?dolomite 1, ?limestone 2 (BM, RL file 6035).
28 Heinrich 1936: Taf. 9-13; Limper 1988.
29 See the materials of the seals in catalogues such as Porada *et al.* 1948, Legrain 1951, Wiseman 1962, Buchanan 1966, *idem* 1981: nos 133-199, and note Hallo's remark in the introduction to this last work (*ibid.*: ix): "marble was most characteristic of the earliest periods, calcite [and shell !] of the Early Dynastic period".

Figure 31.   Votive statuettes from Khafajeh. Limestone/calcite/gypsum. Early Dynastic III.

stones. This applies also to nearly all Early Dynastic stelae,[30] wall-plaques[31] and decorated maceheads,[32] including rare royal monuments ('Vulture stele' and macehead of Eannatum; Mesilim macehead, Ur-Nanše wall-plaques). Early Dynastic cylinder seals too are predominantly light stones (and shell at coastal sites like Ur). Statuary presents a more complex picture. The large series of 'worshippers' and other *ex voto* dedications (Fig. 31), best represented in the temples of the Diyala and Mari, again illustrate an overwhelming reliance on local light-coloured stones.[33] These also account for most of the larger 'royal' and official statuary. Darker exotic stones – principally diorites, dolerites and gabbros – do not appear until the end of Early Dynastic III and are then restricted, as their inscriptions indicate, to statues of rulers and high officials – a sure indication of their prestige value.[34] In the Akkadian period,

---

30 Börker-Klähn 1982: nos 116-26.
31 Boese 1971: catalogue.
32 *E.g.* Amiet 1980a: pls 333 (Eannatum), 302 (Mesilim). The macehead of Rimuš in the British Museum (BM 134905) was recently analysed as calcite (BM, RL file 6035).
33 Of approximately 320 ED 'worshipper' statues catalogued by Braun-Holzinger (1977: 77-86) only 13 (= 4%) are of non-calcareous igneous stones and 6 of these are the official statues cited below. Of the remaining examples, some of which are fragmentary and may also be of officials, 2 are of basalt (from Adab and Jebel-el Beida), 2 of 'diorite' (Tello and Leiden), 1 of 'dark stone' (Tello), 1 of porous grey-green stone (Uruk) and 1 of 'dolerite' (Louvre).
34 'Diorite' statues of Enmetena from Ur (Woolley 1955: pl. 40), Dudu of Lagaš (Amiet *et al.* 1980: no. 58; Braun-Holzinger 1977: 82 calls this "volcanic black stone"), Lupad of Umma, from Ur (Spycket 1981:

and probably earlier, these materials seem to have been obtained primarily from the Gulf (see below).

There are a handful of possible exceptions, such as the statue from Ubaid inscribed by Kurlil, carved from hard greenstone, and the fragment of an Early Dynastic III statue of very similar stone bearing a land sales inscription.[35] This material, though very rarely used for sculpture, is one of the standard stones of the Jemdet Nasr-Early Dynastic II stone vessels, which were most likely imported from highland Iran (below pp. 218f.). It is tempting to consider inner Iran as the source of Kurlil's stone also, whence it could have been washed down one of the Tigris tributaries or perhaps transported over land. Such an origin gains further support from Spycket's stylistic dating of the statue to Early Dynastic II, the peak period of stone vessel use in Sumer, suggesting that it was later 'usurped' and inscribed by Kurlil.[36]

Most of the plain stone vessels and other undecorated objects and building stone of light, calcareous stones in third-millennium Sumer doubtless represent Sumerian workmanship using stone from the local sources accessible by boat. Whether these and other stones available in the Zagros were also brought from the east is presently unclear.

The hard, lustrous marbles were favoured for the finer cylinder seals and animal amulets in the late Protoliterate period giving way in Early Dynastic times to limestone, calcite and (in ED III) to shell.[37] In Sumer bituminous limestone seems to be largely restricted to Uruk, where it was used for vessels and small sculpture in the Jemdet Nasr and Early Dynastic periods.[38] A beautiful translucent, green calcite (crystaline calcium carbonate), often called 'aragonite' in French publications, was used sparingly in the Late Uruk period for amulets, pictographic tablets and, in the Early Dynastic period, for statuettes and vessels.[39] In the Akkadian period it was used also for fine relief carving (Fig. 17).[40] A less transparent green calcite with distinctive ochre-coloured veining occurs rarely from Late Uruk times for statuettes[41] and other small items. It becomes more common in the Early Dynastic period, especially for sub-conical bowls, at Susa. Vessels of this stone (also called 'onyx' and, in French publications, 'aragonite') are less common in Sumer but appear there among temple dedications (notably at Nippur) and grave offerings.

Already in the late prehistoric period a range of more distant materials was also exploited, especially at Uruk IV-III where, in addition to the usual light stones, there is granite, basalt, obsidian, bituminous limestone, slate/schist, variously coloured marbles, green calcite ('aragonite') and 'serpentine'.[42] It is tempting to associate this variety of materials with the widespread network of Late Uruk colonies

---

105f. [for ED III date], pl. 67), Dada-ilum from Ur (Woolley 1955: pl. 41c [U.2732]; Spycket 1981: 106 & n. 330 [for late ED-Akk date]) and Enannatum I (Braun-Holzinger 1977: 83 [Bibliothèque Bodmer, Geneva]).

35 Hall & Woolley 1927: pl. IX; Hall 1928: 15 (WA118074). X-ray diffraction analysis of Kurlil showed "a significant proportion of chlorite ... (It is) probably an altered intermediate/basic volcanic rock" (BM report, courtesy of J.E. Curtis).

36 Spycket 1981: 106.

37 Buchanan 1966: 4, 22, 52, 72.

38 Lenzen 1961: 25.

39 Amulets: Weiss ed. 1985: no. 28. Tablets: André-Leichnam *et al.* 1982: 52 no. 8. Statuettes: *e.g.* Orthmann *et al.* 1975: pl. II (Nippur). Vessels: *e.g.* Woolley 1934: pl. 174:U.10480 (Ur). From the illustrations it is not clear whether the Nippur statuette and Ur bowl are calcite or gypsum. The bowl is a distinctive form which seems to copy metal prototypes.

40 Börker-Klähn 1982: nos 22-24.

41 *E.g.* Orthmann *et al.* 1975: pl. I.

42 Heinrich 1936: 17ff.; Limper 1988.

in Syria (*cf.* some of the same stones used at Brak)[43] and Iran. Vessels in the dark igneous and metamorphic rocks were probably brought from the inner Zagros where these stones are abundant, a distance of some 300km.[44] A handful of 'alabaster' vessels from Archaic Uruk may mark the first evidence of trade with more distant highland Iran.[45] On the other hand, a north-western origin is more plausible for the basalt of the large 'Lion Hunt' stele and some other late prehistoric sculptures[46] and probably also for the 'serpentine' which was commonly used for Late Uruk cylinder seals but virtually disappears in Uruk III after the collapse of the Euphrates settlements.[47] Shale/slate/schist were used, especially for decorative inlays, inlaid vases and various enigmatic inscribed and decorated objects.[48] Similar use of these materials at Tell Brak[49] may indicate a northern origin. The 'steatite' used for decorated stone vessels and sculpture[50] probably relate rather to the Jemdet Nasr-Early Dynastic II presence in eastern Arabia and Oman, where this material was obtained later in the millennium, or to Iran.

The so-called 'piedmont seals' of heat-treated steatite bearing stylized naturalistic and geometrical designs[51] were no doubt manufactured from Iranian stone since they are found principally along the piedmont of the Zagros mountains, the greatest concentrations occuring at Susa and the Diyala sites. They are very rare in Sumer. These seals were widely used in highland Iran as far east as Shahr-i Sokhta[52] and the examples from Mesopotamia are probably to be regarded as Iranian imports.

There are no temple deposits comparable to those of Uruk for the succeeding initial Early Dynastic period and any comparison must take account of this change in the nature of the evidence. In the cemeteries at Ur, Kiš and Khafajeh stone vessels are abundant, reaching a peak towards the end of the 'Jemdet Nasr' cemetery at Ur, now dated from Jemdet Nasr to Early Dynastic II or Early Dynastic I.[53] At this point stone vessels completely out-number pottery, one grave (JNG/221) containing as many as 35 stone vessels.[54] Dark igneous and metamorphic rocks, both hard marble, granite and diorite and soft steatite/chlorite/setpentine, are well represented, as well as the local limestones.[55]

Among the vessels from the Early Dynastic III (and later) 'Royal Cemetery' at Ur the dark igneous stones are largely abandoned in favour of mottled or banded

---

43 Mallowan 1947: pls III-V, VII-XXI.
44 Schüller 1963: 56f. *Cf.* Morgan 1900: 35 who argued that the Iranian igneous rocks were too distant to have been exploited by the lowlanders and considered it likely that they came instead from Armenia, India or the Red Sea (*ibid.*: 37).
45 *E.g.* Heinrich 1936: Taf. 25:W14819h, 30:W14910; below p. 222.
46 Börker-Klähn 1982: nos 1-3, 13, 14; Curtis 1986. *Cf.* the basalt ($NA_4.HAR=erū$) grindstones which were regularly brought down by boat from the north in the OB period (Degraeve 1991: 10-15).
47 Reliable statistics can be given only for collections which have been recently published with geological identifications. In the Yale collection (Buchanan 1981) 8 of 27 Late Uruk cylinders (nos 133-159) are 'serpentine', against only 4 of 39 in local JN style (nos 160-199). In other collections serpentine may be described as 'steatite' or 'greenstone' (Buchanan 1966: xx), all of which are dark and greasy; *cf.*, on this basis, the 'steatite' Uruk seals in Wiseman 1962, Buchanan 1966 *etc.* 'Serpentine' was regularly used for Syrian seals from the 5th mill. on.
48 Inlays: Heinrich 1936: Taf. 32-34. Vases: *ibid.*: Taf. 26. Other: 'Blau Monuments' (Amiet 1980a: pls 232-5); bird from Khafajeh (Moortgat 1969: pl. 37).
49 Mallowan 1947: pl. III.
50 Woolley 1955: pl. 35 (vessel); *ibid.*: pl. 37 (sculpture).
51 Collon 1987: 20-23; Pittman n.d. [1].
52 Amiet 1979.
53 Kolbus 1983; Gockel 1982.
54 Woolley 1955: 116f.
55 Materials listed by types in Woolley 1955: 155-57.

yellow-brown and white calcite.[56] This distinctive stone is largely restricted to certain recurrent types which were probably imported, like the igneous vessels before, as finished articles, though from different regions (below pp. 219, 239-43). This is true also of the steatite which occurs in distinctive plain and decorated vessels (the *séries ancienne* and *récente* of Miroschedji)[57] and occasionally in sculpture.[58] Shale/schist continues for decorated inlay backgrounds, wall-plaques and other specialised uses.[59]

The Akkadian period sees a number of important changes. For the first time, hard dark igneous/metamorphic stones become the standard medium for monumental royal sculpture (Fig. 32). Of the twenty-six Akkadian monuments, mainly from Susa, in the Louvre, nineteen (73%), including all but one of the seven with royal inscriptions, are of dark stones usually identified as 'diorite'.[60] Only seven are of light stones.[61] Four of the dark pieces, as well as two stele fragments from Sippar, have recently been analysed, one of Sargon, four of Maništušu and one of an unidentified Akkadian ruler.[62] All are "olivine-gabbros, none from precisely the same specimen but likely from the same geological intrusion or set of intrusives".[63] The inscription on three of the Maništušu statues relates how, after defeating Anšan and Šherihum, the king campaigned "across the (Lower) Sea", and, after further conquests, "quarried their black stones, loaded them onto ships, and moored them at the quay of Agade".[64] Since no place name is given,[65] the location of this mining operation cannot be proved but there are a number of clues. The expression "across the (Lower) sea" was apparently used of both Arabia and Iran, but in this case the fact that Maništušu "crossed" the sea from Anšan and Šerihum in Iran, makes a location in Oman the more likely option.[66] Olivine gabbro is available on both side of the Gulf, in Oman and in south-central Iran.[67] Maništušu's reference to "silver/precious metal mines" in the same region has been thought to favour an Iranian locale but the evidence is not conclusive.[68]

Inscriptions of Naram-Sin and Gudea indicate that they also obtained dark stones from the Gulf.[69] The origin of these materials is now explicitly given as Magan and the material is specified as *esi*-stone, usually translated "diorite". Literary compositions also attribute *esi*-stone to Magan.[70] The inscription at the bottom of a statue from Susa relates that Naram-Sin:

---

[56] Woolley 1934: 379.
[57] Miroschedji 1973.
[58] Amiet 1986b: 14, Taf. 4:1.
[59] Backgrounds: Langdon 1924: pls XXXVI, XXXIX. Wall-plaques: Watelin 1934: pl. XXVIII.
[60] Amiet 1976a: nos 1-6, 11-14, 16, 17, 20-22, 28-30; Scheil 1902: pl. I:2.
[61] Amiet 1976a: nos 15, 18, 19, 23, 25-27.
[62] *Ibid.*: no. 2 (Sargon); nos 11, 14, *AKI*: Man. 1 Texts C-D (Sippar stelae) (Maništušu); Scheil 1902: pl. I:2 (unidentified).
[63] Heimpel 1982: 65; *idem* 1987: 69.
[64] Quoted with references above p. 104.
[65] *Pace* D.T. Potts 1986b: 273, Magan is not explicitly mentioned in the text on this or any other of the statues analysed by Heimpel 1982.
[66] Glassner 1987: 23 n. 134; *idem* in press. On the reading "crossed" (and the alternative "readied") see above p. 104f., n. 103.
[67] Heimpel 1982: 67; *idem* 1987: 69f.
[68] See above pp. 105, 163.
[69] *AKI*: NS 3; Stat. A ii:6-iii:3.
[70] *EN* 8-9 (Attinger 1984: 12) and *Lugal-e*, 472 (van Dijk 1983: vol. I, 112 = Jacobsen 1987: 259).

Figure 32. Sargonic stele from Susa. Diorite. Ht. 46.2 cm.

conquered Magan and captured Maniu[m], lord of Magan. In their mountains
he quarried stones of diorite (?), transported them to Agade, his city, and
made a statue of himself (and) dedicated it to (... [a deity])[71]

Unfortunately, the stone type of this piece has not been scientifically analysed.[72]

It is plausible to suppose that the Gulf was likewise the origin of most of the
other dark stone used by Sargon and his successors for which no inscriptional
evidence of sources exists. Heuzey observed long ago that many of the dark stone
statues of Gudea are well smoothed and rounded even on the seemingly unworked
areas, and suggested that they were not mined but collected from outcrops eroding
into the Gulf, where they had been smoothed into boulders by the sea.[73] This applies
equally to the Akkadian monuments. Rimuš states that blocks (perhaps: "objects") of
"diorite, *duši*-stone and (other) stones" were also brought back as part of the "booty of
Parahšum (Marhaši)".[74] There is less textual evidence regarding the dark "soft stones"
(steatite/chlorite/serpentine), whose ancient names are in any case less certain. An
Ur III Gulf merchant dedicated "steatite (objects)(?)" (na4al-ga-miš) and a stone used to
make bowls with "thin hands (handles?)(?)" (na4bur-šu-sal), perhaps those of the *série*

[71] NS 3:30-48 = Amiet 1976a: no. 29. Translation after Westenholz in D.T. Potts 1986b and J.A. Black (pers.
comm.); *cf.* Amiet 1976a: 128, von Soden *AHw*, sub *usû(m)* (*CAD* A: *abnu* (a) for tentative translation of
E.SIG-*im* as 'diorite').
[72] Amiet 1976a: 128 gives the material, as for almost all these pieces, as "diorite".
[73] Heuzey 1885.
[74] Rimuš C10:41-45; Oelsner 1989: 404.

récente, as part of his tithe to Nanna upon returning from Magan.[75] On the other hand, no third-millennium records indicate that dark stones were imported from the north-west, despite the Akkadians' many military operations in those regions.[76] The materials typically used by local rulers in northern Iraq and Syria in the late third and early second millennia are limestone and basalt, suggesting that these, rather than diorite-dolerite, were the principal exploited rock-types of the region.[77]

In this connection it is significant that the means of transport used by Sargonic kings and later rulers for importing stones, when specified, is always by boat. Large blocks for statuary would have been too heavy to haul long distances over land, and the possibility of their exploitation in Sumer clearly depended on adequate shipping facilities, whose development may have been accelerated by Akkadian maritime military expansion in the Gulf. These stones are effectively booty, and their inscriptions are more elaborate versions of the dedications on stone 'booty vases'. Thus they remain essentially a royal monopoly under the Akkadians.

A heightened appreciation of the qualities of various stones also led the Akkadians to select carefully among the calcareous rocks for finer works. A smooth, shiny surface was highly prized and they clearly appreciated the beautiful translucent, green calcite/gypsum used for the fine reliefs showing bound prisoners from Nasriyah and Susa (Fig. 17).[78]

Also at this time serpentine became popular again for fine cylinder seals. In the British Museum collection the percentage of serpentine increases from 8% in Early Dynastic III to 46% in Akkadian times.[79] Likewise in the Marcopoli collection serpentine increases from 3 of 14 (=21%) in the Early Dynastic period (not subdivided) to 20 of 31 (=66%) in the Akkadian period.[80] It is noteworthy that the two periods when serpentine is particularly prominent in south Mesopotamian glyptic – during Late Uruk and Akkadian times – correspond to periods of military and cultural expansion along the Euphrates into Syria where this material had long been one of the most popular stones for glyptic.[81] It seems not unlikely therefore that the serpentine of Sumer came from Syria rather than Iran.[82]

Collon remarks on the almost total replacement of serpentine by chlorite for seals in the post-Akkadian and Ur III periods. In the British Museum collection chlorite rises from 1.6% in the Akkadian period to 44% in post-Akkadian times and 55.5% in Ur III, paralleled by an equally dramatic decline in serpentine. A similar

---

[75] *UET III*: 751; Leemans 1960: 21; Heimpel 1987: 50, 80 A43. *Cf.* also the na4šu-man ("stone with two (?) hands [handles?]") cited with esi-stone among the produce of Magan in *EN*; this stone is listed in H*h* immediately after na4šú-u, which term a Kassite inscription ascribes to a serpentine macehead (*MSL X*: 14, 27; D.T. Potts 1993a).

[76] Booty from these regions generally consists of metals and/or timber. The text NS C5:76-81 reports the setting up of a diorite statue, presumably in Akkad, after the defeat of Riš-Adad of Armanum, but it is not stated where the stone came from.

[77] Exceptions, such as the 'diorite' man from Aššur (Moortgat 1969: pl. 143) and the stele of Naram-Sin at Pir Hussein, are either Akkadian monuments or come from Akkadian strongholds, and are as likely to be imports from southern workshops.

[78] Börker-Klähn 1982: nos 22-24, describing them as "alabaster"; Amiet (1976a: 27) describes the Susa reliefs as "albâtre vert ou aragonite".

[79] Collon 1982: 14, 26; Collon & Geller 1983: 205.

[80] Teissier 1984.

[81] *E.g.* Braidwood & Braidwood 1960: *passim.*

[82] Further testing of this hypothesis is hindered by the unreliable or ambiguous identifications of stones in most catalogues. Buchanan's 'steatite' is apparently a "broken down serpentine" (Buchanan 1966: 72; *cf.* Hallo in Buchanan 1981: xx who suggests for this the term 'serpentinite'). Kohl had claimed that the Iranian material traditionally called "steatite" is in fact mainly chlorite (Kohl *et al.* 1979); but Amiet remarks that this use of "chlorite" is incorrect, that it is really "serpentine" (Amiet 1977: 98; *idem* 1980b: 156).

pattern can be seen in the seals from Tell Asmar and Nippur.[83] At the same time chlorite vessels of the *série récente* were being imported into Mesopotamia from the Gulf which now also supplied Sumer's copper. The evidence of later third-millennium stones thus complements the metal analyses in suggesting an increasing dependence on the Gulf at the expense of any remaining river trade with Syria (serpentine) or overland trade with Iran. It is notable in this connection that after the early second millennium, when the Gulf trade declines, lapis lazuli and other eastern stones virtually disappear from the seal repertory and are replaced by haematite from eastern Anatolia.[84]

The dark stone statuary of the post-Akkadian period indicates that the Gulf supply channels were maintained, presumably now by trade rather than military intervention.[85] As before, their use seems to be restricted essentially to the royal family.

Most of the attributable extant statues are from the dynasty established at Lagaš by Ur-Baba, principally those of Gudea. Of twenty-five almost certainly genuine Gudea (and Gudea-like) figures,[86] mostly excavated or acquired in the nineteenth century, almost three-quarters are of dark stones usually described as 'diorite'.[87] The full break-down is as follows:

Stone type[88]	*Number*
diorite	13[89]
gabbro diorite	1[90]
microdiorite	2[91]
dolerite	2[92]
uralite-quartz-dolerite	1[93]
paragonite	1[94]
steatite	1[95]
alabaster, gypseous chlorite	1[96]
limestone	1[97]
unspecified (Nippur)	1[98]

The uralite-quartz-dolerite was identified analytically.[99] Other stone descriptions which suggest that analytical identifications have been made include the "alabaster" Ur-Ningirsu and the Boston head of "green diorite with hornblende component".[100]

---

[83] Collon 1982: 14, 110, 130 (BM); Meyer 1981: Table 23 (Asmar, Nippur).
[84] Collon 1986: 10f.
[85] Aside from Anšan, Gudea makes no claim to have conquered the regions from which he obtained stone and other building material for the E-Ninu.
[86] These are the statues and fragments listed as genuine by Johansen 1978: 40, plus Gudea statues M (pls 75-76), N (pls 64-70) and O (pls 55-63) and the statue of his son Ur-Ningirsu (pls 118-119), all of which are vindicated to varying degrees by their inscriptions (Alster in Johansen 1978: 49-56 [statue M], 56f. [statues N and O], 58f. [Ur-Ningirsu]), plus the statue AO 29.155 published by Amiet 1987.
[87] The unreliability of many of these visual identifications is illustrated by the fact that a "steatite" head in Philadelphia (CBS 16664) belongs to a "diorite" statue in Baghdad (IM 2909) (Johansen 1978: 26).
[88] Stone types follow Johansen 1978 unless otherwise specified.
[89] Statues, A, B, E, F, G, H, I, K, BM 98065, Boston Mus. of Fine Arts 26,289, HSM 8825, AO 12, AO 13.
[90] Statue C (Amiet 1987: 170).
[91] Statue D, AO 29.155 (Amiet 1987).
[92] Statue N (Amiet 1987: 169; *cf.* earlier descriptions as calcite (Spycket 1981: 191 n. 35) and diorite (Orthmann *et al.* 1975: 177)), Cleveland Mus. of Art 63.154.
[93] Statue U.
[94] Statue M.
[95] Statue O.
[96] Ur-Ningirsu (Amiet 1987: 169).
[97] Statue S.
[98] Johansen 1978: 13.

Figure 33.   Statue of Gudea from Girsu(?). Dolerite/diorite(?). Ht. 73.6 cm.

Five more probably genuine Gudeas include two each of 'diorite' and 'dolerite' and one of 'steatite'.[101] A further unpublished Gudea fragment was analysed as "equigranular quartz diorite".[102]

The remaining ten pieces of questionable authenticity[103] break down as follows:[104]

diorite	3
diorite or gabbro	1
diorite, gabbro or guartz	1
greenish stone (diorite ?)	1
steatite	2
alabaster	1
unspecified	1

---

99   Sollberger 1968: 142 n. 5.
100 Johansen 1978: pls 118-119; Amiet 1987: 169 (Ur-Ningirsu); Johansen 1978: pls 92-93, p. 26 (Boston).
101 Listed Johansen 1978: 41.
102 Heimpel 1982: 65f. (AO 26647), presumably acquired rather than excavated.
103 Those listed by Johansen 1978: 40 (all of which he considers fakes) with the exceptions cited in note 86. Unfortunately, the New York seated Gudea (pls 84-87), one of the few pieces which has been geologically analysed (diorite or gabbro; see below main text), is also suspect (Alster in Johansen 1978: 57f.).
104 The identifications of the items listed second and third in this list (diorite/gabbro/quartz), both in New York, were established analytically (Johansen 1978: 24, 28, n. 75).

Gudea's inscriptions celebrating the building of the E-Ninu for Ningirsu relate that the esi-stone for his statues came from Magan, where Naram-Sin had mined this same material.[105] The analysis of one Gudea statue as diorite confirms that this was included in the range of stones known to the Sumerians as esi-stone. It is hardly surprising that the Akkadian statues analysed as olivine-gabbro were also called by the same name, since modern visual identifications of these statues have failed to distinguish them. Diorite (and dolerite) occurs in Oman,[106] the probable location of Magan, but Heimpel reports the opinion of a geologist that the blocks found there are too small for such statuary, and suggests for their origin instead the region 50 miles north-north-east of Bandar Abbas, where larger blocks of diorite and gabbro are available. However, this argument from silence can hardly preclude the identification of Oman with Magan, as Heimpel believes.[107] Even if it were accepted, since it is unclear whether and how much of the Iranian littoral was included under this designation the locale of Gudea's source of diorite would still to this extent remain uncertain.

Steible's recent attempt to establish a relative chronology of Gudea's inscriptions[108] makes it possible to trace in the statues Gudea's increasing use of Maganite diorite. A group of relatively small works in heterogeneous stones (statues M, N, O) date earliest in the sequence. An intermediate group of small statues in dolerite and diorite (P, I, Q) reflect a period of limited access to the stones of Magan. Last come a group of life-size and colossal diorite statues (A-H, K) reflecting Gudea's extravagant exploitation of Maganite esi-stone, flaunted also in the accompanying inscriptions.

'Steatite', also probably from the Gulf or south-central Iran, was now used for couchant androcephalic bulls, statues, reliefs and also for decorated vessels and lamps, though some of these last may well be Iranian imports.[109]

Gudea also provides evidence, unique in the third millennium, for the procurement of 'common' stones in the north-west. These are:

(1) "large (blocks) of na-stone (^{na_4}na-gal)" (limestone?), for stelae, from "Umanum the mountain of Menua (and) from Basalla the mountain of Mardu (people)".[110]

(2) "alabaster in blocks", for lion sculptures, from "Tidanum the mountain of Mardu (people)".[111]

(3) a type of bitumen and "red clay" (?), for use in building the E-Ninu, from "Madga the mountain of Iluruda".[112]

(4) "... na-stone (^{na_4}na-lu-a)" (possibly: "numerous (blocks) of limestone"), for building the foundation of the E-Ninu, brought from Mt Barme in boats.[113]

(5) "nir-stone blocks" (for a macehead decorated with three lions' heads) from Meluhha.[114]

---

[105] Stat. A, ii:6-iii:3; Pettinato 1972: 137 and n. 818 for parallel passages.
[106] Heimpel 1982: 67 n. 23; Ratnagar 1981: 15; Hauptmann 1985: 17, Abb. 5, 6.
[107] Heimpel 1982: 67; *cf.* Amiet 1986: 180.
[108] Forthcoming in *JCS*, reported by Azarpay 1990: 660f.
[109] *E.g.* Amiet 1980a: pl. 403, dedicated by Ur-gar (bulls); *ibid.*: pl. 53 (statues); *ibid.*: pl. 396 (reliefs). For vessels see below pp. 250ff. Note also the 'steatite' lamp cover from Girsu with intertwined serpents (*ibid.*: pl. 402), a motif best paralleled on the wood gaming board from Shahr-i Sokhta (Piperno & Salvatori 1983: 179-85, citing comparanda).
[110] Stat. B, vi:3-12; *NBWI*: I 164ff, II 21, n. 54.
[111] Stat. B, vi:13-20; *NBWI*: I 166; for "alabaster in blocks" *cf.* Pettinato 1972: 77 s.v. ^{na_4}nu$_{11}$-gal.
[112] Stat. B, vi:51-54, 57f.; *NBWI*: I 168; for "red clay" *cf.* Pettinato 1972: 78.
[113] Stat. B, vi:59-63; *NBWI*: I 168, II 26 n. 76; for translation *cf.* Pettinato 1972: 75.

Figure 34. 'Libation vase' of Gudea from Girsu. Serpentine/steatite. Ht. 23 cm.

(6)   excavated "alabaster (^{na4}nu$_{11}$-gal)" for a macehead decorated with three lions' heads, brought from Uringiriaz on the Upper Sea.[115]

(7)   "alabaster (^{na4}nu$_{11}$-gal) from the "alabaster mountain (kur-nu$_{11}$)".[116]

Of the places cited, only Basalla (=Basar/Jebel Bishri in Syria)[117] can plausibly be located with any precision. The references to "the mountain of Mardu (people)" confirm a generally north-western orientation.[118] It is noteworthy that the only clearly specified stone-type (excluding bitumen) is a light-coloured material ("alabaster") – no dark stones are mentioned – and that this is said to have been excavated (mu-ba-al)[119] and transported (as was also nir-stone) in blocks – clear indications that he had the material mined rather than relying on intermediaries. It is significant also that the "numerous(?) na-stones (limestone?)" are said to have been transported by "boats".

In the Ur III period (and into the second millennium) hard, dark igneous and metamorphic stones continued to be exploited for royal statuary, as is illustrated by

---

[114] Stat. B, vi:29-32; *NBWI*: I 166.
[115] *NBWI*: I Gudea 44 ii:2-iii:4.
[116] Cyl. A, xvi:24; *NBWI*: II 22, n. 55.
[117] *RGTC 1*: 26.
[118] Umanum and Menua, not otherwise known, are presumed to lie in the north-west (*RGTC 1*: 121, 165); Tidanum is fixed approximately by its connection with Amurru (*ibid.*: 157); Madga's supposed proximity to Kimaš (*RGTC 2*: 113) has been undermined by a new reading of the relevant text (Edzard & Röllig 1976-80: 593); this also brings into question Mt Barme's suggested location near Nuzi (*RGTC 1*: 26).
[119] Gudea 44: iii:1.

Figure 35.   Statue of Narunte with linear Elamite inscription of Puzur-Inšušinak. Susa, ca. 2100 BC.
Limestone. Ht. 1.09 m.

rare survivals like the statue of Šulgi from Ur.[120] Interestingly, all of Puzur-
Inšušinak's extant monuments are, by contrast, of limestone, suggesting that the
Akkadian kings' monopoly of such materials was maintained also under the kings of
Ur (Fig. 35).[121] Hard dark stones were used also for particular classes of smaller
sculpture in the round and utilitarian items, notably duck-weights, while the equally
dark but softer 'steatites' continued to be exploited for small to medium-sized
sculpture such as androcephalic bulls and even tablets. On the other hand, Ur III
stelae and relief carving, of which much more has survived than three-dimensional
work, reverted almost exclusively to local limestones.[122]

    As in the Akkadian and post-Akkadian periods, there is nothing among the
common stones worked in Sumer in the Ur III period that could not have been
acquired in Sumer (limestones *etc.*) and along the Gulf. Certainly there is nothing to
suggest overland trade in unworked stone with the Iranian plateau, and perhaps
even the Zagros Mountains should be questioned as a major source. Exports from
the eastern highlands seem to have been restricted to relatively small quantities of
semi-precious stones and finished products, especially vessels.

---

[120] Woolley 1974: pl. 47b; *cf.* also pls 45g, h, 46b-d, 49a.
[121] Amiet 1976a: nos 32, 33, 35-40, 61, 62; Scheil 1902: 4ff., pl. 2; *idem* 1908: 9f., pl. III:1,2 (stelae).
[122] *E.g.* Amiet 1980a: pls 400, 401 (bulls); Kärki 1986: Anon. nos 16, 17, 19 (tablets); Amiet 1980a: pls 391-
    2, 394-5, 397-8 (limestone reliefs).

Of imported finished stonework other than stone vessels there is very little evidence. Isolated finds include a fragmentary steatite(?) sculpture of an open-mouthed serpent with oval cavities for inlays in its body from a Jemdet Nasr context at Uruk; and a steatite sculpture of an animal with circular inlay cavities and intertwined serpents from Girsu.[123] Both pieces clearly derive from what Amiet has called the 'trans-Elamite' style of highland Iran, which also produced the *série ancienne* vessels (below pp. 250ff.).

(b) Susa

At Susa the emphasis on the use of local stones of the Zagros foothills, to which its location provided direct access, is more marked than in contemporary Sumer. Leaving aside the Akkadian monuments brought to Susa as booty, and 'steatite' vessels and seals which arrived as finished products from highland Iran and the Gulf, the dark igneous and metamorphic rocks of the inner Zagros and Gulf regions are almost totally absent from late fourth and third-millennium contexts. The emphasis in local stone-work – vessels, amulets, statuary and relief sculpture – is entirely on light-coloured limestone and especially gypsum, stones which were available in the foothills of Luristan and as boulders in the rivers running down into Susiana.[124] The finest gypsum, the favoured material, is translucent and white, but much is a more opaque grey, occasionally verging to green or pink.[125] This is the standard material for Uruk-style four-lugged jars, miniature vessels and zoomorphic amulettes, and for the series of Sumerian-inspired Early Dynastic 'worshipper' statuettes and plaques.[126] These very light-coloured materials are supplemented only by bitumen and bituminous limestone, whose use for decorative purposes in the third millennium seems to be restricted largely to Susiana (and Uruk), unlike the gypsums which were also used widely in Sumer. Both varieties were locally available, bitumen being abundant in Susiana, and bituminous limestone occurring throughout the hills of the Pusht-i Kuh.[127] The plastic qualities of hot bitumen, which was usually mixed with ground calcite, made it an excellent medium for decorative work. The principal extant series include decorated vessels, stands and plaques of the Early Dynastic II-III period, and a group of beautiful vessels with zoomorphic relief decoration or zoomorphic handles produced in the final third and early second millennia.[128] Bitumen was less rarely exploited for such purposes in Sumer and bituminous limestone not at all. Although adequate supplies of bitumen existed near Hit and Abu Gir in Akkad the inscription on the bitumen plaque of Dudu (Fig. 14) indicates that the material was brought from the Elamite border town of Urua.[129] The

---

[123] Lenzen 1961: 24f., Taf. 14a-g (Uruk) (the implications of this piece for the chronology of the *série ancienne* are discussed below, p. 257); Amiet 1986b: 14, Taf. 4:1 (Girsu).

[124] Morgan 1900: 46, 48; Carter 1984: 122.

[125] Amiet 1986: 127.

[126] Amiet 1976c; Pelzel 1977.

[127] Marschner & Wright 1978; Morgan 1900: 46.

[128] Amiet 1986: 123f., figs. 62-65; 1966: figs. 117-22 (ED II-III); Amiet 1966: figs 185, 200-11; Börker-Klähn 1970: 68-90 (zoomorphic vessels). One zoomorphic vessel (Amiet 1966: no. 203) has been recently analysed as bituminous stone (Lahanier 1977: 48, analysis 2307).

[129] Bitumen sources: Marschner & Wright 1978a. Dudu plaque: Amiet 1980a: pl. 327; *ABWI*: Ent. 76=*SARI 1*: La 5.28; it is called "bitumen" by Amiet (1980a: 447) and so it appears to the naked eye, though the Louvre label describes it as "bituminous stone", as does Orthmann *et al.* 1975: 189.

few decorated bitumen vessels in Sumer[130] were probably imported as finished articles from Susiana.

Susa's preference for gypsum and bituminous limestone was particularly strong from the Proto-Elamite period to near the end of Early Dynastic III, giving the local stonework an almost totally 'black and white' aspect. Before this time, under Late Uruk influence, harder coloured marble provided some variety, especially for animal amulets and other small objects. Proto-Elamite and Early Dynastic cylinder seals continue to show some variety, reflecting their more disparate origins. The nearest possible source for a group of Proto-Elamite (and rarely Early Dynastic) cylinders of pale green volcanic tuff are deposits near Tepe Sialk, in Kerman north of Tepe Yahya and near Birjand, north-west of Shahr-i Sokhta.[131]

In the late Early Dynastic III period, other calcareous stones make their appearance, especially among vessels. Banded yellow and white calcite first appears in a datable context among the vessels of the Early Dynastic III *Vase à la Cachette*.[132] Similar vessels continue to appear in tombs at Susa down to the end of the third millennium and, as we have seen, many are also attested in Sumer. These vessels have no local antecedents, but can be paralleled on the Iranian plateau and in Central Asia (below pp. 239-43), suggesting that they were finished imports, perhaps from south-eastern Iran where the only known manufacturing centre (Shahr-i Sokhta) is located.[133] The material was never used for recognisably local vessels or other stonework. As always, however, the argument from silence should be treated with caution, especially since the Chalcolithic vessels from Tell es-Sawwan are made from a similar (more local?) material and banded calcites are said to exist in Luristan (see above).

Another distinctive calcite which makes it appearance at about the same time (late ED III) – and seems in this case to be Susian – is the translucent banded green stone in which the layers are often separated by thin veins of opaque ochre-coloured deposit.[134] This very attractive material was used sparingly in Late Uruk and Proto-Elamite stonework.[135] Like the yellow and white calcite, it is particularly popular for vessels though not in the same range of shapes. These were deposited in graves on the *Donjon* and continue to appear in burials at Susa for the rest of the third and early second millennia. On rare occasions it was used for larger sculpture, *e.g.* the monumental horns inscribed by the eighth-century king Šutruk-Nahhunte,[136] suggesting that the source was not far distant from Susa. It is said to occur near Shahr-i Sokhta[137] but nearer supplies certainly existed. It is less common in Sumer, being noticeable only at Nippur and Girsu, where bowls of this material were popular for dedications and to a lesser extent in the Royal Tombs at Ur.

Morgan also mentions small quantities of a 'green marble' at Susa, more or less translucent. His statement that it is deposited by thermal spring suggests what

---

[130] Decorated bitumen vessels occur at Ur (Woolley 1955: pl. 36 [U.210]; inspection in the British Museum showed that this is not "black steatite" as claimed *ibid.*: 167), and at Kiš (Langdon 1924: pl. XXXII:4; inspection in the Ashmolean Museum showed that this is not "black stone" as there stated).

[131] Sax & Middleton 1989. *Cf.* Lahanier 1976 where this material is described as "heulandite" and "mordenite". Lahanier tested 17 3rd-mill. cylinders of this material: 11 from Proto-Elamite Susa, 1 plus 2 fragments from late ED Susa and 4 from Proto-Elamite Shahr-i Sokhta.

[132] Amiet 1986: 126f.

[133] Casanova 1982; Amiet 1986: 127.

[134] Morgan 1900: 48; Heuzey 1903: 31f.

[135] In addition to the items cited above, p. 181, note the vessel of "translucent green alabaster" from Tepe Farukhabad (Wright ed. 1981: 158).

[136] *MDP* III: pl. XIX; for inscription König 1965: no. 71.

[137] Tosi 1983: 167.

the French excavators later frequently describe as 'aragonite', from which many of the Susa stone vessels were carved.[138] Morgan notes that such springs exist in the Pusht-i Kuh, though samples of this stone were known to him only from the region of Urmia.

In the later third millennium, some raw chlorite/steatite/serpentine may have been imported from the Gulf regions to be fashioned into objects like the decorated chlorite macehead dedicated by a maritime merchant.[139] Otherwise the dark stone objects present in small numbers at Susa in the very late third and early second millennia tend to be recognisably foreign products. Some, such as the *série récente* vessels, 'Persian Gulf' stamp seals, hybrid Harappan seals and chert Indus weights are matched by similar finds in Sumer.[140] They clearly derive from the intense sea-borne trade with the Gulf and beyond, in which Sumer seems to have played the leading role,[141] as is confirmed by the fact that the weights and seals have to do with the regulation of trade.[142]

Some other finds at Susa, however, are not paralleled further west; they derive rather from Susa's close political and cultural association with the plateau and the wide network of 'inter-Iranian' exchange to which this gave access. These include:

(1)   Miniature 'gypsum' columns of unknown purpose, presumably ritual.[143] Identical pieces are known from Tepe Hissar and Tureng Tepe in the north-east, Seistan in the south-east and in Central Asia, where they occur also in 'steatite' and marble.[144]

(2)   A small stylized human figurine similar to pieces from Tepe Hissar.[145]

(3)   Bitumen cylinder seals in the Anšanite 'common style', presumably from Tal-i Malyan where this type is now well attested. Amiet dates them to the early Sukkalmah period. Some bitumen copies of Gulf-type seals also may have come from Anšan.[146]

(c) Greater Iran and the Persian Gulf

The use of stones in these regions is strongly oriented to one or two types which, to the extent that sufficient geological information is available, can be shown to be those available nearest to the site. Practicability of transport, rather than any abstract system of preferences, seems to have dictated the pattern of exploitation. Calcite, as the most widely distributed stone type, is also the most extensively

---

138   Morgan 1900: 48f. The 'aragonite' of these vessels is a green (or yellow) banded stone. Similar yellow banded stone vessels have been visually identified by the Dept. of Earth Sciences, Oxford, as calcite. The stone described elsewhere by Amiet (1980a: pl. 36 [Nippur statuette], caption) as aragonite is not this material but the unbanded translucent green stone which is reserved primarily for fine relief carving, not for vessels. It is not stated which, if either, class of objects has been scientifically identified as aragonite.

139   Amiet 1986: 220, fig. 80.

140   Miroschedji 1973 (vessels); Amiet 1986: 150, figs 90:1-7 ('Persian Gulf' seals); *ibid.*: 143, n. 9; fig. 94 (hybrid Harappan seals; these seals of un-Harappan form with Harappan motifs and/or inscriptions may originate in the Gulf, rather than in Sumer and Susa [as Amiet 1986: 143, n. 9; *cf.* Brunswig *et al.* 1983]); Ratnagar 1981: 184-86; Amiet 1986: 143, fig. 93 (Indus weights).

141   There are also Harappan objects at Susa which are not yet paralleled in Sumer: a Harappan-style (?) sculptured head (Amiet 1986: 144, fig. 95) and a female figurine (*ibid.*: 148 & n. 1, fig. 98) closely matched by clay figurines in Afghanistan and Pakistan.

142   Note the 'Persian Gulf' seal impression on a Susa document (Amiet 1986: fig. 90:2).

143   Amiet 1986: 147f., 165, 185f., figs 157-8.

144   Dales 1977a (south-east Iran); Pottier 1984: nos 283-88; Amiet 1977: 101, figs 10, 11 (Central Asia).

145   Amiet 1986: 148, fig. 98 (Susa); Schmidt 1937: pl. XLVI:H.2263, pls XXXIII, XLVII:H.3832, 3500, 5178 (Hissar).

146   Amiet 1986: 153, fig. 113:1-3 (Susa); *ibid.*: 153 (Malyan); *ibid.*: 150, fig. 90:8-10 (bitumen Gulf-type seals).

exploited across Iran and into Afghanistan and Central Asia. There is direct evidence that vessels were made from local calcite deposits at Shahr-i Sokhta, in the Kur river basin and possibly also at Shahdad and Tepe Hissar.[147] At Tal-i Qarib in the Kur basin, a stone vessel dump contained vessels of local travertine (calcite), some of it a "pale green colour" and others of plaster.[148] Tepe Yahya likewise made full use of its local deposits of chlorite for vessels and almost all other decorative and utilitarian stonework, both for local consumption and, in the case of *série ancienne* vessels, also for export.[149] Local deposits of bitumen were exploited at Tal-i Malyan for seals.[150] A pale green volcanic tuff of which the major known sources are north of Yahya, south and west of Tepe Sialk and north-west of Shahr-i Sokhta, was used for Proto-Elamite (and rarely ED) cylinder seals.[151] Although mostly known from Susa they were probably made in highland Elam.

Along the Arabian side of the Gulf (Failaka, Tarut, Eastern Arabia, Bahrain, the United Arab Emirates, Oman) vessels, stamp seals and other stone objects are made almost exclusively from steatite/chlorite, which was available in Arabia and the Oman peninsula.[152] The harder dark stones, such as gabbros, were apparently not exploited on any scale by the local inhabitants, despite their export to Sumer. Calcite, though available in Arabia,[153] occurs only rarely, principally as vessels which seem to be imports from (south-)eastern Iran (below p. 235 n. 103).

2. THE ORIGINS AND EXPLOITATION OF SEMI-PRECIOUS STONES

A wide variety of semi-precious stones was used in third-millennium Mesopotamia for jewellery and other small-scale decorative work. Chief amongst these are lapis lazuli and carnelian, with lesser quantities of quartz (rock crystal, jasper), chalcedony (agate, onyx, sardonyx), obsidian, haematite, chrysoprase *etc.*

Some of these materials were available in Syro-Anatolia, but the primary source areas seem to have lain to the east in Iran and beyond. A number of sites in these regions (Malyan, Shahdad, Sokhta II and Hissar) have yielded evidence of bead production using carnelian, chalcedony, lapis, turquoise and other stones. Most of these are widespread in Greater Iran and it is not yet possible to trace their sources. Only lapis lazuli and carnelian can plausibly be attributed to specific supply zones. Later texts from Ur mention various semi-precious stones brought back from Dilmun,[154] many deriving from lands further along the Gulf, including Meluhha. Fourteen semi-precious stones, which together receive a blessing in *Lugal-e*,[155] are implied, like all the other stones in this composition, to 'inhabit' the eastern mountains. These include lapis lazuli, carnelian, agate (?), chalcedony, jasper and 'fish eyes' ([na4]e-gi-zà-ga).

---

[147] Ciarla 1979; *idem* 1981 (Sokhta); Sumner 1986: 200f. (Kur basin); Amiet 1986: 127 (Shahdad).
[148] Alden 1979: 116f., fig. 57; Sumner 1986: 200.
[149] Kohl 1974: 101-08.
[150] Amiet 1986: 153, fig. 112-14.
[151] Sax & Middleton 1989.
[152] Zarins 1978: 67; Kohl *et al.* 1979.
[153] Beale 1973: 136.
[154] Leemans 1960: 33f.
[155] van Dijk 1983: 120-22; Jacobsen 1987: 233-72.

Transporting the small blocks or pebbles in which these materials occur presented no major practical problems. Since Neolithic times, wide-ranging exchange networks had distributed Anatolian obsidian and Central Asian turquoise throughout the Near East and these same channels could be used to distribute other stones. As in earlier times, the third-millennium trade in semi-precious stones to Sumer probably dealt principally in unworked blocks. Virtually all semi-precious stonework from Mesopotamia would therefore have been given its present form locally. Along with the general practice of cutting down old or broken objects, this explains the extreme rarity of finished imports in Sumer – a mere handful of items distinguished by their unusual shapes (*e.g.* a Turkmenian stepped-cross bead at Susa)[156] or technique (*e.g.* 'etched' carnelian beads).

One material conspicuously absent from the repertory of Sumerian semi-precious stones is turquoise, whose principal source in early times seems to have been the inner Kyzyl Kum in Central Asia.[157] Having been popular in Mesopotamia in the Neolithic and Chalcolithic periods, turquoise seems to fall out of use entirely by the end of the fourth millennium. A possible explanation for this anomaly, based on the broader pattern of third-millennium trade, is considered below (p. 281).

We turn now to the evidence relating to carnelian and lapis lazuli, two of the most widely exploited stones in third-millennium Sumer, and the only ones for which there is a sufficient basis to attempt to determine the major trade routes.

(a) Carnelian

Carnelian was imported to Sumer principally as raw lumps but also in lesser quantities as finished products, including the distinctive etched beads. The superior craftsmanship of carnelian beads compared to those of lapis lazuli at Kiš[158] may be an indication of foreign manufacture, but most beads were doubtless produced locally. There is evidence of such production, using a distinctive percussion technique for disc/ring beads, in the Larsa region. Examples of this bead type are known from Ur, Kiš and Mari, and from Susa and Tepe Sialk in Iran.[159] Surveys at Uruk have likewise yielded evidence of Late Uruk-Early Dynastic I carnelian working using flint borers.[160] Microlythic beadworking tools have also been found in surveys at Lagaš.[161] The stone *šammu* (= emery?), called "carnelian-piercing" in *Lugal-e*,[162] was presumably used as an abrasive in the drilling process.

As well as its staple use for beads (Fig. 37) and amulets (and in later periods cylinder seals), large numbers of which survive, carnelian was also employed sparingly for larger objects such as tablets.[163] Documentary evidence extends the list to vessels and other luxury items and shows that it was used in cult statues.[164]

The Mesopotamians distinguished various types of carnelian, as they did with many other stones. The lexical text *abnu šikinšu* lists "the stone which is like boxthorn, carnelian is its name; carnelian which is speckled with black, Meluhha carnelian is its name; carnelian which is speckled with mustard, 'mustard-like' carnelian is its name; carnelian which is speckled [with black], 'mustard-like'

---

[156] Amiet 1986: fig. 100a.
[157] Tosi 1974b: 148-50, 159.
[158] Mackay 1925: 699f.
[159] Chevalier *et al.* 1982: 55.
[160] Müller 1963; Aue 1985: 62; Eichmann 1985: 95f.; Finkbeiner 1985: 30.
[161] Carter 1990: 95.
[162] Heimpel *et al.* 1988: 199.
[163] van Driel 1973.
[164] *CAD S*: 122-24, *samtu* b)-d).

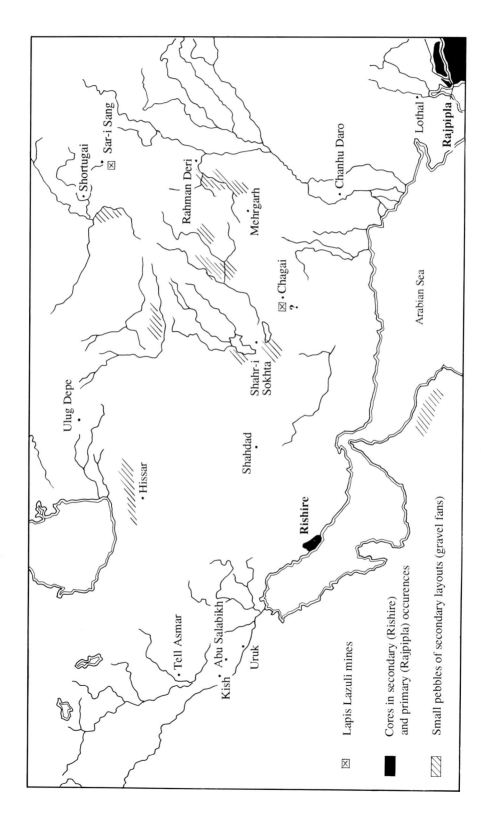

Figure 36.   Map showing major sources of carnelian and lapis lazuli (after Tosi 1976-80: fig. 2).

carnelian [is its name]; [carnelian] which is speckled [with] white, Meluhha carnelian is its name; carnelian which is speckled with yellow, Marhaši carnelian is its name".[165]

Carnelian occurs as a primary deposit in veins and nodules and secondarily in alluvial fans and gravel beds. These latter are said to occur "most abundantly all over the Iranian plateau, the Hindu Kush [whence pebbles were washed down the Himand river to Seistan], around the Central Asian depressions as well as south-eastern Arabia and the eastern desert of Egypt."[166] These yield mainly pebbles which are suitable only for small beads, and were probably exploited chiefly for local consumption. Larger pieces of Sumerian carnelian, particularly the long tubular beads, must have come from 'primary layouts', of which far the largest are in southern Gujarat. Tosi is surely correct in arguing that this source, "although at the very eastern limit of the protohistorical trade network, was already exploited during the IIIrd millennium".[167] Gujarat carnelian presumably reached Sumer by boat. The only other confirmed source of large carnelian blocks is also on the Gulf coast, at Bushire (Fig. 36).[168]

The carnelian supplies of the Indo-Iranian borderlands were exploited from very early times. Production sites with phtanite borers have been excavated at Mehrgarh I-III and Mundigak I3-4.[169] Carnelian from Gujarat, as well as secondary layouts in Iran and Afghanistan, probably supported the bead-making industries attested widely in third-millennium Iran by tools, debitage and unworked lumps at Shahr-i Sokhta II, Tal-i Malyan and Shahdad.[170] At Sokhta II-III six graves with bead-makers' micro-drills were found. One grave (Gr. 77) from phase 5 contained also raw materials, including chalcedony (*i.e.* carnelian) at varoius stages of processing.[171]

Textual evidence confirms that Sumer was supplied by eastern sources of carnelian (^{na4}gug), especially those in or controlled by Meluhha.[172] Royal inscriptions, lexical lists and literary compositions concur in citing this as the primary, if not the exclusive, origin of Sumerian carnelian.[173] Lexical lists also mention the carnelian of Dilmun, Marhaši and Gutium,[174] but of these only Marhaši may possibly be placed far enough east to be connected with any of the primary source zones (Bushire?). Dilmun, which appears again as the source of carnelian offered to the temple of Ningal by maritime merchants,[175] was certainly merely a transit stations. A similar

---

[165] *abnu šikinšu* ll. 5-9; Horowitz 1992: 114.

[166] Tosi 1976-80: 448; for Shahdad see also Salvatori & Vidale 1982: 8: "[carnelian is] certainly plentiful in … the Shahdad area". Previously it has been widely stated that the nearest eastern carnelian is in the Hindu Kush and India (Tosi 1969: 374; Lamberg-Karlovsky & Tosi 1973: 46, Map 3; Beale 1973: 136f.).

[167] Tosi 1976-80: 448f.; Ratnagar 1981: 106, 128f. end map.

[168] Tosi 1976-80: 449; Whitehouse 1975.

[169] Jarrige 1981: 108f.; Lechevallier 1984: 46.

[170] Lamberg-Karlovsky & Tosi 1973: 46; Tosi 1976-80: 449-52 (Sokhta); Sumner 1986: 204 (Malyan); Salvatori & Vidale 1982: 8f. (Shahdad).

[171] Piperno 1979: 125, 132; *idem* 1976.

[172] Ratnagar's reference to Magan as a source of carnelian (1981: 39, 41f.) seems to be based on a mistranslation of *EN*.

[173] H*h* XVI:128 (*MSL X*: 8); *Lipšur* 33 (Reiner 1956: 133); *EN* BII:3 (Attinger 1984: 13); Hymn to Ninurta (M. Cohen 1975: 31); Gudea Cyl. A, xvi:22; Cyl. B, xiv:13; hymns to Inanna (Sjöberg 1976: 188; *idem* 1988: 169); stones list (Cavigneaux 1976: 122 no. 7:4); *abnu šikinšu* (Horowitz 1992: 114); Diri VI A:22´; medical text (as amulet) (*CAD S*: 122, 3´).

[174] CAD S: 121f. *samtu* [a]); H*h* XVI: 127, 129f.; *malku-šarru* I:219 (Dilmun); Steinkeller 1982: 250f. n. 46 (Marhaši); *abnu šikinšu* (quoted above).

[175] *UET V*: 286, 546, 548, 678; Leemans 1960: 23ff.; *malku-šarrum* I 219.

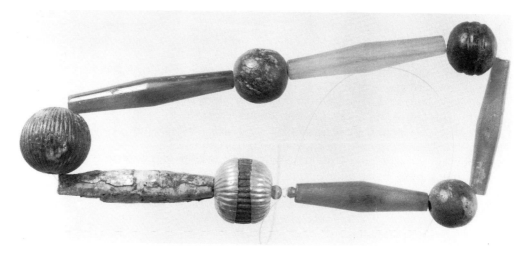

Figure 37.   Beads of carnelian (bi-conical) and lapis lazuli (spherical) from Ur. Early Dynastic III.

explanation is likely in the case of Gutium. The flint drills found in Sumer and references to "carnelian piercing" *šammu* stone (emery?),[176] confirm that carnelian was worked in Mesopotamia. Carnelian and other exotic materials are hardly ever mentioned in third-millennium economic texts. Rare exceptions are the "four long NIM-stones" and "340 small carnelians" delivered by a Sargonic institutional merchant (damgàr).[177] Movement along the Gulf is confirmed by numerous carnelian beads at Umm an-Nar and many sites in Oman.[178]

Ratnagar and Chakrabarti have reviewed evidence for the sources and working of carnelian in the Indus region, and for the export of beads, principally with 'etched' decoration, to Sumer.[179] The etched beads have been catalogued by Reade.[180] These occur in Mesopotamia at Tell Brak, Aššur, Ešnunna, Nippur, Kiš, Lagaš, Abu Salabikh and (far the greatest concentration) Ur, in contexts ranging from Early Dynastic III to the early second millennium. Although more examples are published from the west than the Indus itself, there can be no doubt that they derive from that region, where the stone was available and the technology of heating and 'bleaching' carnelian (and steatite) had a long history.[181] There are a few pieces with unusual designs that may be of Sumerian manufacture.[182]

Etched beads are so far very rare in the Gulf (Umm an-Nar, Hili North Tomb A, Ajman).[183] They are better represented in Iran where isolated examples come from Susa, Kalleh Nisar (Luristan), Tepe Hissar IIIC, Shah Tepe IIA$_2$ and Tepe Yahya IVA, and further east at Mundigak.

The carnelian found on sites on the Iranian plateau and in Central Asia must have been traded overland from the sources in and around Afghanistan. As far as

---

[176] Heimpel *et al.* 1988: 197, 199.
[177] Foster 1983: 161 no. 18.
[178] Hafit, Hili, Amlah, Tawi, Silaim and Ajman (Frifelt 1991: 112ff., 116).
[179] Ratnagar 1981: 128-30; Chakrabarti 1982.
[180] Reade 1979: 8-23; add Hansen 1978: 76 (al-Hiba), Amiet 1986: fig. 92 (Susa); Frifelt 1991: 116, fig. 288 (Umm an-Nar).
[181] Tosi 1976-80: 452.
[182] Reade 1979: 24f.
[183] Frifelt 1991: 116, fig. 238.

Mesopotamia is concerned, however, all indications suggest that carnelian arrived by sea, principally from Meluhha.

(b) Lapis lazuli

(i) Patterns of exploitation.   The semi-precious stone lapis lazuli (hereafter 'lapis') is attested in Mesopotamia in secure stratigraphical contexts from the Late Ubaid period (Gawra XIII), though it may have first appeared considerably earlier.[184] Lapis occurs as veins in a calcite matrix and is thus available only in relatively small blocks. These were used in the third millennium principally for beads, inlay-work and cylinder seals.[185] Lexical and literary texts mention larger objects[186] but these have rarely survived: a spouted cup, whetstone and dagger handle from Ur, and lapis foundation tablets from Mari and elsewhere are rare exceptions.[187] Its beauty, rarity and hardness (Mohs 5.5) made lapis the most highly prized of all Mesopotamian stones, becoming a *leitmotiv* of Sumerian luxury decoration, especially in combination with gold and carnelian. It was lavished on the most important temples (and palaces?) and conspicuously consumed in sumptuous burials, epitomised by the 'Royal Tombs' at Ur (Figs 37-39). Different qualities of the stone were carefully distinguished and cheaper artificial substitutes were later devised.[188] 'Lapis-like' was a standard metaphor in literary descriptions of great wealth, a synonym for all things bright and splendid, especially the beard or other features of heroes and deities.

Texts frequently mention unworked lapis "lumps".[189] The largest amount cited is two-thirds of a talent, which an Ur jeweller used in one year.[190] This is clearly how the bulk of the lapis consumed in Mesopotamia arrived. Raw pieces have been recovered in excavations in Syria at Late Uruk Jebel Aruda, 23.26 kg. in the Palace at Ebla, at Susa and, in later periods, in Mesopotamia.[191] It was scrupulously recycled, larger objects being cut down to smaller ones and eventually to beads.[192] This accounts for the fact that all figurative and other elaborate lapis work is recognisably local in style and subject matter.

Fluctuations in the use of lapis in third-millennium Mesopotamia are obscured by the unevennes of the evidence. Periods better represented through excavation have inevitably yielded the largest quantities of lapis. This can largely be

---

[184] Herrmann 1968: 29 (Gawra). To the pieces from Arpachiyeh (surface find) and Nineveh (level IIc or III; Late Ubaid) cited by Herrmann (1968: 29), add now (1) a cylindrical bead and pendant from Samarra (Herzfeld 1930: 4, Taf. XLV), though Herzfeld elsewhere denies the existence of any lapis in these graves (1933: 29); and (2) beads from Yarim Tepe level 8 dating to the early Hassuna period (Merpert *et al.* 1976: 40). Together these finds provide adequate grounds for leaving open the option of a pre-Ubaid commencement of trade. If confirmed, the beads from Yarim Tepe would require a complete rethinking of the date and circumstances of the earliest exchange. It is possible, however, that some or all of this early 'lapis' is in fact azurite with which lapis is apparently often confused in the Indus (Fairservis 1983: 2).

[185] Röllig 1983a; Herrmann 1968: 29-53 (Ubaid-Akkadian); Herrmann & Moorey 1983; Rosen 1990: 21-45 (Ubaid-Ur III).

[186] Röllig 1983a: 488f.; cf. Biggs 1966: 175; H*h* XVI; *CAD S*: 122 b).

[187] Woolley 1934: pls 151, 174 (Ur); Parrot 1956: 52ff. (Mari tablet); *SARI 1*: Ki. 8, Um. 4.1; cf. *The Epic of Gilgameš* I i:25 (A. Shaffer 1983: 307 n. 2) (other tablets).

[188] S. Cohen 1973: 157f., 286f.; Oppenheim *et al.* 1970: 10 (could some denote azurite?). Substitutes: *ibid.*: 10f.

[189] *Ibid.*; Cohen 1973: 157f; Pettinato 1972: 78 with refs.

[190] *UET III*: 1498; Heimpel 1987: 51.

[191] Aruda – van Driel & van Driel-Murray 1979: 19f.: "a few pieces of rough unworked lapis lazuli". Ebla – Matthiae 1985: pl. 36; Pinnock 1986. Susa – Morgan 1905b: 124. Mesopotamia – Herrmann & Moorey 1983: 491.

[192] Note the diminution in average size of lapis cylinder seals from ED III to Ur III and OB (Herrmann 1968: 51; Bussers 1984: 72; Collon 1986: 10); also the poor quality (locally made?) lapis beads at Kiš (Mackay 1929: 185) and their reduction in size from ED III to Akkadian (Herrmann 1968: 51).

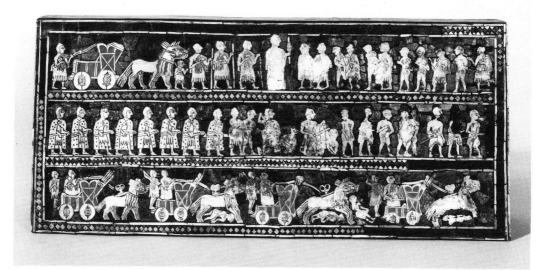

Figure 38. The 'Standard of Ur', battle scene. Lapis lazuli, limestone and shell. Early Dynastic III. Ht. 20.3 cm.

compensated by considering proportions of lapis to non-lapis objects of a given class, rather than absolute figures. But another imbalance remains, for which it is necessary to allow not only for the quantity but also for the quality of the excavated contexts: this is the exceptional richness of certain finds, particularly the 'Royal Tombs' at Ur (Fig. 38). A period known from its royal burials cannot be compared directly with another represented principally from habitations or inferior graves. Recycling introduces a further bias which will tend to inflate the figures for later periods at the expense of earlier ones.

In reviewing variations in quantities of extant lapis during the third millennium, Herrmann refers to the proportions of lapis to non-lapis seals.[193] As an attempt to quantify this variation, Tables 5.1-5.3 summarise the proportion of lapis seals (expressed as percentages of the total corpus of all materials) of the Jemdet Nasr to Old Babylonian periods from excavations at Ur, the Diyala sites and Susa, and from the collections of the British Museum, the Ashmolean Museum, Yale and North America (see Tables for references). Table 5.4 combines the figures from the excavations and collections into 'sub-totals' and then adds these latter to form 'grand totals' indicating the overall percentages of lapis seals for each period. In this table the Ur figures are given both including and excluding the material from the 'Royal Cemetery' (presented separately in Table 5.1) to make readily apparent the affect of these extraordinary finds on the general picture at Ur and elsewhere. (All references in this discussion to 'Ur' without further qualification exclude the 'Royal Tombs'). Seals were selected for the practical reason that they alone can be sufficiently closely dated and are common enough to provide an adequate quantitative basis for chronological analysis. However, it should be emphasised that some periods are

---

[193] Herrmann 1968: 49 (ED III), 52 (Akk).

Figure 39.   Lapis lazuli cylinder seal and impression from Ur. Early Dynastic III. Ht. 4.0 cm.

much better represented than others, and only those percentages based on reasonably large samples can be given any weight. Moreover, since the pattern of lapis use for seals may not correspond to changes in fashion in beads, inlays *etc.*, these categories also should be analysed before generalisations are accepted.

All excavations and collections show low percentages of lapis seals in the Jemdet Nasr period, yielding a grand total of only 0.9%. Early Dynastic I draws a complete blank,[194] though the grand total of 94 from this period is rather low. Excavations and collections both yield a figure of 5% for Early Dynastic II, but again on a fairly restricted basis of 127 seals. All sources show a substantial rise from Early Dynastic II to III,[195] with the sole exception of Susa where both periods failed to yield a single lapis cylinder – a startling discrepancy to which we shall return. For the British Museum, Yale and North American collections this period also constitutes the all-time peak lapis percentage. Likewise at Ur, Early Dynastic III, with 15% (19% counting the transitional pieces), is marginally ahead of Akkadian at 14% (or 17% with its transitional pieces). In the 'Royal Cemetery' as many as 47% of the cylinders were of lapis at this time (Table 5.1 (a)), even more with the transitional pieces (b). This probably represents the true peak, rather than the Ur III period which yields a higher figure (57%) based on a sample less than half the size (see below). In the Diyala also an anomalous Ur III peak is caused by a single example out of a miserly total of 11. In the Ashmolean, similarly spurious peaks occur in Early Dynastic II and post-Akkadian on single examples from dismissably low samples of 16 and 19 respectively. Less easy to explain away is the evidence from Susa. Here, as in the 'Royal Cemetery', the high-point is reached in Ur III, though neither of these is based on particularly large samples (55 and 30 respectively). If Susa's rise is genuine, it may reflect increased access to Mesopotamian lapis under the imperial Ur III

---

[194]   Unless one assigns to this period some of the Brocade-style seals from Ur (Legrain 1951: nos 51, 53, 61). Herrmann 1968: 37 cites only one seal from this period.

[195]   *Cf.* Herrmann's total of 138 lapis seals from this period (1968: 48).

TABLE 5.1

Lapis Lazuli Cylinder Seals from the 'Royal Cemetery' at Ur

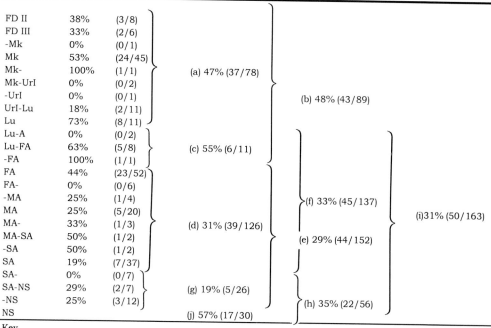

FD II	38%	(3/8)
FD III	33%	(2/6)
-Mk	0%	(0/1)
Mk	53%	(24/45)
Mk-	100%	(1/1)
Mk-UrI	0%	(0/2)
-UrI	0%	(0/1)
UrI-Lu	18%	(2/11)
Lu	73%	(8/11)
Lu-A	0%	(0/2)
Lu-FA	63%	(5/8)
-FA	100%	(1/1)
FA	44%	(23/52)
FA-	0%	(0/6)
-MA	25%	(1/4)
MA	25%	(5/20)
MA-	33%	(1/3)
MA-SA	50%	(1/2)
-SA	50%	(1/2)
SA	19%	(7/37)
SA-	0%	(0/7)
SA-NS	29%	(2/7)
-NS	25%	(3/12)
NS		

(a) 47% (37/78)

(b) 48% (43/89)

(c) 55% (6/11)

(d) 31% (39/126)

(e) 29% (44/152)

(f) 33% (45/137)

(g) 19% (5/26)

(h) 35% (22/56)

(i) 31% (50/163)

(j) 57% (17/30)

Key

(a) Definitely ED
(b) 'Greater ED III', *i.e.* definitely ED III plus (c)
(c) Transitional ED III-Akkadian
(d) Definitely Akkadian
(e) 'Greater Akkadian I', *i.e.* definitely Akkadian (d) plus transitional Akkadian-Ur III (g)
(f) 'Greater Akkadian II', *i.e.* definitely Akkadian (d) plus transitional EDIII-Akkadian (c)

(g) Transitional Akkadian-Ur III
(h) 'Greater Ur III', *i.e.* definitely Ur III (j) plus transitional Akkadian-Ur III (g)
(i) 'Greatest Akkadian', *i.e.* definitely Akkadian (d) plus transitional ED III-Akkadian (c) and transitional Akkadian-Ur III (g)
(j) Definitely Ur III

Notes

Percentages of lapis seals for each period are followed (in brackets) by the absolute figures from which they are derived, expressed as the ratio: number of lapis seals/total number of seals of that period.

Dating follows Nissen 1966 whose chronological abbreviations are used. Collon's (1982) re-dating of the BM seals generally agrees, but reduces the number of Ur III (-NS and NS) lapis seals by 6, assigning 1 (U.8584) to Akkadian and the others (U.15303, 11580, 11592, 11442, 7957) to Post-Akkadian — Ur III. This lowers the Ur III percentage, bringing it more in line with the evidence from other sources.

Chronological Divisions. Nissen (1966) divides the seals into narrow chronological divisions as listed in this table. In addition, the seals from the major periods are here bracketed to give some impression of the overall commonness of lapis. This increases the statistical basis which, in the case of many of Nissen's divisions, is very low indeed. More importantly, it shows the extent to which seals of uncertain or transitional date might affect the general picture depending on whether they are assigned to one or other of the relevant periods. Thus, for example, brackets (a) and (d) give the percentages for all the definitely Early Dynastic III and Akkadian seals respectively, while (b) shows what happens if all the transitional Early Dynastic III-Akkadian seals are assumed to be Early Dynastic III, and (f) shows the result if they are assumed, on the contrary, to be Akkadian. And so on *mutatis mutandis* for the other brackets. It is reassuring that these contrary assumptions generally alter the result very little (1%-2%). Further calculations (not represented here) show that even under the more extreme assumption that all and only the lapis seals of some transitional category belong to one or other of the respective major periods (while all and only the non-lapis seals belong to the other period) still does not greatly change the outcome. For example, Early Dynastic III reaches a maximum of 51% (43/84) and a minimum of 45% (37/83) while Akkadian exhibits extremes of 39% (50/137) and 26% (39/152).

TABLE 5.2

Lapis Lazuli Cylinder Seals from Selected Excavations

Ur (excluding the 'Royal Cemetery')[1]

Late Prehistoric	9.5%	(4/42)			
Early Dynastic I	0%	(0/4)			
Early Dynastic II	0%	(0/3)			
Early Dynastic III	15%	(7/46)	}		
EDIII-Early Akk.	100%	(2/2)	} 19%	(9/48)	
Akkadian	14%	(8/58)	}		
Akkadian-Post Akk.	100%	(2/2)	} 17%	(10/60)	
Post Akkadian	0%	(0/20)			
Post Akk.-Ur III	5%	(2/38)			
Ur III	2%	(3/134)			
Ur III-Isin-Larsa	0%	(0/6)			

The Diyala (Asmar, Khafajeh, Agrab)[2]

Jemdet Nasr	1%	(4/385)
Early Dynastic I	0%	(0/59)
Early Dynastic II	0%	(0/49)
Early Dynastic III	5%	(4/76)
Early Dynastic	5%	(3/57)
Akkadian	2%	(4/139)
Gutian	0%	(0/3)
Ur III	9%	(1/11)
Isin-Larsa	4%	(2/56)
Old Babylonian	2%	(1/43)

Susa[3]

Susa A (I)	0.3%	(1/269)			
Susa B (II)	0%	(0/26)			
Susa Ca-b					
stamps	0%	(0/193)	}	0%	(0/194)
cylinders	0%	(0/1)	}		
Jemdet Nasr	0.5%	(1/176)	}		
Susa Cc-Da	0%	(0/34)	}	0.2%	(1/504)
Proto-Elamite, misc	0%	(0/294)	}		
Early Dynastic II	0%	(0/6)			
Early Dynastic III	0%	(0/14)			
Akkadian-Post Akk.	1%	(2/159)			
Ur III	11%	(6/55)			
Sukkalmahh-Old Bab.	3%	(2/65)			
Sukkalmahh-Elamite	1%	(2/174)			
Mid-2nd millennium	0%	(0/17)			
Middle Elamite	0%	(0/40)			

Notes

[1] Seals published in Legrain 1951. Dating after Moorey (pers. comm.) and Collon (1982 and pers. comm. via Moorey).
[2] Seals published in Frankfort 1955 whose datings are followed here.
[3] Seals published in Amiet 1972 whose datings are followed here. More recent revisions in the 4th-early 3rd mill. sequence may require adjustments in the figures for these periods.

TABLE 5.3

Lapis Lazuli Cylinder Seals from Selected Collections

British Museum[1]			*Various North American Collections*[2]		
Jemdet Nasr	2%	(2/97)	Jemdet Nasr	0%	(2/97)
Early Dynastic I	0%	(0/4)	Early Dynastic I	0%	(0/4)
Early Dynastic II	7%	(1/15)	Early Dynastic II	8%	(1/13)
Early Dynastic III	20%	(20/99)	Early Dynastic III	21%	(14/68)
Akkadian	7%	(17/243)	Akkadian	6%	(7/122)
Post Akkadian	16%	(12/75)	Post Akkadian	13%	(2/15)
Ur III	1%	(2/165)	Ur III	14%	(4/28)
			Isin-Larsa	5%	(1/19)
			Old Babylonian	2%	(6/253)

Ashmolean Museum[3]

Jemdet Nasr	0%	(0/64)		
Post-Jemdet Nasr	6%	(1/16)		
Early Dynastic	0%	(0/37)		
Early Dynastic/EDI	0%	(0/15)		
Early Dynastic II	6%	(1/16)		
Early Dynastic III	3%	(2/61)		
Early Akkadian	4%	(1/28)	1%	(1/95)
Mature Akkadian	0%	(0/67)		
Post Akkadian	5%	(1/19)		
Ur III	4%	(1/26)		
Late Ur III-Old Bab.	0%	(0/15)		
Old Babylonian	0%	(0/92)		

Yale Collection[4]

Jemdet Nasr	0%	(0/72)		
Early Dynastic I	0%	(0/8)		
Early Dynastic II	0%	(0/27)		
Early Dynastic III	16%	(13/82)		
Early Akkadian	9%	(4/46)	4%	(4/94)
Akkadian	0%	(0/48)		
Post Akkadian	4%	(1/26)		
Ur III	1%	(1/86)		
Late Ur III-				
Isin-Larsa	3%	(1/44)		
Early Old Babylonian	18%	(2/11)	3%	(3/97)
Old Babylonian	1%	(1/86)		

Notes
1 Seals published in Wiseman 1962 (down to ED III) and Collon 1982 (Akkadian-Ur III). Only the dating for this later material can be considered reliable. Of these seals 203 are from Ur and thus partly duplicate the evidence presented in Tables 5.1. and 5.2.
2 Seals published in Porada and Buchanan 1948 whose datings are followed here. Many now require revision.
3 Seals published in Buchanan 1966 whose datings are followed here.
4 Seals published in Buchanan 1981 whose datings are followed here.

TABLE 5.4

Lapis Lazuli Cylinders from Excavations and Collections Combined[1]

Period	Combined Excavations		Combined Collections		Grand Total	
Jemdet Nasr	1%	(9/931)	0.7%	(2/267)	0.9%	(11/1198)
Early Dynastic I	0%	(0/63)	0%	(0/31)	0%	(0/94)
Early Dynastic II	5%	(3/66)	5%	(3/61)	5%	(6/127)
	0%	*(0/58)[2]*				
Early Dynastic III	22%	(48/214)	16%	(49/310)	18%	(97/524)
	8%	*(11/136)*				
Akkadian	11%	(53/482)	5%	(29/548)	8%	(82/1030)[3]
	4%	*(14/356)*				
Post Akkadian	0%	(0/23)	12%	(16/135)	10%	(16/158)
Ur III	12%	(27/230)	3%	(8/305)	7%	(35/535)
	5%	*(10/200)*				
Isin-Larsa	3%	(4/121)	3%	(2/78)	3%	(6/199)
Old Babylonian	1%	(3/217)	2%	(9/442)	2%	(12/659)

Notes

1   Seals of uncertain or transitional date are omitted from the calculations in this table. Since the Ur seals in the BM are counted twice (in the combined excavations and combined collections), the grand totals for periods ED II-Ur III will be slightly inflated.

2   Figures in italics exclude the evidence from the 'Royal Cemetery' at Ur.

3   Compare Herrmann's estimate (1968: 52) of 78 lapis seals out of the 1696 catalogued by Boehmer (1965), giving a proportion of 5%. She notes however that not all of the collections used by Boehmer were available to her, so the real figure will be somewhat higher.

government.[196] The combined figures for Early Dynastic III from excavations (22% or, without the 'Royal Cemetery', 8%) and collections (16%), and the resulting grand total (18%) (which should flatten out statistically unsound aberrations), all agree in making this the all-time highpoint of lapis use for cylinder seals.

All sources except Susa show a sharp drop from Early Dynastic III to Akkadian.[197] The grand total of 8% is less than half that for Early Dynastic III. Such a dramatic change, especially when based on such large totals (524 [ED III] and 1,030 [Akk]), is very suggestive.[198] The collections rise sharply while the excavations drop to zero in post-Akkadian times, reflecting the uncertainties in dating seals of this period. No conclusions can yet be drawn, but the possibility of some strengthening of trade under the Guti and Sumerian princes like Gudea should perhaps be considered. The combined excavation and collection figures for the Ur III period are almost the same as for Akkadian times, joining to yield a grand total of 7%. The general rarity of lapis during the Ur III period and after is reflected in the virtual restriction of its use for seals to high officials.[199] Percentages hover around the 3% mark in the Isin-Larsa and Old Babylonian periods, attesting a further reduction in lapis use in the early second millennium.

---

196 Alternatively, it may be that Ur derived some special benefit from a lapis route running through Susa at this time. In this connection it may be noted that the quantity of lapis used as inlay on the walls of the 'Mausolea' may have rivalled or even surpassed the extravagence of the 'Royal Tombs'.

197 See Table 5.4, n. 3.

198 Pinnock's (1986: 224) argument against an Akkadian decline in lapis use on the basis of the finds from Ebla is not compelling. In any case, the Ebla blocks may rather date to the late ED III period.

199 Bussers 1984: 72f.

Although many details remain unclear, a pattern begins to emerge from these figures which largely confirms the conclusions of Herrmann. After a relatively modest consumption of lapis in Sumer in the early third millennium, there is a dramatic influx in Early Dynastic III. This represents the highest ever level of lapis use for seals. Thereafter, the amount of lapis in circulation approximately halves in the Akkadian period, and this seems to hold good even if the 'Royal Cemetery' is excluded.[200] Lapis levels remain about the same for the rest of the millennium showing, if anything, a gradual diminution in Ur III. An apparent surge in the post Akkadian period remains to be confirmed.

In Iran the consumption of worked lapis, evidenced almost exclusively by beads, is nowhere as extensive as in Sumer. It is so far first attested in the fourth millennium. Early finds come from Susa I, Tepe Giyan VC, Tepe Yahya VB, Tepe Sialk III and IV1 and Zaghe near Qazvin.[201] Slightly later it is attested also at Jemdet Nasr-period Susa, in Tepe Hissar IIA-III tombs, at Yahya IVC and at Middle Banesh Malyan.[202] Probably the largest quantities of lapis in third-millennium Iran so far are from the poorly dated burials at Shahdad.[203] Lapis appears from the first settlement at Shahr-i Sokhta, period I, becoming most common in periods II-III.[204]

A number of sites have produced evidence of local production of beads and other small objects. There are drill bits with lapis traces, lapis waste flakes and raw lumps weighing up to 0.5 kg at Shahr-i Sokhta II-III; drills, beads and blocks at Shahdad; at Tepe Hissar surveys and excavation have revealed widespread evidence of lapis bead manufacture – both lapis in various stages of production and a range of flint tools – concentrated in Hissar terminal I-II, including the dump of a lapis cutter's workshop from late Hissar IIB; and raw lumps and unfinished beads have been recovered from Banesh-period Tal-i Malyan.[205] The grave of a lapis worker with his materials and tools was found at Shahr-i Sokhta.[206] These tools match closely those of a bead maker at Ur. Yet while the technology of bead drilling was consistent across third-millennium Iran and into Sumer,[207] only the simplest undiagnostic bead shapes represented at Shahr-i Sokhta match those of Sumer.[208] Shahr-i Sokhta's beads were apparently intended for local consumption, as is confirmed by their presence in graves.[209] Tosi suggests that trimmed blocks were also traded to the west.[210] Among the excavated seals from Iran, only one (from Shahr-i Sokhta) is of lapis.[211]

In the Indus basin lapis is remarkably scarce in the third millennium. Moreover, according to Fairservis, a proportion of this so-called lapis is actually

[200] In this the results diverge from Herrmann (1968: 49f.) who challenged previous claims for such a decline.
[201] Susa – Amiet 1972: no. 14 (stamp seal). Giyan – Contenau & Ghirshman 1935: 42, pl. 38:31, 42 (stamp seals). Yahya – Lamberg-Karlovsky & Tosi 1973: 47, fig. 94 (bead). Sialk – Ghirshman 1938: 56, 69-71, pl. XXX ('treasure'); Amiet 1986: 68f. for date. Zaghe – Majidzadeh 1982.
[202] Susa – Mecquenem 1943: 15f. Hissar – Schmidt 1937: 122, 133. fig. 134 (beads, amulets). Yahya – Lamberg-Karlovsky 1972: 97 (bead). Malyan – Sumner 1986: 204.
[203] Hakemi 1972.
[204] Tusa 1977: 259 (period I); Tosi 1974: 17; Piperno 1981: 320 (periods II-III).
[205] Sokhta - Tosi 1974: 17; Lamberg-Karlovsky & Tosi 1973: 46; Tosi & Piperno 1973. Shahdad - Salvatori & Vidale 1982. Hissar - Tosi & Piperno 1973; Tosi 1974b: 154-58; Bulgarelli 1979; Dyson 1987: 653; Tosi 1989: 15f.; Tosi & Vidali 1990: 98. Malyan - Sumner 1986: 204.
[206] Sokhta - Tosi & Piperno 1973: 18f., Gr. 12. Ur - Woolley 1934: 206f., PG/958; *cf.* Piperno 1976; *idem* 1979: 132f.
[207] Gwinnet & Gorelick 1981.
[208] Tosi & Piperno 1973: 23.
[209] Piperno 1979: 131, fig. 4.
[210] Tosi 1974: 17; *idem* & Piperno 1973: 23.
[211] Dyson & Harris 1986: 83.

azurite.[212] In 1968 Wheeler could cite a total of only eleven beads (including two unfinished), an inlay fragment and a gaming piece from the three major sites of Mohenjo-daro, Harappa and Chanhu-daro.[213] Little more can be added today: a pendant from Harappa and beads from Lothal, Somnath, Pabumath, Pandi Wahi, Karchat, and Jhuknar.[214]

On the other hand, evidence of lapis in the pre-Indus period has increased dramatically. Wheeler noted strings of lapis beads from Nal.[215] Stein had also found a few beads at Kulli and a pin-head at Mehi, while a bead came from Damb Sadaat II.[216] Many more pre-Indus sites have recently yielded lapis artefacts. The earliest finds, at Mehrgarh I (site MR 3), show the use of lapis beads extending back as far as the seventh millennium, even earlier than the unconfirmed Hassuna-period lapis from Yarim Tepe.[217] Thereafter, sporadic finds at Mehrgarh indicate the continuation of lapis exploitation through the sixth-fifth millennia.[218] In level VI, dated to the late fourth-early third millennium, "enormous quantities" of lapis beads were recovered.[219] At Mundigak, lapis appears from the fourth millennium, in level I3; lapis beads continue to occur through levels II and III (mainly III6), and in level IV2, dated to *ca.* 2400 BC, approximately contemporary with Shahr-i Sokhta II-III.[220] A significant increase in the proportion of lapis is noticeable from levels III to IV, in which an engraved lapis 'button' was also found.[221] Other pre- or early-Indus sites which have produced lapis beads are Balakot I (4 beads, early third millennium), Serai Khola II (1 bead, plus 11 surface finds), Lewan, Damb Sadaat II, Said Qala, Amri I, Jalipur II and Rahman Dheri.[222] The latter two Early Indus sites yielded "large amounts" of worked and unworked lapis,[223] indicating local fashioning or a transit trade in raw lumps. The discovery of microlithic flint and phtanite borers used for making beads at Mehrgarh I-III and Mundigak I3-4 shows that this technology had a long local history before its spread across Iran in the third millennium.[224] During the third millennium these were supplemented at Mehrgarh and Mundigak by drills of copper.[225]

The redating of the Southern Turkmenian sequence has also pushed back the earliest use of lapis in Central Asia to at least the early fourth millennium (Geoksjur

---

[212] Fairservis 1983: 2.
[213] Wheeler 1968: 79.
[214] Harappa - Vats 1940: 59. Lothal - Rao 1973: 116. Other sites - Ratnagar 1981: 132-35.
[215] Wheeler 1968: 80; Hargreaves 1929: 32, 34, 43, pl. XVa.
[216] Mehi - Stein 1931: 123, pl. XXXII. Damb Sadaat - Fairservis 1956: 230.
[217] Lechevallier & Quivron 1981: 82, 89; Jarrige 1984: 22 for date; *idem* 1985: 285.
[218] Mehrgarh II - Allchin & Allchin 1982: 107; Jarrige 1984: 22 for date.
[219] Ratnagar 1981: 135; for dating see Jarrige 1979: 533.
[220] Casal 1961: 240, fig. 138:2 (cylindrical bead); de Cardi 1984: 63 and Jarrige 1984: 28 for date (level I3). Casal 1961: 240, fig. 138:3, 10, 18; F. Shaffer 1978: 144; Allchin & Allchin 1982: 126 for date (level II-IV2).
[221] F. Shaffer 1978: 146; Casal 1961: 229 (button).
[222] Balakot - Dales 1979: 255. Serai Khola - Halim 1972: 16, fig. 4:7. Lewan - Allchin & Allchin 1982: 152. Damb Sadaat - Fairservis 1956: 230; Agrawal 1971: 16, 71. Said Qala - F. Shaffer 1978: Table I. Amri - Casal 1964. Jalipur - Mughal 1972: 124, pl. XXVIII:6; *idem* 1974: 112; Dales 1977: 78. Rahman Dheri - Durrani 1981: 204.
[223] Dales 1977: 78.
[224] Jarrige 1984: 108f.; *idem* 1985: 285ff. figs 1-4; Lechevallier 1984: 46; Tosi & Vidali 1990.
[225] Jarrige 1985: 290, figs 2, 4. The earliest flint drills (7th to 5th mill.) are replaced *ca.* 4000 BC (Period III) by phtanite (a type of green jasper) paralleled at Mundigak and Amri; by the 3rd millennium (Period VII) these had been superceded by copper drills, again paralleled at Mundigak IV1 (Jarrige 1985: 285ff., figs 1-4). The earliest workshop so far excavated, dating to the first half of the 4th mill., is at Mehrgarh 2 (Tosi & Vidali 1990). Working was probably done on wooden boards of the type found perforated with drill holes at Shahr-i Sokhta.

and Khapous, Namazga II period).[226] The use of lapis continued through the third millennium along the Kopet Dagh, and spread with the expansion of settlement to Margiana and southern Bactria in the late third-early second millennia.[227]

Lapis is rare along the Gulf. A figurine from Tarut is assigned stylistically to the Early Dynastic II period.[228] There are only a few lapis beads on Umm an-Nar sites on the Oman peninsula. From Qalat al-Bahrain and Barbar Temples I-II come some beads and three conical gamesmen and from Tarut some "chunks". From Failaka comes an inscribed lapis vessel (?) sherd, probably dating to the second millennium.[229]

(ii) Sources and trade routes.   Although analytical tests have begun to distinguish between various known lapis deposits, no definitive criterion for identifying the source(s) of Mesopotamian lapis has been established.[230] Any judgement, therefore, is still a matter of choosing between the geological options on the basis of archaeologically attested distributions. Even this procedure will be invalidated if it should turn out that a significant proportion of the material presently identified as lapis is azurite.[231]

Since Herrmann it has been generally accepted that all Near Eastern lapis came from the mines in the Kerano-Munjan area of Badakhshan, these being the nearest geologically confirmed deposits (Fig. 40). Darius the Great explicitly defines this region, *i.e.* Sogdiana, as the origin of lapis imported for his palace at Susa.[232] Herrmann reviewed medieval textual evidence for closer sources in Mazanderan, Kerman and Azerbaijan but concluded that, although the latter two areas at least probably contained lapis deposits, they were not exploited in antiquity.[233] The use of lapis deposits in the Pamirs and around Lake Baikal is dismissed on grounds of inaccessibility and distance.[234]

The Badakhshan source was certainly a major, if not necessarily the only, source of Near Eastern lapis. These mines must also have supplied the early Central Asian settlements to the north and north-west and perhaps also the pre-Indus sites to the south. The early exploitation of lapis in these regions, before its confirmed presence in Mesopotamia, provides the background of local mining and trade through which we may begin to understand how the Mesopotamians were able to gain knowledge of, and acquire a taste for, this very distant material – a process which remained obscure while evidence of early lapis use was restricted to western

---

[226] Sarianidi 1971: 12; Kohl 1984: 90 and 213 for dates.

[227] Kopet Dagh – Kohl 1984: 101 (Namazga III), 108 (Nam. IV), 120, 130, 132 (Nam. V); Gupta 1979: 155, 170, 203. Margiana – Kohl 1984: 148 (beads); Sarianidi 1981a: fig. 11. Southern Bactria – Pottier 1984: 60, nos 275, 325 (inlays).

[228] D.T. Potts in press [b].

[229] Oman – Frifelt 1979: 577; *idem* 1991: 116. Bahrain – Mortensen 1970; Ratnagar 1981: 133. Tarut – Frifelt 1991: 116f. Failaka – D.T. Potts 1990: 293, C-G1.

[230] Herrmann 1968: 29 reports that three scientific tests failed to distinguish Afghan from Baikal lapis. Measuring the ratios of sulphur isotopes, Keisch (1972: 96-98) was able to distinguish between lapis from Afghanistan, Chile, Siberia and artificial ultramarine. Hogarth and Griffin (1976) report differences in the percentages of MgO and K_2O in lapis from Afghanistan, Russia, Italy, the Pamirs, Baikal and Burma. Tosi's claim (1974b: 148) that "thin section analyses and sulphur isotope determinations have allowed [us] to assume the origin of the finished products and wasters of lapis-lazuli collected at Ur, Hissar and Shahr-i Sokhta and examined so far to be attributed to Badakshan" has proven premature, since analyses are not available for the now likely alternative(s) in Baluchistan (and Kerman?).

[231] Fairservis 1983: 2.

[232] Herrmann 1968: 27f.

[233] *Ibid.*: 28f.

[234] Herrmann (*ibid.*: 28) notes the possible use of the Baikal source for poor quality lapis seals.

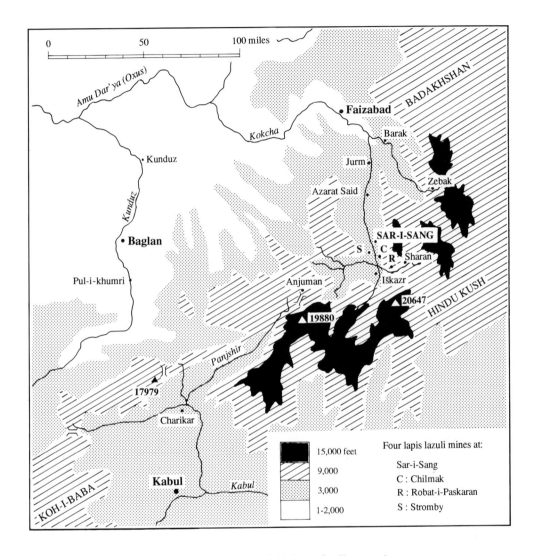

Figure 40. Map showing sources of lapis lazuli in Badakhshan (after Herrmann).

Iran and Mesopotamia.[235] The actual logistics of the early lapis trade, however, remain unclear. Did the Sumerians initiate procurement expeditions?; or did they continue to rely on the intermediaries through whom they had presumably encountered lapis in the first place? A literary text from Abu Salabikh perhaps suggests the latter when stating that "the garaš-merchant from the (eastern-) mountain(s) (garaš-kur) brought lapis lazuli and silver".[236]

---

[235] Herrmann 1966: 235; Tosi 1974: 6f.; Ratnagar 1981: 238f.
[236] Biggs 1966: 175; S. Cohen 1973: 27 n. 156.

The exploitation of these seams in the third millennium, for which there was previously no direct evidence, has been confirmed by the discovery of raw lapis at Shortugai I on the Oxus.[237] This much was to be expected. More surprising is that the material culture of the settlement concerned (period I) is entirely Harappan.[238] Shortugai I was apparently a Harappan colony, established primarily to procure lapis.[239]

The discovery of Shortugai renders even more anomalous the scarcity of lapis in mature Indus sites to the south. Three explanations suggest themselves: (1) the lapis was sent south but because of the particular patterns of use, recycling or chance has not been recovered in excavation; (2) it was transported south but nearly all sent on to Sumer and/or Iran;[240] or (3) the Harappans established themselves at Shortugai not to supply or trade through the Indus, but to trade directly with some other region(s), perhaps Central Asia or Mesopotamia via the Khorasan Road. The textual evidence of lapis from Meluhha, whose products came by ship along the Gulf, supports (2) or some compromise between (2) and (1).

Geological evidence of a second lapis source within a reasonable distance of Sumer has come to light recently with the collection of samples from a seam in the Chagai hills south-west of Quetta on the Afghan-Pakistani border.[241] The Quetta lapis is said to be greenish-blue, a feature elsewhere shown to be due to the presence of diopside.[242] This may have been the origin of the lapis exploited by the early inhabitants of the Indo-Iranian border-lands, and perhaps continued to be drawn upon in the mature Indus period. The discovery of this new source highlights the inadequacy of existing geological information and cautions against dismissing documentary evidence of lapis in other areas of Iran. For Kerman in particular there is the testimony of local inhabitant, as yet unconfirmed, that lapis exists near Sirjan.[243] Such a source would explain the large quantities of lapis consumed at Shahdad. Beale cites an unconfirmed report of lapis in north-west India.[244]

The primary documentary evidence for the sources of lapis derives from literary texts (epic poems and lexical lists) and one royal inscription (of Gudea). Aratta and Meluhha are cited as sources a number of times; various other places are cited once.

These references are helpful only to the extent that it is possible independently to establish the locations of the key geographical entities. As things stand, however, only Meluhha is reasonably securely fixed (as the Indus region; above pp. 35ff.). The location of Aratta, the chief lapis source in Sumerian literature, remains highly uncertain as do those of most other lapis suppliers. The problem of transit-trade complicates matters further. A text referring to lapis "from/of GN" is no guarantee that it was mined in that area; indeed, in some cases this is demonstrably not the

---

[237] Francfort & Pottier 1978. Lyonnet 1981: 71f. argues from ceramic evidence for an earlier (Chalcolithic) settlement of the Taluqan plain, and suggests that this also may have been partly concerned with obtaining lapis.

[238] Analyses have shown that the pottery is not imported but locally made (Echallier 1981: 118), suggesting that Harappans themselves (including potters) settled there.

[239] Lyonnet 1977: 31-33; Francfort & Pottier 1978: 58; Francfort 1984. The suggestion that Shortugai was also founded to procure copper remains unproved; the slag recovered is probably only from melting, not smelting (Francfort 1984: 309).

[240] *Cf.* Ratnagar 1981: 135f.

[241] Berthoud *et al.* 1982: 41 n. 21.

[242] Moorey pers. comm.

[243] Hakemi 1972: 14; Morgan 1900: 49; *idem* 1905a: 53; *idem* 1905b: 118.

[244] Beale 1973: 137.

case.[245] Lapis, like metal, was an important form of wealth, regularly hoarded in temples. The literary nature of most relevant texts introduces another dimension of uncertainty. The testimony of epics, especially on matters peripheral to the main narrative, cannot be assumed to be accurate. Finally, it must be recognised that the textual evidence is incomplete. At Ebla, for example, no texts record the trade, receipt or working of lapis despite the significant quantities of raw blocks found there.[246]

Thus cautioned, what do the texts relate as to the probable source(s) of Mesopotamian lapis? An Ur III literary text describes lapis as "characteristic of ... (*LAK* 384), the far-away mountain land".[247] In the Enmerkar-Lugalbanda cycle the people of Aratta are repeatedly associated with the quarrying and fashioning of stones from the mountains.[248] As regards lapis in particular, they "cut pure/shiny[249] (?) lapis lazuli (^{na_4}za-gin-duru$_5$) from the lumps"[250] and it is generally implied to be among the stones they mined. One passage from *Enmerkar and the Lord of Aratta* is more explicit and seems to associate the Arattans directly with lapis extraction when it refers to an earlier time when "[gold, si]lver, copper, tin, lumps of lapis lazuli [and mountain stones] – all these were not brought down from their mountain (sources). (The people of Aratta) were not bathing for the festivals ...".[251] Lapis is one of the goods Enmerkar demands from the lord of Aratta, which is appropriately called the "mountain of silver and lapis lazuli", kur-kù-^{na_4}za-gìn-na.[252] This epithet was later applied to Mt Biqni,[253] which seems to lie in the area inhabited by the Medes[254] and is usually identified with the Kuh-i Alwand or Demavend.[255] The "house of lapis lazuli", é-za-gìn, is used ambiguously either as an epithet of Aratta or to describe a building within it.[256]

The Arattans, then, are definitely portrayed as working lapis and probably also as mining it. On a literal view, this would require the identification of Aratta with Badakhshan, Baluchistan or Kerman.[257] Aratta is once implied to be accessible from Uruk by boat.[258] Taken at face value, this is consistent only with Baluchistan which could be reached via the Gulf; but this is probably pressing a poetical text too far. The description of the geography between Uruk and Aratta on the more usual overland route – the journey through Anšan (Fars) and over the (proverbial?) seven mountains (the Kerman range?) – is sufficiently vague to be consistent with all three options (though it would imply a southern route to Badakhshan, perhaps via Seistan, rather than along the Khorasan road). Distance counts against Badakhshan if the epics are to be taken at all seriously; it is hardly plausible to imagine emissaries repeatedly travelling, and grain later being sent, the 1,500 miles to Badakhshan and back again, a round trip by caravan of about six months even with camels.[259]

---

[245] See below on the lapis brought to Nippur from Elam, Marhaši and Dilmun; also probably the lapis of Tukriš. Compare the many other materials which came "from Dilmun" but in fact derive from further afield.
[246] Pinnock 1986: 224f.
[247] Michalowski 1988: 164.
[248] *ELA* 39-41, 49-50, 80-81; *EL* 409f.
[249] On the meaning of duru$_5$ as 'wet-looking, shiny' see Sjöberg 1988: 171.
[250] *ELA* 40.
[251] *ELA* 18-20.
[252] *ELA* 481; Cohen 1973: 287.
[253] Thompson 1931: 21, 47.
[254] Röllig 1983a: 488.
[255] *E.g.* König 1938: 29.
[256] *ELA* 26; *cf.* Cohen 1973: 52 n. 41; *EE* 149, 162.
[257] Sarianidi 1971: 15 (Badakhshan); Majidzadeh 1976 (Kerman, though denying the existence of lapis there).
[258] *EE* 148f. [=168f.], Berlin 1979: 49; *cf.* Cohen 1973: 52 n. 41.
[259] *Cf.* Herrmann 1968: 36 n. 75.

If the tradition of Arattan lapis has an historical basis the Kerman deposits, though not confirmed by modern reconaissance, deserve serious consideration. These would most naturally be traded overland through Fars (Anšan) to Susa and Sumer, as was the lapis of Aratta. This takes on special relevance since the new evidence from Shortugai suggests that the lapis of Badakhshan was handled by the Harappans, and is thus likely to have reached Sumer by ship (as did other Meluhhan goods) rather than over land.

This leads conveniently to the evidence concerning Meluhha which is somewhat more straighforward. A hymn to Ninurta cites "carnelian and lapis lazuli from the land of Meluhha".[260] Likewise Gudea cites "blocks of lapis lazuli ... bright carnelian from (the land of) Meluhha", though it is unclear in this case whether the lapis as well as the carnelian is being attributed to this source.[261] Meluhha is probably also the intended reference in the hymn to Inanna *Inninšagurra* when it refers to "the high mountain land, the land of carnelian and lapis lazuli".[262] If, as seems likely, third-millennium Meluhha was part of the Indus region, these references imply that lapis was travelling to Sumer from Pakistan. By analogy with the well-attested Gulf trade, the most likely means of transport would be up the Gulf by ship. The plausibility of such a trade route has been greatly enhanced by the discovery of the Harappan colony at Shortugai.

As regards this Badakhshan lapis, Meluhha was simply an entrepôt. But the newly discovered lapis of Baluchistan, a region which, from a Mesopotamian perspective, could easily have been considered part of Meluhha, may also have been mined and traded westward. The Sumerians would have had no reason to distinguish (if indeed they were able to do so) between this material mined within Meluhha and other supplies channeled through it.[263]

Other places are rarely cited as sources of lapis. The blessing on Dilmun in *Enki and Ninhursag* admonishes Tukriš to send "gold (from) Harali and lapis lazuli, [...]", perhaps also from some further region.[264] An Early Dynastic (?) literary text preserved in Ur III copies likewise states: "May Tukriš, the mountain land of great food offerings, bring to you gold, kù-NE-a and lapis lazuli" and again: "May X, the faraway mountain land, bring to you lapis lazuli and sù-ág, (products) that are characteristic of (this) mountain land".[265] Hymns to Innana mention "lapis lazuli from kur-muš (mountain crests?)" and relate how "the high mountain land, the land of carnelian (and) lapis lazuli, bowed down before you".[266]

Lapis is also cited as booty. In *Enki and the World Order* lines 246f. Enlil brings to Nippur as booty "their (*i.e.* Elam's and Marhaši's) silver and lapis lazuli (kù na4za-gin-bi) ... ".[267] A Šulgi hymn (D) relates how the king after defeating the Guti loaded "pure lapis lazuli (kù-za-gin)" into leather bags as booty.[268] The *Lipšur* Litany lists the mountain/land of Dapara, otherwise unknown, as the "home of lapis lazuli".[269] Hittite sources mention lapis from a mountain with the Anatolian-sounding

[260] M. Cohen 1975: 31; *cf.* Muhly 1973: 449 n. 543.
[261] Cyl B, xiv:13. *Cf.* Pettinato 1972: 78 who assumes that it is not.
[262] Sjöberg 1976: 188 l. 110; *idem* 1988: 172.
[263] Note, however, the Marhašian lapis which has 'green spots' (Steinkeller 1982: 250, n. 47). Could this be the (diopside-rich?) greenish lapis of Baluchistan?
[264] BII:1-2; Attinger 1984: 13; Kramer 1963: 279.
[265] Michalowski 1988: 164, 163.
[266] Sjöberg 1988: 169, 172; *idem* 1975: 189 l. 110.
[267] Benito 1969: 126. This expression is translated alternatively as "precious metals and stones" (Pettinato 1972: 80, 125), "bright lapis lazuli" (Cohen 1973: 286f.) or "pure lapis lazuli" (Klein 1981: ll. 348-50).
[268] Klein 1981: ll. 348-50.
[269] Reiner 1956: 133; Röllig 1983a: 488.

name Takniyara.[270] However, there is no geological evidence of lapis in Anatolia and this, like the other places cited above, is probably merely the origin of hoarded lapis supplies, not a primary source zone. An origin in "the (eastern) mountain(s)" is also implied by the fragmentary Abu Salabikh literary text quoted above (p. 209). An Ebla version of an Old Akkadian Šamaš myth implies that some lapis was thought to arrive by boat: "the mountains/lands (kur-kur) yielded lapis lazuli and silver ... the property of traders ... (which) he loaded (?) on his boats".[271] In this connection it may be noted that in the Larsa period lapis was paid as a tithe to the temple of Ningal by maritime merchants returning from Dilmun.[272]

The precise routes of any overland lapis trade between the eastern lapis source(s) and Mesopotamia cannot be plotted with any certainty. Geography constrains the options to some extent:[273] the major deserts had to be skirted and, where there was a choice, easily navigable rivers (Hilmand, Indus?) were probably preferred to roads. But more specific tracking is rarely possible. The presence of lapis at a site provides only an approximate indication of where the trade ran. Not every lapis-using centre was necessarily an entrepôt; indeed, the evidence of lapis in Iran relates to local working and consumption, not transit trade which, by its very nature, usually leaves no trace. It is thus dangerous to reconstruct routes of supply simply by drawing lines between the handful of third-millennium settlements which have produced lapis, especially since these are virtually the only sites of the period which have been excavated.

Until the mid-1960s, when all major finds of lapis concentrated in northern Iran, it was reasonable to posit a single route through these regions, if not yet particular towns; but since lapis has now been found equally across southern Iran, lines can be drawn in any number of ways.[274] In such circumstances the solution clearly does not lie in distribution maps alone. To have any chance of determining the overland route(s) of the lapis trade, not only the presence or absence of lapis but also relative quantities, which will reflect the scale and direction of movement, must be taken into account. But since lapis is a luxury commodity, and is likely to be concentrated in particular areas of settlements and cemeteries, reliable estimates will require much larger site exposures than are yet available.

Herrmann proposed an overland trade route from Badakhshan along the Khorasan Road to Mesopotamia, originally branching off north to Tepe Gawra (Late Ubaid to Late Uruk), and later diverted by the Sumerians and Elamites (Susians) via Sialk IV and Susa to Sumer, where the majority of Jemdet Nasr and later finds concentrate.[275] She noted a marked reduction in lapis in Early Dynastic I contexts and attributed the resumption of trade in Early Dynastic II to the initiative of Enmerkar, related in *Enmerkar and the Lord of Aratta*.[276]

New evidence has modified and supplemented this picture in some respects. Unworked lapis at Late Uruk Jebel Aruda (see above) indicates that the dearth in Sumer at that time (and earlier) is probably fortuitous; for it is unlikely that the south was deprived of material available in the colonies. Likewise, the Early Dynastic I break has been made somewhat less severe by the redating of many of the 'Jemdet

---

[270] Röllig 1983a: 488.
[271] W. Lambert 1989: 11, 33 ll. 3-5.
[272] Leemans 1960: 23ff.
[273] Herrmann 1966: 187f.
[274] *Cf.* Tosi 1974: map 1.
[275] Herrmann 1968: 36f., 53.
[276] *Ibid.*: 37, 53f.

Nasr' graves at Ur to this period.[277] Susa's role in the supply of lapis to the lowlands remains to be documented. Although links between Sumer and Susa were often close, the proportion of lapis seals at Susa in the third millennium (and indeed in all periods) is conspicuously low compared to Sumer (see Table 5.2).

The discovery of lapis-working debris and tools at Tepe Hissar II[278] confirms the movement of some raw lapis, presumably from Badakhshan, along the Khorasan Road; and it remains possible – though proof is lacking – that some of this material continued westward to Mesopotamia. The main emphasis of recent discoveries, however, has been on southern Iran, suggesting the existence of alternative route(s) along the Gulf.[279] The Harappans were actively involved in mining lapis in Badakhshan and presumably brought the material south to the Indus itself, though not primarily for their own consumption. The scarcity of lapis on mature Indus sites suggests rather that most was shipped west to Sumer, where it was known as the "lapis lazuli of Meluhha". Some raw lapis also reached Shahr-i Sokhta where it was trimmed from the matrix and worked into beads.[280] This lapis was assumed by Tosi to have come along the Hilmand from Badakhshan, but the Quetta mines must now also be considered as a possible source.

The discoveries at Shahr-i Sokhta, concentrated in period II, have given rise to much speculation about a southern overland lapis route, continuing through Kerman and then via Fars (or Sialk) to Susa, paralleling the Khorasan Road which Tosi argues was not used for lapis until Early Dynastic II-III.[281] Tosi argues that some lapis was "semi-processed" at Shahr-i Sokhta to reduce its weight and sent on to Mesopotamia. While some such trade may have occurred as far west as Shahdad and Tal-i Malyan (even this will be doubtful if a Kerman source is confirmed), the evidence at Shahr-i Sokhta relates directly to production of beads for local consumption. In any case, this is a long and difficult way of reaching Sumer. It is more natural to assume that the bulk of Sumer's lapis, whether from Badakhshan or Quetta, came by ship up the Gulf. In this case, Iranian sites like Shahr-i Sokhta and Shahdad may be viewed primarily as consumers, sending on only what they did not want themselves; it is unlikely that any significant proportion of this stone reached as far as Susa.

The emphasis on Gulf lapis in the later third millennium may relate to developments near the source zone. Dales notes that lapis-using Early Indus sites from Mundigak through northern Baluchistan were all abandoned at a point which he places on corrected radiocarbon evidence at *ca.* 2500 BC, *i.e.* approximately contemporaneous with the Early Dynastic III rise in Sumerian consumption and the *floruit* of the Gulf trade. This was followed by the rise of the Mature Indus civilization and "a dramatic shift in the avenues of contact to the south, into southern

---

277 On Kolbus' redating (1983: Abb. 2) the graves with lapis beads are distributed as follows: JN (Group I) – JNGs 201, 210, 295, 325, 337, 347; ED Ia (Group II) – JNGs 309, 315; ED Ib (Group III) – JNGs 161, 179, 218, 225, 279, 285, 296, 301; ED II (Group IV) – JNGs 154, 155, 220, 221, 261. Note also a bead from a Luristan tomb of Haerinck's Phase II (Haerinck 1987: 35), which his high chronology dates to ED I, and the rosettes from Archaic Uruk (Heinrich 1936: 44, pls 32f, 34e).
278 Bulgarelli 1979; Tosi & Piperno 1973: 21f.; Dyson 1987: 653.
279 Pinnock's (1986: 222) suggestion that it went south-west to Shahr-i Sokhta and thence north-west to Hissar seems unlikely.
280 Tosi & Piperno 1973: 20f.
281 *E.g.* Tosi 1974: 13f., 17; Tosi & Piperno 1973: 16f. (map), 23.

Baluchistan and along the Indian Ocean coast".[282] Was the lapis which had been consumed locally now being exported to Sumer?[283]

3. CONCLUSIONS

There is considerable variation during the course of the late fourth and third millennia in the types of stones commonly used in Mesopotamia. Notwithstanding imbalances in the evidence, it seems likely that some periods witnessed a much wider exploitation of exotic stone types than others, particularly the Late Uruk and Akkadian periods. The Ur III period would probably show similar variety if more evidence had survived. The Early Dynastic III period is more notable for the quantities than for the range of stones used.

From highland Iran seems to have come only finished stonework, particularly plain and decorated stone vessels, and perhaps small quantities of semi-precious stones – but not raw blocks of common stones. The explanation for this pattern is probably largely a matter of simple logistics. It was not cost-effective to haul heavy stone blocks long distances over land, when much of the stone would be wasted in production. Better, wherever possible, to trade the fashioned product. When raw blocks were desired these would be brought from areas accessible by boat, particularly along the Tigris-Euphrates into Syro-Anatolia (basalt, obsidian *etc.*), along the Karun to Susa ('aragonite', yellow banded calcite), and down the Gulf (various hard dark stones, steatite/chlorite *etc.*). The calcareous stones used widely in all periods in Sumer were acquired along the Euphrates near Uruk and north of Baghdad. The hard dark stones exploited from the late Early Dynastic III period for official statuary were probably collected or mined along the Gulf littoral. In Akkadian times the acquisition of such stones became an aspect of booty-taking, and their conspicuous use a mark of prestige. The Gulf remained the principal source of foreign common stones in the Ur III period, steatite becoming especially prominent at this time.

Semi-precious stones (especially lapis, carnelian and agate) were also taken as booty when Iranian cities were sacked. As regards trade in these materials, however, textual evidence suggests that most activity was conducted by sea along the Gulf. The major carnelian deposits lay conveniently along this route (Gujarat, Bushire). Recent evidence presents a more complex picture of the sources and trade routes of lapis than has previously been envisaged. There was clearly westward lapis trade both by sea and by land. Caravans supplied a substantial Iranian consumption, and this, rather than transit trade with Mesopotamia, may have been their primary object. Judging by textual evidence, the sea route from Meluhha was the main vehicle of lapis trade into Sumer. Susa, lying at the western extreme of the overland route, understandably received little or nothing through that channel, but its exclusion from Gulf lapis supplies before the Ur III period must rather have a political explanation.

---

[282] Dales 1973: 166f.; *idem* 1977.
[283] Dales, writing before the discovery of Shortugai, argued rather that the lapis supplies from the north were cut off. On this view Sumerian lapis came in through other channels, perhaps overland via Seistan (Dales 1973: 167). His dating of the Shahr-i Sokhta and Turkmenian abandonments to 2500 BC is much too high.

Chapter 6

Stone Vessels

Of all the classes of artefacts which survive on Mesopotamian sites, stone vessels are of the greatest immediate relevance in the attempt to trace trade and exchange between Sumer and the east. Excepting the vessels made from sedimentary rocks available in Sumer and the Tigris-Euphrates valleys, all had to be imported or made from imported stone. Moreover, if imported as finished products, stone vessels could not, like those of metal, be indefinitely repaired, reworked and recast. Even as sherds they retain decorative and technological features distinctive of their original production. In this they differ even from other stone products such as jewellery-stones, which were regularly cut down and reshaped. Finally, unlike monumental sculpture and other larger stone objects, vessels are light and strong enough to be easily transported and redistributed over wide areas.

Early studies of the origins of Mesopotamia's stone vessels naturally focused on those regions where typological parallels could be demonstrated: principally Egypt for plain calcite types, and the Indus Valley and Iran for the more elaborate "steatite" pieces.[1] Not all these links have proved significant. Reisner discredited the supposed connections between Egyptian and Mesopotamian calcite types, at least as indicating a common origin, by showing that, on closer scrutiny, there are consistent differences in rim forms and other details.[2] On the other hand, excavations during the past twenty years in Iran and the Gulf have fully confirmed that those regions were manufacturing centres for many of the most distinctive stone vessel types found on Mesopotamian sites. Foremost among these are undecorated calcite vessels, presently best attested in south-east Iran and Bactria,[3] and various plain and decorated vessels of soft dark steatite/chlorite/serpentine.

Typological evidence for the eastern origins of some of these types is supplemented in the Akkadian period by the testimony of contemporary inscriptions. A number of vessels of that period bear royal dedications in Old Akkadian, many celebrating foreign conquests. Some of these indicate the vessels' place of origin. Pieces from the "booty of Elam" and the "booty of Magan" have been known for many years, and their importance as proof of foreign manufacture has often been noted (Fig. 41).[4] In the early publications, however, many vessels were not illustrated or adequately described, and their forms therefore remained unknown. Meanwhile,

---

1   Heuzey 1903: 32; Woolley 1928: 186; Petrie, cited by Woolley 1934: 379 (Egypt); Mackay 1932 (Indus).
2   Reisner 1931; Woolley 1934: 379f. The same applies to the Egyptian parallels cited by Glob (1958) and Mortensen (1970: 396; idem 1986: 184) for the tall calcite vases found in the Barbar Temple on Bahrain; these vessels belong rather to the Mesopotamian-Iranian type (D.T. Potts 1983: 129-31). The possibility of some *influence* from Egypt on Sumer should perhaps be left open. Such a view, originally expressed by Woolley (1934: 380), has recently been advanced by Vértisalji and Kolbus (1985: 95, n. 141) who claim to see typological parallels between vessels of IIIrd Dynasty Egypt and ED I Sumer and attribute the more sophisticated techniques of manufacture evident in the ED II period to itinerant Egyptian craftsmen working in Mesopotamia (*ibid.*: 99).
3   D.T. Potts 1986a.
4   *E.g.* Woolley 1955: 51, though he incorrectly equates Elam with Susa.

fresh evidence has continued to appear. Whereas ten years ago only one vessel from the 'booty of Magan' had been illustrated, and this only in an inadequate photograph (Table 6.1: B1a), it and two other "Maganite" vessels can now be described accurately. Furthermore, understanding of the historical geography of the regions east of Mesopotamia, including the two areas cited as sources of booty, has made significant advances in recent years (see Ch. 1). Elam, long identified with Susiana (northern Khuzistan) and the neighbouring Zagros mountains, is now known to have been centred rather on Fars, well into the Iranian plateau; while regarding Magan, archaeological evidence has steadily been accumulating in support of its identification with the Oman peninsula.

Section 2 of this chapter brings together the stone vessels and fragments with Sargonic royal inscriptions and reassesses the arguments for their centres of production in the light of this improved archaeological and historical-geographical evidence. Conclusions regarding the inscribed vessels are used to complement the archaeological evidence for the origins of the much larger corpus of typologically identical uninscribed pieces from southern Mesopotamian sites reviewed in section 1. Finally, consideration is given to the means by which these vessels arrived in Mesopotamia. Recent studies have tended to interpret their presence within the framework of a major highland-lowland trade network which, it is argued, linked third-millennium Sumer and Akkad with the surrounding highlands.[5] However, the royal inscriptions on the Sargonic vessels, together with other textual and archaeological clues, suggest that other factors besides trade may have been equally important.

1. UNDECORATED VESSELS

(a) The production of plain stone vessels in Mesopotamia and Iran

In Mesopotamia, as in the Near East generally, stone vessels have a long history before the third millennium. They were used before the invention of pottery in the Neolithic period and occur in the earliest Chalcolithic settlements of southern Mesopotamia.[6] Banded calcite vessels and statuettes are particularly prominent among grave goods in the Samarra-period town of Tell es-Sawwan I. After a lull in the Ubaid and Early Uruk periods (represented by cemeteries at Ubaid, Eridu and Susa I), plain vessels reappear at Uruk in significant quantities in Late Uruk and Jemdet Nasr times, especially in the temple deposits.[7]

Throughout the third millennium vessels are found primarily in funerary and temple contexts, neither of which can be assumed to provide a reliable indication of their currency in everyday life. In temples they served both as ritual equipment and as votive offerings, probably containing foods, aromatics or other delicacies.[8] In Early Dynastic administrative texts stone bowls (bur) also appear among the taxes delivered to the household of the city ruler and unlike clay vessels (dug) these seem not to have contained foodstuffs.[9]

The high-point in the use of plain stone vessel for grave gifts in Sumer, as evidenced by the cemeteries at Ur ('Jemdet Nasr Cemetery'), Kiš ('Y' Cemetery) and

---

[5] *E.g.* Kohl 1979; *idem* 1982.
[6] Bielinski 1987.
[7] Heinrich 1936: Taf. 21, 24; Strommenger 1963; Schüller 1963; Adams 1981: 79, table 5.
[8] *SARI 1*: Ki 3.2 n. 1 (ritual equipment). Note, however, *ABWl*: En I 18 which states that the vessel is "for crushing garlic".
[9] Bauer 1972: Fö 176 I:1, 2ff., Fö 176 V:11, 12, Fö 159 II:1.

Khafajeh, seems to fall in the early third millennium (ED I-II). Most are simple sub-conical bowls in hard, dark igneous and metamorphic stones. At Ur such vessels become common in burials of late Early Dynastic I reaching a peak in the less numerous Early Dynastic II graves,[10] a situation mirrored in the Diyala where almost half of all stone vessels from Jemdet Nasr to Early Dynastic IIIa may be attributed to Early Dynastic II.[11] In the 'Jemdet Nasr' cemetery the proportion of igneous stones decreases and that of limestone and gypsum increases from Jemdet Nasr to Early Dynastic II. In Early Dynastic Ia, when stone vessels were not yet common, imitations in metal and pottery appear; these die out as stone becomes abundant in Early Dynastic II.[12]

Stone vessels continue to appear in the Early Dynastic III graves of the 'Royal Cemetery' at Ur, especially in the rich 'Royal Tombs',[13] but they now form a lesser proportion of the total grave goods. Moreover, the forms and materials represented are different. A proportion of local limestone-gypsum continues, but the dark igneous stones give way to a new repertory dominated by banded calcite (often called "onyx" or "marble onyx" in French publications).[14] The incidence of stone vessels at Ur continues to decline in the Akkadian and Ur III periods.[15] This probably reflects a genuine decrease in the currency of stone vessels in everyday life, even allowing for some change in burial customs. On the other hand, stone vessels remain prominent in sacral contexts at Ur, Nippur and Girsu, especially as inscribed dedications.

A detailed typological study of Mesopotamian stone vessels has yet to be undertaken and remains a difficult prospect in view of the poor stratigraphical status of the evidence, most of it from cemeteries (Ur, Kish, Tello). Much work has been done on the material from Ur[16] but residual stratigraphical uncertainties combined with the unreliable quality of the type drawings limit the progress that can be made without reexamination of the primary material or further excavation.

During the third millennium there is a notable correlation between shapes and stone types. Particular forms of vessels are consistently made from certain types of stone, and often by a particular method of manufacture, suggesting not only that shapes were adapted to the properties of the stone, but also that certain shapes are specific to particular regions or workshops. Sub-conical bowls tend to be made of dark igneous rocks in Jemdet Nasr-Early Dynastic II. In Early Dynastic III a banded calcite appears which is used for these bowls and also for cylindrical vases, flasks, and carinated bowls (Fig. 41:1, 2, 4; Table 6.5). (Sub-)hemispherical bowls are more often limestone. Shouldered jars in the 'Jemdet Nasr' cemetery at Ur are made almost exclusively from gypsum,[17] as are shell-shaped lamps and other local forms.[18]

---

[10] Vértesalji & Kolbus 1985: 89; Kolbus 1983 for dates. Gockel 1982 gives the cemetery a shorter range, assigning all the graves to the middle of ED I. This is apparently endorsed by Nissen as fitting better with the palaeography of the tablets in the 'Seal Impression Strata' (Nissen 1986b: 317).

[11] Vértesalji & Kolbus: 89, n. 124.

[12] *Ibid.*: 89.

[13] Woolley 1934: 379; rarely also in Kiš Cemetery 'A': Mackay 1929: 199.

[14] *E.g.* Heuzey 1903: 29, 31f. These observations are based primarily on visual identifications, as are most identifications in excavation reports. These must be treated with caution; those of Woolley, Langdon and de Genouillac are often demonstrably wrong. Few scientific analyses have been made, among which the following may be noted: 23 vessels from the Royal Cemetery at Ur – all calcite (BM, Research Lab. file 6035); 2 vessels from the JN Cemetery at Ur – both gypsum (*ibid.*); and 87 vessels from Susa – 67 calcite and 20 gypsum (Cassanova 1982).

[15] Woolley 1934: 379; Nissen 1966: Taf. 10-11; Karstens 1987.

[16] Nissen 1966; Kolbus 1983; Gockel 1982; Karstens 1987.

[17] Below note 32.

[18] Woolley 1934: 379.

The peoples of highland Iran had direct access to abundant stone supplies which they used for making vessels from Neolithic times. Calcite and steatite/chlorite, as the most abundant and most easily worked materials, came increasingly to form the basis of the Iranian vessel industries, and by the third millennium these two stones dominate production across the plateau and into Central Asia.[19] Production centres have been identified at three Iranian sites.

(1) Shahr-i Sokhta. A number of partly finished wasters show that the calcite vessels common at Shahr-i Sokhta in periods I to late III/early IV were made at the site.[20] There are at least three nearby supplies of stone.[21] The less common vessels of the same type at Mundigak, which has no close sources of calcite, were probably imported from Shahr-i Sokhta.[22] Parallels with material from Sumer are discussed below. Tepe Graziani, 5 km east of Shahr-i Sokhta, seems to have been a specialised production centre; many vessel blanks were found there in surveys.[23]

(2) Tepe Yahya. Large quantities of chlorite debitage attest the production of plain and decorated vessels during period IVB4-1.[24] The chlorite was derived from local outcrops.[25]

(3) Tal-i Qarib (Kur River Basin). Surveys in the Kur basin have suggested the existence of a network of production and exchange in the Early Banesh period centred on Qarib, where an ancient dump produced vessel fragments of banded travertine, grainy limestone and lime plaster (some of the latter with coloured paste inlay). The plaster vessels were locally produced,[26] the others apparently being brought in from workshops nearer the raw material. It is suggested that Qarib acted as a distribution centre.[27]

(b) Local and Foreign Production

In the case of many decorated vessels, the use of characteristically Sumerian motifs provides unequivocal proof of local manufacture. Archaeological evidence for local production of plain vessels includes Late Uruk and Early Dynastic workshops at Uruk, unfinished vessels at Fara and the recovery of borers used for hollowing-out the interior of the vessel from late fourth and third millennium contexts at Uruk, Ur and Kiš.[28] Pictorial evidence is ambiguous[29] but administrative and literary texts list stone-workers and stone vessels in the context of local activities. Some Early Dynastic dedication inscriptions state that the dedicant had the vessel made and a

---

[19]   Kohl 1974; Ciarla 1979; *idem* 1981 (Iran); Pottier 1984 (Central Asia).
[20]   Ciarla 1979; *idem* 1981.
[21]   Tosi 1969: 368; Ciarla 1979: 321, 323f.
[22]   *Ibid.*: 326ff.
[23]   Tosi 1989: 24.
[24]   Kohl 1974; *idem* 1975; *idem* 1979; Lamberg-Karlovsky 1988.
[25]   Kohl *et al.* 1979. An unfinished "alabaster" bowl reported from Tepe Yahya V (Lamberg-Karlovsky 1972: 97) seems not to be cited in the final report (Beale *et al.* 1986).
[26]   Blackman 1982.
[27]   Alden 1982: 620; Sumner 1986: 200.
[28]   Nöldeke 1939: 17f., Taf. 27; Finkbeiner 1985: 30 (Uruk); Heinrich 1931: 21, Abb. 19 (Fara). At Ur borers begin in rubbish levels above the 'JN Cemetery', providing a *terminus a quem* of ED II, and continue through the remainder of the 3rd mill. (Woolley 1955: 14, fig. 5, pl. 13:U.16405; Woolley & Moorey 1982: 40). One example in the Ashmolean Museum (Ash. 1935.764) was recently analysed by the Dept. of Earth Sciences, Oxford as "impure algal limestone". At Uruk 94 borers were found in contexts ranging from ED (probably also Uruk III) to NB (Wartke 1979: 259f., n. 23). At Kiš there are two unpublished borers (V 918, IM 1661), examined by the writer in the Iraq Museum (June 1983). IM 1661 is very like Wartke 1979: Abb. 4a-b, but squatter. For general discussions and Egyptian parallels see Wartke 1979 (esp. p. 258), Møller 1984 (esp. pp. 94-96) and Eichmann 1987.
[29]   One of the 'Blau Monuments' (Amiet 1980a: fig. 232) seems to show men drilling stone vessels with a bow drill.

hymn mentions "my (house) whose stonecutter (bur-gul) used to carve stone bowls".[30] There is textual evidence for the use of emery (*šammu*) in the manufacture of 'alabaster' objects. A few vessels of a very distinctive shape which copy metal forms may also be regarded as local products.[31]

While definite identification of locally manufactured plain stone vessels among the extant corpus is not always possible, it may safely be assumed that the vast majority were made in stone derived from the nearest available sources (*i.e.* the light-coloured calcareous stones of western Sumer, the Tigris-Euphrates valleys and the westernmost Zagros mountains,[32] as is confirmed by the fact that almost all unfinished vessels are in these materials. However, since these stones are very widely distributed beyond this area across the Iranian plateau, it cannot be assumed that all such vessels were locally produced. Indeed, inscriptions prove that some were not. A large cylindrical "calcite" vessel, dedicated to Enlil by Enmetena, states that "he had (this) massive stone bowl (bur) brought down from the mountains (kur)",[33] though whether by plunder or exchange is not stated.

As to the identification of foreign vessels, the converse hypothesis – that vessels in hard, dark igneous and metamorphic stones, only available at considerable distances from Sumer, were imported as finished products – is a reasonable starting point. This applies particularly to the hard dark vessels – mainly simple sub-conical bowls – which form the bulk of the stone vessels in Sumerian burials of the earlier third millennium, before the Gulf regions were widely exploited for stones. Hauling unworked stone over land from the inner Zagros, where the material probably originated,[34] would not have been cost effective, since so much of the block would be wasted in production.[35] In the relatively small sample of Ubaid period stone vessels, mainly from northern Mesopotamian sites, three-quarters are of limestone and only four of granite, steatite and calcite.[36] Some third-millennium vessels may, however, have been imported in a semi-finished state.[37] It is significant that the hard dark stones were not widely exploited for vessels, or other objects, in the later third millennium when Gulf shipping is best attested.

As yet, however, direct evidence of highland production in the early third millennium has not come to light. The only confirmed manufacturing centres (at Tepe Yahya and Shahr-i Sokhta) were based on other materials (chlorite and calcite) and seem to concentrate somewhat later. Dark stone vessels, indeed stone vessels of any kind, are conspicuously absent from the third-millennium graves of the Pusht-i Kuh,

---

[30]   *ABWI:* En I 18, Ean 62 (dedications); *PSD* B: 184, bur A, Bilingual 1 (hymn).

[31]   *E.g.* Woolley 1934: pl. 174: U.10480.

[32]   One type which almost certainly drew on these closest sources is the shouldered jar, one of the most common types of the late 4th to early 3rd mill. at Ur (types JN 53-58), Kiš and elsewhere in Sumer. Virtually all are cut from mottled or veined greyish-white translucent gypsum and limestone (the same as is used for many vessels, miniature vessels and amulets in the Uruk-JN period). The interior was not drilled but roughly gouged out with a sharp tool, leaving deep vertical or oblique grooves on the interior which were not smoothed off. It is notable that the few better-made examples of this form from Late Uruk-JN period Susa and Ur are in a different material – opaque limestone/marble – and have drilled interiors. The form seems to have a long history, appearing in 'calcaire' in a Chalcolithic grave at Dum Gar Parchineh (Vanden Berghe 1975: 50, fig. 4:3) and at Ubaid Tell Songor A (Bieliński 1987: pl. II:5).

[33]   Hilprecht 1896: nos 115-17; Legrain 1926: pl. 1; *ABWI:* Ent. 32 ii:1´-4´; *cf. PSD* B: s.v. bur A.

[34]   Schüller 1963. Syria and south-east Turkey represent other possibilities not considered by Schüller; note also that his comments on sources of calcareous stones ignore the local supplies cited above (p. 177).

[35]   Porada's suggestion that the cylinders of stone created by using tubular drills for hollowing out the interiors of stone vessels were used for cylinder seals (Porada 1977: 7) reinforces this suggestion, since the seals of the Late Uruk to ED periods were overwhelmingly light-coloured, calcareous stones, not the hard dark stones of most contemporary bowls.

[36]   Bielinski 1987: 265.

[37]   Heinz 1989: 207f.

Luristan, and Tepe Giyan, as they are also from the contemporary settlements (Godin and Giyan). Only a vessel from Tepe Hissar III, identical in form and material to many from Kiš and Ur, may indicate the existence of a production site somewhere in the 'volcanic belt' of the inner Zagros mountains near the Khorasan road.[38]

A handful of vessels are of distinctive shapes which find such close parallels outside of Sumer that they can be assumed to be imports. One problematic case is a miniature pedestal vase from Proto-literate Uruk paralleled in undated finds from Bactria, 'Astrabad', Shahdad and Quetta.[39] Rather less distinctive is a calcite spouted, sub-conical bowl from Uruk which is closely paralleled in shape and material at Shar-i Sokhta I.[40] The tall cylindrical calcite vessels of the mid-late-third millennium (Fig. 41:1; Table 6.5:1) were originally compared to similar types from Egypt which was therefore identified as their likely origin but closer study has shown consistent differences in rim forms and other details which indicate different sources.[41]

(c) Sumer and Susa

The corpus of third millennium stone vessels from Susa overlaps considerably with that of Sumer – more so than the pottery or even the metalwork. This is due only partly to the export of highland forms to both regions (discussed below). There is also evidence of exchange in apparently lowland types, both from Susa to Sumer and, in the Late Uruk period, *vice versa*. As in Sumer, the local industry was based on the nearest available stones: white and grey gypsum and limestone, here supplemented more often by bitumen and bituminous limestone. Indeed, Susa's proximity to these materials led to an even narrower range of exploitation than in Sumer, so that the harder, darker stones of the inner Zagros and the Gulf are virtually absent. This is particularly apparent in the Early Dynastic II-III period when the stone vessels (as indeed all non-jewellery stonework) are almost exclusively 'black' (bitumen/ bituminous stone) and 'white' (gypsum/limestone). As in Sumer, soft dark stones (steatite, chlorite, serpentine) appear in the last centuries of the millennium, but even these are mostly finished imports in recognisably foreign styles.

The evidence again comes principally from graves, which are here less closely datable.[42] Stone vessels were recovered principally on the Acropolis, the *Ville Royale* and the *Donjon*.[43] The main concentration seems to be mid to late third millennium.[44] Aside from the third-millennium calcite vessels, which have been the

---

38   Schmidt 1933: 423, pl. CXXXIX:H.391; *cf.* Woolley 1955: pl. 35 (U.19241); Watelin 1934: pl. XXII, lower.
39   Heinrich 1936: Taf. 25a (Uruk). *Cf.* Amiet 1986b: 16, Taf. 7:4; Pottier 1984: nos 217, 218; Jarrige ed. 1988: 199, fig. A17 (Bactria); Rostovtzeff 1920: pl. III:7 (Astrabad); Hakemi 1971: pl. XIIIB (Shahdad); Jarrige ed. 1988: 127, Figs 168-69 (Quetta). Casanova (1982: 38 n. 34) refers to further examples at Dashly 3 and Altyn-tepe (Namazga V). Note also similar vessels (with a more splayed foot) in pottery at Mehrgarh VII (Jarrige & Lechevallier 1979: 517f., fig. 35), where they are said not to be local.
40   Heinrich 1936: Taf. 30b (Uruk); Tosi ed. 1983: pl. LXXVIII:93 (Sokhta).
41   Heuzey 1903: 32; Woolley 1928: 186; Petrie, cited in Woolley 1934: 379. *Cf.* (demonstrating a non-Egyptian origin) Reisner 1931; Woolley 1934: 379f. Similar counter arguments apply to the Egyptian parallels cited by Glob (1958) and Mortensen (1970: *idem* 1986: 184) for the tall calcite vases found in the Barbar Temple on Bahrain; these vessels belong rather to the "Mesopotamian" type (D.T. Potts 1983: 129-31). The possibility of some influence from Egypt on Mesopotamia should perhaps be left open, as Woolley (1934: 380) maintained. Such a view has recently been developed by Vértesalji and Kolbus who claim to see typological parallels between vessels of IIIrd Dynasty Egypt and ED I Sumer (1985: 95, n. 141) and (less plausibly) attribute the more sophisticated techniques of manufacture evident in the ED II period to itinerant Egyptian craftsmen working in Mesopotamia (*ibid.*: 99).
42   Le Breton 1957: 109-12, 119f., figs 28-32; 40:4-7; 42; Amiet 1986: 57, 98, 125, 126f.; Casanova 1982.
43   Mecquenem 1934: 188-206 (Acropolis); *ibid.*: 206-18 (Ville Royale); *idem* 1943: 70-126 (Donjon).
44   But *cf.* Le Breton 1957: 109.

subject of a detailed study,[45] only a small part of the material recovered in the early excavations is published and the reports give no detailed statistics.

The principal materials used for vessels in the Late Uruk (Susa II) period are sandstone and gypsum (hydrous calcium sulphate, "albâtre gypseux"), the latter ranging in colour from translucent white to dull grey.[46] Shapes include a number of Sumerian forms: tall spouted jugs[47] and four-lugged jars.[48] Amiet now dates the miniature versions of these and other zoomorphic forms and painted multiple vessels to this period rather than Proto-Elamite times, when they were deposited in two depôts on the Acropolis.[49] A few similar miniature vessels are known from Sumer but many types are apparently distinctive of Susiana.[50]

Le Breton states that "the practice of including stone vessels among grave furnishings is especially characteristic of Cb, as it is of Jemdet Nasr art generally".[51] However, the dark stone bowls typical of Sumer at this time (JN-ED II) are conspicuously absent from the Louvre Susa collection, and the gypsum shouldered jars of Early Dynastic Ib-II are matched by only a few Susian pieces.[52]

Vessels of the Early Dynastic period in the local tradition are cut principally from gypsum ("albâtre gypseux") and coarse calcite ("calcaire assez grossier").[53] They are not numerous and the forms are simple.[54]

From the late Early Dynastic period the local industry is supplemented by vessels of banded yellow and white calcite (calcium carbonate, Amiet's "albâtre fin, rubané blanc et jaune, appelé 'marbre onyx' ou 'albâtre antique'"; often called "aragonite" by Mecquenem and other French authors).[55] Gypsum becomes relatively rare.[56] The calcite is represented by a new repertory of forms which first appear in the *Vase à la Cachette*.[57] These include sub-conical bowls, cylindrical vases, carinated bowls and bottles with a sharply defined vertical neck. These new forms occur in the same material in the 'Royal Cemetery' at Ur and elsewhere in Sumer (Table 6.5).[58] Both at Susa and in Sumer they continue to appear down to the end of the millennium, when some were inscribed as dedications or 'booty' (see below). There can be little doubt that the Sumerian and Susian examples derive from the same source(s), probably in eastern Iran.

[45] Casanova 1982.
[46] Le Breton 1957: fig. 28; Amiet 1986: 127.
[47] Le Breton 1957: fig. 28:19; *cf.* Heinrich 1936: Taf. 22, 26, 27. 1 ex. of grey-white calcite/gypsum inspected in the Louvre (Sb509α).
[48] Mecquenem 1943: fig. 20:14; Le Breton 1957: fig. 28:23, 26-34; Le Brun 1978: fig. 37:5-6. 4 full size exx. (2 with pedestal base), 17 small exx. and many miniature exx. of calcite, gypsum and limestone inspected in the Louvre. These were also introduced to colonies on the Upper Euphrates, *e.g.* Weiss ed. 1985: nos 30, 31.
[49] Amiet 1986: 57; Mecquenem 1934: figs 19-20; Le Breton 1957: figs 32 (depôt), 28-30; Le Brun 1971: fig. 54:1, 2, 4; *idem* 1978: fig. 37:5, 6; Amiet 1976c: 62f.
[50] Le Breton 1957: 112. *E.g.*, multiple vessels with engraved zig-zags and obliques red and black painted stripes (Mecquenem 1943: fig. 20:2, 3).
[51] Le Breton 1957: 109.
[52] Above note 32. 2 exx. of gypsum with gouged interiors are Sb638α and Sb12015 (inspected in Louvre); *cf.* Ur types JN 53-58. The Susa II/III precursors of this type (*e.g.* Le Breton 1957: fig. 28:24-25 [=Sb4067, A7459?]) tend to be made of limestone with drilled interiors.
[53] Amiet 1986: 125.
[54] Mecquenem 1934: fig. 60:13, 14, 26; *idem* 1943: figs 10-11; Le Breton 1957: 119f., figs 40:4-7; 42; Amiet 1966: no. 104; Carter 1980: Figs 18:1-2, 4-5, 22:1.
[55] Amiet 1986: 127; Mecquenem 1934: 216; Casanova 1982: 5-8.
[56] Of the 116 "alabaster" vessels of the late 3rd-mill. Louvre collection only 20 (12%) are of gypsum (Casanova 1982: 5, table 1). The rare gypsum versions of the carinated bowls may be local copies of the calcite imports.
[57] Le Breton 1957: fig. 40:4-7 (= Mecquenem 1934: fig. 21:7), fig. 42.
[58] Below notes 67, 120.

In the *Ville Royale* graves Mecquenem notes that stone vessels are "très nombreux; ce sont en général des écuelles de gypse et d'arragonite".[59] Under this latter term he included not only the yellow-white banded calcite but also a green banded variety, often with thin opaque layers of ochre or red. Like the yellow-white calcite, this attractive and distinctive stone first appears at Susa around Early Dynastic III and is most popular during the second half of the third millennium. At Susa it is employed exclusively for sub-conical bowls with a straight or slightly convex profile and simple tapering rim.[60] Of a total of eighty-seven sub-conical bowls from Susa, thirty-two (37%) are of this material.[61] They are consistently well made, more regular and better finished than the usual Sumerian and Susian light-coloured calcareous stone vessels. Identical bowls occur in Sumer, the greatest known concentrations being among temple dedications at Nippur (inspected in the Iraq Museum) and Lagaš,[62] but nowhere are they as common as at Susa. Its use in much later periods for monumental sculpture (see below) suggests a source relatively close to Susa, though there are also sources on the Iranian plateau, including near Shahr-i Sokhta, where very similar vessels were made and most recent studies have assumed that the Susian examples derive from some such distant eastern centre of production.[63] In any case, it was probably *via* Susa, the highlands' conduit onto the floodplains, that the Sumerian examples were obtained.

Within the Susa corpus some correlations between stone type and form may be noted. The carinated bowls, cylindrical jars, necked jars and a sub class of the sub-conical bowls[64] are overwhelmingly in brown/yellow-white banded calcite while the remainder of the sub-conical bowls (a total of 77) are almost half green calcite (32) with very few of the brown/yellow-white banded variety (8).[65] This may indicate different highland origins for these two groups or preferential use of certain stone sources by the highland craftsmen, or both. As noted above, it is also possible that the green calcite bowls are local Susian products.

Susian calcite types which are paralleled in Sumer but not in the highlands include flasks with an S-shaped profile[66] and necked bottles.[67] These may be lowland types made in Sumer or at Susa from stone acquired in the Zagros. But while the material of the flasks is rather different from that of the 'highland' types, being generally a mottled yellow/brown-white rather than banded stone, that of the Susian necked bottles is banded yellow-white calcite identical to the carinated bowls, cylindrical jars and some of the sub-conical bowls,[68] for which a highland origin is virtually assured. Moreover, both types make their appearance around the same time as the 'highland' calcite types (a necked bottle appears in the *Vase à la Cachette*); and in Akkadian times flasks received royal inscriptions which in some cases (the

---

[59]   Mecquenem 1934: 216.
[60]   Mecquenem 1934: figs 21:7, 60:14, 26; Le Breton 1957: fig. 42:1, 2; Casanova 1982: 7, table 1.
[61]   Casanova 1982: table 1 types X-XVIII.
[62]   Heuzey (1903: 29, 31f.) calls this "une très belle sorte de marbre-onyx [*i.e.* calcite], plus ou moins veiné ou roubanné ... diaprée de zones blanches ou brunes, parfois même teintée légèrement en vert, c'est un matière de luxe". Most are dedicated to Baba; one is inscribed as booty, probably royal (name lost) (*ibid.*: 30, fig. 25; *ABWI*: AnLag 1). Note also an *e.g.* inscribed by ŠKš (also booty?) (Sweet in Muscarella 1981: 30).
[63]   Tosi 1983; Ciarla 1981 (Sokhta). For eastern origin of Susian vessels see *e.g.* Casanova 1982; Amiet 1986.
[64]   Casanova's series X, which has a relatively wide base and slightly concave profile.
[65]   Casanova 1982: 7, table 1.
[66]   Below note 120.
[67]   Susa – Casanova 1982: series VI; Mecquenem 1943: fig. 71:14; Le Breton 1957: fig. 42:7. *Cf.* Ur – Woolley 1934: pls 248f., RC 79, 91a-b, pl. 178b:U.104961 ("grey and white marble"), pl. 180:U.8380. Kiš – Mackay 1929: pl. LVI:4.
[68]   Casanova 1982: 7.

fragments are too small for definite identification) may identify them as "booty of Elam" (Table 6.1:A1h, A4a). While at present these two forms cannot be demonstrated to be highland types, therefore, it is best to regard the issue as open.

A few Susian types can be paralleled in highland Iran but not yet in Sumer.[69] These are presumably highland imports which did not penetrate further west than Susa – a phenomenon we have seen paralleled in metalwork.

2. INSCRIBED VESSELS

Historical inscriptions occasionally refer to stone vessels imported into Sumer from various eastern lands, including Parahšum/Marhaši, or brought back as booty.[70] But beyond the gross and highly speculative divisions in terms of materials established above, the identification of such imports on typological grounds remains highly problematic. A large proportion of the plain vessels of third-millennium Sumer are bowls of various simple, undiagnostic forms whose parallels with foreign types are of dubious significance. A few common types where the similarity extends also to material and techniques of manufacture will be considered below. First however, it is appropriate to consider the vessels which may be identified as imports on more definitive, non-typological grounds, *viz.* through their inscriptions.

The practice of inscribing stone vessels with dedications was well established by the Akkadian period. The earliest historically datable examples – which are also the earliest attributable royal inscriptions – are two fragments inscribed by or for "[En]mebaragesi, king of Kiš", whose reign is assigned to the Early Dynastic II period.[71] Lapidary inscriptions, as indeed texts generally, are much more abundant in the Early Dynastic III period. Finds from Nippur, Girsu, Adab and other Sumerian sites attest the large numbers of vessels inscribed as offerings to the gods which were increasingly deposited in temples at this time.[72] The same practice is observed also in the north at Mari.[73] Stone vessels were apparently particularly appropriate offerings to the gods, in contrast to metal vessels which are only rarely attested.[74] Heinz lists some 135 different inscriptions which appear on Early Dynastic stone vessels eight of which are also decorated.[75] (On the other hand, while metal vessels with inscriptions identifying their owners are known from graves very few of stone have been recovered).[76] Stone vessels remain popular as inscribed dedications in the Akkadian and Ur III periods.[77] The inscriptions typically record an offering to a deity "for the life

69   *E.g.* bowl with convex profile, flat everted rim and low ring base: Casanova 1982: series III:40, *cf.* Khurab – Stein 1937: fig. 262, pls VI, XXXII:18; Mundigak IV1-3 – Casal 1961: fig. 134:6; Southern Bactria – Pottier 1984: no. 199.
70   Amiet 1986: 147; Steinkeller 1982: 251f.; Pettinato 1982: 56, 59, obv. iii:4; Davidović 1984.
71   Jacobsen in Delougaz 1940: 146, fig. 126:2; Nissen 1965: 1-5; Edzard 1959.
72   These inscriptions are conveniently collected in Braun-Holzinger 1991 (ED-OB); *ABWI* (ED) and Heinz 1989; note also Meyer 1981: 397, Grégoire 1981: no. 3.
73   Fales 1983.
74   A notable exception is the silver vessel of Enmetena (*ABWI* I: 250f., Ent 34). See A. Westenholz 1979: 21 n. 14 on other aspects of dedication conventions. Only great kings dedicated to Enlil; ensis of Nippur and lesser mortals dedicated to Ninlil, Inanna *etc.*
75   Heinz 1989: 223f., 203.
76   Woolley 1934: pl. 163 (metal); *ABWI*: AnUr 2, AnUr 4. (stone).
77   For inscriptions see *AK* (Akkadian), *NBWI* (Ur III).

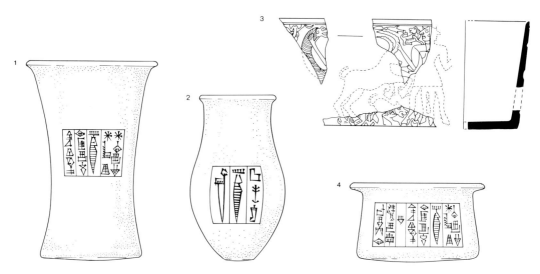

Figure 41. Booty vessels of Rimuš (2, 3) and Naram-Sin (1, 4) from Elam and Parahšum (2, 3) and Magan (4, ?1). Calcite (1, 2, 4) and steatite/chlorite (3). From ?Drehem (1), Girsu (2), Ur (3) and unprovenanced (4). Not to scale.

of' (nam-tì-la-šè) the dedicant, his/her spouse or children, or a ruler.[78] There are well over one hundred fragments from a least half that many stone vessels which bear Lugalzagesi's inscription.[79] Westenholz suggests that these may have been offered by ensis for Lugalzagesi's coronation at Nippur.[80] Many sherds of dedication vessels were recovered from Ur, especially below the Kurigalzu floor in the Enunmah[81] and in temples at Nippur. The context of the vessels from Ur well illustrates the tendency for temple holdings to be kept within the god's precinct long after their original dedication, even when broken. Thanks to this practice, much evidence has been preserved from the Sargonic and other periods for which few stratified contexts are available.

The use of stone vessels as votive offerings seems to have been particularly popular among certain Sargonic rulers. Royal dedications are attested also in the Early Dynastic and Ur III periods, but neither group is numerically or proportionately as large as the Sargonic corpus. In the existing sample (see Tables 6.1 and 6.3), vessels inscribed by Rimuš (a total of approximately 107) are far the most common; Naram-Sin is also well represented (a total of approximately sixteen vessels). On the other hand, there are no known vessels inscribed by Sargon[82] and only one vase each of Maništušu and Šarkališarri.[83] None of these latter inscriptions provides any indication of the vessels' origins. A long vessel inscription of Naram-Sin preserved in an Old Babylonian copy shows that very large vessels were sometimes dedicated and that these were prized pieces: "Whoever shall do away with the inscription of Naram-Sin ... and shall set his name on the vessel of Naram-Sin, saying, 'It is my vessel', or

[78] Heinz 1989: 215-8, table 4.
[79] *ABWI*: Uruk: Luzag 1.
[80] A. Westenholz 1987: 156.
[81] Woolley 1974: 51.
[82] A vase dedicated to Sargon is Sollberger 1965: no. 10; Nagel & Strommenger 1968: 172 n. 41.
[83] Hilprecht 1896: no. 118 (Man.); Sweet in Muscarella 1981: 30 (Škš). An ancient squeeze with an inscription of Šarkališarri may be from another stone vessel of this king (Hilprecht 1903: 517).

shall show it to an outsider or to another man, saying, 'Erase his name, set (on it) my name', may Ištar (*etc.*) ...the great gods in their totality lay upon him a great curse".[84]

Occasionally Early Dynastic III dedication inscriptions describe vessels as booty.[85] Enšakušanna's vessel is from a campaign against Kiš but others may be eastern.[86] This practice was applied more widely by the conquering Akkadian kings, especially Rimuš and Naram-Sin, a number of whose vessels state that they were dedicated "from the booty of GN", now invariably foreign lands (Fig. 41). Particular importance attaches to these booty inscriptions, which provide a unique means of identifying vases of foreign origin. It must be conceded at the outset, however, that such inscriptions do not guarantee that these vessels, less still all those of the same forms, were manufactured in the regions specified. They may have been previously plundered from elsewhere, or traded. But where the 'labels' are consistent (*i.e.* assign the same origin to typologically similar vessels) and are not contradicted by other evidence, it is a reasonable working hypothesis that most booty vessels derive from the vicinity of their stated origin. The inscriptions of Rimuš and Naram-Sin thus provide a useful starting point for identifying a minimal corpus of foreign stone vessels in southern Mesopotamia.

(a) Rimuš

The inscriptions of Rimuš, second king of Akkad, which occur on stone vessels are listed in Table 6.1.

More than twenty vessels,[87] virtually all from the Ekur, carry Rimuš's inscription A: "To Enlil (or Sin), Rimuš, king of Kiš, when he had conquered Elam and Parahšum, from the booty of Elam, dedicated (this)". Other vessels carry shortened versions of this text (Inscriptions B and C) which refer to the conquest of Elam and Parahšum but do not explicitly state that the vessel concerned comes from the booty there taken. A large number of fragments carry just the king's name and title "king of Kiš" (Inscription D).

Table 6.2 illustrates the shapes of the known Rimuš vessels, with comments on stone types and manufacturing techniques. The vases specified as coming from Rimuš's "booty of Elam" (Inscription A) are tall cylindrical vases (type 1), a shorter thinner-walled cylindrical bowl/vase (type 2), sub-conical bowls (type 3) and probably also flasks (type 5). The forms of many other vessel fragments bearing this inscription cannot be identified in the present state of publication. All the Inscription A vessels that have been inspected or are reliably described are of calcite, which may vary in colour from white to yellow or pale brown, and is usually attractively banded. This is variously described in the literature as "alabaster", "onyx", "marble", "dolomite" and "gypsum".[88]

The one vessel with *inscription B* is unhelpfully described as a "vase". It is said to be made of "diorite", but this identification should be regarded with caution since neither this piece nor the one other inscribed Sargonic vessel supposedly carved from that material (Table 6.1: C1b) is illustrated.

---

[84] Foster 1990: 33 pericope 12.

[85] *ABWI*: AnLag 1; Uruk: Enšak 2.

[86] AnLag 1 is a familiar type of low sub-conical bowl with slightly convex profile carved from "marbre-onyx [*i.e.* calcite] rubanné de veines blanches" (Heuzey 1903: 29, fig. 25), a stone type which we have seen is thought to be eastern.

[87] The total may be much greater; see Table 6.1, n. 2.

[88] The "red marble" bowl (Table 6.1: A1f) may be an exception to this pattern. 3rd-mill. vessels in the Ashmolean Museum of the same shape and visually similar stone type as Rimuš's inscription A vessels have been analysed by the Department of Earth Sciences, Oxford University, as calcite.

TABLE 6.1
Rimuš Inscribed Stone Vessels – Inscriptions[1]

Inscription A: "To Enlil/Sin, Rimuš, King of Kiš, when he had conquered Elam and Parahšum, from the booty of Elam, dedicated (this)"

(1) Nippur[2]

(a) large con. bowl/ vase	dolomite (?) (H)	Hilprecht 1893: no. 5, pl. III:4, 5
(b) cyl. vase (1)	white marble (H)	Hilprecht 1893: pl. III:6
(c) cyl. vase (1)	white marble (H)	Hilprecht 1893: pl. III:8
(d) cyl. vase (1)	white marble (H)	Hilprecht 1893: pl. III:9
(e) cyl. vase (1)	white marble(?) (H)	Hilprecht 1893: pl. III:10
(f) con. bowl (3)	red marble (H)	Hilprecht 1893: pl. III:7
(g) cyl. vase (1)	white marble(?) (H)	Hilprecht 1893: pl. III:11
(h) jar, convex profile (5?)	white-blue marble (H)	Hilprecht 1893: pl. III:12
(i) cyl. vase (1)	white marble (H)	Hilprecht 1896: no. 62, pl. xx
(j) "vase"	?	Gelb 1961: 195 (Orig. inscr. 1e); Goetze 1968: 54 (2N-T445)
(k) bowl	"white stone"	Biggs & Buccellati 1969: no. 43
(l) bowl	limestone (M)	Biggs & Buccellati 1969: no. 44
(m) cyl. vase (1)	banded calcite	Braun-Holzinger 1991: G197A, Taf. 10
(n) con. bowl	"alabaster"	Braun-Holzinger 1991: G197A2
(o) large con. bowl	?	Braun-Holzinger 1991: G197A4
(p) ?	?	Braun-Holzinger 1991: G197A8
(q) cyl. vase/con. bowl	"alabaster"	Braun-Holzinger 1991: G197A9
(r) cyl. vase (1)	"alabaster"	Braun-Holzinger 1991: G197A10
(s) bowl/cyl. vase	"brown veined limestone"	Braun-Holzinger 1991: G197A11
(t) bowl (?)	"red-brown veined stone"	Braun-Holzinger 1991: G197A13
(u) ?	"limestone"	Braun-Holzinger 1991: G197A14
(v) large con. vessel	"alabaster"	Braun-Holzinger 1991: G197C
(w) ?	"white stone"	Braun-Holzinger 1991: G200D

(2) Ur

(a) con. bowl (3)	banded calcite	Gadd & Legrain 1928: no. 10 (U7807); T.F. Potts 1989: fig 1
(b) "vase"	"calcite"	Gadd & Legrain 1928: no. 22 (U.6333)
(c) cyl. vase, b/s (1)	yellow-white veined calcite	Sollberger 1965: 25 no. 7 (U.263); T.F. Potts 1989: fig. 2

(3) Tutub

(a) bowl	"alabaster"	Jacobsen in Delougaz 1940: 149 no. 8

(4) Tell Brak

(a) round profile jar (5?)	banded calcite	Mallowan 1947: 27, 66,[3] 197, pl. L:4

(5) Sippar

(a) cyl. vase/bowl (2)	banded calcite	King 1899: pl. 4 (BM 91020); T.F. Potts 1989: fig. 3
(b) con. bowl (3)	banded calcite	Walker & Collon 1980: 98, no. 23; T.F. Potts 1989: fig.4

Inscription B: "[To Sin/Enlil, Rimuš, King of Kiš, when Elam and Parahš]um he had [con]quered, [ded]icated (this)"[4]

(1) Nippur

(a) con.(?) bowl	diorite(?) (B-H)	Hilprecht 1893: pl. 5:10

Inscription C: "Rimuš, King of Kiš, conqueror of Elam and Parahšum"

(1) Ur

(a) bowl, *sér. anc.* (4)	"steatite"	Woolley 1955: pl. 36 (U.231); Gadd & Legrain 1928: no. 9; here Fig. 41:3[5]
(b) "bowl"	"diorite"	Sollberger 1965: 25 (U.3291); Woolley 1955: 171

(2) Provenance unknown

(a) bowl, *sér. anc.* (4)	"steatite"	Klengel & Klengel 1980: Abb. 1, 3

Inscription D: "Rimuš, King of Kiš"

(1) Girsu

(a) con. bowl (3)	banded calcite	Heuzey & Sarzec 1884-1912: LVI, pl. 5, fig. 4
(b) flask (5)	banded calcite?	*Ibid*: pl. 44bis, fig.2; Braun-Holzinger 1991: Taf. 10:G202B; here Fig. 41:2
(c) ?	"beige-brown alabaster"	Heuzey & Sarzec 1884-1912: LVI (AO189)
(d) con. bowl (3)	banded calcite?	Shileico 1915: 9f.
(e) globular jar (6)	limestone?	unpubl. (Istanbul ES T941)

(2) Nippur

(a) cyl. vase (1)	"white marble"	Hilprecht 1893: pls 5:7, V
(b) bowl ?	grey-white limestone (B-H)	Hilprecht 1893: pl. 5:8
(c) round bodied jar	"white marble"	Hilprecht 1893: 20 n. 3, 48, pl. 5:9
(d) "vase"	calcite (M)	Goetze 1968: 54, 57 (5N-T567)
(e) "vase"	calcite (M)	Goetze 1968: 54, 57 (6N-T1033a)
(f) cyl. vase (1)	"alabaster"	Braun-Holzinger 1991: G202I1
(g) bowl	"black stone"	Braun-Holzinger 1991: G202I2
(h) tall narrow vase	"alabaster"	Braun-Holzinger 1991: G202I3
(i) cyl. vase (1)	"calcite"	Braun-Holzinger 1991: G202I4
(j) thin-walled vase	"alabaster"	Braun-Holzinger 1991: G202I5
(k) thin-walled bowl	"alabaster"	Braun-Holzinger 1991: G202I6
(l) ?	"red-brown veined stone"	Braun-Holzinger 1991: G202I7
(m) thick-walled vessel	"alabaster"	Braun-Holzinger 1991: G202I8
(n) ?	"alabaster"	Braun-Holzinger 1991: G202I9
(o) cyl. bowl	"alabaster"	Braun-Holzinger 1991: G202I10
(p) bowl	"red-brown marble"	Braun-Holzinger 1991: G202I11
(q) con. bowl (?)	"red-beige veined stone"	Braun-Holzinger 1991: G202I12
(r) bowl	"red-brown veined stone"	Braun-Holzinger 1991: G202I13
(s) con. bowl	"red-brown veined stone"	Braun-Holzinger 1991: G202I14
(t) bowl	"white limestone"	Braun-Holzinger 1991: G202I15
(u) shallow bowl	"grey-white veined stone"	Braun-Holzinger 1991: G202I16
(v) cyl. vase (1)	?	Braun-Holzinger 1991: G202I17
(w) large vessel	"limestone"	Braun-Holzinger 1991: G202I18
(x) cyl. vase (1)	banded calcite	Braun-Holzinger 1991: G202I19
(y) cyl. vase (1)	banded calcite	Braun-Holzinger 1991: G202I20
(z) ?	?	Braun-Holzinger 1991: G202I21
(aa) bowl	?	Biggs & Buccellati 1969: no. 51

(3) Ur

(a) cyl. vase (1)	banded calcite	Gadd & Legrain 1928: no. 8, pl. II; T.F. Potts 1989: fig. 5
(b) cyl. vase (1)	banded calcite	Sollberger 1965: 25 no. 5 (U.264); T.F. Potts 1989: fig. 6
(c) bowl	"white calcite"	Sollberger 1965: 25 no. 5 (U.18308)
(d) globular jar (6)	white limestone (B-H)	Sollberger 1960: 75 no. 92 (U.207);[6] Braun-Holzinger 1991: Taf. 10:G202L

(4) Uruk

(a) bowl	banded calcite?	Nöldeke et al. 1936: 20, Taf.25c

(5) Sippar

(a) con. bowl (3)	banded calcite	King 1899: pl. 4 (BM12161); T.F. Potts 1989: fig. 7

(6) Kiš?

(a) con. bowl (3)	banded calcite	Grégoire in Moorey 1978: Fiche 3, D11, fig. 3

(7) Tutub

(a) "vase"	"calcite"	Jacobsen in Delougaz 1940: 150 no. 10

(8) Tell Brak

(a) cyl. vase (1)	banded calcite	Loretz 1969: no. 83[8]

(9) Provenance unknown

(a) cyl. vase[9] (1)	"grey limestone"	Stephens 1937: no. 97
(b) globular jar (6)	"grey limestone"	Stephens 1937: no. 98, pl. XLIII
(c) con. vessel (3)	"alabaster"	Messerschmidt 1907: Taf. 6:10

E: Inscription Uncertain

(1) Nippur

(a) vase (Insc. C?)	?	Goetze 1968: 54, 57 (6N-T1033)
(b) bowl (Insc. C/D?)	"white stone"	Biggs & Buccellati 1969: no. 45
(c) vase/macehead	"alabaster"	Braun-Holzinger 1991: G205C1
(d) ?	white limestone	Braun-Holzinger 1991: G205C2
(e) cyl. vase/con. bowl	"alabaster"	Braun-Holzinger 1991: G203/3
(f) ?	?	Braun-Holzinger 1991: G203/4
(g) bowl	"limestone"	Braun-Holzinger 1991: G203/5
(h) con. bowl	"red-brown limestone"	Braun-Holzinger 1991: G203/6
(i) thick-walled vessel	"red-brown stone"	Braun-Holzinger 1991: G203/7
(j) bowl	"red-brown veined stone"	Braun-Holzinger 1991: G203/8
(k) low bowl/lid	?	Braun-Holzinger 1991: G203/9
(l) small bowl	"white limestone"	Braun-Holzinger 1991: G203/10
(m) bowl	"white limestone"	Braun-Holzinger 1991: G203/11
(n) low bowl	?	Braun-Holzinger 1991: G203/12

Inscription A or B

(o) ?	"white limestone"	Braun-Holzinger 1991: G200A5
(p) ?	?	Braun-Holzinger 1991: G200A6
(q) bowl	"limestone"	Braun-Holzinger 1991: G200A7
(r) ?	?	Braun-Holzinger 1991: G200A8
(s) large cyl. vase	"white limestone"	Braun-Holzinger 1991: G200A9
(t) ?	"red-beige veined stone"	Braun-Holzinger 1991: G200A10

(u) large cyl.(?) vase	"grey-white veined stone"	Braun-Holzinger 1991: G200A11
(v) ?	"white limestone"	Braun-Holzinger 1991: G200A12
(w) large cyl. vase	?	Braun-Holzinger 1991: G200A13
No royal name preserved		
(x) ?	"dark stone"	Braun-Holzinger 1991: G205C3
(y) ?	"white stone"	Braun-Holzinger 1991: G205C4
(z) ?	?	Braun-Holzinger 1991: G205C5
(aa) con. bowl	?	Braun-Holzinger 1991: G205C6
(2) Tutub		
(a) bowl (Insc. A/B)	"alabaster"	Jacobsen in Delougaz 1940: 150 no. 9
(3) Ur		
(a) sm. bowl (3)	banded calcite	Sollberger 1965: 35 no. 41 (U.1167); T.F. Potts
(Insc. C/D)		1989: fig. 9
(4) Susa		
(a) cyl. vase (1)	banded calcite (?)	Amiet, pers. comm.[10]

Notes

1   The following abbreviations are used in this and Table 6.3:

     b/s   body sherd
     con.   (sub-)conical
     cyl.   cylindrical
     sér. anc.   *série ancienne*
     sér. rec.   *série récente*
     sm.   small

     Numbers in brackets in the shape column refer to the types illustrated in Table 6.2. A reference is given only when the
     shape is certain. (H), (M) and (B-H) in the stone-type column refer to the authority followed: Hirsch 1963, Meyer 1981 and
     Braun-Holzinger 1991 respectively. Stone identifications in quotes are those of the respective authors cited in the
     reference. The remainder, without quotes, are the writer's judgements from photographs or first-hand inspection.
     Inscriptions correspond to the listing in *AKI* as follows: A=Rimuš 1-2; B=Rimuš 3; C=Rimuš 5; D=Rimuš 6.

2   There may be more Rimuš inscriptions from Nippur which remain unpublished; at least 61 fragments were recovered from
     the "Temple of Bel" alone (Hilprecht 1893: 20). Since the first 5 lines of Inscription A are shared with Inscription B and a
     macehead inscription (Gadd & Legrain 1928: no. 10, pl. D), the identification of the many incomplete inscriptions is
     uncertain.

3   Note that the text as there quoted is incorrect.

4   The beginning of this inscription is reconstructed after Inscription A.

5   Hallo 1957: 22 n. 6 notes that the title preserved on this fragment (the name itself is lost) was claimed by Sargon also.
     However, the lack of any other known vessels of that king makes such an attribution unlikely.

6   Incorrectly listed by Sollberger as a macehead.

7   Purchased by the Kiš expedition.

8   Lorentz's reference (p. 13) to Mallowan 1947: pl. L:4 is incorrect. That is another sherd listed here as A4a. *Pace* Finkel
     1985: 201, these cannot belong to the same vessel since Inscription A does not begin "Rimuš king of Kiš", as is preserved on
     fragment D8a.

9   Stephens reports that this vessel has the same form as D2a above.

10   Sb 17824, h. 8.5cm, diam. 8.5cm. According to information kindly supplied by Dr P. Amiet, this fragment is from a vase "de
     même type [as Naram-Sin B1a], avec seulement 2 signes de la fin de l'inscription A.MU ... la graphie est agadéenne et la
     module assez semblable". Among known Sargonic inscriptions the formula A.MU(.RU), "dedicated (this)", occurs only on
     Rimuš's inscriptions A and B, and never on those of Naram-Sin.

Two of the three vessels with *inscription C* are steatite/chlorite bowls with low-relief decoration in the style of the *série ancienne* or Intercultural Style (Fig. 41:3).[89] The third, an undecorated "bowl" (shape not further described), is the second supposedly "diorite" piece mentioned above.

Vessels with *Inscription D* – "Rimuš, King of Kiš" – are the most widespread in the existing sample. Some are of the same shapes attested for Inscription A: *viz.* tall cylindrical vases (type 1) and sub-conical bowls (type 3). In addition, the flask is here definitely attested (type 5) along with a larger, squatter jar with everted rim (type 6).

Discussion of the origin of Rimuš's inscribed stone vessels must start with inscription A which specifies its bearers as coming from the "booty of Elam", presumably from the Elam-Parahšum-Zahara campaign described in detail in his

89   Miroschedji 1973 ("*série ancienne*"); Kohl 1974, 1975, 1982 ("Intercultural Style").

inscriptions (above pp 100ff.).[90] Although, as these inscriptions relate, Parahšum too was conquered by the king, and, as Rimuš's account of this campaign informs us, stone booty was taken from there also, that region is never cited as the source of booty vessels. In all Rimuš's extant vessel inscriptions in which an origin is explicitly stated, that origin is given as Elam.

In terms of modern geography, however, this provides only a very general indication of the source of the inscription A vessels. For, as has been discussed above (pp. 14ff.), the place name "Elam", as used by third-millennium Mesopotamian scribes, was in a crucial respect ambiguous: it could serve to designate not only the highland kingdom of Elam proper in Fars, but also the lowland territory of Susiana, which was for much of the third millennium the western limit of Elamite culture and periodically also the boundary of her political control. Indeed, lying closer to Sumer, Susiana enjoyed much stronger relations with the west than did highland Elam, a fact which is largely responsible for the long-current misperception of Susa as the 'capital' of Elam.

This ambiguity is compounded by the fact that Rimuš's account of the Elam-Parahšum-Zahara campaign describes military incidents both "in the midst of Parahšum" and "between Awan and Susa at the Middle River" (*i.e.* in Susiana). Thus, his booty may have comprised objects, including stone vessels, from either or perhaps both of these widely separated regions. On the basis of the inscriptions, therefore, it is possible only to confirm the testimony of the vessels themselves that they are broadly "Elamite"; whether they came from highland Elam-Parahšum or from lowland Elam (Susiana) remains unclear.

At this point it is appropriate to consider the evidence of typological comparisons which may help in deciding between these alternatives. In recent years vessels of the same forms and material (banded calcite) as those inscribed by Rimuš as booty have come to light far to the east of Mesopotamia at sites in central Iran, the Indo-Iranian borderlands and Central Asia. Of these, the most distinctive are the tall cylindrical vases (Tables 6.2:1, 6.5:1), which have so far been found at Shahdad and Shahr-i Sokhta in Iran, and in Bactria and southern Turkmenia. A similar technique of manufacture is indicated by the 'ompholos' on the bottom of the interior created by the drilling process. This feature appears on vessels as far afield as Ur and Bactria.[91] The discovery of vessels at various stages of completion at Shahr-i Sokhta shows that production was undertaken at that site, exploiting the nearby calcite deposits.[92] Sub-conical bowls (Tables 6.2:3, 6.5:3) have a similar distribution from Iran and the Gulf to Bactria. Such natural forms were probably very widespread, and it is not yet possible to attribute the examples recovered in Mesopotamia to a particular sub-region.[93] But the orientation of these finds strongly favours a generally eastern origin, somewhere in the calcite-rich highlands of south-central or eastern Iran.

As described above, the French excavations at Susa have also yielded vessels of banded calcite, including tall cylindrical vases and sub-conical bowls identical to those inscribed by Rimuš, presumably originating in the same regions of inner Iran

---

90   A passage from the end of inscription C6:138-51 confirms that booty from the conquered lands was taken back to Agade. Significantly, the text qualifies the list with the same form of words as on the vessels: "when he had conquered Elam and Parahšum ...".
91   *E.g.* Pottier 1984: no. 204.
92   Ciarla 1979; *idem* 1981. There is also evidence of possible alabaster vessel production on Tarut (Howard-Carter 1987: 103).
93   According to Ciarla and Tosi (Howard-Carter 1987: 86; Ciarla 1985) the similar Failaka sherds are of east Iranian type and material.

TABLE 6.2
Rimuš Inscribed Stone Vessels — Shapes[1]

(1) *Tall cylindrical vases with straight or slightly convex profile and everted rim.* Almost exclusively cut from white-yellow-pale brown banded calcite; the bands usually run vertically, accentuating the tall form; interior drilled.

EXAMPLES (at least 14)
    Table 6.1:A1b-e, g, i, m, r, A2c, D2a, f, i, v, x-y, D3a-b, D8a, D9a, E4a

(2) *Shallow (?) cylindrical bowl/vase with broad everted rim.* Smaller and thinner walled than type 1 and probably not as tall; vertically banded greyish-white-yellow calcite; interior drilled.

EXAMPLES (1)
    Table 6.1:A5a

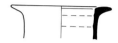

(3) *Sub-conical bowls, usually with slightly concave profile.* Almost exclusively in the same calcite as type 1, but usually cut with the bands running horizontally; drilled interior.

EXAMPLES (at least 9)
    Table 6.1:A1f, A2a, A5b, D1a, d, D5a, D6a, D9c, E3a (and possibly A1a, k-l, A3a, D2b-c, D3c, D4a)

(4) *Cylindrical "steatite" bowls of the série ancienne.* Interior chiselled (?) and smoothed.

EXAMPLES (2)
    Table 6.1:C1a, C2a

(5) *Flask or small jar.* White and yellow-pale brown banded or mottled calcite; interior drilled.

EXAMPLES (at least 1)
    Table 6.1:D1b (and possibly A1h, A4a)

(6) *Squat jar with everted rim.* Banded calcite (?);[2] interior drilled.

EXAMPLES (3)
    Table 6.1:D1e, D3d, D9b

Notes
1   Vessels are listed only when the shape can be confidently determined either on the basis of personal inspection or from previous publications. For the majority of vessels the shape is not specified or only vaguely described, or the fragments are insufficient for attribution.
2   D9b is described as "grey limestone" but the banding evident in the photograph suggests calcite.

or Central Asia. It is unlikely, however, that Rimuš's booty of Elam was taken from Susa; for, while Susian spoil might legitimately have been considered "Elamite", one would in that case expect vessels of the limestone and gypsum which dominates production in Susiana[94] to be represented among the booty which received inscriptions. As it is, however, they are completely absent.[95]

Unlike inscription A, *inscriptions B and C* do not explicitly designate the bearers as "booty". However, their conspicuous references to the conquest of Elam and Parahšum imply that these vessels also were brought back in the wake of that campaign. Such an origin is also demonstrable on typological grounds in the case of two cylindrical "steatite" vessels with inscription C, which are decorated in low relief in the style of the *série ancienne*. The principal area of production of that style, widely distributed in the mid- and late third millennium from Syria to Central Asia and the Indus Valley,[96] seems to have been highland Iran.

It is noteworthy, moreover, that none of the four vessels bearing inscriptions B and C is made from the light-coloured calcites which completely dominate the much larger inscription A corpus. Is this an accident of discovery, or does it reflect a genuine difference of origin? In particular, might the dark-coloured inscription B and C vessels represent the booty of Parahšum? It is interesting in this connection that the colophon to one Old Babylonian account of Rimuš's Elam-Parahšum campaign relates that "the diorite (ESI), *duhšû*-stone (DUH.ŠI) and (other) stones (or: stone objects ?) (NA₄.NA₄) which I[(l)] took, (were) the booty of Parahšum".[97] As Steinkeller suggests, "there is a good chance ... that these two bowls [*i.e.* the *série ancienne* vessels bearing inscription C] were among the spoils brought back by Rimuš from that campaign"[98] – more particularly, if this line of reasoning is correct, from Parahšum. Steinkeller also draws attention to the reference to vessels and other small objects of a stone called *marhu/ašu*, whose name indicates an origin (or supposed origin) in Marhaši/Parahšum. Steinkeller's suggestion that *marhašu* be identified as chlorite/steatite would strengthen the connection between that land and the inscribed *série ancienne* vessels.[99] It remains unclear, however, why they would not have been explicitly designated as "booty of Parahšum".

The typological similarity of the vessels bearing inscription D – "Rimuš, king of Kiš" – to those with inscription A suggests that, like the latter, some of these are Elamite booty. The predominant types are again tall cylindrical vases and sub-conical bowls of banded calcite, whose highland Iranian connections have been noted above (Table 6.2:1,3). The flask (Table 6.2:5) and the squat jar with everted rim (Tables 6.2:6; 6.5:4) are not closely matched beyond Susiana.

(b) Naram-Sin

The inscriptions of Naram-Sin, fourth king of Agade, which occur on stone vessels are listed in Table 6.3.

---

[94] Amiet 1986: 125, 127.
[95] Moreover, the tall cylindrical vases which are the most common Rimuš type (Table 6.2:1) are rare at Susa.
[96] Below note 173.
[97] C10:41-46 with collation by Oelsner.
[98] Steinkeller 1982: 254; *cf.* previously Klengel & Klengel 1980: 51, arguing the same origin for the vase in Berlin (Table 6.1:C2a).
[99] Steinkeller 1982: 251. An inscription of Šarkališarri claims to be a copy of the text on a foundation tablet of this stone (^na4 *na-rú-a* ^na4 *mar-huš-a*) (Frayne 1984: 24, ll. 72f.). A NB text refers to "alabaster" of Marahši (*CAD* M, Part I: 281 sub *marhušu*), which in that period should be calcite. For an alternative identification of serpentine as NA₄.MUŠ=*aban ṣēri* ("serpent stone") see Degraeve 1991: 6.

TABLE 6.3
Naram-Sin Inscribed Stone Vessels – Inscriptions[1]

Inscription A: "Naram-Sin, king of the four quarters, bowl (from) the booty of Magan"[2]

(1) Ur

(a) goblet, *sér. réc.* (6)	chlorite	Woolley 1955: 168; idem 1974: 88 [U.282+283]; Sollberger 1965: 35 no. 42; T.F. Potts 1989: fig. 10
(2) Provenance unknown		
(a) "vase"	"alabaster"	Rawlinson 1861: pl. 3 no. VII (lost in Tigris)
(b) cyl. bowl (2)[3]	banded calcite	Sweet in Muscarella (ed.) 1981: 80f. no. 33; here Fig. 41:4

Inscription B: "Naram-Sin, king of the four quarters, f[rom the booty of Magan(?)]"

(1) Susa

(a) cyl. vase (1)	banded calcite	Scheil 1902: 1, pl. 1:1

Inscription C: "Naram-Sin, the mighty, king of the four quarters, conqueror of Armanum and Ebla"

(1) Girsu

(a) shell-shaped lamp (7)	"green marble"	de Genouillac 1913: 101; Matthiae 1985: fig. 82

Inscription D: "Naram-Sin, king of the four quarters"

(1) Girsu

(a) shouldered jar (5)	calcite/gypsum	Heuzey & Sarzec 1884-1912: LVII, pl. 44:1
(b) "flask"	"brown limestone"	Braun-Holzinger 1991: G213J (AO156)
(c) ?	"alabaster"	Braun-Holzinger 1991: G213H (AO197)
(2) Puzriš-Dagan		
(a) cyl. vase (1)	banded calcite	Nassouhi 1925: 91; here Fig. 41:1
(3) Ur		
(a) bowl (4)	"black & white granite"	Gadd & Legrain 1928: no. 24A, pls E:24, IV:24A; T.F. Potts 1989: fig. 11
(4) Provenance unknown		
(a) bowl (3)	"red marble"	Stephens 1937: no. 96, pl. XLIV
(b) ?	"alabaster"	Braun-Holzinger 1991: G213I (AO8536)

Inscription E: "[Naram-Sin], king of the four quarters, [for] Enlil in Ni[ppur] dedica[ted] (this)"

(1) Nippur

(a) jar (?)[4]	"alabaster"	Legrain 1926: no. 18; Braun-Holzinger 1991: G215

F: Inscription uncertain

(1) Ur

(a) "vase"	"alabaster"	Gadd & Legrain 1928: no. 277
(2) Tutub		
(a) bowl	"alabaster"	Jacobsen in Delougaz 1940: 149 no.7
(3) Provenance unknown		
(a) "vase"	"alabaster"	King 1912: pl. 8 (BM 104418)

Notes

1   Numbers in brackets in the shape column refer to the types listed and illustrated in Table 6.4. A reference is given only when the shape is clear. Inscriptions correspond to the listing in *AKI* as follows: A = NS13; B = NS13B; C = NS11; D = NS14; E = NS9; F = NS12, NS15, NS14G.

2   The inscription of this type on the vase published in Stephens 1937: no. 95 is a modern forgery; *cf.* Nagel 1966: 16; D.T. Potts 1986b: 280-82. Braun-Holzinger (1989: 132; 1991: 161) argues that inscription A2b also is a fake and that vase A2a in fact bore Inscription B, but see T.F. Potts 1989: 132.

3   Sweet suggests that A2a and A2b may be the same vessel.

4   Braun-Holzinger 1991: G215: vessel with "gewölbte Wandung und abgesetztem Rand".

Inscription A indicates that its bearers are bowls (bur) "(from) the booty of Magan", paralleling Rimuš's "booty of Elam". The beginning of inscription B is the same and goes on to state where its bearers came "f[rom]", but the name of the source is lost. Comparison with other Sargonic royal inscriptions, where "from" is almost invariably followed by "the booty of GN"[100] suggests that this text too specified a source of booty. Inscription A supplies the likely place name: Magan. Inscription C refers to Naram-Sin's much-celebrated conquest of Armanum and Ebla. Inscription D gives just his name and title "king of the four (world-)quarters", to which Inscription E adds that the object is a dedication for Enlil at Nippur.

The published reconstructable vessels of Naram-Sin are illustrated in Table 6.4. Of the three surviving vessels from the "booty of Magan", one (Table 6.3:A2b, Table 6.4:2) is a banded calcite bowl of roughly cylindrical form with straight, slightly inward-leaning sides and an everted rim. The other (A1a), from Ur, comprises two fragments from the base and lower sides of a roughly cylindrical, flat-based goblet of Miroschedji's *série récente*, group C.[101] It is decorated with rows of dotted double circles of which only the lowermost row is preserved. Of the vessel lost in the Tigris (A2a) we know only that it was a "vase" of "alabaster" (calcite?).

The *inscription B* booty vessel, probably also from Magan, is "cylindrique, mais légèrement cintré", almost certainly a tall cylindrical vase (Table 6.4:1).[102] Like Rimuš's vessels of that type, it is made from calcite ("albâtre").

The one known vessel with *inscription C* is a "green marble" shell-shaped lamp (Table 6.4:7), the only royally inscribed example of that form.

The four vessels which carry *inscription* D include another tall cylindrical calcite vase (D2a; Table 6.4:1), as well as three types which are new to the inscribed Sargonic repertory: a flaring "granite" bowl (D3a, Table 6.4:4), a squat, heavy marble bowl with everted rim (D4a, Table 6.4:3) and a tall, shouldered gypsum/calcite jar (D1a, Table 6.4:5).

The vessel with *inscription E* is said to have a rounded profile and everted rim (presumably a jar) while those with incomplete inscriptions (F) are not assignable to specific types.

Of Naram-Sin's inscribed stone vessels, the vases from the "booty of Magan" (inscriptions A and B) are most directly relevant to the question of origins. The Susa fragment (Table 6.3:B1a) seems to be from a tall cylindrical vase, the same type earlier inscribed by Rimuš as booty of Elam. The best typological connections, as we have seen, are with eastern Iran and the adjacent regions. Likewise, the fully preserved cylindrical bowl (A2b) – which is in effect a squatter version of the vase – finds many close parallels at sites in south-central Iran, the Indo-Iranian borderlands, Bactria and southern Turkmenia (Table 6.5:2), again with evidence of local manufacture at Shahr-i Sokhta. In Oman (=Magan), on the other hand, evidence of vessel production is restricted to chlorite types (see below). Although calcite occurs in Oman there is as yet no evidence of its working. Indeed, very few calcite vessels have been recovered from the southern side of the Gulf and those that do occur are presumably mostly imports from the north.[103]

---

[100] In particular Rimuš's inscription A. For other instances of the fomula *in* NAM.RA.AK X[ki] see also Goetze 1968: 54 (NBC 10736) (Rimuš) and Grayson 1972: 2 (Ass. 20377) (Ititi).

[101] Miroschedji 1973: 37.

[102] P. Amiet, pers. comm. Sb 17825, ht 6.5 cms, varying in thickness from 2.0 (bottom) to 1.3 cms; *cf.* the poor photograph in Scheil 1902: pl. 1:1.

[103] The principal finds are: Oman – Hili (Vogt 1985: 157); Hili Grave A (*ibid.*, Taf. 72:1-4); Amlah site 1 (de Cardi *et al.* 1976: 139, fig. 23:2). Umm an-Nar – Cairns I, V, IX, X (Thorvildsen 1962: 210, 217; Vogt 1985: 157; Frifelt 1991: 105, fig. 221). Bahrain – Barbar Temple IIa, some tall cylindrical vases "and

By contrast, the third reconstructable vessel from Naram-Sin's "booty of Magan", the *série récente* chlorite goblet (A1a), must derive from the southern side of the Gulf.[104] It was probably made in Oman, where this series was manufactured from local chlorite deposits.[105] Pieces similar to the Naram-Sin vessel have been recovered there in burials, as well as in the U.A.E. and on Bahrain and Tarut islands.[106]

The restoration of the text has two important consequences: first, it confirms that production of the *série récente* had begun as early as the Akkadian period;[107] and, secondly, it shows that Naram-Sin's "booty of Magan" included vessels not only from Iran but also from the southern side of the Gulf, very probably from Oman.

On the face of it, therefore, the evidence of Naram-Sin's booty vessels neatly confirms other arguments that have been advanced in support of the view that third-millennium Magan included territories on both sides of the Gulf.[108] But there is cause for caution. Nothing in Naram-Sin's account of the Magan campaign (above pp. 112f.) provides any hint that the king's conquest involved campaigns on both sides of the Gulf. It is at least as plausible to suppose that Naram-Sin's booty was taken on one side of the Gulf only, to which vessels from the other had previously been transported.[109] Indeed, there is independent evidence of such movement in both directions: Iranian calcite vessels have been found in Oman and on Failaka, Umm an-Nar, Tarut and Bahrain islands;[110] and Omani chlorite vessels of the *série récente* occur in Iran.[111] As was argued above, historical considerations favour Oman.

---

fragments of a number of others" from the 'foundation deposits' (Glob 1958; D.T. Potts 1983: 129-31) (this deposit was assigned to Temple III in the original stratigraphy; for the revised sequence see Andersen 1986, Mortensen 1986); three tombs near Ali, "alabaster vessels" (one a "small conical bowl") (Frifelt 1986: 129). Tarut – disturbed contexts (Burkholder 1984: nos 16a (miniature), 21a (limestone), 29a; D.T. Potts 1989: fig. 17). Failaka – "perhaps a dozen fragments" of "alabaster" vessels, all but 2 "typologically imputable to the Hilmand Centre with conical, hemispheroid and cylinder-conical profiles", 1 "globular" vessel with Tepe Yahya parallel (Ciarla 1985: 398; Howard-Carter 1987: 86). Note also the Iranian chlorite vessel at Hili North Tomb A (Vogt 1985a: 32, pl. 29:11).

[104] T.F. Potts 1989: 134, fig. 10. Although the geographical name in the final line is entirely broken away, it may confidently be restored as "Magan", since that is the only place name which occurs in this context in vessel inscriptions of Naram-Sin (see Table 6.3).

[105] Miroschedji 1973: 38 (group C); Kroll in Wesigerber 1981: 212-14; Abb. 46, 47.

[106] Tarut – Zarins 1978: pls 64 (undecorated goblets), 71:547. Bahrain – Mughal 1983: fig. 24:7, pl. LI:6 (decorated), figs 25:1, 3 (plain). ed-Dur – Boucharlat *et al.* 1988, fig. 2:3. Tell Abraq – D.T. Potts 1991: figs 25-26. Maysar-1 – Kroll in Weisgerber 1981: Abb. 46:11 (with lid). Shimal Tomb SH 99 – Häser 1987: fig. 33:7 (unpierced lugs). This last is the closest in shape to the Ur vessel, though not enough of the latter is preserved to tell whether it too had lugs. It is notable that most of these parallels are Wadi Suq-period types, which are usually dated to the very end of the 3rd or early 2nd mill., not as early as the Akkadian period. *Cf.* also the same decoration on other vessel forms, especially rectangular compartmented boxes and concave-profile goblets: *e.g.* Zarins 1978: pl. 71:107, 197, 551; Cleuziou & Vogt 1983: fig. 10:1-4; Vogt 1985a: Pl. 27:14, 16, 17, 19, 22; Miroschedji 1973: figs 8:10, 9:2-3; Mughal 1983: fig. 25:4.

[107] This starting date was argued on the basis of archaeological evidence from Ur by Miroschedji (1973: 27 n. 115, 41) and D.T. Potts (in press [b]). The Akkadian dating of the vessel from PG 473 is confirmed by its association with a pottery vessel of type RC 67 which Pollock assigns a *floruit* in her phase I (=ED IIIb) of the Royal Cemetery (Pollock 1985: 138). To the evidence for the continuing currency of the *série récente* during the Ur III period cited by Miroschedji and D.T. Potts (*loci cit.*) add Sollberger 1965: 6, no. 26 (U.280), a bowl with concentric circle decoration and an inscription of Šulgi.

[108] Eilers 1983; D.T. Potts 1986a: 272-75, 284f.

[109] Glassner (1989: 188f.) suggests that calcite vessels might have reached Oman as presents (ni-šu-tag$_4$) offered by merchants to the local king.

[110] Above note 103.

[111] At Susa – Miroschedji 1973: figs 8:7-10, 9:2-3, pls VI:f, g, i, VII:h; Bushire – Pézard 1914: pl. VIII:4, 5; and Tepe Yahya – Lamberg-Karlovsky 1973: fig. 5F (period IVA); *idem* 1988: 52, figs 3:H-L, 4:Z-DD; D.T. Potts in press [a]: fig. IIk.; Kohl 1974: 220f.; *idem* 1979: 72; *idem* 1982: 27; Miroschedji 1973: 28, 30 n. 134.

TABLE 6.4
Naram-Sin Inscribed Stone Vessels — Shapes

TYPE 1 *Tall cylindrical vase.* Banded calcite; interior drilled.

EXAMPLES (2)
        Table 6.4:B1a, D2a

TYPE 2 *Cylindrical bowl, slightly narrowing towards the top, with everted rim.* Horizontally banded calcite; interior drilled.

EXAMPLES (1)
        Table 6.4:A2b

TYPE 3 *Shallow bowl with convex profile and everted rim.* "Red marble".

EXAMPLES (1)
        Table 6.4:D4a

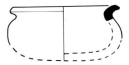

TYPE 4 *Sub-conical bowl, slightly convex upper and concave lower profile.* "Black and white granite"; interior drilled.

EXAMPLES (1)
        Table 6.4:D3a

TYPE 5 *Tall shouldered jar with everted rim.* Gypsum/calcite, not banded.

EXAMPLES (1)
        Table 6.4:D1a

TYPE 6 *Chlorite/steatite goblet decorated with incised concentric circles (série récente).* Interior drilled.

EXAMPLES (1)
        Table 6.4:A1a

TYPE 7 *Shell-shaped lamp.* "Green marble".

EXAMPLES (1)
        Table 6.4:C1a

Of Naram-Sin's other vessel inscriptions only C refers to a foreign conquest, *viz.* the defeat of Armanum (Aleppo?)[112] and Ebla. By analogy with Rimuš's inscription B and C vessels, one might expect a vessel celebrating Naram-Sin's Armanum-Ebla victory to be booty from that campaign. But in the case of the only extant example this must be considered unlikely, for it is a lamp in the characteristic Sumero-Akkadian form of a cut shell (Table 6.3:C1a; Table 6.4:7). Such vessels, often decorated with a bearded bull, are attested widely on southern Mesopotamian sites from the the mid-third millennium,[113] but they are not reported from excavations in Syria. At most one may speculate that the lamp may have been fashioned from stone brought back to Sumer as booty from the north-west. It is one of only three extant vessels with Sargonic royal inscriptions said to be made from coloured "marble" (the others are Table 6.1:A1f and Table 6.3:D4a), a material widely available in Syro-Anatolia. No firm conclusions are possible until these geological identifications are confirmed.

Inscriptions D and E provide no direct clues as to their bearers' origins. However, on typological grounds one of the inscrption D vessels (Table 6.3:D2a, Table 6.4:1) may be assigned an eastern origin. It is a tall cylindrical calcite vase, very similar in shape and material to many of Rimuš's vessels from the booty of Elam (Table 6.2:1). As in those cases, typological connections suggest an origin in south-central Iran or the Indo-Iranian borderlands. The same applies also to the calcite vessels of Naram-Sin whose inscriptions are too incomplete for identification (Table 6.3:F).

The Inscription D vessel from Ur (Table 6.3:D3a) is black and white granite, a material which suggests an origin in the northern or eastern highlands. The simple shape makes further specification difficult.[114]

The remaining two vessels of Naram-Sin represent Mesopotamian forms and may be considered local products. One is a squat red "marble" (limestone?) bowl with an everted rim, a form sometimes decorated in low relief during the Ur III period (Table 6.4:3).[115] The other is a tall shouldered jar, a recurrent Mesopotamian form with local antecedents dating back at least to Late Uruk times (Table 6.4:5). This example is carved from locally available white gypsum/calcite.

3. CALCITE VESSELS FROM HIGHLAND IRAN

Outside the reigns of Rimuš and Naram-Sin there are virtually no inscriptions on third-millennium stone vessels which mark their bearers as foreign objects.[116] However, the booty vessels provide some basis for identifying the much larger numbers of uninscribed examples of the same forms and materials as imports from the east. Indeed, those inscribed vessels represent some of the most popular forms in Sumer-Akkad during the Early Dynastic III to Old Babylonian periods. A common origin for the inscribed and uninscribed examples is assured by the fact that, while the materials of vessels differs considerably between types, there is a remarkable degree of intra-type correlation between shape on the one hand, and material and

---

[112] Edzard *et al.* 1977: 18.
[113] *E.g.* Woolley 1934: 377, pl. 182.
[114] It is similar to many vessels from the 'Jemdet Nasr' cemetery at Ur (*e.g.* types JN 42, 43) and so may be an heirloom.
[115] *Cf.* Woolley 1955: pl. 36:U.232.
[116] An exception is the large cylindrical "calcite" vessel of Enmetena cited above.

method of manufacture (especially the drilling of the interior) on the other, whether they are inscribed or not.

While not all the uninscribed examples of types identified by the Sargonic rulers as booty of Elam or Magan need have originated in those lands, these designations provide convenient labels under which provisional groupings of foreign types may be attempted. They should be understood only as rough guides, to be replaced or refined as fresh evidence becomes available. It is essential always to keep in mind that this evidence, whether archaeological or inscriptional, usually bears directly only on a vessel's final or penultimate provenance, which is not necessarily its place of production. As we have seen, the best parallels for "Elamite" calcite types lie well beyond the limits of historical Elam in eastern Iran, Afghanistan and Central Asia.

(a) 'Elamite' Types

Among Rimuš's booty vessels, the most common forms are the tall cylindrical vase and the sub-conical bowl, both of which were manufactured in banded calcite. They first occur in significant numbers in southern Mesopotamia in the Early Dynastic III period,[117] notably in the 'Royal Cemetery' at Ur, and continue through to Old Babylonian times (Table 6.5:1).[118] Their appearance marks part of a broader phenomenon which saw the introduction into southern Mesopotamia and Khuzistan of considerable numbers of banded and mottled calcite vessels in a limited range of distinctive forms. Other recurrent types include: (1) Low cylindrical or slightly tapering bowls – essentially a squat version of the tall cylindrical vases (Table 6.5:2); the best typological parallels for the rare examples of this type from Sumer and Susiana are likewise found in eastern Iran, Bactria and southern Turkmenia. This general region is again perhaps the most likely origin, despite Naram-Sin's identification of at least one such vessel as booty of Magan (Table 6.3:A2b; also A2a?). (2) Carinated bowls with a slightly everted rim, the profile usually convex below and concave above the carination (Table 6.5:5); although not yet attested inscribed, these are often found in the same contexts as the other calcite forms, and, like them, have close parallels in eastern Iran, Bactria and southern Turkmenia. Rarely this shape is carved from a black limestone with globular white inclusions; close parallels of this distinctive variant are known from Shahdad, Failaka and Girsu, where one such bowl was dedicated by Ur-Baba, Gudea's father-in-law.[119] (3) Flasks of the form which was sometimes inscribed with the name and title of Rimuš (Table 6.1:D1b) and perhaps also as Elamite booty (Table 6.1:A1h, A4a).[120] These

---

[117] Some already inscribed (Heinz 1989: 203, fig. 11; Fales 1983 [Mari]).

[118] At Ur the most common form of tall cylindrical vase (type RC3) occurred in no less than 13 graves (Woolley 1934: 518). They were still used in Ur III times as funerary equipment (mausolea) and for dedications, and continue to appear in OB contexts.

[119] Shahdad – Hakemi & Sajjidi n.d.: fig. 4 top left. Failaka – Ciarla 1985: 398, fig. 5. Girsu – Balty *et al.* 1988: 73 bott. left.

[120] Ur – Hall & Woolley 1927: pls XLVI:3 (TO11), LXII: type XXXIX (Ubaid); Woolley 1934: pls 177:U.8936, 179a:U.7654, U.7649, 179b:U.8030; 249-49: types RC 60b, 85-87, 89 (some vessels catalogued as other types, notably RC 92, are also actually of these types); Reisner 1931: figs 1, 3:15. Kiš – Mackay 1929: pls XXXVIII:10.3, LVI:3. Girsu – Heuzey & Sarzec 1884-1912: pl. 44bis, fig. 2; de Genouillac 1934: pl. 9* (TG1437). Mari – Parrot 1956: pl. LII:M568. Tepe Gawra VIIIC – Speiser 1935: pl. LXXVI:20. Susa – Mecquenem 1943: fig. 70:36; Le Breton 1957: fig. 42:6, 9; Casanova 1982: series VI (18 vessels of this type from Susiana, 15 of them made of mottled yellow and white calcite (Sb 612α, 4008, 4088, 11826, 11884-11890, 11892, 12029, 14655; and, from Aliabad, 6469 and 6526), the rest of grey-white gypsum, were inspected by the author in the Louvre). Less close parallels occur at Shahr-i Sokhta – Ciarla 1981: fig. 3b, pear-shaped, bi-conical; Tosi (ed.) 1983: pl. LXXVIII:fig. 95.

TABLE 6.5
Principal Types of Calcite Vessels in Sumer (ED III – Ur III) with Eastern Parallels[1]

(1) *Tall cylindrical vases, usually with slightly convex base and everted rim* (Woolley's "spill vases"). Carved from yellow-white banded calcite, usually cut with the bands running vertically, perhaps to accentuate the height; the interior always bored using a stone disc-drill in the final stages which leaves clear abrasions and undulation on the walls.

MESOPOTAMIA[2]
> Ur – Hall & Woolley 1927: pl. LXI: types II, III (Ubaid); Woolley 1934: 518, pls 177a:U.8949, 178c:U.7645, 241: types RC 2-6; *idem* 1955: pl. 34:U.19015, U.19108; *idem* 1974: pl. 51: Ur III types I, II; Woolley & Mallowan 1976: pl. 100:9; Reisner 1931: fig. 2:1-6; Heinz 1989: 203, fig. 11; T.F. Potts 1989: figs 2, 5, 6
> Girsu – de Genouillac 1934: pls 9[*] (TG1441), 55:3a (TG 1337), 56:2f (TG 1441); *idem* 1936: pl. 85:3 (TG 1407)
> Nippur – McCown *et al.* 1967: pl. 29:1; Gibson *et al.* 1978: fig. 9:2
> Sippar – Walker & Collon 1980: pl. 27:33
> Mari – Fales 1983
> Brak – T.F. Potts 1989: fig. 8.

COMPARANDA
> Susa (rare) – Mecquenem 1934: fig. 21:7; 76:47; Amiet 1977: 96f.; *idem* 1986: 127; Casanova 1982: series IV nos 41-49[3]
> Shahdad – Hakemi 1972: pls XII-XIII
> Shahr-i Sokhta – Ciarla 1979: Tab. 6 (lower part of vessel only)
> Kulli – Stein 1931: pl. XXIII Kul. V.IX.1
> Quetta – Jarrige ed. 1988: nos 165-6
> Mundigak IV3 – Casal 1961: fig. 134:22 (4 exx.)
> South Turkmenia – Masson & Sarianidi 1972: pl. 35
> Bactria – Pottier 1984: nos 204, 205, 207
> East Arabia – Burkholder 1984: nos 16a (miniature), 21a (limestone), 29a
> Tarut – D.T. Potts 1989: fig. 17
> Bahrain – Mortensen 1970: fig. 7 left, middle

(2) *Cylindrical bowls with everted rim, slightly convex base, sometimes slightly narrowing to the top.* This is essentially a squatter, broader version of type (1), made using similar stone and technique, except that the stone is usually cut with the bands running horizontally.

MESOPOTAMIA
> Ur – Woolley 1934: pl. 241: RC 1, 7, 9, 11, pls 176:U.12696, 180a:U.8331; *idem* 1974: 93, pl. 51 Ur III type III
> Kiš – Langdon 1934: pl. XXXIV:1, 2
> Nippur – McCown *et al.* 1967: pl. 107:11

COMPARANDA
> Shahdad – Hakemi 1972: pl. XIII:C, D
> Shahr-i Sokhta II-III & Mundigak – Tosi 1969: fig. 40:h, i; Tosi 1983: 179, fig. 16, 2nd row right, 4th row 3rd from left; Ciarla 1981: fig. 3 (b, cylinder-cone); D.T. Potts 1986b: pl. XXIX
> Seistan (Gardan Reg. 109) – Fairservis 1961: fig. 29:i-k; fig. 37:45-6
> Khurab – Stein 1937: pls XIX:Bii229, XXXII:14
> Mundigak – Jarrige & Tosi 1981: fig. 3a 1st, 2nd, 5th from right
> Bampur – Stein 1937: pl. VIII:bott. left; de Cardi 1971: fig. 47:12
> Anau Tepe – Schmidt in Pumpelly 1908: pl. 45:12
> South Turkmenia (Nam. IV) – Masson & Sarianidi 1972: pl. 35
> Bactria – Amiet 1977: fig. 7:1-3; Pottier 1984: nos 203-6

(3) *Sub-conical bowl, profile varying from slightly convex to slightly concave.* Almost always cut with the bands running horizontally.

MESOPOTAMIA

  Ur – Hall & Woolley 1927: pl. LXI: type XVIII (Ubaid); Woolley 1934: pl. 176:U.11818, U.12673, pls 241-43: types RC 13, 14, 16, 19, 20a, 24, 25 (all also in other materials); *idem* 1955: type JN 27; *idem* 1974: pl. 51: Ur III type V
  Girsu – Heuzey & Sarzec 1884-1912: pl. 44b:1; *idem* 1903: figs 24-28; Sweet in Muscarella 1980: 30
  Sippar – Walker & Collon 1980: pl. 27:21
  Nippur – unpublished; inspected in Iraq Museum

COMPARANDA

  Susa – Mecquenem 1934: figs 21:7, 60:26; *idem* 1943: fig. 71:11; Le Breton 1957: figs 40:4, 42:1, 2, 5; Stève & Gasche 1971: pl. 15:15; Casanova 1982: series X-XVI
  Aliabad – Gautier & Lampre 1905: figs 288, 290, 293
  Shahr-i Sokhta – Ciarla 1981: figs 3a (cones), 4a, 4f, 4i, 8, 12; Tosi (ed.) 1983: 179f., figs 16-17
  Mundigak – Jarrige & Tosi 1981: fig. 3a, 3rd from right
  Bactria – Pottier 1984: no. 195
  Tarut – Burkholder 1984: no. 16c; D.T. Potts 1989: fig. 15 right

(4) *Small jars.* Although sometimes made from the same banded calcite as types (1) to (3), these are usually in a poorer quality mottled yellow-white calcite with irregular limestone veins; the interior is drilled, as with the other types, either in a straight cylinder or further undercut to follow the line of the exterior profile.

MESOPOTAMIA

  Ur – Woolley 1934: pl. 246ff.: types RC 61, 62, 88, 90b,[4] pls 176:U.11786, 177:U.8980, U.8948, 178:U.10502 (spouted)
  Girsu – de Genouillac 1934: pl. 9*:TG1442

COMPARANDA

  Susa – Casanova 1982: sub-types B1, B2, series V no. 54[5]
  Aliabad – Gautier & Lampre 1905: fig. 291
  Tepe Hissar – Schmidt 1937: pl. LIX:H.1847
  Bactria – Pottier 1984: nos 209-11.
  Mundigak – Casal 1961: fig. 134:9
  Altyn Tepe – Piotrovsky (ed.) 1979: no. 73

(5) *Carinated bowls, usually with concave upper and convex lower profile.* Cut with bands running horizontally or vertically; drilled interior.

MESOPOTAMIA

  Ur – Woolley 1934: pls 178:U.7648, 179:U.8216, pls 245f.: types RC 54, 59, 64-66; Woolley 1955: pl. 69: type RC 109; Reisner 1931: fig. 3:21-22
  Nippur – McCown *et al.* 1967: pl. 107:10
  Abu Salabikh – Postgate (ed.) 1985: fig. 141: Gr. 1:48, pl. XXVIIIa

COMPARANDA[6]

  Susa – Mecquenem 1943: fig. 71:10; Le Breton 1957: fig. 42:3, 4; Stève & Gasche 1971: pl. 15:16; Casanova 1982: series I-II
  Shahdad – Hakemi 1972: pl. XII:D, no. 143; Hakemi & Sajjidi n.d.: fig. 4 (top left)
  Seistan – Fairservis 1961: fig. 29:a-b, o-q
  Bampur – Stein 1937: pl. XXXII:17
  Tepe Hissar IIIC – Schmidt 1937: pl. LIX:H.3615, fig. 125
  Bactria – Pottier 1984: nos 193, 196-98[7]
  Tarut – Burkholder 1984: no. 18c
  Failaka – Ciarla 1985: fig. 5

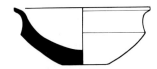

Notes

1   The following information is based on the excavation reports and observations on the Ur, Kiš and Susa material in Baghdad, London and Philapelphia. For Ur note Woolley's remark (1934: 379) that the following types occur exclusively in calcite: "spill vases" types RC 1-12 (type 10 is actually 'steatite' and should not have been included) and jars types RC 85-92. For further information on ED manufacturing techniques see Heinz 1989: 208f.

2   Note also copies in clay, *e.g.* Woolley 1974: pl. 48c (Šulgi).

3   Note also the ceramic version Mecquenem 1934: 213, fig. 54.

4   Some vessels catalogued as other types, e.g. RC 72, are also of this form.

5   A further 11 vessels of this general shape inspected in the Louvre (Sb 470α, 475α, 643α, 11975-77, 11979-80, 11982, 12022, and one vessel with no visible number) may be of earlier (Susa II-III) date. These have drilled interiors and are made from pure light-coloured limestone, not the mottled calcite/limestone typical of the Mesopotamian examples.

6   Note also from Tepe Yahya VA(?) Lamberg-Karlovsky & Tosi 1973: fig. 93 bott. right (not cited in Lamberg-Karlovsky & Beale 1986); if correctly stratified, this is far the earliest context for this type.

7   *Cf.* in metal Sarianidi 1977: fig. 24 top, 2nd from left.

---

currently have no good highland parallels and are therefore not included in Table 6.5; they were apparently not produced at Shahr-i Sokhta and may represent another highland region altogether. An origin in or near Sumer is unlikely since they appear there at the same time and in the same contexts as other Iranian types. Moreover, in terms of shape they fall within a typologically continuous series which extends from tall slim flasks to squat jars, the next type to be considered. (4) These globular jars are more problematic. Their closest parallels east of Susa – general analogues which are hardly compelling in such a simple form – are vessels from Tepe Hissar (1 example) and Bactria (Table 6.5:4). Since calcite vessels appear at Hissar only in period IIIC[121] and no evidence of local manufacture has been found there,[122] the Hissar example is probably best regarded as an import from Bactria/Turkmenia. As for the Mesopotamian examples, however, an origin so far east requires further proof, especially for so natural a shape. Lastly one may include in this category (5) the necked bottles of banded calcite which appear along with these types in Sumer and at Susa (lacking highland parallels they are excluded from Table 6.5).[123]

None of these types has local antecedents and, although deposits of banded calcite are reported from the western folds of the Zagros mountains, the present distribution of parallels suggests that they were made in regions well east of Mesopotamia, whither they arrived as finished products. It is interesting that these types do not extend to the Indus, where stone vessels (mainly local gypsum) are rare. They appear at approximately the same time at Susa and in the Deh Luran Plain,[124] where Amiet regards them as imports from south-eastern Iran.[125] Rare finds on the southern side of the Gulf[126] raise the possibility that the Mesopotamian examples arrived by boat, after having travelled south from their highland production centres.

It is unclear whether the concentration of early examples of calcite types in graves at Ur and in Susiana, giving way in the Akkadian and Ur III periods to temple dedications, reflects a genuine trend or just differences in the excavated contexts from period to period.

---

121   Schmidt 1937: 212.

122   Tosi 1989: 24.

123   Above note 67.

124   Table 6.5 and note 120. The earliest closely datable context is the *Vase à la Cachette*, assigned on glyptic evidence to ED III (Amiet 1986: 125).

125   Amiet 1986: 125.

126   Above note 103.

The parallels cited above should not be taken to indicate the exact origins of their Mesopotamian analogues. Many of the more natural, simple forms (*e.g.* sub-conical bowls, cylindrical vases, globular jars) were clearly widespread on the Greater Iranian plateau and could have arrived in Mesopotamia from any one (or combination) of a number of regions. Even some of the more distinctive shapes (*e.g.* carinated bowls) have broad highland distributions which render impossible any particular source provenance attribution. Vast tracts between the known sites remain largely unexplored and unexcavated. As the only known manufacturing centre, the tendency has been to assign types to Shahr-i Sokhta but this should be resisted, especially since the parallels with that site are presently restricted to the most simple and natural bowl forms. None of the more distinctive types (carinated bowls, tall vases) has been found there; nor have Shahr-i Sokhta's more distinctive necked jars and footed vessels[127] yet been found in Mesopotamia. A more local production centre also should not be excluded: that there was an accessible source of the greenish calcite/gypsum is suggested by an oval bowl with lugs from the tomb of Pu-abi at Ur, exactly copying a Sumerian metal form.[128]

(b) 'Maganite' Types

The inscriptions on chlorite/steatite vessels of the *série récente* identifying one as "booty of [Magan]" and another as a dedication by Ur-Baba, perhaps the Gulf merchant of that name,[129] conveniently complement archaeological evidence for the manufacture of such vessels in the Oman peninsula, and support the attribution of the dozen or so uninscribed examples from Sumerian sites[130] to the same source.

As we have seen, the present distribution of typological parallels raises serious doubts regarding any attribution of the cylindrical calcite bowls and vases of the types labelled as "booty of Magan" to manufacturing centres on the southern side of the Gulf. Nor is there presently evidence to connect any other stone vessel types with Magan in particular, although it remains possible that some of the types to be discussed next may prove to come from centres within the domain of historical Magan.

4. UNDECORATED 'STEATITE' VESSELS FROM IRAN AND THE PERSIAN GULF[131]

Under this heading may be considered some earlier undecorated stone vessels from Sumerian sites for which typological evidence suggests origins in the Gulf littoral or Iran, though they had fallen out of currency before the Sargonic period when booty inscriptions, which might have confirmed such sources, began to be applied. Most of these are best represented in Sumer in the "Jemdet Nasr Cemetery" at Ur, of which the true end-date fell in Early Dynastic I or, in the chronology followed here, Early Dynastic II.[132] A few appear first in the Early Dynastic III "Royal

---

[127] *E.g.* Ciarla 1981: fig. 4:j-p.
[128] Woolley 1934: pl. 174 U.10480.
[129] Miroschedji 1973: 28 n. 116; Amiet 1986: fig. 88; *cf.* D.T. Potts, in press [b].
[130] Below notes 258, 266.
[131] The term 'steatite' is here used to refer conveniently to all stones of the steatite-chlorite-serpentine group which cannot be distinguished confidently by eye.
[132] Gockel 1982 (ED I); Kolbus 1983 (ED II).

Cemetery"; none remained popular in Mesopotamia much beyond the end of that period.[133] Together with the better-known decorated styles assigned by Miroschedji to the *séries ancienne* and *récente* (see below), these plain steatite types dominate the vessel industries of southern Iran and the Gulf. The raw material occurs in both regions.[134] Production of plain vessels has been documented at Tepe Yahya IVB$_{4-1}$ in Iran and at Maysar-1 in Oman where they occur with the *séries ancienne* and *récente* respectively.[135]

The types concerned (see Table 6.6) are bowls and goblets carved from dark green-grey stones, principally steatite/chlorite: bag-shaped goblets; (sub-) hemispherical bowls; square-based, cylindrical goblets; bell-shaped bowls; sub-conical, slightly concave-profile bowls; concave-profile, quasi-cylindrical goblets; bag-shaped bowls. All find close parallels among the more than three hundred plain stone vessels recovered (along with many decorated types of the *séries ancienne* and *récente*) in non-archaeological excavations at al-Rufayah on Tarut Island.[136] Close analogues for some types are also known from Umm an-Nar Island and Hili in Oman, and, in Iran, from Susa, Tepe Yahya, Shahdad and Shahr-i Sokhta. The Gulf examples are described in recent publications as "chlorite" or "steatite". Woolley, however, listed Ur vessels of these types as occurring also in "diorite" and "basic diorite".[137] If this is confirmed, the material of the Gulf vessels also should be re-examined, for grey-green (altered) igneous rocks which take a high polish can superficially resemble steatite.[138] Whatever their true geological identification(s), it seems plausible to suppose that the very similar vessels from Sumer, the Gulf and Iran derive from the same source(s); and, in particular, that the Mesopotamian examples came through the Gulf.

Adopting Kolbus' chronology for the 'Jemdet Nasr Cemetery' at Ur, the earliest examples of these types appear there in the Early Dynastic Ia period, continuing into Early Dynastic II.[139] This makes them roughly contemporary with the so-called 'Jamdet Nasr' pottery found in Oman; for, as D.T. Potts has recently shown, there are sound reasons for believing that that corpus also continues down into the Early Dynastic period.[140] The possibility thus presents itself that the dark-stone vessels in Sumer and the Sumerian pottery vessels in Oman are complementary aspects of one and the same process of exchange.

Of the dark soft-stone types found in Sumer the most common are *bell-shaped bowls*, which also seem to be the latest in the sequence. Among twenty-six examples

---

[133] Heavy sub-hemispherical bowls (Table 6.6:2) occur at Ur in graves assigned to the Akkadian and Larsa periods (Woolley 1934: 518 [type RC 36]; Woolley & Mallowan 1976: 243, U.16723).

[134] Kohl *et al.* 1979.

[135] Kohl 1974; Lamberg-Karlovsky 1988 (Yahya); Kroll in Weisgerber 1981 (Maysar).

[136] Zarins 1978; D.T. Potts 1986: 149.

[137] Woolley 1955: 156.

[138] Woolley's descriptions should not be accepted without confirmation. U.19408 from ED II JNG 221, a vessel of type JN 32 catalogued by Woolley as "steatite" (1955: 206), proved on inspection in the Iraq Museum to be a hard igneous rock, what he elsewhere calls "(basic) diorite". On the other hand, two *série récente* vessels (Woolley 1934: pl. 245:52, 53), almost certainly of steatite/chlorite, are twice described by him as "basic diorite" (1934: 380, 541 [U.9020]), though one of them is elsewhere correctly called "steatite" (*ibid.*: 559 [U.10547]).

[139] Ur type JN 31 comes exclusively from graves assigned by Kolbus to ED II (JNGs 220, 221, 234, 246 [Woolley 1955: 156; Kolbus 1983: Abb. 2 Group IV; Vértesalji & Kolbus 1985: 107]). The very similar type RC32 occurs in only two graves which Nissen dates to RT (*i.e.* ED III) (Nissen 1966: Taf. 10). Kolbus places one example of type JN 32 in each of ED Ia (U.19848; JNG 298), ED Ib (U.19653; JNG 248) and ED II (U.19408; JNG 221; Kolbus 1983: 11, Abb. 2), though she cites this latest period as its "main occurrence" (Vértisalji & Kolbus 1985: 107). The more numerous examples of type JN28 fall in ED Ib-II (JNGs 174, 221, 224, 301; *ibid.*).

[140] D.T. Potts 1986: 129-34.

TABLE 6.6
Undecorated Dark Stone Vessels from Sumer and Eastern Parallels

(1) *Bag-shaped goblets*
Stones: "diorite, basic diorite" (JN 31), "steatite" (RC 32)

MESOPOTAMIA
> Ur – Woolley 1955: pl. 66: type JN 31; *idem* 1934: pl. 243: type RC 32 (2 exx.: U.8763, U.10503)

COMPARANDA
> Tarut – Zarins 1978: pl. 64:73, 75, 78, 81-83, 92, pl. 72B:76, pl. 74A:23 (= Golding 1974: fig. 4:3); D.T. Potts 1986a: pl. 2b (left & centre)

(2) *(Sub-)hemispherical bowls*
Stones: "basic black diorite"[1]

MESOPOTAMIA
> Ur – Woolley 1934: pl. 244: type RC 36; Woolley & Mallowan 1976: pl. 100:5 (U.6880)[2]
> Girsu – Genouillac 1936: pl. 85:2

COMPARANDA
> Tarut – Burkholder 1984: no. 20b
> Susa – Miroschedji 1973: fig. 7
> Shahr-i Sokhta – Tosi (ed.) 1983: 179, figs 16-17

(3) *Square-based cylindrical goblets*
Stones: "diorite"[3]

MESOPOTAMIA
> Ur – Woolley 1955: pl. 66: type JN 32

COMPARANDA
> Tarut – Zarins 1978: pl. 64:21; Burkholder 1984: no. 28a; D.T. Potts 1986a: pl. 2b (right)

(4) *Bell-shaped bowls*
Stones: chlorite[4]

MESOPOTAMIA
> Ur – Woolley 1934: pl. 245: type RC 49-51

COMPARANDA
> Tarut – Zarins 1978: pls 64:33, 65:587, 74a:593, cat. nos 334, 417, 497, 585; Burkholder 1984: nos 15a, 18b, 28c
> Hili North, Tomb A – Vogt 1985a: pl. 27:12
> Wadi Suq – Frifelt 1975a: fig. 18e
> Tepe Yahya – Lamberg-Karlovsky 1970: fig. 23, pl. 24:B; *idem* 1973: fig. 5:J; Lamberg-Karlovsky & Tosi 1973: fig. 96; Kohl 1974: pl. LXa
> Shahdad – Hakemi 1972: pls IXB, IXE; Hakemi & Sajjidi n.d.: fig. 4 bott. right

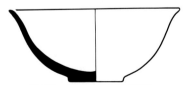

(5) *Sub-conical, slightly concave profile bowls*
Stones: "steatite"(?), "diorite"[5]

MESOPOTAMIA

Ur – Woolley 1955: pl. 65: type JN 28

COMPARANDA

Tarut – Zarins 1978: pl. 64:86 = D.T. Potts 1989: fig. 7

(6) *Concave profile, quasi-cylindrical goblets*
Stones: chlorite(?), "dark steatite"[6]

MESOPOTAMIA

Ur – U.19536, U.19213a (Woolley 1955: pl. 34; inspected in the I.M.)
Abu Salabikh – AbS 2157 (Gr. 213, unpubl.)

COMPARANDA

Tarut – Zarins 1978: pls 64:72, 65:325; D.T. Potts 1989: figs 8-9
Bahrain, Sar al-Jisr – Mughal 1983: Fig. 50:6
Umm an-Nar, Gr. 1 – Frifelt 1991: fig. 220
Hili – Frifelt 1970: 358, fig. 3:B (Gr. 1059); *idem* 1971: fig. 3B; Vogt 1985: pl. 27:11 (Tomb A)
Shimal – Häser 1987: 106, fig. 47:6
Shahdad – Hakemi 1972: pl. IXA, X:B
Tepe Yahya – Lamberg-Karlovsky 1970: fig. 23:U; Kohl 1974: pl. LXIa

(7) *Bag-shaped bowls*
Stones: "diorite"[7]

MESOPOTAMIA

Ur – Woolley 1955: pl. 69:RC 114

COMPARANDA

Tarut – Zarins 1978: pl. 64:75, 82, 92

Notes

1   U.6880 (OB type 5). No material given for type RC 36.
2   Note that vessel U.16723, listed as another type 5 vessel by Woolley & Mallowan 1976: 185 n. 12, is in fact the type 6 v (as the description *ibid.*: 243 indicates and confirmed by J.E. Curtis). The vessel U.6651, listed by Woolley & Mallowan as 6, is in fact the type 7 vessel.
3   Woolley 1955: 156 lists the stones of these vessels as "diorite, steatite". However, the one "steatite" vessel, U.19408, insp by the author in the Iraq Museum, is a harder (altered igneous?) material; it is definitely not steatite.
4   A vessels of type RC 51 from Ur, now in the Ashmolean Museum (Ash. 1933.240) has been analysed by the Dept. of Sciences, Oxford as chlorite.
5   Stone types listed in Woolley 1955: 156 are "diorite, basic diorite, limestone, calcite, steatite". Of the two vessels list "steatite", one is not really this type (see next note), the other (U.18683) is from a JNG 221, dated ED II by Kolbus (198 Abb. 2). Six of the remaining eight JN 28 vessels which are described by Woolley (those from JNGs 173, 174, 244 wer registered and are therefore nowhere described) are said to be of "diorite".
6   U.19536, from a plundered grave and therefore of no chronological value, is misleadingly catalogued as type JN 28 (W 1955: 209). Inspection in the Iraq Museum showed that it is cylindrical vessel, identical to the Tarut parallels cited b Dimensions: h. 5.8-5.9; rim diam. 8.0; base diam. 7.7. cms. Visually identified as chlorite. U.19213a, from a plundered grave, is misleadingly catalogued as type RC 8 (Woolley 1955: 202); it is said to be "dark steatite".
7   U.19112, from a plundered PJ/B grave, is said to be "diorite"; otherwise the stones represented in this type are not specif

excavated by Woolley at Ur, twenty fall in the range Early Dynastic IIIa-b, four more appearing in the Akkadian and post-Akkadian periods.[141] Woolley noted that these vessels, some of which are very large, are carved exclusively from "steatite". Exactly similar bowls represent the standard plain bowl type at Tepe Yahya in periods IVB and IVA, dated by the excavator to the mid- and late third millennium.[142] Their discovery in the Gulf (Tarut, Hili, Wadi Suq) supports Kohl's suggestion that the examples found in Sumer, especially the larger vessels, arrived by sea.[143]

The other Jemdet Nasr types listed by Woolley as occurring in steatite – *viz.* low, open bowl types JN 17, 19, 21, 23 and jar types JN 60, 61 – are not paralleled closely at Tarut[144] and probably come from elsewhere in the Gulf or Iran.

On the basis of this evidence it may be suggested that the use of plain Gulf and/or Iranian steatite vessels in the 'Royal Cemetery' at Ur concentrates in the latter half of the Early Dynastic period. An earlier start is probable but cannot yet be demonstrated. Importation probably continued also through the later third millennium for which the evidence of graves, their primary archaeological source in Sumer, is less extensive.

5. DECORATED VESSELS

Decorated stone vessels occur in Sumer throughout the period with which this study is concerned. As would be expected over such a time range, the repertory is very diverse in iconography, style and stone type. Unlike plain vessels, most locally produced decorated vessels may be confidently identified as such on the basis of their unambiguously Sumero-Akkadian decoration. These distinctions are reinforced in the vast majority of cases by the material of manufacture: the locally available light-coloured limestone, less often gypsum, sandstone or calcite. Although ignorance of contemporary Iranian iconography initially hindered recognition of highland imports, excavation and casual finds during the 1960s and 70s in Iran, and more recently in the Gulf states, has also made the identification of foreign pieces less subjective, although finer regional and stylistic distinctions remain problematic. Again stone-types provide welcome support: almost all stylistically alien decorated vessels are made from soft dark green-grey chlorite/steatite/serpentine. Considerable numbers of such vessels entered Sumer from the east in the third millennium, representing one of the largest groups of unambiguously foreign-manufactured objects in Sumer. On the other hand, it is interesting to note that no distinctively northern or north-western types have yet been recognised.

(a) Decorated vessels in late fourth- and third-millennium Sumer

Decorated vessels were made in Sumer during Late Uruk times, and a proportion of the local products continued to be decorated throughout the third millennium. The vast majority of vessels in primary contexts have been recovered from temples; fewer examples come from graves and less again from domestic levels.

Two very different styles are prominent among the material from the Archaic levels of the Eanna sanctuary at Uruk. The first, almost always in light-coloured

---

[141] Kohl 1974: 263-5.
[142] Woolley 1934: 379 (Ur); Kohl 1974: 218f., 264 (Yahya). But for dating see below on D.T. Potts' lower chronology which starts period IVB4-1 (= old IVB1) after 2200, ending around 2000 BC, with IVA in the early 2nd mill. (D.T. Potts in press [a]).
[143] Kohl 1974: 220.
[144] An approximate analogue to JN60 is Zarins 1978: pl. 69:54.

limestones, is characterised by animals (lions, bulls, sheep) carved in relief. Bowls typically carry a file of animals in low relief taking up almost the whole exterior surface.[145] One Uruk jug also has lions carved in the round on the shoulder.[146] Small receptacles may be totally overwhelmed by the much larger supporting sculptures.[147] A variety of shapes – tall vases, troughs and bowls – show more complex cultic and pastoral scenes in low relief, sometimes in multiple registers.[148] Although no vessels of these kinds have been discovered at Susa, Porada attributes one jar in Boston, showing a row of bulls above mountain sheep or ibexes, to that site on the basis of stylistic connections with Proto-Elamite glyptic and the species of sheep, which are not otherwise known on Mesopotamian vessels. Similar stylistic considerations lead her to question whether the large 'lion jug' from Uruk is not also Susian.[149] In both cases, however, the issue must be left open since other explanations for the Susian connections are certainly possible.

A second Uruk series is characterised by inlaid decoration, dominated by rosettes and 'eyes' in various coloured stones (limestone, schist) and shell, set into vessels of bituminous limestone[150] or grey-green schist, often with a separate neck and/or spout in lighter stone.[151] Within Sumer the use of bituminous limestone seems to be restricted largely to Uruk. Vessels from other sites in this style are cut from fine grained slate-like stone (*e.g.* BM 118468) and grey-green igneous stones, including a bowl from Khafajeh Sin Temple IV.[152] The Khafajeh bowl parallels in shape and material many plain vessels from the 'Jemdet Nasr' cemetery at Ur. Like these it was probably imported and the decoration added in Sumer.

Animals in relief continue to dominate decorated vessels in the Early Dynastic period. These are known principally from finds in the temples of the Diyala sites, and from graves in the 'Jemdet Nasr' cemetery at Ur (a bat-lamp, ram bowl, leaf-pattern bowl and two animal-file bowls).[153] Miniature vessels may be supported by animals in the round.[154]

The repertory expands in the Early Dynastic III period. Gypsum shell-shaped lamps now often carry an androcephalic bull.[155] A basalt vase showing a vegetation goddess, incribed by Enmetena,[156] is often assumed to be local work[157] though its unusual iconography and material raise the possibility of a foreign origin. Similar vegetation deities appear on Akkadian glyptic both in Mesopotamia and Iran.[158]

Until the end of the Early Dynastic period, locally produced decorated vessels occur almost exclusively in soft calcium-based stones, with rare exceptions in 'steatite', basalt *etc.* In the Akkadian period these materials began to be supplemented by the hard, dark stones which were now preferred for monumental

---

[145] *E.g.* Amiet 1980a: pl. 225; Woolley 1955: pl. 35 (U.18118); Møller 1984: figs 1-3; Porada 1976: pl. 2c (jar).
[146] Amiet 1980a: pls 29, 224.
[147] *Ibid.*: pls 30, 227, 230; Moortgat 1969: pl. 15-16; Contenau 1931: fig. 445; Porada 1976: pls 1-2b.
[148] Amiet 1980a: pls 27, 231, 236; Møller 1984: fig. 11 (Agrab).
[149] Porada 1976: 2f., pl. 2c.
[150] Thus they are described by Heinrich 1936: 36, 38; but see note 205. Others are not given geological designations.
[151] *E.g.* Heinrich 1936: Taf. 25-28.
[152] Orthmann *et al.* 1975: pl. X.
[153] Frankfort 1935: figs 24, 51; Behm-Blanke 1979: Taf. 25-29 (Diyala sites); Woolley 1955: pl. 31 (U.18524, U.19378, U.20000) (Ur).
[154] *Ibid.*: pl. 31 (U.19426); Møller 1984: fig. 14 (Fara).
[155] Woolley 1934: pl. 182a-b.
[156] Orthmann *et al.* 1975: pl. 87a; *ABWI*: Ent. 33.
[157] Heinz 1989: 207; *cf.* Girsu limestone plaque with the same goddess: Amiet 1980a: pl. 337.
[158] Boehmer 1965: figs 532-3, 536-8 *etc.* (Mesopotamia); Amiet 1986: figs 132-3; Sotheby's 1992: no. 97 (Iran).

Figure 42. Stone vase fragment showing bound prisoner. Uruk. Steatite(?). Ht. 5.8 cm.

sculpture. As in glyptic art, there is also a notable expansion in subject matter. Unfortunately, dating depends on stylistic analysis rather than stratigraphical criteria, since undisturbed Akkadian levels have hardly ever been encountered, and never with objects of this quality. Most examples come from the large mass of broken stone vessels and other temple refuse sealed under the floors of rooms 11 and 12 in the Enunmah at Ur, dated by inscribed bricks of Kudur-Mabuk and Kurigalzu in the associated walls to the second millennium.[159] Among those attributed to the Akkadian period are vessels showing a series of flowing vases (in limestone/marble) and another in which these are held by the *lah(a)mu*-hero with six-locks (in "dark steatite").[160] From Uruk comes a "brown steatite" vessel with vertical tubular lugs showing a bound prisoner led by a rope attached to a nose-ring (Fig. 42).[161] His distinctive hair accurately represents the highland Iranian style, well known from *série ancienne* chlorite vessels.[162] The famous Nasriyeh relief showing a file of

---

[159] Woolley 1955: 51; *idem* 1974: 51.
[160] Woolley 1955: pl. 36 (U.449) (flowing vases); *ibid.*: pl. 35 (U.224) (*lah(a)mu*-hero). For this identification of the curly-haired hero, see Wiggermann 1982 and Lambert 1985.
[161] Amiet 1976a: no. 24.
[162] Amiet 1976a: 25 & n. 77 bis; *cf.* Amiet 1986: fig. 73.

Meopotamian prisoners (Fig. 17) provides a likely indication of the overall character of the scene, probably representing a Mesopotamian victory against a highland state.

In the post-Akkadian and Ur III periods the repertoire of subjects broadens further; the surface of the vessel is now treated as a field for decoration, just like any other relief sculpture. Thus vessels attest many of the same subjects as free-standing reliefs, plaques and stelae: historical 'narratives', aspects of everyday life such as musicians,[163] as well as mythological and cultic scenes.

(b) Decorated vessels from Iran and the Persian Gulf

From Early Dynastic III to the early second millennium decorated vessels of 'steatite' formed part of a widespread network of 'exchange' linking Sumer with highland Iran and the Gulf. Along with the plain calcite types considered above, they are the only sizeable body of material from this traffic that has survived in Mesopotamia and thus provide a unique insight into the scope and mechanisms of Mesopotamian interaction with her eastern neighbours at this time. Deservedly, the steatite series have been the focus of much recent attention, especially by Kohl. As fresh information has continued to accumulate, and some explanations of this phenomenon are open to question, the series are given detailed attention here.

The decorated vessels of foreign origin from Mesopotamia are almost all carved from secondary metamorphic minerals varying in colour from grey-green to almost black, or rarely brown. Being relatively soft, these are easily carved and serve as an excellent medium for complex relief decoration. Usually identified as "steatite" (rarely "bituminous limestone")[164] in early reports, analyses have shown that most of these vessels are in fact chlorite.[165] For convenience this term will be used here but it should be understood as elliptical for chlorite/steatite/serpentine.[166]

In organising the chlorite vessels from Susa Miroschedji divided them into a *série ancienne* and a *série récente*.[167] Although the chronological implications of this terminology must be qualified, Miroschedji's designations are retained here, in preference to Kohl's "Intercultural Style" (= *série ancienne*) which belies the earlier style's distinctively Iranian character. While Miroschedji applied these terms specifically to the vessels from Susa, they may naturally be extended to embrace all examples in the respective styles.[168]

(i) The série ancienne. The *série ancienne* (Figs 43-45) was first encountered in excavations in southern Mesopotamia and Susa, and some scholars originally considered these lowlands its principal production centre.[169] However, the *série ancienne*'s essentially non-Sumerian style and wide distribution as far east as the

---

[163] Moortgat 1969: pl. 200 ("steatite").
[164] Nöldeke *et al.* 1940: 22f., Taf. 35a.
[165] Kohl *et al.* 1979; see however Blackman 1989, demonstrating that the soft-stone used for non-vessels at Tepe Hissar is talc (steatite).
[166] There seems still to be some disagreement as to the correct identification and/or designation of these materials. Kohl *et al.* 1979 seem to assume that all such vessels are either chlorite or steatite. But Amiet (1977: 98; *idem* 1980b: 156) claims that the use of the term "chlorite" for the vessels of Iran and Central Asia is incorrect, that they are in fact serpentine which, however, he says is composed of chlorite crystals. It is presently unclear to what extent this disagreement is substantive and to what extent merely terminological.
[167] Miroschedji 1973.
[168] Kohl's definition of the 'Intercultural Style' rightly excludes the vessels with simple geometric patterns, often on compartmented boxes, found in south-eastern Iran (Kohl 1974: 225; included in the catalogue of Durrani 1964). These seem to date to the later 3rd and early 2nd millennia.
[169] *E.g.* Hall & Woolley 1927: 68f.; Durrani 1964: 96; Frankfort 1954: 19.

*Figure 43.   (1) Série ancienne bowl from Khafajeh(?). Steatite/chlorite. Early Dynastic III. Ht. 10.3 cm.   (2)
Série ancienne double bowl from Susa, Temple of Inšušinak. Steatite/chlorite. Ur III period(?). Wth. 18.3 cm.*

Indus eventually led most scholars to favour an eastern origin, as the Rimuš inscription suggested.[170] This was confirmed in the late 1960s by the discovery of a chlorite production centre at Tepe Yahya in Kerman, where many of the most common types and motifs were represented at various stages of manufacture.[171] Some types at least were also produced at Tarut in the Gulf, where unfinished vessels have been recovered in earth moving operations (Fig. 44:2, 3).[172]

Over six hundred objects of the *série ancienne*, the vast majority vessels (as well as six handled 'weights', five plaques and one sculpture), have been found at sites stretching from Palmyra in the west to Mohenjo-daro in the east and from the Gulf in the south to Fergana in the north.[173]

The grouping of all these widely separated vessels under the heading of a single 'series' (Miroschedji) or 'style' (Kohl) is more an indication of the ignorance which still prevails in all details of regional and chronological variation than a reflection of genuine stylistic homogeneity.[174] Although the simple stylized repetitive motifs show considerable uniformity from the Indus to Syria, the more complex figurative scenes illustrate a variety of subjects and styles which are united only by their general 'un-Sumerianness' and similarity of material.[175] While it may prove possible to separate these into groups on internal evidence, they cannot yet be assigned geographical or chronological limits.[176]

The most common shape is a cylindrical vessel with a straight or slightly concave profile (Figs 43, 44); these range from tall vases ('jars') to bowls. A sub-conical variant has more or less straight sides narrowing towards the top. There are also flaring and round bottom bowls, as well as rare globular jars (only Tarut and Mari), boxes and 'cornets'.[177]

The *série ancienne* motifs are listed by Kohl under twelve headings with fourteen secondary designs: combatant serpents (or snake and feline/eagle; Figs 44:3, 45:1); palm-tree; scorpion; figured motifs (Figs 43:1, 44:2, 45:2); Imdugud;

---

[170] Woolley 1928: 186; *idem* 1935: 96; *idem* 1955: 51; Mackay 1932; Piggott 1950: 117; Mallowan 1971: 254; Porada 1965a: 36f.

[171] Lamberg-Karlovsky 1970: 39-61; *idem* 1973: 311-15; *idem* 1988: 52, pl. I; Kohl 1974; *idem* 1975; *idem* 1978; *idem* 1982.

[172] Zarins 1978: 67, pls 72b:110; 75a:505; Kohl *et al.* 1979: 140.

[173] See site list in Lamberg-Karlovsky 1988: 55-68 and add: (1) 'Hut-pot' sherd (bored for reuse as pendant) from Uruk: Boehmer 1984a: 131, Taf. 5:31. (2) Lamberg-Karlovsky (following Kohl 1974: 685) list only 4 hut-pots, 1 matt-weave and a hut-pot/figured fragment from the Danish excavations on Failaka; more are published by Howard-Carter 1989. From photographs of a selection of 46 of these fragments supplied by Dr. P. Kjærum the following motifs were identified: guilloche (2 sherds), bevelled square (1); combatant serpent (1), 'hut-pot' (7), 'mat-weave' (1), imbricate (4) and whirl (2); there are also 28 figurative pieces, most, if not all, of 2nd-mill. date which, though carved in the same material, are stylistically distinct from the *série ancienne* (many carry purely Mesopotamian motifs). The total number of fragments of figurative vessels including those of the *série ancienne* is well over one hundred. Some fragments are published in Calvet & Salles 1986: figs 25:99, 26:103. (3) Sherd inscribed and reused as brick-stamp of Hammurabi; Hilprecht 1893: no. 27. (4) The sherd listed by Lamberg-Karlovsky as no. 528 (unprov.) is from Kiš. (5) 'Whirl' fragment from Kamtarlan II, level 2; Schmidt *et al.* 1989: pl. 128:F. (6) Handled 'weight', Levy collection; von Bothmer ed. 1990: no. 27. (7) Vessels, Metropolitan Museum of Art, New York, ex Schimmel collection; unpublished. (8) Figured goblet with Sumerian inscription: Amiet 1987: fig. 73. (9) Uruk, fragment reused as pendant; Limper 1988: no. 137. (10) Tarut; D.T. Potts 1989: figs 11-12. (11) Gonur Tepe, Margiana, possible hut-pot frag.; Hiebert & Lamberg-Karlovsky 1992: fig. 3.

[174] *Cf.* Kohl 1974: 144f., where the 'Intercultural Style' is defined formally by the juxtaposition of motifs on the same vessels, and Miroschedji 1973: 21f.

[175] *Cf.* Lamberg-Karlovsky 1988: 55, who argues that the iconography relates to death.

[176] Frankfort's claim (1970: 42) that all figurative decoration had ceased by ED III is not supported by the evidence; see *e.g.* the two vessels inscribed as "booty of Elam" by Rimuš discussed above. Kohl suggests that some unusual figured scenes, *e.g.* the British Museum 'Zebu vase' (Fig. 43:1) and the Rimuš vase from Ur (Fig. 41:3), may be late pieces.

[177] Kohl 1974: 202-9; Lamberg-Karlovsky 1988: 46.

rosette; guilloche (intertwined serpents); 'hut pot', hut/temple facade (door with concave lintel; Fig. 43:2); mat (basket-weave; Figs 43:2, 44:1); imbricate; 'whirl' (hair or fur?); bevelled square (bricks?).[178] It should be emphasised that Kohl's fourth category – figured motifs – is a much broader grouping than the others, encompassing all figurative decoration (except the few recurrent motifs listed separately).

Regarding the distribution of these motifs,[179] the serpent, bevelled square and 'hut pot' are particularly widespread, the latter being the most common motif over all, attested at sixteen sites.[180] However, there is very little evidence for particular patterns of use or distribution in individual motifs. In general, the greatest numbers of motifs are represented at the sites which have produced most pieces; that is to say, there is no clear indication that particular schemes were preferred in particular regions or that sites used only vessels with particular motifs.[181] Kohl justly concludes: "None of the twelve motifs can be considered specific to a geographical region".[182]

Kohl's analysis points to only two possible correlations: the hut and the simple geometrical motifs are more common in Iran than in the Gulf, while the complex figurative scenes and naturalistic pattern designs (scorpions, palm tree *etc.*) are more common in Mesopotamia (especially the Diyala) and the Gulf than in Iran.[183] Kohl was inclined to see this as fortuitous since all these motifs occur at the Tepe Yahya production centre,[184] but it may also reflect differences in the nature of the excavated contexts. In Mesopotamia patterned vessels tend to occur in burials while figurative vessels come principally from temples, of which none has yet been excavated in third-millennium Iran (except possibly the Burned Building at Tepe Hissar III).[185] The Imdugud motif may be attributed in all probability to Sumerian influence, though the question of where the vessels concerned were carved remains open. It is notable that none is reported from Sumer itself. The 'whirl' pattern, one of the commonest motifs, occurs also on an unprovenanced silver vessel, suggesting that some motifs may have been copied from metal prototypes.[186]

Vessels with all the above-listed motifs, except Imdugud and rosettes, are represented in the highland production centre at Tepe Yahya IVB4-1. It is not stated, however, which designs are attested in unfinished form. Sources of chlorite around Tepe Yahya were certainly exploited for this production, though the signs of old working cannot now be dated.[187] Direct evidence of local production is restricted to period IVB,[188] but finds from other periods illustrate its exploitation also for beads, sculpture and many other decorative and utilitarian goods.[189]

Raw chlorite lumps and a vessel with an unfinished guilloche design, as well as many finished vessels, have been recovered from Tarut,[190] which also had access

---

178 Kohl 1974: 145-202, 210f.; *cf.* Lamberg-Karlovsky 1988: 46f.
179 See maps in Kohl 1979: figs 1-2. Note the addenda cited in note 173 above.
180 Kohl 1974: 147, 177, 182.
181 *Ibid.*: 212, 227; Lamberg-Karlovsky 1988: 46-52.
182 Kohl 1974: 227.
183 *Ibid.*: 165, 212f.
184 *Ibid.*: 227.
185 Dyson 1972; Dyson & Remsen 1989: 96f.
186 Sotheby's 1992a: no. 160.
187 Kohl 1974: 104.
188 Lamberg-Karlovsky 1988: 52.
189 Kohl 1974: 24-99.
190 Zarins 1978: pl. 72b:110.

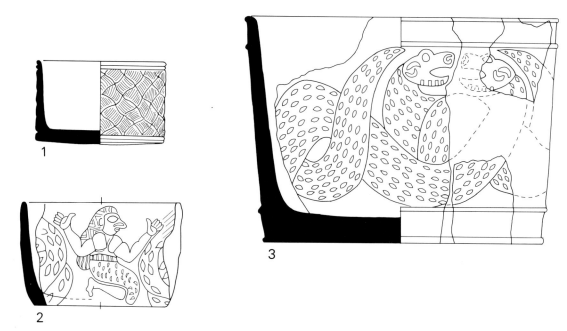

Figure 44. Série ancienne vessels from Susa (1) and Tarut (2, 3). Late third to early second millennium. Not to scale.

to supplies of chlorite/steatite on the Arabian mainland. Here, unlike Tepe Yahya, the lathe was used in production.[191]

X-ray diffraction analyses of the stone types of roughly one-third of the known corpus from Iran, the Gulf and Mesopotamia, along with samples from possible source areas around Tepe Yahya, confirm the stylistic impression that other manufacturing centres existed.[192] To some extent these can be sorted according to the stone types: chlorite vs steatite; and, within chlorites, by their minerological 'fingerprints'. Tepe Yahya used chlorite almost exclusively, but at other sites, especially Tarut, Failaka and Adab, a wider range of materials are present, notably steatite (available both in Iran and in Arabia 150-200 miles south-west of Riyadh) and chlorite schist from a variety of sources. Together these non-chlorite sherds account for almost one-fifth of the tested corpus.[193] Otherwise, Kohl suggests three possible groups which may have drawn on the same production centre(s): a 'Sumerian group' which accounts for most artefacts from Ur, Nippur, Kiš and Khafajeh, as well as fragments from Shahr-i Sokhta, Damin and Bampur;[194] and two Arabian groups, A and B, which together account for most of the material from the Arabian penninsula. On the basis of possible links between material at Tepe Yahya, Susa and Mari, Kohl suggests a connecting trade route by-passing Sumer.[195]

---

[191] *Ibid.*: 67, pl. 72b:501; *cf.* the Khafajeh vessel, Frankfort 1935: fig. 53; Kohl 1974: 244.
[192] Kohl *et al.* 1979.
[193] *Ibid.*: 136.
[194] *Ibid.*: 143ff.; Kohl 1977: 113.
[195] Kohl *et al.* 1979: 147.

The attribution of the vessels found in Mesopotamia to specific sources remains problematical. The stone analyses make clear that various centres, drawing on different sources of stone, were producing almost identical vessels. The stones exploited at Tepe Yahya, themselves quite varied,[196] are not closely matched among finds from Mesopotamia. Sumer evidently relied principally on another source, which is to some extent analytically distinguishable in the tested sample.[197] Kohl conjectures that this source may have been in Persian Makran,[198] but this is highly speculative. While Yahya remains the only confirmed production centre it is not even possible to estimate reliably the approximate area within which the style was manufactured. As noted above, the booty inscriptions of Rimuš on two of the vessels from Sumer raise the possibility that those pieces were brought back from Elam or Parahšum; but the great stylistic variety that characterises the figured scenes in the corpus as a whole precludes any assignment of the uninscribed figured vessels to these or any other particular region(s) of Greater Iran. The Rimuš vessels are themselves very different and may represent widely separated 'schools'. The unprovenanced bowl carries a standard feline-serpent combat scene, while the Ur vessel bears a number of unique motifs (horned demon, ibex, dog) represented in a highly distinctive style. So even if they were taken as booty from Elam or Parahšum it remains possible that either or both vessels originated elsewhere. The discovery of large quantities of *série ancienne* vessels on Tarut and Failaka Islands again highlights the importance of the Gulf as a principal channel of supply into southern Mesopotamia, rather than the overland routes envisaged by Kohl.[199]

(ii) Chronology of the série ancienne.   How these vessels came to Mesopotamia, and what their significance may have been are dependent on the question of dating. Only when the chronological limits of the series are fixed can its presence or absence in the lowlands be assessed in relation to other data on Mesopotamian-Iranian relations. In practice, however, the issue of dating has generally been approached from the other direction, basing the chronology of the *série ancienne* on the Mesopotamian evidence. To make any progress by this method, assumptions must be made which pre-judge crucial issues from the Iranian prespective. This was understandable, and indeed unavoidable, while the bulk of the known corpus, and the only part that could be independently dated, came from Mesopotamia. It was quite naturally also the first line of approach on the material from Tepe Yahya IVB4-1, especially since these levels, unlike IVC, did not yield Mesopotamian objects which could be used to date the local assemblage. It seemed obvious that the date of the workshop at Yahya IVB4-1 should be founded on the dates of its supposed exports to Sumer. In retrospect, however, it is possible to see some pitfalls in this method. Modifications to the high Yahya chronology proffered by the excavator have been suggested by a number of scholars in the past twenty years, the most recent and radical by D.T. Potts.[200]

In 1974 Kohl assembled evidence bearing on the chronology of the *série ancienne*.[201] Of the 113 artefacts in his corpus from Mesopotamia, Kohl identified

---

[196] *Ibid.*: 146.
[197] *Ibid.*: 143ff.
[198] Kohl 1978: 464.
[199] Zarins 1978; Kjærum pers. comm. Kohl (1974: 325; 1978: 464, 467) acknowledges that some vessels travelled along the Gulf, but gives priority to "direct movement of goods between the highland and lowland zones" (1978: 467, fig. 4).
[200] D.T. Potts in press [a].
[201] Kohl 1974: 243-52.

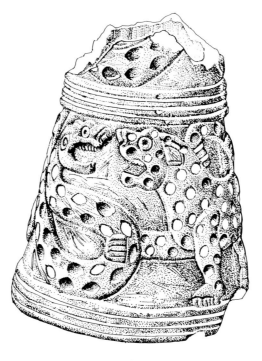

1

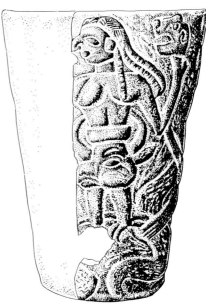

2

Figure 45.   (1) Série ancienne vase from Nippur, Temple of Inanna VIIB. Early Dynastic III. Steatite/chlorite. Ht. 14.2.   (2)   Série ancienne vase with Sumerian dedication inscription, from Iran(?). Early Dynastic III. Steatite/chlorite. Ht. 15.0 cm.

twenty vessels from documented contexts which he took to represent the period of their initial importation from Iran; five from Ur, three from Nippur, two from Khafajeh and ten from Mari. After examining the stratigraphical evidence, Kohl concluded that seventeen of the twenty objects date to the period from Early Dynastic II to IIIa, to which range he therefore restricts the *floruit* of the series as a whole. This stratigraphical evidence is confirmed by a sherd from Adab inscribed by Mesilim, a king of Kiš historically dated to Early Dynastic II or IIIa.[202] To this evidence may now be added a vessel from Iran with an Early Dynastic III Sumerian dedication inscription.[203] Arguing that a uniform style is unlikely to have had a long lifespan, Kohl assigned the production deposits at Tepe Yahya IVB the same range.

That *série ancienne* vessels were reaching Mesopotamia during the Early Dynastic II-IIIa period is certainly correct; most if not all of the contexts Kohl cites clearly fall within that range. But its upper and lower limits are by no means secure.

Kohl rightly warns against the relevance of stylistic parallels between Jemdet Nasr-Early Dynastic I Sumerian art and the *série ancienne* which is an essentially Iranian style.[204] However, one early piece, which seems not to have been noticed, is harder to explain away. This is a fragmentary serpent sculpture in "bituminous limestone" (chlorite?)[205] from a Jemdet Nasr context at Uruk.[206] The serpent is open-mouthed and its body has oval cavities for inlays, exactly as in the 'combatant snake' motif of the *série ancienne*. Although this is a sculpture (perhaps attached to a frieze)[207] rather than a vessel, it demonstrates that one of the standard motifs of the *série ancienne* was in existence, and was being exported (?) to Sumer, already in the late fourth millennium. This at least raises the possibility that the origins of the style reach back further than Early Dynastic II.[208] In this connection, the steatite handled 'weight' from Ur with 'eye' and rosette decoration reminiscent of the Archaic inlaid stone vessels may also be noted.[209]

There is a stronger case for extending the series down beyond Early Dynastic IIIa, a revision which has important consequences for this study. Of the twenty vessels cited by Kohl, ten (*i.e.* half the "well-stratified" pieces) come from temples and associated structures at Mari, where they were found in the heavy destruction level attributed to Lugalzagesi, Sargon or Naram-Sin, *i.e.* the very end of the Early Dynastic IIIb or early Akkadian period.[210] The discovery of a similar destruction level

---

[202] Delougaz 1960: pl. IXa; *ABWI*: Kiš:Mes. 3.

[203] Amiet 1986: fig. 73. Note also the fragmentary ED inscription on a cylindrical vessel with imbricate pattern, Brussels 0.1324: ⌜x (erín?)⌝-mu / [...]-si/u$_5$.

[204] Kohl 1974: 257, 259-62, 266; *cf.* Porada 1971: 329f.

[205] *Série ancienne* vessels are also described as "bituminous limestone" (Nöldeke *et al.* 1939: 20, Taf. 24:1; *idem* 1940: 22f., Taf. 35a).

[206] Lenzen 1961: 24f., Taf. 14a-g.

[207] *Ibid.*: 25.

[208] Note also the ?Early Dynastic Girsu sculpture in chlorite with circular cavities and intertwined serpents (Amiet 1986b: 14, Taf. 4:1).

[209] Durrani 1964: pl. IX. These weights begin at Susa in light-coloured stones in the Susa II (Late Uruk) period (Amiet 1986: figs 13-16).

[210] Parrot 1974: 87; *idem* 1956: 40f.; *idem* 1962: 170f.; Archi 1985a: 49f.; Charpin 1987: 95f. Only Sargon explicitly claims the conquest of Mari, though Lugalzagesi and Naram-Sin both campaigned in the north-west as far as the Mediterranean (Upper Sea), and are thus assumed to have secured this city, which lies on the natural route. A *terminus ante quem* for the destruction of Mari is provided by a group of copper vessels bearing inscriptions of the daughters of Naram-Sin in a post-destruction stratum above the Temple of Dagan in the area of the "maison rouge" (Parrot 1955: 195; *idem* 1974: 90). Like Mari, Ebla was conquered by (or at least submitted to) both Sargon and Naram-Sin, and may also have been taken by Lugalzagesi. Brak, on another road to the north-west, now provides evidence of two close destructions before the Naram-Sin palace (Area CH, phases 7 and 6) which the excavators plausibly attribute to Lugalzagesi and Sargon (J. Oates 1985: 143).

at Ebla, though again not attributable to any one of these conquerors in particular, confirms the scale of devastation which afflicted the north-west at this time.

Moreover, Kohl does not take into account the two *série ancienne* vessels with inscriptions of Rimuš celebrating his conquest of Elam and Parahšum (Table 6.1:C1a, C2a). Although neither was 'stratified' in Akkadian levels,[211] they must once have had such a context.[212]

Kohl also omits from consideration for chronological purposes some equally well 'stratified' vessels from post-Akkadian contexts, assuming from their rarity that they are heirlooms. The possibility that exotic objects like the *série ancienne* vessels, especially those stored in temples, may be heirlooms is indeed very real. But when the total number of securely dated pieces is so small, assumptions on such matters can prejudice the issue rather than resolve it. Indeed, if the destruction at Mari is attributed to Sargon or Naram-Sin, the emphasis of the contexts of discovery changes from Early Dynastic III to the Akkadian period. In this case the Rimuš vases are quite at home, and later occurrences begin to look more plausible. These include a double vessel from the Temple of Inšušinak at Susa which was built by Šulgi (Fig. 43:2),[213] and a vessel from Inanna Temple IV at Nippur, also dating to the Ur III period. A vessel from "the neighborhood of shrine of Bur-Sin [Amar-Suen] on Temple Hill" may also be relevant.[214] Another fragment at Uruk was found below an Ur III structure.[215] Still later, one vessel at Ur was found above Larsa-period housing in area EM and a fragment was reused as a brick inscription stamp of Hammurabi. Above all, numerous *série ancienne* sherds were recovered from Failaka sites F3 and F6, which were founded in the Ur III period and flourished in the Old Babylonian and Kassite periods,[216] indicating continued use well into the second millennium. It may be significant that these later finds are concentrated in the Gulf and nearby settlements.

Further uncertainties arise in applying the Mesopotamian dates to the Iranian production zone in general, and to the debris from the manufacturing centre of Tepe Yahya IVB in particular. The style may have begun in Iran earlier, and continued after, its period of prominence in Mesopotamia. Moreover, 'exchange' of whatever kind between these regions may have been periodically inhibited by political or economic factors at either end of the chain, factors which might now be impossible to detect. With respect to Yahya in particular, it cannot be assumed that production there lasted for the entire period of the style's popularity in Greater Iran as a whole, nor even the heyday of Sumerian 'trade'. The mineralogical analyses of Yahya and Mesopotamian vessels give no particular ground for assuming that Yahya was productive while vessels were reaching Sumer in greatest numbers (ED II-III). Similarly, there is no guarantee that the IVB4-1 levels of production debris represent the only period of *série ancienne* manufacture at Tepe Yahya.[217] The workshop areas

---

[211] Kohl (1974: 247; *idem* 1975: 30; *cf.* previously Miroschedji 1973: 25) erroneously attributes 3 *série ancienne* vessels, including one of the Rimuš vases, to a "Sargonid stratum", following a careless statement of Woolley (1935: 96). As the catalogue entries in Woolley 1955 indicate, however, they came from the surface of the mound (U.7072) and the Enunmah deposit below the Kurigalzu floor (U.231, U.224).

[212] Kohl himself uses the distinctive style of the Rimuš vessel from Ur (Fig. 41:3; U.231) as a basis for dating it slightly after the main series, though not as late as the Akkadian period, and thus to explain its Akkadian inscription (Kohl 1974: 248f.). He also considers the possibility that one Khafajeh vase is a local copy (1974: 268), as does Amiet also for some pieces from Mari (1993: 28).

[213] Amiet 1966a: fig. 149.; Mecquenem 1911: 67f. for construction by Šulgi.

[214] Peters 1897: caption to pl. opp. p. 140; *cf.* Kohl 1974: 151.

[215] *Ibid.*: 194.

[216] Kjærum 1980: 45; Calvet & Salles 1986: figs 25:99, 26:103; Ciarla 1985.

[217] As now conceded by Lamberg-Karlovsky 1988: 52f.

may have moved periodically to accomodate demographic changes in the settlement.[218] Chlorite was used extensively in all periods of Yahya's history, yet the IVB4-1 deposits are the only workshop levels encountered in the limited excavations undertaken. Workshops for other periods must exist elsewhere on the site, but as to the range of their production the domestic deposits excavated so far are at best an incomplete guide. And since virtually no domestic deposits contemporary with the IVB4-1 refuse have been excavated,[219] it is doubly difficult to gauge whether the lack of *série ancienne* fragments in earlier levels, and their paucity later (in IVA),[220] signifies the absence of production during those times.

These doubts, prompted by the archaeological range of finds in Mesopotamia and Failaka, become more acute when combined with suggested lowerings of the high Yahya chronology. As attention has shifted from the *série ancienne* vessels to other aspects of Yahya IVB-A material culture, particularly the glyptic and pottery, the chronology of those periods has been successively down-dated.[221] As a result, it now seems likely that the Mesopotamian exports, though providing an important general point of reference, do not reflect the date of the material from this site in particular.

The glyptic from the pre-chlorite workshop levels includes a stamp seal showing a bull-man whose profile human head is typical of the early Akkadian period (*Akkadisch Ic*);[222] and cylinder seals with seated deities sprouting either horns and wings or vegetation,[223] which also first appear in Mesopotamia in Akkadian times.[224] There is also an early 'Persian Gulf' stamp seal, a type which seems to begin in that region only in the late third millennium.[225]

Amiet explains the Persian Gulf seal as an intrusion[226] but eventually accepts the contexts of the Akkadian-influenced cylinder seals and bull-man as sound, thus

---

[218] *Cf.* the South Hill at Tepe Hissar, where one area of the site was used first for metalworking, then for lapis lazuli working, then as a graveyard, then pottery manufacturing and then again as a graveyard, all within the early 3rd mill. (Tosi & Bulgarelli 1989).

[219] Lamberg-Karlovsky 1978a: 478.

[220] According to Lamberg-Karlovsky (1988: 47) the distribution of finds by levels was as follows: IVB4-2 16.2%, IVB1 52.7%, IVB6 2.7%, IVB5 6.8%, IVA4 6.8%, IVA3 5.4%, IVA2 5.4%, IVA1 4.1%. Thus period IVA as a whole accounted for 21.7% (apparently 27 objects; *ibid.*: 52) of all finds. *Cf.* previously Kohl (1974: 69, 73; Lamberg-Karlovsky 1973: fig. 5:A, B, E, pl. XXXII:a) who states that only 8 sherds were recovered in period IVA and 2 each in periods III/II and I/IA. Kohl explains these as rubbish survival from later building activity or heirlooms. The period III/II and I/IA finds must have been reallocated to period IV, since the total for periods IVB-A is 100%. Note however that the caption to Lamberg-Karlovsky 1988 pl. IVb says "surface [find]" and that the catalogue lists also fragments from IVC (no. 452) and IVC2 (no. 482).

[221] Miroschedji 1973: 23-25; Carter 1984: 205f.; Amiet 1986: 132f.

[222] Lamberg-Karlovsky 1971: fig. 2E; *cf.* Amiet 1976b: 2; Amiet 1986: 133; D.T. Potts in press [a]; Boehmer 1965: nos 94, 99, 101, 102 *etc.*

[223] TY 33 (Lamberg-Karlovsky 1973: pl. XXVI:c [bottom]) from IVB6 and TY 32 (*idem* 1971: fig. 2:A, pl. VI) from IVB5.

[224] D.T. Potts 1981; Miroschedji 1973: 24; Amiet 1974: 106; Amiet 1986: 133; D.T. Potts in press [a]; Boehmer 1965: 66-8, figs 377, 379, 382 (winged astral deities) and 94-97, figs 532-3, 536-8 *etc.* (vegetation deities).

[225] Lamberg-Karlovsky 1971: fig. 2:D; *idem* 1973: pl. XXVIa; *cf.* also pl. XXVIb (double-sided stamp seal with feet and scorpion). Published seals of this type are listed by D.T. Potts 1990: 162f. (add Kjærum 1983: no. 294?). The first (dated) 'Persian Gulf' seals appear in Ur III graves (PG 1847, 401) at Ur (D.T. Potts 1990: 167; *idem* in press [b]) and in level 21 of City II at Qal'at al-Bahrain which is dated by an Isin-Larsa tablet (Brunswig *et al.* 1983: 107f., but see note 235 for an alternative chronology). They continue to level 18, whereafter 'Dilmun'-type seals take over.

[226] Note in this connection a copper disc of Dashli 3 (= Namazga V-VI) type, there dated *ca.* 2000 BC, found at Tepe Yahya IVC (Lamberg-Karlovsky 1984). Since found inside a pot, Lamberg-Karlovsky argues that it cannot be intrusive.

forcing the date of subsequent chlorite production (IVB4-1) into the late Akkadian period at the earliest.

This unhappy compromise relieves rather than resolves the stratigraphical anomalies. A more radical line is taken by D.T. Potts.[227] In a comprehensive review of the chronology of periods IVC and IVB, Potts argues that, leaving aside the *série ancienne* chlorite, everything else in the IVB (and IVC1) assemblage indicates a date in the late third millennium, *ca.* 2200-2000 BC, rather than Kohl's range of 2600-2500 BC.[228]

After period IVC2, securely dated to the Proto-Elamite period, Potts postulates a hiatus of several hundred years until period IVC1, dated by its 'Indo-Baluch' red-on-black ware, black-on-grey ware, snake-cordoned ware, hollow-footed chalices and comb-incised ware, which occur at widespread sites of the late third millennium in Mesopotamia (Khafajeh ED II-III: hollow-footed chalices only), Iran (Sokhta IV, 'proto-imperial' Susa), Pakistan (Mehrgarh VII), the Gulf (Hili 8 period f, Umm an-Nar sites in Oman, Bahrain pre-Barbar, City I and City II), as well as a copper wheel-headed pin with parallels in Bactria. The succeeding period IVB6 has the same pottery types as well as the cylinder seal with winged seated goddess[229] and, most important for dating, the Akkadian-related bull-man stamp seal (TY 36). In the next level, IVB5, along with similar pottery, appears the 'Persian Gulf' stamp seal; a cylinder seal (TY 32) with Akkadian-style winged and now also vegetation deities; *série recente* chlorite vessels (see below); an incised grey-ware sherd,[230] best dated in the 'Burnt Building' of Shahr-i Sokhta IV, *ca.* 2200-1800 BC; a small flat-sided calcite bottle[231] with late third-millennium parallels in chlorite and calcite at Susa, Shahdad, Hissar III and in Bactria;[232] and a shaft-hole axe of a type dated to the late third and early second millennia.[233]

All these finds come before period IVB4-1 in which the *série ancienne* production debris occurs. These levels also produced similar pottery and two chlorite stamp seals (TY 40 and unnumbered) with parallels in Margiana and Bactria[234] which Potts places again in the centuries around 2000 BC. He argues that the assemblage from IVC1 through IVB1 is largely uniform and thus can adequately be accommodated in the two or so centuries he assigns to it.

Noting the discrepancy between this scheme and the previous chronology Potts summarises the dilemma:

> If the sub-phases IVB4-1 ... [are] dated to ED II-IIIa, then IVC1, IVB6, and IVB5, which precede them stratigraphically, must be earlier, and hence fit in between IVC2 of Jamdat Nasr and ED I date, and IVB4-1 of ED II-IIIa date. But it was a study of precisely this point in the sequence which first indicated that the dating of the later IVB sub-phases was wrong, for here, in strata earlier than those belonging to the supposed ED II-IIIa horizon, were a whole host of artifacts of late third millennium date occurring before the Intercultural Style chlorite. This included such obviously late pieces as the Persian Gulf-related seal, the pin with Bactrian parallels, a *série récente*

---

[227] D.T. Potts in press [a].
[228] Kohl 1979: 62.
[229] TY 33. Dyson & Harris 1986: 104 list this as level "IVC1/IVB6".
[230] Lamberg-Karlovsky & Tosi 1973: 43, figs 147-50.
[231] D.T. Potts in press [a].
[232] Amiet 1980b: pl. II:a, c (Bactria), b, d (Susa); Schmidt 1937: pl. LX:H.3498; Hakemi 1972: pl. IXD.
[233] D.T. Potts in press [a]: fig. II:m; *cf.* Deshayes 1960: 79f.
[234] Sarianidi 1981: fig. 3.

chlorite bowl, an alabaster jar [*i.e.* square-based bottle] with many parallels in late third and early second millennium contexts, a stamp seal with a strongly Akkadian bull-man, a piece of incised grey-ware, and many pottery types, among which we have often mentioned the black-on-red/orange ware so identical to a type known in phase F at Hili 8 around 2200 BC. In Mesopotamian terms, therefore, artifacts of Akkadian and Ur III date were found in strata which must be earlier than those with the carved chlorite of assumed ED II-IIIa date.

After rejecting the possibility of some stratigraphical anomaly (*e.g.* that the 'Persian Gulf room' was cut down into earlier levels, or, as Amiet argues, that the seals have fallen down from above) Potts takes the only other course:

> The conclusion I have drawn, therefore, is that the technique of carving chlorite in the Intercultural Style can only have begun at Tepe Yahya in the late third millennium, probably in the Akkadian period, and lasted into the Ur III period, ending around 2000 BC.

As has been shown above, this is not inconsistent with evidence from Sumer, where the *série ancienne* still occurs in the Akkadian and Ur III periods. Regarding Yahya IVB in particular, Potts' chronology depends ultimately on the dating of his comparanda, which come mostly from the Gulf, south-central and eastern Iran, and Central Asia. While the chronology of these regions is hardly more secure than that of Yahya itself, and no case based solely on them could be considered sound,[235] this cannot be said of the parallels with Akkadian glyptic, which is well fixed, at least in the terms of the Mesopotamian sequence. The bull-man in particular is convincingly Akkadian and can hardly be interpreted as the product of an earlier, indigenous Iranian iconography.[236] At present, it is on the basis of these parallels that Potts' chronology is to be preferred.

The down-dating of the *série ancienne* at Tepe Yahya throws new light on the rare presence of the *série récente* at that site.[237] The most typical forms present in period IVB are square-based bottles, both plain and with dotted-circle decoration, hemispherical bowls with wavey lines below the rim (well attested in the Bampur V-VI horizon) and a compartmented box.[238] Other classic *série récente* types – including

---

[235] The absolute chronologies of all these regions, and their relative positions against Mesopotamia, remain very insecure. Recent debate continues to range between options many centuries apart. D.T. Potts (in press [b]) argues consistently for a low chronology of the Gulf regions, including the Umm an-Nar horizon. A pivotal fixed point in his dating of the Bahrain sequence is the Isin-Larsa tablet from basal City II, level 21 (see note 225), along with the first 'Persian Gulf' seal. Højlund (1986), however, defends a higher chronology on the basis of ceramic parallels with Failaka, assuming that the tablet was out of context.

[236] Winged and vegetation deities appear also at Shahdad and on other unprovenanced Iranian seals (Amiet 1986: figs. 132-137) which could perhaps be seen as expressing an indigenous highland iconography which was absorbed into the Mesopotamian repertory during the Akkadian period.

[237] Lamberg-Karlovsky 1988: 52, figs 3:H-L, 4:Z-DD.

[238] Square-based bottles – Lamberg-Karlovsky 1970: fig. 21:R, pl. 24:E, F; Kohl 1979: 72; *idem* 1982: 27. Hemispherical bowls (this is presumably what D.T. Potts (in press [a]) refers to as "a *série récente* chlorite bowl") – Lamberg-Karlovsky 1970: fig. 23:T, pls 23:E, 24:A; *idem* 1988: figs 3:H (now redated IVA), 4:BB (IVB6); others previously unpublished and dated by Lamberg-Karlovsky to IVA are *ibid.*: figs 3:L, 4:Z; D.T. Potts in press [a]: fig. IIk; Kohl 1974: 220f.; *cf.* parallels cited by Kohl 1974: 220f., D.T. Potts in press [a]: 215f. and Miroschedji 1973: 28. Compartmented box – Miroschedji 1973: 30, n. 134. See also the open-work 'hut-door' miniature vessel base (Lamberg-Karlovsky 1973: fig. 5:H; *idem* 1988: pl. 5 bottom, fig. 2:H; *cf.* Hakemi 1972: pl. XV; Miroschedji 1973: 33-35, fig. 12). Miroschedji includes this in the *série*

dotted circle bowls – appear in period IVA, assigned by Potts to the early second millennium.[239] In his most recent discussion, Lamberg-Karlovsky states that all of the *série récente* (including the wavey-line bowls) dates to period IVA,[240] though some of these pieces at least were previously assigned by him and others to IVB,[241] as does still his catalogue for two bowls with wavey-line decoration.[242]

These occurrences, anomalous on the Kohl/Lamberg-Karlovsky chronology, become entirely plausible on Potts' lower dating which makes the production of the *série ancienne* and *série récente* overlap for the last two centuries of the millennium. This then raises the question: If the *série ancienne* was still being produced, why does it become so much less common in Mesopotamia in the later years of the millennium? We shall return to this after considering the *série récente*.

(iii) The série récente.   The *série récente*, as defined stylistically by Miroschedji from the Susa corpus, has little in common with the earlier group except material, and even this is now typically a grey stone rather than the green or black of the *série ancienne*.[243] Low-relief decoration covering the entire surface gives way to much simpler geometric (very rarely naturalistic) motifs arranged in zones, principally dotted circles and parallel lines, executed by linear incision (Figs 46). The cylindrical vessels which account for most of the *série ancienne* production continue, but are now far outnumbered by a different repertory of forms, notably hemispherical bowls and various boxes. These typological differences are matched by a chronological discrepancy, at least as regards Mesopotamia, where the dated examples of this series cluster in the Ur III period and after.

Unlike the *série ancienne*, typological groups within the *série récente* have divergent patterns of distribution which suggest the general location of their respective centres of production. Miroschedji distinguished four principal groups which may still serve as a useful typological starting point:

A) Incised decoration:
    1. Geometric motifs: hatched triangles, chevrons, single dotted circles. Attested on square boxes with lids, jars, cylindrical vessels and small square-based bottles.
    2. Naturalistic decoration.
    3. Wavy line(s) below rim of hemispherical bowls.
B) Incised cross-hatched triangles on compartmented boxes and cylindrical vessels.
C) Double dotted circle decoration on hemispherical bowls and compartmented boxes, all in light grey 'steatite' (Fig. 46).
D) Undecorated vessels of light and dark 'steatite'.[244]

---

récente, though on what grounds is unclear. Note also the cover of a square box cited *ibid.*: 31, n. 140; Lamberg-Karlovsky 1971: fig. 3:S.
[239] Dotted circle, sub-hemispherical bowls (Lamberg-Karlovsky 1988: fig. 4:CC, DD); cylindrical vessel with rows of nested chevrons (*ibid.*: fig. 3:I), a late type characteristic of Baluchistan (Kohl 1974: 81f., 225f.).
[240] Lamberg-Karlovsky 1988: 52.
[241] *Ibid.*: no. 489, fig. 3:H (wavey-line bowl), there dated IVA$_4$ = *idem* 1970: fig. 23:I, pl. 24:A, there dated IVB.
[242] *Ibid.*: 68 no. 399, fig. 4:BB (IVB$_6$); no. 478 (IVB$_{4-2}$) = *idem* 1970: fig. 23:T, pl. 23:E.
[243] Amiet 1986: 146. Some simple geometric motifs appear in both groups: hatched triangles and wavey lines. The dotted circle, *leitmotiv* of the *série récente*, though not found on the *série ancienne* itself, is attested on vessels of ED III-Akk. date found in direct association with them at Mari (Parrot 1956: pl. XLIX).
[244] Miroschedji 1973: 36ff.

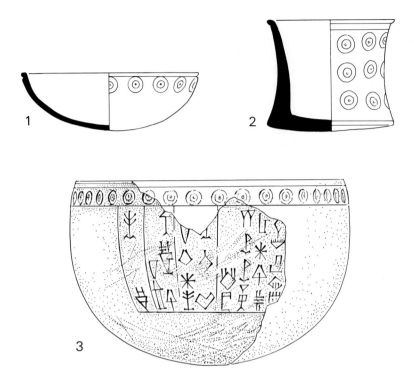

Figure 46. Série récente vessels. (1) and (2) from Susa. Late third to early second millennium. Not to scale. (3) from Girsu, bearing dedication inscription of Ur-Baba, son of the merchant Šeš-Šeš. Reign of Amar-Suen(?). Diam. 16.2 cm. All chlorite/steatite.

Miroschedji showed that group A is concentrated in southern Iran, with A 3 particularly common in the east (Baluchistan), while B is restricted to Baluchistan and C to the Persian Gulf.

Further excavation in Oman in the past twenty years has confirmed the assignment of group C to the southern coast of the Gulf and a later phase of this series (the so-called *séries intermédiaire* and *tardive*), virtually unattested at Susa, has been recognised in Oman, taking production into the early second millennium.[245] On the other hand, clandestine excavations in Bactria have extended the distribution of group A into Central Asia,[246] which may represent a fourth major production centre. Miroschedji's group A 1 is far the largest and least homogenous, and certainly includes material from different regions.

However, since evidence of local manufacturing has been found at only two sites (Tepe Yahya and Maysar 1), the identification of production centres must still proceed principally on the distributions of known examples of each type. Some of these have no strong concentration in a particular region and thus cannot confidently be assigned to any group. This applies, for example, to the square-based bottles of Iran and Bactria (Fig. 47:2), miniature vessels on sculptured 'hut' bases (Fig. 47:1) and the lidded vessels with hatched triangles (perhaps from Baluchistan,

---

[245] Vogt 1985a: 31f. (group C); Cleuziou 1978-79: 40f., 68f.; *idem* 1981: 287, figs 9, 10; Kroll in Weisgerber 1981: 212-214, Abb. 46-47; Häser 1990; D.T. Potts 1990: 249-52 (*séries intermédiaire* and *tardive*).

[246] Pottier 1984: figs 30-31, 42, pl. XX; Sarianidi 1986: 156 right.

like the round unlidded vessels and compartmented boxes). The discoveries in Bactria illustrate the dangers of applying this procedure uncritically, even with well-attested types, while so much of Greater Iran remains effectively unexplored. Many other production centres no doubt remain to be discovered.

With these reservations in mind the following groups may be tentatively distinguished.

(1)   *The Gulf group* (including Miroschedji's group C). This may be divided into earier (*récente*) and later (*intermédiaire-tardive*) sub-phases on the basis of tomb groups and the stratigraphical typology established at Hili 8 (periods IIf, h [early] and III [late]), Hili 3 (early) and Maysar 1 (early) and 9 (late). However, it remains to be proven that these changes occurred simultaneously throughout Oman; they may reflect developments peculiar to some sites only. On the basis of five C[14] readings from Hili 8, periods IIf and h, and four from Maysar 1,[247] the division between the sub-phases is placed at about 2000 BC.[248]

The *série récente* corpus has grown substantially in recent years. While in 1979 Frifelt estimated a total of only "fifty odd pieces from Umm an-Nar island and Hili in Buraimi plus an additional dozen or so from other Umm an-Nar places in Oman"[249] now some hundreds of vessels are known. At Hili North tomb A alone Vogt reports "more than 80 chlorite objects".[250]

The early Gulf group is characterised by double dotted circle decoration, often set around the rim of a vessel below a horizontal line or between a set of parallel lines; more rarely horizontal lines cover the whole vessel. Characteristic shapes are (sub-)hemispherical bowls[251] and 'goblets', with or without a groove for a lid with knob handle, and compartmented rectangular boxes, sometimes with lids. All of these types are attested at the production site of Maysar 1[252] and elsewhere in Oman[253] as well as the islands of the Gulf,[254] Iran[255] and Baluchistan[256] as far east as the Indus[257] and west to Sumer.[258]

---

[247] Cleuziou 1978-79: 68; *idem* 1980: 32. (Hili); Weisgerber 1981: 251 (Maysar).
[248] Kroll in Weisgerber 1981: 212; Cleuzieu 1978-79: 35.
[249] Frifelt 1979: 49.
[250] Vogt 1985a: 31f., pl. 27:10-24.
[251] Known from Umm an-Nar tombs in Oman (including Hili North Tomb A), Hili 8 (IIf), Tarut, Bahrain, Failaka, Ur, Girsu (Fig. 46:3), Susa (Fig. 46:1), Tepe Yahya and Mohenjo Daro (Vogt 1985a: 31f.).
[252] Weisgerber 1980: 83, Abb. 39, 40; *idem* 1981: 212f., Abb. 46. Vogt 1985a: 32 reports that the sub-hemispherical bowls from Maysar are less well executed than at Hili, suggesting a different source.
[253] Amlah 1 and 2a – de Cardi *et al.* 1976: 139f., fig. 23; Bat - Frifelt 1975a: fig. 28e; Bilad al-Maaidin – Weisgerber 1981: 211, Abb. 43:1, 3; ed-Dur – Boucharlat *et al.* 1988: fig. 2:2; Hili 1 – Frifelt 1970: 370, fig. 3a; *idem* 1975a: fig. 17d; *idem* 1979a: fig. 23; Hili 8, period IIf – Cleuziou 1978-79: fig. 41:1, 2; Hili north, Tomb A – Cleuziou & Vogt 1983: fig. 10; Vogt 1985a: pl. 27:10-24; Samad – de Cardi *et al.* 1976: 156; Cleuziou 1978-79: 41; Tawi Silaim – de Cardi *et al.* 1977: 23, fig. 4; Umm an-Nar – Frifelt 1970: 375; Vogt 1985a: 31f.
[254] Failaka – Govt. of Kuwait n.d.; Vogt 1985a: 31f.; Tarut – Zarins 1978: pl. 71:37, 104, 107, 331, 332, 384, 365, 547, 551, 565, 586; Burkholder 1984; D.T. Potts 1989: fig. 18. Bahrain – Bibby 1972: 183; Ratnagar 1981: 118 (unpubl).
[255] Susa – Miroschedji 1973; Bushire – Pézard 1914: pl. VIII:4, 5; Shahdad – Hakemi 1972: pls IX:D, X:A, XI:D, XIV, XV:A-C; Tepe Yahya – Lamberg-Karlovsky 1970: pl. 24:A, E, F; figs 21:R, 23:J; *idem* 1973: fig. 5:D, F, H; *idem* 1988: 52, Figs 3:H-L, 4:Z-DD; D.T. Potts in press [a]: fig. IIk
[256] Ratnagar 1981: 118 cites Bampur, Khurab, Katukan, Mehi, Dasht Valley, Shahi Tump; however, not all of this material belongs to the Gulf Group.
[257] Mohenjo-daro – Marshall 1931: 369, pl. CXXXI:36, 37; Cleuziou & Tosi 1989: fig. 12.
[258] Ur – Woolley 1934: pl. 245:52, 53; *idem* 1974: pl. 49:1; Woolley & Mallowan 1976: pl. 100:1; Miroschedji 1973: 30 n. 132; Girsu – Heuzey & Sarzec 1884-1912: pl. 44bis: 3, 5; Genouillac 1936: 115 (TG 2437, 3676), 117 (TG 514); Amiet 1986: fig. 88; Uruk – Ratnagar 1981: 119 (W.19817G); Larsa (late ?) – Huot *et al.* 1983: fig. 36b; Abu Hatab (Kisurra) – Heinrich & Andrae 1931: pl. 173:1

The late Gulf group or *séries intermédiaire* and *tardive* is characterised by conical (rarely globular) four-lugged suspension vessels with multiple zones of dotted circles (now usually single rather than double), and sets of horizontal and alternate oblique lines.[259] Round lids with a knob handle and dotted circles continue from the early group. Dotted circle bowls[260] now tend to have hatching around the rim and may have an open spout.[261] Most come from Wadi Suq period burials.

The *séries intermédiaire* and *tardive* have been found in large quantities all over the Oman peninsula[262] and Gulf islands,[263] less commonly on mainland Arabia,[264] Iran[265] and in Sumer.[266]

The overwhelming predominance of the late Gulf group in Oman leaves little doubt as to its place of origin. "Four-lugged vessels of the conical type are so numerous and ... so much restricted to the Oman peninsula that I think it is reasonable to consider them as local production".[267] Cleuziou plausibly regards the few similar pieces from Bahrain and Bushire as imports.

The Gulf group is typically made from light grey chlorite which is widely available in the Hajjar mountains. Recent mineralogical sampling of a range of twenty *série récente* and *tardive* vessels and twenty-one chlorite sites in Oman confirmed the assumption of local exploitation and found evidence of ancient (undated) mining at a site near Yanqul.[268]

(2)   *The Baluchistan or "Kulli" group* is characterised by decoration in rows of hatched or cross-hatched triangles, and nested chevrons, often on cylindrical compartmented boxes and quasi-cylindrical concave-profile vessels. This decoration is closely related to the contemporary grey-incised ware which has a similar distribution in south-east Iran and Oman.[269] Unfinished stone vessels are reported from Mehi.[270]

(3)   *The Iranian group.* Under this heading is grouped a wide range of material which probably derives from Greater Iran, though from which province(s) is unclear. Southern Iran probably accounts for a considerable part of the corpus but since so many of the types attested there were exchanged over much of Greater Iran and Bactria it is very difficult to relate types to particular sub-regions. On the basis of their popularity at Shahdad (to which may be added Tepe Yahya),[271] Amiet attributes

[259] Amiet 1986: 147; Cleuziou 1978-79: 40f., fig. 41; *idem* 1981: 290; *idem* 1986: 155, n. 6.; D.T. Potts 1990: 249-52.
[260] Weisgerber 1981: Abb. 47:2.
[261] Zarins 1978: pl. 71:246; Frifelt 1975a: fig. 24:d; Cleuziou 1981: 287.
[262] Bat – Frifelt 1976: fig. 5 (top row, left); *idem* 1975a: fig. 28f.; Hafit, cairn 4 – Frifelt 1970: fig. 14; Hili 3, Hili 8, period III – Cleuziou 1978-79: fig. 41:5, 6; *idem* 1981: fig. 9:1; Maysar 9 – Weisgerber 1981: 214, Abb. 47); Masirah – Vogt 1985: 238; Qattarah – Cleuziou 1978-79: 44 (bottom); *idem* 1981: 287, fig. 10:4, 5; Qusais – Cleuziou 1978-79: 40; Shimal – de Cardi 1971: fig. 52; Cleuziou 1981: fig. 10:1; Donaldson 1984: fig. 11:4; Wadi Sunaysl grave 1112 – Frifelt 1975a: fig. 25b; Wadi Suq graves 1122, 1123, 1126 – Frifelt 1975a: figs 24a-c, 72, 73.
[263] Tarut – Zarins 1978: pl. 71:40, 75b, 129, 136, 246, 252, 300, 550, 594; Failaka – Frifelt 1975a: 380; Ciarla 1985: figs 1-2; D.T. Potts in press [b]; Kjærum pers. comm.; Bahrain – Ratnagar 1981: 118 (520SP; unpubl.); Mughal 1983.
[264] Farid el-Aqrash – Cleuziou 1981: 287.
[265] Susa? – Miroschedji 1973: fig. 11:8; Bushire – Pézard 1914: pl. VIII:2; Shahdad – Hakemi 1972: pl. IX:C, XI:B.
[266] Ur – Woolley & Mallowan 1976: 224 (U.6651), pl. 100:6 ("diorite"); Ubaid (intrusive?) – Hall & Woolley 1927: pl. LXII:XXXV; Uruk? – Ratnagar 1981: 118f, "3 examples, one with lug; unpubl."
[267] Cleuziou 1981: 290.
[268] David *et al.* 1990.
[269] Miroschedji 1973: 29f.
[270] Piggott 1950: 112; During-Caspers in de Cardi 1970: 320.
[271] Lamberg-Karlovsky 1988: pl. V bottom.

to Kerman the small square-based bottles and miniature vessels on a house-shaped support (*cf.* Fig. 47:1, 2).[272] The square box lids (sometimes with zoomorphic handles), four-compartmented boxes and hemispherical bowls with undulating lines below the rim may also belong here.[273] A feature peculiar to the Iranian (and Bactrian?) group(s) is the occasional appearance of naturalistic motifs in a simple linear style very different from the *série ancienne*, on bottles and cylindrical bowls (Fig. 47:3).[274] Amiet suggests that the chlorite vessels of Kerman may be the vessels of Marhaši mentioned in late third and second millennium texts.[275]

(4)   In the *Bactrian group* may be placed heart- and crescent-shaped boxes which are presently attested only in this region.[276] It is unclear how many other types attested there and across Iran to Susa, such as small square-based bottles and square compartmented boxes *etc.*, are indiginous to Central Asia.[277] Motifs attested include standard dotted circles and (cross-)hatched triangles.[278] Serpents are particularly prominent among naturalistic themes (Fig. 47:3).[279] A winged deity, trees, guilloche, 'whirl', hearts and Akkadian-type mountains also occur.[280] It is uncertain how far these novelties reflect features of a local school or simply the result of the greater size of the Bactrian corpus.

These groupings allow some tentative observations on the likely patterns of exchange. The 'Baluchistan' group moved east to Mohenjo-daro and west to Shahdad, Tepe Yahya and Susa,[281] but it is not found south of the Gulf, in Bactria or in Sumer. A large number of types attested from Bactria through Shahdad to Susa testify to a wide-ranging exchange network extending across the Iranian plateau from Susa to Bactria. Its influence was felt also at Tepe Hissar, Shahr-i Sokhta and Tepe Yahya where copies and adaptations were made in local calcite.[282] But while the parameters of this trade are now reasonably clear, its source(s) and direction remain poorly defined. The scale of redistribution itself hinders the definition of regional styles, without which the pattern of trade cannot be traced. What may be remarked, however, is that the general extent of distribution is very similar to that of late third to second millennium metalwork, especially the elaborate weapons and ceremonial objects (above pp. 169ff.). And as in that case, many stone vessels probably originated in Bactria. They do not generally penetrate beyond Susa into Sumer, and only exceptionally south of the Gulf.[283]

---

[272] Amiet 1986: 147, 167.

[273] A piece from Maysar 9 (Weisgerber 1981: Abb. 57:4) may be related to this type.

[274] In addition to Miroschedji's group A 2 note the cylindrical bowl with incised animals from Shahdad (Hakemi 1972: no. 166, col. pl.).

[275] Amiet 1986: 147; *cf.* Steinkeller 1982: 251 for bowls of *marhašu*-stone, whose name probably derives from 'Marhaši'.

[276] Pottier 1984: nos 306-310; Ligabue & Salvatori n.d.: pls 84-85.

[277] *Ibid.*: nos 131-153; *cf.* Amiet 1980b: 155-66 (square-based bottles); Pottier 1984: nos 226, 311 (compartmented boxes).

[278] *Ibid.*: no. 147 (dotted circles), figs 18-19 (hatched triangles).

[279] *Ibid.*: nos 149, 225, 231, 312.

[280] *Ibid.*: nos 150, 145, 308, fig. 42., nos 225, 306.

[281] Marshall 1931: pl. CXXXI:36, 37; Hakemi 1972: pls XI:C; *idem* & Sajjidi n.d.: figs 5-6; Lamberg-Karlovsky 1973: fig. 5:D; Miroschedji 1973: figs 8:1, 9:1, pl. VII:d, f, g.

[282] Tepe Hissar – Schmidt 1937: pl. LX (left), figs 128, 130; Shahr-i Sokhta – Tosi 1968: fig. 93; *idem* 1969: figs 234-5 (bottles); Mari – Parrot 1956: pl. LII:635; Tepe Yahya – D.T. Potts in press [a]: 215f., fig. II:1 (square-based bottle).

[283] A distinctive bottle with dotted circles occurs at Tarut (Golding 1984: pl. 25; *cf.* Pottier 1984: no. 152) and a square-based miniature bottle with incised dotted circle of Bactrian type at Hili North Tomb A (Vogt 1985a: 32, pl. 28:11).

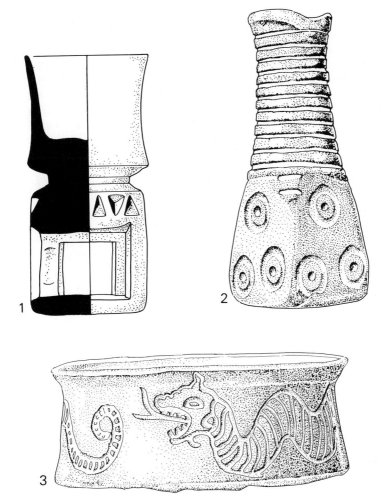

Figure 47.   Chlorite/steatite vessels from Susa (1) and Bactria (2, 3). Late third to early second millennium. Not to scale.

That region is dominated rather by the Gulf group centred on the Oman peninsula where such vessels were produced at Maysar 1, and are a recurrent feature of late third-second millennium burials. During the early phase (and to a lesser degree in the late phase) these vessels were also sent west along the islands of the Gulf to Sumer and Susa, representing a second corridor of exchange. This movement was clearly sea-borne, occurrences beyond Oman being restricted principally to the coastal sites, all (except Bushire) on the southern shore. Two Gulf-style globular suspension vessels from Shahdad[284] represent the only overlap with the Iranian land-based exchange network other than Susa. This latter city alone among excavated sites enjoyed regular access to both networks.

---

[284] Hakemi 1972: pls IXC, XIB. These may belong to the late phase; *cf.* Cleuziou 1978-79: 41; *idem* 1981: 290.

Vessels of the *série récente* have been found in Sumer at Ur, Ubaid, Girsu, Uruk, Larsa and Abu Hatab (Kisurra). Most are typical products of the early Gulf group: hemispherical bowls[285] with a row of dotted double circles below the rim, and round, knob-handled lids with dotted circles,[286] both of which continue into the later repertoire. The fragmentary Naram-Sin booty vessel from Ur also belongs to this group.[287] It is a 'goblet' of which examples with similar decoration (usually with slightly inward-leaning sides) are attested in Oman, Tarut and Susa.[288] The inscription carved on the base – "⌈Naram-Sin⌉ [ki]ng of the fo[ur] quar[ters], bo[wl] [from the booty of Magan]"[289] – provides both the earliest reliable date for this series[290] and confirmation that it comes from Magan (Oman).

Bowls from Ur and Ubaid which differ from the usual hemispherical shape in having also spouts[291] are paralleled in the late phase[292] and may reflect influence from Iran where this form has a long history. There are no close parallels for two bowls from Ur: one with dotted circles and an undulating line, and another with a disc (?) base and carinated everted rim above a row of dotted circles.[293] Rectangular bi-compartmented boxes with a groove for a lid[294] (undecorated versions of Miroschedji's group B) are not a Gulf type (where boxes typically have dotted circles and often no lid) and may derive from Kerman or Baluchistan (or Bactria?).

There is relatively little of the late Gulf group in Sumer. Ratnagar reports some unpublished sherds from Uruk which she describes as having "convex sides, ... incised circle or line motifs in registers", one with lugs. This sounds like a suspension vessel. The round lids cited above may also belong in this later range.[295] Likewise at Susa the only possible late phase piece is a single sherd which may be the lug from a suspension vessel.

The earliest datable vases of the *série récente* in Sumer appear in the Akkadian period. Two dotted circle bowls[296] of Miroschedji's group C,[297] come from Middle Akkadian graves at Ur[298] while an incised sherd from Susa has Akkadian-

---

285 Ur – Woolley 1934: pl. 245:52, 53; Woolley & Mallowan 1976: 234 (U.15470), pl. 100:1. Girsu – Heuzey & Sarzec 1884-1912: pl. 44 bis:5; Amiet 1986: fig. 88; Genouillac 1936: 115 (TG 2437, 3676), 117 (TG 514, "green marble"). Larsa – Huot *et al.* 1983: 209, fig. 36b. Uruk – Ratnagar 1981: 119 (W.19817G; unpubl.).

286 Ur – Woolley 1974: 89 (U.405), pl. 49:1. Girsu – Genouillac 1936: 117 (TG 3676B; "Marble"). Abu Hatab – Heinrich & Andrae 1931: pl. 173:1.

287 T.F. Potts 1989: fig. 10, above p. 236.

288 D.T. Potts 1991: figs 25-26; Boucharlat *et al.* 1988: fig. 2:3; Vogt 1985a: pl. 27:19, 22 (Oman); Zarins 1978: pl. 71: 107, 331, 547, 551; for shape (undecorated) pl. 64: 21, 73, 75, 78 (Tarut); Miroschedji 1973: fig. 8:10 (concave profile).

289 Although the GN is missing it may be confidently restored as Magan, since this is the only place that appears in this context in Naram-Sin's other inscriptions (Table 6.3:Inscr. A).

290 *Cf.* Frifelt 1991: 105 who still begins the *série récente* in Ur III.

291 Above note 266.

292 Zarins 1978: pl. 71: 246.

293 Woolley 1934: pl. 176, bottom row, 2nd from right, unnumbered; Woolley & Mallowan 1976: 225 (U.6839), pl. 100:2.

294 Ur – Miroschedji 1973: 30, n. 132 (unpubl.). Girsu – Heuzey & Sarzec 1884-1912: pl. 44 bis:3; also possibly Genouillac 1936: 116 (TG 2437, "marble").

295 *Cf.* Cleuziou 1981: fig. 10:4, 5.

296 U.9020 from PG 473 (Woolley 1934: 541 ["basic diorite"]; pl. 245:53 [= Basmachi 1950: pl. 5:11]); U.10547 from PG 899 (Woolley 1934: 559 ["grey steatite"], pl. 245:52, incorrectly drawn as having single dotted circles [= Basmachi 1950: pl. 5:12]; note that the tomb catalogue [Woolley 1934: 499] incorrectly describes this vessel as type RC 54).

297 Thus Miroschedji 1973: 27, including them among bowls with double dotted circles. However, as the photographs in Basmachi 1950: pl. 5:11, 12 show, U.9020 has single dotted circles, which would connect it rather with Miroschedji's group A 1, though none of these are bowls.

298 For the Middle Akkadian date of these graves see Nissen 1966: 170, 177. PG 899 contained no other grave goods. PG 473 yielded also an Early Akkadian seal (Woolley 1934: pl 204, no. 154 = Boehmer 1965:

style trees.[299] This early starting date is confirmed by the Naram-Sin 'goblet' fragment from Ur discussed above. Previously the earliest datable inscribed vessel was a dotted-circle bowl from Girsu dedicated by Ur-Baba.[300] Three other vessels also carry Ur III inscriptions.[301] The origin of the style in the Gulf must be somewhat earlier than its Akkadian starting date in Sumer, but by how much is presently a matter of speculation.[302]

Vessels of the *série récente* continue to appear in Sumer in Ur III, Isin-Larsa and Old Babylonian contexts. Indeed these periods account for most of the known examples.[303] At Susa square-based bottles are said to occur in Ur III contexts.[304] In Bahrain vessels appear from level 26 of City I, now dated to the Ur III period.[305] A late phase vessel comes from a City II grave.[306] At Shahdad 'steatite' vessels are said to end before the late burials containing a Linear Elamite inscription and Elamite-related (?) potters' marks.[307]

6. MECHANISMS OF EXCHANGE: TRADE VS BOOTY

The question of how the foreign vessels discussed above arrived in Mesopotamia is unlikely to be answerable in terms of any single exchange mechanism. Each group and period must be assessed separately and conclusions regarding one corpus should not be applied uncritically to another. For a start, the data are very uneven. For most types and periods there is no documentary evidence and speculation must proceed largely on the basis of archaeological distributions and contexts. The booty inscriptions that do exist provide a uniquely direct guide to how

---

no. 358 [Akkadisch Ib/c]) and a jar of type RC 67 which Pollock (1985: 138) assigns to her phase II (= ED IIIb) of the Royal Cemetery. This evidence must take precedence over the absolute dates assigned to the typology of the *série récente* in Oman on the basis of C^{14} readings (see above) which would yield lower dates for at least one of these vessels. U.10547, with a row of dotted double circles between parallel lines, conforms to the standard pattern of the "early phase" (*cf.* Weisgerber 1981: Abb. 43:3, 46:5, 6, 9, 12) except for its slightly flaring profile. However U.9020 is a "late"-type bowl with deep grooves above a row of dotted circles (*cf.* Zarins 1978: pl. 71:129, 300; Weisgerber 1981: Abb. 47:2). The last-cited example from grave 80 at Maysar 9 also shares with the Ur vessel single rather than double dotted circles. The other examples of single dotted circle vessels are also assigned to the late phase (Zarins 1978: pl. 71:136, 246; Frifelt 1975a: fig. 24:a-c, 25:b). One possible exception is Frifelt 1975a: fig. 28:f from an Umm an-Nar grave at Bat. Single dotted circles also occur on the square-based bottles of Iran and Bactria.

299 Miroschedji 1973: pl. VII:a.

300 Amiet 1986: fig. 88; Miroschedji 1973: 28 n. 116. This dating assumed that the Ur-Baba concerned was the same as the merchant (**damgar**) Ur-Baba mentioned on a tablet dated to the reign of Amar-Suen (*CT X:* pl. 43, 14315 i 13) but this is by no means certain since Ur-Baba is one of the most common names among Ur III merchants (listed by Neumann 1979: 24).

301 (1) AO 3285 (Heuzey & Sarzec 1884-1912: pl. 44 bis:5; Miroschedji 1973: 27f. n. 116): dotted circle bowl from Girsu with dedication inscription to an otherwise unknown [en]-si [...]-ra-ni. (2) Bi-compartmented box with dedication inscription in script attributable to the second half of the Ur III period (Miroschedji 1973: 30, n. 131). (3) U.280 (Sollberger 1965: no. 26): bowl with concentric circles, inscribed for Šulgi.

302 Hall & Woolley 1927: pl. LXII:XXXV publish a spouted hemispheric bowl with dotted circle decoration as a type vessel for the 'Early dynastic' cemetery at Ur but since this graveyard continued in use into Ur III times (*e.g.* grave C19; *ibid.*: 191) such a high dating must be regarded as unlikely. (The text and grave list seem to make no mention of this vessel which would allow a date by association with the other grave goods.)

303 Ur – Woolley & Mallowan 1976: pls 100:1 (Larsa grave), 100:6 (Giparu, Larsa period); Woolley 1974: pl. 49:6 (Enunmah room 12, pre-Kurigalzu sack debris), U.282+283 (Enunmah, room 11). Uruk – Ratnagar 1981: 119 (Sin-kašid palace); *ibid.* (Larsa-OB period). Larsa – Huot *et al.* 1983: 209 (surface find).

304 Mecquenem 1934: 231, fig. 80.

305 D.T. Potts in press [b]; *cf.* Amiet 1986: 176.

306 Cleuziou 1981: 291.

307 Hinz 1971: 21-24 (inscription); D.T. Potts 1981a; Miroschedji 1973: 41; Amiet 1986: 163 (potters' marks).

those vessels were acquired, but it should be noted that the reliance on inscriptional evidence itself introduces a new bias, for not all mechanisms of exchange are as likely to be recorded in helpful labels. The non-existence of trade inscriptions in the manner of the booty inscriptions, for instance, is not itself an argument against the existence of such trade.

From the Early Dynastic III period on, the contexts in which plain and decorated stone vessels are found indicate that they were objects of considerable prestige and 'value'. This applies particularly to the elaborately decorated *série ancienne*, which is concentrated heavily in temples,[308] where it was dedicated by kings of Sumer (Mesilim) and Agade (Rimuš), and in richer graves.[309] The *série récente* likewise was dedicated in temples by kings (Naram-sin, Šulgi) and a local ruler (as well as a merchant (?) and private citizens), though it also occurs in humble burials at Ur.[310] Plain vessels, often of attractively banded foreign calcites, became standard offerings to deities by private citizens and royalty alike from the Early Dynastic III to Ur III periods. In Early Dynastic III, plain calcite and 'steatite' vessels are also prominent among the grave furniture of the richer burials in the Royal Cemetery at Ur. Thereafter, they occur primarily in sacral contexts, though this may also reflect changes in the nature of the excavated contexts.

Stone vessels were not imported into Mesopotamia to fill a gap in local production; both plain and decorated forms were made in Sumer throughout the third millennium exploiting the local supplies of calcareous stones. The attraction of foreign vessels depended rather on the aesthetic appeal of their harder, darker stones

---

[308] Well stratified at the following sites: Mari - Temple of Ištar (M.131+190, 144, 165, 171, 184, 185, 267, 268+333, 323) and associated Priests' Quarters (M.150, 282+284, 402) (Parrot 1956); Temple of Ninni-zaza (M.2349, 2625, 2627, 2628, 2979) (Parrot 1967); Temple of Šamaš (M.2226, 2151-53, 2182, 2879); Temple of Ištarat (M.2961) (Parrot 1967). **Nippur** - Temple of Inanna VIII, VIIb and IV (one vessel from each; Kohl 1979: fig. 5; *idem* 1974: 162, 245, 690, pl. XLIIIa). Note also Peters 1897: pl. opp. p. 140 (from shrine of Amar-Suen?). Khafajeh - Sin Temple IX (2 vessels, plus 1 from an unspecified level; Frankfort 1935: figs 53-56; *cf.* Delougaz 1960: 94; note also Ratnagar 1981: 119, table 2.4, which cites pieces from "oval temple ED I-II (ED) [= Temple Oval I-II?] (KH. IV. 60) unpublished" and "Oval I (ED) (KH. IV. 37 Unpublished)". Ur - Enunmah, destruction debris below the Kudur-Mabuk and Kurigalzu floors in rooms 11 and 12 (Woolley 1955: 51; *idem* 1974: 51). Susa - Temple of Inšušinak (Amiet 1986: fig. 70; Mecquenem 1911 for context).

[309] Delougaz 1960: pl. IXa; *ABWI*: Mes. 3; for Rimuš see above. The *série ancienne* has been found in Mesopotamian burials only at Ur. Two of the three are 'Royal Tombs'. (1) PG 337, containing U.8950 and U.8951 (Woolley 1934: 539). These were part of a group of stone vessels found immediately above the grave, not in it (*ibid.*: 45), but Woolley was confident that they belonged with the material from the grave, having been dropped by robbers or left as offerings during the filling of the shaft. The whole group of vessels was given a separate grave number (PG 497) (*ibid.*: 427, 431). This grave does not exist apart from this group, and Woolley's catalogue entry (*ibid.*: 539) is thus not, *contra* Kohl (1974: 246), a mistake, but only a reflection of his original caution. (2) PG 800 (Tomb of Puabi), containing U.10522, U.10523 (Woolley 1934: 558, pl. 178). (3) PG 1633, containing U.14058 (Woolley 1934: 589); this was a simple trench grave. All burials date to ED IIIa. A few vessels from domestic contexts at Ur (U.7145, from above Larsa period houses in area EM; Woolley 1955: 173), Mari (M.543, 660, 661, 665, 666, from houses north and east of Priests' Quarters; Parrot 1956) and Khafajeh (unpublished fragment from "ED houses (KH. V. 83)"; Ratnagar 1981: 119, table 2.4) may represent secondary uses or contexts, as do those from a dump at Adab (Delougaz 1960: 94).

[310] (1) Table 6.3:A1a (Naram-Sin). (2) U.280 (Sollberger 1965: 6, no. 26): bowl with concentric circle decoration and inscription of Šulgi. (3) AO 3285 (Heuzey & Sarzec 1884-1912: pl. 44bis:5; Miroschedji 1973: 27f. n. 116): bowl with concentric circle decoration from Girsu, with dedication inscription mentioning an otherwise unknown [en]si [...]-ra-ni. (4) Amiet 1986: fig. 88; D.T. Potts 1990: 109: bowl with concentric circle decoration and dedication inscription of Ur-Baba, perhaps a merchant. (5) Bi-compartmented box with dedication inscription in script attributable to the second half of the Ur III period (Miroschedji 1973: 30, n. 131). Uninscribed bowls appear in two Middle Akkadian graves at Ur: U.9020 in PG/473, misleadingly listed as "basic diorite" (Woolley 1934: 541); U.10547 in PG/899, incorrectly listed as type RC 54 (*ibid.*: 499; *cf.* 559) and wrongly drawn with single rather than double circles (*ibid.*: pl. 245:52; *cf.* photograph in Basmachi 1950: pl. 5:12).

and especially on what might be called generally their exoticism. It seems that they were desired precisely because they were manifestly foreign – a factor which, in the context of temple dedications and booty vases, could carry important religious and political connotations. A vessel brought back as spoil was tangible proof of a ruler's conquests and therefore constituted a particularly appropriate offering to the gods who had ensured his victory. Likewise, the Sargonids' preference for royal statuary in hard, dark igneous stones, and the popularity of steatite/chlorite/serpentine for small statuary and decorated vessels of local manufacture during the Ur III period, reflect not only an aesthetic preference but also the prestige which attached to the conspicuous consumption of these exotic materials. The 'value' of such objects was clearly very closely tied to the context of their 'use', in which cultural and religious considerations were paramount, and often depended crucially on the means of acquisition. This has little or nothing to do with commercial value; there is little evidence to suggest what the 'price' of such objects might have been, or, indeed, whether they would have commanded a price at all.

It has been generally assumed that the foreign stone vessels found in Sumer arrived principally by trade. This view has been developed most fully by Kohl in relation to the 'steatite' *série ancienne* or Intercultural Style. Kohl argues that these vessels, along with other highland raw materials and prestige fashioned goods, were sent from the Iranian plateau to Sumer in return for lowland agricultural produce. By this means the highlanders supplemented their modest agricultural yields while the Mesopotamians acquired desirable exotic commodities which were used to reinforce, and give expression to, political and social relationships. In Kohl's view, the success of this trade encouraged yet greater economic specialization in the highland manufacturing centres like Tepe Yahya, which increasingly directed their efforts away from production for consumption to production for exchange, eventually becoming dependent on caravans of lowland agricultural produce to meet their basic subsistence requirements.[311]

> ... isolated mountain communities were inexorably drawn into the web of trade. Initially benefiting, they soon came to depend increasingly upon the trade when their own economies had become so specialized in the production of commodities for exchange that they could no longer readily adapt to their own internal crises; when this happened, they exchanged their products at the rate deemed fair by the urban centres.[312]

Few would agree with all the details of Kohl's position[313] but the general assumption that most of the foreign stone vessels found in Mesopotamia arrived there by trade has gone essentially unchallenged.

There can be no doubt that Mesopotamia relied heavily on direct or indirect trade with the surrounding highlands for supplies of metals, stones, timber and other raw materials. However, there is little evidence to suggest that stone vessels constituted part of that exchange. Considering first the *série ancienne* vessels, it may be noted that they are not cited as objects of trade in existing third-millennium texts, either in the economic documents recording trade in commodities and finished artefacts along the Gulf, or in the few literary texts which seem to concern overland

---

[311] Kohl 1978: 470-74.
[312] Kohl 1978: 474.
[313] See the comments published with Kohl 1978: 476-85.

trade with Iran. This is not, of course, conclusive proof that such trade did not exist, as Foster remarks concerning the Akkadian period.[314] But it gives grounds for caution, especially when combined with the testimony of Rimuš's inscriptions on vessels C1a and C2a. These inscriptions – the only documentary evidence which bears directly on how the *série ancienne* arrived in Mesopotamia – imply, on the contrary, that the vessels were brought back as booty from Elam/Parahšum. The question then arises how many other vessels of the series – and indeed of the other decorated and plain types found on Mesopotamian sites – may have arrived as trophies of war. Circumstantial evidence suggests that the proportion may have been much greater than is presently appreciated. Temples, where far the greatest concentrations of the *série ancienne* occur, were the traditional repositories of foreign spoil; and two of the three burials in which they were recovered at Ur are 'Royal Tombs', which might also be expected to have contained the fruits of foreign expeditions.

The importance of booty-taking as against trade may also account for the increasing rarity of the *série ancienne* after the Akkadian period, a fact which becomes particularly puzzling if D.T. Potts' lowering of the end date of production at Tepe Yahya to *ca.* 2000 BC is accepted. Under the Third Dynasty of Ur the main focus of military activity shifted from Elam and south-central Iran, where the Akkadians and probably also the Sumerians before them had campaigned extensively, towards the Hurrian and Amorite frontiers along the central Zagros and in the north-west.[315] With this reorientation the opportunity for acquiring vessels of the *série ancienne* as booty in or near the main centres of production greatly diminished. The observed fall-off is therefore to be expected.

The large quantities of *série ancienne* vessels which have been recovered from the Gulf, notably on Tarut and Failaka Islands, suggest that some genuine trade did take place between the highland production centres and these entrepôts. Moreover, the variety of stone types represented at the island ports (including much genuine steatite at Tarut)[316] indicates that they received vessels from many different sources in Iran. It was probably at entrepôts such as these, where merchants came to acquire copper and other important raw materials, that any incidental trade in *série ancienne* vessels with Mesopotamia was transacted. The absence of any reference to such acquisitions in textual records of the Gulf trade might be taken as an indication of its relatively small scale and minor economic importance, though the silence of Sargonic texts regarding other imported materials (see above) urges caution. In any case, there can be little doubt that whatever trade in *série ancienne* vessels took place in the Gulf was dependent on the existence of a regularized structure serving the economically primary trade in raw materials, and would not otherwise have occured.

Within Iran the situation may have been very different. The evidence recovered from Tepe Yahya IVB4-1 suggests a scale of production beyond the demands of local

---

[314] Foster 1977: 37f.

[315] Only Šulgi claims the conquest of Anšan (year formula 35), whence he brought back booty including 8 stone vessels (see below, note 326). The he-goat received by Šu-Sin as the "tribute (gún) of Anšan" does not imply any real sovereignty (Michalowski 1978: 35, 46; Steinkeller 1982: 253, n. 60). Campaigns against other regions in or around Greater Elam are rare, the year names being devoted overwhelmingly to campaigns on the "Hurrian frontier" (Hallo 1978: Appendix II): Amar-Suen and Šu-Sin claim the conquest of Huhnuri, which the latter describes as the "bolt of the land of Anšan (var. Elam)" (Sollberger 1976: 5f.), perhaps in south-east Khuzistan (Edzard & Farber 1974: 77f.). Šu-Sin fought against six lands of Šimaški (= Burujird Valley of Luristan [Stolper 1982: 46; *idem* 1984: 20] or Kerman [Vallat 1985: 50f.] ?) (Sollberger & Kupper 1971: 152-55, IIIA4e-g). On the other hand, there is considerable evidence of diplomatic relations with these and other eastern regions.

[316] Kohl *et al.* 1979: 140, 147.

consumption. Yahya and similar centres may well have traded a significant proportion of their produce with other Iranian settlements in return for goods or materials to which they did not have ready access. The diffusion of these vessels throughout Greater Iran forms part of a large body of evidence for a network of "échanges inter-iraniens" which has recently been comprehensively reviewed by Amiet.[317] Here too the mechanisms of exhange responsible for the movement of goods may have been more complex than the essentially economic relations envisaged by Amiet. Without relevant documentary evidence it is very difficult to judge. Whatever the truth of that matter, a surprising feature of the highland Iranian network is the extent to which Mesopotamia seems to have been excluded. Many of the distinctive stone and metal artefact-types documented by Amiet appear in a far-flung circuit linking Bactria through south-eastern and southern Iran all the way to Susa – but they rarely penetrate any further into the lowlands, stopping, it seems, at the western limit of Elamite control and culture.

Less of the *série récente* has been recovered from Sumer than of the *série ancienne*; however it arrived, it seems to have constituted only a steady trickle. Again there is no textual evidence that these vessels were objects of trade, and the inscription of Naram-Sin on a goblet from Ur proves that some, at least, were brought in as booty, this time from Magan. Others of the *série récente* bowls which were dedicated at temples in Sumer may likewise have been acquired in their land of origin, forcibly or by purchase, specifically for that purpose. On the other hand, it is possible that some of the smaller closed vessels (bottles, boxes *etc.*), which are not well represented in Sumer, were traded, but incidentally, as the containers of unguents, perfumes or other perishables.[318] The compartmented boxes and small round vessels with handled lids may be the "bowls with thin hands/handles (?)" (na4bur-šu-sal) made from the type of stone dedicated to Nanna by a Gulf merchant returning from Magan.[319]

But while the *série récente* vessels themselves probably were not traded, or only incidentally, their presence in Sumer during precisely the centuries which witnessed the *floruit* of Gulf trade can hardly be coincidental. Mesopotamian traders plying the Gulf for copper and other raw materials might naturally have acquired such vessels as by-products of their ventures in the ports of the islands and Oman, to be kept as momentos or curiosities, or for dedication upon their return to Mesopotamia.[320] If the Ur-Baba who dedicated a bowl at Girsu was the merchant of that name,[321] this vessel may plausibly be interpreted as an offering made upon his safe return from one such expedition. The small quantities of the *série récente* recovered from Sumer can easily be accommodated by unregulated, essentially uncommercial acquisition along these lines (in addition to the limited booty-taking attested under Naram-Sin). It is, then, not implausible to see in the currency of the *série récente* in Sumer an indirect reflection of the increasing emphasis of Mesopotamian trade on the Gulf, which has been documented above for the exploitation of stones and metals. Furthermore, it may be possible to account for the rarity in Mesopotamia of the *séries intermédiaire* and *tardive*, which succeeded the

---

[317] Amiet 1986.

[318] Amiet 1986: 164. Remains of lead oxide reported from small bottles at Shahdad have been taken to suggest unguents (Miroschedji 1973: 33).

[319] Above p. 185 n. 75.

[320] Howard-Carter's suggestion (1989: 263) that the chlorite vessels found at Failaka travelled *from* Sumer *to* the Gulf is highly unlikely.

[321] Amiet 1986: fig. 88; D.T. Potts 1990: 109.

série récente in the early second millennium,[322] as an effect of the reduction of direct Mesopotamian trade with Oman (Magan) after the Ur III period.[323]

Undecorated vessels present a more complex picture which seems to change significantly during the course of the millennium. The large quantities of plain vessels deposited in the graves of Sumer (Ur, Girsu) and Akkad (Kiš, the Diyala sites) in the Jemdet Nasr to Early Dynastic II periods, many of them relatively humble interments, suggests a situation of general availability in which trade may plausibly be considered a factor. From the Early Dynastic III period on, however, textual and archaeological evidence point increasingly to the importance of booty-taking. The bowls of dark igneous stones common in the cemeteries of the early third millennium tend to disappear, suggesting that any trade in these vessels was drying up. Their place was taken, in smaller quantities, by the vessels of banded and mottled calcite. The appearance of these types in Sumer in the Early Dynastic III period is roughly contemporaneous with the earliest historical testimony of campaigns into Iran by Sumerian rulers.[324] Certainly by the Sargonic period, as the booty inscriptions indicate, such vessels featured among the vast spoils taken by the kings of Agade in their numerous eastern campaigns, though the royal narratives never mention objects of such insignificant economic value.[325] As has been noted above, military activity in south-central Iran diminished under the empire of Ur, thereby reducing the opportunities for siezing vessels near the primary production centres. An archival list of booty taken by Šulgi in a campaign against Anšan and deposited in temples in Sumer shows, however, that stone vessels continued to feature among the spoils of the few expeditions that were undertaken.[326] None of the known vessels of this period has been inscribed as booty, but the predominance of sacral contexts is again suggestive.

Trade and booty certainly do not exhaust the options which should be considered in an investigation of this kind. Gift-giving and other unregulated means of non-commercial exchange, which are more difficult to trace in the archaeological record, almost certainly played some role in the movement of stone vessels into Mesopotamia in the third millennium. Another potentially more tangible mechanism which ought not to be ignored is tribute. Unfortunately, however, there is no significant textual evidence for the nature of tribute payments until the Ur III period. At that time, the gún (ma-da) or "provincial tax/tribute" levied on the highland regions under Sumerian control (mostly temperate areas of the Zagros mountains)

---

[322] On the definition of these series see D.T. Potts 1990: 249-52; *idem* in press (c). Apart from spouted bowls, possibly belonging to the *série tardive*, at Ur and Ubaid noted by Potts, no definite examples of these series from Mesopotamia are known to the author. Possible additions are the fragments from Uruk cited by Ratnagar (1981: 119): "3 examples [of convex sided vessels with or without lids, and with incised circle or line motifs in registers], one with lug; W.16755, W.19817G; ? Date Larsa and OB. All unpublished". The piece with a lug is probably from one of the 'suspension vessels' which typify these late series (*e.g.* Cleuziou 1981: 287, fig. 9:1, fig. 10).

[323] Oppenheim 1954: 14f.; Muhly 1973: 14f.; D.T. Potts 1978: 45f.; below p. 290 n. 79.

[324] Note, *e.g.*, the *Sumerian King List* description of (En)mebaragesi as "he who carried away as spoil the 'weapon' of the land of Elam" (Jacobsen 1939: 82-4). Some of Eannatum's inscriptions also refer to conquests of Elam and other eastern locations (*ABWI*: Ean. 1, 2/68, 3/4, 5, 11, 22). Unfortunately, nothing is known of the exploits of the Meskalamdug dynasty at Ur, in whose burials many of these pieces were recovered. Note, however, the proverb regarding the legendary king Nanna of Ur (=Aannepadda?) that he captured Simuru(m) but was unable to choke(?) it (Kramer & Gurney 1976: 38f.).

[325] In addition to the evidence of the stone vessels themselves, note the records of booty taking by Rimuš in Elam and Parahšum (gold, copper and slaves [Rimuš C6, quoted above]), by Maništušu across the Lower Sea (mining stones, metals [Man. 1, C1]), and by Naram-Sin in Magan (mining stones [NS 3]).

[326] Pettinato 1982: 56, 59 line iii:4: "8 stone vessels (na$_4$ bur)". Note also the many metal vessels and objects (no vessels) of stone in the lists published by Davidović 1984, which probably record booty from the same campaign (texts B & C) and from a war of Amar-Suen (text D).

was paid principally in livestock,[327] rather than in stones, metals or other highland raw materials. The goods demanded of these and other conquered territories in earlier times may, of course, have been different; but for the Ur III period at least, there is nothing in the available evidence to suggest that stone vessels featured significantly as tribute.

---

[327] Michalowski 1978; Steinkeller 1987: 30f., 40.

Chapter 7

Conclusions

1. THE RANGE AND ORIENTATION OF SUMERIAN / AKKADIAN TRADE IN THE THIRD MILLENNIUM

Southern Mesopotamia's dependence on trade has long been recognised as an important factor not only in her economy, but also in her culture and history generally. In the period that concerns us here, a number of recent studies have argued that trade and exchange played a crucial rôle in the social and political developments relating to early state formation in Sumer, Susiana and highland Iran, and in determining the nature of subsequent relations between these regions.[1] Iran is typically assumed to have been one of Sumer's chief trade partners, supplying stones, metals, timber, horses and other commodities which were unavailable in the Tigris-Euphrates alluvium. This view has been developed most fully by Kohl, taking as his point of departure the Iranian *série ancienne* chlorite vessels produced in highland Iran, and widely distributed throughout the Near East.[2] Kohl argues that these vessels were only the "tip of an iceberg", vestiges of a much more varied and extensive highland-lowland trade in which raw materials were exchanged for lowland agricultural produce.[3] On Kohl's view, such trade encouraged economic specialization, particularly in the highland manufacturing centres like Tepe Yahya, which increasingly directed their efforts away from production for consumption to production for exchange, eventually becoming dependent on Sumerian imports to meet their basic subsistence requirements. Against those who see this trade as directed essentially towards elite demand for luxury items, Kohl argues that Mesopotamian-Iranian trade "cannot be discussed as the relatively unimportant exchange of status markers among participating elites .. [Rather] the highland communities came to rely exclusively upon such goods, such as textiles and possibly foodstuffs, they received from Mesopotamia and Khuzistan".[4]

The evidence presented in this study suggests that the extent and importance of overland trade with Greater Iran in the third millennium may have been over-estimated. From the Early Dynastic III period onwards, texts and archaeological evidence alike indicate that the vast bulk of Sumer's requirements in raw materials, and her more modest demand for finished goods, arrived by sea along the Gulf. Copper was derived overwhelmingly from Oman (Magan), often via Bahrain (Dilmun); lapis lazuli, carnelian, gold, silver and tin came largely through the same channels from the Indus (Meluhha), which probably drew heavily on Afghanistan; dark stones for statuary came from Magan and other coastal regions of the Gulf. Timber, not

---

[1]   *E.g.* Johnson 1973; Wright & Johnson 1975; Kohl 1978: 473; *idem* 1979; Yoffee 1981.
[2]   Kohl 1974, 1978, 1979, 1982, 1987.
[3]   Kohl 1978: 465, 474; *idem* 1987: 15f.
[4]   Kohl 1987: 14.

considered in this study, was likewise imported from the Gulf, as well as from Susa (also by boat) and the north-west, especially the Amanus (the 'Cedar Mountain'),[5] whence logs were floated down the Euphrates.[6] Clear instances of these materials coming from the eastern highlands are extremely rare.[7]

Most striking of all is the fact that, among all the third-millennium economic documents and letters recording or mentioning trade with foreign regions, none refers to caravan trade with the eastern highlands.[8] Trade with Iran is recorded in non-literary texts very rarely and only as far as border towns such as Der (Badra)[9] and Susa;[10] and the Susa trade was conducted by boat along the Karun river, thus constituting an extension of the Gulf network.[11]

Finished products tell a similar story in the Early Dynastic III period and after. As Carter has remarked, "the list of identifiable finished goods from Elam [in Mesoptoamia] is not impressive".[12] Highland-manufactured metalwork and stonework is conspicuously absent from the lowlands, with the sole exception of stone vessels. Even in this case, the relevance of trade is questionable. Inscriptions on examples of both major highland Iranian groups (the *série ancienne* and plain calcite forms), and on others made in the Gulf (the *série récente*), suggest that many were brought to Sumer as booty. Any direct trade or casual exchange involving Mesopotamian merchants that did occur probably took place not in highland Iran but in the Gulf (Tarut, Failaka), where some of the greatest concentrations of the *série ancienne* and examples of the main calcite forms occur. Along with the Gulf types – the *séries récente-tardive* and plain 'steatite' forms – these vessels would have

---

5   *RGTC 1*: 140.
6   Leemans 1960: 116, 125-27; Pettinato 1972: 164.
7   These include: copper from Abullat in Kimaš, cited by Gudea; and (from the north) the gold and silver mines near [Mar]daman (= Mardin?), cited by Šu-Sin. Lack of alternative coastal supplies argues for an overland trade in the arsenical-coppers of Anarak-Talmessi (and perhaps Armenia), and silver from the Taurus ('Silver mountain'). Arguments that the Sumerians referred to woodlands in the east, as well as the north-west, as the 'Cedar Forest', from which they derived much timber (Hansman 1976: 25-30), are not compelling.
8   Note, however, the early 2nd-mill. trade with Simurrum, in the Hurrian frontier, cited below; and the Susian (?) trade-colony with lowland pottery, seals and tablets of OB/Sukkalmah date at Chogha Gavaneh in Luristan (Amiet 1986: 154, 210).
9   Leemans 1960: 116. *DP* 513 records the export of slaves and resins to Der in exchange for silver (here probably a medium of exchange rather than itself the object of trade) brought back to Lagaš.
10   Textual evidence for trade between Susa/Elam and Sumer in the ED periods involves principally barley, oil and wool being sent to Elam where they were exchanged for silver, livestock and timber (*Nik* 85, 214, 292, 310, 313 [edited Selz 1989: 302, 444, 521, 537-40; Lambert 1953: 63]; *DP* 423 [*ibid.*: 64f.]; *cf.* discussion in M. Lambert 1981). Some, however, deal with non-local materials. In *Nik* 310 (Selz 1989: 537-40) "tin (for?) bronze (nagga-zabàr)" and barley are remitted to an ensi of Urua (URUxA^ki). The source of this tin is not specified; while often assumed to be coming to Sumer from Elam, the other entries in the text list commodities dispursed to people setting out *to* Elam. *RTC* 21 (Lambert 1953: 114f.) lists among the items deposited in the palace by a garaš-merchant (nam-garaš), wood and a "foreign lahan (or: lahan of the mountains) (la-ha-an kur-ra)" (a lahan was a type of vessel used for beer, milk etc. [*CAD L*: 39f. s.v.]). These goods form part of the "business commissions of an Elamite (?) boat (má-nim)." Akkadian texts from Susa (Foster in press) cite the following items, possibly as articles of trade: copper, tin, silver, wool, grain, emmer, barley, fruit, plants and pottery (Scheil 1913: nos ?4, 8, 12, 13, 16+55, 17, ?19, 21, 26, ?31, 35, 63). Ur III trade texts from Sumer mention "sesame-ship(s) from Susa" (AS4; Sigrist & Butz 1986: 29). Other texts cite labourers, sheep and he-goats (*ibid.*).
11   Lambert 1953: 64 (*DP* 423); Leemans 1960: 175; Gelb in Weiss 1986: 161f. (ED); Foster in press (Akk). Foster (in press), discussing the records of Ummaite merchants residing at Susa in the Akkadian period notes that boats and boatmen are mentioned a number of times (*ibid.*: n. 22) but resists the natural assumption that they were involved in trade. Even if trade between Susa and Sumer travelled overland it is hardly likely, as Foster suggests, that overland trade extended also to Dilmun, Magan and Meluhha. The people from these places recorded at Susa no doubt arrived as part of the maritime movement which Sargon boasts docked at the quai of Agade.
12   Carter 1990: 89.

found their way to Sumer in the wake of the sea-borne trade in copper and other raw materials. Nothing in the existing data suggests direct overland trade between Sumer and highland Iran, as imagined by Kohl.

Present evidence concerning the late fourth and early third millennia indicates a more complex situation in which Sumer drew on a variety of different source areas for both raw materials and finished products. Already the Gulf featured prominently. As far back as the Ubaid period, pottery from eastern Arabia suggests the exploitation of distant marine resources (fish, pearls?).[13] After a gap covering most of the Uruk period, texts of the late fourth millennium suggest that some copper and textiles may then have been arriving in Sumer from Dilmun (the copper presumably mined in Oman). Sumer's involvement with these regions marginally later is confirmed by the Jemdet Nasr-Early Dynastic III-related pottery from burials in eastern Arabia (including inland sites like Sabkha Hammam and Umm ar-Ramadh) and Oman.[14] Of this material, which has been shown by analysis to be of Mesopotamian manufacture,[15] D.T. Potts justly remarks: "That the impetus for such contact was connected to a Babylonian desire for Omani copper, regardless of how this was effected, seems likely".[16] The earliest dated remains of copper smelting in Oman belong to the later third millennium, but there is circumstantial evidence of production in the Hafit period (early third millennium).[17] Hafit graves have also produced carnelian and agate[18] – materials recorded in later times coming along the Gulf. As to the nature of the return trade – if indeed there was any – there is very little clear evidence. The Jemdet Nasr-Early Dynastic III pottery may have been used to transport liquids, but suggestions that these settlements relied extensively on imported Mesopotamian grain are unfounded [19]

On the other hand, analyses of copperwork from Susa (Le Breton's periods B and C) and the Hamrin (ED I) have been taken to indicate trade with inner Iran (Anarak, Bardsir/Kashan). Unfortunately, a similar range of analyses is not yet available for the pre-Early Dynastic II/III copperwork of Sumer, so its sources remain more speculative. But intimate relations with the highland source areas and connecting trade routes in earlier times are illustrated by the colonies established in the Uruk IV period at Godin Tepe and Tepe Sialk. Jemdet Nasr-type pottery at Proto-Elamite sites such as Tepe Yahya may reflect continuing involvement with these regions during the following period also. The lowland forms represented in Iran are consistently different from the Sumerian pottery in eastern Arabia, perhaps suggesting some functional difference.[20]

Also perhaps from Iran (or Syria?) came the vessels of dark igneous stones, common in Jemdet Nasr to Early Dynastic II burials in Sumer. No similar vessels are known from the Gulf, so if these are indeed Iranian it must be supposed that they travelled overland through the Zagros passes. Sumerian literary compositions

---

[13]   J. Oates et al. 1977; D.T. Potts 1978: 34f., 42f.; *idem* 1990: 37-54.

[14]   D.T. Potts 1986a; *idem* 1993b: 180f., noting that a bulla and some sherds from near Dhahran may even be Late Uruk.

[15]   Mynors 1983.

[16]   D.T. Potts 1986a: 134.

[17]   Sherds from the Maysar production site have been dated to the JN period; some Hafit tomb fields are along potential trade routes from copper mines to the coast; and there are some small copper objects in Hafit graves and in the earliest phase of Hili 8, period I (D.T. Potts 1986a: 133f.; *idem* 1990: 84).

[18]   D.T. Potts 1978: 35f.

[19]   During-Caspers 1989; Edens 1992: 127.

[20]   D.T. Potts 1978: 35, 43.

relating to early times also portray the Iranian highlands as supplying lapis, gold, silver and perhaps tin, though this evidence needs to be treated with caution.

It appears, then, that the course of the third millennium witnessed an increasing emphasis on sea-borne trade along the Gulf at the expense of overland exchange with highland Iran. From the Early Dynastic III period on there is virtually nothing among the metals, stones and timbers used in Sumer which could not have been obtained (and, where there is evidence, usually was obtained) in or through the Gulf, or along the Euphrates. This was not the result of a dramatic shift in or after the Proto-Elamite period (as argued by Alden),[21] since the origins of the sea-trade can now be traced back to Uruk times. The demise of Proto-Elam, like the earlier loss of the Euphrates colonies, no doubt accelerated this trend; but it cannot be held primarily responsible. With remarkable prescience, Oppenheim long ago speculated: "We may well assume that the frequency and intensity of contact [between Sumer and the Gulf] had reached a peak early in the third millennium".[22]

The trend towards Gulf trade is attributable principally to economic considerations; in paticular, the fact that bulk transport was much cheaper by boat than by equid caravan. Political factors contributed too (see below), but were probably secondary. Just as Anatolian copper could not compete with Omani supplies in the early second millennium, so the differential costs of transport from Iran *vis-à-vis* the Gulf in the period considered here would have made highland materials uncompetitive in regions which had access to Gulf shipping, *i.e.* all of the Tigris-Euphrates-Karun basin. The lower 'price' of Gulf materials no doubt depended to some extent on the efficiency of extraction and primary processing facilities at source, and the maintainence of supply lines to the major ports, perhaps originally organised under Sumerian or Akkadian supervision. The growth of trade no doubt led in turn to greater prosperity in these source zones, reflected there in the development of urban and funerary architecture.[23]

Mesopotamia's apparent lack of involvement in the large-scale exploitation of Iranian materials and goods is all the more conspicuous and significant because, within Iran, the third millennium was a period of unprecedented internationalism based on inter-regional exchange. The first major manifestation of this phenomenon, in the Proto-Elamite period, saw a lowland connection maintained in the Uruk IV/III-type pottery, sealings *etc.* which appear as far afield as Kerman and Seistan. But thereafter the situation changed dramatically. In the centuries following the demise of the Proto-Elamites a variety of distinctive highland Iranian products – including miniature 'columns' and decorated vessels of stone; elaborate hammers, axes and compartmented stamp seals of copper; and so on – were distributed in identical forms from Bactria through central Iran to Susa.[24] But – and this is the interesting point – there they stopped. Excepting the stone vessels and a handful of metal goods, none occurs in Sumer. The sea-borne Gulf network and the Iranian land-based network seem to have been essentially mutually exclusive. Only Susa participated directly in both, due to its uniquely equivocal position – geographically part of the alluvium, yet culturally and historically tied to highland Elam.

---

[21] Alden 1982.
[22] Oppenheim 1954: 14.
[23] D.T. Potts 1978: 45; *idem* 1990: 94-102.
[24] Objects of highland Iranian origin from Susa include: stone miniature 'columns'; flat shaft-hole Lut-type axes; Bactrian(?) beads and pendants; calcite vases; *série ancienne* vases; chlorite miniature square-based bottles with dotted circle decoration; miniature metal vase on 'hut-pot' base (Amiet 1986: 143f., 147f., figs 96-108; *idem* 1986b: 15f.; Maxwell-Hyslop 1989: 135-38).

Possible explanations may now be suggested for some apparent anomalies. First, there is the conspicuous absence of turquoise in Mesopotamia after the fourth millennium – all the more striking in view of its widespread exploitation in prehistoric times. Tosi notes this anomaly and rightly argues that there must be some systematic explanation.[25] Since lapis and turquoise were traded and worked at Shahr-i Sokhta II-III,[26] which he regards as a major entrepôt for Sumerian lapis, Tosi is forced to explain the lack of turquoise in Sumer by "a weak demand on the main consumer markets" due to unknown "ideological factors".[27]

But the pattern of third-millennium trade which has emerged from this study suggests an alternative explanation. A key factor is its origin. Tosi argues compellingly that the Irano-Afghan sources of turquiose (Kerman, Nishapur, Herat) were not worked in or before the third millennium. The earliest supply zone seems rather to have been the inner Kyzyl Kum in Central Asia,[28] whence were supplied the early urban centres of southern Turkmenia (Namazga III-V periods), but not, it seems, the Indus, where turquoise finds remain extremely rare.[29] As an essentially inland resource, therefore, turquoise fell outside the 'catchment area' of the Gulf network. So, as Mesopotamia came to rely on sea-borne trade at the expense of the old overland routes, turquoise disappeared. Within Iran, on the other hand, it was still distributed through the flourishing highland exchange network, and thus continues to appear at Shahr-i Sokhta, Tepe Hissar II-III (where a stepped-cross bead confirms its Turkmenian origin), Shahdad and even at Kaftari Tal-i Malyan.[30]

The same phenomenon in reverse seems to occur with tin. Tin appears in the third millennium (in the form of bronze) in Mesopotamia, the Gulf, Susa and Luristan; yet it is all but absent from highland Iran, the region closest to the likely sources. Clearly, Afghan tin was not free to move equally by land and sea in all directions. But why? Textual evidence from Mesopotamia, suggesting that the metal arrived there by sea from Meluhha, supplies a plausible answer: *viz.* that the eastern tin exploited in the Near East (whatever its precise source) was controlled principally by the Meluhhans and others who plied the waters of the Gulf. For in this case it is natural that tin should appear only in regions served by the sea-based network of which they were a major partner (or, like Luristan, with close links to these regions – in this case Susa); and thus that it should by-pass highland Iran. There need not have been any political barrier or other prohibition on overland tin-trade between Afghanistan and Iran. In regions which had ready access to the arsenical coppers of Anarak-Talmessi the greater expense of bringing tin by caravan from the east (even supposing camels were available) would have sufficed to deter any significant exchange. Some places distant from both alloying materials (*e.g.* Tepe Yahya) seem to have made do with pure copper.

---

25 Tosi 1974b: 154.
26 *Ibid.*: 154-58; Bulgarelli 1981.
27 Tosi 1974b: 159.
28 *Ibid.*: 148-50, 159.
29 Ratnagar 1981: 154.
30 Schmidt 1937: 229, Fig. 134 (Hissar); Asthana 1984: 360 (Shahdad); Sumner 1986: 204; *idem* 1988: 318 (Malyan).

2. TRADE AND POLITICS

A recurrent theme in work on Mesopotamia's foreign relations has been the relationship between trade and politics. This forms the basis of Alden's interest in Proto-Elam, Algaze's analysis of the Uruk colonies and underlies much of Kohl's work on third-millennium trade in Western Asia.[31] To what extent were trade and politics (in the broad sense of all military and diplomatic activities) connected? How far did economic motives determine military strategy, or *vice versa*?

It is often suggested that the desire to control the sources of raw materials of neighbouring regions and their supply routes was the mainspring of Mesopotamian military expansion. Thus Hinz relates recurrent Mesopotamian-Elamite hostility to the desire for highland resources:

> Mesopotamia needed the products of the Elamite highlands, timber, metallic ore (lead, copper, tin and silver), stone (alabaster, diorite and obsidian), semi-precious stones and also horses. The countless campaigns of the Sumerians and Akkadians against Elam were due to the need to control these important materials.[32]

Similarly, Hallo claims that the 'Hurrian frontier' further north

> ... posed a massive barrier to the north-Iranian trade routes leading to such sought-after raw materials as tin, lapis lazuli and perhaps chlorite. It was therefore a prime target of Mesopotamian military activity by both Sargonic and Ur III kings ...[33]

These assertions are typical of many more that have been made both by archaeologists and by historians, all claiming to see evidence of economic motives behind the military expansion of the kings of Agade and Ur.[34]

In support of these claims it may be observed that there is a demonstrable correlation between the orientation of military and cultural expansion on the one hand, and the range and sources of raw materials consumed in Sumer on the other. The unprecedented variety of stones and metals exploited in the Late Uruk period clearly relates to the cultural, and probably political, expansion which can be traced through lowland colonies in Syria, Anatolia and Iran. One such stone, used extensively for seals in the Late Uruk period, is serpentine, long exploited for the same purpose in Syro-Anatolia. The incidence of serpentine seals decreases dramatically in the Jemdet Nasr period and does not rise significantly until the Akkadian dynasty, likewise a time of Mesopotamian penetration in the north-west. Similarly, the dramatic increase in the use of hard dark stones for sculpture,

---

[31] Alden 1982; Algaze 1989; Kohl 1974, 1978, 1982, 1987.
[32] Hinz 1971: 645.
[33] Hallo 1978: 71.
[34] See, *e.g.*, Bottéro 1967: 110 (Sargon); M. Lambert 1974: 11 (Naram-Sin); Michalowski 1976: 116f. (Ur III); Larsen 1979: 79, 99 (Akkadian empire). These claims are all based principally on textual evidence. Kohl, drawing also on archaeological material, sees the Akkadian empire as an attempt to salvage by force of arms the extensive nework of ED II-III exchange with Iran, disrupted (on his view) by the growth of urban cultures in Turkmenia (Namazga V) and the Indus. Recently, Hiebert & Lamberg-Karlovsky (1992: 4) take the opposite view that "increased trade and commerce was an effect rather than a cause of territorial expansion".

especially royal statuary, by the Akkadians is matched by the escalation of military activity under the Sargonids in the Gulf (Magan, coastal Iran). Both Maništušu and Naram-Sin record mining stones after successful military operations in these regions.

But if some gross correlations are clear, the crucial distinction between cause and effect, or motive and outcome, remains impossible to draw with any confidence. Were the Akkadians and other conquerors drawn to these regions because of their raw materials? Or did they consume their resources because these regions had been conquered (for whatever reason), and could therefore be exploited on favourable terms? To this question neither inscriptions nor archaeological evidence provides a clear answer. *A priori*, it is plausible to suppose that both would have played some part – *i.e.* that the desire to control sources of raw materials would have been one factor in the decision where to direct military efforts; and also that any valuable resources in regions conquered for non-economic reasons would have been exploited nonetheless. Assessing the relative importance of these factors in particular cases, however, is rarely possible, since the rhetoric of imperialism casts as thick a veil over intentions as it does over their success. The best case that can be made for anything approaching a 'trade empire' – and even this is circumstantial – applies to the north-west, where there is both textual evidence for awareness of the region's raw materials (*cf.* Sargon's references to 'the Silver mountain' and 'the Cedar Forest') and archaeological confirmation of attempts to control the main routes of supply (Naram-Sin's palace at Brak).

Regarding Iran, however, the evidence reviewed in this study indicates a degree of correlation between trade and cultural (and military?) expansion only in the Late Uruk period, when lowland colonies were established in Iran (Susa II, Tepe Sialk IV₁, Godin V), and a wide variety of highland raw materials were consumed in Sumer (various igneous and metamorphic stones, carnelian [and lapis?], copper, silver, lead, gold). It is unfortunately not clear from existing analyses whether Sumer, like Susa, drew on Iranian copper at this time; the only source mentioned in a contemporary text is Dilmun (*i.e.* probably from Oman) and even this citation is open to doubt. After the Late Uruk period, evidence of overland trade with Iran (with the possible exception of arsenical copper) decreases to such an extent that the relevance of any economic motive for military activity becomes highly questionable. As indicated above, from at least the Early Dynastic III period the bulk of Sumer's imports seems to have come along the Gulf. There is virtually no textual or archaeological evidence for raw materials coming by trade from or through the regions of attested military conflict – Elam, Marhaši, the 'Hurrian frontier' *etc.* Indeed, as D.T. Potts has argued, escalating hostility between Sumer and these eastern regions must have constituted a major impediment to any regularized overland trade.[35] To the extent that economic considerations may be seen to have played any rôle in eastern conflicts, it was through the taking of booty (see below). Mesopotamian rulers often boast of looting conquered Iranian cities, but none relate mining raw materials (as in the Gulf) or establishing secure trade routes (as Lugalzagesi and Sargon "made straight the road" to the north-west). In the Ur III period the tribute and taxes imposed on territories in the Zagros mountains were levied principally in livestock, not in the raw materials one would expect from regions plying gold, lapis or other highland resources. Likewise in the Akkadian period, taxes in Mesopotamia were paid for the most part in local produce.[36] Rare Early Dynastic III and Old Babylonian texts recording trade

---

[35] D.T. Potts 1982a: 35.
[36] Bridges 1981: 363ff.; Foster in press.

with eastern regions (*e.g.* Der [Badra] and Simurrum [in the Hurrian highlands] respectively) show that oils, resins and perfumes originating in Syro-Anatolia were exported from Sumer to these places where they were exchanged for silver (*i.e.* money) or slaves (Gutians and others).[37] As we have seen above,[38] trade with Susa ('Elam') was principally in barley and wool for silver, livestock and timber. No texts report the purchase of exclusively highland commodities.

Moreover, the historical evidence itself clearly indicates that the overwhelming priority of political relations with Iran was to secure the borders against attack. The pattern of conflict in the Akkadian and Ur III periods, culminating in the devastating invasions which brought those empires to an end, underlines the essentially defensive military strategy that it was necessary to adopt towards the east. Episodes of conquest and expansion must be set in the general context of constant pressure, both from powerful highland states (Elam, Marhaši, Šimaški, numerous Hurrian kingdoms *etc.*) and from the semi-nomadic marauders of the Zagros (Guti, Lullubi), who were ever ready to exploit any sign of weakness in the lowland leadership. Inaction, in this situation, was an invitation to disaster, and isolationism no real option.

From the Iranian perspective, where political events cannot be independently perceived through textual records, speculation has centred around what might more accurately be called the politics *of* trade. In this vein, Alden argues that the Proto-Elamites restricted the flow of goods to Mesopotamia to inflate prices, but in fact eventually drove them to seek other supplies along the Gulf. Muhly, on the other hand, relates that shift to "political disturbances [which] blocked the overland route through the Zagros mountains".[39]

As has been argued above, Alden's view makes little economic or archaeological sense;[40] if trade was important to the Proto-Elamite economy they would hardly have restricted the flow of goods to the extent that it died altogether. As is intimated by Muhly, the connection seems rather to be the reverse, at least in the historical periods. As the third millennium progressed, the rise of Elam and other highland powers[41] openly or potentially hostile to Mesopotamian interests represented an increasingly serious barrier to overland trade with the east.[42] This can only have reinforced the economic arguments favouring the reorientation of trade to the Gulf, as had earlier the collapse of the Uruk IV colonies on the Upper Euphrates[43] and in Iran. The Elamites themselves may in any case have had little to profit from such trade. The lowlands could offer them only foodstuffs and secondary products, most of which they produced already in their own fertile intermontane valleys, albeit on a smaller scale.

---

[37]   Leemans 1960: 89-96, 116; *ibid.*: 127 for Syro-Anatolian origin of oils, resins *etc.*
[38]   Above note 10.
[39]   Alden 1982; Muhly 1973: 230.
[40]   Many commentators have pointed out the implausibility of transporting bulky agricultural goods long distances over land; or that highland centres ever allowed themselves to become dependent on external food supplies. *Cf.* the criticisms of Kohl 1978, published following that article, by Lamberg-Karlovsky (pp. 478-80), D.T. Potts (481f.) and Watkins (485).
[41]   Among these highland places may be included the 'Yanik' and other peoples who forced out the inhabitants of Luristan and Kurdistan with whom Late Uruk Sumer had maintained relations, apparently severing all contact with the lowlands (Young 1986: 221f.).
[42]   Alster (1983: 51) sees evidence of Elamite hostility to the Gulf trade in the passage of *EWO* (below note 53) where, after blessing Meluhha and Dilmun, the poet describes how Elam and Marhaši were destroyed and looted by "the king given power by Enlil".
[43]   Mellaart 1978: 10; D.T. Potts 1978: 43.

Susa illustrates particularly well the decisive rôle political affiliations could play in third-millennium Iranian trade. In the Early Dynastic III to Ur III periods, while the city was mostly under Mesopotamian control, water-borne trade between the two is well attested. In the Old Babylonian period, when Susa reverted to Elamite control, trade with her erstwhile suzerain ceased. "There is no evidence at all from the texts of [Babylonian] trade with these countries [Mutiabal and Elam] in the Old Babylonian period".[44]

Beyond Iran, a number of culture-historical developments, whose political dimension has been irretrievably lost, may be related to changes in the pattern of trade only speculatively. Among these, the most important was perhaps the diffusion of southern Turkmenian (Namazga) culture to Seistan and Baluchistan (Namazga III), and later to Margiana, Bactria and Afghanistan (Namazga V/VI).[45] Without texts the precise nature and implications of these expansions are likely to remain obscure, but control of natural resources may reasonably be considered an important factor. It is at least becoming clear that the balance of overland trade across Iran, long perceived as a flow of materials exclusively to the west, involved a more complex cross-current of movements in which the eastern polities of Seistan, Turkmenia and Bactria carried considerable weight. Indeed, the major drain may have been in the opposite direction, towards the urban settlements of third-millennium Turkmenia.

3. TRADE AND BOOTY

While trade has featured prominently in discussions of Iranian materials and artefacts found in Sumer, less attention has been paid to the question of booty and other forms of non-commercial exchange.[46] Yet the texts present precisely the opposite emphasis. Trade, strictly speaking, is hardly mentioned, but royal inscriptions, administrative texts, dedication inscriptions and literary texts all testify to the seizure of booty by Mesopotamian rulers in eastern campaigns. Easterners likewise raided the lowlands, their depredations being well illustrated by the Akkadian monuments later taken to Susa by Šutruk-Nahhunte. Indeed, plundering conquered territories of their removable riches, especially temple and palace treasures, was standard practice throughout the ancient Near East.[47] While texts recording trade in foreign materials are virtually unknown in the Akkadian period,[48] Rimuš boasts of the 30 minas of gold, 3600 minas of copper and 360 slaves he took as booty from Elam and Parahšum.[49] In another inscription he cites the "diorite, *dušû*-stone and (other) stones" which he took as the booty of Parahšum[50] and archaeological discoveries show that he also plundered vessels of calcite and carved 'steatite'. Other vessels were brought back by Naram-Sin as the "booty of Magan", where he also mined stone for statues. Likewise, Šu-Sin took gold, silver, copper, tin and bronze as booty from the lands of Šimaški; while Ibbi-Sin took gold after

---

44   Leemans 1960: 175.

45   An important recent development is the discovery of a Namazga V/VI settlement at Sibri near Mehrgarh, which itself has a cemetery of the same culture (Santoni 1984).

46   Notable exceptions are D.T. Potts 1982a: 35f.; Heinz 1989: 207 (stone vases) and Foster in press.

47   A typical example is *SARI 1*: Uk 4.1: Enšakušana "having sacked their cities [*i.e.* Kiš and Akšak] ... [he] dedicated their statues, the precious metals and lapis lazuli, their timber and treasure, to Enlil at [N]ippur".

48   Foster 19777: 37f.; *idem* in press.

49   *AKI*: Rimuš C6: 138-51.

50   C10: 41-45; Oelsner 1989: 404.

defeating Susa, Adamdun and Awan.[51] Most informative are the recently identified lists of booty taken by Šulgi from Anšan and by Amar-Suen from some other place(s), and assigned to temples in Sumer.[52] These include objects in various metals (gold, silver, tin, copper, bronze) and stones (lapis, carnelian, agate, chalcedony, alabaster), as well as lumps of unworked steatite (?), carnelian, 'red carnelian', chalcedony, lapis, agate *etc*.[53] Craftsmen too were considered booty and brought back to work for their new masters; in *Enmerkar and Lugalbanda* the metalsmiths and stoneworkers of Aratta, along with their tools of trade, are taken prisoner by the king of Uruk.[54]

It seems likely, therefore, that what movement there was of highland Iranian goods and materials into Mesopotamia depended principally on booty-taking. Gift-exchange, *ad hoc* purchases and tribute may have played more minor rôles, but trade seems to have been minimal. Iran thus stands in contrast to the Gulf and Syro-Anatolia, with which Mesopotamia maintained regular trading relations, based either on secure military control (Syria), or, more often, on mutual economic benefit between regions with complementary resources (Dilmun, Magan, Meluhha). A clear distinction thereby emerges between the limited movement of Iranian finished objects into the lowlands, and the extensive network of genuine trade within Greater Iran, though these different exchange mechanisms sometimes involved the same materials and artefacts (*e.g.* decorated steatite vessels).[55]

This is not to deny the economic importance of booty. On the contrary, in a society where the wealth of the state and temple households consisted largely of hoarded supplies of precious materials, additions to these reserves from foreign campaigns would have been events of major economic significance. But whereas trade could be regularized and to some extent controlled, booty-taking was by nature unpredicatable and thus a more precarious basis for long-term economic security.

4. THE SUMERIAN 'HORIZON'

Recent excavation and historical research has greatly expanded the range of Sumerian and Akkadian cultural, economic and political contact – what might be called the Sumerian 'horizon' – or, following Michalowski,[56] their mental map. Twenty-five years ago Sumerian relations with Iran were hardly conceived as extending beyond Susa and perhaps also Tepe Sialk. The vessels and other stone objects discussed above, with the exception of lapis and possibly carnelian, were assumed to have originated no further afield that the Zagros mountains, or the westernmost fringe of the plateau. It now appears likely that some of the elaborate carved steatite vessels found in Sumer came ultimately from Kerman, and the calcite vessels from south-east Iran or Bactria. A more varied range of objects at Susa, which fell under Mesopotamian control for most of the later third millennium, illustrate even stronger cultural (and economic?) connections with the periphery of the Lut desert, Seistan, southern Turkmenia and southern Bactria. This last region

---

[51] Kärki 1986: SS 20a; *IRSA*: IIIA4e, f (Šu-Sin); Kärki 1986: IS 9, 10; *IRSA*: IIIA5b-c (Ibbi-Sin).
[52] Pettinato 1982; Davidovic 1984.
[53] Pettinato 1982: 67f. Note also *EWO* 242-47 (Kramer & Maier 1989: 47): "Elam (and) Marhaši ... who are all-devouring, given power by Enlil attacked their houses, attacked their walls. Their silver, lapis lazuli [and] storehouse he brought to Nippur for Enlil, king of all the lands".
[54] *EL*: 409f.; Wilcke 1969: 126-29.
[55] In the Iranian network also raw materials were probably the primary objects of exchange, finished artefacts being acquired more casually and often for non-economic reasons.
[56] Michalowski 1986.

Figure 48. Bactrian statuette of a seated woman (goddess?) in kaunakes-like garment. Steatite/chlorite and limestone. Late third to early second millennium.

also provided a window on still more distant lands as far as China, whence came silk and whither were sent compartmented stamp seals in the late third or early second millennium.[57] The arena within which exchange may be seen to have taken place has been greatly expanded.

The extent of early Sumerian 'presence' abroad, often implying full-scale colonization, has also increased dramatically through the discovery of colonies along the Upper Euphrates into Anatolia, and at Godin Tepe and Tepe Sialk in Iran.[58] A slightly later presence in eastern Arabia extended the links down the Gulf originally established in the Ubaid period. This expanded pattern of long-distance contact provides a context within which Sumer's influence on late Predynastic Egypt[59] and her later trading relations with the Indus no longer appear isolated and exceptional. More generally, it suggests that the extent of direct Sumerian interaction with other regions of the Near East from at least the late fourth millennium may have been much greater than previously imagined.[60] This applies to political relations as well as trade and cultural contacts. Akkadian and Ur III texts record diplomatic contacts and military conflicts with a number of eastern states of the Gulf (Magan) and highland Iran (Aratta, Elam, Marhaši and Šimaški). With the Elamite capital Anšan now reliably located as far east as Fars, it is not impossible that others of these places, which are implied to lie still further afield, will prove to have been as distant as Seistan, Afghanistan, southern Turkmenia, Bactria or Baluchistan, regions among which the archaeological data evidences particularly active long-distance movements

---

[57] Amiet 1986: 192, 213.
[58] Algaze 1989.
[59] Moorey 1990.
[60] In this connection various discoveries indicating long-distance movements may be noted: a chlorite *série ancienne* handled weight from Soch, Fergana (Brentjes 1971), Harappan etched carnelian beads in Thailand, Southeast Asian spices from 2nd-mill. Mesopotamia (Kohl 1987: 23) and East African copal in Akkad (Meyer *et al.* 1991).

of goods. Military actions of such range would not stand entirely alone; tradition also ascribes to Sargon an expedition against Purušhanda in central Anatolia.[61]

If the balance of trade flowed into Mesopotamia, the direction of cultural influence within the Sumerian horizon was generally the reverse. The palpable material rewards of the Sumerians' urban bureaucratic lifestyle made it a natural object of admiration and imitation among their neighbours, on whom its impact can be traced first in Proto-Elam and, from the mid-third millennium, also in Syria (Ebla) and perhaps southern Turkmenia.[62] Even in regions which did not have the agricultural basis for urban life, the pervasive influence of Sumerian material culture is evident in the diffusion of characteristically Sumerian objects, motifs and practices, albeit in modified forms: the use of cylinder seals across Iran (Tal-i Malyan, Tepe Yahya, Shahdad, Tepe Hissar) to Bactria, sometimes with Mesopotamian motifs; statuettes of 'worshipper' with clasped hands at Shahdad and of women in *kaunakes*-like garments in Bactria (Fig. 48); Sumerian motifs on metalwork from Gorgan (the 'Astrabad treasure'), Afghanistan (the Fullol hoard) and Bactria, and on a gaming board decorated with entwined serpents from Shahr-i Sokhta; and, more speculatively, the ziggurat-like stepped structures in Gorgan and southern Turkmenia.[63]

In none of these cases, however, do we see the same wholesale imposition of Sumerian culture as in Late Uruk Syria and Iran, nor even the direct copying of selected motifs which occurred in Egypt. As in late-third-millennium Syria, best illustrated by the discoveries at Ebla, Sumerian forms and ideas were creatively modified and adapted according to local tastes. This is hardly surprising, since much of Sumer's influence on the distant eastern regions of Greater Iran was doubtless effected through intermediaries.

Sumer's widespread contacts fit into a broader pattern of long-distance connections at this time. At Shahr-i Sokhta I (phase 10), where the easternmost Proto-Elamite tablet has been found, there is also Namazga III pottery from southern Turkmenia.[64] Towards the end of the third millennium we again see the material culture of the Turkmenia-Margiana-Bactria complex (now surely settlers) at Sibri, Nausharo, Khurab and elsewhere in Baluchistan, and isolated finds of this type across south-central Iran;[65] Indus(-type) artefacts on southern Turkmenian and Bactrian sites;[66] various Iranian-Indus connections,[67] including Indus-type artefacts at Iranian sites as far inland as Shahdad (etched carnelian beads and Indus-type copper mirror)[68] and Yahya (Indus-type seal impression);[69] Indus artefacts in the Oman penninsula and Bahrain;[70] ceramic links between Oman and south-eastern

[61] J. Westenholz 1983: 329.
[62] Masson 1968.
[63] Cylinder seals – Dyson 1987: 657f.; D.T. Potts 1981; Amiet 1978: fig. 15; *idem* 1986: 190, 199f. Worshipper statuettes – Hakemi 1972: no. 344; Amiet 1986: figs 129-30. Sumerian motifs – *e.g.* bearded bull, *kaunakes* garment, antithetical rampant beasts, master-of-animals, entwined serpents (Tosi & Wardak 1972; Maxwell-Hyslop 1982; Amiet 1983; *idem* 1986: 186, 201-03, fig. 149, 196, 202; Ligabue & Salvatori (ed.) n.d.: pl. 73; Piperno & Salvatori 1983: 179-85 [Sokhta gaming board]). Stepped structures – Amiet 1986: 188; Deshayes 1977; Sarianidi 1985.
[64] Such pottery is also found at Mundigak II, Deh Morasi Ghundai II/III and in the Quetta valley (Hiebert & Lamberg-Karlovsky 1992: 11).
[65] Amiet 1986; Jarrige in Jarrige ed. 1988: 111-28; Hiebert & Lamberg-Karlovsky 1992. Interestingly, there is no clear evidence of Iranian imports in late 3rd mill. Turkmenia-Margiana-Bactria.
[66] Cleuziou 1984: 390-94; Kohl 1987: 16.
[67] Heskel 1984; Amiet in Jarrige ed. 1988: 194f.
[68] Asthana 1984.
[69] Lamberg-Karlovsky 1986: 193, 204.
[70] Kohl 1987: 16; Lamberg-Karlovsky 1986: 193; D.T. Potts 1990: 150, 187; *idem* 1993b: 189.

Iran/Afghanistan;[71] as well as a scattering of iconographical borowings between Syro-Anatolia, Mesopotamia, the Gulf, Iran and Central Asia.[72] The complex multi-directional nature of this network defies any simple core-periphery distinction, at least in economic terms. As Kohl has remarked: "the Bronze Age world system of the late third and early second millennia B.C. was characterised not by a single core region linked to less developed peripheral zones, but by a patchwork of overlapping, geographically disparate core regions or foci of cultural development, each of which primarily exploited its own immediate hinterland".[73]

From the pattern of foreign contact that has emerged in the past twenty years it is becoming increasingly clear that Sumer's horizon was not a circle centred on southern Mesopotamia, but an irregular and highly directional perimeter dominated by two major corridors penetrating far into foreign, and sometimes hostile, territory. These corridors were defined essentially by the major arteries of water communication: the Tigris-Euphrates corridor running north-west to Syro-Anatolia and the Mediterranean; and the Gulf corridor leading past the Gulf states to the Indus, and around Arabia to Egypt.[74] Together these river- and sea-lanes provided access to virtually all the areas of early Sumerian 'presence' or settlement: the Upper Euphrates and Tigris rivers, eastern Arabia and probably also Egypt. The only apparent exceptions are Godin V and Tepe Sialk IV₁ in highland Iran, whose association with Sumer rather than Susa is anyway uncertain. Likewise, all Mesopotamia's major trading partners were located along these corridors: the Gulf communities and Indus civilization in the east; and perhaps already the 'cedar forest' and 'silver mountain' in the west. After the Proto-Elamite period, significant Sumerian penetration of land-locked highland Iran seems only to have occurred during military campaigns. Essentially, therefore, all the more distant boundaries of the Sumerian horizon were defined by water. Highland Iran was preeminently a land of mystery and fable, more prominent in literatary than economic texts.[75]

The elucidation of the importance of the Gulf corridor for Sumerian trade throughout the third millennium has been one of the major results of archaeological and textual research in these regions in recent years. References to metals, textiles and tax officials connected with Dilmun in Archaic Uruk texts[76] show that contact was established long before Ur-Nanše, whose shipment of Dilmun timber was previously the earliest attested contact.[77] How far along the Gulf beyond Dilmun Sumer's horizon extended in Uruk IV/III times can presently only be guessed; but certainly by the Early Dynastic III period trade contact with Magan and Meluhha had been established, and constituted an important aspect of Sumer's raw materials supply network. Thus a fragmentary but tantalising literary text from Ebla and Abu Salabikh implies an already flourishing Gulf trade when it describes how "foreign trade he (Ea) gave to the traders. The lands yielded lapis lazuli and silver, sissoo wood, cedar, cyprus, juniper ... perfumed oil, vegetable oil, honey, aromatics he

---

71 Cleuziou & Vogt 1985; Blackman *et al.* 1989; Wright 1989.
72 Amiet 1986: *passim*; Pottier 1984: *passim*; Howard-Carter 1987: 77, 81f. (Margianan 3-toed monster in Gulf glyptic); Brunswig *et al.* 1983: 109 (Turkmenian seals in the Indus); D.T. Potts 1993b: 189; Sarianidi 1993: 34 (Bactria-Margiana and Syro-Anatolian bird-men).
73 Kohl 1987: 16.
74 The Egypt connection was also – and perhaps primarily – through Syria (Moorey 1990).
75 Moorey 1993.
76 Englund 1983a; Nissen 1986a; Howard-Carter 1987: 59f.
77 *IRSA*: IC3c-e. Note the alternative identification of this early Dilmun as a place in Sumer, above p. 35 n. 224.

loaded (?) on boats".[78] Despite a possible contraction of the range of direct commercial contact from Meluhha to Magan and eventually to Dilmun during the Akkadian to Old Babylonian periods,[79] the economic importance of the Gulf trade to Sumer only increased as the third millennium progressed, and Iran became ever more trenchantly hostile. Until about 1800 BC, when the cities of the Indus and the trade they sponsored collapsed, the Gulf remained the chief arena of Sumerian contact with the cultures of the east.

---

[78] W. Lambert 1989: 33.

[79] According to this view, originally argued by Oppenheim (1954: 14f.) and since widely adopted by other scholars (*e.g.* Muhly 1973: 224f.; D.T. Potts 1978: 45f.; Weisgerber 1984-85: 7f.), direct trade extended all the way to Meluhha under the Sargonids, contracting to Magan in Ur III times, and then to Dilmun in the OB period. It is not entirely clear, however, that this reconstruction, based on a handful of scattered references and archives, each with its own interests and orientation, reflects the general pattern of trade rather than particular features of these archives. As Leemans (1960: 55) judiciously comments: "The information in all these periods concerns mainly or only the activity of one person or body... The question arises as to how far the inferences may be generalized". Different traders may have specialized in different commodities or regions depending on where and with whom they were able to establish favourable terms of exchange (*cf.* Lambert's argument [1981: 176f.] that Lagaš held a monopoly on trade with the east by agreement with Uruk after Enmetena helped Lugal-kineše-duddu gain control of Uruk). Much more evidence is required before sound generalizations can be made. Moreover, Oppenheim's account freely combines the testimony of various public and private documents which are of varying credibility. When separated from the rest, the contemporary administrative and economic texts – probably the most reliable guides – suggest a consistently strong connection with Dilmun from Late Uruk to OB times. Magan's only significant appearance (in the archive of Lu-Enlilla) may as validly be attributed to his enterprise *vis-à-vis* the other traders represented in the Ur archives as to any change in the general pattern of trade. Otherwise, most references to Magan, and nearly all those to Meluhha (Limet 1960: 88), occur in royal inscriptions (*e.g. AKI*: Sargon C2; *NBWI*: Urnammu 26) whose irregular survival hardly provides an adequate basis for assessing changes in the range of contact.

References Cited

Abbreviations

The following abbreviations are used in the list of references cited:

AASOR	*Annual of the American Schools of Oriental Research*
AfO	*Archiv für Orientforschung*
AJA	*American Journal of Archaeology*
AMI	*Archäologische Mitteilungen aus Iran*
AOAT	*Alter Orient und Altes Testament*
ASJ	*Acta Sumerologica Journal*
BAR	*British Archaeological Reports*
BASOR	*Bulletin of the American Schools of Oriental Research*
BSOAS	*Bulletin of the School of Oriental and African Studies*
DAFI	*Cahiers de la délégation archéologique française en Iran*
FAOS	*Freiburger Altorientalische Studien*
JAOS	*Journal of the American Oriental Society*
JCS	*Journal of Cuneiform Studies*
JEOL	*Jarbericht ... "Ex Oriente Lux"*
JESHO	*Journal of the Economic and Social History of the Orient*
JNES	*Journal of Near Eastern Studies*
JOS	*Journal of Oman Studies*
JRAS	*Journal of the Royal Asiatic Society*
MAD	*Materials for the Assyrian Dictionary*
MARI	*Mari annales de recherches interdisciplinaires*
MASI	*Memoirs of the Archaeological Survey of India*
MCS	*Manchester Cuneiform Studies*
MDOG	*Mitteilungen der Deutschen Orient-Gesellschaft*
MDP	*Mémoires de la délégation en Perse* (and similar titles of the Mission Archéologique en Iran)
OIC	*Oriental Institute Communications*
OIP	*Oriental Institute Publications*
PBS	*Publications of the Babylonian Section* (of the University Museum, University of Pennsylvania)
PSAS	*Proceedings of the Seminar for Arabian Studies*
RA	*Revue d'Assyriologie et d'Archéologie orientale*
RAI	*Rencontre assyriologique internationale*
RlA	*Reallexikon der Assyriologie und vorderasiatische Archäologie*
SANE	*Sources from the Ancient Near East*
SAOC	*Studies in Ancient Oriental Civilization*
WZKM	*Wiener Zeitschrift für die Kunde des Morgenlandes*
ZA	*Zeitschrift für Assyriologie und vorderasiatische Archäologie*

References Cited

ADAMS, R. McC.
1962 'Agriculture and Urban Life in Early Southwestern Iran', *Science* 136, 109-22.
1974 'Anthropological Perspectives on Ancient Trade', *Current Anthropology* 15, 239-258.
1981 *Heartland of Cities: Surveys of Ancient Settlement and Land Use on the Central Floodplain of the Euphrates*, Chicago.

ADAMS, R.McC., NISSEN, H.J.
1972 *The Uruk Countryside: The Natural Setting of Urban Societies*, Chicago.

AGRAWAL, D.P.
1971 *Copper Bronze Age in India*, New Delhi.
1982 'The Indian Bronze Age Cultures and their Metal Technology', in F. Wendorf & A.E. Close (eds), *Advances in World Archaeology 1*, New York, 213-64.
1984 'Metal Technology of the Harappans', in Lal & Gupta (eds) 1984, 163-67.
1985 *The Archaeology of India*, Scandinavian Institute of Asian Studies, Monograph 46, London & Malmö.

AINSWORTH, W.
1838 *Researches in Assyria, Babylonia and Chaldaea, forming part of the labours of the Euphrates Expedition*, London.

ALDEN, J.R.
1982 'Trade and Politics in Proto-Elamite Iran', *Current Anthropology* 23, 613-640.
1987 'The Susa III Period', in Hole (ed.) 1987, 157-70.

ALGAZE, G.
1983-84 'Private Houses and Graves at Ingharra, A Reconsideration', *Mesopotamia* XVIII-XIX, 135-93.
1986 'Habuba on the Tigris: Archaic Nineveh Reconsidered', *JNES* 45, 125-37.
1986a 'Kurban Hüyük and the Chalcolithic Period in the Northwest Mesopotamian Periphery: A Preliminary Assessment', in Finkbeiner & Röllig (eds) 1986, 274-311.
1986b *Mesopotamian Expansion and its Consequences: Informal Empire in the Late Fourth Millennium B.C.*, Ph.D. Dissertation, Chicago.
1989 'The Uruk Expansion: Cross-cultural Exchange in Early Mesopotamian Civilization', *Current Anthropology* 30, 571-91, 601-08.

ALLAN, J.W.
1979 *Persian Metal Technology 700-1300 A.D.*, Ithaca.

ALLCHIN, B., ALLCHIN, F.R.
1982 *The Rise of Civilization in India and Pakistan*, Cambridge.

ALLCHIN, B. (ed.)
1984 *South Asian Archaeology 1981*, Cambridge.

ALLOTTE DE LA FÜYE, F.-M.
1908-20 *Documents presargoniques*, Paris

ALSTER, B.
1975 *Studies in Mesopotamian Proverbs*, Mesopotamia: Copenhagen Studies in Assyriology 3, Copenhagen.
1983 'Dilmun, Bahrain and the alleged Paradise in Sumerian Myth and Legend', in Potts (ed.) 1983, 39-74.
1985 Review of Cooper 1983a, *Welt des Orients* 16, 159-62.
1990 'Lugalbanda and the Early Epic Tradition in Mesopotamia', in T. Abusch, J. Huehnergard & P. Steinkeller (eds), *Lingering Over Words: Studies in Ancient Near Eastern Literature in Honor of William L. Moran*, Atlanta, 59-72.

AMIET, P.
1966 'Il y a 5000 ans les élamites inventaient l'écriture', *Archéologia* 12 (Sept.-Oct. 1966), 16-23.
1966a *Elam*, Auvers-sur-Oise.
1967 Review of Buchanan 1966, *RA* 61, 181-84.
1970 'Une masse d'armes présargonique de la Collection Foroughi', *RA* 64, 9-16.
1971 'La glyptique de l'Acropole (1969-1971). Tablettes lenticulaires de Suse', *DAFI* 1, 217-233.
1972 *Glyptique susienne des origines à l'époque des perses achéménides*, *MDP* XLIII, 2 vols, Paris.
1973 'Glyptique élamite à propos de documents nouveaux', *Arts Asiatiques* XXVI, 3-64.
1973a 'En Iran Central, la civilisation du désert de Lut', *Archéologia* 60, 20-27.
1974 'Antiquités du désert de Lut, I. À propos d'objets de la collection Foroughi', *RA* LXVIII, 97-110.
1975 'A Cylinder Seal Impression found at Umm an-Nar', *East and West* 25, 425-426.
1976 *Collection David-Weill, Les antiquités du Luristan*, Paris.
1976a *L'art d'Agadé au Musée du Louvre*, Paris.
1976b 'Antiquités du désert du Lut. - II', *RA* LXX, 1-8.
1976c 'Contribution à l'histoire de la sculpture archaïque de Suse', *DAFI* 6, 47-82.
1977 'Bactriane proto-historique', *Syria* LIV, 89-121.
1977a 'Pour une interprétation nouvelle du répertoire iconographique de la glyptique d'Agadé', *RA* LXXI, 107-16.

1978 'Antiquités de Bactriane', *La Revue du Louvre et des Musées de France* XXVIII, 153-64.
1979 'Les sceaux de Shahr-i Sokhta', in Lohuizen-de Leeuw (ed.) 1979, 3-6.
1979a 'Archaeological Discontinuity and Ethnic Duality in Elam', *Antiquity* LIII, 195-204.
1980 *La glyptique mésopotamienne archaïque*, 2nd revised edition, Paris.
1980a *Art of the Ancient Near East*, translated by J. Shepley & C. Choquet, New York.
1980b 'Antiquités de serpentine', *Iranica Antiqua* XV, 155-66.
1983 'Iconographie de la Bactriane Proto-Historique', *Anatolian Studies* 33, 19-27.
1985 'La période IV de Tépé Sialk reconsidérée', in Huot *et al.* (eds) 1985, 293-312.
1985a 'À propos de l'usage et de l'iconographie des sceaux à Suse', *Paléorient* 11/2, 37f.
1986 *L'âge des échanges inter-iraniens 3500-1700 avant J.-C.*, Paris.
1986a 'L'usage des sceaux à l'époque initiale de l'histoire de Suse', in Huot (ed.) 1986, 17-24.
1986b 'Au-delà d'Elam', *AMI* 19, 11-20.
1987 'Une statue de Gudea', *La Revue du Louvre* 1987, 169-71.
1987a 'Approche physique de la comptabilité à l'époque d'Uruk. Les bulles-enveloppes de Suse', in Huot (ed.) 1987, 331-34.
1987b Review of Kohl 1984 and Pottier 1984, *RA* 81, 174-76.
1988 *Suse, 6000 ans d'histoire*, Paris.
1993 'The Period of Irano-Mesopotamian Contacts 3500 - 1600 BC', in Curtis (ed.) 1993, 23-30.

AMIET, P., TOSI, M.
1978 'Phase 10 at Shahr-i Sokhta: Excavations in Square XDV and the late 4th Millennium B.C. Assemblage of Sistan', *East and West* 28, 9-31.

AMIET, P. *et al.*
1980 *Sumer, Assur, Babylone, Chefs-d'oeuvre du Musée de Baghdad*, Paris.

ANDRÉ-LEICHNAM, B., TALLON, F.
1985 'Une herminette inscrite du Luristan', in Huot *et al.* (eds) 1985, 347-53.

ANDRÉ-LEICHNAM, B. *et al.*
1982 *Naissance de l'écriture, cunéiformes et hiéroglyphes*, Paris.

ARCHI, A.
1979-80 'Les dieux d'Ebla au III millénaire avant J.C. et les dieux d'Ugarit', *Annales archéologiques syriennes* 29/30, 167-70.
1985 'Mardu in the Ebla Texts', *Orientalia* 54, 7-13.
1985a 'Rois de Mari et d'Ebla au IIIe millénaire', *MARI* 4, 47-51.
1987 'gin DILMUN "sicle pesé, standard"', *RA* 81, 186f.

ARNE, T.J.
1945 *Excavations at Shah Tepé, Iran*, Stockholm.

ASTOUR, M.
1978 'Les hourrites en Syrie du nord: rapport sommaire', *Revue Hittite et Asianique* 36, 1-22.

AUE, C.
1985 'Uruk-Warka XXXVII: Survey des Stadtgebietes von Uruk II. Zu den Bauaufnahmen dieser Kampagne', *Baghdader Mitteilungen* 16, 59-65.

AZARPAY, G.
1990 'A Photogrammetric Study of Three Gudea Statues', *JAOS* 110, 660-65.

BALTY, J.C. *et al.*
1988 *Musées Royaux d'Art et d'Histoire Bruxelles, Antiquité*, Brussels.

BARNETT, R.D.
1985 'Lachish, Askelon and the Camel: A Discussion of its use in Southern Palestine', in J. Tubb (ed.) *Palestine in the Bronze and Iron Ages*, 15-30.

BARRELET, M.-T. (ed.)
1981 *L'archéologie de l'Iraq: Perspectives et limites de l'interpretation anthropologique des documents*, Paris.

BARTON, G.A.
1913 *The Origin and Development of Babylonian Writing*, *Beiträge zur Assyriologie* IX.

BASMACHI, F.
1950 'Sculptured Stone Vases in the Iraq Museum', *Sumer* VI, 165-176.

BAUER, J.
1972 *Altsumerische Wirtschaftstexte aus Lagaš*, Studia Pohl 9, Rome.

BAZIN, D., HÜBNER, H.
1969 'Copper Deposits in Iran', *Geological Survey of Iran*, No. 13.

BEALE, T.W.
1973 'Early Trade in Highland Iran: A View from a Source Area', *World Archaeology* 5/2, 133-148.

BEALE, T.W. *et al.*
1986 *Excavations at Tepe Yahya, Iran 1967-1975*, Cambridge, Mass.

BECKER, M.J.
1985 'Soft-Stone Analysis', in Donaldson *et al.* 1985, 102-121.

BEHM-BLANCKE, M.R.
1979 *Das Tierbild in der altmesopotamischen Rundplastik*, Baghdader Forschungen Band I, Mainz am Rhein.

BEHM-BLANKE, M.R., *et al.*
1981 'Hassek Hüyük: Vorläufiger Bericht über die Ausgrabungen der Jahre 1978-1980', *Istanbuler Mitteilungen* 31, 11-93.

BEHRENS, H., LODING, D., ROTH, M.T.
1989 *DUMU-E₂-DUB-BA-A: Studies in Honor of Åke W. Sjöberg*, Philadelphia.

BEHRENS, H., STEIBLE, H.
1983 *Glossar zu den altsumerischen Bau- und Weihinschriften*, FAOS 6, Wiesbaden.

BELLELLI, G.M.
1989   'Reflections on an "Unexcavated" Precious Vase with Zoomorphic Decoration', *Iranica Antiqua* XXIV, 87-108.

BENITO, C.A.
1969   'Enki and Ninmah' and 'Enki and the World Order', Ph.D. Dissertation, Ann Arbor.

BERLIN, A.
1979   *Enmerkar and Ensuḫkeśdanna, A Sumerian Narrative Poem*, Philadelphia.
1983   'Ethnopoetry and the Enmerkar Epics', *JAOS* 103, 17-24.

BERTHOUD, TH., CLEUZIOU, S., HURTEL, L.P., MENU, M., VOLFOVSKY, C.
1982   'Cuivres et alliages en Iran, Afghanistan, Oman au cours des IVe et IIIe millénaires', *Paléorient* 8/2, 39-54.

BERTHOUD, TH., CLEUZIOU, S.
1983   'Farming Communities of the Oman Penisula and the Copper of Makkan', *JOS* 6, 239-46.

BEYER, D.
1989   'Un nuveau temoine des relations entre Mari et le monde iranien aux 3eme millénaire', *Iranica Antiqua* XXIV, 109-20.

BIBBY, T.G.
1972   *Looking for Dilmun*, London.

BIELIŃSKI, P.
1987   'Les vases en pierre de Tell el-Saadiya et des autre sites Obéidiens', in Huot (ed.) 1987, 261-75.

BIGGS, R.D.
1966   'Le lapis-lazuli dans les textes sumériens archaïques' *RA* 60, 175-176.
1969   *Cuneiform Texts from Nippur, The Eighth and Ninth Seasons*, Assyriological Studies 17, Chicago.
1974   *Inscriptions from Tell Abu Salabikh*, OIP 99, Chicago.
1981   'Ebla and Abu Salabikh: The Linguistic and Literary Aspects' in L. Cagni (ed.) *La Lingua di Ebla*, Naples, 121-133.

BING, J.D.
1977   'Gilgameš and Lugalbanda in the Fara Period', *Journal of the Ancient Near Eastern Society* 9, 1-4.

BISCIONI, R. *et al.*
1974   'Archaeological Discoveries and Methodological Problems in the Excavations of Shahr-i Sokhta', in J.E. van Lohuizen-de Leeuw & J.M.M. Ubaghs (eds), *South Asian Archaeology 1973*, Leiden, 12-52.

BISCIONI, R., SALVATORI, S., TOSI, M.
1977   'Shahr-i Sokhta: The Protohistoric Settlement and the Chronological Sequence', in Tucci (ed.) 1977, 103-12.

BLACKMAN, J., MÉRY, S., WRIGHT, R.P.
1989   'Production and Exchange of Ceramics on the Oman Penninsula from the Perspective of Hili', *Journal of Field Archaeology* 16, 61-77.

BLACKMAN, M.J.
1980   'Long Range and Local Exchange Patterns in Southern Iran', in Sumner (ed.) 1980, 4 pp.
1982   'The Manufacture and Use of Burned Lime Plaster at Proto-Elamite Anshan (Iran)', in Wertime & Wertime (eds) 1982, 107-15.
1989   'Mineral Talc Samples from Tappeh Hesār, 1976', in Dyson & Howard (eds) 1989, 125.

BOEHMER, R.M.
1965   *Die Entwicklung der Glyptik während der Akkad-Zeit*, Berlin.
1966   'Die Datierung des Puzur/Kutik-Inšušinak und einige sich daraus ergebende Konsequenzen', *Orientalia* 35, 345-76.
1967   'Zur Datierung des Epirmupi', *ZA* 58, 302-10.
1984   'Kalkstein für das urukzeitliche Uruk', *Baghdader Mitteilungen* 15, 141-47.
1984a   'Uruk-Warka XXXVI: Survey des Stadtgebietes von Uruk', *Baghdader Mitteilungen* 15, 113-40.

BOESE, J.
1971   *Altmesopotamische Weihplatten*, Berlin.

BORGER, R.
1971   'Gott Marduk and Gott-König Šulgi als Propheten, Zwei prophetische Texte', *Bibliotheca Orientalis* 28, 3-24.

BÖRKER-KLÄHN, J.
1970   *Unterschungen zur altelamischen Archäologie*, Berlin.
1982   *Altvorderasiatische Bildstelen und vergleichbare Felsreliefs*, Mainz am Rhein.

BOTTÉRO, J.
1961   'Inventaire des tablettes', in H.J. Lenzen, *XVII. vorläufiger Bericht ... Uruk-Warka*, Berlin, 45-56.
1967   'The First Semitic Empire', in J. Bottéro, E. Cassin, J. Vercoutter (eds), *The Near East: The Early Civilizations*, trans. R.F. Tannenbaum, New York.

BOUCHARLAT, R., HAERINCK, E., PHILLIPS, C.S., POTTS, D.T.
1988   'Archaeological Reconaissance at ed-Dur, Umm al-Qaiwain, U.A.E.', *Akkadica* 58, 1-26.

BOVINGTON, C.H., DYSON, R.H., MAHDAVI, A., MASOUMI, R.
1974   'The Radiocarbon Evidence for the Terminal Date of the Hissar IIIC Culture', *Iran* XII, 195-199.

BOVINGTON, C., MAHDAVI, A., MASSOUMI, R.
1983   'Radiocarbon Evidence for a Chronology for S.E. Iran from the mid 4th to mid 3rd millennium B.C.', in Tosi (ed.) 1983, 349-55.

BOWEN-JONES, H.
1968   'Agriculture', in Fisher (ed.) 1968, 565-598.

BRAIDWOOD, R.J., BRAIDWOOD, L.S.
  1960   *Excavations in the Plain of Antioch I:
          the Earlier Assemblages, Phases A - J*,
          OIP LXI, Chicago
BRAIDWOOD, R.J., HOWE, B.
  1960   *Prehistoric Investigations in Iraqi
          Kurdistan*, SAOC 31, Chicago.
BRANDES, M.A.
  1980   'Modelage et imprimerie aux debuts de
          l'écriture en Mésopotamie', *Akkadica* 18,
          1-30.
  1979   *Siegelabrollungen aus den archaischen
          Bauschichten in Uruk-Warka*,
          Wiesbaden.
BRAUN-HOLZINGER, E.A.
  1977   *Frühdynastische Beterstatuetten*,
          Berlin.
  1984   *Figürliche Bronzen aus Mesopotamien*,
          Munich.
  1987   'Nochmals zu Naramsins "Beute von
          Magan"', *Oriens Antiquus*, 285-90.
  1991   *Mesopotamische Weihgaben der
          Frühdynastischen bis Altbabylonischen
          Zeit*, Heidelberger Studien zum Alten
          Orient 3, Heidelberg.
BRENTJES, B.
  1960   'Das Camel im Alten Orient', *Klio* 38,
          23-52.
  1971   'Ein elamischer Streufund aus Soch,
          Fergana (Usbekistan)', *Iran* IX, 155.
  1986   'Neue Daten zur Turkmenischen
          Frühzeit', *AMI* 19, 41-47.
BRETON, L. LE
  1957   'The Early Periods at Susa,
          Mesopotamian Relations', *Iraq* XIX, 79-
          124.
BRICE, W.C.
  1962-3 'The Writing System of the Proto-Elamite
          Account Tablets of Susa', *Bulletin of the
          John Rylands Library* 45, 15-39.
  1966   *South-West Asia, A Systematic Regional
          Geography*, London.
  1978   'Synopses' and 'Conclusion', in Brice
          (ed.) 1978, 82f., 211f., 275f., 350-56.
  1979   'The Pictographic Tablets from Jemdet
          Nasr', in O. Carruba (ed.), *Studia
          Mediterranea Piero Meriggi dicata*, vol. I,
          Pavia, 65-74.
BRICE, W.C. (ed.)
  1978   *The Environmental History of the Near
          and Middle East Since the Last Ice Age*,
          London.
BRUNSWIG JR, R.H., PARPOLA, A., POTTS, D.T.
  1983   'New Indus and Related Seals from the
          Near East', in Potts (ed.) 1983, 101-15.
BUCCELLATI, G.
  1966   *The Amorites of the Ur III Period*,
          Naples.
BUCHANAN, B.
  1954   'The Date of the So-Called Second
          Dynasty Graves of the Royal Cemetery
          at Ur', *JAOS* 74, 147-53.
  1966   *Catalogue of Ancient Near Eastern Seals
          in the Ashmolean Museum. Volume I,
          Cylinder Seals*, Oxford.

  1967   'The Prehistoric Stamp Seal: A
          Reconsideration of Some Old
          Excavations', *JAOS* 87, 265-79, 525-40.
  1981   *Ancient Near Eastern Seals in the Yale
          Babylonian Collection*, New Haven &
          London.
BULGARELLI, G.M.
  1977   'Stone-working Techniques and Bone
          Industry', in Tucci (ed.) 1977, 273-276.
  1979   'The Lithic Industry of Tepe Hissar at
          the Light of Recent Excavation', in
          Taddei (ed.) 1979, 39-54.
  1981   'Turquoise Working in the Helmand
          Civilization: Some Observations', in
          Härtel (ed.) 1981, 65-69.
BULLIET, R.W.
  1975   *The Camel and the Wheel*, Cambridge
          Mass.
BURKHOLDER, G.
  1971   'Steatite Carvings from Saudi Arabia',
          Artibus Asiae XXXIII, 306-322.
  1984   *An Arabian Collection*, Artifacts from the
          Eastern Province, Boulder City, Nevada.
BURTON BROWN, T.
  1951   *Excavations in Azarbaijan, 1948*,
          London.
BUSSERS, H.
  1984   'Glyptique de Tell ed-Der', in L. de Meyer
          (ed.), *Tell ed-Der, Progress Reports
          (Second Series)*, Leuven, 63-79.
BUTZ, K.
  1983   'Dilmun in Wirtschaftstexten der Ur III-
          Zeit', in Potts (ed.) 1983, 91.
CALDWELL, D.H.
  1976   'The Glyptic of Gawra, Giyan and Susa,
          and the Development of Long Distance
          Trade', *Orientalia* 45, 227-250.
CALDWELL, J.R.
  1968   'Ghazir, Tell-i', *RlA* III, 348-55.
CALDWELL, J.R. (ed.)
  1967   *Investigations at Tal-i Iblis*, Springfield.
CALDWELL, J.R., SHAHMIRZADI, S.M.
  1966   *Tal-i Iblis: The Kerman Range and the
          Beginnings of Smelting*, Springfield.
CALMEYER, P.
  1969   *Datierbare Bronzen aus Luristan und
          Kirmanshah*, Berlin.
CALOI, L., COMPAGNONI, B., TOSI, M.
  1978   'Preliminary Remarks on the Faunal
          Remains from Shahr-i Sokhta', in
          Meadow and Zeder (eds) 1978, 87-90.
CALVET, Y., SALLES, J.-F.
  1986   *Failaka Fouilles Français 1984-1985*,
          Travaux de la Maison de l'Orient 12,
          Lyon & Paris.
CAMERON, G.C.
  1936   *History of Early Iran*, Chicago.
CANAL, D.
  1978a   'Travaux à la terrasse haute de
          l'Acropole de Susa (1)', *DAFI* 9, 11-55.
  1978b   'La haute terrasse de l'Acropole de
          Suse', *Paléorient* 4, 169-176.
CARDI, B. DE
  1970   *Excavations at Bampur, A Third
          Millennium Settlement in Persian
          Baluchistan*, New York.

1971 'Archaeological Survey in the Northern Trucial States', *East and West* 21, 225-89.

1975 'Survey and Excavations in Central Oman, 1974-75', *JOS* 1, 109-111

1984 'Some Third and Fourth Millennium Sites in Sarawan and Jhalawan, Baluchistan, in Relation to the Mehrgarh Sequence', in B. Allchin (ed.) 1984, 61-68.

CARDI, B. DE *et al.*
1976 'Excavations and Survey in Oman, 1974-1975', *JOS* 2, 101-187.

1977 'Excavation and Survey in the Sharqiyah, Oman', *JOS* 3, 17-34.

CARTER, E.
1978 'Suse "Ville Royale"', *Paléorient* 4, 197-211.

1979 'Elamite Pottery, ca. 2000-1000 B.C.', *JNES* 38, 111-28.

1980 'Excavations in Ville Royale I at Susa: The Third Millennium B.C. Occupation', *DAFI* 11, 11-134.

1984 'Archaeology', in Carter & Stolper 1984, 103-230.

1985 'Notes on Archaeology and Social and Economic History of Susiana', *Paléorient* 11/2, 43-48.

1987 'The Piedmont and the Pusht-i Kuh in the Early Third Millennium B.C.', in Huot (ed.) 1987, 73-83.

1990 'Elamite Exports', in Vallat (ed.) 1990, 89-99.

1991 Review of Kohl 1984, *AJA* 95, 167-70.

CARTER, E., STOLPER, M.W.
1976 'Middle Elamite Malyan', *Expedition* 18/2, 33-42.

1984 *Elam: Surveys of Political History and Archaeology*, Near Eastern Studies 25, Berkeley and Los Angeles.

CASAL, J.M.
1961 *Fouilles de Mundigak*, 2 vols, Paris.
1964 *Fouilles d'Amri*, 2 vols, Paris.

CASANOVA, M.
1982 *Etude de la vaiselle d'albâtre d'Iran et d'Asie Centrale de la seconde moitié du IIIe millénaire*, unpublished thesis, Université de Paris I, Pantheon-Sorbonne.

CAVIGNEAUX, A.
1976 *Die sumerisch-akkadischen Zeichenlisten Überlieferungsprobleme*, PhD thesis, Munich.

CHAKRABARTI, D.K.
1982 '"Long Barrel-Cylinder" Beads and the Issue of Pre-Sargonic Contact between the Harappan Civilization and Mesopotamia', in G.L. Possehl (ed.), *Harappan Civilization: A Contemporary Perspective*, Delhi, 265-70.

CHAMLOU, GH.
1972 'Explorations archéologique dans la region de Minab', *Bastan Chenassi va Honar-e Iran* 9-10, 84-86.

CHARLES, J.A.
1980 'The Coming of Copper and Copper-base Alloys and Iron: A Metallurgical Sequence', in Wertime & Muhly (eds) 1980, 151-81.

CHARVÁT, P.
1974 'Pre-Sargonic Adab', *Archív Orientální* 42, 161-166.

1976 'The Oldest Royal Dynasty of Ancient Mesopotamia', *Archív Orientální* 44, 346-352.

1978 'The Growth of Lugalzagesi's Empire', in B. Hruška & G. Komoróczy (eds), *Festschrift Lubor Matouš*, Budapest, 43-49.

1979 'Early Ur', *Archív Orientální* 47, 15-20.

1984 Review of Foster 1982, in *Bibliotheca Orientalis* XLI (1/2), 136-141.

CHEVALIER, J., INIZAN, M.L., TIXIER, J.
1982 'Une technique de perforation par precussion de perles en cornaline (Larsa, Iraq)', *Paléorient* 8/2, 55-65.

CHRISTIAN, V.
1940 *Altertumskunds des Zweistromlandes I*, Leipzig.

CIARLA, R.
1979 'The Manufacture of Alabaster Vessels at Shahr-i Sokhta and Mundigak in the 3rd millennium B.C.: A Problem of Cultural Identity', in Gnoli & Rossi (eds) 1979, 319-35.

1981 'A Preliminary Analysis of the Manufacture of Alabaster Vessels at Shahr-i Sokhta and Mundigak in the 3rd Millennium B.C.', in Härtel (ed.) 1981, 45-63.

1985 'Bronze-Age Crafts at Failaka: Some Preliminary Observations on Stone Vase Fragments', *East and West* 34, 396-406.

CIVIL, M.
1967 'Šū-Sîn's Historical Inscriptions: Collection B', *JCS* XXI, 24-38.

1979 'Sur l'inscription de Lugalannemundu', *RA* 73, 93.

1983 'Enlil and Ninlil: The Marriage of Sud', *JAOS* 103, 43-64.

1985 'On Some Texts Mentioning Ur-Nammu', *Orientalia* 54, 27-45.

1989 'The Statue of Šulgi-ki-ur$_5$-sag$_9$-kalam-ma. Part I: The Inscription', in Behrens *et al.* (eds) 1989, 49-64.

CLEUZIOU, S.
1978-79 'The Second and Third Seasons of Excavation at Hili 8', *Archaeology in the United Arab Emirates* II-III, 30-69.

1980 'Three Seasons at Hili: Towards a Chronology and Cultural History of the Oman Peninsula in the 3rd millennium B.C.', *PSAS* 10, 19-32.

1981 'Oman in the Early 2nd Millennium B.C.', in Härtel (ed.) 1981, 279-93.

1986 'Dilmun and Makkan during the Third and early Second Millennia B.C.', in al Khalifa & Rice (eds) 1986, 143-55.

1989   'The Chronology of Protohistoric Oman as Seen from Hili', in Costa & Tosi (eds), 1989, 47-78.

1989a   'Excavations at Hili 8: a preliminary report on the 4th to 7th campaigns', *Archaeology in the United Arab Emirates* 5, 61-87.

CLEUZIOU, S., BERTHOUD, TH.
1982   'Early Tin in the Near East: A Reassessment in the Light of New Evidence from Afghanistan', *Expedition* 25/1, 14-19.

CLEUZIOU, S., TOSI M.
1989   'The South-eastern Frontier of the Ancient Near East', in Frifelt & Sørensen (eds) 1989, 15-47.

CLEUZIOU, S., VOGT, B.
1983   'Umm an-Nar Burial Customs: New Evidence from Tomb A at Hili North', *PSAS* 13, 37-52.

1985   'Tomb A at Hili North (United Arab Emirates) and its Material Connections to Southeast Iran and the Greater Indus Valley', in J. Schotsmans & M. Taddei (eds), *South Asian Archaeology 1983*, Istituto Universario Orientale Dipartimento di Studi Asiatici, Series Minor XXIII, Naples, 249-77.

CLUTTON-BROCK, J.
1981   *Domesticated Animals from Early Times*, London.

1986   'Osteology of the Equids from Sumer', in Meadow & Uerpmann (eds) 1986, 207-229.

CLUTTON-BROCK, J., BURLEIGH, R.
1978   'The Animal Remains from Abu Salabikh: Preliminary Report', *Iraq* XL, 89-100.

COHEN, M.E.
1975   'ur.sag.me.šár.ur₄. A Širnamšubba of Ninurta', *Die Welt des Orient* VIII, 22-36.

1976   'A New Naram-Sin Date Formula', *JCS* XXVIII, 227-232.

COHEN, S.
1973   *Enmerkar and the Lord of Aratta*, Ph.D. Dissertation, Ann Arbor.

COLBOW, G.
1987   *Zur Rundplastik des Gudea von Lagaš*, Münchener Vorderasiatische Studien 5, Munich.

COLLON, D.
1977   'Ivory', *Iraq* XXXIX, 219-222.
1981-82 Review of Brandes 1979, *AfO* XXVIII, 177-81.
1982   *Catalogue of the Western Asiatic Seals in the British Museum, Cylinder Seals II: Akkadian - Post-Akkadian - Ur III Periods*, London.
1986   *Catalogue of Western Asiatic Seals in the British Museum, Cylinder Seals III: Isin-Larsa and Old Babylonian Periods*, London.
1987   *First Impressions: Cylinder Seals in the Ancient Near East*, London & Chicago.

COLLON, D., GELLER, M.J.
1983   Review of Buchanan 1981, *Bibliotheca Orientalis* 40, 204-10.

COLLON, D., READE, J.
1983   'Archaic Nineveh', *Baghdader Mitteilungen* 14, 33-41.

COMPAGNONI, B.
1978   'The Bone Remains of *Equus hemionus* from Shahr-i Sokhta', in Meadow and Zeder (eds) 1978, 105-118.

COMPAGNONI, B., TOSI, M.
1978   'The Camel: Its Distribution and State of Domestication in the Middle East during the Third Millennium B.C. in Light of Finds from Shahr-i Sokhta', in Meadow & Zeder (eds) 1978, 91-103.

CONTENAU, G.
1927   *Manuel d'archéologie orientale*, Vol. I, Paris.

1931   *Manuel d'archéologie orientale*, Vol. II, Paris.

1949   'Introduction', *MDP* XXXI, 1-3.

CONTENAU, G., GHIRSHMAN, R.
1935   *Fouilles de Tépé Giyan*, Paris.

COOPER, J.C.
1980   'Apodotic Death and the Historicity of "Historical" Omens', in B. Alster (ed.), *Death in Mesopotamia*, (26e RAI), Mesopotamia 8, Copenhagen, 99-105.

1983   *Reconstructing History from Ancient Inscriptions: The Lagaš-Umma Border Conflict*, SANE 2/1, Malibu.

1983a   *The Curse of Agade*, Baltimore and London.

1984   'Studies in Mesopotamian Lapidary Inscriptions III', *Iraq* XLVI, 87-93.

1986   *Sumerian and Akkadian Royal Inscriptions I: Presargonic Inscriptions*, New Haven.

COOPER, J., HEIMPEL, W.
1983   'The Sumerian Sargon Legend', *JOAS* 103, 67-82.

COSTA, P.M., TOSI, M. (eds)
1989   *Oman Studies: Papers on the Archaeology and History of Oman*, Serie Orientale Roma LXIII, Rome.

COSTANTINI, L., TOSI, M.
1977   'Population and Natural Resources in Prehistoric Seistan', in Tucci (ed.) 1977, 287-293.

1978   'The Environment of Southern Seistan in the Third Millennium B.C., and its Exploitation by the Proto-urban Hilmand Civilization', in Brice (ed.) 1978, 165-183.

CRADDOCK, P.T.
1984   'Tin and Tin Solder in Sumer: Preliminary Comments', *MASCA Journal* 3/1, 7-9.

1985   'The Composition of the Metal Artifacts', in Donaldson *et al.* 1985, 97-101.

CRAWFORD, H.E.W.
1973   'Mesopotamia's Invisible Exports in the Third Millennium B.C.', *World Archaeology* 5, 232-241.

1974 'The Problem of Tin in Mesopotamian Bronzes', *World Archaeology* 6, 242-247.

CRAWFORD, V.E.
1954 Babylonian Inscriptions in the Collection of James B. Nies, vol. IX, New Haven.
1977 'Inscriptions from Lagash, Season Four, 1975-76', *JCS* 29, 189-222.

CROS, G.
1910-14 *Nouvelles fouilles de Tello*, Paris.

CROWFOOT PAYNE, J.
1968 'Lapis Lazuli in Early Egypt', *Iraq* XXX, 58-61.

CURCHIN, L.
1977 'Eannatum and the Kings of Adab', *RA* LXXI, 93-95.

CURTIS, J.E.
1986 'A Basalt Sculpture Found at Warka', *Baghdader Mitteilungen* 17, 131-34.
1988 'A Reconsideration of the Cemetery at Khinaman, South-East Iran', *Iranica Antiqua* XXIII, 97-124.

CURTIS, J.E. (ed.)
1982 *Fifty Years of Mesopotamian Discovery*, London.
1993 *Early Mesopotamia and Iran: Contact and Conflict 3500-1600 BC*, London.

DALES, G.F.
1973 'Archaeological and Radiocarbon Chronologies for Protohistoric South Asia', in N. Hammond (ed.), *South Asian Archaeology*, Cambridge, 157-69.
1977 'Shifting Trade Patterns between the Iranian Plateau and the Indus Valley in the Third Millennium B.C.', in Deshayes (ed.) 1977, 67-78.
1977a 'Hissar IIIC Stone Objects in Afghan Seistan', in Levine & Young (eds) 1977, 17-27.
1979 'The Balakot Project: Summary of Four Years Excavations in Pakistan', in Taddei (ed.) 1979, 241-273.

DAMEROW, P., ENGLUND, R.K.
1989 *The Proto-Elamite Texts from Tepe Yahya*, Cambridge, Mass.

DAVEY, C.J.
1988 'Tell edh-Dhiba'i and the Southern Near Eastern Metalworking Tradition', in Maddin (ed.) 1988, 63-68.

DAVID, H., TEGYEY, M., LE METOR, J., WYNS, R.
1990 'Les vases en chlorite dans la péninsule d'Oman: une étude pétrographique appliquée à l'archéologie', *Comptes-Rendus de l'Académie des Sciences* 311, Ser. II, 951-58.

DAVIDOVIĆ, V.
1984 'Testi di Ur III concernenti bottino di guerra?', *Annali* (Istituto Universario Orientale) 44, 177-205.

DAYTON, J.E.
1971 'The Problem of Tin in the Ancient World', *World Archaeology* 3, 49-70.
1978 *Minerals, Metals, Glazing and Man*, London.

DEGRAEVE, A.
1991 'Je t'écris au sujet d'une pierre ...', *Akkadica* 74-75, 1-18.

DEIMEL, A.
1923 *Die Inschriften von Fara II, Schultexte aus Fara*, Leipzig.
1925-50 *Šumerisches Lexikon*, IV vols, Rome.

DELAPORTE, L.
1920 *Catalogue des cylindres, cachets et pierres gravées de style oriental I. Fouilles et missions*, Paris.

DELOUGAZ, P.P.
1940 *The Temple Oval at Khafajah*, OIP LIII, Chicago.
1952 *Pottery from the Diyala Region*, OIP LXIII, Chicago.
1960 'Architectural Representations on Steatite Vases', *Iraq* XXII, 90-95.
1967 *Private Houses and Graves in the Diyala Region*, OIP LXXXVIII, Chicago.

DELOUGAZ, P.P., KANTOR, H.J.
1972 'New Evidence for the Prehistoric and Protoliterate Culture Development of Khuzistan', *Memorial Volume. The Vth International Congress on Iranian Art and Archaeology, 1968, Teheran*, vol. I, 14-33.
1973 'Choga Mish', *Iran* XI, 189-191.

DE MAIGRET, A.
1976 *Le Lance nell'Asia anteriore nell'età del Bronzo*, Studi Tipologico, Rome.

DESHAYES, J.
1958 'Marteaux de bronze iraniens', *Syria* XXIV, 284-293.
1960 *Les Outiles de bronze de l'Indus au Danube (IVe au IIe millénaire)*, II vols, Paris.
1967 'Tureng Tepe', *Archéologia* 18, 32-37.
1970 'Tureng Tépé', *Iran* VIII, 207f.
1975 'Les fouilles récentes de Tureng Tépé: La terrasse haute de la fin du IIIe millénaire', *Comptus Rendus de l'Académie des Inscriptions et Belles-Lettres 1975*, 522-530.
1976 'Tureng Tépé', *Iran* XIV, 169-171.
1977 'A propos des terrasses hautes de la fin du IIIe millénaire en Iran et Asie Centrale', in Deshayes (ed.) 1977, 95-111.

DESHAYES, J. (ed.)
1977 *Le plateau iranien et l'Asie centrale des origines à la conquête islamique. Leurs relations à la lumière des documents archéologique*, CNRS, Paris.

DIAKONOFF, I.M., STAROSTIN, S.A.
1986 *Hurro-Urartian as an Eastern Caucasion Language*, Munich.

DIJK, J. VAN
1960 'F. Inschriftliche Funde', in H.J. Lenzen, *XVI. vorläufiger Bericht ... Uruk-Warka*, Berlin, 57-60.
1969 'Les contacts ethnique dans la Mésopotamie et les syncrétismes de la religion sumérienne', in S.S. Hartman (ed.), *Syncretism* (Scripta Instituti

Donerriani Aboensis, vol. 3), Stockholm, 171-206.

1971   *Nicht-Kanonische Beschwörungen und sonstige literarische Texte*, Berlin.

1978   'Išbi'Erra, Kindattu, l'homme d'Elam, et la chute de la ville d'Ur', *JCS* 30, 189-208.

1978a 'Fremdsprachige Beschwörungstexte in der südmesopotamischen literarischen Überlieferung', in Nissen & Renger (eds) 1978, 97-110.

1983   *LUGAL UD ME-LÁM-bi NIR-ĜÁL, Le récit épique et didactique des Traveaux de Ninurta, du Déluge et de la Nouvelle Création*, II vols, Leiden.

DITTMANN, R.
1986   'Susa in the Proto-Elamite Period and Annotations on the Painted Pottery of Proto-Elamite Khuzestan', in Finkbeiner & Röllig (eds) 1986, 171-96.

1986a 'Seals, Sealings and Tablets: Thoughts on the Changing Pattern of Administrative Control from the Late-Uruk to the Proto-Elamite Periods at Susa', in Finkbeiner & Röllig (eds) 1986, 332-366.

1986b *Betrachtungen zur Frühzeit des südwest-Iran. Regionale Entwicklungen vom 6. bis zum frühen 3. vorchristlichen Jahrtausend*, Berliner Beiträge zum Vorderen Orient 4, Berlin.

DOLUKHANOV, P.M.
1981   'The Ecological Prerequisites for Early Farming in Southern Turkmenia', in Kohl (ed.) 1981, 359-385.

DONALDSON, P. et. al.
1985   'Prehistoric Tombs of Ras al-Khaimah', *Oriens Antiquus* XXIV, 85-142.

DONBAZ, V., FOSTER, B.R.
1982   *Sargonic Texts from Tello in the Istanbul Archaeological Museum*, Philadelphia.

DONBAZ, V., HALLO. W.W.
1976   'Monumental Texts from Pre-Sargonic Lagaš', *Oriens Antiquus* XV, 1-9.

DORNEMANN, R.H.
1980   'Tell Hadidi: An Important Centre of the Mitannian Period and Earlier', in J.Cl. Margueron (ed.), *Le Moyen Euphrate*, Strasbourg.

DOSSIN, G.
1962   'Bronzes inscrits du Luristan de la collection Foroughi', *Iranica Antiqua* II, 149-164.

1970   'La route de l'étain en Mésopotamie au temps de Zimre-Lim', *RA* 64, 97-106.

VAN DRIEL, G.
1973   'On "Standard" and "Triumphal" Inscriptions', in M.A. Beek *et al.* (eds) *Symbolae Biblicae et Mesopotamicae Francisco Mario Theodoro de Liagre Böhl Dedicatae*, Leiden, 99-106.

1982   'Tablets from Jebel Aruda', in G. van Driel *et al.* (eds) *Zikir Šumin: Assyriological Studies Presented to F.R. Kraus on the Occasion of his Seventieth Birthday*, Leiden, 12-25.

1983   'Seals and Sealings from Jebel Aruda', *Akkadica* 33, 34-62.

VAN DRIEL, G., VAN DRIEL-MURRAY, C.
1979   'Jebel Aruda 1977-1978', *Akkadica* 12, 2-28.

1983   'Jebel Aruda, The 1982 Season of Excavation, Interim Report', *Akkadica* 33, 1-26.

DUCHENE, J.
1986   'La localisation de Ḫuḫnur', in de Meyer *et al.* (eds) 1986, 65-73.

DURAND, J.-M.
1984   'Le nom de l'Elam dans les archives de Mari', *MARI* 3, 277f.

DURAND, J.-M., BONECHI, M.
in pr. 'Un text littéraire archaïque de Mari'.

DURANTI, S.
1979   'Marine Shells from Balakot, Shahr-i Sokhta and Yahya: Their Significance for the Trade and Technology in Ancient Indo-Iran', in Taddei (ed.) 1979, 317-344.

DURING-CASPERS, E.C.L.
1971   'New Archaeological Evidence for Maritime Trade in the Persian Gulf during the Late Protoliterate Period', *East and West* 21, 21-44.

1972   'La hachette trouvée du la sépulture E de Khurab, dans le Balouchistan Persan, examen retrospectif', *Iranica Antiqua* IX, 60-64.

1972a 'The Bahrain Tumuli', *PSAS* 5, 9-19.

1972b 'Harappan Trade in the Arabian Gulf in the Third Millennium B.C.', *Mesopotamia* VII, 167-191.

1972c 'Etched Carnelian Beads', *Bulletin of the Institute of Archaeology* 10, 83-98.

1982   'Sumerian Traders and Businessmen Residing in the Indus Valley Cities. A Critical Assessment of the Archaeological Evidence', *Annali* (Istituto Orientali di Napoli) 42, 337-79.

1989   'Some Remarks on Oman', *PSAS* 19, 13-31.

DURING-CASPERS, E.C.L., GOVINDAKUTTY, A.
1978   'R. Thapar's Dravidian Hypothesis for the Location of Meluhha, Dilmun and Makkan', *JESHO* XXI, 113-45.

DURRANI, F.A.
1964   'Stone Vases as Evidence of Connection between Mesopotamia and the Indus Valley', *Ancient Pakistan* 1, 51-96.

1981   'Rehman Dheri and the Birth of Civilization in Pakistan', *Bulletin of the Institute of Archaeology* 18, 191-207.

DYSON, R.H.
1960   'A Note on Queen Shub-ad's "Onagers"', *Iraq* XXII, 102-4.

1965   'Problems in the Relative Chronology of Iran, 6000-2000 B.C.', in Ehrich (ed.) 1965, 215-56.

1969   'Preliminary Report on Work carried Out During 1968 by the Hasanlu Project in Azerbaijan', *Bastan Chenassi va Honar-e Iran* 2, 14-18.

1972 'The Burned Building of Tepe Hissar IIIB: A Restatement', *Bastan Chenassi va Honar-e Iran* 9-10, 57-83.

1977 'Tepe Hissar, Iran Revisited', *Archaeology* 30, 418-420.

1987 'The Relative and Absolute Chronology of Hissar II and the Proto-Elamite Horizon of Northern Iran', in O. Aurenche, J. Evin, F. Hours (eds), *Chronologies in the Near East*, BAR International Series 379, vol. 2, Oxford, 647-78.

DYSON, R.H., HARRIS, S.M.
1986 'The Archaeological Context of Cylinder Seals Excavated on the Iranian Plateau', in M. Kelly-Buccellati (ed.) 1986, 79-110.

DYSON, R.H., HOWARD, S.M. (eds)
1989 *Tappeh Hesār. Reports of the Restudy Project, 1976*, Firenze.

DYSON, R.H., REMSEN, C.S.
1989 'Observations on Architecture and Stratigraphy at Tappeh Hesār, in Dyson & Howard (eds) 1989, 69-109.

ECHALLIER, J.C.
1981 'La production des céramiques protohistoriques de Shortugaï (Afghanistan), Études pétrographique', *Paléorient* 7/2, 115-19.

EDENS, C.
1992 'Dynamics of Trade in the Ancient Mesopotamian "World System"', *American Anthropologist* 94, 118-39.

EDWARDS, I.E.S., GADD, C.J., HAMMOND, N.G.L. (eds)
1970 *The Cambridge Ancient History Vol. I, Part 2: Early History of the Middle East*, Cambridge.

EDZARD, D.O.
1957 *Die "Zweite Zwischenzeit" Babyloniens*, Wiesbaden.
1959 'Enmebaragesi von Kiš', *ZA* 53, 9-26.
1959-60 'Neue Inschriften zur Geschichte von Ur III unter Šūsuen', *AfO* XIX, 1-32.
1973 'Zwei Inschriften am Felsen von Sar-i-Pul-i-Zohab: Anubanini 1 und 2', *AfO* XXIV, 73-77.
1975 'Hurriter, Hurritisch', *RlA* IV, 507-14.
1976-80 'Išbi-Erra' *RlA* V, 174f.
1980-83 'Königslisten und Chroniken. A. Sumerisch', *RlA* VI, 77-86.
1984 *Hymnen, Beschwörungen und Verwandtes aus dem Archiv L. 2769*, Archivi Reali di Ebla Testi V, Rome.
1989 'Mardaman', *RlA* VII, 357.
1991 'Sargon's Report on Kish. A Problem in Akkadian Philology', in M. Cohen & I. Ehp'al (eds), *AH ASSYRIA! ... Studies in Assyrian History and Ancient Near Eastern Historiography Presented to Hayim Tadmor*, Scripta Hieroslymitana XXXIII, Jerusalem, 258-63.

EDZARD, D.O., FARBER, W.
1974 *Répertoire géographique des textes cunéiformes 2: Die Orts- und Gewässernamen der Zeit der 3. Dynastie von Ur*, Weisbaden.

EDZARD. D.O., FARBER, W., SOLLBERGER, E.
1977 *Répertoire géographique des textes cunéiformes 1: Die Orts- und Gewässernamen der präsargonischen und sargonischen Zeit*, Wiesbaden.

EDZARD, D.O., KAMMENHUBER, A.
1972-75 'Hurriter, Hurritisch', *RlA* IV, 507-14.

EDZARD, D.O., RÖLLIG, W.
1976-80 'Kimaš', *RlA* V, 593.

EHRICH, R.H. (ed.)
1954 *Relative Chronologies in Old World Archaeology*, Chicago.
1965 *Chronologies in Old World Archaeology*, Chicago & London.

EICHMANN, R.
1985 'Uruk-Warka XXXVII: Survey des Stadtgebeites von Uruk III. Die Steingerätfunde', *Baghdader Mitteilungen* 16, 67-97.
1987 'Uruk-Warka XXXVIII. Oberflächenfunde III. Steingefässbohrer', *Baghdader Mitteilungen* 18, 107-15.

EILERS, WH.
1983 'Das Volk der Maka vor und nach den Achämeniden', *AMI Ergänzungsband* 10, 101-19.

ELIOT, H.W.
1950 *Excavations in Mesopotamia and Iran*, Cambridge, Mass.

ENGLUND, R.
1983 'Exotic Fruits', in Potts (ed.) 1983, 87-89.
1983a 'Dilmun in the Archaic Uruk Corpus', in Potts (ed.) 1983, 35-37.

EPSTEIN, C.
1985 'Laden Animal Figurines from the Chalcolithic Period in Palestine', *BASOR* 258, 53-62.

EPSTEIN, H.
1971 *The Origin of Domestic Animals of Africa*, New York.

ESIN, U.
1982 'Die Kulturellen Beziehungen zwichen Ostanatolien und Mesopotamien sowie Syrien anhang einiger Grabungen und Oberflächenfunde aus dem oberen Euphrattal im 4. Jt. v. Chr.', in Nissen & Rengen 1982 (eds) 1982, 13-22.

FADHIL, A.
1983 *Studien zur Topographie und Prosopographie der Provintzstäde der Königreichs Arraphe*, Baghdader Forschungen 6, Mainz am Rhein.

FAIRSERVIS, W.A.
1956 *Excavations in the Quetta Valley, West Pakistan*, New York.
1961 *Archeological Studies in the Seistan Basin of Southwestern Afghanistan and Eastern Iran*, New York.
1983 Review of Ratnagar 1981, *Quarterly Review of Archaeology* 4/4, 1f.

FALES, F.M.
1983 'An Archaic Text from Mari', *MARI* 2, 269f.

FALKENSTEIN, A.
1936   *Archaische Texte aus Uruk*, Berlin.
1951   'Zur Chronologie der sumerischen Literatür', *Compte rendu de la 2e RAI*, Paris, 12-27.
1963   'Zu den Inschriftfunden der Grabung in Uruk-Warka 1960-1961', *Baghdader Mitteilungen* 2, 1-82.
1965   'Fluch über Akkade', *ZA* 57, 43-124.
1966   *Die Inschriften Gudeas von Lagaš*, 2 vols, Rome.

FALKOWITZ, R.S.
1983   'Notes on Lugalbanda and Enmerkar', *JAOS* 103, 103-14.

FEIGIN, S.I.
1939   'The Oldest Occurrence of Niqum', *JAOS* 59, 107f.

FERIOLI, P., FIANDRA, E.
1979   'The Administrative Functions of Clay Sealings in Protohistorical Iran', in Gnoli & Rossi (eds) 1979.

FERIOLI, P., FIANDRA, E., TUSA, S.
1979   'Stamp Seals and the Functional Analysis of their Sealings at Shahr-i Sokhta II-III (2700-2200 B.C.)', in Lohuizen-de Leeuw (ed.) 1979, 7-26.

FINET, A. *et al.*
1979   'Bilan provisoire des fouilles belges du Tell Kannas', *AASOR* 44, 79-96.
1983   *Lorsque la royauté descendit du ciel... Les fouilles belges du Tell Kannâs sur l'Euphrate en Syrie*, Morlanwelz.

FINKBEINER, U.
1985   'Uruk-Warka XXXVII: Survey des Stadtgebietes von Uruk. Vorläufiger Bericht über die 3. Kampagne 1984', *Baghdader Mitteilungen* 16, 17-58.
1986   'Uruk-Warka: Evidence of the Ğemdat Nasr Period', in Finkbeiner & Röllig (eds) 1986, 33-56.

FINKBEINER, U., RÖLLIG, W. (eds)
1986   *Ğamdat Nasr: Period or Regional Style?*, Beiheft zum Tübinger Atlas des Vorderen Orients, Reihe B, Nr. 62, Wiesbaden.

FINKEL, I.L.
1985   'Inscriptions from Tell Brak 1984', *Iraq* XLVII, 187-201.

FINKELSTEIN, J.J.
1963   'Mesopotamian Historigraphy', *Proceedings of the American Philosophical Society* 107/6, 461-472.

FISH, T.
1932   *Catalogue of Sumerian Tablets in the John Rylands Library*, Manchester.
1954-55 'Towards a Study of Lagaš "Mission" or "Messenger" Texts', *MCS* 4, 78-108 and MCS 5, 1-26.

FISHER, W.B.
1971   *The Middle East. A Physical, Social and Regional Geography*, revised edn, London.

FISHER, W.B. (ed.)
1968   *The Cambridge History of Iran I: The Land of Iran*, Cambridge.

FORBES, R.J.
1964   *Studies in Ancient Technology IX: Metals*, Leiden.
1972   Revised edition of Forbes 1964.

FOREST, J.-D.
1980   'Première campagne de fouilles à Kheit Qasim', in Barrelet (ed.) 1980, 181-92.

FÖRTSCH, W.
1916   *Altbabylonische Wirtschaftstexte aus Zeit Lugalanda's und Urukagina's*, Vorderasiatische Schriftsdenkmäler 14, Leipzig.

FOSTER, B.R.
1977   'Commercial Activity in Sargonic Mesopotamia', *Iraq* XXXIX, 31-43.
1982   *Umma in the Sargonic Period*, Hamden.
1982a   'Archives and Record-Keeping in Sargonic Mesopotamia', *ZA* 72, 1-27.
1982b   'The Siege of Armanum', *Journal of the Ancient Near Eastern Society* 14, 27-36.
1983   'Selected Business Documents from Sargonic Mesopotamia', *JCS* 35, 147-75.
1985   'The Sargonic Victory Stele from Telloh', *Iraq* XLVII, 15-30.
1990   'Naram-Sin in Martu and Magan', *Annual Review of the RIM Project* 8, 25-44.
1990a   'The Gutian Letter Again', *NABU 1990* no. 2, 31.
in pr. '"International" Trade at Sargonic Susa (Susa in the Sargonic Period III)', *Jahrbuch für Wirtschaftsgeschichte*.

FOUADI, A.H. AL
1976   'Bassetki Statue with an Old Akkadian Royal Inscription of Naram-Sin of Agade', *Sumer* 32, 63-75.
1983   'Inscriptions and Reliefs from Bitwāta', *Sumer* 34, 122-29.

FRANCFORT, H.-P.
1984   'Commentaries', in Kohl 1984, 249-265.
1984a   'The Early Periods of Shortugai (Harappan) and the Western Bactrian culture of Dashly', in Allchin (ed.) 1984, 170-75.

FRANCFORT, H.P., POTTIER, M.-H.
1978   'Sondage préliminaire sur l'établissement protohistorique Harappéen et post-Harappéen de Shortugaï', *Arts Asiatiques* 34, 29-86.

FRANKFORT, H.
1928   'Sumerians, Semites and the Origins of Copper-Working', *Antiquaries Journal* VIII, 217-35.
1933   *Tell Asmar, Khafaje and Khorsabad*, OIC 16, Chicago.
1935   *Oriental Institute Discoveries in Iraq, 1933/34*, Chicago.
1936   *Progress of the Work of the Oriental Institute in Iraq 1934/35*, OIC 20, Chicago.
1951   *The Birth of Civilization in the Near East*, London.
1954   *The Art and Architecture of the Ancient Orient*, London.

1955   Stratified Cylinder Seals from the Diyala Region, OIP LXXII, Chicago.
1970   The Art and Architecture of the Ancient Orient, 4th ed, revised by R. Levy, Hammondsworth.

FRANKFORT, H.P., LLOYD, S., JACOBSEN, TH.
1940   The Gimilsin Temple and the Palace of the Rulers at Tell Asmar, OIP XLIII, Chicago.

FRANKLIN, A.D., OLIN, J.S., WERTIME, T.A. (eds)
1978   The Search for Ancient Tin, Washington D.C.

FRAYNE, D.R.
1982   'New Light on the Reign of Išbi-Erra', Vorträge gehalten auf der 28. Rencontre Assyriologique Internationale in Wien, AfO Beiheft 19, Horn, 25-32.
1984   'Notes on a New Inscription of Šar-kali-šarrī', Annual Review of the Royal Inscriptions of Mesopotamia Project 2, 23-27.
1990   Old Babylonian Period (2003-1595 BC), Royal Inscriptions of Mesopotamia, Early Periods 4, Toronto, Buffalo & London.
1991   'Historical Texts in Haifa: Notes on R. Kutscher's "Brockmon Tablets"' (review of Kutscher 1989), Bibliotheca Orientalis XLVIII 3/4, 378-409.
1992   Review of Gelb & Kienast 1990, JAOS 112, 619-38.
in pr. a 'The Early Dynastic List of Geographical Names: Its Inner Structure', AOS.

FRIBERG, J.
1978-79 The Third Millennium Roots of Babylonian Mathematics, I: A Method for the Decipherment, through Mathematical and Metrological Analysis, of Proto-Sumerian and Proto-Elamite Semi-Pictographic Inscriptions, Göteborg.
1984   'Numbers and Measures in the Earliest Written Records', Scientific American 250/2, 78-85.

FRIFELT, K.
1970   'Jamdat Nasr Graves in the Oman', KUML 1970, 374-83.
1971   'Excavations in Abu Dhabi (Oman)', Artibus Asiae XXXIII, 296-99.
1975   'A Possible Link Between the Jemdet Nasr and the Umm an-Nar Graves of Oman', JOS 1, 57-80.
1975a   'On Prehistoric Settlement and Chronology of the Oman Peninsula', East and West 25, 359-424.
1976   'Evidence of a Third Millennium B.C. Town in Oman', JOS 2, 57-73.
1979   'Oman during the Third Millennium B.C.: Urban Development of Fishing/Farming Communities?', in Taddei (ed.) 1979, 567-587.
1979a   'The Umm an-Nar and Jemdet Nasr of Oman and their Relations Abroad', in Lohuizen-de Leeuw (ed.) 1979, 43-57.

1991   The Island of Umm an-Nar 1: Third Millennium Graves, The Carlsberg Foundation's Gulf Project, Moesgaard.

FRIFELT, K., SØRENSEN, P. (eds)
1989   South Asian Archaeology 1985, Papers from the Eighth International Conference of South Asian Archaeologists in Western Europe, held at Moesgaard Museum, Denmark, 1-5 July 1985, Scandinavian Institute of Asian Studies Occasional Paper 4, London.

FRYE, R.N.
1984   The History of Ancient Iran, Munich.

FUJII, H. et al.
1981   'Preliminary Report of Excavations at Gubba and Songor', al-Rafidan II, 131-242.

GADD, C.J.
1929   History and Monuments of Ur, London.
1971   'The Cities of Babylonia', 'The Dynasty of Agade and the Gutian Invasion', 'Babylonia c. 2120-1800 B.C.', in Edwards et al. (eds) 1971, 93-144, 417-63, 595-643.

GADD, C.J., LEGRAIN, L.
1928   Ur Excavations, Texts I: Royal Inscriptions, London.

GAILANI, L. AL
1965   'Tell edh-Dhiba'i', Sumer XXI, 33-40.
1975   '"Steatite" Stone Vessels from Mesopotamia and Elsewhere', Sumer XXXI, 41-48.

GARELLI, P.
1963   Les assyriens en Cappadoce, Paris.
1980   'Les empires Mésopotamiens', in M. Duverger (ed.), Le Concept d'Empire, Paris, 29ff.

GASCHE, H.
1973   La poterie élamite du deuxième millénaire a. C., MDP XLVII, Paris.

GAUTIER, J.E., LAMPRE, G.
1905   'Fouilles de Moussian', MDP VIII, 59-148.

GELB, I.J.
1944   Hurrians and Subarians, SAOC 22, Chicago.
1949   'The Date of the Cruciform Monument of Maništušu', JNES VIII, 346-48.
1955   Old Akkadian Inscriptions in Chicago Natural History Museum, Chicago.
1956   'New Light on Hurrians and Subarians', Studi orietalistici in onore de Giorgio Levi della Vida I, Rome, 378ff.
1959   'Hurrians at Nippur in the Sargonic Period', in R. von Kienle et al. (eds), Festschrift Johannes Friedrich, Heidelberg, 183-94.
1960   'Sumerians and Akkadians in the Ethno-Linguistic Relationship', Genava VIII, 258-71.
1961   Old Akkadian Writing and Grammar, MAD 2, 2nd ed., Chicago.
1971   'On the Alleged Temple and State Economies in Ancient Mesopotamia', in

Studi in onore di Edoardo Volterra, vol. VI, Milano, 137-54.

1973 'Prisoners of War in Early Mesopotamia', *JNES* 32, 70-98.

1987 'Compound Divine Names in the Ur III Period', in F. Rochberg-Halton (ed.), *Language, Literature and History: Philological and Historical Studies Presented to Erica Reiner*, AOS, New Haven, 125-38.

GELB, I.J., KIENAST, B.
1990 *Die altakkadischen Königsinschriften des dritten Jahrtausend v. Chr.*, FAOS 7, Stuttgart.

GELLER, M.J.
1992 Review of Gibson & Biggs (eds) 1987, *ZA* 81, 144-46.

GENOUILLAC, H. DE
1913 'Inscriptions diverse', *RA* X, 101f.
1924-25 *Premières recherches archéologiques à Kich*, II vols, Paris.
1934 *Fouilles de Telloh I: époques présargoniques*, Paris.
1936 *Fouilles de Telloh II: époques d'Ur III Dynastie et de Larsa*, Paris.

GERASIMOV, I.P.
1978 'Ancient Rivers in the Deserts of Soviet Central Asia', in Brice (ed.) 1978, 319-44.

GERMAIN, A.
1868 'Quelques mots sur l'Oman et le Sultan de Muskate', *Bulletin de la Société de géographie* 5/16, 339-64.

GHIRSHMAN, R.
1934 'Une tablette proto-élamite du plateau iranien', *RA* XXXI, 115-19.
1938-39 *Fouilles de Sialk près de Kashan*, II vols, Paris.
1954 *Iran*, Hammonsworth.

GIBSON, McG.
1974 'The Twelfth Season at Nippur', *Expedition* 16/4, 23-32.
1976 Review of Stève & Gasche 1971, *JNES* XXXV, 131-33.
1987 'The Round Building at Razuk: Form and Function', in Huot (ed.) 1987, 467-74.

GIBSON, McG. (ed.)
1981 *Uch Tepe I*, Hamrin Report 10, Chicago and Copenhagen.

GIBSON, McG., BIGGS, R.D. (eds)
1987 *The Organization of Power: Aspects of Bureaucracy in the Ancient Near East*, SAOC 46, Chicago.

GILBERT, A.S.
1983 'Specialised Nomadic Pastoralism in Western Iran', *World Archaeology* 15/1, 105-19.

GIMBUTAS, M.
1965 'The Relative Chronology of Neolithic and Chalcolithic Cultures in Eastern Europe North of the Balkan Peninsula and the Black Sea', in Ehrich (ed.) 1965, 459-502.

GLASSNER, J.-J.
1983 'Naram-Sîn poliorcète: les avatars d'une sentence divinatoire', *RA* LXXVII, 3-10.
1985 'Sargon "Roi du combat"', *RA* 79, 115-26.
1987 *La Chute d'Akkadé, l'Évenement et sa Mémoire*, Berliner Beiträge zum Vorderen Orient 5, Berlin.
1988 'La chute d'Akkadé: addenda et corrigenda', *NABU* 1988 (no. 3, September), 34.
1989 'Mesopotamian Textual Evidence on Magan/Makan in the Late 3rd Millennium B.C.', in Costa & Tosi (eds), 181-91.
in pr. 'Dilmun, Magan and Meluḫḫa: Some Observations on Language, Toponymy, Anthroponymy and Theonymy', in J.E. Reade (ed.), *The Indian Ocean in Antiquity*, London.

GLOB, P.V.
1958 'Alabaster Vases from the Bahrain Temple', *KUML* 1958, 138-45.

GNOLI, G., ROSSI, A.V. (eds)
1979 *Iranica*, Napoli Istituto Universario Orientale, Seminario di Studi Asiatici, Series Minor X, Naples.

GOCKEL, W.
1982 *Die Stratigraphie und Chronologie der Ausgrabungen des Diyala-Gebietes und der Stadt Ur in der Zeit von Uruk/Eanna IV bis zur Dynastie von Akkad*, Rome.
1983 'Ur und Al-'Ubaid', *Akkadica* 32, 32-52.

GOETTLER, G.W., FIRTH, N., HUSTON, C.C.
1976 'A Preliminary Discussion of Ancient Mining in the Sultanate of Oman', *JOS* 2, 43-55.

GOETZE, A.
1947 'Historical Allusions in Old Babylonian Omen Texts', *JCS* 1, 253-65.
1953 'Hulibar of Duddul', *JNES* XII, 114-23.
1953a 'An Old Babylonian Itinerary', *JCS* VII, 51-72.
1953b 'Four Ur Dynasty Tablets Mentioning Foreigners', *JCS* VII, 103-07.
1961 'Early Kings of Kish', *JCS* XV, 105-11.
1963 'Šakkanakkus of the Ur III Empire', *JCS* XVII, 1-32.
1968 'Akkad Dynasty Inscriptions from Nippur', *JAOS* 88, 54-59.
1970 'Early Dynastic Dedication Inscriptions from Nippur', *JCS* XXIII, 39-56.

GOFF(-MEADE), C.L.
1968 'Luristan in the first half of the first millennium B.C.', *Iran* VI, 126-32.
1971 'Luristan Before the Iron Age', *Iran* IX, 131-51.

GOLDING, M.
1974 'Evidence for pre-Seleucid Occupation of East Arabia', *PSAS* 4, 19-31.

GOMI, T.
1984 'On the Critical Economic Situation at Ur in the Reign of Ibbisin', *JCS* 36, 211-42.

GORDON, C.H., RENDSBERG, G.A., WINTER, N.H. (eds)
1987   *Eblaitica: Essays on the Ebla Archive and Eblaite Language*, Winona Lake.

GORDON, E.I.
1960   'A New Look at the Wisdom of Sumer and Akkad', *Bibliotheca Orientalis* XVIII 3/4, 122-52.

GOVERNMENT OF KUWAIT (anonymous)
n.d.   *Archaeological Investigations in the Island of Failaka 1958-64*, Kuwait.

GRAYSON. A.K.
1972   *Assyrian Royal Inscriptions 1: From the Beginning to Ashur-resha-ishi I*, Wiesbaden.
1974-77 'The Empire of Sargon of Akkad', *AfO* XXV, 56-64.
1975   *Babylonian Historical-Literary Texts*, Toronto and Buffalo.
1975a   *Assyrian and Babylonian Chronicles*, Texts from Cuneiform Sources V, New York.

GRAYSON, A.K., SOLLBERGER, E.
1976   'L'insurrection générale contre Naram-Suen', *RA* LXX, 103-28.

GREEN, M.W.
1978   'The Eridu Lament', *JCS* 30, 127-67.
1980   'Animal Husbandry at Uruk in the Archaic Period', *JNES* 39, 1-35.
1984   'Early Sumerian Tax Collectors', *JCS* 36/1, 93-95.
1984a   'The Uruk Lament', *JAOS* 104, 253-79.

GREEN, M.W., NISSEN, H.J.
1987   *Zeichenliste der Archaischen Texte aus Uruk*, Archaische Texte aus Uruk 2, Berlin.

GRÉGOIRE, J.-P.
1981   *Inscriptions et archives administratives cunéiformes (1e partie)*, Rome.

GREPPIN, J.A.C.
1991   'Some Effects of the Hurro-Urartian People and their Language upon the Earliest Armenians', *JAOS* 111, 720-30.

GRILLOT, F., GLASSNER, J.-J.
1991   'Problèmes de succession et cumuls de pouvoir: une querelle de famille chez les premièrs sukkalmah?', *Iranica Antiqua* XXVI, 85-99.

GUNTER, A.C. (ed.)
1990   *Investigating Artistic Environments in the Ancient Near East*, Washington DC.

GUPTA, S.P.
1979   *Archaeology of Soviet Central Asia and the Indian Borderlands*, II vols, Delhi.

GURNEY, O.R.
1955   'The Sultantepe Tablets IV. The Cuthaean Legend of Naram-Sin', *Anatolian Studies* 5, 93-113.
1957   'The Sultantepe Tablets VI. A Letter of Gilgamesh', *Anatolian Studies* VII, 127-36.

GURNEY, O.R., KRAMER, S.N.
1976   *Sumerian Literary Texts in the Ashmolean Museum*, Oxford Editions of Cuneiform Texts V, Oxford.

GÜTERBOCK, H.G.
1934/38 'Die historische Tradition und ihre literarische Gestaltung bei Babyloniern und Hethitern bis 1200', *ZA* NF 8, 1-91 and NF 10, 45-149.
1939-41 'Keilschrifttexte nach Kopien von T.G. Pinches. 11. Bruchstücke eines altbabylonischen Naram-Sin-Epos', *AfO* XIII, 46-50.

GWINNETT, E.J., GORELICK, L.
1981   'Beadmaking in Iran in the early bronze age', *Expedition* 24/1, 10-23.

HAERINCK, E.
1987   'The Chronology of Luristan, Pusht-i Kuh in the Late Fourth and first half of the Third Millennium B.C.', *Préhistoire de la Mésopotamie*, CNRS, Paris, 55-72.

HAKEMI, A.
1972   *Catalogue de l'exposition: Lut, Xabis (Shahdad)*, Teheran.

HAKEMI, A., SAJJIDI, S.M.S.
n.d.   'Shahdad Excavations in the Context of the Oases Civilizations', in Ligabue & Salvatori (eds) n.d., 143-53.

HALIM, M.A.
1972   'Excavations at Sarai Khola, Part II', *Pakistan Archaeology* 8, 1-112.

HALL, H.R.
1928   'Babylonian Antiquities', *BMQ* II, 15.

HALL, H.R., WOOLLEY, C.L.
1927   *Ur Excavations I: Al-'Ubaid*, London.

HALL, M.E., STEADMAN, S.R.
1991   'Tin and Anatolia: Another Look', *Journal of Mediterranean Archaeology* 4, 217-34.

HALLER, A., ANDRAE, W.
1955   *Die Heiligtümer des Gottes Assur und der Sin-Šamaš-Tempel in Assur*, WVDOG 67, Berlin.

HALLO, W.W.
1956   'Zariqum', *JNES* 15, 220-25.
1957   *Early Mesopotamian Royal Titles*, American Oriental Series 43, New Haven.
1960   'A Sumerian Amphictony', *JCS* XIV, 88-114.
1961   'Royal Inscriptions of the Early Old Babylonian Period: A Bibliography', *Bibliotheca Orientalis* XVIII, 4-14.
1962   'The Royal Inscriptions of Ur: A Typology', *Harvard Union College Annual* 33, 1-43.
1964   'The Road to Emar', *JCS* XVIII, 57-88.
1971   'Gutium', *RlA* III/9, 709-20.
1972   'The House of Ur-Meme', *JNES* 31, 87-95.
1973   'The Date of the Fara Period: A Case Study in the Historiography of Early Mesopotamia', *Orientalia* 42, 228-38.
1975   'Towards a History of Sumerian Literature', in S.J. Lieberman (ed.), *Assyriological Studies 20 (Jacobsen Festschrift)*, Chicago, 181-203.
1978   'Simurrum and the Hurrian Frontier', *Revue hittite et asianique* XXXVI, 71-83.

1983 'Lugalbanda Excavated', *JAOS* 103, 165-80.

1983a 'The First Purim', *Biblical Archaeologist* 46/1, 19-29.

HALLO, W.W., VAN DIJK, J.J.A.

1968 *The Exaltation of Inanna*, New Haven & London.

HALLO, W.W., PORADA, E., SCHLOSSMAN, B.L.

1976 *Ancient Mesopotamian Art and Selected Texts, The Pierpont Morgan Library*, New York.

HANSEN, D.P.

1963 'New Votive Plaques from Nippur', *JNES* 22, 145-66.

1965 'The Relative Chronology of Mesopotamia Part 2. The Pottery Sequence at Nippur from the Middle Uruk to the end of the Old Babylonian Period', in Ehrich (ed.) 1965, 201-13.

1973 'Al-Hiba 1970-1971: A Preliminary Report', *Artibus Asiae* XXXV, 62-70.

1978 'Al-Hiba. A Summary of Four Seasons of Excavation 1968-1976', *Sumer* 34, 72-85.

in pr. Sections on the Jemdet Nasr and Early Dynastic periods, in R.W. Ehrich (ed.), *Chronologies in Old World Archaeology*, 3rd edn, Chicago.

HANSEN, D.P., DALES, G.F.

1962 'The Temple of Inanna Queen of Heaven at Nippur', *Archaeology* 15, 75-84.

HANSMAN, J.

1967 'Charax and the Karkheh', *Iranica Antiqua* VII, 21-58.

1972 'Elamites, Achaemenids and Anshan', *Iran* X, 101-24.

1973 'A Periplus of Magan and Meluhha', *BSOAS* 36/3, 554-87.

1976 'Gilgamesh, Humbaba and the Land of the Erin-trees', *Iraq* XXXVIII, 23-35.

1978 'The Question of Aratta', *JNES* 37, 331-36.

HARGREAVES, H.

1929 *Excavations in Baluchistan 1925*, Calcutta.

HARPER, P.O. *et al.*

1984 *Ancient Near Eastern Art, The Metropolitan Museum of Art Bulletin*, (Spring 1984), New York.

HARRISON, J.V.

1968 'Geology', in Fisher (ed.) 1968, 111-85.

HÄRTEL, H. (ed.)

1981 *South Asian Archaeology 1979*, Berlin.

HÄSER, J.

1990 'Soft-Stone Vessels of the 2nd ml. BC in the Gulf Region', *PSAS* 20, 43-54.

HASTINGS, A., HUMPHRIES, J.H., MEADOW, R.H.

1975 'Oman in the Third Millennium BCE', *JOS* 1, 9-55.

HAUPTMANN, A.

1985 *5000 Jahre Kupfer in Oman. Bd. 1: Die Entwicklung der Kupfermetallurgie vom 3. Jahrtausend bis zur Neuzeit*, (Der Anschnitt Suppl. vol. 4), Bochum.

1987 'Kupfer und Bronzen der südostarabischen Halbinsel', *Der Anschnitt* 39.

HAUPTMANN, A., WEISGERBER, G.

1980 'The Early Bronze Age Copper Metallurgy of Shahr-i Sokhta (Iran)', *Paléorient* 6, 120-23.

HAUPTMANN, A., WEISGERBER, G., KNAUF, E.A.

1985 'Archäometallurgische und bergbauarchäologische Unterschungen im Gebiet von Fenan, Wadi Arabah (Jordanien)', *Der Anschnitt* 37, 163-95.

HAUPTMANN, A., WEISGERBER, G., BACHMANN, H.G.

1988 'Early Copper Metallurgy in Oman', in Maddin (ed.) 1988, 34-51.

HAWKINS, J.D.

1979 'The Origins and Dissemination of Writing in Western Asia', in P.R.S. Moorey (ed.) *The Origins of Civilization, Wolfson College Lectures 1978*, Oxford, 128-65.

HEIMPEL, W.

1982 'A First Step in the Diorite Question', *RA* 76, 65-67.

1987 'Das Untere Meer', *ZA* 77, 22-91.

1988 'Magan', *RlA* VII, 195-99.

HEIMPEL, W., GORELICK, L., GWINNETT, A.J.

1988 'Philological and Archaeological Evidence for the Use of Emery in the Bronze Age Near East', *JCS* 40, 195-210.

HEINRICH, E.

1931 *Fara, Ergebnisse der Ausgrabungen der Deutschen Orient-Gesellschaft in Fara und Abu Hatab 1902-03*, Berlin.

1934 'Arbeiten in Eanna, im Stadtgebiet und im Südbau', in Nöldeke *et al.*, *Fünfter vorläufer Bericht ... Uruk-Warka*, Berlin, 5-38.

1936 *Kleinfunde aus den archaischen Tempelschichten in Uruk*, Berlin.

1982 *Die Tempel und Heiligtümer im alten Mesopotamien*, 2 vols, Berlin.

HEINRICH, E., ANDRAE, W.

1931 *Fara. Ergebnisse des Ausgrabungen der Deutschen Orient-gesselschaft in Fara und Abu Hatab 1902/03*, Berlin.

HEINZ, M.

1989 'Die Steingefässe aus Süd- und Mittlemesopotamien als Inschriftenträger der frühdynastischen Zeit', *Baghdader Mitteilungen* 20, 197-224.

HENRICKSON, E.F.

1985 'The Early Develpment of Pastoralism in the Central Zagros Highlands (Luristan)', *Iranica Antiqua* XX, 1-42.

HENRICKSON, R.C.

1983-84 'Giyan I and II Reconsidered', *Mesopotamia* XVIII-XIX, 195-220.

1984 'Šimaški and Central Western Iran: The Archaeological Evidence', *ZA* 74, 98-122.

1985 'The Chronology of Central Western Iran 2600-1400 B.C.', *AJA* 89, 569-81.

1986   'A Regional Perspective on Godin III Cultural Development in Central Western Iran', *Iran* XXIV, 1-55.
1987   'Godin III and the Chronology of Central Western Iran circa 2600-1400 B.C.', in Hole (ed.) 1987, 205-27.

HERRMANN, G.
1966   *The Source, Distribution, History and Use of Lapis Lazuli in Western Asia from the earliest times to the end of the Seleucid era*, unpubl. D.Phil. thesis, Oxford.
1968   'Lapis Lazuli: The Early Phases of its Trade', *Iraq* XXX, 21-57.

HERRMANN, G., MOOREY, P.R.S.
1983   'Lapislazuli. B. Archäologisch', *RlA* VI, 489-92.

HERZFELD, E.
1930   *Die vorgeschichtliche Töpfereien von Samarra*, Berlin.
1933   'Aufsätz zur altorientalischen Archäologie', *Archäologische Mitteilungen aus Iran* V, 1-124.
1941   *Iran in the Ancient East*, London & New York.

HESKEL, D., LAMBERG-KARLOVSKY, C.C.
1980   'An Alternative Sequence for the Development of Metallurgy: Tepe Yahya, Iran', in Wertime *et al.* (eds) 1980, 229-65.

HEUZEY, L.
1885   'Un gisement de diorite, à propos des statues chaldéennes', *RA* I, 121-23.
1903   'La construction du roi Our-Nina', *RA* 5, 26-32.

HEUZEY, L., SARZEC, E. DE
1884- *Découvertes en Chaldée*, 2 vols, Paris.
1912

HIEBERT, F.T., LAMBERG-KARLOVSKY, C.C.
1992   'Central Asia and the Indo-Iranian Borderlands', *Iran* XXX, 1-15.

HILLEN, C.
1953   'A Note on Two Shaft-Hole Axes', *Bibliotheca Orientalis* 10, 211-15.

HILPRECHT, H.V.
1893/96 *Old Babylonian Inscriptions, Chiefly from Nippur. Babylonian Expedition of the University of Pennsylvania, Series A: Cuneiform Texts*, Vol. I, 2 Parts, Philadelphia.
1903   *Explorations in Bible Lands*, Edinburgh.

HILZHEIMER, M.
1941   *Animal Bones from Tell Asmar*, SAOC 20, Chicago.

HINZ, W.
1962   'Zur Entzifferung der elamischen Strichschrift', *Iranica Antiqua* II, 1-17.
1967   'Elams Vertrag mit Naram-Sîn von Akkade', *ZA* 58, 66-96.
1969   *Altiranische funde und Forschungen*, Berlin.
1971   'Persia, c. 2400-1800 B.C.', in Edwards *et al.* (eds) 1971, 644-80.
1971a   'Eine altelamische Tonkrug-Aufschrift vom Rande der Lut', *AMI* NF4, 21-24.
1971b   'Großregent', *RlA* III, 654f.
1972   *The Lost World of Elam*, New York.
1975   'Ḫuḫnur', *RlA* IV, 488f.

HINZ, W., KOCH, H.
1987   *Elamisches Wörterbuch*, AMI Ergänzungsband 17, 2 vols, Berlin.

HIRSCH, H.
1963   'Die Inschriften der Könige von Agade', *AfO* XX, 1-81.

HOCH, E.
1979   'Reflections on Prehistoric Life at Umm an-Nar (Trucial Oman) Based on Faunal Remains from the Third Millennium', in Taddei (ed.) 1979, 589-638.

HOGARTH, D.D., GRIFFIN, W.L.
1976   'New Data on Lazurite', *Lithos* 9, 39-54.

HØJLUND, F.
1986   'The Chronology of City II and III at Qala'at al-Bahrain' in Khalifa and Rice (eds) 1986, 217-24.

HOLE, F. (ed.)
1987   *The Archaeology of Western Iran: Settlement and Society from Prehistory to the Islamic Conquest*, Washington DC & London.

HOLZER, H.F., MOMENZADEH, M.
1971   'Ancient Copper Mines in the Veshnoveh Area, Kuhestan-e-Qom, West-Central Iran', *Archaeologica Austriaca* 49, 1-22.

HOMÈS-FREDERICQ, D.
1983   'Lampe', *RlA* VI, 460-63.

HOROWITZ, W.
1992   'Two Abnu šikinšu Fragments and Related Materials', *ZA* 82, 112-22.

HOUGHTON, W.
1878   'On the Origin or Picture Origin of the Characters of the Assyrian Syllabary', *Transactions of the Society of Biblical Literature* VI, 454-83.

HOWARD-CARTER, T.
1987   'Dilmun: At Sea or not at Sea?', *JCS* 39, 54-117.
1989   'Voyages of Votive Vessels in the Gulf', in Behrens *et al.* (eds) 1989, 253-66.

HRUŠKA, B.
1983   'Dilmun in den vorsargonischen Wirtschaftstexten aus Šuruppak and Lagaš', in Potts (ed.) 1983, 83-85.

HUBER, P.J.
1982   *Astronomical Dating of Babylon I and Ur III*, Occasional Papers on the Near East, Vol. I, Issue 4, Malibu.

HUOT, J.-L.
1969   'La diffusion des épingles à tête à double enroulement', *Syria* XLVI, 57-98.
1971   'Une double hache du Luristan', *Iran* 9, 153-55.

HUOT, J.-L. (ed.)
1987   *Préhistoire de la Mésopotamie*, CNRS, Paris.

HUOT, J.-L. *et al.*
1983   *Larsa et 'Oueili, travaux de 1978-1981*, Editions Recherche sur les Civilizations, Mémoire no. 26, Paris.

HUOT, J.-L., YON, M., CALVET, Y. (eds)
1985   *De l'Indus aux Balkans, Recueil à la mémoire de Jean Deshayes*, Paris.

ISMAIL, B.K., ROAF, M.D., BLACK, J.A.
1983   "Ana in the Cuneiform Sources', *Sumer* XXXIX, 191-94.

JACOBSEN, TH.
1939   *The Sumerian King List*, Assyriological Studies No. 11, Chicago.
1941   Review of S.N. Kramer, Lamentation over the Destruction of Ur, in *American Journal of Semitic Languages and Literatures* LVIII, 219-24.
1953   'The Reign of Ibbi-suen', *JCS* 7, 36-47.
1960   'The Waters of Ur', *Iraq* XXII, 174-85.
1970   *Towards the Image of Tammuz and Other Essays on Mesopotamian History and Culture*, ed. by W.L. Moran, Cambridge, Mass.
1978-79 'Ipḫur-Kīši and his Times', *AfO* XXVI, 1-14.
1987   *The Harps that Once ... Sumerian Poetry in Translation*, New Haven & London.

JARRIGE, J.-F.
1981   'Economy and Society in the Early Chalcolithic/Bronze Age of Baluchistan: New Perspectives from Recent Excavations at Mehrgarh', in Härtel (ed.) 1981, 93-114.
1984   'Chronology of the earlier periods of the Greater Indus as seen from Mehrgarh, Pakistan', in Allchin (ed.) 1984, 21-28.

JARRIGE, J.-F. (ed.)
1988   *Les cités oubliées de l'Indus: Archéologie du Pakistan*, Paris.

JARRIGE, J.-F., HASAN, H.U.
1989   'Funerary Complexes in Baluchistan at the End of the Third mill. in the Light of Recent Discoveries at Mehrgarh and Quetta', in Frifelt & Sørensen (eds) 1989, 150-66.

JARRIGE, J.-F., TOSI, M.
1981   'The Natural Resources of Mundigak', in Härtel (ed.) 1981, 115-42.

JARRIGE, J.-F., LECHEVALLIER, M.
1979   'Excavations at Mehrgarh, Baluchistan: Their Significance in the Prehistorical Context of the Indo-Pakistani Borderlands', in Taddei (ed.) 1979, 463-535.

JASIM, S.A., OATES, J.
1986   'Early Tokens and Tablets in Mesopotamia: New Information from Tell Abada and Tell Brak', *World Archaeology* 17, 348-62.

JÉQUIER, G.
1900   'Traveaux de l'hiver 1898-1899', *MDP* I, 111-38.
1905   'Fouilles de Susa 1899-1900, 1900-1901, 1901-1902: Description des monuments', *MDP* VII, 9-41.

JESUS, P.S. DE
1980   *The Development of Prehistoric Mining and Metallurgy in Anatolia*, B.A.R. International Series 74, i and ii, Oxford.

JOHANSEN, F.
1978   *Statues of Gudea, Ancient and Modern, Mesopotamia*, Copenhagen Studies in Assyriology 6, Copenhagen.

JOHNSON, G.A.
1973   *Local Exchange and Early State Development in Southwestern Iran*, University of Michigan, Museum of Anthropology, Anthropological Papers 51, Michigan.
1975   'Locational Analysis and the Investigation of Uruk Local Exchange Systems', in Sabloff & Lamberg-Karlovsky (eds) 1975, 285-339.
1976   'Early State Organization in Southwestern Iran: Preliminary Field Report', in F. Bagherzadeh (ed.), *Proceedings of the IVth Annual Symposium on Archaeological Research in Iran*, 190-223.
1981   'Spatial Organization of Early Uruk Settlement Systems', in Barrelet (ed.) 1981, 233-63.
1987   'The Changing Organization of Uruk Administration on the Susiana Plain', in Hole (ed.) 1987, 107-39.

JONES, A.H.M.
1966   *The Decline of the Ancient World*, New York.

JONES, T.B., SNYDER, J.W.
1961   *Sumerian Economic Texts from the Third Ur Dynasty: A Catalogue and Discussion of Documents from Various Collections*, Minneapolis.

JORDAN, J.
1931   *Zweiter vorläufiger Bericht ... Uruk*, Berlin.
1932   *Dritter vorläufiger Bericht ... Uruk*, Berlin.

KAMMENHUBER, A.
1976   'Historisch-Geographische Nachrichten aus der althurrischen åberlieferung, dem altelamischen und den Inschrift der Könige von Akkad für die Zeit vor dem Einfall der Gutäer (ca. 2200/2136)', in J. Harmatta & G. KomorÐczy (eds), *Wirtschaft und Gesellschaft im Alten Vorderasien*, Budapest, 156-247.

KANTOR, H.J.
1975   'Excavations at Chogha Mish', *Oriental Institute of the University of Chicago, Report for 1974/75*, 17-26.
1976   'Excavations at Chogha Mish', *Oriental Institute of the University of Chicago, Report for 1975/76*, 12-21.
1976a   'The Excavations at Choqa Mish, 1974-75', in F. Bagherzadeh (ed.), *Proceeding of the IVth Annual Symposium on Archaeological Research in Iran*, Teheran, 23-41.
1977   'Excavatios at Chogha Mish', *Oriental Institute of the University of Chicago, Report for 1976/77*, 15-24.

1979 'Chogha Mish and Chogha Bonut', *Oriental Institute of the University of Chicago, Report for 1978/79*, 33-39.

1982 'Chogha Mish', *Oriental Institute of the University of Chicago, Report for 1981/82*, 53-58.

1983 'Chogha Mish', *Oriental Institute of the University of Chicago, Report for 1982/83*, 28-30.

KÄRKI, I.
1986 *Die Königsinschriften der dritten Dynastie von Ur*, Studia Orientalia 58, Helsinki.

KARSTENS, K.
1987 *Typologische Unterschungen an Gefässen aus altakkadischen Gräbern der Königsfriedhofes in Ur*, Münchener Vorderasiatische Studien 3, Munich.

KEISCH, B.
1972 *Secrets of the Past: Nuclear Energy Applications in Art and Archaeology*, U.S. Atomic Energy Commission.

KEUN DE HOOGERWOERD, R.C.
1889 'Die Häfen und Handelsverhältnisse der Persischen Golfs und des Golfs von Oman', *Annalen der Hydrographie und maritimen Meteorologie* 17, 189-207.

KHALIFA, S.H.A. AL, RICE, M. (eds)
1986 *Bahrain Through the Ages: The Archaeology*, London.

KHOLPIN, I.N., KHOLPINA, L.I.
1989 'Double-spiral Headpins in the Middle East', in de Meyer & Haerinck (eds) 1989, 99-109.

KIENAST, B.
1965 'Zu einigen Datenformeln aus der frühen Isinzeit', *JCS* 19, 45-55.

KING, L.W.
1899 *Cuneiform Texts* VII, London.
1907 *Chronicles Concerning Early Babylonian Kings*, 2 vols, London.
1912 *Cuneiform Texts* XXXII, London.

KIRKBY, M.J.
1977 'Land and Water Resources of the Deh Luran and Khuzistan Plains', in F. Hole, *Studies in the Archaeological History of the Deh Luran Plain*, Memoirs of the Museum of Anthropology, University of Michigan, No. 9, Michigan, 251-88.

KJÆRUM, P.
1980 'Seals of "Dilmun-type" from Failaka, Kuwait', *PSAS* 10, 45-53.

1983 *The Stamp and Cylinder Seals, Failaka/Dilmun, The Second Millennium Settlements*, Vol. 1:1, Moesgaard.

KLEIN, J.
1980-83 'Krieg, Kriegsgefangene', *RlA* VI, 241-46.
1981 *Three Šulgi Hymns*, Ramat-Gan.
1983 'The Capture of Agga by Gilgameš (GA 81 and 99)', *JAOS* 103, 201-04.

KLENGEL, H.
1965 'Lullubum. Ein Beitrag zur Geschichte der altvorderasiatischen Gebergsvölker', *Mitteilungen des Instituts für Orientforschung* XI, 349-71.

1988 'Lullu(bum)', *RlA* VII, 164-68.

KLENGEL, H., KLENGEL, E.
1980 'Zum Fragment eines Steatitgefäßes mit einer Inschrift der Rimuš von Akkad', *Rocznic Orientalistyćzny* XLI, 45-51.

KOHL, P.C.
1974 *Seeds of Upheaval: The Production of Chlorite at Tepe Yahya and an Analysis of Commodity Production and Trade in Southwest Asia in the Third Milennium*, Harvard Ph.D Dissertation, Ann Arbor.

1975 'Carved Chlorite Vessels: A Trade in Finished Commodities in the mid-third Millennium', *Expedition* 18/1, 18-31.

1975a 'The Archaeology of Trade', *Dialectical Anthropology* 1, 43-50.

1976 '"Steatite" Carvings of the Early Third Millennium B.C.', *AJA* 80, 73-75.

1977 'A Note on Chlorite Artifacts from Shahr-i Sokhta', *East and West* 27, 111-28.

1978 'The Balance of Trade in Southwestern Asia in the Mid-Third Millennium B.C.', *Current Anthropology* 19, 463-92.

1979 'The "World Economy" of West Asia in the Third Millennium BC', in Taddei (ed.) 1979, 55-85.

1979a 'Reply', *Current Anthropology* 20, 166f.

1981 'The Namazga Civilization: An Overview', in Kohl (ed.) 1981, vii-xxxviii.

1982 'The First World Economy: External Relations and Trade in West and Central Asia in the Third Millennium B.C.', in Nissen & Renger (eds) 1982, 23-31.

1984 *Central Asia: Palaeolithic Beginnings to the Iron Age*, Éditions Recherche sur les Civilizations, Synthèse no. 14, Paris.

1987 'The ancient economy, transferable technologies and the Bronze Age world-system: a view from the north-eastern frontier of the ancient Near East', in Rowlands *et al.* (eds) 1987, 13-24.

KOHL, P.C., HARBOTTLE, G., SAYRE, E.V.
1979 'Physical and Chemical Analyses of Soft Stone Vessels from Southwest Asia', *Archaeometry* 21, 131-59.

KOHL, P.C. (ed.)
1981 *The Bronze Age Civilization of Central Asia: Recent Soviet Discoveries*, New York.

KOLBUS, S.
1982 'Unter dem Schutt aus einem der ersten Handelskontore von Ur: wohin datiert der sog. Gemdet-Nasr-Friedhof?', *Akkadica* 30, 1-11.

1983 'Zur Chronologie des sog. Gamdat Nasr-Friedhofs in Ur', *Iraq* XLV, 7-17.

KOMORÓCZY, G.
1982 'Die Beziehungen zwischen Mesopotamien and dem iranischen Hochland in der Sumerischen Dichtung', in Nissen & Renger (eds) 1982, 87-96.

KÖNIG, F.W.
 1938 'Bikni', *RlA* II, 28f.
 1965 *Die elamischen Königsinschriften*, AfO Beiheft 16, Graz.
KRAMER, S.N.
 1932 'New Tablets from Fara', *JAOS* 52, 110-32.
 1944 *Sumerian Literary Texts from Nippur in the Museum of the Ancient Orient at Istanbul*, AASOR 23, New Haven.
 1963 *The Sumerians: Their History, Culture and Character*, Chicago.
 1963a 'Dilmun: Quest for Paradise', *Antiquity* XXXVII, 111-15.
 1964 'The Indus Civilization and Dilmun, the Sumerian Paradise Land', *Expedition* 6, 44-52.
 1969 'Lamentation over the Destruction of Nippur: A preliminary Report', *Eretz-Israel* 9, 89-93.
 1977 'Commerce and Trade: Gleanings from Sumerian Literature', *Iraq* XXXIX, 59-66.
 1983 'The Ur-Nammu Law Code: Who Was Its Author?', *Orientalia* 52, 453-56.
 1987 'Ancient Sumer and Iran', *Bulletin of the Asia Institute* 1, 9-16.
 1991 'Lamentation over the Destruction of Nippur', *ASJ* 13, 1-26.
KRAMER, S.N., MAIER, J.
 1989 *Myths of Enki, The Crafty God*, New York & Oxford.
KRAUS, F.R.
 1955 'Provinzen des neusumerischen Reichs von Ur', *ZA* 51, 45ff.
 1963 'Altbabylonische Quellensammlungen zur altmesopotamischen Geschichte', *AfO* XX, 153-55.
KUPPER, J.-R.
 1957 *Les nomades en Mésopotamie au temps des rois de Mari*, Paris.
 1967 'Rois et *šakkanakku*', *JCS* XXI, 123-25.
 1969 'Le pays de Simaški', *Iraq* XXXI, 24-27.
KUTSCHER, R.
 1968-69 'Apillaša, Governor of Kazallu', *JCS* XXII, 63-65.
 1979 'A Note on the Early Careers of Zariqum and Šamši-illat', *RA* 73, 81f.
 1986 'Akkadian *šadādum/šadādum* = "To Camp"', *ZA* 76, 1-3.
 1989 *Royal Inscriptions. The Brockmon Tablets at the University of Haifa*, Haifa.
LAESSØE, J.
 1959 'Akkadian *annakum*: "tin" or "lead"?', *Acta Orientalia* 24, 83-94.
LAHANIER, CH.
 1976 'Note sur l'emploi de l'heulandite et de la mordenite dans ls fabrication de sceaux cylindres proto-élamite', *Annales du Laboratoire de Recherche des Musées de France 1976*, 65f.
 1977 'Analyse d'objets en bitume provenant de Suse', *Annales du Laboratoire de Recherche des Musées de France 1977*, 47ff.

LAL, B.B., GUPTA, S.P. (eds)
 1984 *Frontiers of the Indus Civilization*, New Delhi.
LAMBERG-KARLOVSKY, C.C.
 1967 'Archaeology and Metallurgical Technology in Prehistoric Afghanistan, India and Pakistan', *American Anthropologist* 69, 145-62.
 1970 *Excavations at Tepe Yahya, Iran 1967-69, Progress Report 1*, American School of Prehistoric Research, Bulletin No. 27, Cambridge, Mass.
 1971 'The Proto-Elamite Settlement at Tepe Yahya', *Iran* IX, 87-96.
 1971a 'Proto-Elamite Account Tablets from Tepe Yahya, Southeastern Iran', *Kadmos* 10, 97-99.
 1972 'Tepe Yahya 1971: Mesopotamia and the Indo-Iranian Borderlands', *Iran* X, 89-100.
 1973 'Urban Interaction on the Iranian Plateau: Excavations at Tepe Yahya 1967-1973', *Proceedings of the British Academy* LIV, 282-319.
 1976 'The Third Millennium at Tappeh Yahya: A Preliminary Statement', *Proceedings of the IVth Annual Symposium on Archaeological Research in Iran, 1975*, 71-84.
 1977 'Foreign Relations in the Third Millennium at Tepe Yahya', in Deshayes (ed.) 1977, 33-43.
 1978 'The Proto-Elamites on the Iranian Plateau', *Antiquity* LII, 114-20.
 1978a Comment on Kohl 1978, *Current Anthropology* 19, 478-80.
 1982 Comment on Alden 1982, *Current Anthropology* 23, 631-33.
 1982a 'Dilmun: Gateway to Immortality', *JNES* 41, 45-50.
 1984 'An Idea or Pot-luck', in Lal & Gupta (eds) 1984, 347-51.
 1985 'The longue durée of the Ancient Near East', in Huot *et al.* (eds) 1985, 55-72.
 1986 'Third Millennium Structure and Process: From the Euphrates to the Indus and the Oxus to the Indian Ocean', *Oriens Antiquus* XXV, 189-219.
 1988 'The "Intercultural Style" Carved Vessels', *Iranica Antiqua* XXIII, 45-95.
LAMBERG-KARLOVSKY, C.C., TOSI, M.
 1973 'Shahr-i Sokhta and Tepe Yahya: Tracks on the Earliest History of the Iranian Plateau', *East and West* 23, 21-58.
LAMBERG-KARLOVSKY, C.C. *et al.*
 1976 'Tepe Yahya Project', *Iran* XIV, 172-76.
LAMBERT, M.
 1953 'Textes commerciaux de Lagash', *RA* XLVII, 57-69, 105-20.
 1968 'Masses d'armes de pierre au nom de Naramsîn', *Orientalia* 37, 85f.
 1970 'Note brève', *RA* 64, 189.
 1974 'Les villes du sud-Mésopotamie et l'Iran au temps de Naramsin', *Oriens Antiquus* XIII, 1-24.

1975 'Mesag le prince et Mesag le šabra (la vie économique à l'époque d'Agadé)', *Rivista degli Studi Orientali* 49, 159-84.

1979 'Le prince de Susa Ilish-Mani, et l'Elam de Naramsin à Ibisîn', *Journal Asiatique* CCLXVII, 11-40.

1981 'Ur-Emuš "Grand-Marchand" de Lagash', *Oriens Antiquus* XX, 175-85.

LAMBERT, M, TOURNAY, O.P.
1951 'La statue B de Gudéa', *RA* XLV, 49-66.
1952 'Les statues D, G, E, et H de Gudéa', *RA* XLVI, 75-86.

LAMBERT, W.G.
1985 'The Pair Laḫmu-Laḫamu in Cosmology', *Orientalia* 54, 189-202.
1989 'Notes on a Work of the Most Ancient Semitic Literature', *JCS* 41, 1-33.

LANDSBERGER, B.
1965 'Tin and Lead: The Adventures of two Vocables', *JNES* 24, 285-96.

LANGDON, S.
1924 *Excavations at Kish I (1923-24)*, Paris.
1925 Review of Scheil 1923, *JRAS* 1925, 169-73.
1928 *The Herbert Weld Collection in the Ashmolean Museum, Pictographic Inscriptions from Jemdet Nasr*, Oxford Editions of Cuneiform Texts VII, Oxford.
1934 *Excavations at Kish IV (1925-1930)*, Paris.

LANGSDORFF, A., McCOWN, D.
1942 *Tall-i-Bakun A, Season of 1932*, Chicago.

LARSEN, C.E., EVANS, G.
1978 'The Holocene Geological History of the Tigris-Euphrates-Karun Delta', in Brice (ed.) 1978, 227-44.

LARSEN, M.T.
1976 *The Old Assyrian City-State and its Colonies*, Mesopotamia, Copenhagen Studies in Assyriology 4, Copenhagen.
1979 'The Tradition of Empire in Mesopotamia', in Larsen (ed.) 1979, 75-103.
1982 'Caravans and Trade in Ancient Mesopotamia and Asia Minor', *Bulletin of the Society for Mesopotamian Studies* 4, 33-45.

LARSEN, M.T. (ed.)
1979 *Power and Propaganda*, Mesopotamia 7, Copenhagen.

LE BRETON, L.
1957 'The Early Periods at Susa, Mesopotamian Relations', *Iraq* XIX, 79-124.

LE BRUN, A.
1971 'Recherches stratigraphiques à l'Acropole de Suse', *DAFI* 1, 163-216.
1978 'Le niveau 17B de l'Acropole de Suse (Campagne de 1972)', *DAFI* 9, 57-154.
1978a 'La glyptique du niveau 17B de l'Acropole (campagne de 1972)', *DAFI* 8, 61-79.
1978b 'Suse, Chantier "Acropole 1"', *Paléorient* 4, 177-92.

1985 'Le niveau 18 de l'Acropole de Suse. Mémoire d'argile, mémoire du temp', *Paléorient* 11/2, 31-36.

LE BRUN, A., VALLAT, F.
1978 'L'origine de l'écriture à Suse', *DAFI* 9, 11-59.
1989 'Des chiffres et des signes sur l'argile', *Dossiers: Histoire et archéologie* 138, 36f.
1982 Comments on Alden 1982, *Current Anthropology* 23, 633.

LECHEVALLIER, M.
1984 'The Flint Industry of Mehrgarh', in Allchin (ed.) 1984, 41-51.

LECHEVALLIER, M., QUIVRON, G.
1981 'The Neolithic in Baluchistan: New Evidence from Mehrgarh', in Härtel (ed.) 1981, 71-92.

LEEMANS, W.F.
1960 *Foreign Trade in the Old Babylonian Period*, Leiden.
1960a 'The Trade Relations of Babylonia and the Question of Relations with Egypt in the Old Babylonian Period', *JESHO* III, 21-37.
1966 'Cuneiform Texts in the Collection of Dr Ugo Sissa', *JCS* 20, 34-47.
1968 'Old Babylonian Letters and Economic History. A Review Article with a Digression on Foreign Trade', *JESHO* XI, 171-226.
1977 'The Importance of Trade', *Iraq* XXXIX, 1-10.

LEGRAIN, L.
1921 *Empreintes de cachets élamites*, *MDP* XVI, Paris.
1926 *Royal Inscriptions and Fragments from Nippur and Babylon*, PBS XV, Philadelphia.
1937 *Ur Excavations Texts III: Business Documents of the Third Dynasty of Ur*, London & Philadelphia.
1951 *Ur Excavations X: Seal Cylinders*, Oxford.

LEGRAIN, L., WOOLLEY, C.L.
1936 *Ur Excavations III: Archaic Seal Impressions*, London.

LENZEN, H.
1950 'Die Tempel der Schicht Archaisch IV in Uruk', *ZA* 49, 1-20.
1958 *XIV. vorläufiger Bericht ... Uruk-Warka*, Berlin.
1961 *Uruk vorläufiger Bericht ... XVII*, Berlin.
1964 *XX. vorläufiger Bericht ... Uruk-Warka*, Berlin.
1965 *XXI. vorläufiger Bericht ... Uruk-Warka*, Berlin.

LEVINE, L.D.
1973 'Geographical Studies in the Neo-Assyrian Zagros - I', *Iran* XI, 1-27.
1974 'Geographical Studies in the Neo-Assyrian Zagros - II', *Iran* XII, 99-124.

LEVINE, L.D., YOUNG JR, T.C. (eds)
1977 *Mountains and Lowlands: Essays in the Archaeology of Greater Mesopotamia*, Bibliotheca Mesopotamia 7, Malibu.

LEWIS, B.
1980   *The Sargon Legend: A Study of the Akkadian Text and the Tale of the Hero Who was Exposed at Birth*, ASOR Dissertation Series no. 14, Cambridge, Mass.

LEWY, H.
1968   'A Contribution to the Historical Geography of the Nuzi Texts', *JAOS* 88, 150-62.

1971   'Assyria, c. 2600-1816 B.C.', in Edwards *et al.* (eds) 1971, 729-70.

LIEBERMAN, S.J.
1968-69   'An Ur III Text from Drehem Recording "Booty from the Land of Mardu"', *JCS* XXII, 53-62.

1980   'Of Clay Pebbles, Hollow Clay Balls and Writing: A Sumerian View', *AJA* 84, 339-58.

LIGABUE, G., SALVATORI, S. (eds)
1988   *Bactria: an Ancient Oasis Civilisation from the Sands of Afghanistan*, Venice.

LIMET, H.
1960   *Le travail du métal au pays de Sumer au temps de la IIIe dynastie d'Ur*, Paris.

1972   'L'étranger dans la société sumérienne', in D.O. Edzard (ed.), *Gesellschaftsklassen im Alten Zweistromland und in den angrenzenden Gebieten*, Munich, 123-38.

1972a   'Les métaux à l'époque d'Agade', *JESHO* 15, 3-34.

LIMPER, K.
1988   *Perlen, Kelten, Anhängen, Grabungen 1912-1985*, Ausgrabungen in Uruk-Warka Endberichte 2, Mainz am Rhein.

LISITSINA, G.N.
1981   'The History of Irrigation Agriculture in Southern Turkmenia', in Kohl (ed.) 1981, 350-58.

LITTAUER, M.A., CROUWEL, J.H.
1979   *Wheeled Vehicles and Ridden Animals in the Ancient Near East*, Leiden.

LIVERANI, M.
1988   'The Fire of Haḫḫum', *Oriens Antiquus* XXVII, 165-72.

LLOYD, S. *et al.*
1942   *A Guide to the Iraq Museum Collections*, Baghdad.

LODING, D.
1981   'Lapidaries in the Ur III Period', *Expedition* 23, 6-14.

LOHUIZEN-DE LEEUW, J.E. VAN (ed.)
1979   *South Asian Archaeology 1975*, Leiden.

LOON, M.N. VAN
1971   Review of V.M. Masson, *Sredniana Aziia i Drevnii Vostok*, Moscow and Leningrad, 1964, in *JNES* 30, 226-32.

1977   'Archaeological Evidence of Trade in Western Asia: Problems and Prospects', in B.L. van Beck *et al.* (eds) 1977, *Ex Horreo*, Amsterdam, 1-8.

1981   Review of Stève and Gasche 1971, *Bibliotheca Orientalis* XXXVIII 5/6, 707-16.

LORETZ, O.
1969   *Texte aus Chagar Bazar und Tell Brak, Teil 1*, AOAT 3/1, Vluyn.

LUCAS, A.
1962   *Ancient Egyptian Materials and Industries*, 4th ed. revised by J.R. Harris, London.

LUCKENBILL, D.D.
1924   *The Annals of Sennacherib*, OIP II, Chicago.

1926-27   *Ancient Records of Assyria and Babylonia*, 2 vols, Chicago.

1930   *Inscriptions from Adab*, OIP XIV, Chicago.

LYONNET, B.
1977   'Découverte de sites de l'âge du bronze dans le N.E. de l'Afghanistan: leurs rapports avec la civilisation de l'Indus', *Annali* 37, 19-35.

1981   'Établissements chalcolithiques dans le Nord-Est de l'Afghanistan: leur rapports avec les civilisations du bassin de l'Indus', *Paléorient* 7/2, 57-74.

McALPINE, D.W.
1981   'Proto-Elamo-Dravidian: The Evidence and its Implications', *Transactions of the American Philosophical Society* 71/3.

McCOWN, D.E.
1942   *The Comparative Stratigraphy of Early Iran*, SAOC 23, Chicago.

1954   'The Relative Stratigraphy and Chronology of Iran', in Ehrich (ed.) 1954, 56-68.

McCOWN, D.E., HAINES, R.C., BIGGS, R.D., CARTER, E.F.
1978   *Nippur II: The North Temple and Sounding E*, OIP XCVII, Chicago.

McCOWN, D.E., HAINES, R.C., HANSEN, D.P.
1967   *Nippur I: Temple of Enlil, Scribal Quarter and Soundings*, OIP LXXVIII, Chicago.

McGUINESS, D.M.
1982   'The Family of Giri$_x$-zal', *RA* 76, 17-25.

MACKAY, E.
1925   'Sumerian Connexions with Ancient India', *JRAS* 1925, 697-701.

1929   *A Sumerian Palace and the 'A' Cemetery at Kish, Mesopotamia*, Field Museum of Natural History, Anthropological Memoirs 1, 67-218.

1931   *Report on Excavations at Jemdet Nasr, Iraq*, Field Museum of Natural History, Anthropological Memoirs 1/3, 219-303.

1932   'An Important Link Between Ancient India and Elam', *Antiquity* VI, 356f.

McKERRELL, H.
1978   'The Use of Tin-Bronze in Britain and the Comparative Relationship with the Near East', in A.D. Franklin *et al.* (eds), *The Search for Tin*, Washington, 7ff.

McNEIL, R.C.
1971   *The 'Messenger Texts' of the Third Ur Dynasty*, PhD dissertation, Ann Arbor.

MADDIN, R. (ed.)
    1988   *The Beginning of the Use of Metals and Alloys*, Cambridge Mass. & London.

MAEDA, T.
    1981   '"King of Kish" in Pre-Sargonic Sumer', *Orient* XVII, 1-17.

MAEKAWA, K.
    1979   'The Ass and the Onager in Sumer in the Late Third Millennium B.C.', *Acta Sumerologica* 1, 35-62.

MAJIDZADEH, Y.
    1976   'The Land of Aratta', *JNES* 35, 105-13.
    1979   'An Early Prehistoric Coppersmith Workshop at Ghabristan', *AMI Ergänzungsband* 6, 82-92.
    1982   'Lapis lazuli and the great Khorasan Road', *Paléorient* 8/1, 59-69.

MALFOY, J.-M., MENU, M.
    1987   'La metallurgie du cuivre à Suse aux IVe et IIIe millénaires', in Tallon 1987, 355-73.

MALAMAT, A.
    1970   'Northern Canaan and the Mari Texts', in A. Saundars (ed.), *Near Eastern Archaeology in the 20th century, Essays in Honor of Nelson Glueck*, New York, 164-77.

MALLOWAN, M.E.L.
    1947   'Excavations at Brak and Chagar Bazar', *Iraq* IX, 1-266.
    1970   'The Development of Cities from al-'Ubaid to the End of Uruk 5', in I.E.S. Edwards, C.J. Gadd & N.G.L. Hammond (eds), *The Cambridge Ancient History, vol. I, Pt 1*, Cambridge, 327-462.

MARSCHNER, R., WRIGHT, H.T.
    1978   'Asphalts from Ancient Sites in Southwest Iran', *Paléorient* 4, 97-112.
    1978a   'Asphalts from Middle Eastern Archaeological Sites', in G. Carter (ed.), *Archaeological Chemistry II*, Advances in Chemistry Series 171, 150-171.

MARSHALL, J.
    1931   *Mohenjo-Daro and the Indus Civilization* II, London.

MARTIN, H.P.
    1982   'The Early Dynastic Cemetery at Al-'Ubaid, A Re-evaluation', *Iraq* 44, 145-85.

MASIMOV, I.S.
    1981   'The Study of Bronze Age Sites in the Lower Murghab', in Kohl (ed.) 1981, 194-220.

MASON, K. *et al.*
    1944   *Iraq and the Persian Gulf*, Naval Intelligence Handbook, Oxford.
    1945   *Persia*, Naval Intelligence Handbook, Oxford.

MASSON, V.M.
    1968   'The Urban Revolution in South Turkmenia', *Antiquity* XLII, 178-87.

MASSON, V.M., KIIATKINA, T.P.
    1981   'Man at the Dawn of Civilization', in Kohl (ed.) 1981, 107-34.

MASSON, V.M., SARIANIDI, V.I.
    1972   *Central Asia: Turkmenia before the Achaemenids*, London.

MATTHIAE, P.
    1985   *I tesori di Ebla*, Milan.

MAXWELL-HYSLOP, K.R.
    1971   *Western Asiatic Jewellery, c. 3000-612 B.C.*, London.
    1977   'Sources of Sumerian Gold', *Iraq* XXXIX, 83-86.
    1982   'The Kosh Tapa-Fullol Hoard', *Afghan Studies* 3/4, 25-37.
    1987   'British Museum "Axe" No. 123268: A Bactrian Bronze', *Bulletin of the Asia Institute* 1, 17-26.

MEADOW, R.H.
    1984   'A Camel Skeleton from Mohenjo-daro', in Lal & Gupta (eds) 1984, 133-39.

MEADOW, R.H., ZEDER, M.A. (eds)
    1978   *Approaches to Faunal Analysis in the Middle East*, Peabody Museum Bulletin 2, Cambridge, Mass.

MEADOW, R.H., UERPMANN, H.-P. (eds)
    1986   *Equids in the Ancient World*, Wiesbaden.

MECQUENEM, R. DE
    1905   'Offrandes de fondation du Temple de Chouchinak', *MDP* VII, 61-130.
    1911   'Constructions élamites du tell de l'Acropole de Suse', *MDP* XII, 65-78.
    1912   'Catalogue de la céramique peinte susienne conservée au Musée du Louvre', *MDP* XIII, 105-58.
    1924   'Fouilles de Suse (Campagnes 1923-1924)', *RA* XXI, 105-18.
    1928   'Notes sur la céramique peinte archaïque en Perse', *MDP* XX, 99-132.
    1934   'Fouilles de Suse (1929-1933)', *MDP* XXV, 177-237.
    1943   'Fouilles de Suse (1933-1939)', *MDP* XXIX, 3-161.
    1949   'Épigraphie Proto-Élamite', *MDP* XXXI, 5-150.
    1953   'Têtes de cannes susiennes en métal', *RA* 47, 79-82.

MEEKS, N.D., TITE, M.S.
    1980   'The Analysis of Platinum-Group Element Inclusions in Gold Antiquities', *Journal of Archaeological Science* 7, 267ff.

MELLAART, J.
    1981   'Anatolia and the Indo-Europeans', *Journal of Indo-European Studies* 9 (1/2), 135-49.
    1982   'Mesopotamian Relations with the West, Including Anatolia', in Nissen & Renger (eds) 1982, 7-12.
    1982a   'Archaeological Evidence for Trade and Trade Routes between Syria and Mesopotamia and Anatolia during the Early and the Beginning of the Middle Bronze Age', *Studi Eblaiti* V, 15-32.

MELLINK, M.J.
    1992   'Archaeology in Anatolia', *AJA* 96, 119-50.

MERPERT, N. *et al.*
1976 'The Investigations of Soviet Expedition in Iraq, 1973', *Sumer* 32, 25-61.
MERIGGI, P.
1971-74 *La scrittura proto-elamica I-III*, Rome.

MERHAV, R. *et al.*
1981 *A Glimpse into the Past: The Joseph Ternbach Collection*, Jerusalem.
MESSERSCHMIDT, L.
1907 *Vorderasiatische Schriftdenkmäler der Königlichen Museen zu Berlin I*, Leipzig.
MEYER, C.A.
1981 *Stone Artifacts from Tutub, Eshnunna and Nippur*, Ph.D. Dissertation, Chicago.
MEYER, C.A., TODD, J.M., BECK, C.W.
1991 'From Zanzibar to Zagros: A Copal Pendant from Eshnunna', *JNES* 50, 289-98.
MEYER, L. DE, GASCHE, H., VALLAT, F. (eds)
1986 *Fragmenta Historiae Elamicae, Mélanges Offerts à M.J. Stève*, Paris.
MEYER, L. DE, HAERINCK, E. (eds)
1989 *Archaeologia Iranica et Orientalis: Miscellanea in Honorem Louis Vanden Berghe*, vol. 1, Ghent.
MICHALOWSKI, P.
1975 'The Bride of Simanum', *JAOS* 95, 716-19.
1976 *The Royal Correspondence of Ur*, Yale Ph.D. Dissertation, Ann Arbor.
1978 'Foreign Tribute to Sumer During the Ur III Period', *ZA* 68, 34-49.
1980 'New Sources Concerning the Reign of Naram-Sin', *JCS* 32, 233-46.
1983 'Königsbriefe', *RlA* VI, 51-59.
1983a 'History as Charter: the Sumerian King List Revisited', *JAOS* 103, 237-48.
1984 Review of S.N. Kramer, Sumerian Literary Tablets and Fragments in the Archaeological Museum of Istanbul 2, Ankara, 1976, in *JCS* 36, 123-26.
1985 'Third Millennium Contacts: Observations on the Relationship Between Mari and Ebla', *JAOS* 105, 293-302.
1986 'Mental Maps and Ideology: Reflections on Subartu', in Weiss (ed.) 1986, 129-56.
1986a 'The Earliest Hurrian Toponymy: A New Sargonic Inscription', *ZA* 76, 4-11.
1987 'Charisma and Control: On Continuity and Change in Early Mesopotamian Bureaucratic Systems', in Gibson & Biggs (eds) 1987, 55-68.
1988 'Magan and Meluḫḫa Once Again', *JCS* 40, 156-64.
1988a Review of Gordon *et al.* (eds) 1987, in *BASOR* 270, 100f.
1989 *The Lamentation Over the Destruction of Sumer and Ur*, Winona Lake.
1990 'Early Mesopotamian Communicative Systems: Art, Literature and Writing', in Gunter (ed.) 1990, 53-69.
1990a 'The Skekel and the Vizir', *ZA* 80, 1-8.

MICHALOWSKI, P., WALKER, C.B.F.
1989 'A New Sumerian "Law Code"', in Behrens *et al.* (ed.) 1989, 383-96.
MIEROOP, M. VAN DE
1987 *Sumerian Administrative Documents from the Reign of Išbi-Erra and Šū-ilišu*, BIN 10, New Haven.
1987a *Crafts on the Early Isin Period: A Study of the Isin Craft Archive from the Reign of Išbi-Erra and Šū-ilišu*, Leuven.
MILLER, J.I.
1969 *The Spice Trade in the Roman Empire*, Oxford.
MIROSCHEDJI, P. DE
1972 'Un objet cultuel (?) d'origine Iranienne provenant', *Iran* X, 159-61.
1973 'Vases et objets en stéatite susiens du Musée du Louvre', *DAFI* 3, 9-42.
1974 'Tépé Jalyan, une nécropole du IIIe millénaire av. J.C. au Fars oriental (Iran)', *Arts asiatiques* 30, 19-64.
1980 'Le dieu élamite Napirisha', *RA* 74, 129-43.
1981 'Le dieu élamite au serpent et aux eaux jaillissantes', *Iranica Antiqua* XVI, 1-25.
MØLLER, E.
1984 'Reliefstrnkar fra Mesopotamien' in P.J. Frandsen & J. Laessøe (eds), *Mellem Nilen og Tigris*, Copenhagen, 83-100.
MOOREY, P.R.S.
1966 *An Archaeolgoical and Historical Investigation of the 'Luristan Bronzes'*, D.Phil. thesis, Oxford.
1970 'Pictorial Evidence for the History of Horse-Riding in Iraq before the Kassites', *Iraq* 32, 36-50.
1971a *Catalogue of the Ancient Persian Bronzes in the Ashmolean Museum*, Oxford.
1971b 'Towards a Chronology of the Luristan Bronzes', *Iran* IX, 113-29.
1978 *Kish Excavations 1923-1933*, Oxford.
1979 'Unpublished Early Dynastic Sealings from Ur in the British Museum', *Iraq* 41, 105-20.
1982 'Archaeology and pre-Achaemenid Metalworking in Iran: A Fifteen year Retrospective', *Iran* XX, 81-101.
1982a 'The Archaeological Evidence for Metallurgy and Related Technologies in Mesopotamia, c. 5500-2100 B.C.', *Iraq* XLIV, 13-38.
1984 'Where did they bury the kings of the IIIrd Dynasty of Ur?', *Iraq* XLVI, 1-18.
1985 *Materials and Manufacture in Ancient Mesoptamia: The Evidence of Archaeology and Art. Metals and Metalwork, Glazed Materials and Glass*, BAR International Series 237, Oxford.
1986 'The Emergence of the light, horse-drawn chariot in the Near East c. 2000-1500 B.C.', *World Archaeology* 18, 196-215.
1987 'On Tracking Cultural Transfers in Prehistory: The Case of Egypt and Lower Mesopotamia in the Fourth Millennium

B.C.', in M. Rowlands *et al.* (eds) 1987, 36-46.

1988 'Early Metallurgy in Mesopotamia', in Maddin (ed.) 1988, 28-33.

1989 'The Hurrians, the Mittani and Technological Inovation', in de Meyer & Haerinck (eds) 1989, 273-86.

1990 'From gulf to Delta in the Fourth Millennium BCE: The Syrian Connection', *Eretz-Israel* (Amiran Festschrift) 21, 62*-69*.

1993 'Iran: A Sumerian El-Dorado?', in J.E. Curtis (ed.) 1993, 31-43.

MOOREY, P.R.S., BUNKER, E.C., PORADA, E., MARKOE, G.

1981 *Ancient Bronzes, Ceramics and Seals: The Nasli M. Heermaneck Collection of the Ancient Near East, Central Asiatic and European Art*, Los Angeles.

MOOREY, P.R.S., SCHWEITZER, F.

1972 'Copper and Copper Alloys in Ancient Iraq, Syria and Palestine: Some New Analyses', *Archaeometry* 14, 177-98.

MOORTGAT, A.

1940 *Vorderasiatische Rollsiegel, Ein Beitrag zur Geschichte der Steinschneidekunst*, Berlin.

1969 *The Art of Ancient Mesopotamia*, London & New York.

MORGAN, J. DE

1900 'Matières minérales employées à Suse dans l'antiquité', *MDP* I, 33-49.

1905 'État des travaux à Suse en 1904', *MDP* VII, 1-8.

1905a 'Découverte d'une sépulture Achéménide à Suse', *MDP* VIII, 29-58.

1905b *Mission scientifique en Perse III*, Paris.

1912 'Observations sur les couches profondes de l'Acropole à Suse', *MDP* XIII, 1-26.

1927 *La préhistoire orientale 3, L'Asie antérieure*, Paris.

MORTENSEN, P.

1970 'On the Date of the Temple at Barbar in Bahrain', *KUML* 1970, 385-98.

1986 'The Barbar Temple: its chronology and foreign relations reconsidered', in Khalifa & Rice (eds) 1986, 178-85.

MUGHAL, M.R.

1972 'A Summary of Excavations and Explorations in Pakistan (1971 and 1972)', *Pakistan Archaeology* 8, 113-58.

1983 *The Dilmun Burial Complex at Sar: The 1980-82 Excavations in Bahrain*, Bahrain.

MUHLY, J.D.

1973 *Copper and Tin: the Distribution of Mineral Resources and the Nature of the Metals Trade in the Bronze Age*, Hamden.

1976 *Supplement to Copper and Tin*, Hamden.

1980 'The Bronze Age Setting', in Wertime & Muhly (eds) 1980, 25-67.

1980-83 'Kupfer. B. Archäologisch', *RlA* VI, 348-64.

1985 'Sources of Tin and the Beginnings of Bronze Metallurgy', *AJA* 89, 275-91.

1988 'The Beginnings of Metallurgy in the Old World', in Maddin (ed.) 1988, 2-20.

1993 'Early Bronze Age Tin and the Taurus', *AJA* 97, 239-53.

MUHLY, J.D., WERTIME, T.A.

1973 'Evidence for the Sources and use of tin During the Bronze Age of the Near East: A Reply to J.E. Dayton', *World Archaeology* 5/1, 111-22.

MUHLY, J.D., BEGEMANN, F., ÖZTUNALI, Ö, PERNICKA, E., SCHMITT-STRECKER, S., WAGNER, G.A.

1991 'The Bronze Age Metallurgy of Anatolia and the Question of Local tin Sources', in E. Pernicka & G.A. Wagner (eds), *Archaeometry '90, International Symposium on Archaeometry, 2-6 April 1990, Heidelberg*, Basel, Boston & Berlin, 209-20.

MÜLLER, A. VON

1963 'Feuersteingerät und Perlenfabrikation. Auswertungsmöglichkeiten eines Oberflächenfundplatzes in Uruk-Warka', *Berliner Jahrbuch für Vor- und Frühgeschichte* 3, 187-95.

MUSCARELLA, O.W. (ed.)

1981 *Archäologie zur Bibel*, Mainz am Rhein.

MYNORS, H.S.

1983 'An examination of Mesopotamian ceramics using petrographic and neutron activation analysis', in A. Aspinall & S.E. Warren (eds), *The Proceedings of the 22nd Symposium on Archaeometry*, Bradford, 377-87.

NAGEL, W.

1964 *Djamdat Nasr-Kulturen und Frühdynastische Buntkeramiker*, Berliner Beiträge zur Vor- und Frühgeschichte 8, Berlin.

1966 'Frühe Großplastik und die Hochkulturkunst am Erythraïschen Meer', *Berliner Jahrbuch für Vor- und Frühgeschichte* 6, 1-54.

1970 'Eine Kupferschale mit Inschrift des Königs Manistussu', *Acta praehistorica et archaeologica* I, 195.

NAGEL, W., STROMMENGER, E.

1968 'Reichsakkadische Glyptik und Plastik im Rahmen der mesopotamisch-elamischen Geschichte', *Berliner Jahrbuch für Vor- und Frühgeschichte* 8, 137-206.

NASSOUHI, E.

1925 'Un vase en albâtre de Naram-Sin', *RA* XXII, 91.

NEUMANN, H.

1979 'Handel und Händler in der Zeit der III. Dynastie von Ur', *Altorientalische Forschungen* VI, 15-67.

NICHOLAS, I.M.

1981 'Investigating an Ancient Suburb: Excavations at the TUV Mound, Iran', *Expedition* 23, 39-47.

1990   *The Proto-Elamite Settlement at TUV*, Malyan Excavation Reports I, Philadelphia.

NISHIMURA, S., SASAJIMA, S., TOKIEDA, K., TOSI, M.
1983   'Fishon-Track Ages of the Remians from Shahr-i Sokhta, Iran', in M. Tosi (ed.) 1983, 345-348.

NISSEN, H.J.
1966   *Zur Datierung des Königsfriedhofes von Ur*, Beiträge zur Ur- und Frühgeschichtlichen Archäologie des Mittelmeer-Kulturraumes Bd. 3, Bonn.
1967   'Die Tafeln der XXIII Kampagne', in H.J. Lenzen *et al.*, *XXIII. vorläufiger Bericht ... Uruk-Warka*, Berlin, 37-39.
1968   'Die Tafeln der XXIV. Kampagne', in H.J. Lenzen *et al.*, *XXIV. vorläufiger Bericht ... Uruk-Warka*, Berlin.
1974   'Tontafeln und Verwandtes', in H.J. Lenzen *et al.*, *XXV. vorläufiger Bericht ... Uruk-Warka*, Berlin.
1982   Comment on Alden 1982, *Current Anthropology* 23, 634f.
1985   'The Emergence of Writing in the Ancient Near East', *Interdisciplinary Science Reviews* 10/4, 349-61.
1985a   'Problems of the Uruk Period in Susiana, Viewed from Uruk', *Paléorient* 11/2, 39f.
1985b   'Ortsnamen in den archaischen Texten aus Uruk', *Orientalia* 54, 226-33.
1986   'The Archaic Texts from Uruk', *World Archaeology* 17, 317-34.
1986a   'The Occurrence of Dilmun in the Oldest Texts of Mesopotamia', in al Khalifa & Rice (eds) 1986, 335-39.
1986b   'The Development of Writing and of Glyptic Art', in Finkbeiner & Röllig (eds) 1986, 316-31.

NISSEN, H.-J., RENGER, J. (eds)
1982   *Mesopotamien und seine Nachbarn*, Berlin.

NÖLDEKE, A. *et al.*
1932   *Vierter vorläufiger Bericht ... Uruk*, Berlin.
1936   *Siebenter vorläufiger Bericht ... Uruk-Warka*, Berlin.
1937   *Achter vorläufiger Bericht ... Uruk-Warka*, Berlin.
1939   *Zehnter vorläufiger Bericht ... Uruk-Warka*, Berlin.
1940   *Elfter vorläufiger Bericht ... Uruk-Warka*, Berlin.

NOUGAYROL, J.
1951   'Un chef-d'oeuvre inédit de la littérature babylonienne', *RA* 45, 169-83.

OATES, D.
1982   'Excavations at Tell Brak, 1978-81', *Iraq* XLIV, 187-204.
1985   'Excavations at Tell Brak, 1983-84', *Iraq* XLVII, 159-73.
1987   'Excavations at Tell Brak 1985-86', *Iraq* XLIX, 175-91.

OATES, J.
1985   'Tell Brak and Chronology: The Third Millennium', *MARI* 4, 137-44.
1986   'Tell Brak: The Uruk/Early Dynastic Sequence', in Finkbeiner & Röllig (eds) 1986, 245-71.

OATES, J., DAVIDSON, T.E., KAMILI, D., McKERREL, H.
1977   'Seafaring Merchants of Ur?', *Antiquity* LI, 221-34.

OELSNER, J.O.
1989   'Einige Königsinschriften des 3. Jahrtausends in der Hilprecht-Sammlung Jena', in Behrens *et al.* (eds) 1989, 403-08.

OGDEN, J.M.
1977   'Platinum Group Metal Inclusions in Ancient Gold Artefacts', *Journal of the Historical Metallurgy Society* 11, 53ff.

OPPENHEIM, A.L.
1954   'The Seafaring Merchants of Ur', *JAOS* 74, 6-17.
1967   *Letters from Mesopotamia*, Chicago and London.
1976   'Trade in the Ancient Near East', *Fifth International Congress of Economic History*, Vol. 5, Moscow, 125-49.
1977   *Ancient Mesopotamia, Portrait of a Dead Civilization*, revised ed. completed by E. Reiner, Chicago.
1978   'Man and Nature in Mesopotamian Civilization', *Dictionary of Scientific Biography*, vol. XV, Supplement 1, New York, 634-66.

OPPENHEIM, A.L. *et al.*
1970   *Glass and Glassmaking in Ancient Mesopotamia*, Corning, New York.

ORTHMANN, W.
1976-80   'Kaniš, kārum. B. Archäologisch', *RlA* V, 378-82.

ORTHMANN, W. *et al.*
1975   *Der Alte Orient*, Propyläen Kunstgeschichte 14, Berlin.

OWEN, D.I.
1981   Review of Edzard & Farber 1974, in *JCS* 33, 244-70.
1991   *Neo-Sumerian Texts from American Collections*, Materiali per il Vocabulario Neosumerico XV, Rome.

OZDOGAN, M.
1977   *Lower Euphrates Basin, 1977 Survey*, Istanbul.

PALMIERI, A.
1981   'Excavations at Arslantepe (Malatya)', *Anatolian Studies* 31, 101-19,

PARPOLA, S., PARPOLA, A., BRUNSWIG JR, R.H.
1977   'The Meluhha Village: Evidence of Acculturation of Harappan Traders in Late Third Millennium Mesopotamia?', *JESHO* 20, 129-64.

PARR, P.A.
1974   'Ninḫilia: Wife of Ayakala, Governor of Umma', *JCS* 26, 90-111.

PARROT, A.
1948   *Tello: vingt campagnes de fouilles*, Paris.
1955   'Les fouilles de Mari, dixième campagne', *Syria* XXXII, 185-211.
1956   *Le temple d'Ishtar*, Mission archéologique de Mari I, Paris.

1962   'Les fouilles de Mari, Douzième campagne', *Syria* 39, 151-79.
1965   'Les fouilles de Mari', *Syria* XLII, 1-24.
1967   *Les temples d'Ishtarat et de Ninni-zaza*, Mission archéologique de Mari III, Paris.
1974   *Mari, capitale fabuleuse*, Paris.

PARROT, A., NOUGAYROL, J.
1948   'Un document de fondation hurrite', *RA* 42, 1-20.

PEAKE, H.
1928   'The Copper Mountain of Magan', *Antiquity* II, 452-57.

PELZEL, S.M.
1977   'Dating the Early Dynastic Votive Plaques from Susa', *JNES* 36, 1-15.

PERKINS, A.L.
1949   *The Comparative Archaeology of Early Mesopotamia*, SAOC 25, Chicago.

PERNICKA, E., WAGNER, G.A., MUHLY, J.D., ÖZTUNALI, Ö.
1992   'Comment on the Discussion of Ancient Tin Sources in Anatolia', *Journal of Mediterranean Archaeology* 5, 91-98.

PETERS, J.P.
1897   *Nippur II, Second Campaign*, New York & London.

PETTINATO, G.
1972   'Il commercio con l'estero della Mesopotamia meridionale nel 3. millennio av. Cr. alla luce delle fonti letterarie e lessicali sumeriche', *Mesopotamia* VII, 43-166.
1978   'L'Atlante Geografico nel Vicino Oriente Antico attestato ad Ebla ed ad Abu Salabikh (I)', Orientalia 47, 50-73.
1982   'Il tesoro del nemico elamita, ovvero, il bottino della guerra contro Anšan di Šulgi', *Oriens Antiquus* XXI, 49-72.
1983   'Dilmun nella Documentazione Epigrafica di Ebla', in Potts (ed.) 1983, 75-82.

PÉZARD, M.
1914   Mission à Bender-Bouchir, documents archéologiques et épigraphiques, *MDP* XV, Paris.

PÉZARD, M., POTTIER, E.
1926   *Catalogue des antiquités de la Susiane (Mission J. de Morgan)*, Paris.

PIGGOTT, S.
1950   *Prehistoric India*, Hammondsworth.

PIGGOTT, V.C.
1980   'Research at the University of Pennsylvania on the Development of Ancient Metallurgy. Section I: Research at MASCA', *Paléorient* 6, 105-10.
1989   'Archae-Metallurgical Investigations at Bronze Age Tappeh Hesār, 1976', in Dyson & Howard (eds) 1989, 25-33.

PIGOTT, V.C., HOWARD, S.M., EPSTEIN, S.M.
1982   'Pyrotechnology and Culture Change at Bronze Age Tepe Hissar', in Wertime & Wertime (eds) 1982, 215-36.

PINNOCK, F.
1986   'The lapis lazuli trade in the third millennium B.C. and the evidence of the royal palace at Ebla', in M. Kelly-Buccellati (ed.), *Insight Through Images: Studies in Honor of Edith Porada*, Malibu, 221-28.

PIOTROVSKY, P.P. (ed.)
1979   *Avant les Scythes. Préhistoire de l'art en U.R.S.S.*, Paris.

PIPERNO, M.
1976   'Grave 77 at Shahr-i Sokhta: further evidence of technological specialisation in the 3rd millennium B.C.', *East and West* 26, 9-15.
1979   'Socio-economic Implications from the Graveyard of Shahr-i Sokhta', in M. Taddei (ed.) 1979, 123-39.
1981   'Bead-making and boring techniques in 3rd-millennium Indo-Iran', in M. Tosi (ed.) 1981, 319-25.

PIPERNO, M., SALVATORI, S.
1982   'Evidence of Western Cultural Connections from a Phase 3 Group of Graves at Shahr-i Sokhta', in Nissen & Renger (eds) 1982, 79-85.
1983   'Recent Results and New Perspectives from the Research at the Graveyard of Shahr-i Sokhta, Seistan, Iran', *Annali* (Istituto Universario Orientale) 43, 173-91.

PIPERNO, M., TOSI, M.
1975   'The Graveyard at Shahr-i Sokhta, Iran', *Archaeology* 28, 186-97.

PITTMAN, H.
1980   'Proto-Elamite Glyptic Art from Malyan: Work in Progress', in Sumner (ed.) 1980, 4 pp.
1984   *Art of the Bronze Age, Southeastern Iran, Western Central Asia and the Indus Valley*, New York.
n.d. [1]   'Piedmont Seals'. Lecture delivered at Columbia University, 13 November 1990.
n.d. [2]   'The Origins of Writing: A New Piece in the Puzzle'. *From Minos to Sardanapalus: Near Eastern and Aegean Archaeology at Columbia*, seminar at Columbia University, 9 February 1991.

PLANHOL, X. DE
1968   'Geography of Settlement', in Fisher (ed.) 1968, 409-67.

POEBEL, A.
1909   *Babylonian Legal and Business Documents from the Time of the First Dynasty of Babylon, chiefly from Nippur*, Philadelphia.
1914   *Historical Texts*, PBS 4/1, Philadelphia.
1914a   *Historical and Grammatical Texts*, PBS 5, Philadelphia.

POLLOCK, S.
1985   'Chronology of the Royal Cemetery at Ur', *Iraq* XLVII, 129-58.

PORADA, E.
1965   'The Relative Chronology of Mesopotamia. Part I: Seals and Trade', in Ehrich (ed.) 1965, 133-200.
1965a   *Ancient Iran*, Baden-Baden.
1971   'Excursus: Comments on Steatite Carvings from Saudi Arabia and other

parts of the Ancient Near East', *Artibus Asiae* XXXIII, 323-31.

1971a 'Remarks on Seals Found in the Gulf States', *Artibus Asiae* XXXIII, 331-37.

1976 'Problems of Style and Iconography in Early Sculptures of Mesopotamia and Iran', *Essays in Archaeology and the Humanities, In Memoriam Otto J. Brendel*, Mainz.

1977 'A Cylinder Seal with a Camel in the Walters Art Gallery', *The Journal of the Walters Art Gallery* XXXIV, 1-6.

1981 'Stamp and Cylinder Seals of the Ancient Near East', in Moorey *et al.* 1981, 187-234.

1982 'Remarks on the Tôd Treasure in Egypt', *Societies and Languages of the Ancient Near East, (Festschrift Diakonoff)*, Warminster, 285-303.

PORADA, E., BUCHANAN, B.
1948 *Corpus of Ancient Near Eastern Seals in North American Collections*, New York.

PORADA, E. *et al.*
1958 *Man in the Ancient World, An Exhibition of pre-Christian Objects from the Regions of the Near East, Egypt and the Mediterranean*, New York.

POSTGATE, J.N.
1986 'The Equids of Sumer, Again', in Meadow & Uerpmann (eds) 1986, 194-206.

1986a 'The Transition from Uruk to Early Dynastic: Continuities and Discontinuities in the Record of Settlement', in Finkbeiner & Röllig (eds) 1986, 90-106.

POTTIER, E.
1912 'Étude historique et chronologique sur les vases peints de l'Acropole de Suse', *MDP* XIII, 27-103.

POTTIER, M.-H.
1984 *Matériel funéraire de la Bactriane méridionale de l'âge du bronze*, Éditions recherche sur les civilizations, mémoire 36, Paris.

POTTS, D.T.
1977 'Tepe Yahya and the End of the 4th Millennium on the Iranian Plateau', in Deshayes (ed.) 1977, 23-31.

1978 'Towards an Integrated History of Culture Change in the Arabian Gulf Area: Notes on Dilmun, Makkan and the Economy of Sumer', *JOS* 4, 29-51.

1981 'Echoes of Mesopotamian Divinity on a Cylinder Seal from South-eastern Iran', *RA* 75, 135-42.

1981a 'Potter's Marks at Tepe Yahya', *Paléorient* 7/1, 107-22.

1982 'The Road to Meluhha', *JNES* 41, 279-88.

1982a 'The Zagros Frontier and the Problem of Relations between the Iranian Plateau and Southern Mesopotamia in the Third Millennium B.C.', in Nissen & Renger (eds) 1982, 33-55.

1983 'Barbar Miscellanies', in Potts (ed.) 1983, 127-39.

1983a 'Dilmun: Where and When?', *Dilmun* 11, 15-19.

1984 'On Salt and Salt Gathering in Ancient Mesopotamia', *JESHO* XXVII, 225-71.

1985 'Reflections on the History and Archaeology of Bahrain', *JAOS* 105, 675-710.

1986 'Dilmun's Further Relations: the Syro-Anatolian evidence from the third and second millennia B.C.', in al Khalifa & Rice (eds) 1986, 389-98.

1986a 'Eastern Arabia and the Oman Peninsula during the Late Fourth and Early Third Millennia B.C.', in Finkbeiner & Röllig (eds) 1986, 121-68.

1986b 'The Booty of Magan', *Oriens Antiquus* XXV, 271-85.

1989 *Miscellanea Hasaitica*, Carsten Niebuhr Institute Publications 9, Copenhagen.

1990 *The Arabian Gulf in Antiquity I: From Prehistory to the Fall of the Archaemenid Empire*, Oxford.

1991 *Further Excavations at Tell Abraq. The 1990 Season*, Copenhagen.

1993 'Rethinking Some Aspects of Trade in the Arabian Gulf', *World Archaeology* 24, 423-40.

1993a 'Soft Stone from Oman and Eastern Iran in Cuneiform Sources?', *Circulation des marchandises et des biens,* in R. Gyselen (ed.), *Res Orientales* V, 9-14.

1993b 'The Late Prehistoric, Protohistoric and Early Historic Periods in Eastern Arabia (ca. 5000-1200 B.C.)', *Journal of World Prehistory* 7/2, 163-212.

in pr. a 'Chapter 8: A Chronological and Culture Historical Summary', in D.T. Potts, *Excavations at Tepe Yahya, Iran, 1967-1975: Periods IVC and IVB (3000-2000 B.C.)*, Cambridge, Mass.

in pr. b 'The Chronology of the Archaeological Assemblages from the Head of the Arabian Gulf to the Arabian Sea (8000-1750 B.C.)', R.W. Ehrich (ed.), *Chronologies in Old World Archaeology*, 3rd ed., Chicago.

POTTS, D.T. (ed.)
1983 *Dilmun: New Studies in the History of Bahrain*, Berliner Beiträge zum Vorderen Orient, Bd. 2, Berlin.

POTTS, T.F.
1989 'Foreign Stone Vessels of the Late Third Millennium B.C. from Southern Mesopotamia: Their Origins and Methods of Exchange', *Iraq* LI, 123-64.

1993 'Patterns of trade in third-millennium B.C. Mesopotamia and Iran', *World Archaeology* 24, 379-402.

1993a 'The Stone Vessels', in A.R. Green (ed.), *Abu Salabikh Excavations 4. The 6G Ash-Tip and its Contents: Cultic and Administrative Discard from a Temple?*, London, 159-61.

POWELL, M.A.
1981 'Three Problems in the History of Cuneiform Writing: Origins, Direction of Script, Literacy', *Visible Language* XV, 419-40.
1985 Review of Foster 1982, *JAOS* 105, 144f.
1990 'Identification and Interpretation of Long Term Price Fluctuations in Babylonia: More on the History of Money in Mesopotamia', *Altorientalische Forschungen* 17, 76-99.
1991 'Narām-Sîn, Son of Sargon: Ancient History, Famous Names, and a Famous Babylonian Forgery', *ZA* 81, 20-30.

PRAG, K.
1978 'Silver in the Levant in the 4th millennium B.C.', in P.R.S. Moorey & P.J. Parr (eds), *Archaeology in the Levant*, Warminster, 36-45.

PRITCHARD, J.B. (ed.)
1969 *Ancient Near Eastern Texts Relating to the Old Testament*, 3rd ed., Princeton.

PUMPELLY, R.
1908 *Explorations in Turkestan, Expedition of 1904*, Washington.

QUARANTELLI, E. (ed.)
1985 *The Land Between the Two Rivers*, Turin.

RAO, S.R.
1973 *Lothal and the Indus Civilization*, Bombay.

RAPP, G.
1988 'On the Origins of Copper and Bronze Alloying', in Maddin (ed.) 1988, 21-27.

RASHID, S.A., ALI-HURI, H.A.
1982 *The Akkadian Seals of the Iraq Museum*, Baghdad.

RATNAGAR, S.
1981 *Encounters, The Westerly Trade of the Harappa Civilization*, Delhi.

AL-RAWI, F.N.H.
1990 'Tablets from the Sippar Library I: The "Weidner Chronicle": A Suppositious Royal Letter Concerning a Vision', *Iraq* LII, 1-13.

RAY, J.D.
1986 'The Emergence of Writing in Egypt', *World Archaeology* 17, 307-16.

RAWLINSON, H.C.
1861 *The Cuneiform Inscriptions of Western Asia* I, London.

READE, J.
1979 *Early Etched Beads and the Indus-Mesopotamia Trade*, British Museum Occasional Paper 2, London.
1992 'An Early Warka Tablet', in B. Hrouda, S. Kroll & P.Z. Spanos (eds), *Von Uruk nach Tuttul, ein Festschrift für Eva Strommenger*, Munich & Vienna, 177-79.

REINER, E.
1956 'Lipšur Litanies', *JNES* XV, 129-49.
1965 'The Earliest Elamite Inscription?', *JNES* XXIV, 337-40.
1969 'The Elamite Language', *Altkleinasiatische Sprachen, Handbuch*

der Orientalistik, Erste Abteilung, II. Bd., 1. und 2. Abschnitt, Lieferung 2, Leiden & Köln, 54-118.
1973 'The Location of Anšan', *RA* 67, 57-62.
1974 'New Light on Some Historical Omens', in K. Bittel *et al.* (eds), *Anatolian Studies Presented to H.G. Güterbock on the Occasion of his 65th Birthday*, Istanbul, 257-61.

REISNER, G.A.
1931 'Stone Vessels found in Crete and Babylonia', *Antiquity* V, 200-12.

RENGER, J.
1977 'Legal Aspects of Sealing in Ancient Mesopotamia', in McG. Gibson & R.D. Biggs (eds), *Seals and Sealing in the Ancient Near East*, Bibliotheca Mesopotamica 6, Malibu, 75-88.

RIPINSKY, M.M.
1974 'The Camel in the Archaeology of North Africa and the Nile Valley', *Popular Archaeology* III (6/7), 10-15.
1985 'The Camel in Dynastic Egypt', *Journal of Egyptian Archaeology* 71, 134-41.

ROAF, M.D.
1982 'The Hamrin Sites', in Curtis (ed.) 1982, 40-47.
1983 'A Report on the Work of the British Archaeological Expedition in the Eski Mosul Dam Salvage Project from November 1982 to June 1983', *Sumer* XXXIX, 68-94.

ROBERTS, J.J.M.
1972 *The Earliest Semitic Pantheon*, Baltimore and London.

ROSEN, L. VON
1990 *Lapis Lazuli in Archaeological Contexts*, Studies in Mediterranean Archaeology Pocket Book 93, Jonsered.

RÖLLIG, W.
1975 'Heirat, politische', *RlA* IV, 282-87.
1983 'Kupfer. A. Philologisch', *RlA* VI, 345-48.
1983a 'Lapislazuli. A. Philologisch', *RlA* VI, 488f.

RÖMER, W.H.PH.
1985 'Zur Siegesinschrift des Königs Utuḫeĝal von Unug (±2116-2110 v. Chr.)', *Orientalia* 54, 274-88.

ROSTOVTZEFF, M.
1920 'The Sumerian Treasure of Astrabad', *Journal of Egyptian Archaeology* VI, 4-27.

ROWLANDS, M., LARSEN, M.T., KRISTIANSEN, K. (eds)
1987 *Centre and Periphery in the Ancient World*, Cambridge.

RUBINSON, K.S.
1991 'A Mid-Second Millennium Tomb at Dinkha Tepe', *AJA* 95, 373-94.

SABLOFF, J.A., LAMBERG-KARLOVSKY, C.C. (eds)
1975 *Ancient Civilization and Trade*, Albuquerque.

SAFAR, F., ALI MUSTAFA, M., LLOYD, S.
1981 *Eridu*, Baghdad.

SAJJIDI, M.
1979 'The Proto-Elamite Period on the Izeh Plain', in Wright (ed.) 1979, 93-98.

SALONEN, A.
1956   *Hippologica Accadica*, Helsinki.
1968   *Agricultura Mesopotamica nach sumerisch-akkadischen Quellen*, Helsinki.
SALVATORI, S.
1979   'Sequential Analysis and Architectural Remains in Central Quarters of Shahr-i Sokhta', in Taddei (ed.) 1979, 141-48.
SALVATORI, S., VIDALE, M.
1982   'A Brief Surface Survey of the Protohistoric Site of Shahdad (Kerman, Iran), Preliminary Report', *Rivista di Archeologia* VI, 5-10.
SANTONI, M.
1984   'Sibri and the south cemetery of Mehrgarh: third millennium connections between the northern Kachi Plain (Pakistan) and Central Asia', in Allchin (ed.) 1984, 52-60.
SARIANIDI, V.I.
1971   'The Lapis Lazuli Route in the Ancient East', *Archaeology* 24, 12-15.
1977   'Ancient Horasan and Bactria', in Deshayes (ed.) 1977, 129-42.
1979   'New Finds in Bactria and Indo-Iranian Connections', in Taddei (ed.) 1979, 643-59.
1981a   'Margiana in the Bronze Age', in Kohl (ed.) 1981, 165-93.
1981b   'Seal-Amulets of the Murghab Style', in Kohl (ed.) 1981, 221-55.
1985   'Monumental Architecture in Bactria', in Huot *et al.* (eds) 1985, 417-32.
1986   *Die Kunst des Alten Afghanistan*, Leipzig.
1993   'Excavations at Southern Gonur', *Iran* XXXI, 25-37.
SAYRE, E.V., YENER, K.A., JOEL, E.C., BARNES, I.L.
1992   'Statistical Analysis of the Presently Accumulated Lead Isotope Data from the Near East', *Archaeometry* 34, 73-105.
SAX, M., MIDDLETON, A.P.
1989   'The Use of Volcanic Tuff as a Raw Material for Proto-Elamite Cylinder Seals', *Iran* XXVII, 121-23.
SCHAEFFER(-FORRER), C.F.A.
1949   *Ugaritica* II, Paris.
1978   'Ex Occidente Ars', *Ugaritica* VII, Paris, 475-551.
SCHACHT, R.
1987   'Early Historic Cultures', in Hole (ed.) 1987, 171-203.
SCHARFF, A.
1929   *Die Altertümer der Vor- und Frühzeit Ägyptens*, vol. 2, Berlin.
SCHEIL, V.
1900   *Textes élamites-sémitiques, MDP* II, Paris.
1902   *Textes élamites-sémitiques, deuxième série, MDP* IV, Paris.
1905   *Textes élamites-sémitiques, MDP* VI, Paris.
1908   *Textes élamite-sémitiques, quatrième série, MDP* X, Paris.
1911   *Textes élamite-anzanites, quatrième série, MDP* XI, Paris.
1913   *Textes élamite-sémitiques, cinquième série, MDP* XIV, Paris.
1923   *Textes de comptabilité proto-élamite (nouvelle série), MDP* XVII, Paris.
1931   'Dynasties élamites d'Awan et de Simaš', *RA* 28, 1-8.
1932   *Actes juridiques susiens, MDP* XXIII, Paris.
1935   *Textes de comptabilité proto-élamites, troisième série, MDP* XXVI, Paris.
1939   *Mélanges épigraphiques, MDP* XXVIII, Paris.
SCHLOSSMAN, B.
1968   *Animal Art of the Ancient Near East.*
SCHMANDT-BESSERAT, D.
1977   'An Archaic Recording System and the Origin of Writing', *Syro-Mesopotamian Studies* 1/2, 1-70.
1979   'On the Origins of Writing', in D. Schmandt-Besserat (ed.), *Early Technologies*, Malibu, 41-45.
1980   'The Envelopes that Bear the First Writing', *Technology and Culture* 21, 371-74.
1981   'From Tokens to Tablets: A Re-Evaluation of the So-Called "Numerical Tablets"', *Visible Language*, XV, 321-44.
1984   'Before Numerals', *Visible Language* XVIII, 48-60.
1986   'Tokens at Susa', *Oriens Antiquus* XXV, 93-125.
1988   'Tokens at Uruk', *Baghdader Mitteilungen* 19, 1-175.
SCHMIDT, E.F.
1933   'Tepe Hissar Eacavations 1931', *The Museum Journal* XXIII, 323-483.
1937   *Excavations at Tepe Hissar, Damghan*, Philadelphia.
SCHMIDT, E.F., VAN LOON, M.N., CURVERS, H.H.
1989   *The Holmes Expedition to Luristan*, OIP 108, Chicago.
SCHNEIDER, N.
1936   *Die Zeitbestimmungen Wirtschaftsurkunden von Ur III*, Analecta Orientalia 13, Rome.
SCHÜLLER, A.
1963   'Die Rohstoffe der Steingefäße der Sumerer aus der archaischen Siedlung bei Uruk-Warka', in H.J. Lenzen *et al.*, *XIX. vorläufiger Bericht ... Uruk-Warka*, Berlin, 56-58.
SEELIGER, T.C., PERNICKA, E.
1985   'Archäometallurgische Unterschungen in Nord- und Ostanatolien', *Jahrbuch des Römisch-Germanischen Zentralmuseums Mainz* 32, 597-659.
SELZ, G.J.
1989   *Altsumerische Verwaltungstexte aus Lagaš*, Teil I, FAOS 15/1, Stuttgart.
SEUX, M.-J.
1967   *Épithètes royales akkadiennes et sumériennes*, Paris.

SHAFFER, A.
  1983   'Gilgamesh, the Cedar Forest and Mesopotamian History', *JAOS* 103, 307-13.
SHAFFER, F.R.
  1978   'The Later Prehistoric Periods', in F.R. Allchin (ed.), *The Archaeology of Afghanistan*, London, 71-186.
SHAFFER, J.G.
  1978   *Prehistoric Baluchistan*, Delhi.
  1982   'Harappan Commerce: An Alternative Perspective', in S. Pastner & L. Flam (eds), *Anthropology in Pakistan*, Ithaca.
SHENDGE, M.J.
  1983   'The Use of Seals and the Invention of Writing', *JESHO* XXVI, 113-36.
SHERRATT, A.G.
  1981   'Plough and Pastoralism: Aspects of the Secondary Products Revolution', in I. Hodder *et al.* (eds), *Patterns of the Past: Studies in Honour of David Clarke*, Cambridge, 261-305.
SHILEICO, V.K.
  1915   *Votivnïya nadpisi Shumeriiskikh pravitelei*, Petrograd.
SIGRIST, M.
  1986   'Les couriers de Lagaš', in de Meyer *et al.* 1986, 51-63.
  1988   *Isin Year Names*, Institute of Archaeology Publications Assyriological Series II, Berrien Springs, Michigan.
  1990   *Messenger Texts from the British Museum*, Potomac.
SIGRIST, M., BUTZ, K.
  1986   'Wirtschaftliche Beziehungen zwischen der Susiana und Südmesopotamien in der Ur-III-Zeit', *AMI* 19, 27-31.
SIGRIST, M., GOMI, T.
  1991   *The Comprehensive Catalogue of Published Ur III Tablets*, Bethesda, Maryland.
SJÖBERG, A.W.
  1972   'A Commemorative Inscription of King Šusîn', *JCS* 24, 70-73.
  1976   'in-nin šà-gur₄-ra A Hymn to the Goddess Inanna by the en-Priestess Enheduanna', *ZA* 65, 161-253.
  1988   'A Hymn to Inanna and her Self-Praise', *JCS* 40, 165-86.
SJÖBERG, A.W. *et al.*
  1969   *The Collection of the Sumerian Temple Hymns*, TCS III, Locust Valley & New York.
SMITH, S.
  1928   *Early History of Assyria to 1000 B.C.*, London.
  1932   'Notes on the Gutian Period', *JRAS* 1932, 295-308.
  1936-7   'Early Sculptures from Iraq', *British Museum Quarterly* XI, 116-21.
SMITH, S.A.
  1887   *Miscellaneous Assyrian Textes of the British Museum*, Leipzig.
  1936   'Early Sculptures from Iraq', *BMQ* XI, 116-21.

SNELL, D.C.
  1977   'The Activities of Some Merchants of Umma', *Iraq* XXXIX, 45-50.
  1982   *Ledgers and Prices: Early Mesopotamian Merchant Accounts*, New Haven.
SOLLBERGER, E.
  1954-56   'Sur la chronologie des rois d'Ur et quelques problèmes connexes', *AfO*, XVII, 10-48.
  1960   'Notes on the Early Inscriptions from Ur and el-'Obed', *Iraq* XXII, 69-89.
  1965   *Ur Excavations, Texts VIII: Royal Inscriptions, Part II*, London.
  1967-68   'The Cruciform Monument', *Jaarbericht ... "Ex Oriente Lux"* 20, 50-70.
  1968   'Notes sur Gudéa et son temps', *RA* 62, 137-45.
  1969   'The Rulers of Lagaš', *JCS* 21, 279-91.
  1970   'The Problem of Magan and Meluhha', *Bulletin of the Institute of Archaeology* 8-9, 247-50.
  1971   'Gunidu and Gursar', *RlA* III, 700.
  1976   'Ibbi-Suen', *RlA* V, 1-8.
  1982   'A New Inscription of Šar-kali-šarrī', in M.A. Dandamayev *et al.* (eds), *Societies and Languages of the Ancient Near East*, Warminster, 345-48.
  1984   'The Cuneiform Scripts', *The Society for Mesopotamian Studies Bulletin* 7, 6-18.
SOLLBERGER, E. KUPPER, J.-R.
  1971   *Inscriptions royales sumériennes et akkadiennes*, Paris.
SOTHEBY'S
  1992   *Western Asiatic Cylinder Seals & Antiquities from the Erlenmeyer Collection (Part I), London, 9th July 1992*, London.
  1992a   *Antiquities and Islamic Works of Art, New York, June 25 1992*, New York.
SPAR, I.
  1987   *Tablets, Cones and Bricks of the Third and Second Millennia B.C.*, Cuneiform Texts in the Metropolitan Museum of Art I, New York.
SPEISER, E.A.
  1935   *Excavations at Tepe Gawra, Vol. I: Levels I to VIII*, Philadelphia.
  1952   'Some Factors in the Collapse of Akkad', *JAOS* 72, 97-101.
  1967   *Oriental and Biblical Studies*, ed. by J.J. Finkelstein & M. Greenberg, Philadelphia.
SPYCKET, A.
  1981   *La statuaire du Proche-Orient ancien*, Leiden.
STARR, I.
  1986   'The Place of the Historical Omens in the System of Apodoses', *Bibliotheca Orientalis* XLIII 5/6, 628-42.
STECH, T., PIGOTT, V.C.
  1986   'The Metals Trade in Southwest Asia in the Third Millennium B.C.', *Iraq* XLVIII, 39-64.
STEIBLE, H.
  1982   *Die altsumerischen Bau- und Weihinschriften*, FAOS 5, Wiesbaden.

1991   *Die neusumerischen Bau- und Weihinschriften*, FAOS 9, Stuttgart.

STEIN, A.
1931   *An Archaeological Tour of Gedrosia*, MASI 43, Calcutta.
1937   *Archaeological Reconnaissances in North-Western India and South-Eastern Iran*, London.
1940   *Old Routes of Western Iran*, London.

STEINKELLER, P.
1980   'The Old Akkadian term for "Easterner"', *RA* LXXIV, 1-9.
1982   'The Question of Marhaši: A Contribution to the Historical Geography of Iran in the Third Millennium B.C.', *ZA* 72, 237-65.
1984   'Communication', *RA* 78, 83-88.
1986   'Seal of Išma-Ilum, son of the Governor of Matar', *Vicino Oriente* VI, 27-40.
1987   'The Administrative and Economic Organization of the Ur III State: The Core and the Periphery', in Gibson & Biggs (ed.) 1987, 19-41.
1987a   Review of Foster 1982, *WZKM* 77, 182-95.
1987b   'On the Meaning of zabar-šu', *ASJ* 9, 347-49.
1987c   'The Name of Nergal', *ZA* 77, 161-68.
1988   'On the Identity of the Toponym LÚ.SU(.A)', *JAOS* 108, 197-202.
1988a   'The Date of Gudea and his Dynasty', *JCS* 40, 47-53.
1989   'Man-ištūšu. A. Philologisch.', *RlA* VII, 334f.
1989a   'Marḫaši', *RlA* VII, 381f.
1990   'More on LÚ.SU(.A)=Šimaški', *NABU* (no. 1, March), 10f.
in pr. a Review of A.Westenholz 1987a.
in pr. b 'History of Mesopotamia (Third Millennium BC)', *Anchor Bible Dictionary*, New York.

STEPHENS, F.J.
1937   *Votive and Historical Texts from Babylonia and Assyria*, YOS IX, New Haven, London & Oxford.

STÈVE, M.J.
1989   'Des sceaux-cylindres de Simaški?', *RA* 83, 13-26.

STÈVE, M.J., GASCHE, H.
1971   *L'Acropole de Suse*, MDP XLVI, Paris.

STÈVE, M.J. *et al.*
1980   'La Susiane au IIe millénaire: à propos d'une interprétation des fouilles de Suse', *Iranica Antiqua* XV, 49-154.

STOLPER, M.W.
1976   'Preliminary Report on Texts from Tal-e Malyan 1971-4', *Proceeding of the 4th Annual Symposium on Archaeological Research in Iran*, 89-97.
1982   'On the Dynasty of Šimaški and the Early Sukkalmaḫs', *ZA* 72, 42-67.
1984   'Political History', in E. Carter & M.W. Stolper, *Elam: Surveys of Political History and Archaeology*, Near Eastern Studies 25, Los Angeles.

1985   'Proto-Elamite Tablets from Tall-i Malyan', *Kadmos* 24, 1-12.
1987   'Awan', in E. Yarshater (ed.), *Encyclopaedia Iranica* III/2, London & New York, 113f.

STRANGE, G. LE
1905   *Lands of the Eastern Caliphate*, Cambridge.

STROMMENGER, E.
1963   'Archaische Siedlung', in H.J. Lenzen *et al.*, *XIX. vorläufiger Bericht .... Uruk-Warka*, Berlin, 45-55.
1977   'Habuba Kabira am syrischen Euphrat', *Antike Welt* 8/1, 11-20.
1980   'The Chronological Division of the Archaic Levels of Uruk-Eanna VI to III/II: Past and Prsent', *AJA* 84, 479-87.
1980a   *Habuba Kabira, Eine Stadt vor 5000 Jahren*, Mainz.
1989   'Man-ištūšu. B. Archäologisch', *RlA* VII, 335-39.

STROMMENGER, E. *et al.*
1973   'Vierter vorläufiger Bericht ... Habuba Kabira ...', *MDOG* 105, 6-68.

SUMNER, W.N.
1972   *Cultural Development in the Kur River Basin, Iran*, Ph.D. Dissertation, Ann Arbor.
1974   'Excavations at Tal-i Malyan, 1971-72', *Iran* XII, 155-80.
1976   'Excavations at Tall-i Malyan (Anshan) 1974', *Iran* XIV, 103-15.
1977   'Tal-i Malyan', *Iran* XV, 177-79.
1980   'The Malyan Project: Introduction', in Sumner (ed.) 1980, 1-16.
1985   'The Proto-Elamite City Wall at Tal-i Malyan', *Iran* XXIII, 153-61.
1986   'Proto-Elamite Civilization in Fars', in Finkbeiner & Röllig (eds) 1986, 199-211.
1988   'Malyān, Tall-e (Anšan)', *RlA* VII, 306-20.
1989   'Anshan in the Kaftari Phase: Patterns of Settlement and Land Use', in de Meyer & Haerinck (eds) 1989, 135-61.

SUMNER, W.M. (ed.)
1980   *Problems of Large Scale, Multi-disciplinary Regional Archaeological Research: The Malyan Project*, xerox.

SÜRENHAGEN, D.
1974-75 'Zwei neuerworbene Steatitgefäße', *Acta praehistorica et archaeologica* 5/6, 165-70.
1981   'Ahmad al-Hattu 1979/80', *MDOG* 113, 35-51.
1986   'The Dry Farming Belt: the Uruk Period and Subsequent Developments', in Weiss (ed.) 1986, 7-43.

SZARZYŃSKA, K.
1988   'Records of Garments and Cloths in Archaic Uruk/Warka', *Altorientalische Forschungen* 15, 220-30.

TADDEI, M. (ed.)
1979   *South Asian Archaeology 1977, (Papers from the Fourth International Conference of South Asian*

Archaeologists in Western Europe), 2 vols, Naples.

TALLON, F.
1987   *Métallurgie susienne I: De la fondations de Suse au XVIIIe siècle avant J.C.*, Notes et documents des Musées de France 15, Paris.

TAYLOR, J.W.
1983   'Erzgebirge Tin: A Closer Look', *Oxford Journal of Archaeology* 2, 295-98.

TEISSIER, B.
1984   *Ancient Near Eastern Cylinder Seals from the Marcopoli Collection*, Los Angeles & London.
1987   'Glyptic Evidence for a Connection Between Iran, Syro-Palestine and Egypt in the Fourth and Third Millennia', *Iran* XXV, 27-53.

TEREKHOVA, N.N.
1981   'The History of Metalworking Production among the Ancient Agriculturalists of Southern Turkmenia', in Kohl (ed.) 1981, 313-24.

THAPAR, B.K.
1975   'A Possible Identification of Meluhha, Dilmun and Makkan', *JESHO* XVIII, 1-42.

THOMPSON, R.C.
1931   *The Prisims of Esarhaddon and of Ashurbanipal*, London.

THOMPSON, R.C., HUTCHINSON, R.W.
1929   'The Excavations on the Temple of Nabû at Nineveh', *Archaeologia* 79, 103-48.

THOMSEN, M.L.
1984   *The Sumerian Language*, Mesopotamia: Copenhagen Studies in Assyriology 10, Copenhagen.

THORVILDSEN, K.
1962   'Burial Cairns on Umm an-Nar', *KUML* 1962, 208-19.

THUREAU-DANGIN, F.
1907   'Une incursion élamite en territoire sumérien', *RA* 6, 139-42.
1927   'Tablettes à signes picturaux', *RA* 24, 23-29.

THUREAU-DANGIN, F., DUNAND, M.
1936   *Til-Barsip*, Paris.

TOSI, M.
1968   'Excavations at Shahr-i Sokhta, Preliminary Report on the First Season, Oct.-Dec. 1967', *East and West* 18, 9-66.
1969   'Excavations at Shahr-i Sokhta, Preliminary Report on the Second Season, Sept.-Dec. 1968', *East and West* 19, 283-386.
1974   'The Lapis Lazuli Trade Across the Iranian Plateau in the 3rd Millennium B.C.', *Gururājamañjarikā. Studi in onore di Giuseppe Tucci*, Naples, 3-22.
1974b   'The Problem of Turquoise in Protohistoric Trade on the Iranian Plateau', *Studi di Paletnologia, Paleoantropologia, Paleontologia e Geologia del Quaternario* NS 2, 147-62.

1974c   'The Northeastern Frontier of the Ancient Near East', *Mesopotamia* VIII-IX, 21-76.
1974d   'Some Data from the Study of Prehistoric Culture Areas on the Persian Gulf', *PSAS* 4, 145-71.
1975   'Notes on the Distribution and Exploitation of Natural Resources in Ancient Oman', *JOS* 1, 187-206.
1976   'Shahr-i Sokhta', *Iran* XIV, 167f.
1976-80 'Karneol', *RlA* V, 448-52.
1977   'Archaeological Evidence for Protostate Structures in Eastern Iran at the End of the 3rd Millennium B.C.', in Deshayes (ed.) 1977, 45-66.
1979   'The Proto-urban Cultures of Eastern Iran and the Indus Civilization. Notes and Suggestions for a Spatio-temporal Frame to Study the Early Relations between India and Iran', in Taddei (ed.) 1979, 150-71.
1982   'The Development of Urban Societies in Turan and the Mesopotamian Trade with the East: the evidence from Shahr-i Sokhta', in Nissen & Renger (eds) 1982, 57-77.
1983   'Development, Continuity and Cultural Change in the Stratigraphic Sequence of Shahr-i Sokhta', in Tosi (ed.) 1983, 127-80.
1984   'The Notion of Craft Specialization and its Representation in the Archaeological Record of Early States in the Turanian Basin', in M. Spriggs (ed.), *Marxist Perspectives in Archaeology*, Cambridge, 22-52.
1986   'The Archaeology of Early States in Middle Asia', *Oriens Antiquus* XXV, 153-87.
1989   'The Distribution of Industrial Debris on the surface of Tappeh Hesār as an Indication of Activity Areas', in Dyson & Howard (eds) 1989, 13-24.
1989a   'Protohistoric Archaeology in Oman: The First Thirty Years (1956-1985)', in Costa & Tosi (eds) 1989, 135-61.

TOSI, M. (ed.)
1983   *Prehistoric Seistan I*, Istituto Italiano per il Medio ed Estremo Oriente, Reports and Memoirs XIX 1, Naples.

TOSI, M., BULGARELLI, G.M.
1989   'The Stratigraphic Sequence of Squares DF 88/89 on South Hill, Tappeh Hesār', in Dyson & Howard (eds) 1989, 35-53.

TOSI, M., PIPERNO, M.
1973   'Lithic technology behind the ancient lapis lazuli trade', *Expedition* 16/1, 15-23.

TOSI, M., VIDALI, M.
1990   '4th Millennium BC Lapis Lazuli Working at Mehrgarh, Pakistan', *Paléorient* XVI, 89-99.

TOSI, M., WARDAK, R.
1972   'The Fullol Hoard: A New Find from Bronze-Age Afghanistan', *East and West* 22, 9-17.

TUCCI, G (ed.)
1977   *The Burnt City in the Salt Desert*, Venice.

TUSA, S.
1977   'Seals and Seal Impressions', in Tucci (ed.) 1977, 259-61.

TYLECOTE, R.F.
1976   *A History of Technology*, London.

UNGER, E.
1928   'Aratta', *RIA* I, 140.

VAIMAN, A.A.
1972   'A Comparative Study of the Proto-Elamite and Proto-Sumerian Scripts', *Vestnik Drevnei Istorii*, 124-33 (Russian with English summary).

1989   'Beiträge zur Entzifferung der Archaischen Schriften Vorderasien. Erste Teil.', *Baghdader Mitteilungen* 20, 91-133.

1990   'Beiträge zur Entzifferung der Archaischen Schriften Vorderasien. Zweiter Teil.', *Baghdader Mitteilungen* 21, 91-123.

VALLAT, F.
1971   'Les documents épigraphiques de l'Acropole (1969-1971)', *DAFI*, 235-45.

1973   'Les tablettes proto-élamite de l'Acropole (campagne 1972)', *DAFI* 3, 93-103.

1978   'Le matériel épigraphique des couches 18 à 14 de l'Acropole', *Paléorient* 4, 193-95.

1980   *Suse et l'Elam*, Recherche sur les grandes civilizations, mémoire 1, Paris.

1980a   'Documents épigraphiques de la Ville Royale I (1972 et 1975)', *DAFI* 11, 135-39.

1984   'Une inscription cunéiforme de Bouchir', *Dédalo* 23, 258ff.

1985   'Éléments de géographie élamite (Résumé)', *Paléorient* 11/2, 49-54.

1986   'The Most Ancient Scripts of Iran: The Current Situation', *World Archaeology* 17, 335-47.

1990   'Réflections sur l'époque des sukkalmah', in Vallat (ed.) 1990, 119-127.

VALLAT, F. (ed.)
1990   *Contribution à l'histoire de l'Iran: Mélanges offerts à Jean Perrot*, Éditions Recherche sur les Civilisations, Paris.

VANDEN BERGHE, L.
1959   *Archéologie de l'Iran ancienne*, Leiden.
1972   'La chronologie de la civilisation des bronzes du Pusht-i Kuh, Luristan', in F. Bagherzadeh (ed.), *Proceedings of the Ist Annual Symposium on Archaeological Research in Iran (1972)*, Teheran, 1-6.

1975   'Fouilles au Luristan: La necropole de Dum Gar, Parchineh', in F. Bagherzadeh (ed.), *Proceedings of the IIIrd Annual Symposium on Archaeological Research in Iran*, Teheran, 45-62.

1979   *Bibliographie analytique de l'archéologie de l'Iran*, Leiden.

1982   *Luristan: een verdwenen bronskunst uit West-Iran*, Gent.

VANDEN BERGHE, L., HAERINCK, E.
1984   'Prospection et fouilles au Pusht-i Kuh, Luristan', *AfO* XXXI, 200-209.

VATANDOOST-HAGHIGHI, A.
1977   *Aspects of Prehistoric Iranian Copper and Bronze Technology*, Ph.D Thesis, University of London.

VATS, M.S.
1940   *Excavations at Harappa*, 2 vols, Delhi.

VEENHOF, K.R.
1972   *Aspects of Old Assyrian Trade and its Terminology*, Leiden.

1982   'The Old Assyrian Merchants and their Relations with the Native Population of Anatolia', in Nissen & Renger (eds) 1982, 147-60.

VÉRTESALJI, P.P., KOLBUS, S.
1985   'Review of Protodynastic Developments in Babylonia', *Mesopotamia* XX, 53-109.

VIDALI, M.L., VIDALI, E., LAMBERG-KARLOVSKY, C.C.
1976   'Prehistoric Setlement Patterns around Tepe Yahya: A Quantitative Analysis', *JNES* 35, 237-50.

VINOGRADOV, A.V., KUZMINA, E.E.
1970   'Moules de fonderie trouvé à Liavliakan', *Sovetskaya Arkheologiya 1970* no. 2, 125-35 (Russian with French summary).

VIROLLEAUD, C., LAMBERT, M.
1968   *Tablettes économiques de Lagash (époque de la IIIe dynastie d'Ur) copiées en 1900 au Musée impérial Ottoman*, Paris.

VITA-FINZI, C.
1978   'Recent Alluvial History in the Catchment of the Arabo-Persian Gulf', in Brice (ed.) 1978, 255-61.

VOGT, B.
1985   *Zur Chronologie und Entwicklung der Gräber des späten 4.-2. Jtsd. v. Chr. auf der Halbinsel Oman: Zusammenfassung, Analyse und Würdingung publizierte wie auch unveroffentlichter Grabungsergebnisse*, doctoral thesis, Göttingen.

1985a   'The Umm an-Nar Tomb A at Hili North: A preliminary report on three seasons of excavation, 1982-1984', *Archaeology in the United Arab Emirates* IV, 20-37.

VOIGT, M.M., DYSON JR, R.H.
in pr. 'The Chronology of Iran, ca. 8000-2000 B.C.', in R.W. Ehrich (ed.), *Chronologies in Old World Archaeology*, 3rd ed., Chicago.

VON BOTHMER, D. (ed.)
1990   *Glories of the Past: Ancient Art from the Shelby White and Leon Levy Collection*, New York.

WARTKE, R.B.
1979   'Steinborer aus Uruk', *Altorientalische Forschungen* VI, 257-61.

WATELIN, L.CH.
1934   *Excavations at Kish* IV (1925-1930), Paris.

Wäfler, M.
  1980   'Der Becher MBQ 26/35-62 (=71 MBQ59)', *MDOG* 112, 9-11.
Waetzoldt, H.
  1981   'Zur Terminologie der Metalle in den Texten aus Ebla', in E. Cagni (ed.), *La Lingua di Ebla*, Naples, 363-78.
Waetzoldt, H., Bachmann, H.G.
  1984   'Zinn- und Arsenbronzen in den Texte aus Ebla und aus dem Mesopotamien des 3. Jahrtausends', *Oriens Antiquus* 23, 1-18.
Walker, C.B.F., Collon, D.
  1980   'Hormuzd Rassam's Excavations for the British Museum at Sippar in 1881-1882', in L. de Meyer (ed.), *Tell ed-Dēr III: Sounding at Abū Habbah (Sippar)*, Leuven.
Webster, R.
  1983   *Gems: Their Sources, Description and Identification*, 3rd edn revised by B.W. Anderson, London.
Weidner, E.
  1931-32   Review of Thompson & Hutchinson 1929 etc., *AfO* VII, 278-82.
Weidner, E., Christian, V.
  1927-28   'Das Alter der Gräberfunde aus Ur', *AfO* V, 139-50.
Weisgerber, G.
  1980   '... und Kupfer in Oman', *Der Anschnitt* 32, 62-110.
  1981   'Mehr als Kupfer in Oman - Ergebnisse der Expedition 1981', *Der Anschnitt* 33, 174-263.
  1981a   'Evidence of Ancient Mining Sites in Oman: A Preliminary Report', *JOS* 4, 15-28.
  1983   'Copper Production During the Third Millennium BC in Oman and the Question of Makan', *JOS* 6, 269-76.
  1984   'Makan and Meluhha - third millennium B.C. copper production in Oman and the evidence of contact with the Indus Valley', in Allchin (ed.) 1984, 196-201.
  1984-85   'Dilmun - A Trading Entrepot: Evidence from Historical and Archaeological Sources', *Dilmun* 12, 5-10.
  1987   'Archaeological Evidence of Copper Exploitation at 'Arja', *JOS* 9, 145-72.
Weisgerber, G., Haupmann, A.
  1988   'Early Copper Mining and Smelting in Palestine', in Maddin (ed.) 1988, 52-62.
Weiss, H.
  1977   'Periodization, Population and Early State Formation in Khuzistan', in Levine & Young (eds) 1977, 347-69.
Weiss, H. (ed.)
  1985   *Ebla to Damascus: Art and Archaeology of Ancient Syria*, Washington D.C.
  1986   *The Origins of Cities in Dry-Farming Syria and Mesopotamia in the Third Millennium B.C.*, Guilford.
Weiss, H., Young, T.C.
  1975   'The Merchants of Susa: Godin V and Plateau-Lowland Relations in the Late Fourth Millennium B.C.', *Iran* XIII, 1-17.

Wellsted, J.R.
  1838   *Travels in Arabia*, London.
Wertime, T.A.
  1964   'Man's First Encounter with Metallurgy', *Science* 146 (no. 3649), 1257-67.
  1973   'The Beginnings of Metallurgy: A New Look', *Science* 182, 875-887.
Wertime, T.A., Muhly, J.D. (eds)
  1980   *The Coming of the Age of Iron*, New Haven & London.
Wertime, T.A., Wertime, S.F. (eds)
  1982   *Early Pyrotechnology. The Evolution of the First Fire-Using Industries*, Washington.
Westenholz, A.
  1974-77   'Old Akkadian School Texts, Some Goals of Sargonic Scribal Education', *AfO* 25, 95-110.
  1975a   *Old Sumerian and Akkadian Texts in Philadelphia Chiefly from Nippur, Part 1: Literary and Lexical Texts and the Earliest Administrative Documents from Nippur*, Bibliotheca Mesopotamica I, Malibu.
  1975b   *Early Cuneiform Texts in Jena*, Copenhagen.
  1979   'The Old Akkadian Empire in Contemporary Opinion', in Larsen (ed.) 1979, 107-24.
  1984   Review of Foster 1982, *AfO* 31, 76-81.
  1987   'Lugalzagesi', *RlA* VII, 155-57.
  1987a   *Old Sumerian and Old Akkadian Texts in Philadelphia II. The 'Akkadian' Texts, the Enlilemaba Texts, and the Onion Archive*, Casten Niebuhr Institute, Copenhagen.
Westenholz, A., Oelsner, J.
  1983   'Zu den Weihplattenfragmenten der Hilprecht-Sammlung Jena', *Altorientalische Forschungen* 10, 209-16.
Westenholz, J.G.
  1983   'Heroes of Akkad', *JAOS* 103, 327-36.
  1984   'Kaku of Ur and Kaku of Lagash', *JNES* 43, 339-42.
Wheeler, R.E.M.
  1968   *The Indus Civilization*, 3rd ed., Cambridge.
Whitehouse, D.
  1975   'Carnelian in the Persian Gulf', *Antiquity* XLIX, 129f.
Whiting, R.M.
  1976   'Tiš-atal of Nineveh and Babati, uncle of Šu-sin', *JCS* 28, 173-82.
  1987   'Four Seal Impressions from Tell Asmar', *AfO* 34, 30-35.
  1987a   *Old Babylonian Letters from Tell Asmar*, AS 22, Chicago.
Wiggermann, F.A.M.
  1982   '"Exit Talim!" Studies in Babylonian Demonology', *Jaarbericht ... "Ex Oriente Lux"* 27, 90-105.
Wilcke, C.
  1960   'Drei Phasen des Niedergangs des Reiches von Ur III', *ZA* 50, 54-69.
  1969   *Da Lugalbandaepos*, Wiesbaden.

1974-77 'Die Keilschrift-Texte der Sammlung Böllinger', *AfO* 25, 84-94.

WILHELM, G.
1988 'Gedanken zur Frühgeschichte der Hurriter und zum hurritisch-urartäischen Sprachvergleich', in V. Haas (ed.), *Hurriter und Hurritisch, Konstanzer Altorientalische Symposien 2*, Konstanz.
1989 *The Hurrians*, trans. J. Barnes, Warminster.

WILLIAMS, G.R.
1981 'Geological Notes on Rocks, Fossils and Objects of Antiquarian Interest Excavated from the Ruins of Eridu', in Safar *et al.* 1981, 311-16.

WILLIES, L.
1990 'An Early Bronze Age Tin Mine in Anatolia, Turkey', *Bulletin of the Park District Mines Historical Society*, 11/2, 91-96.
1992 'Reply to Pernicka *et al.*: Comment on the Discussion of Ancient Tin Sources in Anatolia', *Journal of Mediterranean Archaeology* 5, 99-103.

WISEMAN, D.J.
1962 *Catalogue of the Western Asiatic Seals in the British Museum I, Cylinder Seals, Uruk - Early Dynastic Periods*, London.

WOOLLEY, C.L.
1928 *The Sumerians*, London.
1934 *Ur Excavations II: The Royal Cemetery*, London.
1935 *The Development of Sumerian Art*, New York.
1939 *Ur Excavations V: The Ziggurat and its Surroundings*, London.
1955 *Ur Excavations IV: The Early Periods*, London.
1961 *Mesopotamia and the Middle East*, London.
1974 *Ur Excavations VI: The Ur III Period*, London.

WOOLLEY, C.L., BARNETT, R.D.
1952 *Carchemish III: The Excavations in the Inner Town*, London.

WOOLLEY, C.L., MALLOWAN, M.E.L.
1976 *Ur Excavations VII: The Old Babylonian Period*, London.

WOOLLEY, C.L., MOOREY, P.R.S.
1982 *Ur 'of the Chaldees'*, London.

WRIGHT, H.E.
1955 'Geological Aspects of the Archaeology of Iraq', *Sumer* XI, 83-94.

WRIGHT, H.T.
1978 'The Comparative Stratigraphy of Fourth Millennium Khuzistan', *Paléorient* 4, 233-34.
1979 'Comments on the Geography of the Izeh Plain', in Wright (ed.) 1979, 35-38.
1979a 'The Uruk Period on the Izeh Plain', in Wright (ed.) 1979, 59-63.
1980 'Problems of Absolute Chronology in Protohistoric Mesopotamia', *Paléorient* 6, 93-98.
1981 'The Southern Margins of Sumer: Archaeological Survey of the Area of Eridu and Ur', in Adams 1981, 295-345.
1987 'The Susiana Hinterlands during the Era of Primary State Formation', in Hole (ed.) 1987, 141-55.

WRIGHT, H.T., JOHNSON, G.A.
1975 'Population, Exchange and Early State Formation in Southern Iran', *American Anthropologist* 77, 267-89.
1985 'Regional Perspectives on Southwest Iranian State Development', *Paléorient* 11/2, 25-30.

WRIGHT, H.T. *et al.*
1975 'Early Fourth Millennium Developments in Southwestern Iran', *Iran* XIII, 129-47.
1980 'Time and Process in an Uruk Rural Center', Barrelet (ed) 1980, 265-82.

WRIGHT, H.T. (ed.)
1979 *Archaeological Investigations in Northeastern Xuzestan, 1976*, Ann Arbor.
1981 *An Early Town on the Deh Luran Plain: Excavations at Tepe Farukhabad*, Ann Arbor.

WRIGHT, R.P.
1989 'New Perspectives on Third Millennium Painted Grey Wares', in Frifelt & Sørensen 1989, 137-49.

YAKAR, J.
1984 'Regional and Local Schools of Metalwork in Early Bronze Age Anatolia', *Anatolian Studies* XXXIV, 59-86.

YANG, Z.
1986 *A Study of the Sargonic Archive from Adab*, vol. 1, unpublished Ph.D. dissertation, Chicago.

YENER, K.A.
1986 'The Archaeometry of Silver in Anatolia: The Bolkardağ Mining District', *AJA* 90, 469-72.

YENER, K.A., GOODWAY, M.
1992 'Response to Mark E. Hall and Sharon R. Steadman "Tin and Anatolia: Another Look"', *Journal of Mediterranean Archaeology* 5, 77-90.

YENER, K.A., ÖZBAL, H.
1987 'Tin in the Taurus Mountains: the Bolkardağ Mining District', *Antiquity* 61, 220-26.

YENER, K.A., ÖZBAL, H., MINZONI-DEROCHE, A., AKSOY, B.
1989 'Bolkardağ: Archaeometallurgy Surveys in the Taurus Mountains, Turkey', *National Geographic Research* 5, 477-94.

YENER, K.A., ÖZBAL, H., KAPTAN, E. *et al.*
1989a 'Kestel: an Early Bronze Age source of tin ore in the Taurus Mountains, Turkey', *Science* 244, 117-264.

YENER, K.A., SAYRE, E.V., JOEL, E.C., ÖZBAL, H., BARNES, I.L., BRILL, R.H.
1991 'Stable Lead Isotope Studies of Central Taurus Ore Sources and Related Artifacts from Eastern Mediterranean

Chalcolithic and Bronze Age Sites', *Journal of Archaeological Science* 18/5, 541-77.

YENER, K.A., VANDIVER, P.B.,
1993 'Tin Processing at Göltepe, an Early Bronze Age Site in Anatolia', *AJA* 97, 207-38.

1993a 'Reply to J.D. Muhly, "Early Bronze Age Tin in the Taurus" with an appendix by Lynn Willies: Early Bronze Age Tin Working at Kestel', *AJA* 97, 255-64.

YILDIZ, F.
1981 'A Tablet of Codex Ur-Nammu from Sippar', *Orientalia* 50, 87-97.

YOFFEE, N.
1981 *Explaining Trade in Ancient Western Asia*, Monographs on the Ancient Near East 2/2, Malibu.

YOUNG JR, T.C.
1986 'Godin Tepe Period VI/V and Central Western Iran at the End of the Fourth Millennium', in Finkbeiner & Röllig (eds) 1986, 212-24.

YOUNG JR, T.C., LEVINE, L.D.
1974 *The Godin Project: Second Progress Report*, Toronto.

YOUNG, W.J.
1972 'The Fabulous Gold of the Pactolus Valley', *Bulletin of the Boston Museum of Fine Arts* 70, 5ff.

YULE, P.
1982 *Tepe Hissar: Neolithische und kupferzeitliche Siedlung in Nordostiran*, Munich.

ZADOK, R.
1987 'Peoples of the Iranian Plateau in Babylonia during the Second Millennium B.C.', *Iran* 25, 1-26.

ZARINS, J.
1976 *The Domestication of Equidae in Third Millennium B.C. Mesopotamia*, Ph.D. Dissertation, Ann Arbor.

1978 'Steatite Vessels in the Riyadh Museum', *Atlal* 2, 65-93.

1978a 'The Domesticated Equidae of Third Millennium B.C. Mesopotamia', *JCS* 30, 3-17.

1986 'Equids Associated with Human Burials in Third Millennium B.C. Mesopotamia: Two Complementary Facets', in Meadow & Uerpmann (eds) 1986, 164-93.

1992 'The Early Settlement of Southern Mesopotamia: A Review of Recent Historical, Geological, and Archaeological Research', *JAOS* 112, 55-77.

ZEDER, M.A.
1984 'Meat Distribution at the Highland Iranian Centre of Tal-e Malyan', in J. Clutton-Brock & C. Grigson (eds), *Animals and Archaeology 3: Herders and their Flocks*, Oxford, 279-337.

ZERVOS, C.
1935 *L'art de la Mésopotamie*, London.

ZEUNER, F.E.
1963 *A History of Domesticated Animals*, London.

ZIEGLER, C.
1962 *Die Terrakotten von Warka*, Berlin.

Index

Main entries are indicated in bold.